Womanlist

BOOKS BY MARJORIE P. K. WEISER

Ethnic America   *1976*
Fingerprint Owls   *1972*
Museum Adventures   *1967*
Museums U.S.A.   *1965*

WITH JEAN S. ARBEITER

Pegs to Hang Ideas On   *1973*

Womanlist

Marjorie P. K. Weiser

and

Jean S. Arbeiter

ATHENEUM

New York

1981

To
Norman
and
Solomon
with love and thanks

Library of Congress Cataloging in Publication Data

Weiser, Marjorie P. K.
    Womanlist.
    Bibliography: p.
    Includes index.
    1. Women's encyclopedias and dictionaries.
I. Arbeiter, Jean S., joint author. II. Title.
HQ1115.W43   1981   305.4   80–65983
ISBN 0–689–11083–9
ISBN 0–689–11113–4 (pbk.)

Copyright © 1981 by Marjorie P. K. Weiser and Jean S. Arbeiter
All rights reserved
Published simultaneously in Canada by McClelland and Stewart Ltd.
Composition by American–Stratford Graphic Services, Inc., Brattleboro, Vermont
Manufactured by American Book–Stratford Press, Saddle Brook, New Jersey
Designed by Mary Cregan
First Edition

CONTENTS

Preface   *xiii*

I. Out of the Ordinary   3

First Women · A Few for the Record Books · Short People: Twenty
Women 5 Feet 3 Inches and Under · Nineteen Early Starters · Five
Bearded Ladies · And Two Saints with the Same Attribute · Fifteen One
and Only Ones · Four Monuments to Devotion · Eight Who Were Not
What They Claimed · Anything for a Laugh · Missing Persons · Nine
Prophetic Dreamers · Eleven Seers and Psychics · The Second Time
Around? · Lois Gould's List of Women "Whose Endings I Most Envy"

II. What's the Difference?   17

Some Differences Between Eve and Adam · Passing It On · Health Problems—for Women Only · Be-switched · Two Who Did It Without Surgery · And What Can Come of It · A Man's Life · Six Men Who Wanted
to Be Taken for Women · Separate but Not Equal · I Love Men Except
for Their . . . · I Love Women Except for Their . . .

III. Show of Courage   25

Eleven Faces of Heroism · Seven Who Led the Way · Ten Underground
Agents of World War II · Four Who Chose to Go Down with the
Titanic · Twelve Who Overcame Adversity · From Mental Breakdown
to a New Life · Voices of Conscience · Seeking Justice for the In-
dian · Nikki Giovanni's List of Eighteen Great Black Women · Marilyn
French's List of Hope for the Next Decade

IV. Love, and Marriage   36

Barbara Cartland's List of History's Ten Most Romantic Women · Helen
Gurley Brown's List of Women Who Could Have Been the *Cosmo*
Girl · Lovers of Catherine the Great · Three Other Man Fanciers and
Their Conquests · Fifteen Women in the Tangled Love Life of Lord
Byron · The Ancient History of the Oldest Profession · The Etymology of
the World's Oldest Profession · The Courtesan as Celebrity I: The He-
tairae · The Courtesan as Celebrity II: The Grand Horizontals · Four
Papal Mistresses · The Family That Plays Together: Four Daughters of the
Marquis of Nesle, and the King · Eight Who Told All · Doing a Number
on Love, and Marriage · The Value of a Wife · The Uses of Virgin-

ity · Virgin Wives · Advice for Brides · Eight Marital Arrangements with Interesting Possibilities for Women · Unequal Spouses · Seven Husbands of Barbara Hutton · The Rewards of Being Mrs. Tommy Manville · Alice Toklas's List of Wives of Geniuses

V. M *Is for . . . and Other Family Connections*   62

Notable Cases of Maternity · No Pausing for Pregnancy · The Oedipal Connection · Some Mothers of Nine or More · Call Them Mom · Mothers Who May or May Not Be "Unnatural" · Paeans to Mom · Special Deliverers · Seventeen Mothers Out of Wedlock · Founders of the First Birth Control Clinics · Four Abortionists · Five Regularly Advertised Abortifacients of the Nineteenth Century · Joy Adamson's List of "Qualities I Most Respect in Female Animals" · Three Sets of Sisters Who May, or May Not, Be of Assistance · Singing Sisters · Sixteen Sets of Celebrated Sisters · Their Fathers' Daughters · Their Mothers' Daughters · Relatively Speaking, with Tongue in Cheek

VI. *She's the Boss*   80

Room at the Top · Thirteen at the Top · And in the Executive Suite · To Bank on · Ten with Potential · Lobbying for Business · Women Members on the Floor of the New York Stock Exchange · Two Diamond Merchants · Nine Black Businesswomen · Thirteen Who Had Good Business Ideas · Taking Over for Their Husbands · Eight Printing Widows of the Thirteen Colonies · And a Printing Dynasty · Breadwinners of Early America · At Home in a House · Eleven Self-Starters of the Nineteenth Century · Dealing the Cards · Five Commercial Females Who Never Were · Flying the Friendly Skies

VII. *Persons at Work*   96

About Women's Work · Meanwhile, in the Soviet Union · Housework · Five Hints to Young Women in Business · Facts About Secretaries · Firsts for the Working Woman · Fourteen Who Were First on a "Man's Job" · Wearing a Blue Collar · Uncle Sam's First Female Employees · Seven Frontier Women · Nine Fire Fighters · "Let Her Works Praise Her in the Gates": Exhibitors at the Centennial Exhibition of 1876 · Mothers of Invention · Four Flag Women · Working Women of the Comics with Their Very Own Strips · Seventeen Officers of the Law · They Asked What's Cooking · Perfect Attendants—the First Eight Airline Stewardesses · Come Fly with Me · Late Starts and Second Careers · Why Retire? Thirteen Who Didn't

VIII. *Thirsting for Knowledge*   120

Thomas Jefferson's Curriculum for His Daughter Martha · A Diller, a Dollar—Some Very Early Scholars · Nine Dedicated Teachers · Blimey! The First Women's Colleges in England · The First College-Educated American Women · Eleven First Women of American Higher Education · Founding the Seven Sisters · Eleven Super Scholars · Top Numbers in Higher Education · Going Higher in Mathematics · Women in Science · Seeing Stars · Sixteen on the Frontiers of Science · Exploring for Science · Figuring Out What's Good for Us · Women in Medicine Today · The First Licensed Physicians · Nine on Call · Ms. M.D.: Firsts and Founders · Eleven Pioneer Women's Remedies · Ten Physicians with a Mission · Nine Women Urologists · Seven Daughters of Psyche

IX. *Arms and the Woman*   143

Fabled Women Warriors · Fourteen in the Thick of Battle · Five Who Fought for England · Eight Who Fought in the Revolutionary War · They Also Served . . . · I Spy—Eight Undercover Agents of the Civil War · Four Who Wore War Paint · Top Brass: Achievements of American Military Women · First Women in the White House Honor Guard · Nine Policy Makers at the Pentagon in 1979 · Some Lady Hell Cats · Eight Ensigns · First Women in Service · Four Russian Fighter Pilots · Weapons with Feminine Nicknames

X. *The Search for Adventure*   157

The Wild West and the Big Top · Five Sisters of the Road · Living Dangerously · Long-Distance Endurance · Ten Explorers · Climb Every Mountain · Eight Floating Upward · Six Who'll Journey into Space · Thirteen Who Won't · And Two Females Who Have Already Been in Orbit

XI. *That's Entertainment*   170

The First Actresses · Playing the Woman · Hand Me My Doublet and Hose: Actresses Who Portrayed Shakespeare's Heroes · The Family That Acts Together · Crowd Pleasers · Helen Hayes's List of "Roles I Would Have Liked to Play but Never Did" · Behind the Scenes · "Glorifying the American Girl": Six Ziegfeld Follies Beauties and What Became of Them · Seven Rules of the Honky-Tonks · Fourteen Stars Who Started in the Chorus · Six Who Got a Break at the Cotton Club · Strictly Female? · Seven "Dizzy Dames" of Radio · . . . And Some Smart Ones · The Three Longest-Playing Soap Opera Actresses on Radio · Fifteen Who Sang on "Your Hit Parade" · Five Unique Noisemakers · Unseen Voices · Nine Women of "Today" · When Women Ruled the Silver Screen · Ten Silent Directors · All About Eve · A Tribe of Indian Heroines Who Weren't · Divas on the Silver Screen · Twenty-one Directors Today · Songs by Women Lyricists Nominated for Academy Awards · Two-Time Academy Award Winners · A Three-Time Winner · And the Three-Time Winner with the Most Oscar Nominations · Eleven Modern Screenwriters and Their Films · Eight Movie Moguls · Their World of Dance · Eleven Makers of Modern Dance

XII. *Music in the Air*   197

Early to Play · Inspirations · The Women of Chopin's Music · Composing Themselves · Seven Librettists · Pants Roles · Beverly Sills's List of the Most Challenging Roles for a Soprano · Ten on the Podium · Caldwell in Concert · Heading the Opera · And Then I Wrote . . . : Fourteen Popular Favorites by Women · Seven Songs and the Women They Were Written for · Women's Musical Groups · Nine Who Sang the Blues · Twenty Jazzwomen · "Girl Groups" of the Fifties and Sixties • The Brill Building Sound • Twenty with Two or More Gold Singles • Talking Heads: Rock Women Speak • Queens of Country

XIII. *In Their Own Write*   215

Literary Firsts • Six Writers of Long Ago • Three Prose Writers of Early America • Eleven Colonial Poets • Seven Originals: The Women Behind the Tales • Rediscovered Fiction • Eight Best-Selling Novelists • The Lure of Lurid Romance • Getting the Top Dollar • Beloved by Generations of Children • Twenty-one Black Women Who Write About Black Women • All About Men • Queens of Crime • "Cherchez la Femme"—to Catch the Murderer • By Women Published: Sixteen Feminist Publishing Houses in the United States • Magazine Women of the Nineteenth Century • Fourteen Magazine Women Today • Ms. Publisher • By the Script: Twenty-five Women Playwrights

XIV. *For Art's Sake*   239

Three Painters of Antiquity • Known for Their Needlework • Seven Precocious Painters • Académie Women • Uncovered at Last • Drawing from Life • At Their Side • At Easel • Six Revolutionary Artists of Russia • Personal Preference • A Scattering of Sculptors • Fourteen Model Women • Five "Virgins" Who Definitely Weren't • Five Early Collectors of Avant-Garde Art • Thirteen Who Founded Museums • On Top at the Museum • Drawing the Line • Sixteen Master Builders • Frances Benjamin Johnston and Her Feminine Colleagues • Fourteen Photographers

XV. *In the Money*   261

Dollar Princesses • Traveling in Style • Eight Big Spenders • Life of the Party • A List from One of Elsa Maxwell's Scavenger Hunt Parties • Cursed by the Hope Diamond • Nine Gifted Women • Charles Hamilton's List of Most Valuable Women's Autographs • And Nineteen Others • Lucky or Not? Six Widows Who Won the Lottery • Settled at Last

XVI. *Fads and Fashions*   271

Artifice on the Nile • What They Did for Beauty • Seven Undergarments That Changed the Female Form • Ten Beauty Aids That Probably Won't Come Back • Patching It Up • On a Nineteenth-Century Dressing Table • Do-It-Yourself Cosmetics • Seven Rules for Putting on Leg Make-up • Three Make-up Mavens • Trend Setters • Showing Off Fashion—Some Supermodels • Here She Comes—There She Goes: What Happened to Thirteen Miss Americas • It Happened at the Miss America Pageant • Interiors By • Eight Designing Women • In the Rag Game • Nine Fashions Named for Women • Arbiter of Beauty: Florenz Ziegfeld's Standards for Choosing a Ziegfeld Girl • Heartthrobs • No Life Without Rudy

XVII. *Inside and Outside the Law*   287

Firsts at the Bar • Making Legal History • In Justice • Decisions, Decisions • It's Legal—Twelve Laws, Statutes, and Ordinances • "Legal" Holidays · Three Pirates · Seven Bandits of the Old West · Murder Most Foul · The Sting · Six Most Wanted by the FBI · Five "Soap" Murders

XVIII. Victims 306

Sacrificed · Victims of Henry VIII · A Coven of Witches · A Field Hand's Life · Eight Who Were Captured by Indians · From Sweatshop to Death · Ten Who Fell from the Heights · Women: Addiction, Suicide, and Family Violence · A Variety of Victims · Unlucky in Love · Seven Victims Vindicated · Seven Held Hostage

XIX. What's in a Name? 320

A Rose by Every Other Name · The Soup Course · Select Dishes · Sweets and Desserts Named for Women · Our Town · Her Moccasins Trod Here · In Honor of the Queen · Nature Echoes Her Name · Bra-less · Choosing a Name for Baby · Nicknames for Her and Him · The Most Popular Girls' Names · How They Got Their Names · A.K.A. · Mad Monickers · They Gave Their Names · Getting Away from the Man · Himmicanes · Under a Woman's Name: Female Pseudonyms Used by Men · Under a Man's Name · No Married Name

XX. The Ballot—and Beyond 336

Ten American Foremothers · Four on the Continent · And Eight in England · Issuers of the Call for the Seneca Falls Convention of 1848 · Why Women Should Not Be Allowed to Vote · Jailed for the Vote · Carrie Chapman Catt's List of What It Took to Win the Vote · Where U.S. Women First Voted · Sixteen Countries Where Women First Voted · Countries That Last Gave Women the Vote · They Didn't Promise to Obey · Standing by Their Women: Eight Male Feminists of the Past · Alan Alda's Incomplete List of Today's Male Feminists · Asserting Rights Today · And Some in Other Lands · Is It Worth All This Trouble? Keeping Women Down · Women Pro Status Quo · Fighting Words from Women · Karen DeCrow's List of No Place to Go

XXI. In and Around Power 353

Nine Lands That Never Were and the Women Who Ruled Them · Ruling the Holy Land · African Queens · Women of Power in the Sixteenth Century · Modern Matri-Monarchs · Modern Nations Headed by Women · Fifteen Rulers Who Reigned for More than Thirty Years · Founding Mothers: Wives of the Signers of the Declaration of Independence · The Working Lives of Ten Presidents' Wives · Powers Behind the President · Eight Candidates for Highest Office · Legislative Record Setters · Ten Congressional Firsts · Three Actresses Elected to Congress · Unrepresentative Representation · Her Honor, the Mayor · Where the Mayors Were · Five Governors · And Seven Lieutenant Governors · Six Cabinet Secretaries · Forty-two in the Highest Councils · Sixteen International Women · In and Around Power in China · Evil in High Places

XXII.   Women of Faith   *379*

If God Were a Woman . . . · Patron Deities of China · The Women
in Jesus' Life · Prostitutes Who Became Saints · Eight Appearances
of the Virgin Mary · Six Worshiped Women · Chased, Chaste,
and Sainted · All in Order · Friendly Persuaders · Founders of
Faith · Where the Ministers Are · Firsts in the Pulpit · Almost a
Rabbi · My Daughter, the Rabbi · Three Cantors · Who Blew the Shofar? · Grouping for Converts · Seven Churches That Ordain Women · In
Priestly Garb · Six Faith Healers

XXIII.   Games Women Play   *401*

Seven Myths About Women Athletes · Four Demythologizers: Men Who
Studied Women Athletes · Having an Impact on Sport · Oh,
Babe! · Tops at Mid-century · Riding in the Money · Fillies at the Fin-
ish · Uplifting Women · Come Out Fighting · Court Style · Racquet
Bearers · Allison Danzig's List of All-Time Top-Ranking Women Tennis
Players · And Some More Recent Additions · Three Umps · Play
Ball! · Through the Hoop · Teeing Off · And Other Golf Women · Over
Track and Field · Speedsters · Cutting a Fine Figure · Water
Sports · Swimming the Distance · Jaws · Down to the Bare Essen-
tials · Record Breakers · Write in the Locker Room

XXIV.   Words of Wisdom—and Otherwise   *426*

Some Men's Opinions · Advice from the Men · From the Lips of Mae
West · Woman to Women · And What They Advised · Emily Post's
Women · Women Quoted in the First Edition of Bartlett's *Familiar
Quotations,* 1855 · Familiar Words from Unfamiliar Names · Womanly
Wisdom · Excuses, Excuses · The UN Declaration of Women's
Rights · Tombstone Reports: Thirteen Women's Epitaphs · Parting Re-
marks: What They Said Before They Died

XXV.   Honors   *440*

Preserved in Cement · The Most Honored Woman · Thirty Firsts for
Black Women · Awarded the Iron Cross · Outstanding—Ten Women
Who Received Radcliffe College's First Honorary Degrees · Recipients of
the American Psychological Association's Distinguished Scientific
Awards · Elected to the National Academy of Sciences · Commemorated
on U.S. Postage Stamps · Pulitzer Prize Winners · Nobel Prize Win-
ners · *Time*'s "Man" of the Year · Women of the 1970s · *Ms.* Magazine's
Women to Watch in the 1980s · "Busted" in the Hall of Fame · The
Women's Hall of Fame · Westminster Women · Capitol Women · Ven-
usians · National Parks · Recent Winners: A Miscellany

Bibliography   *457*

Index   *461*

*Illustrations will be found on pages 58–61, 116–19, 166–169, 235–238,
302–305, 349–352 and 397–400.*

Why We Wrote This Book

Several years ago, when we were compiling a book of quotations for young people, we noticed a strange phenomenon: only words of wisdom of male origin were, apparently, preserved in print. We had set no "quotas" for our sources, but we found it necessary to make a special effort to locate words written or spoken by women. Examination of the standard quotations books on the reference shelf dramatically confirmed our suspicions: the women had been left out. In every volume we analyzed, only five to seven percent of the "quotees" were women.

Thus, we were not surprised when a popular book of a few years ago contained only twenty lists relating to women. But we were appalled at the sexism of a book that could list male opera singers but not female opera singers, or could list only a single woman among the best actors of all time. So we decided to do something about it.

The result is this book. It celebrates women's accomplishments (for ill as well as good)—and they are many. The world has seen no lack of memorable women's work, but has recorded precious little of it. There is no shortage of women to be discovered, but it has not always been easy to find them. A lot of sleuthing, reading between the lines, tracking down tantalizing hints and slightest mentions, has made our research fun, exhausting, and ultimately rewarding.

Our research proved what we suspected—women have been everywhere, done everything, and in spite of obstacles have had a good time doing it. Most of the women we encountered were a pure joy to read about and write about. Their lives and deeds were fun for us to discover, as we hope they will be for our readers. To share our pleasure, the off-beat, the undeservedly obscure, and the zany, as well as the great and notable, are all included here.

Happily, our detective work showed our subject to be vast—so vast, in fact, that it has not been possible to "enlist" every woman whose name and achievements we discovered. Especially in the areas of literature, music, the visual arts, politics, sports, and the women's movement, it has not been possible to list more than a fraction of the accomplishers. Where there was a large group to select from, we chose a representation of those whose names and achievements were well known, and as many lesser known figures as we could, in recognition of their names and contributions. At least the subject is represented, if not every woman who contributed to its development. Therefore most of our lists are incomplete. Readers can add their own entries, as their special knowledge or the world's progress permits.

This is not a book of women's "firsts," although it contains many of them. "Firsts" can, we admit, become tiresome. But as long as firsts are still happening, they must be recorded. All of today's women are, in some ways, firsts—they are likely to be the first women in their families to do at least one of the following: complete high school or college, earn one or more graduate degrees, be fully self-supporting, have children and a job simultaneously, go back to school after raising a family, get divorced, live with a man without being married to him or live alone, enter a profession, travel widely, own property in their own names, buy themselves furs or jewelry, or go out unescorted in the evening—or all of the above, and more.

Hurdles still keep women from fully equal participation in most of the world's work. The more hurdles stand between women and a goal or activity, the more "firsts" there are to record when the walls are breached. We look forward to a day when it will no longer be necessary to tally the firsts, and when lists such as these will have only pleasantly nostalgic purpose. But until then, may these reminders of the accomplishments to date inspire those that are yet to come.

That includes our daughters, Claire Arbeiter and Nina J. Katz, who were an inspiration; Nina especially contributed useful ideas and points of view to the book as it progressed. Many others aided and encouraged us in this project, including Daniel and Peter Arbeiter. We particularly acknowledge Kenneth D. Schwartz and the late Robert Sonkin for their diligent assistance and unfailing support. We are indebted to those who compiled special lists for this book; acknowledgments accompany their contributions. Particular appreciation is due our agent Charlotte Sheedy, for nurturing this project from its formative stages on, and for her always wise counsel, and to her associates Barbara Held and Linda Nelson. It has been truly a pleasure to work with our editor, Neil Nyren, whose infallible good cheer and good sense resolved many a problem and smoothed many a paragraph. We thank also the entire staff at Atheneum for their thoroughness and professionalism, and our typist Nancy Perkus for her care with the manuscript. Our research was facilitated by the cooperative staffs and excellent reference collections of the New York Public Library, especially those of the Mid-Manhattan, Donnell Art, and Lincoln Center Theater and Music Divisions, the Leonia Public Library, and the Hackensack Public Library. We are especially grateful to the many relatives, friends, and acquaintances—too many to be acknowledged individually—whose expertise in a particular subject was always available to answer a question or make a useful suggestion of still another source to consult, another woman to add to our roster. And last but far from least, our appreciation goes to the supportive men in our private lives, our husbands Norman Weiser and Solomon Arbeiter.

Finally, our information is accurate, to the best of our belief, as of the period in which the research for this book was done, 1978 to mid-1980. Obviously, lives change—and if we had tried to do a last-minute check on everybody's vital statistics the manuscript would never have gotten off to the printer. If we have misplaced anybody's *curriculum vitae* we humbly beg pardon.

Marjorie P. K. Weiser
Jean S. Arbeiter
September, 1980

Womanlist

I ❧ OUT OF THE ORDINARY

FIRST WOMEN
❧

It all starts here . . .

Eve.♀ "And the rib, which the Lord God had taken from man, made he a woman, and brought her unto the man" (Genesis 2:22). Eve, of course, tempted Adam to eat the forbidden fruit, thus condemning humankind to toil and trouble. One wonders if Adam ever regretted losing . . .

Lilith, who, according to an ancient Jewish legend, was Adam's first wife and was created, as he was, from the dust of the earth. She fled from him, however, and refused to return, thus incurring this punishment: every day she stays away, one hundred of her demon children are destroyed. Seeking vengeance, Lilith haunts the earth, inflicting death and disease on human newborns.

Pandora was the first woman of the Greeks, but to her sterling qualities Zeus added one zinger: curiosity. Out of the pretty box the god had warned her *not* to tamper with flew all the plagues of humanity—and with them the tiny, fluttering Hope.

Embla came about because Ask, the first man of the Norse people, suffered, like other primary males, from too much solitude. Odin neatly solved his problem by creating Embla out of a piece of elm wood.

Mashyane was the first woman to be created in an equal-opportunity fashion. According to Persian (Zoroastrian) tradition, when the great god Gayomart was slain, his seed fertilized the earth where he died; forty years later a plant grew on that very spot, divided into two parts, and, presto, the first human couple: Mashyane and her husband, Mashye. They became the mother and father of all human beings.

Hine, the first woman in Polynesian tradition, was fashioned lovingly out of sand and clay by Tane, god of forests and birds. Overwhelmed by her beauty, Tane couldn't resist sleeping with his creation. When Hine realized that her husband was also her father, she fled in horror to the underworld and became its queen. This first act of forbidden love brought both the human race and death into the world.

Mbongwe first saw light when Sekume, the first Bantu man, took matters into his own hands. Finding himself mateless, he created a woman out of a tree.

♀ denotes names that appear in another list; consult index.

A FEW FOR THE RECORD BOOKS
❧

Jane Bunford of Great Britain was the tallest woman ever recorded, at 7 feet 11 inches, though a spinal curvature gave her an effective height of only 7 feet 7 inches. Bunford's hair also achieved the record length of 8 feet. She died at the age of twenty-seven in 1922.

Sandy Allen of Shelbyville, Indiana, is the world's tallest living woman, at 7 feet 7 inches. Allen, who wears size 22 shoes and weighs 440 pounds, stopped growing when she was twenty years old, following surgical removal of a pituitary gland tumor.

Flora Jackson, an American and the heaviest woman on record, reached a weight of 840 pounds before dying in 1965 at the age of thirty-five.

Deborah and *Susan Tripp,* who were exhibited at Peale's Museum in New York in 1829, may have been the heaviest little girls on record. Susan, just under six years of age, weighed 205 pounds, and her sister Deborah, age three, 125 pounds.

Lina Medina, a Peruvian girl, became the youngest mother ever recorded when she gave birth at the age of five. Medina was so young she thought her infant was a doll and played with it.

Alice Stevenson (1861–1973), of Great Britain, aged 112 years, 39 days, is one of many women for whom claims of greatest longevity have been made. The *Guinness Book of World Records* lists nineteen women among twenty-eight authenticated cases of extremely old, old age.

Khfaf Lasuria, though her age is *not* authenticated, is a Soviet Georgian reputed to be at least 130 years old. She won the title of "Farm's Fastest Tea Picker" when she was 100.

Princess Alice, Countess of Athlone, set a different record in 1979: at ninety-six, she had lived longer than any member of Britain's royal family since the Norman Conquest in 1066.

The wife of Tai, an ancient Chinese noblewoman, is probably the world's most perfectly preserved woman. Discovered by a 1973 archaeological expedition, she was found to be in tiptop condition 2,100 years after her burial. She now reposes in a glass display case, on exhibit in the Changsha Museum in China.

SHORT PEOPLE
Twenty Women 5 Feet 3 Inches and Under
❧

Clara Barton,♀ founder of the American Red Cross.

Elizabeth Blackwell,♀ the first woman to get a medical degree in the United States.

Susan Bokonyi, vaudeville dancer, all 3 feet 4 inches of her; in December 1979, at one hundred years of age, she weighed 37 pounds and was still making all her own clothes.

Margery Brown, a pioneer woman pilot who made a two-year flight around the world in the 1930s with an extension on her plane's rudder bar and seated on a large cushion; Brown was 4 feet 11 inches tall.

Mercy Bump, wife of Tom Thumb, 32 inches tall and weighing 29 pounds.

Sarah Caldwell,♀ orchestra conductor.

Nellie Cashman,♀ prospector of the Old West.
Sally Field
Debbie Lawler,♀ stunt woman and racing-car driver.
Brenda Lee,♀ pop singer.
Anita Loos,♀ writer.
Princess Margaret Rose of Great Britain.
Bette Midler
Marilyn Miller,♀ musical comedy star of the 1920s.
Carmen Miranda
Annie Oakley♀
Edith Piaf
Dolly Parton♀
Ida Rosenthal,♀ founder of the Maidenform brassiere company.
Mae West♀

NINETEEN EARLY STARTERS

✹

Maria Agnesi,♀ the eighteenth-century Italian mathematician, published a
   discourse in defense of higher education for women when she was only
   nine years old.
Daisy Ashford wrote a novel, *The Young Visiters* (*sic*), in 1891 at the age of
   nine. Her tale of society, with an introduction by Sir James M. Barrie,
   was published in 1919 to critical acclaim.
Gwendolyn Brooks,♀ the Pulitzer Prize–winning black poet, published her
   first collection of verse, *American Childhood,* when she was thirteen.
Wang Tuan, a nineteenth-century Chinese poet, is said to have begun reading in infancy and started writing verse at the age of seven.
Elizabeth Taylor♀ not only was a child star, but also, at thirteen, wrote and
   illustrated *Nibbles and Me,* an account of her adventures with a pet
   chipmunk.
Deanna Durbin was signed for the movies in 1935 when she was thirteen; her
   youthful trilling in *100 Men and a Girl* and other successes soon lifted
   Universal Pictures out of the red.
Patty Duke achieved Broadway stardom at thirteen, playing Helen Keller♀
   in *The Miracle Worker* in 1959.
Tatum O'Neal became the youngest person ever to win an Oscar, in 1974 for
   Paper Moon, at the age of ten.
Judy Garland♀ was fourteen when she sang "You Made Me Love You" in
   Broadway Melody of 1938.
Janis Ian became a pop star at thirteen when she wrote and recorded "So-
   ciety's Child"; she had thought of the song while waiting for an ap-
   pointment with her high school guidance counselor.
Petulia Clark, an English pop star, had her own BBC show, "Pet's Parlour,"
   in 1943 when she was eleven.
Philippa Duke Schuyler had written more than 200 musical compositions by
   the time she was fourteen in 1946.
Tracy Austin began playing tennis at the age of two, was the subject of a
   cover story for *World Tennis* magazine by the time she was four, and
   played on her first tennis tour in 1977 at the age of fourteen.

Nadia Comaneci, the Rumanian gymnast, was fourteen when she scored three perfect scores of 10 in the 1976 Olympics.

Joy Foster became Jamaica's singles and mixed doubles table tennis champion at the age of eight.

Karen Muir, who broke the world's record for the 100-meter backstroke with a time of 1 minute, 8.7 seconds, at the age of twelve, was the youngest person to ever make or break an athletic record.

Angelica Kauffman,♀ painter of the eighteenth century, was famous for her accomplishments by the time she was eleven.

Clara Petacci began to bombard Italian dictator Benito Mussolini with love letters in 1926, when she was fourteen. "Duce, my life is yours," gushed the teen-ager. Seven years later she became his mistress.

And the all-time early starter: *Shirley Temple* was Hollywood's curly-topped favorite by the age of *three.*

FIVE BEARDED LADIES

Annie Jones, who appeared with Barnum and Bailey from childhood on, had a beard measuring 2 inches.

Grace Gilbert grew whiskers 6 inches long.

Josephine Boisdechene, also known as *Madame Fortune Clofullia,* had a beard of 8 inches, but no mustache. P. T. Barnum also displayed her hairy infant son, called the "infant Esau."

Lady Olga (née *Jane Barnell*) had a mustache, and a beard of 13½ inches. Her career as a sideshow performer lasted longer than that of any other American woman.

Jane Deveree wore the longest beard of all the bearded ladies. According to the *Guinness Book of World Records,* it measured 14 inches.

Their bearded state did not limit the desirability of these five. Most were married, Lady Olga four times.

AND TWO SAINTS WITH THE SAME ATTRIBUTE

St. Galla, young and wealthy, was widowed after one year of marriage. Despite the warnings of the physicians of sixth-century Rome that if she did not remarry she would grow a beard, Galla consecrated her life to God and service to the poor.

St. Wilgeforte or *Vigiforte,* also known as *St. Liberta* or *St. Uncumber,* betrothed against her will to a pagan, prayed to her Christian God to disfigure her in some way so that she would not be attractive to men. A beard grew on her chin. Her lover, revolted, rejected her as she had hoped, and her irate father had her crucified. It's easy to understand why, under the name of St. Uncumber, she has received the prayers of women eager to be free of their husbands.

FIFTEEN ONE AND ONLY ONES

꙰

Berengaria was the only English queen who never visited Britain while she was its ruler. A Spanish princess wed to Richard I, she awaited his return from the Crusades, then joined him in another foreign war, staying with him until his death in 1199.

Vannozza Dei Catanei ♀ may have been the only woman in history to watch her lover sworn in as pope. Catanei was in the audience when her paramour, Rodrigo Borgia, became Pope Alexander VI in 1492.

Elizabeth St. Leger is believed to be the only woman ever initiated into the Freemasons. As a teen-ager she accidentally witnessed a Masonic initiation and was discovered. Her quick-thinking father, Lord Doneraile, saved his daughter from death by swearing her into the order; her portrait used to hang on the wall of almost every Masonic lodge in Ireland. She died in 1775 at the age of eighty.

Mary Walker ♀ was the only woman to win the U.S. Medal of Honor, for her services as a surgeon in the Fifty-second Ohio Regiment during the Civil War. It was presented to her in 1865, three years after the medal was first awarded, by President Andrew Johnson.

Phoebe A. Hanaford ♀ was the only woman minister (ordained 1868) known to have officiated at her own daughter's wedding.

Marie Curie ♀ was the only woman to win the Nobel Prize twice (in 1903 for physics and in 1911 for chemistry). When her older daughter, *Irène Joliot-Curie,* ♀ won the Nobel Prize for chemistry in 1935, the pair became the only mother-daughter Nobel-winning combination.

Lady Evelyn Carnarvon (Beauchamp) was the only woman member of the small band of Egyptologists who entered the tomb of King Tutankhamen when it was opened in November 1922. Her father, the expedition's enthusiastic sponsor Lord Carnarvon, died a few months later of a mysterious mosquito bite, but Lady Evelyn avoided "King Tut's curse."

Mary Campbell of Columbus, Ohio, was the only contestant to win the Miss America contest twice (1922 and 1923).

Jeannette Rankin ♀ was the only member of Congress to vote against the nation's entry into both world wars (April 6, 1919, and December 8, 1941).

Grace Kelly (now Princess of Monaco) is the only film actress ever honored on a postage stamp. The Principality of Monaco issued the commemorative stamp to honor her 1956 marriage to Prince Rainier. It could be purchased only on the day of that event.

Janet Guthrie was, in 1977, the only woman racing driver ever to take part in the Indianapolis 500. She was not assigned a car until shortly before the race was to begin. Keeping secret a broken wrist, she went the distance and finished in eighth place.

Mary Shane, the only woman play-by-play announcer in the major leagues, broadcasts for the Chicago White Sox.

Susan B. Anthony ♀ in 1979 was the first real woman, as opposed to Lady Liberty, to be honored by having her image on a United States coin. The honor turned to ashes within weeks, however, as public acceptance of the dollar proved nil, earning it the title "Susan B. Edsel."

Bette Davis ♀ is the only woman to date to receive the lifetime achievement

Award of the American Film Institute. Other honorees are John Ford, Orson Welles, Alfred Hitchcock, William Wyler, James Stewart, James Cagney, and Henry Fonda.

FOUR MONUMENTS TO DEVOTION

The Hanging Gardens of Babylon, rising from 75 to 100 feet and rated as the second wonder of the ancient world, were built by Nebuchadnezzar about 600 B.C. to please his queen, *Amuhia.*

The Taj Mahal, completed in 1650 in Agra, India, was built as a monument to a perfect love by Shah Jahan when his wife of nineteen years, *Mumtaz Mahal,* died. More than 20,000 laborers quarried the building materials used in its construction.

The Eleanor Crosses were constructed by England's King Edward I in memory of his first wife, *Eleanor of Castile,*♀ who died in 1290. The enormous crosses were set up at each of the twelve places from Lincoln to Charing Cross where her body rested on its way to entombment in Westminster Abbey.

Coit Tower was built by the City of San Francisco when philanthropist *Lillie Hitchcock Coit*♀ left half of her estate to her beloved city upon her death at eighty-three in 1924. She had been a fire buff for almost seventy years—and the landmark tower is shaped like the nozzle of a fire hose.

EIGHT WHO WERE NOT WHAT THEY CLAIMED

Caraboo, Princess of Javasu. In 1817 the English public was agog with news of an exotic-looking woman who had turned up claiming to be Caraboo, Princess of the island of Javasu, off the coast of Sumatra. The "princess" conversed in an unknown tongue and was so convincing that distinguished scholars undertook to "decipher" her language, and she became a darling of society. Eventually she was identified as *Mary Baker,* the daughter of a Devonshire cobbler, who, trying to raise money for passage to America, had hit upon this scheme for attracting both attention and cash. Years later Baker turned up again trying to exhibit herself for one shilling a customer. She ended her days selling leeches to hospitals and drugstores.

The Tutbury Marvel. Anne Moore, a resident of the small English town of Tutbury, claimed, in 1807, that she lived entirely without food. Several "experts" were sent to examine her, and they authenticated her unique claim. Hundreds flocked to see the phenomenon, and in the course of two years Moore collected 250 pounds. Suspicions abounded, however, and in 1813 another "committee," observing her closely, noted that she soon was "suffering from want" and rapidly losing weight. The exhausted Moore finally confessed that for the past six years her daughter had been slipping her small bits of sustenance.

A royal princess. Olive Serres, landscape painter to the Prince of Wales, came up with a claim that was to shake the throne of England. Serres asserted that her grandfather had been secretly married to the sister of a Polish count who later became King of Poland, and that her mother had likewise secretly married the Duke of Cumberland, brother of King George III—putting Serres in line to the throne. When the matter finally came to trial in 1866, however, all the documents the family had carefully assembled turned out to be forgeries and the jury turned down their claim. The fraud and its execution took years of labor on Olive Serres's part; it was to be the great work of her life.

George Washington's nurse. Joice Heth, an aged slave, was claiming to be 161 years old and to have been George Washington's nursemaid when P. T. Barnum spotted her in an "exhibit" in Philadelphia in 1835. He bought her for $1,000, half of it borrowed, and embarked on his career as a master huckster. Heth survived only one year of such show biz and, upon her death, was found to have been not more than 80.

Producer of ectoplasm. Marthe Béraud, under the pseudonym "Eva C," worked as a medium during the early 1900s. Béraud claimed that she was able to create ectoplasm, but examination by the Society for Psychical Research in 1920 showed she produced it by regurgitating paper and fabric—a good enough feat in itself.

The German countess. Mary Clay slipped away from her New England home in 1907 at the age of fourteen and surfaced years later as Marguerite von Graff, the daughter of Countess von Graff, who lived in "Donna Castle" in the Blitzen Mountains of Germany. Before an old classmate unmasked her, Clay amassed a fortune from starry-eyed young men who loved to be around royalty. The masquerade over, she returned to America, where she lived quite nicely on her profits.

Anastasia, Princess of Russia. "Fräulein Unknown" was the name hospital authorities gave to an emaciated young woman dragged from the Landwehr Canal in Berlin in 1920. Because she seemed to be an amnesiac, the frail creature was placed in a mental institution. Two years later, she broke a long silence and claimed to be the Princess Anastasia, the only living child of Czar Nicholas II of Russia. Despite several books, plays, and movies written about her, however, her claim was never officially substantiated, and 10 million pounds still wait in the vault of an English bank for the legitimate heir of the Romanovs.

The daughter of a French king. In 1920 ***Opal Whitely*** brought five cardboard boxes, containing a million tiny pieces of paper, to the offices of *Atlantic Monthly* magazine, claiming they contained a diary she had written at the age of five, whose pages had been torn by a sister in a fit of jealousy. In nine months she pieced together the 150,000-word story of a strange existence as the secret daughter of the last French king, with details of her life growing up in the logging camps of Oregon. When the diary was published, the precocity of its language and ideas led to questions about its validity. Its author disappeared, sending back word that she was variously a maharani in India and the wife of the Prince of Wales. Eventually her cover was blown, and she ended her days in a mental institution.

ANYTHING FOR A LAUGH

※

Lillie Langtry.♀ Her friends always had to be on the lookout for gags from the elegant "Jersey Lily." Once she filled a chamber pot with ink and fixed it over the door so that it would fall on her husband's head as he walked in.

Maria Jeritza. As Tosca, the opera star was required to stab the villain with a dagger. One night she substituted a ripe banana, and by the time the curtain fell, her victim was thoroughly covered with the fruit. His comments were not recorded.

The Duchess of Marlborough. Consuelo Vanderbilt's mother-in-law would slip slices of soap between the cheeses she served at her dinner parties. She guessed, correctly, that her well-born guests would rather eat the stuff than demonstrate bad manners by spitting it out.

Mame Thurber. The mother of humorist James Thurber was a renowned practical joker. In her sixties, she went to visit a friend she had not seen for thirty years. The plan was for Mrs. Thurber to wear a red rose so that the friend could identify her at the railroad station. When Mrs. Thurber arrived, she noticed a woman about twenty years older asleep on a bench, pinned the rose on the sleeping woman, and stepped back to watch the action. The friend arrived, stared in disbelief, and shook the old woman until she awoke. "Why, Mame Thurber," said she to the uncomprehending stranger, "how are you? You look marvelous!"

Carole Lombard.♀ One of the most persistent practical jokers in Hollywood, Lombard particularly enjoyed placing department store mannequins in the beds of assorted prominent men in the film colony. Only Carole had the imagination and energy to serve guests at a black-tie party out of bedpans; fill her house with hay and wear pigtails when entertaining at another formal dinner; and show up at a party on a stretcher with an ambulance in attendance. She also, after husband Clark Gable flopped in the film biography *Parnell,* had "Parnell" stickers made, which she plastered on his food, clothes, and books—as well as on what his secretary termed "unexpected places."

Kathleen Norris. The novelist was staring in a Fifth Avenue window when she recognized another writer, Frank Sullivan, edging up and preparing to goose her. Thinking fast, Norris whirled about, shouting, "Not one penny more! You and your family have had all the money you'll ever get out of me! I've given you everything I have—and still you hound me for more!" Overwhelmed by the stares of the crowd, her victim fled.

Tallulah Bankhead.♀ Arriving at a society party accompanied by a distinguished-looking black man, Bankhead introduced him as Dr. Bechet, Albert Einstein's most valued assistant at Princeton. For some time her companion effectively parried questions about relativity, before finally producing a soprano saxophone and starting to play. He was jazz musician Sidney Bechet.

MISSING PERSONS

———————————————————— ❧ ————————————————————

Anna Fellows left her husband, William S. Fellows, in 1879 after three years of marriage. One day twenty years later, he returned home to find Mrs. F. in the kitchen, nonchalantly preparing dinner. Fellows, who must have been a model of taciturnity, asked no questions, and his wife volunteered no answers. She stayed at home in Cambridge, Massachusetts, for another three years before vanishing forever in 1903.

Grace Martin Perkins, a New England socialite, vanished without a trace in 1898, and a few months later her distraught parents identified a murder victim as their daughter. In the midst of an elaborate funeral, the "deceased" burst into the chapel and angrily berated her parents for making her a laughingstock. She had run off to get married, she revealed, and now her honeymoon was ruined.

Dorothy Harriet Camille Arnold left her Manhattan mansion on December 12, 1910, wearing an enormous "Baker hat," a popular chapeau of the day. A friend spotted her at Brentano's on Twenty-seventh Street, and that was the last anyone ever saw of Dorothy Arnold. The outwardly prim and proper New York heiress was involved in a secret love affair with the scion of an old Boston family. Her lover, the newshounds, and the Pinkertons her father hired for $100,000 never turned up her trail. Reports that she had been seen in more than a hundred cities all proved false. The most common theory, that Arnold had been done in by a quack abortionist, remained just that. The "girl in the Baker hat" was never found. The publicity given to her disappearance inspired a young English woman, *Agatha Christie,*⁹ to consider writing mysteries. Later in her career, Christie too would be a missing person.

*Aimee Semple McPherson,*⁹ who called herself "the world's most pulchritudinous evangelist," was at the height of her million-dollar career when she vanished from the beach at Carmel, California, on May 18, 1926. Sister Aimee presided over a $1.5-million "Temple" in Echo Park, California; a $75,000 radio station; 400 branch churches; and 178 missionary stations. For five weeks ransom notes trickled in; then on June 23, 1926, McPherson was discovered sleeping in Agua Prieta, Mexico. She told a tale of abduction and escape, but police were skeptical because Kenneth G. Ormiston, Sister Aimee's radio operator *and* a married man, had disappeared on the same day as his employer and had been spotted with an unidentified woman in hotel rooms all over California. McPherson and her mother were indicted for fraud, but the charges were eventually dismissed for lack of evidence.

Agnes Tufverson was a successful corporation lawyer who fell madly in love with Captain Ivan Poderjay, a dashing Yugoslav officer. After they wed, she withdrew the $25,000 in her savings account. On December 20, 1933, the honeymooners took a taxi to the pier where they were to board the *Hamburg* for Europe. Agnes Tufverson was never seen again. Two days later, Poderjay sailed on the *Olympic,* alone. Investigation showed the captain to be an experienced bigamist with wives in several countries. He was extradited from Austria to the United States, convicted of bigamy, and sent to Sing Sing for seven years, but he never revealed what, if anything, he had done with Agnes Tufverson.

Amelia Earhart,[9] the noted aviator, vanished on July 2, 1937, in the midst of a flight around the world. Recent evidence suggests that she may have been on a spy mission over Japanese territory. Some think that a young woman captured on Saipan in 1937, taken to Japan, and executed as a spy was Earhart. After her disappearance, her husband, George Putnam, opened a letter she had left with him to be read in the event of her death. "Please know that I am quite aware of the hazards," she wrote. "I want to do it—because I want to do it."

Dorothy Forstein received a telephone call on October 18, 1950, from her husband, Philadelphia magistrate Jules Forstein, telling her he'd be home late. "Be sure to miss me!" murmured his wife, in words that turned out to be prophetic. Later that night when Forstein returned home, his children reported that they had seen a strange man enter Mommy's bedroom, pick her up, and carry her off, remarking enigmatically, "Your mommy has been sick, but she will be all right now." There were no clues whatsoever. Dorothy Forstein is still a missing person.

NINE PROPHETIC DREAMERS

꙳

Queen Maya suspected her son's future greatness even before becoming pregnant because she dreamed that he entered her womb in the form of a white elephant. Later she gave birth to the Buddha in an early example of painless childbirth. The queen was standing in a garden, holding a branch of the saka tree in her right hand, when the infant emerged from her right side with nary a contraction. Seven days later the new mother died of joy.

Calpurnia, wife of Julius Caesar, begged him not to go to the Roman Senate the day after she dreamed that his statue, in Shakespeare's words, "like a fountain with a hundred spouts did run pure blood, and many lusty Romans came smiling and did bathe their hands in it." Needless to say, Caesar ignored her.

Arlette Fulbert was an innocent seventeen-year-old peasant girl when Duke Robert of Normandy spotted her and carried her off to his castle for a wild night of passion. Arlette conceived a child and, with the coming of dawn, dreamed that a giant tree grew out of her body. Its branches covered not only Normandy, but England, too. Years later, her son, the ruler of France, successfully invaded England in 1066 and became known as William the Conqueror.

Eleanor of Aquitaine was distressed when Thomas Agnell, Archdeacon of Wells, came to see her. She told him of a disturbing dream: her son Henry was lying on a couch, his hands folded together, the crown of England glittering on his head, and a second crown, composed of eerie light, framing his pale face. Agnell, whose mission was to inform the queen of her son's death, sadly confirmed the accuracy of her dream.

Marie d'Avignon, as the fourteenth century drew to a close, dreamed of arms and armor that were meant not for her but for "a maid who should restore France." In January 1412 Joan of Arc⁹ was born.

Mrs. W. M. Stoney received a telegram from her soldier son during World War II. "Coming home on leave," it said, and instructed her to meet him at London's Charing Cross Station the next evening. That night in a dream, Mrs. S. saw her son coming out of a telephone booth in what was clearly Waterloo Station. Trusting her dream, she went to Waterloo instead of Charing Cross and found her son emerging from that very phone booth.

Mrs. Joe McDonald. Why had she begun to dream incessantly about a high school friend she had not seen or thought about since 1954, almost twenty years earlier? Disturbed, McDonald wrote to her friend's hometown, scrawling "please forward" on the envelope. Soon she heard from the amazed friend. At the very time of the dreams, the woman had been in the hospital, hovering between life and death.

Thora B. Filkins in 1970 wrote to psychic investigator Dennis Bardens of an unusual dream that had taken place years earlier. The night before she was to take a New York State Regents examination, she dreamed every question, word for word, that would appear on the test. Her dream turned out to be so accurate she got a grade of 96 percent and was first in her class. Several decades later she was still wondering: "Did I cheat?"

Jean Jones dreamed of the numbers 7, 3, and 6 on a Saturday night in 1979 and gave her husband, John, $12 to take to Cincinnati's River Downs race track the next day. Following her dream, he put $6 on three long shots in the tenth race trifecta—and won $64,654. Said Mr. Jones, "I should have known she was going to hit, because she never gives me any money to take to the track."

ELEVEN SEERS AND PSYCHICS

❧

The woman of Endor. King Saul may have regretted asking her the outcome of his impending battle with the Philistines. She predicted defeat for his forces and death for himself and his three sons—and so it happened.

Pythia, the Oracle at Delphi. For more than a thousand years, hers was the human voice through which the god Apollo answered the questions of travelers. Pythia, played by a succession of women, would go into a trance and speak for the god, in tones presumed to be his. At first the oracle was a young virgin from a noble family, but after Delphi was shaken by the scandal of a Pythia being seduced by a handsome Thessalonian, the minimum age went up to fifty. The oracle's record was supposedly infallible from the time of Croesus through the Persian Wars, but because she did not speak ordinary Greek, priests had to translate her words. If things didn't work out, the client was told that there had been an error in translation.

The Druid priestesses. The daughters of the Druid priests of Gaul were gifted with second sight and could make themselves invisible or take on animal forms. How they did it was a dark secret that few cared to probe deeply. It was a Druid priestess who foresaw defeat for Vercingetorix, leader of the Gauls. "The eagles with golden claws [the Romans]," she intoned, "will eat the brains of our people. . . ."

Paranazin. The sister of the Aztec emperor Montezuma habitually dropped off into cataleptic trances. This had its risks—she was once presumed dead and nearly buried alive. More often she emerged with important news. She forecast the arrival of an army of foreign ships that would conquer the empire, a prophecy that came true when the Spanish invaded Mexico in 1519.

Ursula ("Mother") Shipton.♀ In the fifteenth century this seer accurately foretold events in the reigns of future kings James I, Charles I, and Charles II. Shipton was not consistently on target, however, so her prediction that the world will end in 1991 need not be cause for alarm.

Eilley Orrum. The Washoe Seeress was the leading citizen of Virginia City, Nevada, in the boom days of the 1850s. She was able to predict what everyone in those parts wanted to know: where the next strikes would be made. Orrum advised two brothers against going to one site, saying, "I see the earth full of yellow to the north but there is blood on it. Be careful." They did not heed her words and both met violent accidental deaths. A year later gold was discovered on that very spot, which became world famous a short time afterward as the Comstock Lode when vast silver deposits were found there. Orrum herself became fabulously wealthy.

Mollie Fancher. Blind, bedridden, and schizoid (she had six distinct personalities), this woman did a thriving business in prophecy from the bedroom of her Brooklyn home. Between 1865 and 1904, close to 50,000 people came there to consult her about the future. Before leaving the premises, clients were directed to a gift shop on the first floor of the house where Fancher, who never missed a trick, maintained a thriving memorabilia concession.

Hester Dowden. She claimed that the messages she took down in "automatic writing" came directly from the dead. Among the spirits who favored her with their confidences in the early twentieth century were the victims of the *Titanic* and the *Lusitania,* as well as the ever lively Oscar Wilde.

Jeanne Scruggs. Prisoners who tried to escape from the small southern prison camp where her husband was warden didn't stand a chance. Between 1926 and 1946 the warden's wife anticipated at least a dozen breakouts.

Frances ("Frankie") Garcia. A visit to Frankie could be as good as a trip to the bank for the medium's clients, who often learned where unexpected treasures were stashed. Rebecca G. Dulzaides, a Galveston, Texas, widow whose husband had died in 1960, went to see Garcia in 1964 seeking business advice. The medium came up with the following message from the late Mr. D.: "There is property. Sixty-three lots and twelve acres. See lawyer tomorrow." Dulzaides rummaged through his old papers, found a lawyer's card, and collected the deeds that were indeed waiting for her.

Jeanne Dixon. She became a consulting psychic at the age of nine, when she told a discouraged Marie Dressler♀ that she would soon become a movie star. Dixon warned Carole Lombard♀ against plane travel a few weeks before the actress's death in an air crash and foretold the deaths of Franklin Roosevelt, John Kennedy, and Dag Hammarskjöld. Once, when a doubter defied Dixon to pick the winning ticket in a car raffle, she selected the right one, a 14,000-to-1 chance. Among Dixon's predictions for the 1980s: a war in which Asian and African nations will be pitted against the People's Republic of China.

THE SECOND TIME AROUND?

Joan Grant, an English woman born in 1907, believed that she was the reincarnation of Sakeeta, the wife of an Egyptian pharaoh. While on an expedition to the Middle East with her husband, she became convinced that in her earlier incarnation she had dwelled near the ruins of Nefertiti's palace. She published *Winged Pharaoh,* Sakeeta's biography, claiming that it was a reminiscence and not fiction.

Theda Bara,♀ vamp of the silent movies, insisted that she had actually lived before as the serpent of the Nile: "I live Cleopatra, I breathe Cleopatra, I am Cleopatra."

Ruth Simmons is the pseudonym given by hypnotist Morey Bernstein to a patient who, under hypnosis, revealed exact details of the life of Bridey Murphy, an Irish woman who died in 1864. As Murphy, Simmons referred to villages in Ireland so small that they are not on any maps and are known only to local residents—and Simmons had never been to Ireland. She recalled that her husband had purchased foodstuffs from a greengrocer named John Carrigan. A Belfast librarian investigated and found that there had been a John Carrigan with a grocery business at the right address. This and similarly accurate details persuaded Bernstein that Simmons was really Bridey.

Shanta Devi, who lived in Delhi, India, started talking at the age of three about a husband she had once had in the town of Madura, some one hundred miles away. As she grew older, she identified herself as Lugdi, a young Madura housewife who died after the birth of her first child. Lugdi's husband was still alive, and when they met Devi gave him accurate details of their former life together; the interview left him in tears. European and American psychiatrists studied Devi in the early 1960s. One of them, Dr. Ian Stevenson, concluded that she was a genuine case of supernatural reincarnation, one of the forty or so he had authenticated out of hundreds examined.

LOIS GOULD'S LIST OF WOMEN "WHOSE ENDINGS I MOST ENVY"

Amelia Earhart♀ disappeared into mists of legend.
Margaret Mead♀ strode into history at a ripe young age.
Catherine the Great♀ was crushed in passion by a four-footed lover.

Mrs. Isidor Straus ♀ refused a place in a lifeboat to go down on the *Titanic*
with the man she loved.

Virgin Mary ♀ went directly to heaven without really dying.

As for fictional heroines, my favorite exit is that of Marlene Dietrich's ♀
Mata Hari ♀ in *Dishonored.* Refusing the traditional blindfold, she checks
her mirror image, smiles radiantly at her all-male firing squad, and out, in a
blaze of bullets.

Exclusively for *Womanlist*

II ❦ *WHAT'S THE DIFFERENCE?*

SOME DIFFERENCES BETWEEN EVE AND ADAM

❦

- Odds favor the conception of a male and the birth of a male. About 120 males are conceived for every 100 females, and about 105 boy babies are born for every 100 girl babies. But only 103.5 twin boys are born for every 100 twin girls, and 98 triplet boys for every 100 triplet girls.
- Girl babies smile more often than boy babies. And they keep on smiling more, too.
- Adam's rib went a long way: a woman's pelvis is 2 inches wider on the average than that of a man. But men have more blood cells than women, their hearts and other muscles are heavier, and they have larger skulls and brains, also on average. However, there is no evidence that their brains are different in structure and capability.
- Because their lungs and tracheas are larger, most men have greater respiratory capacity than women. Men average 16 breaths per minute, 4 to 6 fewer than most women. Men's pulse rates are also slower, averaging 72 beats per minute compared to 80 for women.
- Women live longer than men. More male than female babies die at birth, and more males die in each succeeding year of life. By age 65 there are only about 7 men to every 10 women. In 1978 life expectancy for men in the United States was 69 years compared to 76.7 years for women, according to the National Center for Health Statistics. (The odds are a little better in Hawaii, where male life expectancy is 73.6 years, female 79.4, the highest in the nation. The lowest life expectancies for both men and women are found in Washington, D.C.: 65.7 for men, 75.3 for women.)
- Women are affected by alcoholic beverages more rapidly than men are.
- More women than men are knock-kneed.
- And women generally:
  - have better manual dexterity
  - are less physically active
  - start to talk earlier
  - have fewer speech problems
  - learn to read earlier
  - note details more carefully
  - learn modern (but not ancient) languages more easily

17

- respond more accurately to shape and color
- are more sensitive to loud sounds
- get higher test scores in grammar, spelling, and language skills
- express their emotions more readily, and
- respond more compassionately to the emotions of others
  than do boys and men.

- In a review of more than 2,000 studies of behavioral and intellectual differences between males and females, Eleanor Emmons Maccoby and Carol Nagy Jacklin, in *The Psychology of Sex Differences,* found:
  - only one area of female superiority: verbal ability
  - three clear areas of male superiority: aggressiveness, visual-spatial coordination, and mathematics ability
  - eight areas in which men and women are considered to be different, but in which there are actually no significant distinctions: sociability, self-esteem, ability to learn by rote, suggestibility, motivation for achievement, analytic ability, responsiveness to visual or auditory stimuli, and susceptibility to genetic or environmental influence.

PASSING IT ON

- All the differences between males and females start from one chromosome. Females have two X chromosomes, males have one X and one much smaller Y. At the moment of conception, the female parent contributes one X chromosome; the male parent, either an X or a Y. Thus, *he* determines the gender of the offspring.
- Until six weeks after conception, all embryos look alike; then testes begin to develop in the male embryo. After twelve weeks, ovaries begin to develop in the female.
- An ovum is 90,000 times larger than a sperm. At birth, a baby girl's ovaries contain 2 million egg follicles, but most of them will not become ova. At puberty there are only about 300,000 left, still many times more than the 300 to 400 ova released during a woman's reproductive lifetime.
- A woman releases only one ovum a month, whereas a man releases hundreds of millions of sperm in every ejaculation. A mature ovum is 1/175 inch in diameter; a sperm is 1/500 inch in length.

HEALTH PROBLEMS—FOR WOMEN ONLY

The National Foundation for Women's Health has been established by Dr. Robert E. Cooke, president of the Medical College of Pennsylvania, to sponsor research on health problems of women, because women are not simply men with different sex organs. "In every cell of the body, the female has a different chromosomal structure, a different amount even of DNA than the male," says Dr. Cooke. He adds, "On top of that comes a large amount of psychological and psychosocial difference as the genetic material interacts with the environment."

The following conditions are more prevalent in women than in men:

Diabetes.

Anorexia nervosa. Only 2 percent of those afflicted with this psychological starvation syndrome are males.

Pellagra. Although no longer a significant disease in the United States, in its heyday at least twice as many women as men died of this niacin-deficiency disease every year from 1920 to 1960, nearly 60,000 women versus 25,000 men.

Osteoporosis, a weakened bone condition, is particularly prevalent in women of middle and older age.

Iron-deficiency anemia, while not as widespread as the television commercials would have us believe, is quite common in women, especially during childbearing years.

Obesity. Four and a half million American women are 50 percent or more overweight, but only 2.5 million men are 30 percent or more overweight.

Depression. Women are from two to six times more likely to suffer from and seek medical attention for depression.

But men are more likely than women to suffer from bronchial asthma, gastric ulcer, gout, hepatitis, and tuberculosis. They also are more likely to get coronary heart disease and to die of cancer.

BE-SWITCHED

In 1976 alone, one thousand people were estimated to have switched gender through a combination of surgery and chemotherapy. Four out of every five persons who seek sex-change operations are born male. A few of the better-known cases:

Christine Jorgensen, born George W. Jorgensen. News of his sex-change operation in Copenhagen in 1952 created a world-wide sensation, even though Jorgensen was not the first to have such surgery. The Bronx-born youth had served in the army and was twenty-six when he underwent five major operations, one minor operation, and 2,000 hormone injections. Because of the resulting publicity, Jorgensen was able to build a moderately successful nightclub act. Twenty-seven years after the operation, she lives in semiretirement in California and says she has no regrets.

Jan Morris, born James Morris. A noted English author and foreign correspondent whose life had leaned toward the adventurous, Morris had belonged to a "fine regiment" in the army and took part in the first successful assault on Mount Everest. Although a father, he had long been uncomfortable as a man. "I was three or perhaps four years old when I realized that I had been born into the wrong body and should really be a girl." At the age of forty-five, with his wife's blessing, he started the long medical procedures. She is now writing as Jan, whose first book was an account of her transformation entitled *Conundrum.*

Renee Richards, born Richard Raskind, a New York ophthalmologist, husband, father, and nationally ranked amateur in men's tennis, who changed his sex in 1974. As Renee, Richards wanted to continue playing pro tennis, but the U.S. Tennis Association demanded she take a chromosome test until a New York State court judged this requirement discriminatory and ordered Richards admitted to tournament play. She finished the 1977 season ranking tenth in earnings among professional women tennis players.

Elizabeth Eden, born Ernest Aron. Aron was so desperate for a sex change that his boyfriend, John Wojtowicz, held up a Brooklyn bank one summer day in 1972 to finance it. The incident was celebrated in the film *Dog Day Afternoon,* and the operation was financed with part of Wojtowicz's $7,500 earnings from the movie. Things have not gone well for Aron since becoming Ms. Eden: in September 1979 she was hospitalized as a result of an overdose of Tuinal and alcohol.

TWO WHO DID IT WITHOUT SURGERY

❧

Tiresias was a soothsayer of Thebes in Greek mythology. Because he witnessed a forbidden sight—snakes coupling—he was changed temporarily into a woman. Since Tiresias was the only mortal who had direct experience of living as both male and female, he was asked to settle an argument between Zeus and Hera as to which sex enjoyed making love more. Without hesitation Tiresias gave his vote to women.

Orlando, the hero of Virginia Woolf's? 1928 novel of the same name, fell asleep one day when he was serving as Charles II's ambassador at Constantinople. One week later he awoke—as a woman.

AND WHAT CAN COME OF IT

❧

In 1979 a robber broke into a London apartment and found the tenant, a forty-eight-year-old woman who lived alone, watching a horror movie on television. She led the intruder into her bedroom and then delivered a stunning right-hand punch to his face. She caught the crook in a half nelson wrestling lock and took him to the building manager, who called the police. The secret of the woman's strength? She was a former bricklayer who had undergone a sex-change operation.

A MAN'S LIFE

❧

One of the most common kinds of imposture has been women disguising themselves as men. A few women have lived their entire lives as members of the opposite sex.

Pope Joan may or may not have really existed. According to a legend widely
believed in the Middle Ages, a woman disguised as a male cleric named
Johannes Anglicus succeeded to the papacy in 853. Her reign, if she had
one, was short. Anatomy turned out to be destiny and exposed her secret. One day she went into labor and delivered a baby in the middle of
St. Peter's Square, and angry onlookers stoned her to death. The child
is supposed to have survived and become a bishop.

Miranda Stuart. His fellow officers found the behavior of the top-ranking
medical officer of the British army disconcerting, even though there was
no doubting the man's surgical skills. Snobbish and quick to take offense, Dr. James Barry had fought more than one duel, emerging victorious despite his slight build. Barry, who had shown bravery at the battles of Waterloo and Balaclava, kept to himself and was so eccentric
that he refused medical treatment during his final illness. Death revealed the reason. Barry, a member of an elite army officer corps for
more than fifty years, was a woman, Miranda Stuart. The deception
had begun when the daughter of a prominent Scotch family decided to
attend the University of Edinburgh, graduating in 1812 as the fifteen-
year-old Dr. Barry. Another secret discovered at her death was that she
had given birth to a child.

Mary East. After her boyfriend, a highway robber, was killed, East created
the identity of James How, posed with another woman as a married
couple, and became an extremely respectable eighteenth-century innkeeper. For fourteen years the Hows were publicans in various English
towns, and James held almost every municipal office. Eventually East
fell prey to blackmail by one who knew her secret, and the truth came
out. The community supported the Hows, arguing that they had "won
the good opinion of all with whom they came in contact."

Chevalier John Theodora Verdieu was a "walking bookseller" and teacher of
languages who died in London in 1802. Upon his death, Verdieu was
discovered to be a woman who had lived in the city under male guise
for twenty years.

Charlotte Parkhurst first put on male clothes to escape from an orphanage in
New Hampshire. After that she became Charley Parkhurst, a familiar
figure in the mountains of California during the gold rush and a crack
stagecoach driver. Her identity went undetected until her death in 1879,
at which time the community of Soquel put up a plaque proclaiming
their town as the site where a woman (Parkhurst) had first voted in a
presidential election, in 1868.

Elsa Jane Forest Guerin, as a young widow, had two reasons to opt for man-
hood: to earn enough money to support her children, and to track down
her husband's murderer. She was to spend thirteen years as a man.
Soon Guerin "began rather to like the freedom of my new character. I
could go where I chose, do many things which while innocent in themselves, were debarred by propriety from association with the female
sex." She found her husband's killer but was unable to apprehend him.
Her economic activities, however, were more successful: she worked a
ranch, traded with Indians, tried mining in Pikes Peak, and eventually
opened a saloon in Denver—all of which made her quite wealthy.

Isabelle Eberhardt roamed the desert of North Africa in the late nineteenth
century disguised as an Arab man named Si Mahmoud. Perhaps the

Russian-born writer had decided that only a male guise would give her complete access to the wild lands she loved. "I wanted to possess this country, and this country has possessed me." A convert to Islam, she was initiated into several male orders and was accepted by the Arabs, although they undoubtedly knew of her deception. A street in Algiers is named after her, and "Si Mahmoud" is the name on her tombstone.

Harold Lloyd is the only name we have for a woman who, around 1910, held a "humble position" in London. By the time she died, she had lived as a man for a quarter of a century, been married and widowed, and was the "father" of an adult daughter. Lloyd was buried under the name by which she had always been known. The postmortem discovery of her true identity was a sensation.

But the honor for the most successful masquerade of all surely belongs to a woman who was known to other pioneers at a fur-trading post in North Dakota as the *"Orkney lad"* until the day in December 1807 when she gave birth to a baby boy.

SIX MEN WHO WANTED TO BE TAKEN FOR WOMEN

Charles Eon de Beaumont (Chevalier d'Eon). Was he or wasn't he? The chevalier was such a slippery character he even fooled some historians about his sex. Born in France in 1728, he was not only a prodigious sword fighter and scholar but also, for almost twenty years, a trusted secret service agent of Louis XV. It was in the latter role that he learned to enjoy a feminine existence. Disguised as a woman, he ingratiated himself into the confidence of Empress Elizabeth of Russia. The chevalier even fought duels dressed as a woman, although on the battlefield he appeared as a man. When he returned to France from London in 1771, Marie Antoinette? demanded that he put on feminine apparel. Thereafter he wore feminine clothing exclusively and styled himself "La Chevalière d'Eon." It's hard to tell whether this kinky decision was Eon's or the preference of his royal employers.

Edward Hyde, Lord Cornbury. Queen Anne's cousin was sent to the colonies in 1702 as the royal governor of New York and New Jersey, probably because his habit of going about in female dress was distressing to the crown. In New York he was able to prowl nightly dressed in garb filched from his wife's closet. A portrait of the governor in drag hangs in the museum of the New-York Historical Society.

Daniel Buckley. A third-class passenger on the sinking ocean liner *Titanic,* Buckley put on a woman's shawl, jumped into a lifeboat with several other men, and huddled there crying. Most of the other men were hauled out of the boat, but Buckley's impromptu disguise worked. He claimed that Mrs. Astor had given him the shawl.

Dora Ratjen was a German "female" high jumper in the 1930s, but after World War II she admitted to being male. "Dora" said the Hitler Youth Movement had forced him to compete as a woman to win medals for the Third Reich. In the late 1960s he was working as a waiter in Bremen, where fellow employees called him Herman.

Lea Caurla, a French athlete, won medals in women's events in the 1946 European championships in Oslo. Soon afterward, she changed her name to Leon when doctors decided she was really a man.

George Cantey. Georgia Black, one of the most respected members of the black community in Sanford, Florida, had twice been married and was the mother of an adopted son. As a widow, she collected a pension from the Veterans Administration. In 1951, as Mrs. Black lay on her deathbed, the truth came out: the attending physician discovered her to be a man. Born George Cantey on a South Carolina plantation, he had rejected his sex at the age of fifteen. Convinced that fate had intended him to be female, he dismissed his male organs as "growths." Even his adopted son had no idea of Black's real sex. The people of Sanford respected "her" memory, however, and were angry at the doctor, who, they felt, had revealed the truth for no good reason.

SEPARATE BUT NOT EQUAL

❧

Men get the glory	*but women get the blame*
Honest man	**Honest woman,** has the added connotation of illicit sex: "he made an honest woman of her."
A man's job, important 9-to-5 work.	**Woman's work,** light stuff, even though it's never done.
Man in the street, represents The People.	**Woman of the streets,** available at a small price.
Master	**Mistress,** has the added connotation of illicit sex.
Sir	**Madam,** has the added connotation of illicit sex.
Stag party, a convivial night out for the boys who will be boys.	**Hen party,** a gossip-filled gathering of chattering women.
Bachelor, an enviable status.	**Spinster,** a pitiable condition.
Doll, a likable, kindhearted person.	**Doll,** has the added connotation of sex object.
Mannish, applied to a woman, means exhibiting positive traits of strength, boldness, or plainness of speech and manner for which men are rightly admired.	**Womanish** or **effeminate,** applied to a man, means not strong or brave, as a man should be; exhibiting negative traits of cowardice, frailty, or frivolity for which women are rightly condemned.
Tomboy, a strong, active, agile girl who will grow out of her passing interest in wholesome, daring male pursuits and learn her passive place in society.	**Sissy,** diminutive of *sister;* a weak sister, a boy whose fear or lack of interest in wholesome, daring male pursuits will bring him to no good end.

Contributed by Ruth Ulmyn

I LOVE MEN EXCEPT FOR THEIR ...

              ℳ

Dependency, the well-known reluctance of many men to do anything alone.

Helplessness, the inability of many men to pick up their socks, wash their underwear, make their beds, sew on their shirt buttons, brew coffee, and cook anything more complicated than toast.

Insecurity, which may lead to the attempted cover-up of verbal abuse, an infinite variety of barbs hurled unerringly at the most vulnerable spots.

Need to dominate, which may lead to mental or physical abuse.

Refusal to let anyone else get a word in edgewise

Lack of sociability

Uncouth behavior and careless personal habits

Fear of sexual failure, which often results in compulsive sexual behavior or (paradoxically) lack of sexual attentiveness.

Fear of assertiveness and independence on the part of women

From a *Womanlist* poll

I LOVE WOMEN EXCEPT FOR THEIR ...

              ℳ

Independence, the ability of many women to do outrageous things competently and on their own.

Helplessness, the inability of many women to make decisions, put nails in the wall, change a flat tire, stand on a ladder, change a light bulb, or carry packages.

Insecurity, which may lead to verbal abuse, the attempted cover-up of an infinite variety of barbs hurled unerringly at the most vulnerable spots.

Need to dominate, which may lead to mental abuse, a constant barrage of sarcastic comments, and orders given in a loud voice.

Refusal to let anyone else get a word in edgewise

Excessive sociability, especially with their female friends and on the telephone.

Careless personal habits

Avoidance of sex

Sexual aggressiveness

Overemotionalism, the tendency of many women to use tears to get their way or to respond to a situation in an excessively dramatic manner.

From a *Womanlist* poll

III ✹ *SHOW OF COURAGE*

ELEVEN FACES OF HEROISM

✹

Lady Godiva sympathized with the unhappy people of eleventh-century Coventry, who suffered under the heavy taxes imposed on them by her husband, Leofric, Earl of Mercia. When she begged him to lift their burden, he offhandedly replied he'd do so only if she rode stark naked through the city on a white horse. Godiva took him at his word.

Pocahontas♀ saved the life of Captain John Smith, a leader of the Jamestown colony, by hurling her body over his in 1607 when her father, Chief Powhatan, and other elders of her tribe were about to kill him. Pocahontas later married John Rolfe, another Virginia colonist, and traveled to England, where she was received with honor.

Flora Macdonald in 1746 helped her hero, the defeated Bonnie Prince Charlie, flee Scotland after his defeat at the Battle of Culloden by disguising him as her serving maid and guiding him to the Isle of Skye—for which Macdonald was imprisoned in the Tower of London until public pressure gained her release. Years later she and her family came to North Carolina, where, riding through the woods on a white horse and addressing troops in Gaelic, she rallied the Scottish colonists to the royalist cause during the War of Independence.

Hannah Duston watched helplessly as her six-week-old infant was slaughtered, then was herself abducted, with other women and children, from her Massachusetts home in 1697 by a band of Indians. But one week later she had her revenge. In a New Hampshire cabin, Duston arose during the night to find all ten of her captors sound asleep; she slew them all with one of their own tomahawks, liberated several other captives, and returned home with the scalps on her belt.

Ida Lewis,♀ the slight daughter of a lighthouse keeper, and eventually a lighthouse keeper herself, in 1858 saved four men whose vessel had capsized in rough seas. She went on to save fifteen lives over a period of forty-eight years.

Clara Maass,♀ an army nurse assisting William Gorgas's attempt to conquer yellow fever in Cuba, deliberately exposed herself to the sting of the *Stegomyia* mosquito in 1901 to test his theory that the mosquito spread the infection. Ten days later she lay dead—and the culprit had been pinpointed beyond a shadow of a doubt.

Edith Cavell,♀ a British nurse in Belgium during World War I, smuggled 200 Allied officers out of the country after it had fallen to the Germans. "There is a higher duty than prudence," she said. Both international acclaim and martyrdom were her rewards. She fell before a German firing squad in 1915.

Hannah Senesh was the only woman in a unit of specially trained Palestinian Jews who parachuted into Eastern Europe in March 1944. Their mission: to rescue Hungarian Jews. The Nazis captured and brutally tortured Senesh, but she refused to reveal any information. Still silent, she met her death before a firing squad.

Vivian Malone was stopped at the door by Governor George C. Wallace when she attempted to attend classes at the University of Alabama in 1963. Malone persisted despite harassment from other students and became, in 1965, the first black woman to graduate from the university.

Amalia Fleming returned to her native Greece after the death of her British husband, Sir Alexander Fleming, the discoverer of penicillin. It was 1967; a junta of colonels ruled Greece, and Lady Fleming found the voice of democracy silenced. Having been a World War II fighter, she threw herself into a new resistance, helped a young poet escape from prison, was captured and tortured, but refused to implicate her friend. Her bravery focused world attention on her cause.

Dorothy Kelly, a flight attendant for Pan American World Airways, risked her life to rescue passengers and crew members after the collision of two 747 planes on the Canary Islands in 1978. For her bravery, the United States Department of Transportation gave her the highest award it had ever issued.

SEVEN WHO LED THE WAY

Harriet Tubman,♀ an escaped slave, led more than three hundred slaves to freedom on the Underground Railroad in the 1850s. Despite a bounty of $40,000 (in nineteenth-century dollars) on her head, Tubman made nineteen clandestine trips to the South and was never caught. She lived to the age of ninety-three.

Frances Willard ♀ was an organizer of the Women's Christian Temperance Union (WCTU) and its second president from 1879 to 1898. Visiting San Francisco in 1883, Willard had a vision—"We are one world of tempted humanity"—and proceeded to expand her organization world-wide, extending its scope to include labor reform and woman suffrage.

Henrietta Szold, born into a prosperous Jewish family, left Baltimore to settle in Palestine in 1909. There she devoted herself to improving medical care and three years later founded Hadassah, now an international women's organization that runs a large health network in Israel. During the Holocaust, Szold, seventy-three years old, traveled to Berlin to negotiate directly with the Nazis and started the "Youth Aliyah," which brought 2,330 European Jewish children to Palestine.

Autherine Lucy was, in 1956, the first black student to enroll at an all-white institution of public education in Alabama. On her first day at the University of Alabama, other students moved away from her; the demonstrations spread; and school officials suspended Lucy "for her own safety." After she brought suit against the university, Alabama's schools finally began to desegregate.

Ethel Percy Andrus, a former teacher, founded the National Retired Teachers Association in 1947, and in the 1950s the American Association of Retired Persons, the first broad-based organization for older Americans, which now has a membership of more than 9 million.

Betty Williams ♀ and *Mairead Corrigan* ♀ are two women of Northern Ireland who decided they had had enough violence. When Williams saw a gunner's car go out of control and slaughter three children on the streets of Belfast, she set out to find one hundred like-minded women to join her, and within two weeks the peace movement in Ulster was born. One of the women who became her co-worker was Corrigan, the dead children's aunt. Williams and Corrigan were awarded the Nobel Peace Prize in 1976.

TEN UNDERGROUND AGENTS OF WORLD WAR II

❧

Christine Granville (Countess Skarbek), a Polish-born countess who had been Miss Poland before the war, transformed herself into one of the crack female agents in France, undertaking three secret trips to Poland and several intelligence missions in the Balkans before 1944. Once, in southern France, she bluffed the Gestapo into freeing two of her captured comrades a scant three hours before they were scheduled to be shot. Granville survived the war, to be murdered in London in 1952 by an Irishman.

Nancy Wake, an Australian journalist, joined the resistance under the name of "Lucienne Carlier" after the fall of France. She was trained in Britain and parachuted back into France, where her exploits included the sabotage of prearranged targets on D-Day and the destruction of the German headquarters at Monthuçon.

Odette Sansom, a British agent, helped organize the resistance in enemy-occupied countries. When arrested in France with co-worker Peter Churchill, she pretended she was his wife and that he had come to France to visit her, concealing the fact that Churchill was really the leader of a spy organization in Vichy. To find out the truth, her captors subjected Sansom to brutal torture, tore her toenails out and seared her back with a red-hot iron, but they could not get her to talk. She was sent to Ravensbrück concentration camp and survived the war.

Violet Szabo, a French citizen living in London, went to work for British intelligence in 1944 and was sent to join a resistance network in France. In June 1944 she was in a group ambushed by a Panzer division. An injured ankle made it impossible for her to flee, but Szabo, an excellent shot, held off the Germans for two hours until she ran out of ammunition. When captured, she refused to divulge any information and, with two other British agents, *Denise Block* and *Lillian Rolfe,* was sent to Ravensbrück. There all three were shot to death on January 26, 1945.

Mathilde Carré ("The Cat") was a French spy and resistance fighter who founded one of the first important intelligence networks of the war and was skilled in extracting information from the enemy. In the winter of 1941 her headquarters was raided and she was persuaded to save her life by becoming a double agent. Shortly thereafter her old comrades were arrested. After liberation, she was tried for treason and condemned to death, a sentence later commuted to life imprisonment.

Marguerite Bervoets, a Belgian professor, was the co-founder of a resistance group in her native country and worked as a spy, courier, and guide until she was caught in 1942. She was taken to Germany, where she was beheaded.

Marie-Louise Henin, a Belgian dental surgeon, worked for the underground press and guided escapees from the Nazis until she was caught. Transported to Germany, she met the same fate as Bervoets.

Anne Brusselmans, an English woman married to a Belgian, helped 180 British and American fliers escape from occupied Belgium over a four-year period. The Gestapo searched her apartment three times but never found enough evidence to arrest her. By war's end she was the sole surviving member of her cell of underground workers.

FOUR WHO CHOSE TO GO DOWN WITH THE *TITANIC*

On April 19, 1912, the *Titanic* sank, with a loss of life estimated from 1,490 to 1,635. The vessel carried enough lifeboats for 1,178, but there were 2,207 passengers on board. Because the dictum of "women and children first" was followed, far more women than men survived the disaster. Four of 143 first-class women passengers were lost, 15 out of 93 from second class, and 81 of 179 from third class. Apparently the rules of chivalry did not extend to steerage passengers.

These four first-class female passengers went down with the *Titanic* by choice:

Mrs. Hudson J. Allison, who refused to leave her husband.

Lorraine Allison, her young daughter, who stayed with the family.

Mrs. Isidor Straus, an older woman, who chose to perish with her mate, saying, "I've always stayed with my husband; so why should I leave him now?"

Edith Evans, who was unmarried and gave up her chance to leave the ship so that Mrs. J. Murray Brown, the mother of a family, could be saved instead.

TWELVE WHO OVERCAME ADVERSITY

Martha Ann Honeywell, who lived in the early nineteenth century, was born without hands and one foot but with a great deal of artistic talent. She supported herself by cutting silhouettes, many of them quite intricate and detailed. Included in each cutout, in tiny cursive letters, were the words "Cut without hands by M. A. Honeywell" or "Cut with the mouth by M. A. Honeywell."

Margaret Haughery was a twenty-three-year-old illiterate domestic servant when death claimed her husband and young child. With what little money she had, she bought two cows and sold milk through the streets of New Orleans; by 1840 she owned a herd of cows and, soon after, expanded her enterprise to include bread-selling routes. As she prospered, Haughery founded charities and orphanages; she gave more than $600,-000 to these institutions in her lifetime. The extent of her generosity was so well known that it was necessary to put only one word on the statue erected to her memory: "Margaret."

Mother (Mary Harris) Jones ♀ was an Irish immigrant whose husband and four children died in the yellow fever epidemic of 1867 and whose dressmaking shop burned down in 1871. From this ill fortune the widow emerged as "Mother Jones," a militant organizer for the United Mineworkers Union. For fifty years she took part in every major strike, helping strikers' families, laying out the dead, and exhorting the men to hang on. But remembering her early losses, Jones never again tried to set up a home. She carried all her possessions with her in a knitted shawl. "My address is like my shoes," she declared; "it travels with me."

Laura Bridgman, Anne Sullivan, ♀ and *Helen Keller* ♀ were linked by circumstance. Bridgman, born blind, deaf, and mute, was a "hopeless case" until Samuel Gridley Howe taught her to communicate at his Perkins Institution. She became a teacher at the institution and remained there all her life, visited by hundreds of curiosity seekers, including Charles Dickens. From Bridgman a young Perkins graduate, the partially sighted Anne Sullivan, learned to teach the deaf and blind. She applied these methods to Helen Keller, another who lived in a world of total isolation because she could neither see nor hear. With Sullivan's aid, Keller learned to understand words, graduated cum laude from Radcliffe in 1904, and later gained world-wide fame as a writer, promoter of social causes, and symbol of courage.

Fannie Merritt Farmer ♀ was forced by ill health to forgo her plans to attend college. Overcoming her disappointment, Farmer taught herself to cook and eventually became the principal of the Boston Cooking School and the leading authority on American cookery by the turn of the century. In later life, confined to a wheelchair after suffering two strokes, she continued to lecture on nutrition and food preparation.

Carrie Jacobs Bond ♀ was seven when she was severely burned, twelve when her devoted father became bankrupt and died, in her early twenties when her first marriage ended in divorce, and thirty-three when her second husband died, leaving his widow and young son penniless. Bond struggled to get along by painting china and writing music (she was self-taught) and songs, churning out melody after melody until finally she struck it rich in 1906 with "I Love You Truly." The song sold over a million copies—and is still popular today.

Wilma Rudolph, ♀ the only American woman to win three Olympic gold medals in track and field, could not walk at all until she was eight years old. One leg had been crippled as the result of double pneumonia and scarlet fever. With determination Rudolph learned to walk and, after she turned to running, there was no stopping her.

Jacqueline Susann ♀ kept secret from all but her husband and a few close friends the fact that she suffered from breast cancer. Her best-selling novels were written in the twelve years following a mastectomy in 1962.

Kitty O'Neil (Hambleton),♀ racing-car driver and stunt woman, has been totally deaf since she was four months old. In 1967 O'Neil came down with spinal meningitis and was expected never to walk again. But she overcame that misfortune too and, in 1976, among other accomplishments, set a new women's speed record.

Ruth Broemmer Rosenbaum doesn't have to leave her wheelchair to excel at athletics. Paralyzed by polio as an infant in 1945, she won gold medals for slalom, shot put, discus, and javelin in the 1972 Para Olympics, an international sporting event for those restricted to wheelchairs.

FROM MENTAL BREAKDOWN TO A NEW LIFE

Dorothea Dix suffered an emotional and physical collapse in 1836 that left her a total invalid for five years. One day a friend asked her to teach a Sunday school class to a group of imprisoned women. The conditions she saw pulled Dix out of her own depression and gave her a cause to fight for. Between 1843 and 1847 Dix traveled 30,000 miles across the country, examining prisons and mental institutions and haranguing state legislatures into improving them. Because of her efforts, 110 asylums and hospitals were built and some of the stigma of mental illness was lifted.

Mary Baker Eddy,♀ from early childhood on, was plagued by inexplicable physical and emotional ailments. After the death of her beloved first husband multiplied her hysterical symptoms, her family had to rock her to sleep like an infant and ply her with morphine to quiet her. In 1862 Eddy fell under the influence of Dr. Phineas P. Quimby, who believed in healing through prayer. She adopted his methods and succeeded in curing herself of a back injury and in eliminating her mental difficulties as well. She converted mind healing into a religion, held the first Christian Science service in 1875, and is honored today as the founder of that faith.

Jane Addams ♀ experienced four years of inactivity and a "nervous depression" so debilitating she sought to shake it off by a trip to Europe. After that 1887 journey, Addams's life was never again without a focus. In London she visited Toynbee Hall, one of the first settlement houses for industrial workers, and determined to start something similar. Her settlement, Hull House in Chicago, was to become the model for a national movement aimed at providing enlightened social welfare policies for workers, women, and children.

Charlotte Perkins Gilman suffered a severe and prolonged depression after the birth of her first child and came to realize that the cause was her feeling of being stifled by conventional marriage and motherhood. She wondered how many other women were being damaged by their traditional roles, became obsessed with the idea that the economic and social structure of society should be changed, and went on to expound her views in influential books on religion, economics, and child care.

Edith Wharton,[9] a member of New York's social aristocracy, was twenty-three when she wed a suitably proper Bostonian, but their leisure-oriented existence did not provide enough mental stimulation. In her late twenties she suffered a nervous breakdown. After her doctor suggested writing as a form of therapy, Wharton threw her intellectual energy into it and, in 1902, when she was forty, published her first novel, *Valley of Decision.* She followed it with a book a year for the remainder of her life.

Bertha Pappenheim, the young daughter of a respected orthodox Jewish family, suffered from a breakdown that baffled Joseph Breuer and his associate, Sigmund Freud, who wrote her up as "Anna O," one of his most renowned case studies of hysteria. The two could do little to help Pappenheim, and her mental health was truly restored only after she cast aside the role of dutiful daughter in search of a husband to become a feminist and social worker. In the early twentieth century Pappenheim founded homes for unmarried mothers and delinquent girls in Germany, worked to eliminate prostitution, and undertook a hazardous investigation of the white slave trade. "Nobody is allowed to remain quiet if he knows that somewhere wrong is being done. To know of wrong and to remain quiet makes one partly guilty."

VOICES OF CONSCIENCE

Anne Hutchinson enraged the Puritans by preaching the right of the individual to freedom of one's conscience. They tried her for heresy, found her guilty, and forced her to leave Massachusetts. With her fourteen children she fled to the religious haven of Roger Williams's Rhode Island and later migrated south to New York, where she was slain by Indians in 1643.

Mary Dyer, a Quaker, challenged Massachusetts authorities by trying to preach her faith there. When threats of death did not stop her, she was banished. But Dyer returned to continue challenging the persecution of her coreligionists and was herself hanged in 1660.

Prudence Crandall admitted a black student to the boarding school she ran in Canterbury, Connecticut, in 1831. After public outrage forced the school to close, Crandall reopened it as an all-black institution. She was harassed and arrested, and eventually a mob set fire to the school. Although Crandall gave up the fight in 1834 after being tried and convicted, her brave stand converted others to the abolitionist cause.

Frances Wright came to the United States from Scotland in 1779 at the age of twenty-three and two years later founded Nashoba, a settlement in Tennessee to train slaves to work for their freedom. She was also associated with Robert Dale Owen in founding the Utopian community at New Harmony, Indiana. In 1829 in New York they established the *Free Enquirer,* a paper advocating women's rights, broad social change, and the abolition of slavery.

Emily Hobhouse criticized British policy in South Africa during the Boer War; in 1900 and 1901 she conducted her own investigations of the concentration camps in which women and children were kept. She aroused public opinion on her return to England, and conditions improved; later she returned to Africa to work for women's education. When she died in 1926, her ashes were sent to South Africa for a state funeral.

Kate Richards O'Hare opposed the entry of the United States into World War I, was indicted under the Espionage Act, and was sentenced to a five-year term in the Missouri State Penitentiary. Appalled at conditions for inmates, she became an advocate of prison reform, a cause to which she devoted the rest of her life. Her sentence was commuted in 1920; she became assistant director of the California Department of Penology in 1939.

Fannie Lou Hamer, a sharecropper, attended her first civil rights rally in Mississippi in 1962. "I never knew we could vote before," she later recalled. "Nobody ever told us." She became a field worker for the Student Nonviolent Coordinating Committee (SNCC) and until her death in 1977 worked to register voters. Because of her dedication to civil rights, Hamer was arrested, shot at, beaten, and dispossessed from the shack she and her family called home.

Mary Church Terrell,♀ born to former slaves during the Civil War, was a founder and first president of the National Association of Colored Women, the first black woman to be appointed to the school board in Washington, D.C., and an organizer of the National Association for the Advancement of Colored People. When she was nearly ninety, she led the first sit-in at a Washington cafeteria and organized additional sit-ins and picket lines to persuade merchants to serve all patrons regardless of color, leading to a Supreme Court ruling that all "respectable, well-behaved persons" must be served.

Rosa L. Parks,♀ a dressmaker, was sitting on a bus in Montgomery, Alabama, on her way home from work on December 1, 1955, when the driver ordered her to get up so that a white passenger could sit down. Parks refused, was arrested and fined $10; disobeying a bus driver's instructions was a misdemeanor in Alabama. The case was carried to the Supreme Court, and Parks's defiance was the start of a decade or more of civil rights protests, leading her to be hailed as the "Mother of the Civil Rights Movement."

SEEKING JUSTICE FOR THE INDIAN

Susette La Flesche was the mission-educated daughter of an Omaha chief. When the Ponca Indians were forcibly removed from their lands and their leaders jailed in 1877, she began lecturing on their behalf, using her Indian name, Inshtatheamba, "Bright Eyes." Among those she impressed was Senator Henry L. Dawes, who, in 1887, sponsored key legislation for the protection of the Indians.

Helen Hunt Jackson was converted to the Indian cause after hearing La Flesche speak and wrote *A Century of Dishonor,* an exposé of the government's record of brutality and broken pledges. The book was ignored, but recalling what her friend Harriet Beecher Stowe ♀ had accomplished, Jackson turned to fiction and in 1884 published *Ramona*, a popular romance detailing the suffering of the Indians of the Southwest, which went through 300 printings and—later—three film versions.

Sarah Winnemucca, a Paiute, saw her baby brother killed in an army massacre of a defenseless Indian camp. She served as a scout for the United States during the Bannock Indian uprising of 1878, but when, at war's end, her own people were driven from their homeland, Winnemucca became outraged. She took to the lecture platform, a striking figure in traditional dress, protesting the repeated deceits of Indian agents. Powerful opponents called her a "drunken prostitute," but she would not be silenced. Winnemucca's strength as a speaker and lobbyist secured many promises from Washington—though these were never kept.

Lorelei Means and **Madonna Gilbert** were among the leaders of the Oglala Sioux and American Indian movement when the village of Wounded Knee, South Dakota, was occupied on February 27, 1973, to protest government policies and the nonactivist program of tribal officials. Under gunfire Means and Gilbert made repeated trips to remove the wounded to a temporary field hospital during the two-and-a-half-month siege. Later they established a Survival School to teach Native American history, traditions, and the Sioux language.

LaDonna Cranford Harris,♀ a Comanche and the wife of former Senator Fred Harris of Oklahoma, founded Americans for Indian Opportunity in 1965, an organization devoted to improving all aspects of life of Native Americans. She has also been an active spokeswoman for poor people's and women's rights.

Kahn-Tineta Horn, a young Mohawk woman who turned from a career as a model and actress to law school and the lecture circuit, prepares legal challenges to further the Indian cause, based on constitutional law relating to treaties and land rights. Unlike other groups struggling for equal rights, Horn points out, Indians are a separate people having specific rights guaranteed by special laws.

NIKKI GIOVANNI'S ♀ LIST OF EIGHTEEN GREAT BLACK WOMEN

Being asked to list great women is analogous to asking a rain cloud which drop she prefers when she knows it's time for rain—or asking a rainbow to pick her favorite color. It has become quite fashionable to extol the virtues and strengths of Black women, but I am an unabashed, unrepentant, unapologetic Black female chauvinist. The history of the Black female is a history of bridges—she has labored in the fields with the men—she has reared her children with the women. She has filled the gap between a "woman's place" and "man's work." The Black American female, over the past 400 years, has given witness against the lie that women are somehow a subspecies of human being; women can and do perform any task, question any assumption, dream any and every dream that is humanly possible; women can do everything—and do everything well.

The eighteen women I have chosen only represent the women I feel have directly captured my imagination through their lives, their work, and their example. The list is in no way complete. My mother, my sister, my grandmother do not appear on my list because most people cannot know them as I have. My best friend in the fifth grade, my English teacher in the eighth, my high school librarian do not appear. My dean of women at college, the friends of my mother who encouraged me do not appear. I could, in reality, make a list of women not on my list. Like the night, I cannot pick the brightest stars—I only share my delight in those which can be viewed by all hemispheres.

Rosa Parks ♀ for her lifelong commitment to equal rights for Black Americans.

Daisy Bates, for her courageous stand in Little Rock.

Harriet Tubman,♀ for walking where angels feared to tread.

Sojourner Truth,♀ for her unparalleled eloquence.

Phillis Wheatley,♀ who dared to sing in a joyless land.

Jeanne Noble, who has written the most complete book of the Black woman, *Beautiful Also Are the Souls of My Black Sisters.*

Bessie Head, the best Black African writer writing in the English language.

Toni Morrison,♀ who is the best female American novelist writing today.

Ida Lewis, for the journalistic vision of Black Americans as an international force. With the founding of *Encore American and Worldwide News,* the first Black newsmagazine, Ms. Lewis's journalistic pursuits have set the standard for excellence in the Black press and the standard for inquiry in the larger community.

Cicely Tyson, for the dignity she brings to every role she plays.

Lena Horne,♀ not only for being one of America's great song stylists but for the contained rage she generates.

Gloria Richardson, who led the struggle in Baltimore when others turned their backs.

Angela Davis,♀ for the power of her persona.

Alma Lewis, for refusing to understand why her dreams could not be realized and making them come true.

Mary McLeod Bethune,♀ for her total commitment to the education of Black youngsters.

Ida B. Wells-Barnett, for her reportage. Mrs. Wells, were she not Black, would have been the foremost American female reporter in this century.

Leontyne Price, for the sheer pleasure of her voice and the passion she brings to each Black spiritual she sings.

Marian Anderson,♀ for her voice, her dignity, her acceptance of her responsibility not to bend under horrendous circumstances . . . to stand on the steps of the Lincoln Monument and sing in a city of hate. Where did she find the strength?

Exclusively for *Womanlist*

MARILYN FRENCH'S LIST OF HOPE
FOR THE NEXT DECADE

❧

- Our government will spend as much money on the upbringing of children as it now spends on the armaments that kill our children.
- Men and women alike will recognize that the future is in our children, and that the most important job of any culture is the nurturance and education of its offspring.
- Persons in power will wield power as a loving parent "controls" a child: with compassion, as necessary, to empower a child for life.
- Women and men will be equally able to live up to their potential: to employ power, to create structures, to possess the richness of the world; to nurture, to be tender, to grieve; to regain access to our human, our mythic, our childhood roots; to feel pleasure without guilt, sex without contamination; and to play.
- Unanimity will cease to be our goal; rather, our goal will be a chorus of disparate voices, a new polyphonic music.

Exclusively for *Womanlist*

IV ❧ *LOVE AND MARRIAGE*

BARBARA CARTLAND'S ♀ LIST OF HISTORY'S TEN MOST ROMANTIC WOMEN
❧

Cleopatra ♀ (69 B.C.–30 B.C.)

Héloïse ♀ (d. 1164). A learned beauty of the Middle Ages, she fell in love at eighteen with the theologian priest Peter Abelard. The pair fled to Paris, where she gave birth to his son and they were secretly married. In revenge, her relatives had Abelard castrated. He became a monk and she an abbess. They were reunited in death, buried alongside each other.

Francesca da Rimini (d. ca. 1285). The lovely Francesca was married, for political reasons, to a man she did not love—Gianciotto, the deformed Lord of Rimini. She and his handsome younger brother, Paolo, became overwhelmed with passion for each other. In the midst of an embrace they were surprised by her husband and murdered. The poet Dante, their contemporary, consigned them to hell in his *Inferno*, but even here Francesca refuses to disavow her love for Paolo.

Diane de Poitiers ♀ (1499–1566). The most beautiful woman in France, Diane de Poitiers was eighteen years older than King Henry II when he fell madly in love with her; from 1547 until Henry's death in 1559, she virtually ruled France. Because of her adoration for her country, however, Diane realized the king had to have legitimate heirs, so on many nights when Henry came to her arms, she would return his passionate kisses, then suddenly say, "Go to your consort and lie with her." When the queen did become pregnant, Diane received from the royal exchequer a gift of 5,500 *livres* for her "good and commendable services . . . for the welfare of the Queen."

Nell Gwynne ♀ (1650–1687) sold oranges outside the King's Theatre and later became an actress. She was piquant, good-tempered, and high-spirited; also exceptionally clean, which was astonishing in that age. Charles II became an assiduous playgoer to see "pretty witty Nell" perform. She became his mistress, giving the king a gentle, unaffected happiness he found with no one else (although there were many others) and a son. One day while driving in Hyde Park her coach was mistaken for that of Louise de Keroualle, a Catholic royal favorite whom the mob hated. Surrounded, Nell stuck her head out of the coach window and shouted, "Desist, good people, I'm the *Protestant* whore!"

Madame de Pompadour♀ (1721–1764). Lovely, graceful, fascinating, witty, sparkling, she outshone all the other women at the court of Louis XV. She could act brilliantly, dance, sing, paint, and even engrave precious stones. It was a scandal for the king to take a bourgeoise as his mistress, but she charmed, amused, and taught him to appreciate art. She worshiped the ground he walked on, and he would have been lost without her.

Emma Hamilton♀ (1765–1815). The exquisitely beautiful daughter of a blacksmith became the mistress of Charles Grenville, who handed her over to his uncle, Sir William Hamilton, British ambassador at Naples. While married to Sir William, she fell in love with the naval hero Horatio Nelson, bore his child, and scandalized all England. Their intense romance ended when Nelson was killed at the Battle of Trafalgar.

Jane Digby, Lady Ellenborough (1807–1881). A great romantic, the greatest beauty of her day, with "blue eyes which could move a saint," her love affairs read like a naughty Almanach de Gotha. Bored by her pompous husband, Lord Ellenborough, she took up with the foreign Prince Schwarzenberg and had the whole House of Lords thundering over her adultery. Pregnant, she fled to her lover's side, only to find that his ardor had cooled. Two daughters later, Jane found herself alone but a celebrity. Ludwig I of Bavaria was her next conquest. When their serene idyll came to an end, she married Baron Carl-Theodore von Vennigen, young, handsome, and rich but, alas, also boring. Count Spyridon Theotoky, noble, poor, proud, and irresistible to women, came to her rescue, fought for Jane in a duel, and carried her away to the burning isles of Greece. His employer, King Otto of Greece (son of Ludwig I), became Jane's lover, much to the queen's irritation. But then Jane fell in love with the chief of the Pallikares, a mountain bandit, until he took a fancy to her maid. Then she took off for the Syrian desert. There, while negotiating for a camel caravan, she encountered Sheikh Abdul Medjuel el Mezrab, blue-blooded, educated, speaking several languages, with glittering, impenetrable black eyes. Jane had met her fourth and last husband, the real great love of her life. For twenty-five years their marriage was wildly, ecstatically passionate, and at age sixty Jane was still irresistibly beautiful. When she died at seventy-four, Medjuel was disconsolate.

Mary Anne Disraeli (1792–1872). The wife of the brilliant politician Benjamin Disraeli, Mary Anne recorded in her diary, "Gloves 2/6—in hand 300 pounds. Married 28.8.39. Dear Dizzy became my husband." Five years earlier, when they met, he had described her as "a pretty little thing, a flirt and a rattle." Twelve years older than her spouse, Mary Anne waited on him like a slave—or a mother. One day when she drove with him to the House of Commons, a footman slammed the carriage door on her fingers. The devoted Mary Anne never murmured lest she distract Dizzy. Afterward, he had the door preserved.

Elizabeth Barrett Browning (1806–1861). To mention her name is enough.

Exclusively for *Womanlist*

HELEN GURLEY BROWN'S ♀ LIST OF WOMEN WHO COULD HAVE BEEN THE *COSMO* GIRL

———————————————— ❧ ————————————————

So many well-known women in history were well known because of a *man* . . . they were his inspiration or helpmate but didn't do it *themselves.* That person wouldn't be a *Cosmopolitan* woman! A few women I can think of who *were* man-loving and attractive as well as achieving (all requisites for the *Cosmo* Girl) are:

Cleopatra ♀
Elizabeth I ♀ (attractive until she got smallpox)
George Sand ♀
Catherine the Great ♀ (she may have overdone the man appreciating)
Madam Chiang Kai-shek ♀
Amelia Earhart ♀
Maria Callas

Exclusively for *Womanlist*

LOVERS OF CATHERINE THE GREAT

———————————————— ❧ ————————————————

"I cannot live one hour without a man." Catherine II ♀ of Russia could command all the lovers she wanted—and there were many she wanted, though not as many as have been attributed to her. In the monarch's later years, the court position of "adjutant general" was created for the current royal favorite. The man (always young) selected by the empress had to pass a medical examination and the scrutiny of two ladies-in-waiting, known as *emprouveuses* because they tested his lovemaking abilities to see if they were adequate for the royal bed. The English ambassador estimated that Catherine spent $900 million on the men she kept. But the job was not an easy one. Catherine's men included:

Emperor Peter III, her cousin and unloving husband, deposed by Catherine in 1762 shortly after he reached the throne. Almost no one in Russia cared for the imbecilic Peter, who spent most of their marriage playing with his toy soldiers, and he does not, strictly speaking, belong on this list, for he was unable to consummate the marriage. As a result, after seven loveless years, Catherine fell into the arms of . . .
Sergei Saltykov, a twenty-six-year-old nobleman renowned for his attraction to women. Worried over the lack of a royal heir, Peter's aunt, the Empress Elizabeth, made sure that the handsome Saltykov crossed Catherine's path. After two miscarriages, Catherine gave birth to a son, almost certainly Saltykov's, who later became Emperor Paul I. Then Saltykov's ardor cooled, and Catherine was broken-hearted. Never again would she give her heart so completely.
Count Stanislas Poniatowski, a young Polish nobleman and one of the best-looking men of his time, became Catherine's second extramarital lover. Better at romance than at grammar, he recalled that "she was at that time of beauty which is ordinarily the height for any woman who has

one." A daughter, Anne, resulted from their affair, while Catherine's royal spouse innocently remarked, "I don't know how it is that my wife becomes pregnant." Poniatowski remained her friend even after Catherine broke off their romance, and in 1763 she helped him become King of Poland.

Gregory Orlov, it is said, was spotted by Catherine one day while she gazed out the window. Orlov and his brothers, a tightly knit clan, helped Catherine carry off her coup d'état and were probably responsible for the murder of Peter III. Gregory Orlov assumed that the grateful empress would marry him, but although she had three children by him, Orlov had to settle for ten years of being a "backstairs husband." When she finally dismissed him from her heart, he was rewarded with 6,000 serfs, 150,000 rubles a year, and a palace of marble. Still, his pride was hurt when the empress replaced him with . . .

Alexander Semeonovich Vassilchikov, a young man of whom Catherine soon tired, sighing that she had never been so unhappy in her life. Vassilchikov was urged to travel for his health. "I was nothing more than a kept woman," he lamented, although he didn't turn down the ample compensation.

Gregory Potemkin first attracted Catherine's attention in 1762, and by the time he moved into her apartments, there was little in Russia he could not have had on demand. Even though they lived together, she wrote him every day, and as her most trusted adviser he shared power. Rumor had it that they were secretly wed, but this was never proved. After their passion cooled, Potemkin continued to be concerned with her love life as the royal procurer. New young favorites were chosen from among his selections, and the fortunate fellows always made sure that Potemkin got his cut.

Peter Alexeyevich Zavadovsky was a Potemkin choice who became Catherine's secretary. He was an outstanding intellectual among the "adjutants general," who were scarcely selected for their brain power.

Alexander Dmitriev-Mamonov was sent to the empress by Potemkin, ostensibly to deliver a watercolor, but really to have her look him over. On the back of the painting Catherine scribbled, "The outlines are good but the choice of colors is less than felicitous," a cryptic comment praising his body but faulting his complexion. Nevertheless, Dmitriev-Mamonov filled the bill and was her favorite for two years until he fell in love with a woman his own age. Catherine wept, and—a truly royal gesture—had the pair married on the spot.

Ivan Rimsky-Korsakov, one of the handsomest of the young lovers, was far from the brightest. He once ordered a library of books just to fit the shelves in his apartments.

Alexander Lanskoy, a particular favorite, could not keep up with the empress even though he plied himself with aphrodisiacs. He expired, either in his mistress's arms or of scarlet fever, depending on which authority one chooses to believe. Lanskoy was twenty-two and his employer fifty-one when he breathed his last. She wept for him for six months.

Plato Zubov, a selection not approved by Potemkin, was twenty-four and the empress sixty when they became lovers. Hard, ambitious, and scheming, he attained great power over her. Zubov's tenure lasted until her death seven years later in 1796.

THREE OTHER MAN FANCIERS AND THEIR CONQUESTS

※

Madame de Staël.♀ "Genius has no sex," she cried, and she dedicated herself to pursuing the demands of the intellect and the heart. Her checkered love life was as unconventional as her belief that a woman had the right to be a thinker and a political force. Although she was no beauty, de Staël attracted men, probably because she lacked neither wealth nor assertiveness. Her best-known relationship was a tempestuous on-again, off-again fifteen-year affair with writer Benjamin Constant, and her list included barons, vicomtes, counts, and grafs; Abbé de Talleyrand; and Albert-Jean-Michel Rocca (John Rocca), her last husband, a young man of no particular intellect who satisfied her need for unfailing devotion. Napoleon, turned off by her political ambitions and "unfeminine" behavior, is not on her list of lovers, although she once had hopes of putting him there.

Ninon de Lenclos.♀ "One needs a hundred times more spirit in order to love properly than to command armies," she said. Being a great courtesan was more than a profession for Ninon de Lenclos—she believed in what she was doing. She lived for love and wrote about the joy of sex before it became a popular subject. Lenclos held the best-attended salon in seventeenth-century Paris, dividing her lovers into "the payers, the martyrs, and the favored." In her later years she conducted a School of Gallantry, where young male aristocrats received hands-on instruction in the arts of love. It is told of Lenclos that one of her natural sons, the Chevalier de Villiers, not knowing of their relationship, fell in love with her when she was sixty-five. She refused him several times, but he was so insistent that she was forced to reveal her identity. Murmuring "Mother," he fled into the garden and fell upon his own sword. Her complete lover list, were it available, would undoubtedly be too long for this book, but her men included Comte Gaspard de Coligny, Abbé Dessiat, Maréchal d'Estrées, Sainte-Evremond, La Rochefoucauld, and the Marquis de Sévigné and his son.

Lola Montez.♀ Entertainment was her life, on the stage and in the boudoir. In the nineteenth century the performances of "Spanish" dancer Montez, born Marie Delores Eliza Rosanna Gilbert, were often attacked as "suggestive, lewd, and immoral"; still, few could resist the opportunity to see her. Her men included Captain Thomas James, her first husband; the Viceroy of Poland; Nicholas, Czar of Russia; composer Franz Liszt; André Henri Dujarier, a newspaper editor and the great love of her life, who was killed in a duel defending her honor; King Ludwig Carl Augustus of Bavaria, who gave Montez the title of Countess Landsfeld and lost his throne because of popular discontent over their affair; Lieutenant George Trafford Heald, her second husband, who later sued Montez for annulment on grounds of bigamy, claiming correctly that she had not been finally divorced from her first husband; Patrick Purdy Hull, her third husband and also her manager; and Dr. Karl Adler, a German geologist and sportsman who met Montez when she toured California.

FIFTEEN WOMEN IN THE TANGLED LOVE LIFE
OF LORD BYRON

---------------------------------- ❧ ----------------------------------

Catherine Gordon Byron, the erratic mother who alternately coddled and rejected him. "I have never been so *scurrilously,* and *violently* abused by any person, as by that woman, whom I think I am to call mother...."

Mary Duff, a distant cousin. He worshiped her from afar at the age of eight.

Mary Chaworth, who was eighteen years old when she became an object of unrequited desire to the fifteen-year-old Byron. "Do you think I could care anything for that lame boy?" she scoffed.

Lady Caroline Lamb, who was drawn to Byron by the threat of danger. "Mad, bad, and dangerous to know," she wrote in her diary after their first encounter. When he ended their passionate liaison, her fervor turned to hatred. She wore buttons reading *"Ne crede Byron"* ("Don't believe Byron") and offered her favors to gentlemen who would challenge him to a duel. He finally escaped her and turned to others, one of whom was ...

Lady Oxford, forty years old when they met. Byron was that cultivated woman's last conquest; he, in turn, conquered ...

Augusta Leigh, his adoring half sister, with whom he may have fathered ...

Elizabeth Medora Leigh, who grew up to bear three children fathered by her brother-in-law. Through all of Byron's adventures he had a confidante in ...

Lady Melbourne, mother-in-law of the tempestuous Lady Caroline Lamb and the poet's friend and adviser. She was instrumental in arranging his marriage to ...

Anne Isabella Milbanke. The pair proved to be incompatible, and in 1816 they divorced, perhaps because she suspected the true nature of his relationship with Augusta Leigh. Milbanke was the mother of Byron's only legitimate child ...

Augusta Ada Byron,♀ who apparently inherited her father's impulsive personality. After an unhappy marriage to the Earl of Lovelace, she used her talents for mathematics and science to develop a system for betting at the races. Not only was the system a failure, but one of her blackmailing lovers tormented her into a breakdown and early death. Her father also had a daughter by ...

Claire Clairmont, sister-in-law of his poet friend Percy Bysshe Shelley, half-sister of Mary Shelley (author of *Frankenstein*), and stepdaughter of feminist Mary Wollstonecraft. ♀ The freethinking Clairmont and Byron became the parents of the angelic ...

Allegra, whom Byron preferred to love from afar. Contrary to Clairmont's wishes, he insisted on placing her in an Italian convent, where she died at the age of five. Clairmont's career inspired Henry James to write *The Aspern Papers,* but that was many years after Byron, dwelling in Italy, had abandoned her for a series of local women, including ...

Marianna Segati, the young wife of his Venetian landlord,

Margarita Cogni, the wife of a Venetian baker, and

Countess Teresa Guiccioli, Byron's last mistress. The nineteen-year-old Guiccioli, her fifty-eight-year-old husband, and the poet constituted a *ménage à trois* in Ravenna. Perhaps his boredom with the countess had a part in his decision to leave and fight in Greece. The move cost Byron his life in 1824, but Guiccioli lived for fifty-five more years, possessed by her lover's memory. She later married a French marquis, and they hung Byron's portrait over their mantel.

This complicated list is far from complete. Byron himself confessed to more than 200 love affairs, not all of them with women.

THE ANCIENT HISTORY OF THE OLDEST PROFESSION

- The establishment of houses of prostitution was an outgrowth of urbanism, since neither space nor women were readily available in the cities, unlike the situation in the countryside.
- The earliest brothel on record may be Ka-Kum, in the Sumerian city of Erech or Uruk, ca. 3000 B.C.
- Kal-Ba, who may be the first of his occupation on record, managed a brothel in Babylon in the reign of King Nebuchadnezzar, about 500 B.C.
- The first brothels in Europe were the nonprofit establishments of Athens in about 600 B.C. The philosopher statesman Solon decided that all male citizens should have access to this public health facility, so the fee was set at one *obol* (cent) per contact.
- A sign on a wall in Pompeii offers for lease a brothel and substantial additional property—nine bars and shops—owned by the Lady Julia Felix. (*Felix*—"happy"—she may have been indeed, with so lucrative an endowment!)
- *Ad Sorores IIII*—"At the Four Sisters"—was the name of a brothel in imperial Rome. You might say that this was the first sorority house.
- The first "red-light districts," so called because ecclesiastic authorities required every brothel to have a red light outside so that it could be recognized, were established about 1234 in Avignon, Toulouse, and Montpellier, France.

THE ETYMOLOGY OF THE WORLD'S OLDEST PROFESSION

Prostitute, from the Latin word *prostitute,* from a word meaning "to expose for sale."

Whore, from Old English *hore,* Icelandic *hora,* Greek *hure,* Gothic *hors,* and Latin *carus,* "dear."

Fille de joie, French, "girl of pleasure."

Doxy, from Middle Flemish *docksey,* "little doll."

Strumpet, probably from a Middle English word.

Harlot, from Old French *herlot,* "young idler."

Courtesan, from Italian *cortigiana,* "woman of the court."

Mistress, an ironic application of the English term of address for any woman.

Paramour, from Old French *par amour,* "by love."

Madame, an ironic application of the French term of address for a married woman.

Bawd, from Middle French *baude,* the feminine form of *baud,* meaning "dissolute."

Whorehouse, from the Saxon *horhus.*

Bawdyhouse, from *baude* plus *hus.*

Brothel, from Old English *breothan,* "to degenerate."

Bordello, from Old French *borde,* "wooden hut," by way of Italian.

Wenchaus, German, from a word that originally meant "child" plus the word for house.

Stewhoulder, stewhouse, Elizabethan English terms, from Late Middle English *stue(n),* "to take a steam bath," and Vulgate Latin *extufare,* "from steam." Bathhouses came to provide a variety of services, and the word *stew* came to mean a disreputable neighborhood.

THE COURTESAN AS CELEBRITY I:
The Hetairae

❧

The *hetairae,* or courtesans, were the highest class of prostitutes in ancient Greece. They were well educated, adept at the arts of pleasing, and their fees averaged 500 gold drachmas per visit. Several of these blond beauties (the hetairae were marked by their bleached hair) became so well known they acquired the status of celebrities, and the populace eagerly followed their exploits. Among them:

Clepsydra, who kept an hourglass at her bedside and sent her lovers away when the sands ran out.

Cyrene, much in demand because she knew twelve different ways of performing intercourse.

Theoris, a favorite of Sophocles, who in his old age fathered an illegitimate child by her.

Lamia, who so captivated Demetrius Poliorcetes, King of Macedon, that he met her demand for 250 talents, or $300,000. He raised the sum by levying a tax on soap. The Athenians joked about the matter, saying that since Lamia required so many suds she must have been even dirtier than everyone thought.

Aspasia,[9] foremost of the Greek courtesans, who was the mistress of Pericles, ruler of Athens. So talented was she that rumor stated she was the actual author of several of his famous orations. Because Aspasia took up a great deal of her lover's time, his enemies argued he was neglecting the state, and she was brought to trial for impiety toward the gods and for procurement. An eloquent defense by Pericles himself brought a vote of acquittal. Aspasia is believed to have posed for Phidias' statue of Athena in the Parthenon.

Lais, who gave herself only to those she truly loved. She turned down an offer of 10,000 drachmas for one night from Demosthenes. Then she gave herself to the poverty-stricken Diogenes, gratis.

Phryne, who was absolutely and literally irresistible to all men, and thus grew enormously wealthy. When Alexander the Great destroyed the walls of Thebes, she offered to pay for their reconstruction if the citizens would erect a plaque reading "Thebes was overthrown by Alexander and rebuilt by Phryne." Her offer was refused. After her death, the sculptor Praxiteles honored her with a gold statue in the Temple of Diana of Ephesus.

THE COURTESAN AS CELEBRITY II:
The Grand Horizontals

⚥

The 1890s in Paris were the supreme epoch of self-indulgence. "The great business at hand was pleasure," Cornelia Otis Skinner has written, "conducted by people who knew the seriousness of that business." Courtesans who were good at their trade grew richer than their wildest dreams. The escapades of these "grand horizontals" were followed eagerly by the public, which dubbed the following headliners *les grand trois*—"the great three."

Liane de Pougy was the star of the trio; her compatriots often referred to her as *"nôtre courtisane nationale."* After the breakup of an early marriage she became a Folies Bergère showgirl, which enabled her to become known to some of the better "protectors" in Paris, including the Prince of Wales. Houses, carriages, jewels, and works of art were showered upon her, and she even traveled to Russia accompanied by her Parisian jeweler, who discreetly showed potential customers the items she admired. In her middle thirties she became religious and entered an order, adopting the appropriate name of Sister Mary Magdalene of the Penitence, but the fervor lasted only one year. She returned to the world and married a Rumanian nobleman, whose family promptly cut him off. Undaunted, the couple retired to a country cottage, where they enjoyed twenty-seven years of marital bliss. At her husband's death, de Pougy returned to the convent.

Caroline Otero, known as "La Belle Otero," was the illegitimate child of a Greek nobleman and a Spanish gypsy woman. By the age of fifteen she had already shed three husbands, and in 1892 she became the star of the Folies Bergère. The Comte Chevedole blew his brains out after squandering his fortune on her, and so many other suitors followed his example that Otero was billed as the "Suicide Siren" when she visited New York. During her life, according to Otero, Cornelius Vanderbilt offered her a yacht, Gabriele D'Annunzio composed a poem in her honor, Pierre Renoir immortalized her on canvas, and Prince Peter of Russia implored, "Ninouchka, ruin me, but never leave me!" In her middle forties, Otero abandoned her career and settled in Nice, where she lost much of her accumulated wealth in gambling.

Emilienne d'Alençon was the most kindhearted of the grand trio, giving generously to charities and caring for an illegitimate child that was not her own. Leopold of Belgium was her first important lover; she later married a titled army officer, enabling her to style herself a countess even though the union did not last. After her last lover was killed in World War I, d'Alençon ended her days as a drug addict.

FOUR PAPAL MISTRESSES

Marozia, the mistress of Pope Sergius III in the tenth century, was the daughter of a papal official. In 931 she plotted to have her illegitimate son become Pope John XI. She was only upholding a family tradition, because . . .

Theodora, Marozia's mother, a noble beauty, had been mistress of Pope John X.

Vannozza Dei Catanei ♀ first met the future Pope Alexander VI when he was Rodrigo Borgia, a lawyer in Valencia; when he was called to serve the Church she followed him to the Vatican. She bore him four children, including Lucrezia ♀ and Cesare Borgia. When she began menopause at the age of forty-four, she was retired on a pension.

Giulia Farnese, at the age of seventeen, succeeded Catanei in the Borgia pope's affections. She gave her lover, who was forty years her senior, three children. Farnese's alliance with the pope was a political ploy, engineered by her brother Alessandro, which bore fruit later when Alessandro succeeded to the papacy himself. She was the model for Guglielmo della Porta's nude statue *Truth,* which rests on top of her brother's tomb, an outstanding example of the triumph of art over real life.

THE FAMILY THAT PLAYS TOGETHER
Four Daughters of the Marquis of Nesle, and the King

Comtesse de Mailly. King Louis XV of France had been barred from the queen's bedchamber. To fill the gap, his advisers literally pushed Madame de Mailly into his arms, her clothing askew. She succeeded in attracting his attention and became the royal mistress, but keeping His Majesty amused was no easy matter. So, perhaps deliberately, de Mailly introduced him to her sister, the . . .

Comtesse de Vintimille du Luc. The king soon fell under the spell of Madame de Vintimille, a very dominating woman. Their tumultuous romance was short-lived, for the comtesse died in childbirth within a year. Her lover grieved for several months, but then turned to the . . .

Marquise de La Tournelle, another sister. A recent widow, she held the king at bay by refusing to yield until he promised to recognize her as his chief mistress, give her the title of duchess, legitimize any children they might have, grant her access to the private royal purse, and stop seeing her older sister, Madame de Mailly. The king agreed to everything, and she became the Duchess of Chatauroux. But her reign as chief mistress turned out to be short-lived. The king fell seriously ill, and the Bishop of Soissons refused to administer the final sacraments until the duchess had been dismissed. Upon his recovery, His Majesty called for the duchess—but it was too late. She had died in the interim. He was desolate, but amused himself occasionally with another sister, the . . .

Duchess of Lauragais. She was, intermittently, mistress of the king, but she never achieved the favored position that her sisters had held.

Louis de Mailly, the Marquis of Nesle, benefited greatly from his daughters' charms. For their services to the crown, all his debts were paid, and he received a nice sum from the royal purse. A fifth Nesle sibling also attracted the royal eye but did not become his mistress. Her husband had taken a unique stand for those times, saying that any slur on his honor would be settled in "royal" blood—and the king did not pursue the matter.

EIGHT WHO TOLD ALL

※

Harriette Wilson. After a dazzling career as one of the leading "fashionable impures" of the eighteenth century, Wilson, having lost her looks and being pressed for cash, decided to publish her memoirs—but not without giving her former lovers a chance to protect their reputations. She notified each that for 200 pounds she would not mention him in her life history. Many gentlemen, delighted to get off the hook, met her price, but one of her most famous customers, the Duke of Wellington, replied, "Publish and be damned!" Her *Memoirs* went into thirty-one editions within a year and earned her a total of 10,000 pounds.

Victoria Woodhull. ♀ Suffragists were reluctant to reveal that their supporter, the Reverend Henry Ward Beecher, was not the paragon of virtue he seemed, but the unconventional Woodhull was angry at other feminist leaders for refusing to support her candidacy for president in 1872. The free-love advocate exposed Beecher's adulterous affair with the wife of a respected friend, but her ploy backfired; she was imprisoned for sending "obscene" literature through the mail. Beecher's trial for adultery ended in a hung jury.

Ann Eliza Webb Young. Mormon leader Brigham Young was sixty-seven years old and Webb twenty-four when she became his nineteenth wife in 1869. Polygamy did not prove to be her style. She filed for divorce, demanding a settlement of $200,000; Young offered $15,000. Infuriated, Webb went on to lecture widely about the horrors of multiple marriage, then put it down on paper in *Wife No. 19, or The Story of a Life in Bondage.* The memoir brought her revenge but no alimony, but the publicity helped to get an antipolygamy law passed in 1882.

Nan Britton. As a teen-ager, Britton harbored a schoolgirl crush on Warren G. Harding and fulfilled her fantasies on a couch in his Senate office. She conceived a child. The affair continued during Harding's presidency, and after his death Britton turned to the Harding family for funds. They refused to pay child support—and she told all in *The President's Daughter.*

Anna Sage. Fearing she would be deported to her native Rumania, the Chicago brothel keeper, in return for a pledge of safety, promised FBI agents she would "finger" her friend, most wanted criminal John Dillinger. In 1934 the "lady in red" pointed him out in the lobby of a movie theater and federal agents shot him.

Elizabeth Ray. Frightened, she said, by the temper of her employer, Representative Wayne Hays of Ohio, Ray confided to two reporters from the *Washington Post*: "I can't type, I can't file, I can't even answer the phone." The only work she did for a $14,000-a-year salary plus expenses, she charged, was the work she did in bed. Hays resigned in August 1976.

Judith Campbell Exner. Exner maintains she would never have written *My Story* (1977), an exposé of her relationships with President John F. Kennedy and Mafia chieftains John Roselli and Sam Giancana, if the press and others had dealt fairly with her after she told all to a Senate committee in 1975. The FBI had learned early of her strange combination of friendships and hounded her, even after she became pregnant. It therefore bore the brunt of her wrath. Exner decided that "It wasn't fair to the child to have him come into this kind of world." She attempted suicide in 1965, recovered, and gave the baby up for adoption.

Judy Chavez. In 1979 the twenty-two-year-old woman published the story of her five-month subsidized romance with Arkady Shevchenko, a former United Nations official who defected from the Soviet Union and whose expenses—including Chavez—were possibly underwritten by the CIA. She earned $5,000 a month for her services—in addition to a luxury sports car, Caribbean vacations, shopping sprees, and other expenses. The CIA declined to comment on the source of Shevchenko's money.

DOING A NUMBER ON LOVE, AND MARRIAGE

- In 1978 there were 1.1 million unmarried couples living together, more than double the number of such couples in 1970.
- In that year too there were as many divorces as there were unmarried households—1.1 million.
- In 1978 there were 48 million married couples, and 2.2 million marriages took place.
- Of the unmarried-and-living-together couples, more than 96,000 women were living with markedly younger men, and more than 223,000 men were living with markedly younger women.
- In 1977, 2,176,000 marriages were performed in the United States, only slightly more than the 2,154,807 of 1976. A record of 2,277,000 marriages was set in 1973.
- Also in 1977, 1,090,000 divorces became final, an increase of 7,000 over the preceding year. The number of divorces in the United States has increased every year since 1962 and more than doubled between 1966 (499,000) and 1976 (1,083,000). But the yearly increases have gotten smaller in every year since 1971. The 1977 divorce rate of 5 per 1,000 population was almost double the rate of 2.6 per 1,000 population of ten years earlier.

- In 1977 Texas led the way to the altar with 161,331 marriages, followed closely by California with 151,346. That year—and in most years—California also had the most divorces, 132,888. At the other extreme, the fewest marriages were posted that year in Delaware—3,999—while North Dakota's 1,982 and Vermont's 1,838 divorces were the least of any state.

THE VALUE OF A WIFE

❧

- The Papuans of New Guinea exchange for a virgin bride five pigs, one cassowary, and $300. A woman who has been previously married, however, is valued at two pigs, one cassowary, and $37.50. How the monetary figures were arrived at is unknown.
- Among the Baganda of Africa, a groom-to-be presents several goats or a cow, beer, bark cloth, and thousands of cowrie shells to the kin of his bride.
- A Kazak man of Central Asia cements his marriage by handing over about forty animals—sheep, cattle, horses, and/or camels—to the family of his bride.
- A Crow Indian man gives meat to his bride's mother and horses to her brothers.
- Among the Kai of New Guinea a boar's tusk and a hog are among the valuables the groom gives to the bride's brothers and maternal uncles. The groom must put in some time working for her father as well.
- Among some of the people of the Amazon Valley, a man presents a pot of tobacco and a pot of coca to the father of his bride.
- In Dahomey, Africa, it takes a series of three payments to make a marital arrangement official. The first accompanies betrothal, which may take place when the future couple are still infants; the groom-to-be's family gives cowrie shells, grain, and cloth to the family of the bride-to-be. When she is a young girl the bride-to-be has the opportunity to accept or reject the match. If she refuses, her family must return the gifts. But if the match is to go through, the future groom must present to the bride's father the precise amount of the fee of the midwife who officiated at her birth. When the marriage finally takes place, the groom must give the bride's ancestors livestock, vegetables, palm oil, and liquor.
- Among the Hopi Indians a wedding cannot be finalized until the groom finishes weaving the special wedding garments to be worn by his bride.

THE USES OF VIRGINITY

❧

Virginity has always been thought to be powerful. It can work magic and do all sorts of good—except, perhaps, for the virgin.

- A virgin can rejuvenate an aging man. Abishag did this job for King David: "Now King David was old *and* stricken in years; and they covered him with clothes, but he got no heat. Wherefore his servants said unto him, Let there be sought for my lord the king a young virgin; and let her stand before the king, and let her lie in thy bosom, that my lord the king may get heat" (1 Kings 1:1–2).

- Only the purity of a virgin can keep a sacred fire going—which accounts for the use of vestal virgins as priestesses by peoples as scattered in time and place as the Romans, the Druids, and the Incas.

- The presence of a virgin causes crops to grow. The Romans would carry a young woman across the fields at planting time to ensure a good harvest. The ancient Mayans had a more complicated procedure: at Chichén Itzá they would sacrifice a virgin (cross-eyed only) by pushing her into a natural well from a high jutting rock. If she fell straight in and disappeared, she was acceptable to the gods and the crops would be good. If the drowned body surfaced, either her eyes weren't crossed enough or she wasn't virginal enough—take your choice. But if, miraculously, she emerged alive, the lucky maiden was welcomed as a goddess and revered for the rest of her well-deserved life.

- Pliny gives a virgin credit for the following phenomena: if she climbs a cherry tree it will die; within a mile of her presence, bees will flee from their hives; at her touch brass will rust and wine turn to vinegar.

- The sacrifice of a virgin can save a community from impending disaster. In folk tales of the Middle Ages, the "damsels in distress" rescued by brave knights had usually been handed right over to their "monster" or "dragon" captors by frightened townsfolk.

- Intercourse with a virgin can cure venereal disease—without infecting the virgin. This medieval belief (or rationale) thrust many young girls into the eager arms of syphilitic men. The continued spread of the disease should have suggested that the "cure" did not work, but perhaps this medical procedure was too popular to give up.

- According to St. Gregory the Great, only a virgin can grasp the horn of the elusive unicorn. The shy creature and a maiden generally appear together in medieval tapestries.

- The Royal Swans on the Thames River gladly eat from the hand of a virgin, but will have no truck with those who are less pure. Hence the saying "She'll never feed another swan," applied to those who have seen better days. One fifteenth-century lady whose virginity had been impugned by rivals at court, stood on the riverbank and offered bread to a swan, which imperiously sailed past her. Disgraced, she threw herself into the river. Later it was discovered that the noblewoman's enemies had put out the creature's eyes so that it would not be able to see her.

- A garter plucked from the left leg of a virgin in the light of the moon is very lucky. This ancient belief was still around during World War I when English flying aces would murmur "Touch your garters" for luck just before takeoff.

- If the bones of virgins are used to build the walls of a fortress, it will be protected against invaders. Children's skeletons are often found today in the ruins of old castles. The "fair lady" of the London Bridge nursery rhyme was probably one such virgin. The bridge started falling, it was rumored, because the twelve-year-old used as part of the foundation had not died a natural death, as required. When the bones of a peasant girl were used as reinforcement, the problem was solved.

- A candle made of virgin fat will protect a thief while he is robbing a holy place. This gory belief was responsible for a thriving trade in candles composed of melted-down virgins in medieval Russia.
- The stone lions in front of New York's Public Library at 42nd Street and Fifth Avenue roar whenever a virgin walks by. For decades the lions have been strangely silent.

VIRGIN WIVES

Isis. ♀ On the night before the Egyptian goddess was to be married to her brother Osiris, he was abducted and torn into little pieces which were scattered throughout the world. With the zeal of a jigsaw-puzzle fan, Isis found the pieces and put her man back together—but nowhere could his genitals be found. Isis stolidly accepted this sad situation, announcing that she would remain forever a virgin bride.

St. Werburga. After being wife in name only for three years to her husband, Ceolred, she took the veil. According to tradition her father, Wulphere, King of Mercia, impressed by his daughter's piety, founded the Abbey Church of Chester, England (A.D. 600), as a convent for her. Ceolred's opinions are not recorded.

Elisabeth Gonzaga. A Renaissance historian writes that the wife of Guidobaldo, Duke of Urbino, was "one of those of whom the apostle speaks, who are married as though they were not. . . . She passed the first two years of her marriage in such a great ignorance of the sacrament in which she was engaged, that she imagined all the other married women were like her."

The Princess of Mantua. She was a sixteen-year-old virgin when she wed the prince in 1583. On their wedding night, her husband discovered that she had an unusually narrow vagina and he could not penetrate her. A clerical and medical hubbub followed, with the unfortunate princess being subjected to a series of useless surgical procedures. The case finally went to the Consistory in Rome, where the Archbishop of Turin and seven high cardinals pronounced her condition the devil's work. Despite his devotion to her, the prince divorced his impenetrable bride, and she spent the rest of her virginal life in a convent.

Catherine the Great. ♀ One of history's best-known collectors of men was actually a virgin during the first seven years of her marriage to Peter III of Russia because he was also in that state. Catherine reports in her memoirs that her childlike spouse had neither the will nor the desire to make love and thought of her mainly as a playmate. She found solace elsewhere.

Marie Carmichael Stopes. ♀ Because she was still a virgin after five years of marriage to Canadian botanist Reginald Ruggles Gates, Stopes read every book in the British Museum on the subject of sex. As a result of her research she divorced Gates, became the first woman expert on the subject, and published *Married Love* (1918), the first sex manual to focus on a woman's pleasure. Her second mate, Humphrey Vernon Roe, proved to be much livelier; together they founded the Mothers' Clinic for Birth Control in London in 1921.

Florence ("Peaches") Browning. When the penniless fifteen-year-old nymphet wed wealthy fifty-one-year-old realtor Edward ("Daddy") Browning in 1926, their marriage was the sensation of the tabloids. It was even more so when the union ended, after only six months—and Peaches claimed her virginity was still intact. "Daddy" Browning confirmed this: "Peaches did not sleep with me. From the very first night she has always slept with her mother."

Lady Ampthill, a British society beauty of the 1920s, was sued for divorce by her husband, the third Baron Ampthill, who charged that the child she was carrying was illegitimate. The Ampthill union, he claimed, had never been consummated. Medical witnesses confirmed this. Lady Ampthill was shown to be, technically, a virgin, even though she was five months pregnant. The legitimacy issue was not completely resolved until 1976, when the fourth Lord Ampthill, issue of this "virgin birth," was admitted to the House of Lords and to the peerage.

ADVICE FOR BRIDES

- When a bride dreams of her wedding day, it means good luck.
- A bride shouldn't marry a man whose last name begins with the same letter as her own:

> Change the name and not the letter,
> Change for the worse and not for better.

- It is good luck for a bride to carry bread in her pocket. With every piece she gives away, she gives away one of her troubles. For each morsel she gives to the poor on her way to the church, a bit of bad luck is avoided.
- A bride will be fortunate if a ray of sunlight falls on her as she emerges from the church:

> Happy the bride the sun shines on,
> Woe to the bride the rain rains on.

- Women who marry in red will wind up fighting with their mates before the year has ended, or their husbands will die.
- After the bride is fully dressed for church, she must not look into a mirror again until the ceremony is over. If she does, things will go badly. She may, however, dress in front of a mirror, but she should leave off some small piece of clothing that can be added at the last minute without using a mirror.
- To find a spider crawling on her wedding dress is a sign of good luck for the bride.

- A bride should have her hair done, and her veil put on, by a woman who is herself happily married.
- Happiness will come to the bride who carries a bit of salt with her when she goes to the church. Devils and witches hate salt because it stands for friendship and loyalty.
- It's unlucky if a bride does not weep on the day of her wedding.
- When a bride breaks something on her wedding day, it means that she will fight with her mother-in-law and her husband will take his mother's part.
- If an ex-lover, with animosity in his soul, kisses the bride on her wedding day, the honeymoon will not be a happy one.
- It's important for a bride to throw away or "lose" the pins on her bridal ensemble. If she keeps even one pin, nothing will go well for her. If one of her bridesmaids is so unwise as to keep a pin, she should not expect to be married for a year.
- A bride must not put her feet on the bare floor on her wedding night. This is certain to bring ill fortune.
- The morning after the wedding, a bride can ask her husband for some money or for any piece of property that appeals to her. He's honor-bound to fulfill her request.
- Standing at the altar, a bride should manage to place her right foot ahead of the groom's. This ensures her future dominance over him.

From *The Folklore of Wedding and Marriage,* selected and edited by Duncan Emrich (New York: American Heritage Press, 1970)

EIGHT MARITAL ARRANGEMENTS WITH INTERESTING POSSIBILITIES FOR WOMEN

꙳

A 1973 anthropological survey of 854 societies found that in the vast majority—83 percent—one man could be married to more than one woman at a time. Polygyny is particularly popular in the traditional societies of Africa, the Mediterranean region, the Pacific Islands, and South America. In only four societies was polyandry, the marriage of one woman to several men, customary:

- Among the Sinhalese of Sri Lanka (Ceylon), one woman may be married to two or more brothers. The first husband must consent to his wife's subsequent husbands and liaisons. Each father legitimates his own children—which would seem to give the mother a great deal to say about the paternity of her offspring.
- Among the Nayar of the Malabar Coast of India, all girls who have come of age (seven to twelve years) are married to a group of older ritual bridegrooms. Each couple remains in seclusion for three days, then the bridegrooms leave, perhaps never to see their brides again. After this marriage ceremony a girl has become a young woman. Later, when she finds—or is chosen by—Mr. Right, she may freely enter into a relationship. In fact, she may have as many visiting husbands as she desires. The husband who visits on any given evening leaves his weap-

ons—Nayar men belong to a military caste—at the door of her room. Any other husbands who show up that night may sleep on the veranda. Otherwise, the men live with their own mothers and sisters, or with their military unit. When a baby is born, one of the mother's husbands acknowledges paternity by paying the fee of the midwife. That is his only obligation.

- Among the Todas of the Nilgiri Hills of southern India, a woman gets married to a man and his brothers at the same time. She may also take as many extra lovers as she wishes, provided the lover has obtained the consent of her husbands and given them generous presents. The "official" father of a woman's children is the husband who has performed a special ceremony with her prior to the child's birth and is not necessarily the biological father.
- In the Marquesas Islands of the Pacific, a woman who is the oldest child, and therefore her family's heir, owns and rules the entire household. She can take and dismiss husbands as often as she pleases. Her chief husband serves as his wife's deputy, caring for the children, cooking, and housekeeping as she orders.

In a few other societies polyandry is permitted under special circumstances:

- In mountainous Tibet, because land is so scarce, a group of brothers often marry one woman so that their children can inherit the family property in its entirety. A woman who has been chosen to be the wife of several brothers has high social status.
- Among the Pende, Lele, and some other peoples of the Congo, a woman is chosen by the members of a village, or promised by her father, to become the "wife of the village." After being chosen for this high-status position, she takes part only in male activities, including hunting, and no longer has to do the women's work. After a while she may choose as many men as she likes to be her husbands and sets up housekeeping with them. She and her children are supported by the entire village, which pays the bride wealth for her sons when they are to be married. Her daughters have particularly high status and can ask a higher bride wealth than usual; their husbands, too, will have status equal to that of a chief.

And, in a few places, women always have the last word:

- Among the Navaho of the southwestern United States, a man goes to live with his wife and her relatives after marriage. When a woman decides she has had enough of a particular husband, she simply packs up his personal belongings and places them outside the entrance of her hogan. Her husband—and the entire community—gets the message. He returns to the hogan of his mother and stays there until he can find some other woman who will have him.
- Among the Cashibos, a Chama people of the Lower Ukayali River in Peru, the women run things. When a girl is ready to settle down, she simply steals the mosquito net of the man she has chosen and moves it to her own dwelling. This constitutes marriage. The husband takes his wife's name and works for his mother-in-law and his wife's family. Even the clothes on his back become the property of his wife. Divorce

is managed quite as easily. The wife simply returns her husband's mosquito net, takes back his clothing, and sends him off to his relatives. It's not unusual for one Cashibo woman to have five or six husbands at one time.

UNEQUAL SPOUSES

Man and wife: note that the wife is never pronounced first.

Better half: usually ironic if referring to a wife.

The farmer takes a wife: the passively taken wife—though she is probably just as industrious and productive as he.

Henpecked husband: a universal term of derision.

Ball and chain: what the henpecked husband drags; rarely applied to a wife's burden.

Wearing the pants: still the prerogative of the male head of the family, despite the clothing revolution.

Contributed by Ruth Ulmyn

SEVEN HUSBANDS OF BARBARA HUTTON ♀

"Poor little rich girl" was the phrase the press used to describe the Woolworth heiress who seemed to get little happiness from either her vast fortune or her titled husbands. A butler told her at the age of nine, "Someday you may be the richest girl in the world, but all that means is that somebody will want to marry you for your money. You're fat and not very pretty, so if anybody does marry you, you'll know it was the money that did it." Love, Hutton hoped, would make her feel good. "Life doesn't make any sense without men," she said of her seven trips to the altar. She died in 1979, a semirecluse with a fortune that had declined from $70 million in 1930 to just $10 million. A goodly amount of it was spent on these gentlemen:

Prince Alexis Mdivani, a Russian nobleman, who married Hutton in 1933, after divorcing his first wife when the heiress met his price: $2 million cash, plus an annual income of $50,000. After the Hutton deal was made, the international playboy cabled his sisters, "I've won the prize. Announce the betrothal." Mdivani started Hutton on what was to become a lifetime regimen of stringent "coffee-only" dieting, and by the time the couple divorced in 1935, she proudly compared her figure to that of Mahatma Gandhi. The prince received a divorce settlement of $3 million.

Count Kurt von Haughwitz-Reventlow, a Danish nobleman, who married Hutton in Reno, Nevada, in 1935. He found her habit of weeping when the scales showed a gain of even an ounce disconcerting, and her flirtations with other men drove the marriage to the rocks. They separated in 1938.

Cary Grant, who married Hutton in 1942, the only one of her husbands to maintain his financial independence. He also wasn't fond of the society crowd; at their divorce hearing in 1945 Hutton explained, "Mr. Grant did not like my home, and on more than one occasion when I had a dinner party and invited friends, he refused to come down to dinner because he was too bored."

Prince Igor Troubetzkoy, Russian nobleman, connoisseur, and racing-car driver, who wed Hutton in 1947. He watched her fight insomnia, devour pack after pack of Chesterfields, and drink fifteen to twenty cups of coffee a day, and two years later the marriage ended. His divorce settlement of $1,000 a month for life, plus substantial property, may have had something to do with his decision to lock away forever his manuscript entitled "My Life with Barbara Hutton."

Porfirio Rubirosa, a Dominican playboy described by one society columnist as the world's "Number One Foreign Co-respondent," who added Hutton to his collection in 1953, jilting Zsa Zsa Gabor to do so. "Barbara looks like she's on a death march," Gabor commented acidly after seeing their wedding photo, and it did turn out that Hutton spent most of the marriage in bed, alone. Their marriage lasted four months, during which time Rubirosa collected his own plane ($200,000) and an $800,000 citrus ranch that guaranteed him an annual income of $200,-000.

Baron Gottfried von Cramm, a German tennis champion, who married Hutton in 1955. Von Cramm was refused admittance to the United States because of an old prison term for homosexual acts. By 1956 the union was over.

Prince Doan Vinh Na Champacak, a Vietnamese nobleman, who married Hutton in 1964. It lasted until 1967. The divorce settlement included a check for $3 million to Prince Doan and, mysteriously, $1 million to his brother, Prince Ronald.

THE REWARDS OF BEING MRS. TOMMY MANVILLE

All his life, multimillionaire Manville, heir to the Johns-Manville asbestos-manufacturing fortune, pursued pleasure and matrimony, but most of his unions were extremely short-lived; the thrill was in the chase. All his brides were physically similar—blond, beautiful, and amply endowed. Undoing the results of his excursions to the altar cost Manville a total of $3 million, but "every penny was well spent," he confided to columnist Ed Sullivan. "I know some of the biggest men in the country who spent a lot more on hobbies and ended up with a lot less."

Florence Huber was a twenty-one-year-old chorus girl and Manville a youth of seventeen when they wed in August 1911. His father promptly disowned him, and the bridegroom was forced to take employment as a chauffeur. The couple separated in 1917 and were divorced five years later. After the reinstated Manville came into his inheritance, he gave Huber more than $100,000.

Lois Arline McCoin started out as secretary to Manville senior and perhaps something more. She and young Manville were wed October 1, 1925, and the union endured until Christmas. In that time she spent more than $50,000 on clothes and furs. The divorce settlement provided her with $19,000 a year—until her premature death in 1929.

Avonne Taylor, a former Follies girl, received $200,000 upon the breakup of her marriage thirty-four days after it began on May 21, 1931.

Marcelle Edwards wed Manville on October 9, 1933, but left him by April 1934. He presented the former chorus girl with a bouquet of orchids as she flew to Reno and negotiated a settlement of $200,000.

Bonita Edwards, a twenty-two-year-old Follies girl (and no relation to Marcelle), married the forty-seven-year-old Manville on November 18, 1941. According to friends, he looked at least sixty. Seventeen days later, she arrived in Reno.

Wilhelmina ("Billy") Connelly Boze wed the industrialist on October 11, 1942. A twenty-two-year-old actress, she proved unique among the Manville wives. After their two-month alliance ended she insisted on an agreement that there would be no alimony, support, or maintenance. But like his other ex-mates, she maintained a warm friendship with the millionaire.

Macie Marie ("Sunny") Ainsworth achieved the shortest of all these brief alliances. Her marriage, performed on August 24, 1943, was over eight hours after the vows were taken. This gave her just enough time to get ready for the trip to Reno. Although Ainsworth was barely twenty, her wedding to Manville was her fifth. She received $75,000 for the experience.

Georgina Campbell, a writer, met Manville while interviewing him. Their union, celebrated on December 13, 1945, ended four weeks later. Campbell opted for a separation instead of a divorce, and Manville agreed, hoping in that way to provide him with "insurance" against another ill-considered alliance. He paid her $1,000 a month until she was killed in a car crash on her way to visit him in 1952.

Anita Frances Roddy-Eden, a twenty-nine-year-old songwriter, married Manville on July 10, 1952. Two weeks later she got a Mexican divorce and accepted $100,000 in lieu of alimony.

Patricia Gaston, a Texas chorus girl, was twenty-seven years younger than her sixty-three-year-old husband. Shortly after their wedding on May 5, 1957, she journeyed to Reno and collected $200,000.

Christina Erdlen's connection to Manville was delayed by the fact that he had to arrange for a quick Mexican divorce for her from her first husband. Finally, the waitress and the playboy married on January 12, 1960. They were still wed when Manville died in 1967, leaving her his considerable estate.

ALICE TOKLAS'S ♀ LIST OF WIVES OF GENIUSES

❦

"The geniuses came and talked to Gertrude Stein and the wives sat with me. How they unroll, an endless vista through the years."

Gertrude Stein,♀ *The Autobiography of Alice B. Toklas*

Fernande, the first long-term mistress of Picasso.
Madame Matisse
Marcelle Braque
Josette Gris
Eve Picasso
Bridget Gibb
Marjory Gibb
Hadley Hemingway
Pauline Hemingway
Mrs. Sherwood Anderson
Mrs. Bravig Imbs
Mrs. Ford Madox Ford

Mercy Bump (32 inches, 29 pounds) and her husband, Barnum attraction Tom Thumb, on their wedding day in 1863. *Library of Congress.* (SHORT PEOPLE)

Amelia Earhart and her mother enjoy a day of triumph in 1928 after she became the first woman to fly across the Atlantic. Nine years later Earhart disappeared over the Pacific. *Library of Congress.* (MISSING PERSONS)

(*Above*): Eilley Orrum, "The Washoe Seeress," foresaw the riches of the Comstock Lode before the first strike was made. She is shown here with her husband, Sandy Bowers. *Nevada Historical Society.* (ELEVEN SEERS AND PSYCHICS)

(*Below left*): Perhaps no man has ever masqueraded as a woman so well as master-spy Charles Éon de Beaumont (La Chevalière d'Éon) pictured here in typical attire. (SIX MEN WHO WANTED TO BE TAKEN FOR WOMEN)

(*Below right*): Hannah Senesh parachuted into Eastern Europe in 1944 in a vain attempt to rescue Hungarian Jews from the Nazis. *Zionist Archives and Library.* (ELEVEN FACES OF HEROISM)

Laura Bridgman, born blind, deaf, and mute, succeeded in learning to communicate. Her example inspired Anne Sullivan, who later taught Helen Keller. *Sophia Smith Collection, Smith College.* (TWELVE WHO OVERCAME ADVERSITY)

(*Above left*): Paiute Indian Sarah Winnemucca protested the brutal treatment of her people in the late nineteenth century. *Nevada Historical Society.* (SEEKING JUSTICE FOR THE INDIAN)
(*Above right*): Newspaperwoman Ida B. Wells-Barnett, shown here with her children, ran a one-woman crusade against lynching. *Reprinted from* The Autobiography of Ida B. Wells-Barnett *by permission of The University of Chicago Press.* (NIKKI GIOVANNI'S LIST OF EIGHTEEN GREAT BLACK WOMEN)

therine the Great of Russia nearing the end of her reign. Her love life continued to be a busy one.
OVERS OF CATHERINE THE GREAT)

V ❧ M *IS FOR ... AND OTHER*
FAMILY CONNECTIONS

NOTABLE CASES OF MATERNITY

❧

Margaret, wife of Henman, Earl of Henneberge, a sharp-tongued countess, once questioned the paternity of a poor woman's twins. The maligned mother prayed to God to send the noblewoman "as many children as there were days in the whole year." Consequently, sometime around 1276, Margaret is supposed to have given birth to 365 children at one time, all of whom perished on the same eventful day.

Dianora Frescobaldi, a lady of the Renaissance, is said to have been the mother "of at least fifty-two children." According to the inscription on a portrait of her by Bronzino, she never produced fewer than three infants from one pregnancy.

Mrs. Ormsby of Chicago, herself one of a set of triplets, gave birth to fourteen children in seven years, including a set of quadruplets born in 1901.

Mrs. Pennock of St. Louis, herself one of twenty-four children, had given birth to three sets of twins by the time she was twenty-one years old.

Madame Fyodor Vassilet, a Russian peasant of the mid-nineteenth century, gave birth to sixteen sets of twins, seven sets of triplets, and four sets of quadruplets. Madame Vassilet is the greatest producer of offspring whose accomplishment has been verified. She became so renowned that she was presented at the court of Czar Alexander II.

Josimar Carnauba of Belém, Brazil, according to the *Guinness Book of World Records,* has thirty-eight children. The fifty-four-year-old woman was married when she was fifteen and by 1977 had produced fourteen sons and twenty-four daughters, all at yearly intervals.

Ruth Kistler, the oldest mother ever recorded, gave birth to a daughter in 1956 when she was 57 years and 129 days of age.

Elzire Dionne gave birth to history's most publicized babies, the Dionne quintuplets,♀ in a Canadian farmhouse on May 28, 1934. More than a thousand tourists a month visited the Dionne farm to ogle the quints and shop at the Dionnes' souvenir stand.

Mary Louise Morris, a thirty-nine-year-old black mother in Virginia, gave birth to her fourth successive set of twins in 1974, bringing her total number of offspring to thirteen. Medical odds on such a sequence of twin births are 1 in 65,610,000.

Susan Rosenkowitz became the mother of sextuplets in Cape Town, South Africa, on January 11, 1974; they were the first complete set of sextuplets to survive. In return for world-wide rights to their children's story, the parents accepted $147,500 from a Johannesburg publisher, and it is reported that an additional $127,360 was produced by articles about the babies by the time they were one year old.

Grete Bardaum in 1975 gave birth out of wedlock to twin sons. One was white, the other black. At a paternity hearing, Bardaum explained the medical rarity by saying she had slept with both a white man and a black man on the same day. Blood tests proved that the fraternal twins resulted from two ova that were, indeed, fertilized by sperm from two different men. The mother has since married and given birth to another set of twins; both children were white.

Myrna Faulkner of San Diego, California, gave birth in November 1978 to a daughter after only twenty-three weeks of pregnancy, the earliest successful premature birth on record. Tiny Mignon Faulkner weighed seventeen ounces and was twelve inches long when she was seven weeks old.

Lesley Brown of Bristol, England, thirty-one years old, had been unable to conceive during ten years of marriage. On July 25, 1978, she gave birth to a five-pound twelve-ounce girl, named Louise, the first authenticated birth of a human infant conceived outside the mother's body (*in vitro,* in laboratory glassware) and implanted in the maternal uterus to continue prenatal development.

Durga Agarwal was the world's second "test tube" baby, born October 3, 1978, to Pravat Kumar and Bella Agarwal in Calcutta, India. The child's name is that of a Hindu goddess who triumphs over evil.

Margaret Martin, a twenty-nine-year-old New Zealand woman who had a hysterectomy eight months earlier, gave birth to a healthy daughter in May 1979. Apparently a fertilized ovum remained in her body and became implanted in her small intestine. The baby was surgically removed four weeks before term and weighed five pounds.

NO PAUSING FOR PREGNANCY

❧

Sacajawea,♀ an Indian guide, was at the beginning of a pregnancy when she agreed to lead the Lewis and Clark expedition across the continent.

Chen Li,♀ a Chinese Communist leader in the 1920s, participated in military action while pregnant.

Colette,♀ later the writer, continued to perform acrobatic routines as a music-hall performer when she became pregnant.

June Irwin was three and one-half months pregnant when she won a bronze medal in platform diving at the 1952 Summer Olympics.

Andrea Mead Lawrence won two gold medals in alpine racing at the 1952 Winter Olympics when in her first trimester.

Mary Bacon, ♀ a jockey, gave birth to a daughter soon after riding her third horse of the day.

Wendy Boglioli, the Olympic swim champion, was in her fifth month of pregnancy when she competed in the preliminary heat of the hundred-yard free-style at the American Amateur Athletic Union national short course meet in April 1978.

Ze'eva Cohen, the Israeli-born choreographer and dancer, continued to perform while pregnant and created the dance *Seed* in which a pregnant dancer is the central figure.

Mary Jones ran the "half marathon" (13.1 miles) of the Dallas White Rock Marathon in December 1976 in two hours and five minutes—near the end of her eighth month of pregnancy.

THE OEDIPAL CONNECTION

Amalie Nathanson Freud, although she was the mother of seven other children, doted on her oldest, Sigmund, and called him *"mein goldener Sigi."* Freud appreciated the benefits: "A man who has been the indisputable favorite of his mother keeps for life the feelings of a conqueror, that confidence of success which frequently induces real success." The Oedipus can be very complex indeed, as the following stories indicate.

Katharine Elisabeth Textor Goethe,♀ a teen-ager herself when her son was born, grew up with the poet as a close companion and playmate. When he became famous she would introduce herself to strangers by saying, "I am Goethe's mother."

Caroline Fleuriot Flaubert, the mother of novelist Gustave Flaubert, lived with him through most of his adult life. He remained a bachelor even after her death. Wrote Flaubert to his mother, "I know very well that I shall never love another as I do you. You will never have a rival, never fear."

Margaret Morrison Carnegie ♀ was so devoted to her son Andrew Carnegie that he swore he would never wed while she lived and kept his word. He married for the first time at the age of fifty-one, six months after his mother's death.

Jessie Wilson. Her son Woodrow remembered unabashedly that he had been tied to her apron strings "till I was a great big fellow." In one of his more controversial studies, Freud used the duo as an example of the Oedipal connection. Fittingly, it was Wilson who, in 1914, put his signature to the resolution proclaiming Mother's Day.

Sara Delano Roosevelt, FDR's "dear Mama," never stopped trying to dominate her son's life. Until he was fourteen she rarely left his side. When he went to Harvard she rented a house in Boston. No woman was good enough for him, but she finally acquiesced to his marriage to distant cousin Eleanor ♀ in 1905. Then she built the couple a house that adjoined her own with a connecting door on the fourth floor.

Mary Hardy MacArthur, Douglas MacArthur's mother, has been described as doting to the point of being dotty. During her son's four years at West Point she lived in a hotel near enough to his dormitory that she would know at what hour he turned off the lights at night. Even when he was army chief of staff, MacArthur went home to have lunch with his mother every day.

Annie Hoover was the major influence in the life of her son J. Edgar Hoover, who never married. They lived together in Washington, D.C., until her death at the age of eighty.

Dolly Sinatra. The priest who presided at her 1977 memorial service recalled that "she lived and died for her son. Every breath she ever breathed, every effort she ever made, every prayer she ever prayed was for her son"—who was, of course, Frank Sinatra.

Mabelle Hollenbeck,♀ the mother of actor Clifton Webb, was seldom separated from him from the time he made his stage debut at the age of six. She counted the house at each of his performances and moved to Hollywood with him, supervising every aspect of his day. After she died, his grief lasted until his own demise in 1966.

Rebekah Baines Johnson♀ determined that since her husband was not successful, her oldest son, Lyndon, would be. She taught him to read when he was two and had him perusing Longfellow by the age of three. Wrote biographer Doris Faber, "She would not allow him the least doubt that he was destined for leading." When he did achieve prominence, she beamed: "You have always justified my expectations, my hopes, my dreams."

SOME MOTHERS OF NINE OR MORE

Niobe, wife of the King of Thebes, was, according to Greek myth, the overly proud mother of seven sons and seven daughters. When she demanded that they be honored in preference to the offspring of Apollo and Diana, the people obeyed and, indignant, Apollo hunted down Niobe's sons while Diana slew Niobe's daughters. Niobe sat unmoving, wailing over her slain children for nine days and nights, then was changed to stone, from which, in the form of a mountain stream, she weeps for them still.

Hecuba, the wife of Priam, King of Troy, had nineteen children, the oldest of whom was Hector, destined to be slain by Achilles during the Trojan War.

Cornelia, a Roman matron of the second century B.C., gave birth to twelve children. Two of them became the famous statesmen the Gracchi—Tiberius and Caius.

Priscilla Mullins had, after John Alden finally spoke for himself and married her in 1621, eleven children.

Empress Maria Theresa called herself the "general and chief mother" of the Hapsburg empire, an apt title. She had sixteen children, among them the ill-starred Marie Antoinette.♀

Queen Charlotte,♀ the wife of George III of England, was the mother of fifteen children, among them two future kings: George IV and William IV.

Sojourner Truth,♀ the black abolitionist and mystic, was the mother of thirteen children.

Lily Martin Spencer had thirteen children and even so managed to become a well-known genre painter in the late nineteenth century. Spouse Benjamin Rush Spencer was an early househusband, devoting himself to domesticity while she earned their bread.

Adeline Younger Dalton had fifteen children. Eleven became respectable citizens, but four became the notorious Dalton Brothers Gang, known for their bank and train robberies.

Queen Victoria,♀ although not overly delighted with pregnancy, did her duty nevertheless and produced nine children. As the century turned, her progeny occupied the thrones of half the countries of Europe, among them grandchildren Kaiser Wilhelm II of Germany, Czarina Alexandra of Russia, and Queen Marie of Rumania.

Annie Oakley (Phoebe Ann Moses),♀ the Wild West sharpshooter, adopted and raised eighteen children.

Lillian Gilbreth, an industrial engineer, and her husband, Frank, applied time-and-motion techniques, plus psychology, to the rearing of their twelve offspring and became immortalized in one son's book, *Cheaper by the Dozen.*

Rose Fitzgerald Kennedy,♀ mother of nine including John, Robert, and Edward Kennedy, has said of child rearing,"My theory is, if you bring up the oldest the way you want the others to go, invariably they'll all follow."

Julie Martinez of Brownfield, Texas, has given birth to twenty-one children in twenty-five years, the most recent in January 1980. Martinez, who was seventeen at the time of her first delivery, has been pregnant a total of 190 months, or nearly sixteen of her forty-two years. Eighteen of her children survive and a dozen still live at home.

Edith Kerns, of Haymarket, Virginia, has been foster mother to 1,218 children. It all started when Kerns, whose husband was killed in 1949, longed for the daughters she never had. A friend put her in touch with local child welfare authorities, and since 1956 her wards have ranged from an abandoned four-day-old baby to eighteen-year-olds. Usually from seven to nine children are with Kerns at any one time.

CALL THEM MOM

Ma Perkins,♀ a lumberyard owner in the soap opera of the same name.

Ma Barker, the mastermind behind the stickups, murders, and kidnappings her four dutiful sons carried out in the 1920s and 1930s. J. Edgar Hoover believed she had "the most resourceful criminal brain of any man or woman I have observed." After a shoot-out with Hoover's agents in 1935, Ma was found dead, her machine gun clutched to her bosom.

Ma Ferguson ♀ became the governor of Texas in 1924, one of the first women to be elected governor of a state. She ran in place of her husband, Pa Ferguson, who had been impeached for corruption and was unable to run again. Ma served a full term, relaxed for a few years, and ran again, serving a second time from 1933 to 1935.

Mother Shipton,♀ born in a cave in England in 1488, was a seer whose predictions are said to have included the steam engine and the telegraph.

Mother Bickerdyke was the name General Grant's troops gave to **Mary Ann Bickerdyke,** a "cyclone in calico" who served as nurse and surgeon on nineteen major battlefields during the Civil War, cut through army red tape to get supplies and treatment for the wounded, and didn't mind stepping on toes to do it. When bureaucrats complained to General Sherman, he sighed, "She outranks me."

Mother Machree was the subject of a popular paean to motherhood composed by Chauncey Olcott and Ernest R. Ball in 1910. Irish tenor John McCormack popularized the song, and there was nary a dry eye in the house when he finished.

Mother Goose may have been a seventeenth-century Boston woman, **Elizabeth Foster,** who married a middle-aged widower named Vergoose, Goose, or Verboose. Thomas Fleet, one of her many sons-in-law, published her rhymes, *Songs for the Nursery* or *Mother Goose's Melodies,* in 1719.

Old Mother Hubbard was the name used by police and public alike for **Margaret Brown,** an agile pickpocket who flourished in New York during the 1890s.

Old Mother Cresswell enjoyed a long career as a prostitute and madame in Restoration London, counting the city's leading gentlemen among her customers. In old age she turned to religion, leaving 10 pounds for a funeral sermon in which only complimentary remarks would be made about her.

Mother Ann ♀ is the name often used for **Ann Lee** (1736–1784), founder of the Shaker sect.

Mother Bunch was a noted London tavern keeper of the late sixteenth century. Many jokes of the period concern her and several plays mention her.

The Mother of Believers is the name by which **Ayesha,** ♀ the second and favorite wife of the prophet Muhammad, is often known.

Mother Bloor, a labor organizer, socialist, and later a founder of the American Communist party, was **Ella Reeve Bloor,** the daughter of a wealthy Republican banker.

Mother Courage is the title character of a play by Bertolt Brecht set in the seventeenth century during the Thirty Years' War—a symbol of the human capacity to survive.

Mother of the Doughboys was the name given to Wagnerian opera singer **Ernestine Schumann-Heink** during World War I in honor of her many concerts for U.S. soldiers. A naturalized American citizen and mother of eight, she had sons fighting for both the Germans and the Allies; one on each side was killed.

Mother Goddam was the brothel-keeping leading character of a 1929 Broadway play, *The Shanghai Gesture.* When it moved to the screen in 1941, the character's name was laundered to "Mother Gin Sling."

Whistler's Mother ♀ is the familiar, but inaccurate, title of a work by James McNeill Whistler portraying **Anna Mathilda McNeill Whistler.** The painting was actually called *Arrangement in Gray and Black.*

Mother Carey's chicken is the name given by sailors to a small web-footed bird also called the stormy petrel. The name probably derives from *mater cara,* Latin for "dear mother." At sea, these birds were believed to bring news of coming storms and were regarded as messengers of the Virgin Mary.♀

Ma Bell is the familiar nickname by which the world's largest corporation, the American Telephone & Telegraph Company, is known, especially to the millions of shareholders to whom Ma has been extremely generous over the years.

MOTHERS WHO MAY OR MAY NOT BE "UNNATURAL"

♀

Medea, abandoned by Jason for another woman, took revenge by murdering the children who had been born to them. This was not Medea's first venture into extreme child abuse. A few years earlier she had helped Jason escape with the Golden Fleece by cutting her little brother into pieces and throwing them on the water so that her father would be forced to stop and gather them for burial.

Procne, understandably outraged on learning that her husband, Tereus, had raped and mutilated her sister, Philomela, killed her son Itys, cut up his body, and served it to Tereus at a sacred feast. When the father called for his son, Procne replied, "If you look for Itys, search for him inside your own body."

Althea had a visit from the Three Fates ♀ upon the birth of her son Meleager. The child's life, they said, would last as long as the log burning on the fire. Althea removed the wood and kept it safe, but when as a grown man Meleager murdered his mother's brothers, who had wronged him, Althea forced herself to throw the log on the fire, thus ending his life.

Agrippina II,♀ the sister of Caligula and mother of Nero, probably poisoned her husband (and uncle), the Emperor Claudius, to bring Nero to power. Once on the throne, Mama's talent for dissension was more than the unbalanced emperor could cope with; in a classic display of filial ingratitude, he had her murdered.

Empress Irene of Byzantium deposed and blinded her son in A.D. 797 and ruled in his stead for five years.

Lucrezia Borgia,♀ the much-married daughter of Pope Alexander VI, had a son, Gennaro, who was raised by fishermen and kept ignorant of his mother's identity. When he spoke out against Borgia vices, Gennaro was jailed and sentenced to be poisoned, but his mother provided him with an antidote. He eventually met his death by poison at a banquet anyway, and as he died, Lucrezia revealed the truth to him.

Adèle Chevalier abandoned her vows as a nun to become the mistress of Abbé Boullan, a satanist and practitioner of the black arts, and bore him at least two children. At a black mass celebrated in January 1860, Chevalier sacrificed one of her children to the devil.

Margaret Garner, a slave, escaped to Cincinnati with her husband and four children, only to be recaptured. As the slave hunters took her husband away, she murdered her three-year-old daughter so that she would not have to live in slavery. Later, while being transported down the Ohio River back to slavery, her baby fell overboard "by accident."

Hetty Green, a nineteenth-century millionaire, was undoubtedly one of the greatest misers of all time. Despite their wealth, she and her children lived in cold-water hovels on scraps and hand-me-downs. When her son Edward injured his leg, she refused to call a physician. By the time she took him to a free clinic, the leg had to be amputated. Green had it buried in the family plot in Bellows Falls, Vermont.

Alice Crimmins, in a custody fight with her ex-husband, allegedly said she would rather see her children dead than with their father. The courts eventually had to decide whether she had made good on that threat. In July 1965, after Crimmins and her boyfriend had reported her children missing, their dead bodies were found and she was arrested for murder. A first, sensational trial was inconclusive, and in April 1971, after a second trial, she was found guilty of first-degree murder in the death of one child and manslaughter in the death of the other. After spending several years in prison, Crimmins was paroled.

PAEANS TO MOM

❧

Abigail Smith Adams.♀ "My mother was an angel upon earth"—John Quincy Adams.

Sarah Pearson West. "The kiss of my mother made me a painter"—artist Benjamin West.

Elizabeth Hutchinson Jackson. "The memory of my mother and her teachings were after all the only capital I had to start in life with, and on that capital I have made my way"—Andrew Jackson.

Nancy Hanks Lincoln. "All that I am or ever hope to be I owe to my angel mother"—Abraham Lincoln.

Abigail May Alcott. "The great deep heart that was a home for all"—Louisa May Alcott.♀

Nancy Elliott Edison. "My mother was the making of me. She was so true, so sure of me; and I felt that I had someone to live for, someone I must not disappoint"—Thomas Alva Edison.

Margaret Morrison Carnegie.♀ "My favorite heroine—my mother"—Andrew Carnegie.

Martha Young Truman. "She's wonderful! They don't make them like that anymore"—Harry S Truman.

Ida Stover Eisenhower. "Her sincerity, her open smile, her gentleness with all and her tolerance of their ways"—Dwight D. Eisenhower.

Rose Fitzgerald Kennedy.♀ "She was the glue, she's not as forceful as my father, but she was the glue"—John F. Kennedy.

Rebekah Baines Johnson.♀ "She was quiet and shy, but she was the strongest person I ever knew"—Lyndon B. Johnson.

Hannah Milhous Nixon. "She was a saint"—Richard M. Nixon.

SPECIAL DELIVERERS
※

Louise Bourgeois Boursier. Until the early seventeenth century, only male midwives attended noble-born women when they gave birth. Midwife Boursier, one of the first women to serve royalty, attended Marie de Medici, wife of Henry IV, for seven confinements, one of which produced the future Louis XIII. For her services Boursier was compensated at the chauvinistic rate of 1,000 ducats for the birth of a boy and 600 for a girl. She was the first midwife to publish a book on obstetrics (1609).

Elizabeth Cellier. This midwife was so appalled at conditions in seventeenth-century England that she decided to keep a record. From 1642 to 1662, 6,000 women perished in childbirth, 5,000 infants were stillborn, and 13,000 aborted, according to her statistics. She claimed that two-thirds of these casualties were the result of the clumsy and unskilled midwifery of her day.

Justine Dittrichin Siegemundin. Siegemundin became a truly scientific midwife, teaching others what she had learned and practicing among the poor. Her fame spread, and in 1688 she was called to Berlin to attend the wife of Frederick I of Prussia. She wrote on midwifery in German instead of the customary Latin so that other women would be able to study and learn from her works.

Angélique Marguérite Boursier du Coudray. Most physicians had little professional knowledge of female anatomy until the daughter of Louise Boursier designed a plaster model of the torso to be used in demonstrating the progress of childbirth. Her book on midwifery, published in 1759, went through five editions.

Marie-Jonet Dugès and *Marie-Louise LaChapelle.* Dugès was midwife in chief at the Hôtel Dieu in eighteenth-century Paris, and her daughter LaChapelle an apt pupil. At age of fifteen, LaChapelle successfully took charge of an extremely difficult delivery. During her career she collected enough data to write a three-volume work on childbirth.

Mary Donnally. This illiterate Irish midwife performed the first successful Caesarean delivery in Great Britain on Alice O'Neal in January 1738, using a razor. The case clearly called for such heroic measures: Donnally was called in after the mother had been in labor for twelve days.

Marie Anne Victoire Gillian Boivin. Thought by many to be the outstanding obstetrician of the nineteenth century, Boivin refused the lucrative offers her reputation brought. She chose instead to work for minimal pay, in a hospital for prostitutes. In 1827 a German university made Boivin an honorary M.D., a tribute rarely given a woman. At retirement her pension was so small that she died in severe want a year later.

Regina and *Charlotte Von Siebold.* Mother and daughter both received the titles of honorary doctor from the University of Giessen in Germany. The younger Von Siebold was so respected she was called to England in the early nineteenth century to deliver the Duchess of Kent of the baby that would become the future Queen Victoria.⁹

Mary Heathman Smith. "Granny Smith" came to Utah from England in 1862. A memorial monument, quoted in part, explains how she endeared herself to her adopted land: "... for thirty years, in storm or sunshine, during the bleakest winter, or the darkest night, with little or no remuneration, she attended the people of Ogden Valley with courage and faithfulness unexcelled. In addition to rearing her own family of nine, under her skill and attention she brought into the world more than 1500 babies. . . ."

SEVENTEEN MOTHERS OUT OF WEDLOCK

Ingrid Bergman ♀
Dorothy Day,♀ Catholic social reformer.
Catherine Deneuve
Bernadette Devlin,♀ Irish activist and politician.
Emily Hahn, writer.
Héloise,♀ twelfth-century intellectual.
Lillie Langtry,♀ actress.
Francesca Annis, actress, shortly after portraying Langtry in a television series.
Gypsy Rose Lee,♀ ecdysiast.
Sylvia Pankhurst,♀ English feminist leader.
Vanessa Redgrave
Grace Slick,♀ rock singer.
Liv Ullmann
Suzanne Valadon,♀ impressionist painter and artists' model.
Marie Walewska,♀ paramour and patriot.
Rebecca West, writer.
Mary Wollstonecraft,♀ feminist theorist.

FOUNDERS OF THE FIRST BIRTH CONTROL CLINICS

Aletta Jacobs,♀ Amsterdam, the Netherlands, 1881. Jacobs, the eighth of eleven children, was the first woman in Holland to become a physician, having · gotten a special permit from the government to attend the university. Upon completing her studies she was horrified to find her patients becoming pregnant over and over again. She was the first to advocate use of the diaphragm and to make it available to all her female patients. Male physicians led the opposition—they feared she would ruin their business.
Margaret Sanger,♀ her sister *Ethel Byrne,* and their friend *Fania Mindell,* Brownsville, Brooklyn, New York City, 1916. Charging 10 cents for each woman advised, the clinic continued its work until the three founders were arrested on the tenth day. They were tried, convicted, and sentenced. In 1918 the state court of appeals upheld the verdict, but interpreted the law so that physicians could dispense birth control information to married women for health reasons, vindicating Sanger.

Marie Carmichael Stopes,[9] London, 1921, with her second husband, Humphrey Vernon Roe. Three years earlier she had written a book on the subject of contraception, *Married Love,* which was published in Great Britain although banned in the United States. Dr. Stopes was a botanist, not a physician.

FOUR ABORTIONISTS
_____ ꙮ _____

Abortion was not uncommon in early-nineteenth-century America; it was generally believed the life of the unborn did not begin until the mother actually felt movement. Newspaper advertisements were freely placed, and those who offered methods of "clearing obstructions" did not lack for customers. After mid-century, however, public opinion became increasingly opposed to the practice, and by the 1880s antiabortion laws were on the books in most states.

Madame Restell (Ann Lohman) was the leading abortionist. In addition to a mansion on New York's Fifth Avenue where she treated "complaints arising from female irregularity," Restell had branches in Boston and other cities, and sent sales representatives out on the road selling "Female Monthly Pills." Because she knew so many secrets, Restell was a dreaded figure among New York's high society. In the 1880s Anthony Comstock, New York's indefatigable commissioner of vice, came to her house posing as a young husband who wanted to negotiate an abortion. When she agreed to perform the operation, he arrested her. She paid the bail money, came home, and slit her throat in her elegantly decorated bathroom.

Catherine Costello, a well-known mid-century abortionist, lived in Jersey City and was a rival of Madame Restell's. To reassure those in need of her services, she advertised that she "officiates personally in every case, so that hesitation or dread need never be apprehended." But there was indeed reason to be wary: In April of 1846, Costello's husband was indicted for selling the corpse of one of his wife's clients.

Sarah Sawyer was known as "The Restell of Boston."

"Sleeping Lucy," a clairvoyant who lived in Vermont, began her small abortion practice in 1842. The enterprise expanded, and she soon had assets said to be worth $1 million.

FIVE REGULARLY ADVERTISED ABORTIFACIENTS OF THE NINETEENTH CENTURY
_____ ꙮ _____

Madame Restell's Female Monthly Pills, "successful for removing female irregularity."

Dr. Peter's French Renovating Pills, "a blessing to mothers."

Dr. Monroe's French Periodical Pills, "sure to produce a miscarriage."

Dr. Melveau's Portuguese Female Pills, "certain to produce miscarriage."
Madame Drunette's Lunar Pills

JOY ADAMSON'S LIST OF "QUALITIES I MOST RESPECT IN FEMALE ANIMALS"

Joy Adamson, who was killed in Kenya in early 1980, was a naturalist who devoted herself to the care of wild animals. More than 13 million readers bought her books about Elsa, a lioness she adopted in 1956: *Born Free, Living Free,* and *Forever Free.* Only such a close and tender observer could have written the following list.

- They are excellent mothers. With infinite patience, they treat each young one individually, differently, according to its character. They take great care and love, discipline, and protect the young until independence. This period is in lions twenty months, in cheetahs seventeen to eighteen months. Even if the mother has regular estrus during this time she will not let a male interfere, let alone mate.
- Altruism. I have often watched cheetah and lion mothers starve in order to let the cubs have food first. Elsa even took a goat we gave her across the river to give it to her rival lioness who had just given birth and therefore could not hunt for a few days. Elsa had been hungry that day but knew we might give her another goat. Thus she helped this rival lioness who had often attacked her, as Elsa had invaded her territory. After Elsa died, the lioness chased Elsa's cubs out of the area and returned to her territory.
- Help to others. Elephants, lions, and porpoises have an elderly female assisting in rearing the young. (Can this be so that in case the mother is killed, the young already know their foster mother?)
- Baby-sitting. Other females take care of the young while mothers feed or hunt. This is done by the giraffe, oryx, chamois, impala.
- Sentiment. I have a wild-living family of colobus monkeys on my grounds which I have watched for seven years. When the father was shot by poachers, the mother and infant mourned for several weeks— sitting close together and staring into space. The face of the mother got deeply furrowed during this period. When Pippa (my cheetah) lost a cub which the vet had removed for treatment, she searched the area for many days, climbing trees to look far away, and was most upset.

Exclusively for *Womanlist*

THREE SETS OF SISTERS WHO MAY, OR MAY NOT, BE OF ASSISTANCE

Think you can use a little more beauty and charm? Consult the Three Graces, responsible for all adornments of mind and body:

Euphrosyne, joy.
Aglaia, brilliance.
Thalia, bloom.

Short of inspiration? Try the Nine Muses:
Calliope, epic poetry.
Clio, history.
Euterpe, lyric poetry.
Melpomene, tragedy.
Terpsichore, choral dance and song.
Erato, love poetry.
Polyhymnia, sacred poetry.
Urania, astronomy.
Thalia, comedy (who should not be confused with the Grace of the same name).

Wondering about your future? The Three Fates ♀ are spinning your destiny right now—but watch out for their shears:
Clotho spins the thread of human life.
Lachesis determines its length.
Atropos, whose name means "inflexible," cuts it off.

SINGING SISTERS

❧

The Andrews Sisters, Patti, Maxene, and LaVerne. (A fourth sister, Nancy, was dismissed from the act because of her "nasal tones.")
The Blossom Sisters, Helen and Dorothy.
The Boswell Sisters, Connee, Vet, and Martha.
The Dandridge Sisters, Dorothy ♀ and Vivian. (Etta, a third member of the act, was not a sister.)
The DeMarco Sisters, Lily, Mary, and Ann.
The Dinning Sisters, Lou, and twins Jean and Ginger.
The Dolly Sisters,♀ Jenny ♀ and Rosie, born Janzieska and Roszieska Deutch.
The Fontane Sisters, Geri, Marge, and Bea.
The Frazee Sisters, Jane and Ruth.
The King Sisters, Donna, Louise, Alyce, and Yvonne Driggs.
The Lane Sisters, Priscilla and Rosemary.
The Lennon Sisters, Peggy, Kathy, Janet, and Diane.
The McGuire Sisters, Dorothy, Phyllis, and Christine.
The Pickens Sisters, Jane, Helen, and Patti.
The Pointer Sisters, Ruth, Anita, Bonnie, and June.

SIXTEEN SETS OF CELEBRATED SISTERS

❧

Harriet Beecher Stowe,♀ author, and *Catharine Beecher,*♀ educator. Harriet wrote *Uncle Tom's Cabin* and other books; Catherine, advocating advanced education for women, opened the Hartford Female Seminary in 1823.

Elizabeth♀ and *Emily Blackwell,* physicians. Elizabeth was the first woman to receive a medical degree in the United States (1849), and Emily followed in her footsteps. Together they founded the New York Infirmary for Women and Children in 1868.

Nadia♀ and *Lili Boulanger,*♀ musicians. Nadia (1887–1979), a conductor, pianist, and noted teacher, became, in 1939, the first woman to conduct the Boston Symphony Orchestra. When Lili, a prize-winning musician and composer, died at the age of twenty-four, she had already composed more than fifty works.

Anne,♀ *Charlotte,*♀ and *Emily Brontë,*♀ novelists. In 1847 alone, Anne published *Agnes Grey;* Charlotte, *Jane Eyre;* and Emily, *Wuthering Heights.*

Minna♀ and *Ada Everleigh,*♀ businesswomen. Accomplished madames, they ran Chicago's most elegant and exclusive brothel in the late nineteenth century.

Margaretta and *Kate Fox,* spiritualists and promoters. The sisters began to communicate with the spirit world in 1847 by means, they said, of mysterious rappings; their brand of spiritualism soon became the rage in the United States and Europe.

Elinor Glyn,♀ novelist, and *Lucille, Lady Duff-Gordon,*♀ fashion designer. Glyn wrote best-selling romances in the 1920s; Lucille designed clothes for the most fashionable women of the same period.

Sarah and *Angelina Grimké,*♀ abolitionists and women's rights advocates. The sisters left their native South Carolina because they could not coexist with slavery. In the cause of abolition, in the 1830s, they became the first women to address "mixed" audiences of males and females.

Edith Hamilton, scholar, and *Alice Hamilton,* physician. Edith, a renowned educator and classicist, was the author of the best-selling *The Greek Way* (1930) and numerous later works. Alice was a pioneer toxicologist and expert on industrial poisons, and the first woman appointed to the medical school faculty of Harvard University (1919).

Aletta Jacobs,♀ physician, *Charlotte Jacobs,* pharmacist, and *Frederique Jacobs,* mathematician. Aletta was the first female physician in Holland and the first person anywhere to open a birth control clinic. Charlotte became Holland's first female pharmacist, and Frederique was the first woman in that country to earn a graduate degree in mathematics.

Ann Landers (Esther Pauline Friedman)♀ and *Abigail Van Buren (Pauline Esther Friedman),*♀ advice-dispensing newspaper columnists and twins who have not always seen eye to eye. They maintained their strong sibling rivalry well into their adult years.

Emma Lazarus, poet and *Josephine Lazarus,* social worker. Emma's sonnet "The New Colossus" ("Give me your tired, your poor . . .") is inscribed on the base of the Statue of Liberty. Josephine devoted herself to the education and training of new immigrants.

Soong Ai-ling, Ching-ling, and *Mai-ling,* the celebrated Soong sisters of China. Born into a politically powerful and wealthy family and educated in the United States, all three married leaders of their nation and were themselves influential. Soong Ai-ling wed a banker and Kuomintang official and was a social worker. Soong Ching-ling, wife of President Sun Yat-sen, broke with the Kuomintang after his death and later became vice-chair of the People's Republic of China, in 1951 receiving the Stalin Prize. Soong Mai-ling, the powerful Madame Chiang Kai-shek,♀ was elected to the legislature and held other positions in her husband's government.

Ann Storer Hogg, Fanny Storer Mechler, Maria Storer Henry, and **Miss Storer (Henry),** actresses. Born in England, they came to North America in 1767 and became the most popular attractions behind the footlights in the American colonies. A critic described Maria, the youngest and most famous of the quartet, as "the best public singer America had known." After she died, her older sister married her bereaved husband.

Frieda, Else, and **Johanna von Richthofen.** Their father, Baron von Richthofen, called them "goddesses three." Frieda believed above all in erotic love and ran away from her husband and children to become the mistress and inspiration of novelist D. H. Lawrence. Else fought her way into the university, became one of the first German women to receive a doctorate, went on to a career in the social sciences, and was the secret lover of sociologist Max Weber. Johanna became the mistress of some of the most brilliant men in pre-Weimar Germany.

And, finding sisterhood—**Helen Matthews** and **Doris Smith** are two sisters who never knew they were related, even though they lived only three blocks apart and worked in the same department store. Chatting during a coffee break, they recently discovered they had the same mother. After forty years without sibling rivalry Matthews says, "It's wonderful having a sister again."

THEIR FATHERS' DAUGHTERS

Hypatia,♀ a distinguished philosopher and mathematician of Alexandria (ca. 370–415), was trained by her father, Theon, a professor of mathematics at the University of Alexandria—where years later she herself taught.

Novella Calderini was educated to be a lawyer by her father, a fourteenth-century professor at the University of Bologna. When she represented their clients in court she wore a veil so as not to sway justice with her beauty. Shakespeare may have had Calderini in mind when he created Portia.

Ninon de Lenclos,♀ the seventeenth century's leading courtesan, was guided into her profession by her father, a musician who did some pimping on the side and did not hesitate to add his stunning daughter to his stable.

Elizabeth Vigée-Lebrun,♀ the most celebrated woman artist of the eighteenth century, was painting portraits of the Parisian aristocracy before she was twenty. Pastel portraitist Louis Vigée trained his daughter when she was a child. It was good that he did, for she soon became the sole support of her widowed mother.

Margaret Fuller,♀ an early-nineteenth-century feminist, was educated in New England by an exacting father who used her as proof of his theory that a girl could be intellectually superior to any boy. Under his guidance the child learned six languages—and put them to good use in her later career as a writer and editor.

Edith Hayllar was the most successful of Victorian painter James Hayllar's four daughters, all of whom became artists.

Judith Gautier, a French poet, novelist, and essayist, and the first woman elected to the Académie Goncourt, was the daughter of novelist Théophile Gautier.

Susan B. Anthony ♀ was the daughter of Daniel Anthony, a Quaker abolitionist who believed that women should be brought up to be the equals of men and treated her accordingly.

Maria Mitchell, ♀ a nineteenth-century professor of astronomy, was first encouraged to search the skies and calculate the orbits and positions of heavenly bodies by her father, William Mitchell, an amateur astronomer.

Marie Curie ♀ was helped by her father, a teacher of mathematics and physics, who recognized early her abilities and insisted that she develop them.

Anna Freud, ♀ the daughter of the founder of psychoanalysis, became one of his disciples, applying his theories to childhood development, and a leading analyst of children.

Fanny Harwood, encouraged by her physician father, in 1912 became the first woman in Britain to be licensed in dental surgery by the Royal College of Surgeons.

Virginia Woolf, ♀ the daughter of English writer Sir Leslie Stephen, was always regarded by him as an intellectual equal. From earliest childhood she was allowed free use of his extensive library and was at home with his friends—Robert Louis Stevenson, John Ruskin, and Thomas Hardy, among others.

Chien-Shiung Wu, ♀ the experimental physicist who disproved the long-accepted Law of Parity, grew up in China in the early twentieth century, where her scholar father insisted she get a university education, rare for a young woman at that time.

Debra Ann Powers, a pilot for United Airlines since 1978, has followed in the footsteps of her father, a senior DC-8 pilot.

Ann, Henriette, and *Caroline Wyeth,* the daughters of painter N. C. Wyeth and sisters of Andrew, are equally creative. Ann is a composer. Henriette is a portrait painter, as is Caroline, who says that her father was her teacher for nineteen years and her severest critic. She had her first public exhibition in 1979 when she was sixty-nine years old. Unlike most other women whose fathers taught and inspired them, however, Caroline's relationship with N. C. was strained. "It's a shame," she said. "If we could have met somehow, we'd have had such a great time."

THEIR MOTHERS' DAUGHTERS

※

Mary Katherine Goddard, ♀ the colonial printer who printed the Declaration of Independence, was inspired by her exceptionally well-educated mother, *Sarah Goddard,* ♀ also a printer.

Rosalba Carriera,♀ in the eighteenth century, first pursued her mother's occupation of lacemaker, then turned to decorating the lids of snuffboxes and finally to painting miniatures, for which she became much in demand; her mother's training gave her fingers the needed dexterity.

Amy Marcy Cheney Beach,♀ a nineteenth-century concert pianist and composer, was trained by her mother, pianist and singer *Clara Imogene (Marcy) Cheney.*

Alice Stone Blackwell,♀ the daughter of feminist leader *Lucy Stone,*♀ was herself a feminist leader active in the women's suffrage movement. So was . . .

Harriot Stanton Blatch,♀ who followed in the footsteps of her mother, *Elizabeth Cady Stanton,*♀ and organized the Equality League of Self-Supporting Women in 1907.

Pearl Starr,♀ *Belle Starr*'s♀ daughter, briefly followed her mother's line of work as a bandit, until she found it more profitable to operate a bawdyhouse.

Irène Joliot-Curie♀ became a physicist like her mother, *Marie Curie,*♀ and like her won a Nobel Prize (1935).

Colette,♀ the French writer, attributed her ability to write with sensitivity about nature to her mother, *Sido.*

Leola Hopkins, the first woman to enlist in the navy after the outbreak of World War II, was the daughter of a corporal in the all-female marine reserve unit of World War I.

Emmeline Pankhurst,♀ the militant British feminist leader, followed the teachings of her mother, a nineteenth-century radical activist, who took the fourteen-year-old Emmeline to a women's suffrage meeting and gave her a cause for life. *Christabel Pankhurst,*♀ Emmeline's oldest daughter, joined her mother in organizing the militant women's suffrage movement in England, while *Sylvia Pankhurst,*♀ Emmeline's youngest daughter, advocated free love and defended unmarried motherhood both in print and in action. Sylvia also led the movement for Ethiopian independence in the 1930s and wrote a biography of her mother.

Margaret Webster, the American actress and co-founder of the American Repertory Theatre, was the daughter of thespians *Dame May Whitty* and Ben Webster. Her 1969 autobiography, *The Same Only Different,* tells her mother's story as well as her own.

Lady Antonia Fraser♀ has written best-selling biographies of Mary, Queen of Scots,♀ Oliver Cromwell, and James I while bringing up six children. Her debt to her mother is clear: the *Countess of Longford* raised eight children while writing biographies of the Duke of Wellington and Queen Victoria.♀

Nora Ephron, the popular essayist, is the daughter of successful screenwriters *Phoebe* and Henry *Ephron. Delia Ephron,* another of their four daughters, is also a best-selling author.

Lynn Anderson, the popular country singer, is the daughter of singer-writer *Liz Anderson,* who has written hits for Merle Haggard and others. Lynn got her first recording break when she traveled with her mother to Nashville in 1965.

Liza Minnelli reminds us strongly, in both looks and style, of her mother, *Judy Garland.*♀

Mimi Sheraton, restaurant critic and food writer, in her book of recipes *From My Mother's Kitchen* unabashedly asserts her indebtedness to her mother, *Beatrice R. Solomon,* a businesswoman and administrative executive as well as a superb cook.

Elaine Grossinger Etess, hotel owner and first woman president of the New York State Hotel and Motel Association, is the daughter of legendary hotelier *Jenny Grossinger,* who turned her family's small hotel into a mammoth operation with its own post office.

RELATIVELY SPEAKING, WITH TONGUE IN CHEEK

❦

Weak sisters: inevitably inferior.

Sob sisters: the same, whether female or not.

Maiden aunt: you can't take her anywhere. A figure of fun, as opposed to a bachelor uncle, who is fun to be with.

Old wives: they tell tales we can dismiss as mere superstition. Genuine folk wisdom stems from old men, otherwise known as "sages."

Mothers-in-law: their husbands are equally tiresome; but fathers-in-law, the old boys who run the networks, can afford better publicity agents.

Contributed by Ruth Ulmyn

VI ❧ SHE'S THE BOSS

ROOM AT THE TOP
❧

Despite the recent advances for women in industry, very few women have made it to the big time in corporate life. In January 1977, according to *Business Week,* there were about 400 women directors in the 1,300 largest companies in the United States—up from 20 five years earlier. In 1978 *Business Week* asked forty-three corporations to identify their top-ranking women. One-quarter did not name any women on the management level. Only seven polled named women in top management positions: General Motors, J. C. Penney, Georgia Pacific, General Mills, Federated Department Stores, General Electric, and General Foods. Most of the women named were in the middle-management range, earning $20,000 to $50,000.
- Of the women who were corporate officers:
  - 1 in 4 held the title of vice-president or higher.
  - 8 percent were vice-presidents.
  - 12.9 percent were corporate secretaries.
  - 45.2 percent were assistant secretaries.
  - 27 percent earned under $20,000.
  - 55 percent earned less than $30,000.
  - 20 percent earned $50,000 or more.
- The typical woman vice-president or other executive officer earned $40,000 a year or more, whereas the average male executive officer received a salary of $50,000 or more.
- According to a 1979 survey, the typical woman corporate officer is married, younger than fifty, has one or more degrees, and comes from a low- or lower-middle-income family.

THIRTEEN AT THE TOP
❧

Nelma J. Andrew heads Midwest Metal Products, Inc., of Kansas City, Kansas. In July 1979 her firm was awarded the largest federal loan guarantee—90 percent of a $3,655,000 bank loan—ever granted to a business owned and operated by a woman, to build and equip a new plant in an inner-city neighborhood, providing some 400 jobs.

Ann Bassett is president of the Bassett Ice Cream Company.

Marisa Bellisario became president of the Olivetti Corporation of America in February 1979. She joined Olivetti in Italy as a systems analyst in 1960 after graduation from Turin University, became head of software development, and later headed the corporate-planning and data-processing divisions.

Ellen R. Gordon, a 1952 Vassar graduate, is president of Tootsie Roll Industries. She is the second woman to be elected to the presidency of a company listed on the New York Stock Exchange.

Nathalie Hocq (pronounced *uk*) became president of Cartier, a world-wide chain of eleven luxury stores, after her father was killed in an auto accident in December 1979. Hocq *fille,* twenty-eight years old, had worked with her father at the Paris Cartier store for six years, heading the jewelry design division for most of that time.

Mary Wells Lawrence founded and was president of the Wells Rich Greene advertising agency and since 1971 has been chairwoman of the board. Her first job: copywriter at a Youngstown, Ohio, department store.

Joan D. Manley was elected chairwoman of the board of the Book-of-the-Month Club, a Time, Inc., subsidiary, in January 1979. Manley is also chairwoman of the board and chief executive officer of Time-Life Books. She was named publisher in 1970 and was, a year later, the first woman to be elected a vice-president of that company. Her first publishing job was as a secretary in the advertising department of Doubleday and Company.

Jane Cahill Pfeiffer was chairwoman of the National Broadcasting Company from 1978 to 1980, having come to the network from IBM. Pfeiffer joined IBM in 1955, six months after college graduation, and by 1972 she was a vice-president.

Lynn D. Salvage ♀ became, at thirty-three, president and chief executive officer of the Katherine Gibbs School, Inc., after having been president of New York's First Women's Bank for three years.

Dorothy Shaver became in 1946 the first woman to head a major department store when she became president of New York's Lord & Taylor, a position she held until her death in 1959.

Geraldine Stutz became president of New York's Henri Bendel department store in 1957—and now owns it.

Anne Burnett Tandy, who died on January 1, 1980, at the age of seventy-four, for years supervised the 208,000-acre northwest Texas 6666 Ranch, as well as two smaller ranches, founded by her grandfather.

Lois Wyse is president of the Wyse Advertising Agency of Cleveland and New York, established by herself and her husband. She has also written about forty books for children and adults. Her first job: reporter for the *Cleveland Press.*

AND IN THE EXECUTIVE SUITE

꙰

Betsey Ancker-Johnson, the first female vice-president of General Motors Corporation and its highest-ranking woman, is in charge of the company's environmental activities staff and represents GM before government agencies. She has also been assistant secretary of commerce for science and technology.

Juliette M. Moran, age sixty-one, is executive vice-president in charge of communication services at GAF Corporation and a board member.

Beverly C. Lannquist is vice-president of Morgan Stanley and Company, a major investment house. She is the only woman chosen by *Institutional Investor* for its All-American Team of top Wall Street analysts.

Stella Russell had crack secretarial skills when she was hired as executive secretary to Norton Simon in 1955. In 1973 she was earning $72,000 a year as vice-president and director of Norton Simon Company.

Virginia Alice Dwyer, age fifty-eight, is the highest-ranking woman at American Telephone & Telegraph. Until 1970 the company had no women as high as level five in its ten-rung management pyramid. In 1978 three women, including Dwyer, held level-six posts. The following year she was appointed vice-president and treasurer, reaching level seven.

Dorothy A. Servis has been general attorney at U.S. Steel Corporation for more than ten years.

Barbara Scott Preiskel, age fifty-four, is senior vice-president and general attorney of the Motion Picture Association of America.

Mary A. McCravey is the highest-ranking woman at the Georgia Pacific Company. She joined the company just out of law school in 1948 and became its corporate secretary in 1956. Her salary is $75,000.

Mercedes A. Bates, age sixty-two, is General Mills, Inc.'s, first woman vice-president, at $50,000 a year.

Reva Korda serves as executive vice-president and creative head of Ogilvy and Mather, Inc. The advertising agency has world-wide billings of $175 million.

Alice Dale Stratton, at forty-four, is district marketing manager at Du Pont Corporation. Stratton, who joined the company in 1955 but didn't get into top management until 1970, was the first woman to have responsibility for a Du Pont sales force. Her yearly salary is $50,000.

Pamela Nelson, thirty-six, and *Marilyn Koester,* thirty-eight, are the highest-ranking women at Sears, Roebuck and Company in Chicago. As national merchandise managers, each takes home $50,000 plus.

TO BANK ON

❧

Priscilla Wakefield started a savings bank in 1799 in the English village of Tottenham. By 1804 it was organized under the name Charitable Bank.

The Bank for Savings on Chambers Street in New York City was the first savings bank in the United States to open its doors to women depositors in 1819. Almost a century later, women represented 40 percent of the total bank depositors in the United States.

Maggie Lena Walker, whose mother was a slave, became head of the St. Luke's Penny Savings Bank of Richmond, Virginia, in 1903. When St. Luke's Bank merged with others, Walker became chairwoman of the

board, participating in its management during the last twenty years of
her life, even when she was confined to a wheelchair.

Mary Bateman founded a women's bank in London in 1913.

Brenda Runyon was the first president of the first women's bank in the
United States, which opened in Clarksville, Tennessee, in 1919 with a
completely female staff. In 1926 the bank merged with another bank,
and the nation was without a women's bank until . . .

The First Women's Bank started doing business on Park Avenue in New
York City in 1975. Founders included *Betty Friedan*[♀] and *Pauline
Trigère; Madeline H. McWhinney* was the first president.

Mary Roebling was president of the Trenton Trust Company in New Jersey
from 1937 to 1972. She was also the first woman governor of the
American Stock Exchange (1958).

Catherine Cleary became president of First Wisconsin Trust Company in
1970. She started with the trust company at the age of thirty-one, after a
few years of practicing law.

Muriel Siebert is superintendent of banks of the State of New York. The financial wizard became the first female member of the New York Stock
Exchange in 1967, the same year she founded her own financial concern, Muriel Siebert and Company.

Sandra S. Jaffee became the first woman senior vice-president at Citibank,
New York, in 1979 amid fifty-three male senior vice-presidents.

Salwa Saleh is the manager of the women's bank that opened its doors in
Abu Dhabi, Saudi Arabia, in 1977. In this branch of the Khalij Commercial Bank, women depositors can take off their veils and learn about
interest and checking accounts. Before it opened, Saudi women could
either use the back doors of the other banks or have their male relatives
handle matters for them.

Madelon D. Talley was appointed director of the New York State Common
Retirement Fund in February 1979. She oversees investment of funds,
marketing of securities, and disposition of investments for the state's
$11.7-billion pension fund.

Judy Hendren Mello became president and chief executive officer of the First
Women's Bank in New York in June, 1980. Previously, Mello had been
vice-president of international treasury management at the Marine
Midland Bank in New York City.

Eve Grover is president of the First Women's Bank of Maryland, which
began operating in 1979. By mid-1980, eight women's banks were
operating in the United States. Says Grover, who has been in banking
for thirty years, "As women become more and more integrated into the
financial community, we are all evolving into full-service, community-
based banks. Our bank might well be the last woman's bank to be
formed."

TEN WITH POTENTIAL

❧

The Financial Women's Association was founded twenty-three years ago
to advance the role of women in the business world. In March 1979 the association gave representatives of the nation's leading corporations a list of ten

women it considered highly qualified to serve on boards of directors. The ten potential directors are:

Amelia Bassin, president of a marketing consulting firm and also of a company that organizes workshops on human resource development.

Marilyn V. Brown, president of her own financial consulting company.

Paula D. Hughes, vice-president and director of Thomson McKinnon Securities, Inc.

Suzanne D. Jaffe, partner in an investment advisory firm.

Marsha A. O'Bannon, assistant vice-president of corporate planning for the New York Stock Exchange.

Lynn D. Salvage,[9] then president and chief executive officer of the First Women's Bank of New York.

Ellen B. Sachar, vice-president and security analyst at Paine Webber Mitchell Hutchins, Inc.

Anita M. Volz, vice-president of European American Bank.

Julia M. Walsh, chairwoman of her own Julia M. Walsh & Sons, a stockbrokerage firm.

Rosalie J. Wolf, vice-president of Donaldson, Lufkin & Jenrette.

LOBBYING FOR BUSINESS

❧

Lobbying in Washington has traditionally been considered a male preserve. Not so any longer. A dozen women representing major industrial companies and trade associations in Washington banded together in 1975 to form Women in Government; in less than five years the group has grown to about 200 members. "The list of companies represented by women on Capitol Hill and before the regulatory agencies reads like a *Who's Who* of American business," said *Business Week* on May 7, 1979. They include:

Metropolitan Life
Sears, Roebuck
General Electric
John Deere
LTV
General Foods
Dresser Industries
Exxon
Mobil
Shell
Atlantic Richfield
Armstrong Cork
CPC International
Bendix Corporation
Procter & Gamble
Association of American Railroads

WOMEN MEMBERS ON THE FLOOR OF THE NEW YORK STOCK EXCHANGE

Leslie Hammond, Merrill Lynch.
Alice Jarcho, Oppenheimer & Company.
Ellen Lee, Bache Halsey Stuart Shields, Inc.
Ingrid Karen Nelson, Greenwich Options Company.
Rosemary Onorato, H. D. Baumer & Company.
Helaine Meryl Zuckerman Stuart, Frankel & Company.

From the New York Stock Exchange, Inc.

TWO DIAMOND MERCHANTS

Eastern European Hasidic Jews dominate the business of polishing, buying, and trading in diamonds. Until very recently women were, by tradition, excluded; the New York Diamond Dealers Club admitted no women, and the DeBeers Central Selling Organization in London, which markets 85 percent of the world's diamonds, permitted no female buyers. However:

Ethel Blitz had been trying to become a diamond merchant since she was eighteen. She is descended from five generations of diamond traders, but it took years for her to find a New York diamond cutter who would teach her the rudiments of cutting a rough diamond. Now at thirty-two, she is a partner in a company that buys rough diamonds, cuts and polishes them, and sells them on the world market. She was the first woman customer accepted by DeBeers. She is also the first woman to gain full membership in the New York Diamond Dealers Club (1,800 male members), but her acceptance letter read "Dear Sir." Recalls Blitz, "I told them to change it. They said I was being too sensitive."

Nicole Polak works in her father's New York industrial-diamond firm, buys from DeBeers, and is so far the only woman admitted to the industrial bourse in Antwerp. "I can't say I'm a pioneer," she says. "I feel more like a princess."

NINE BLACK BUSINESSWOMEN

Madeline Bunch was semiretired in 1972 when she and her family began the Bunch Products Company (Old South Brand beef and pork sausages) in the basement of their home in Santa Rosa, California. The family members worked without pay for two years, but finally succeeded in getting their product into the supermarkets. Today Bunch is vice-president of the successful company.

Jolyn Robichaux, president of the Baldwin Ice Cream Company in Chicago, inherited it from her husband. Unable to find a man to take over, she decided to run the business herself and four years later had nearly tripled its annual income. Robichaux's daughter, Sheila, a business major, works with her.

Jackie Calloway heads Tonganoxie, Inc., a Los Angeles bedspread-manufacturing company she and her mother founded together. They began making custom-made bedspreads in their garage; today the spreads, favorites with celebrities, sell for $800 and up.

Elaine Jenkins founded One America, Inc., in Washington, D.C., in 1969 when she was fifty, putting the entire family savings into the business. The firm specializes in affirmative action planning, rehabilitation counseling, business research and development. By 1974 One America, Inc., had a staff of twenty-two in its Washington office and thirteen in a Houston office.

Ruth Bowen owns the Queens Booking Corporation, a New York theatrical booking agency that handles such clients as Aretha Franklin and Sammy Davis, Jr.

Helen Greenwood Allen is general manager and secretary-treasurer of the Greenwood Transfer and Storage Company, the oldest black business in Washington, D.C., founded by her father in 1922.

Ruth Washington took over the newspaper owned by her husband after he suffered a stroke in 1948, even though she knew nothing about the business. By the mid-1970s the size of the *Los Angeles Sentinel* had doubled, and it was one of the leaders among black newspapers in real estate and classified ads.

Barbara Proctor is president of Proctor and Gardner, a Chicago advertising agency she founded.

Saint Charles Lockett is president and founder of Ethnic Enterprises in Milwaukee, Wisconsin, a packaging and assembly company. Lockett began her career as a hairdresser but switched to welding because the pay was better.

THIRTEEN WHO HAD GOOD BUSINESS IDEAS

Tillie Lewis, the wife of a grocer, got the idea that Italian tomatoes should be grown in America. She persuaded a grower to let her take his seedlings to California, induced West Coast farmers to plant them, opened her own cannery, and soon business was booming. Another successful Lewis idea was for artificially sweetened canned fruit. In 1966 she sold her controlling shares in Tillie Lewis Foods, Inc., to the Ogden Corporation for $9 million.

Ruth Handler and her husband founded the Mattel Toy Company in 1945. Handler had two ideas that would make the company's fortune: buying network time to advertise toys to children and, in 1959, the Barbie Doll. In 1971 the Handlers' share of Mattel stock was valued at more than $285 million. By 1979 more than 112 million Barbies had been sold.

Bertha West Nealey, a South Carolina poet, often entertained her friends at tea, serving a tea made according to her grandmother's old family recipe. One day a friend bubbled, "My dear, your tea was the hit of the party. There was nothing but constant comment." With a friend, Ruth

Bigelow, Nealey established Constant Comment Tea in 1945 and sold her interest in the thriving company twenty years later.

Betty Graham, a Texas secretary, was also an amateur artist. Mixing some new acrylic-based paints in her kitchen one day, she came up with a mixture that seemed to have more than an artistic use. Graham reasoned that it could be used to cover typewriting errors and launched the successful Liquid Paper Company.

Florence Greenberg was searching for a way to insure her blind son's future when she was impressed by the performance of some of her daughter's school friends. She founded Scepter Records to record the Shirelles' ♀ first song, "I Met Him on a Sunday." The record sold a million copies. Other top talents first launched by Scepter include Burt Bacharach and Dionne Warwick.♀

Rose Totino and her husband had a small restaurant in the Midwest. The popularity of her cuisine led them to start a frozen-pizza business with $50,000 they had saved—and the Totinos eventually sold the company bearing their name for $20 million.

Helen Gurley Brown ♀ thought that the ailing *Cosmopolitan* magazine could be converted into a vehicle for the hopes and dreams of the single working woman she had described in her 1962 best seller, *Sex and the Single Woman.* She took over *"Cosmo"* in 1965, filled its pages with zippy, sexy advice, and sent its circulation soaring.

Patricia H. Brennan ran a private postal delivery service in Rochester, New York, for two and a half years, during which time her original clientele of 9 expanded to 357 and she and her husband delivered between 2,800 and 5,000 letters a day. Unfortunately, in 1978 a circuit court ruled Brennan's enterprise unconstitutional, holding that the U.S. Postal Service had a monopoly, even if a private entrepreneur thought she could do better.

Helen Mahler Brachman and *Henrietta Mahler,* sisters-in-law, peddled their homemade French salad dressing to Milwaukee stores during the depression. They subsequently founded Henri's Food Products Company—and when Brachman died in 1980 at the age of eighty-three, her company was posting annual sales of $15 million.

Ernesta G. Procope founded the E. G. Bowman Company, an insurance brokerage firm, in the Bedford-Stuyvesant section of Brooklyn in 1953 to sell personal insurance services. By 1979 her company was the largest black-owned insurance brokerage in the United States, grossing $12 million a year.

Wanda Jablonski is founder and publisher of the *Petroleum Intelligence Weekly,* which for eighteen years has been "must reading for anyone who has to keep informed on the world oil industry," according to experts. A subscription costs $780 a year. Once, King Saud of Saudi Arabia agreed to let Jablonski interview him, sent a plane, and left instructions for her to stay in his harem. When she protested that this was not the kind of interview she had in mind, the reply was: "Madam, where else could he put you up?"

Faline Roberts and her husband determined that American women buy and drink 5 million cases of bottled-in-Britain scotch whiskey annually. They founded Roberts Imports, Inc., to market First Lady, a premium-blended 86-proof scotch. Ads reading "Women's Libation" and "To each her own" are launching the new product.

TAKING OVER FOR THEIR HUSBANDS
꙳

Madame Hon-Cho-Lo was married to a leading Chinese river pirate of the seventeenth century. When he died she assumed full command of his vessel and became known as the Terror of the Yangtze.

Anna Manzolini was the wife of an eighteenth-century professor of anatomy who produced wax figures for anatomical study, using corpses as models. When he fell ill with tuberculosis, his wife took over the modeling enterprise, studied anatomy, lectured in his place, and even did dissections. A few years after his death, she was appointed professor of anatomy in her own right (1766).

Rebecca Lukens inherited an iron mill in eastern Pennsylvania from her husband in 1825 and ran it for twenty-two years as the Brandywine Iron Works and Nail Factory. At her death in 1854 she left an estate of $100,000, a considerable fortune at that time.

Eliza Nicholson inherited the debt-saddled *New Orleans Picayune* newspaper, which she had joined as a $25-a-week literary editor, and successfully turned the venture around.

Elizabeth Bailey was disowned by her family when she eloped with circus musician James Bailey in 1858. He soon became a circus owner; his first circus was so successful that it was bought by P. T. Barnum. But James couldn't stop being a circus proprietor and founded another show. When he became ill in 1885, Elizabeth was prepared to take over. Mollie Bailey's Show was the first circus in the United States owned and operated by a woman.

Miriam ("Minnie") Leslie ♀ lived in flamboyant style with her fourth husband, magazine publisher Frank Leslie, until the financial panic of 1877, when their fortunes tumbled and Leslie died. Minnie legally changed her name to Frank Leslie to answer the lawsuits, closed down the unprofitable magazines, increased the circulation of the survivors—and the Leslie empire was back on its feet. When she died in 1914 at the age of seventy-eight, she left half of her $2-million estate to the women's suffrage movement.

Lydia Pinkham helped her ailing neighbors with a home-brewed remedy consisting of unicorn root, life root, fenugreek seed, pleurisy root, black cohosh, and—the real kicker—18 percent alcohol, which they credited with curing their ills. Not until her husband went bankrupt in the panic of 1873 did Pinkham look upon her "vegetable compound" as a possible moneymaker. Sales of the compound had reached $300,000 a year by the time she died in 1883; by 1898 they had zoomed to $1.3 million.

Henrietta Chamberlain King inherited a Texas ranch from her husband, Richard, but its half-million acres were half a million dollars in debt. The widow thought about selling it, but decided instead to try her hand at running things herself. When she died in 1925 at the age of ninety-two, the holdings of the famous King ranch had reached more than one million acres, and her estate was worth $5.4 million.

Olive Ann Beech was a bookkeeper who married the boss and continued working as secretary-treasurer and director of Beech Aircraft Corporation. In 1940 Walter Beech went into a coma, and his wife, who had just given birth, took over management of the company. During World War II she converted the modest enterprise into a giant defense company; by 1945 Beech sales reached a wartime high of $122 million. After her husband's death in 1950, she assumed the positions of president, chairwoman of the board, and chief executive of the company.

EIGHT PRINTING WIDOWS OF THE THIRTEEN COLONIES

Women ran many of the printing presses of prerevolutionary America, usually inheriting them from their husbands. Historian Elizabeth Anthony Dexter notes, ". . . one is tempted to believe that it was a condition of membership in the craft that all male members should agree to leave widows competent to carry on the business."

Dinah Nuthead, the first woman printer in America, moved her husband's press from St. Mary's, Maryland, to Annapolis after his death in 1695.

Anne Smith Franklin, Benjamin Franklin's sister-in-law, continued her husband's printing business after his death. Her younger son started the *Newport Mercury* in 1758, the first newspaper in Rhode Island, leaving it to his mother when he died four years later.

Cornelia Smith Bradford, the second wife of Andrew Bradford of New York, carried on his business of printing and bookselling beginning in 1742. For a while she published the *American Weekly Mercury* with a male partner, but later managed alone.

Anna Catherina Maul Zenger, John Peter Zenger's widow, continued his publishing activities after his death in 1746.

Elizabeth Timothy was the first woman in America to edit a newspaper, the *South Carolina Gazette,* in 1738. She published the paper for several years before selling out to son Peter, whose widow was some years later to have her own turn at managing it.

Ann Catherine Hoof Green handled most of the government printing in Annapolis, Maryland, after her husband died and also continued publishing his newspaper, the *Annapolis Gazette.*

Clementina Rind published the *Virginia Gazette* for the two years following her husband's death in 1773 until her own in 1775.

Margaret Draper published the *Boston Newsletter,* the first paper in Massachusetts, after the death of her husband, Richard, in 1774 and continued to publish until after the British evacuation of Boston, making the *Newsletter* the last paper in that colony as well.

AND A PRINTING DYNASTY

*Sarah Updike Goddard*⁹ loaned her son, William, 300 pounds in 1762 to establish the *Providence Gazette,* but it did so poorly that he left for New York. After repeal of the Stamp Act, Sarah successfully started the paper again, then she and William undertook a similar enterprise in

Philadelphia. William went on to establish other newspapers, among them the *Maryland Gazette,* of which ...

Mary Katherine Goddard,♀ William's sister, took charge in 1774, when he went off to war, and ran it profitably throughout the Revolution. Goddard was asked to print the Declaration of Independence. In 1784 she returned the venture to William but continued to serve as postmistress of Baltimore for several more years.

BREADWINNERS OF EARLY AMERICA

In colonial and revolutionary times, when their families were in need, women adapted their domestic skills to services that were as essential to the growth of the young nation as their incomes were to the maintenance of their families. Some examples of their enterprise:

Anna Jones distilled a variety of spirits and sold them in her Massachusetts shop, carrying on the business of her late husband.

Ann Page of Pennsylvania, a turner, provided cylindrical articles—mortars and pestles, bench screws, spindles—and made and mended spinning wheels.

Mary Emerson, of Pennsylvania, silvered mirrors, worked as a joiner, a carpenter, and furniture maker, and sold new and used furniture.

Elizabeth Franklin (wife of Benjamin's brother John) continued making and selling soap and candles in Boston after her husband's death.

Margaret Paschal made cutlery to continue her husband's business.

Elizabeth Russell continued her husband's coach-making business.

Ann Smith of Philadelphia returned home from a buying trip to London in 1773 and started a bookstore; however, after her new husband became manager of the enterprise, it "went to the dogs."

Sarah Jewell continued her husband's rope-making business in Philadelphia.

Mary Salmon of Boston shod horses.

Mary Cowley of Philadelphia was a tanner and leather worker.

Hannah Beales of Philadelphia carried on her late father's net-making business.

Mary Jackson of Boston made and sold copper and brass pots and kettles.

Martha Turnstall Smith of Long Island ran a whaling company and went out in the boats herself.

Cornelia Lubbetse DePeyster of New York imported the first salt to the colony.

Mary Spratt Provoost, who had been brought up by her grandmother De-Peyster after her mother died, became a merchant in New York herself after the death of her husband; the first sidewalk in the city was built to lead from her counting house to her offices and house and adjacent streets.

Many women became tavern keepers. In colonial Philadelphia, these women all advertised the hospitality of their establishments in the local gazettes:

Mrs. Jones, at the Plume of Feathers.

Rebecca Pratt, at the Royal Standard.
Widow Withy, at the Blue Anchor.
Mary Jenkins, at the Conestoga Wagon.
Mary Yeats, at the Fountain and Three Tons.
Margaret Berwick, at the Three Mariners.
Margaret Ingram, at the Rose and Crown.
Sarah Raunall, at the Sign of the Siege of Louisbourg, and then at the Sign
   of the Salutation.

Hospitality of a different sort was also available, at a price. *Quaker Fan,*
Katie Crow, and *Man-of-War Nance* all ran brothels in New York City during the Revolutionary War.

AT HOME IN A HOUSE

❧

Irene McCready claimed to be the pioneer who opened the first "parlor
   house" on San Francisco's notorious Barbary Coast.
Ah Toy was imported into San Francisco as a slave prostitute but managed
   to buy her freedom and open her own brothel, becoming the most prosperous dealer in Chinese prostitutes in California. As a service to other
   impoverished Chinese, Ah Toy often paid the cost of shipping their
   dead bodies home to China for burial.
Mattie Silks ran several "parlor houses" in Colorado and reigned as the
   queen of Denver's underworld. She served champagne in her establishments, and she always carried an ivory-gripped pistol in one pocket of
   her gown.
Pearl DeVere ran the Old Homestead in Cripple Creek, Colorado, a house
   whose fame reached one hundred miles to Denver and beyond. To get
   past the uniformed maid at the front door, a client needed not only a
   full wallet but also a formal letter of introduction. When DeVere died
   of an overdose of morphine, the town raised money by public subscription to "give the little girl a real send-off," as one bartender put it.
Mary Ellen ("Mammy") Pleasant, a mulatto, was a mysterious figure who
   often passed for white, especially during her early career as an agent on
   the underground railroad. Her life in San Francisco was less altruistic.
   Here she prospered as a madame, voodoo priestess, and intimate of political figures who were often the victims of her blackmail. Many un-
   solved murders occurred in her infamous house at 1661 Octavia Street.
Julia Bulette, the "Queen of Sporting Row" in Virginia City, Nevada, was
   one of its leading citizens and attracted a high class of miner as clients.
   When she was murdered by a thief in 1867, the whole town turned out
   for her funeral.
Josephine ("Josie") Woods ran the Tiffany of brothels in New York City
   during the 1860s. Noted for the decorum of her clientele, Woods received some of the city's most powerful figures at her annual New
   Year's Day open house. Customers, who had to be recommended to
   gain entry, were received in evening dress only.
Johanna Werner's San Francisco establishment was known for the variety of

experiments that flourished therein. Commented Werner, "Only the rich can afford to be perverse."

Miss Dixie Lee, the most popular madame in Wichita, Kansas, died of "galloping consumption" at the age of twenty-seven, leaving a substantial fortune. A search for an heir turned up her father, a Missouri country minister. He was shocked on learning how his daughter had garnered wealth but accepted the money anyway, leading one wag to remark that "the wages of sin are a damned sight better than the wages of virtue."

Bertha Kahn was the San Francisco madame who invented the catch phrase "Company, girls!"

Maud Nelson, with many aliases behind her, conducted "a questionable resort" at 404 Stockton Street in San Francisco and developed a more than businesslike relationship with Charles Fair, the son of a U.S. senator. Their marriage in October 1893 created a society scandal, but to everyone's surprise, the Fairs lived together in peace and harmony until their death in a car accident nearly a decade later.

Sally Stanford♀ began her career as a bootlegger and speakeasy proprietor before emerging as a leading San Francisco madame in 1949. After Stanford retired from the sporting life she opened a popular restaurant on the Sausalito waterfront, became involved in civic affairs, ran for City Council seven times, and was finally elected mayor of Sausalito in 1972.

ELEVEN SELF-STARTERS OF THE NINETEENTH CENTURY

Marie Gresholtz Tussaud learned the art of modeling in wax from her Swiss uncle, and during the Reign of Terror she got plenty of practice recreating the bodies of its victims in wax. When her marriage ended and she had to support two young sons, she moved to London. There, in 1802, she opened Madame Tussaud's Waxworks, long a tourist attraction.

Sarah Josepha Hale♀ influenced thousands of women as the editor of *Godey's Lady's Book* for more than forty years, from 1837 on. The first popular women's magazine, *Godey's* offered the last word on fashion, manners, issues of the day, and the home. Hale turned to writing to support her five children after the death of her husband.

Harriet Hubbard Ayer was without funds after her divorce. Marketing a face cream she claimed had been invented by Madame Recamier, the peerless beauty of Napoleonic France, Ayer became one of the first manufacturers to put her own name on the label of her product and to get endorsements from such celebrities as Lillie Langtry.♀

Ellen Demorest,♀ an early-nineteenth-century milliner, observed that only the wealthiest women could afford to dress in the latest imported fashions and hit upon the idea of cutting paper dress patterns in standard sizes, so that any woman could create high fashion at home. With her husband, she put out a fashion magazine called *Mme. Demorest's Mirror of Fashion* and ran a thriving mail-order business. She also founded Sorosis, the first real professional women's club, and made it a point to hire members of her own sex, particularly black women, as employees.

Susan King made a fortune of $1 million in New York City real estate in the nineteenth century, perhaps acquiring her skill from her father, a government purchasing agent for the army, who took her along on his business trips when she was a child.

Nellie Cashman ♀ prospected all over the American West and in Alaska and Mexico for fifty years. Always looking for one more strike to explore, she is rumored to have gone as far as South Africa. Cashman acquired many fortunes in her long career but gave away most of her money to causes and needy miners. Her beneficiaries called her the "Saint of the Sourdoughs." The first white woman to go into the wilderness of Alaska alone, she was past seventy when, with a dog sled, she mushed across 750 miles of frozen waste.

Sarah Breedlove Walker was born in poverty in Louisiana and became the first black woman millionaire with a hair-straightening method that her agents sold from door to door. As the money rolled in, she built herself a palatial residence on the Hudson River, designed by a black architect at a cost of $250,000. She was also one of the first black philanthropists, contributing a great deal to charity.

Jenny Lind ♀ earned, at the peak of her popularity, $3 million a year. A sharp businesswoman, the "Swedish Nightingale" got $1,000 per concert on her American tour for P.T. Barnum, plus a share of the profits.

Minna ♀ and *Ada Everleigh* ♀ were the leading American madames of the nineteenth century. In the 1890s their Everleigh Club in Chicago was known for its exclusivity, and those lucky enough to get in had a choice of parlors: Gold, Silver, Copper, Moorish, Chinese, Egyptian, Rose, Green, Blue, and Oriental. The gold-plated piano was always attended by a professional musician in evening dress.

Mary Seymour opened the first business school for women only in the late 1800s, Mary Seymour's Union School of Stenography and Typewriting at 38 Park Row in New York. She also began to publish the *Business Woman's Journal* in 1889.

DEALING THE CARDS

❧

Doña Tules (Doña Gertrudis Barcelo) was a noted monte dealer who ran an elegant gambling house in Santa Fe, New Mexico, around 1830. She parlayed her profits into a position as one of the town's most socially and politically prominent citizens and was rumored to have been the mistress of the territorial governor.

Eleanore ("Madame Moustache") Dumont, a top faro (twenty-one) dealer, was probably the best-known woman in the West in the 1870s. Her nickname came from the fine hairs growing on her lip. Dumont opened a gambling house in Nevada City during the gold rush and ran others throughout the West as well. But one day the cards stopped coming up right for Madame Moustache. In 1879, bankrupt and aging, she committed suicide.

Alice ("Poker Alice") Ivers did not hesitate to pull a gun to protect her winnings at the poker table. She told one opponent, "I could admire a clever crook, but have no use for a clumsy one." Ivers operated professional gaming tables throughout the Colorado territory in the 1870s. She met one of her three husbands, W . G. Tubbs, when he was her rival dealer in Deadwood. The pair retired peacefully to a South Dakota homestead. She went back to the old trade when he died, and lived to a ripe old age.

Madame Vestal (Lurline Monte Verde) was a woman of several careers. During the Civil War she was Belle Siddons, a daring Confederate spy. An army surgeon introduced her to gambling, and after the war she practiced that trade in New Orleans and the West, becoming an expert card dealer specializing in Spanish monte and blackjack. But Vestal's love life was one poor gamble. After losing several lovers, she turned to drugs and alcohol, was arrested in an opium den in San Francisco in 1881, and died soon afterward.

Jane Drake is ranked as the best woman poker player in the country today. She learned how to gamble from her husband and now spends most nights at a poker table in Las Vegas, surrounded by men, playing her hand. The twenty-eight-year-old former actress beat fifty-six others to win the women's title in 1979. She has been studying psychology at the University of Nevada in Las Vegas—paying for her studies with her poker winnings, of course.

FIVE COMMERCIAL FEMALES WHO NEVER WERE

Betty Crocker. Although Betty Crocker never really existed, General Mills still receives a persistent flow of proposals for her. The homemaker was the brainchild of advertising executives in the 1920s. Her surname was selected in honor of William G. Crocker, a recently retired director of the company—Betty was simply the most popular female name of the period. At first the name was used as a signature on answers to customer queries, but Crocker grew so popular she was brought to life by the artist's pen and became a cookbook author.

Aunt Jemima. Chris Rutt and Charles G. Underwood developed a ready-made pancake batter in 1889 and were looking for a marketing angle. At a vaudeville show Rutt saw a pair of comedians in blackface who did a cakewalk to a tune called "Aunt Jemima." One of them wore an apron and a red bandanna. Thus inspired, Rutt created the symbol for his new product, gambling that the public would have confidence in the culinary capability of a southern black cook.

Elsie, the Borden cow. In 1936 the Borden Company ran a series of ads in medical journals promoting the use of condensed milk for infant feeding. Originally, Elsie was part of a bevy of bovines that also included Mrs. Blossom, Bessie, and Clara; Elsie, however, was the cow that caught on. She became a national favorite when one of the journal ads was transformed into a radio commercial a few years later.

Gertrude, the Pocket Books kangaroo. The maternal marsupial made her first appearance in 1939. Her creator, a now-forgotten artist, had been hired to design book covers for the publisher that originated mass-market paperbacks. He was paid $25 for his drawing. Originally, Gertrude was studious-looking and wore spectacles. When Walt Disney revised her image a few years later, he slimmed her down and dispensed with the glasses. These, he said, suggested to the public that pocket books were difficult to read.

Chiquita Banana. One afternoon in 1944 Len MacKenzie and Garth Montgomery wrote a song for the United Fruit Company describing a glamorous banana:

> I'm Chiquita Banana and I've come to say
> Bananas have to ripen in a certain way . . .
> Bananas like the climate of the very, very tropical equator
> So you should never put bananas in the refrigerator.

Chiquita was an immediate favorite and became so well known that United Fruit went on to package other products under her name.

Quoted by permission of Chiquita Brands, Inc.

FLYING THE FRIENDLY SKIES

In 1978, United Airlines decided to get the facts on their women business passengers. The results of their research:

- Businesswomen accounted for 18 percent of the airline's market in 1978.
- The woman business passenger makes about ten round trips each year (male business fliers make eighteen).
- She's likely to be on her way to a convention. Thirty-nine percent of women passengers are traveling on business, compared with 12 percent of male passengers.
- Most flying businesswomen are married. But a larger proportion of businesswomen than businessmen are unmarried. Thirty-seven percent of female and 16 percent of male business travelers are unwed.
- She is thirty-eight years old, he is forty-one.
- Her personal income is $25,600 as compared to his $34,200.
- She owns a car.

VII ❧ PERSONS AT WORK

ABOUT WOMEN'S WORK

❧

- In 1890 (when the U.S. government began keeping records) 3.7 million women had a paying job or wanted one. That was 18 percent of working-age females. Less than 5 percent of married women were in the labor force.
- By 1900, 1 out of every 5 women was in the labor force.
- By 1920, 23 percent of working-age women held paying jobs.
- By 1940, 26 percent of eligible females were employed.
- During World War II, 37 percent of working-age women were in the work force.
- By 1978, half of the eligible U.S. female population either had a job or were looking for one.
- It is predicted that by 1990, 52 million women will be either working or seeking work, and they will constitute 45 percent of the labor force.
- Fifty-eight percent of mothers with school-age children are now working; 41 percent of mothers with children under five years are also employed.
- The Census Bureau lists 441 occupations, of which only 20 account for the employment of nearly all working women. Leading the list are secretaries, elementary-school teachers, and waitresses, in that order.
- Seventy-nine percent of women workers are in clerical occupations. Women account for 96 percent of all typists, but only 1 percent of the repairers of typewriters.
- Women were placed in 60 percent of the new jobs that opened up in the 1970s.
- Fifty percent of all working women have occupations that are 70 percent female; 25 percent work in jobs that are 95 percent female.
- Twelve percent of the nation's doctors are women (up from 6 percent in 1950).
- Ten percent of the country's lawyers are women (up from 4 percent in 1915).
- Women now hold nearly one-quarter of management jobs.
- In 1939, women earned 58 percent of what men earned; in 1959, 59 percent; and in 1979, 57 percent, according to figures from the Equal Employment Opportunity Commission.

- In 1975, a survey of 1,522 women conducted by the National Commission on the Observance of the International Women's Year found that more than a third—35 percent—had no individual income of their own, and nearly a third—31 percent—earned less than $5,000. One-fifth—20 percent—earned from $5,000 to $9,999; 6 percent earned from $10,000 to $14,999; and less than 3 percent earned $15,000 and more.

MEANWHILE, IN THE SOVIET UNION

- Fifty-one percent of the labor force is female.
- Forty-nine percent of all university and college students are women.
- Seventy-one percent of all teachers are women.
- Twenty-five percent of the members of the Supreme Soviet (national legislature) are women.
- One-third of the judges are women.

HOUSEWORK

The International Women's Year survey reported that 49 percent of its respondents listed themselves as homemakers. What does a homemaker do? Translated into job market terms, she could be listed as a:

Chef
Dishwasher
Handyman (or person)
Home maintenance worker
Clothing care specialist
Assistant clerk
Assistant teacher
Health care worker
Provider of personal services
Chauffeur
Bookkeeper
Party planner
Human relations counselor

FIVE HINTS TO YOUNG WOMEN IN BUSINESS

From the first issue of the *Business Woman's Journal,* March–April 1889:

- Never ask for your services more, and never accept for them less, than they are actually worth.

- Never chat during business hours.
- Be as ladylike in your office as you would be in a parlor; and above all things avoid undue familiarity with the clerks with whom you may be associated.
- Never accept gifts or other attentions from your employer unless he has introduced you to the members of his family, and you have been received on a social equality by them.
- In your association with men in business, above all things strive to command their respect.

FACTS ABOUT SECRETARIES

- There are 3.39 million secretaries at work in America.
- About 13 percent of all working women are secretaries.
- Only 1 percent of the nation's secretaries are male.
- The average salary for a secretary is $11,000 per year. Legal or executive secretaries can earn $15,000 to $20,000 per year. Very few receive as much as $35,000.
- There is a nationwide shortage of 80,000 secretaries.
- There are, in the United States, 12,064 executive secretaries who are qualified to be called Certified Professional Secretaries. They have passed a two-day, six-part test administered by the National Secretaries Association.
- National Secretaries' Week was established in 1952, under pressure from the florists of the nation, to honor office workers—and provide another occasion for sending flowers.
- In the 1970s Working Women–National Association of Office Workers was founded, to eliminate sexist assumptions from the job and its public image, and to improve working conditions for its members. In recent years National Secretaries' Week has featured awards for the pettiest office procedures of the year. Samples from the 1980 collection: a secretary was asked to put her boss's galoshes on for him because his knees hurt; another was asked to copy cartoons from *Playboy* to send to his associates. Both refused.

FIRSTS FOR THE WORKING WOMAN

- 1734: The first women's labor organization was established by New York City maids to protest the abuses they suffered from their mistresses' husbands.
- 1824: The first women to participate in a strike were female weavers in Pawtucket, Rhode Island, who were resisting increased hours and reduced wages.
- 1825: The first women's labor organization in a trade was the United Tailoresses Society of New York. Later that year this group conducted the first strike by a women's labor organization.

- 1845: The first government investigation into women's labor conditions was in Massachusetts. The resulting report stated that conditions failed to warrant legislation since health was not being impaired and that reduced hours would affect wages and hurt competition.
- 1867: The first national women's labor organization, the Daughters of St. Crispin, was formed by female shoemakers. The union lasted until 1878.
- 1872: The first antidiscrimination law against women was passed in Illinois.
- 1879: The first state legislation prohibiting the employment of women in coal mines was in Illinois.
- 1891: The first use of the term *collective bargaining* was by Beatrice Potter Webb in *The Co-operative Movement.* And the first law restricting women in manufacturing to an eight-hour day was passed in California.
- 1905: The first law restricting women workers generally to an eight-hour day was passed in Massachusetts.
- 1908: The first Supreme Court decision upholding state legislation that restricted working hours for women was *Muller* v. *Oregon.*
- 1912: The first state minimum wage law for women and children was passed in Massachusetts. Eight other states passed similar measures in 1913, but the Supreme Court declared all such laws unconstitutional.
- 1919: The first states to have equal pay legislation for women were Michigan and Montana.
- 1920: The Women's Bureau was created, under the Department of Labor.
- 1933: The first woman secretary of labor and first woman cabinet officer, Frances Perkins,♀ was also the first secretary of labor who did not belong to a union and the first to have a college education. She served until 1945.
- 1963: The first federal equal pay legislation was the Equal Pay Act.

From U.S. Department of Labor, *Labor Firsts in America* (1977)

FOURTEEN WHO WERE FIRST ON A "MAN'S JOB"

Sadie Orchard. One of the first women to drive a stagecoach regularly in the Wild West, the petite Orchard never dressed in men's clothing. Rather, her attire was that of an English woman on her way to a hunt. She carried a bullwhip instead of a gun, but was effective nonetheless. "No stage was ever robbed while I was driving," she claimed.

Mary Fields. Perhaps the first woman to be hired as the driver of a U.S. mail coach, Fields got the job in the 1880s when in her sixties. Earlier, Fields had been a freight hauler. "She could drink more whiskey than anyone I ever knew," said one admiring male co-worker.

Emma Nutt. Until she became the first woman telephone operator in 1878, it was a "men only" occupation, since they alone were thought capable of handling such complex technology. Nutt was chief operator when she retired after thirty-three years with the phone company.

Marie Luhring. The first woman automotive engineer, Luhring received a Master of Engineering degree from New York's Cooper Union in June 1922 and was the first woman to be elected an associate member of the Society of Automotive Engineers.

Alice L. Marston. Probably the first woman dispatcher at an airport, Marston worked at Concord, New Hampshire, in the 1930s, sometimes meeting planes in temperatures as low as −35 degrees Fahrenheit with snow six feet deep blocking the runways.

Katy Margerum. The supervisor of air freight operations for American Airlines in El Paso, Texas, is the first woman in the industry to have this broad authority over day-to-day operations.

Lynne Degillio. She is the first woman to work as a traffic controller at Kennedy Airport in New York.

Rachel C. Hall. The first woman to work in the final repair station at Chrysler Corporation's Hamtramck, Michigan, assembly plant got the job in 1969 when in her early fifties.

Joni E. Barnett. Appointed director of physical education at Yale University in 1973, Barnett is the first female athletic director at a major university.

Josephine Figliolia Striano. In 1977 she became the first woman to be issued a master plumber's license in New York City.

Candy Dykstra. The first woman to receive a dealership from the Ford Motor Company, and the granddaughter of a former Ford Motor executive, Dykstra offers "the sweetest deals in town" in Eton Rapids, Michigan. The dealership has increased business about 600 percent over its previous owner's volume.

Libby Howie. The first woman to be an art auctioneer for Sotheby in London, after two years on the job, Howie became head of the department of nineteenth- and twentieth-century prints in 1976.

Deirdre Hickey. Her new job began shortly before she pulled a train out of the Port Washington station at 4:35 P.M. on June 6, 1979. The twenty-four-year-old conductor on the Long Island Railroad, the nation's largest commuter line, is the first woman in the U.S. qualified to run yard, freight, and passenger trains. Earlier the same year, *Nancy Marlborough* became the first woman engineer on the LIRR, which also employs 34 women as brakemen (sic) and fare collectors.

WEARING A BLUE COLLAR

*

A regulation issued by the Office of Federal Contract Compliance Programs in April 1978 called for registered apprenticeship and training programs to prepare women for entry into blue-collar areas. Some who already wear blue collars are:

Mamie O'Dell Smith of Tappahannock, Virginia, a truck driver. The great-grandmother has also worked as a riveter, welder, truck assembler, spray painter, bomb builder, and waitress. Truck driving is her favorite, however. Says O'Dell, "I love the driving itself, but it's also the truck stops and meeting the other drivers and swapping views."

Kim Hinderliter, a twenty-three-year-old miner for the Renton Mine of the Consolidation Coal Company in Pennsylvania. Although a mining accident once cost her broken bones and torn muscles, she's dedicated to the challenge of her job: "You can't get bored in a coal mine. It's too dangerous."

Frances Amich, now fifty-six, in the bricklaying business since she was seventeen. The Frankfort, Indiana, woman received a bricklayer's union card in Washington, D.C., in 1939 and acts as her own contractor.

Maureen Hanlon, a professional window cleaner in office buildings and high-rise apartments for Flatiron Window Cleaning in Manhattan. "It's a lot safer here than it is down there."

Ruth Wilson, a thirty-five-year-old mother of eleven, the first woman hired as a street cleaner by the Philadelphia Sanitation Department in 1976. Wilson maintains, "I do the same work as the men and hold my own."

Kathleen Elkins, accepted by Local 5 of the International Brotherhood of Electrical Workers as their first female trainee. Her starting salary was $110 a week but this wage more than tripled after a four-year apprenticeship.

Evelyn Hancock, a welder at the Misener Industries boatyard in Tampa, Florida. She has six grandchildren.

Kathleen Shearer, a bellhop at the Plaza Hotel in New York, the first female occupant of this position in the Big Apple. Her supervisor says he decided to hire Shearer because of her firm handshake, "a good indication of hand and arm strength."

Cathy Monzadellis, hired at the age of twenty-three as the first woman sandblaster in New York City early in 1979. Sandblasters work at great heights, from scaffolds alongside the walls of tall buildings, and Cathy's twenty-six-inch waist required a special safety belt (her co-workers are generally quite burly). The company that employs Monzadellis puts up "Persons Working" signs when she is on a job.

Phyllis Maizel, possessor of a rigger's license from New York City since 1978. It entitles her to erect scaffoldings for window washing and other exterior maintenance work; she is the city's first female rigger.

Shirley B. Eubanks, operator of an offshore platform for the Sun Gas Company. In 1977 the thirty-four-year-old Eubanks earned $24,000.

Barbara Johnson, accepted after two years of waiting into the apprenticeship program of the pipefitters' union in Washington, D.C., in 1976.

Jean Strauss, a sheet-metal apprentice and the only female employee of Aire Sheetmetal, Inc., of Redwood City, California.

Libby Howard, a journeyman carpenter in Washington, D.C., forced to leave construction work because of harassment from male co-workers. She now heads a women's lobbying and support group called Women Working in Construction.

Virginia ("Cookie") Escobar and ***Gwen Wells,*** among fifty-five women who received temporary licenses to work on the docks in New York and New Jersey in early 1979 and among the thirty who lasted the first year. Says Wells, "When you start feeling a little weak, you think about that $10.40 an hour and you keep on throwing bananas."

UNCLE SAM'S FIRST FEMALE EMPLOYEES

❦

The U.S. government first hired women in large numbers in the 1860s. The secretary of the treasury, General Francis Elias Spinner, employed them to cut the paper bills for his department: "A woman can use scissors better than a man and she will do it cheaper." Women also worked under sweatshop conditions at the Government Printing Office, where they sewed books by hand at the rate of 80 cents each; on a good day it was possible to stitch nine volumes. Under the Civil Service Act of 1883 women became eligible to compete with men for government jobs. By 1894, 14 percent of the government's typists were women; by 1914, it was 25 percent.

Clara Barton ♀ claimed to be the first woman to hold a white-collar government job. The future founder of the American Red Cross started as a clerk-copyist at the Patent Office in 1854. The taunts of other employees were fierce, but Barton persisted, becoming a confidential clerk to the superintendent of patents at the unusually high salary of $1,400 a year.

Mrs. Stephen Brown, one of Spinner's employees in the Treasury, was the "greatest living expert" at identifying mutilated currency. An Iowa farmer once sent the department a hardened brown lump, all, he claimed that remained of six $5 bills consumed by his goat. In two hours Brown succeeded in separating the particles of currency and determined that he was telling the truth. She sent the farmer six brand-new bills.

Sophia Holmes, the widow of a black soldier killed in the Civil War, considered herself lucky to have a job as a charwoman in the Treasury Department at $15 a month. One afternoon she found $200,000 in greenbacks lying among the waste papers. Afraid to leave her find, she spent the night in the office and reported it to the authorities in the morning. As a reward she was upgraded to the position of "janitress" and a salary of $660 a year. Holmes thus became the first black woman ever to receive an official appointment in the service of the U.S. government. Needless to say, her salary was considerably less than that of the lowest ungraded man.

Mary Francis Hoyt, a Vassar graduate, had the highest score of any man or woman on the first civil service examination, given in 1883. Her appointment to a $900-a-year clerkship took effect on September 5 of that year.

Alice B. Sanger, a stenographer, was the first woman hired to work at the White House; the year was 1890.

Margaret W. Young held a unique job in the William Taft and Theodore Roosevelt administrations, in the days before multiple-signing pens. Congress authorized her to sign the president's signature to standard documents such as land patents. By 1911 she had signed more than 90,-000 such patents with the name "Theodore Roosevelt" and even more with the appellation "Wm. H. Taft"—all with "per Margaret W. Young" noted below, of course.

SEVEN FRONTIER WOMEN

━━━━━━━━━━━━━━━━ ❧ ━━━━━━━━━━━━━━━━

The West boasted five times as many actresses, nearly four times as many female lawyers, and twice the number of women doctors and journalists as there were back East. Just a few of the early working women of the West:

Julie Shannon, a daguerreotypist in San Francisco in 1850, also served as a midwife.

Madame Bauer of Walla Walla, Washington, was a linguist in the 1850s who gave lessons in French, German, Italian, and Spanish. She knew Hebrew and Latin as well and, as a bonus, taught plain and fancy needlework.

Luzena Wilson started a boardinghouse in a tent in Nevada City, California, but it soon grew into a hotel accommodating 75 to 200 boarders at a time. Wilson sewed for the miners and also loaned them money at 10 percent interest per month. Money poured in, and she replaced her hotel with an even larger one. When fire destroyed this one, she built another that later developed into the town of Vacaville, California.

Clara Brown tried to board the stagecoach to Mountain City, Colorado, where she was planning to open a laundry, but was told that public conveyances were off-limits to blacks. Undaunted, Brown, who was a successful businesswoman, hired a prospector to be her chauffeur.

Katrina Murat, with her husband, ran the mining camp that eventually grew into Denver, Colorado. Her husband's drinking consumed the profits, so they turned to other enterprises. In the mid-1860s Murat presided over the most fashionable restaurant in Virginia City, Nevada; its legendary pies went for an unheard-of $2 or more. The Murats accumulated and lost several fortunes, and in her old age the enterprising Katrina had to be supported by charity.

Abbie Cardozo, a photographer in Ferndale, California, in the 1890s, was also a hairdresser.

Cassie Hill took over the Wells Fargo depot in Roseville, California, after her husband died in 1885, and operated it for twenty-three years.

NINE FIRE FIGHTERS

━━━━━━━━━━━━━━━━ ❧ ━━━━━━━━━━━━━━━━

Molly, a slave owned by a member of New York City's Engine Company Number 11, answered all alarms along with him. Male volunteers were in short supply during a raging blizzard in 1818, so Molly grabbed the drag rope along with the men and helped lug the pumper through almost impassable snow. She was proud to be "as good a fire laddie as many of the boys who bragged at being such."

Marina Betts would join the bucket brigades as soon as a fire broke out in Pittsburgh in the 1820s. Betts's specialty was capturing passers-by as volunteers. Tall and imposing-looking, she was described as a "virago" and a "recruiting sergeant." "Menfolk should be working," she would intone as she commandeered the hapless strangers.

*Lillie Coit,*⁹ a San Francisco heiress, saw her first fire on Telegraph Hill when she was fifteen. She stepped into line, grabbed hold of the rope, and yelled, "Come on, you men! Let's beat 'em." After that, Coit was hooked. She went to every fire attended by Knickerbocker Engine Company Number 5, which made her an honorary member. Until her death she wore a solid gold "5" pinned to her dress and signed her letters "Lillie H. Coit, 5."

Peggy Miller, Vera Musser, Judy Spotts, and *Patty Stouse,* of Centre Hall, Pennsylvania, became in the early 1970s the first women certified as fire fighters in their state.

Dolly Browder, a professional forest-fire fighter, serves on one of the first all-female fire-fighting crews because she loves "the chance to be together and accomplish something." Browder and the other women in her crew work summers for the National Forest Service.

Sister Sophia, a nurse and member of the Sisters of the Holy Family of Nazareth, was in early 1980 unanimously elected by the trustees of the village of Sea Cliff, New York, to be the first woman in the volunteer fire-fighting force of that Long Island community.

"LET HER WORKS PRAISE HER IN THE GATES":
Exhibitors at the Centennial Exhibition of 1876

⚘

America celebrated its one-hundredth birthday with a great Centennial Exhibition in Philadelphia. The Women's Pavilion highlighted the work of inventors, businesswomen, artists, scientists, physicians, and writers. The only requirement for exhibition of a woman's work was that it be "the product of her thought and labor." Over the entrance to the pavilion were the words of the book of Proverbs 31:31, noted in the title above. A few of the contributors:

Emma Allison handled the controls of a steam engine that powered six looms and a printing press, showing that women were capable of entering what had been an all-male domain. To spectators who worried about her safety, Allison replied that running the steam engine took much less energy than running after children and was a lot easier than standing over a kitchen stove.

Mary Nolan exhibited a model house made of "Nolanum," a system of interlocking blocks she had invented for improved ventilation of the home. "Nolanum" blocks were finished on both sides, so that once they were in place the inner wall surface needed no plastering or paper hanging.

Hannah Mountain invented a life-preserver mattress that was given the official approval of the Board of United States Supervising Inspectors of Steamboats.

Martha Coston, left with three small children when her husband died, managed his company which produced phosphorescent flares for signaling distress or warnings. At the Centennial Exhibition, Coston showed her invention, a three-color pyrotechnic light signal, which had been adopted by the American government and at least five foreign governments.

Hannah Suplee's invention was an open-eyed sewing machine needle that could be easily threaded even by those with failing eyesight.

Margaret Colvin created the Triumph Rotary Washer; it promised homemakers a new era of liberation from scrubbing clothes by hand.

Mary Florence Potts devised a flatiron that was double-pointed so that it could be used twice as long without being reheated. Other special features were a removable wooden handle and an inner core of nonconducting material, making the iron cooler to handle.

Jane Wells displayed a baby holder/jumper that was produced in a Chicago factory managed by her husband and staffed mostly by women.

Graceanna Lewis, a member of the Philadelphia Academy of Natural Sciences, exhibited a Chart of the Animal Kingdom. It won her a Centennial medal and praise from prominent male scientists.

Martha Maxwell, a naturalist, had created a diorama that took up a good part of the Kansas-Colorado building. It contained about 300 mammals, 300 birds, and a few reptiles from the Rocky Mountains, all of which Maxwell had shot and mounted.

Elizabeth French, a physician, exhibited a case full of appliances she had patented for electrical treatment of the human body.

Annie Ramborger showed artificial teeth that the Centennial judges commended for their "thoroughness of workmanship and excellence of finish." Three years earlier Ramborger and two other women students had been temporarily expelled from the Pennsylvania College of Dental Surgery when some male students, afraid to compete with their work, threatened to resign if the women were allowed to continue.

Susan Bogart Warner's popular novel *Wide Wide World* (1851) was one of the books shown at the Women's Pavilion. It was the first American novel to sell a million copies.

Edmonia Lewis,♀ a black and Indian sculptor, showed one of the most talked about works of the exhibition, a heroic sculpture called *The Death of Cleopatra.*

Caroline Brooks sculpted a large statue out of butter which was kept on ice throughout the Centennial. Brooks had patented her process and claimed that the butter mold gave her plaster casts "delicacy of texture and finer shades of expression."

MOTHERS OF INVENTION

※

Kansi. At a Feast of Lanterns on a muggy day in ancient Japan, this daughter of a courtier was so warm that, in violation of court etiquette, she removed her mask. To hide the fact that her face was bare, she began fanning herself with the mask. All the other women followed her lead. The actual fan appeared soon afterward, or so it is said.

Sarasvati.♀ According to legend, the beautiful multiarmed Hindu goddess, wife of Brahma, invented the *devanagari,* the Sanskrit alphabet.

Si Ling-chi, Empress of China ca. 2640 B.C., developed the process by which the delicate thread is removed from the cocoon of the silkworm, then established the silk cultivation and weaving industries.

Sibella Masters, an early colonist, developed a new method of cleaning and airing Indian corn. This first American invention received an English patent in the name of Mr. Masters.

Elizabeth Flanagan, an upstate New York barmaid, allegedly created the cocktail—and consequently the cocktail hour—during the American Revolution. She combined rum, rye whiskey, and fruit juice, decorated the glass with a feather snatched from the tail of her Tory neighbor's rooster, and handed it to a French officer. "Vive le coq's tail," said the quick-witted gentleman, naming the drink with his first swig. This was not Flanagan's only claim to immortality; James Fenimore Cooper made her a character in his novel *The Spy.*

Betsy Metcalf created the first straw bonnet made in the United States in 1798.

Margaret Knight was only twelve when she came up with the first of her twenty-seven (or more) known inventions in 1850; she would later be called the "Woman Edison." Her creations ranged from a shoe-cutting machine to a device that folded paper bags with square bottoms. The last patents she was granted before her death in 1914 were for rotary engines and motors for automobiles.

Catherine Littlefield Greene owned a plantation given to her and her late husband, Revolutionary War general Nathanael Greene, in gratitude by the people of Georgia. A conversation with some local planters led her to think of a machine to separate the black cotton seeds from the white fluff, a chore that occupied many hours. She explained her idea to a young schoolteacher from her native New England who boarded with her, and Eli Whitney has been credited ever since with the invention of the cotton gin. Whitney built the working model of the device in a room provided by Greene, who also suggested metal teeth to clutch the seeds but slide through the fine threads.

Ann Harned Manning of New Jersey improved the cutting action of the early-nineteenth-century mower and reaper by suggesting a combination of teeth on cutting blades that could turn in a crosswise or rotary direction; her husband patented the invention.

Sister Tabitha Babbit, a Shaker, invented the circular saw. She got the idea for it one day while watching her spinning wheel.

May Evans Harrington, in 1889, invented a "mustache-guard for attachment to spoons or cups when used in the act of eating soup and other liquid food or drinking coffee."

Cynthia Westover, in the late nineteenth century, constructed a cart that would dump dirt as well as carry it. This invention proved so useful that Westover was made *membre d'honneur* of the Parisian Academy of Inventors.

Ellene Alice Bailey, a resident of Pont Fort, Missouri, at the end of the century invented three different varieties of powder puff, a special needle for sewing on shoes, the first silver whisk broom, a music roll that doubled as a Christmas or Easter card, novelty clocks, special chairs for holding draperies, and a leg protector for furniture made of waterproof cloth.

Susan Stavers. A sailor who boarded in her Boston rooming house criticized her puddings as being too lumpy. In the South Pacific he had seen natives pound tapioca in their mortars—why couldn't she get the same results with a coffee grinder? Stavers did and created Minute Tapioca, a quick-cooking product which she began marketing in 1894.

Ruth Wakefield cut pieces of a chocolate candy bar into her drop-cookie batter one day, thinking the chocolate would melt and "marble" the cookies. Instead, the crunchy bits remained and melted in the mouth. Guests at Wakefield's Toll House Inn in Massachusetts begged for the recipe, and soon the cookie was being baked in homes all over the country. The Nestlé Company began to produce chocolate "morsels" especially for home versions of Wakefield's creation; the recipe is on the package.

Gertrude Rogallo in 1948, with her husband, Francis, invented a new kind of flying machine: the hang glider. The Rogallos and their four children tested the models in a wind tunnel in their attic.

Margaret Rudkin. The first recipient of her old-fashioned bread baked with unbleached flour was her allergic son. When his health improved, his allergist asked Rudkin to make the bread for other patients. The demand became so great that, in the 1950s, the Pepperidge Farm Company was born.

Becky Schroeder, one of the youngest ever to receive a U.S. patent, invented a luminous writing board in 1974 when she was twelve. Schroeder wanted to equip herself to do her homework after lights out.

FOUR FLAG WOMEN

❧

Elizabeth ("Betsy") Griscom Ross,[?] according to historian Linda Grant de Pauw, never did sew the first national flag; that was a tale told by Ross's grandson in 1870. However, she did exist (1752–1836), and she did make flags, for ships and for the Commonwealth of Pennsylvania, and at the time of the Constitutional Convention she was indeed living in Philadelphia.

Mary Young Pickersgill, with the assistance of her daughter *Caroline Pickersgill,* of Baltimore, sewed the flag that was destined to become the Star-Spangled Banner when it flew over Fort McHenry during a battle with the British in 1814, inspiring Francis Scott Key to compose his patriotic verse. The flag now hangs in the Smithsonian Institution in Washington, D.C.

Rebecca M. Winbourne would later become known as the "Betsy Ross of the Confederacy" for making a sample of the flag that was adopted by the Confederate Congress in 1861. Her sample flag was only twelve by fifteen inches and made from dyed flour sacks; but less than two weeks after she was given the go-ahead, Winbourne had a nine-by-twelve-foot version ready for display.

WORKING WOMEN OF THE COMICS WITH THEIR VERY OWN STRIPS

Honors for the most exotic occupation of a female comic-strip character surely go to the Dragon Lady, a hard-boiled but attractive Eurasian opium dealer who was shot to death in the very first sequence of "Terry and the Pirates" but was later miraculously resurrected. She never had a strip of her own, but working women who did include:

Winnie Winkle, created by Martin Branner in 1920, in the first successful strip about a "working gal." Winnie was a spirited stenographer who always dressed in the latest fashion.

Tillie the Toiler, created by Russ Westover in 1921, a curly-haired secretary with Clara Bow lips and a flapper's problems.

Ella Cinders, created by Bill Conselman and Charles Plumb in 1927, a film contract player with enormous Betty Boop eyes.

Connie, created by Frank Godwin in 1927, variously a reporter, detective, and space explorer.

Jane Arden, created by Monte Barrett and Frank Ellis in 1928, also a reporter—far and away the favorite occupation of employed comic-strip heroines.

Dixie Dugan, created by John Striebel and J. P. McEvoy in 1929, a glamorous showgirl at first. As the strip became more family oriented, she settled into life as a secretary.

Lois Lane, created by Jerry Siegel and Joe Shuster for "Superman" in 1938, who succeeded to a strip of her own in 1958. She was a capable and brisk reporter, twenty times as competent as Clark Kent.

Debbie Dean, created by Bert Whitman in 1942, a chic—you guessed it—newspaper reporter!

Brenda Starr, created by Dale Messick ♀ in 1940, a reporter.

Mary Perkins, heroine of "On Stage," created by Leonard Starr in 1957, a star-struck small-town girl who came to New York and made it big as a Broadway actress.

Miss Peach, created by Mel Lazarus in 1957, a schoolteacher kept on her toes by a classroom of neurotic and highly competitive small souls.

Tiffany Jones, created by Pat Tourret and Jenny Butterworth in 1964, a glamorous English model in the mod mode of the period.

Agatha Crumm, created by Bill Hoest in 1978, a tycoon with the savvy of a Rockefeller and a heart about the size of a pea.

SEVENTEEN OFFICERS OF THE LAW

Women have served as police officers for decades, but only recently have they been given the same assignments as men. Barriers that have kept them out of police work are also falling. In September 1973 a court decision in Cleveland enjoined the city's police department from imposing its height requirement of 5 feet 8 inches and weight requirement of 150 pounds; many police departments have now modified the physical requirements that excluded women.

Alice Stebbins Wells persuaded the mayor of Los Angeles to appoint her to the police force in 1910, becoming the first policewoman in the United States. Because of Wells's commitment to the use of policewomen, at least twenty-five cities and twenty states, as well as several foreign countries, had hired women for such jobs by 1916. In 1915 the International Association of Policewomen was formed, with Wells as its first presiding officer.

Mary Sullivan headed New York City's first Bureau of Policewomen, organized in April 1926. She also had her own radio program, "Mary Sullivan, Policewoman."

Winifred Taylor is a detective superintendent and operational head of Scotland Yard's Extradition Department.

Marilynn O'Regan of the Chicago Police Department is deputy chief in the Traffic Division.

Gertrude Schimmel is deputy chief in the New York City Police Department. The highest-ranking woman in the department, she is commanding officer of the Community Affairs Division. New York's force has 10 women lieutenants, 13 women sergeants, 90 woman detectives, and 438 women police officers.

Betty Blankenship and *Elizabeth Coffal* of the Indianapolis Police Department were among the first policewomen to go on patrol. Their success in "Car 47" encouraged departments in other cities to follow suit.

Gail A. Cobb, the first U.S. policewoman to be killed in the line of duty, was a twenty-four-year-old member of the Washington, D.C., force when she was shot by a fleeing gunman in an underground garage. Both of Cobb's parents were also members of the District of Columbia Police Department.

Marty Green, thirty-seven, of the Louisville police force, foiled an armed hijack attempt at Louisville airport in January 1973. Green, dressed as a flight attendant, negotiated with the 170-pound terrorist until he promised to surrender his gun if she would hold his hand. As he relinquished the shotgun, she pulled him into a headlock and judo-tossed him down the ramp, where other police officers waited.

Bettie Jean Eppes, twenty-nine, of the District of Columbia force, knocked down two men who were fighting in a Washington bar after her male partner had been put out of commission. Said Eppes, "The training at the academy was so good that I knew instinctively what to do and I did it automatically."

Regina Robbins, a cum laude graduate of the University of Syracuse, was at the top of her class—120 men and Robbins—at the New York State Troopers' academy.

Mikele Carter, a Miami plainclothes woman, single-handedly brought in one of the FBI's most wanted criminals.

Giovanna Punneo of the San Jose, California, Police Department volunteered to be a decoy after the campus of San Jose State University was terrorized by sexual assaults. One night she felt a knife at her throat. A 240-pound man had grabbed her from behind, muttering, "Come with me or you're dead." Punneo whirled about and shot him in the chest.

Lucille Franckowiak is San Antonio's first woman undercover narcotics agent. In 1978 she filed most of the 73 cases against 117 suspects rounded up for pushing drugs in the city during the previous year.

Jolanta Giergon, Heather-Ann Phyllis, and *Anne Pritchard* were among the first thirty-two women sworn in to the Royal Canadian Mounted Police Force in the fall of 1974.

THEY ASKED WHAT'S COOKING

The earliest publications on cookery were written by men, first because relatively few women could read or write before the eighteenth century; second, because men have always been most concerned with the foods to be served them. Recent studies have suggested that the male palate is more sensitive than that of the female—which perhaps accounts for all those fussy husbands that we know. In this list are some notable cookery books by women of previous centuries.

Hannah Wooley was the first woman whose byline appeared on a cookery book. *The Queen-like Closet or Rich Cabinet,* published in London in 1681, carried as many "receipts" for needlework, medicine, and make-up as for food and was a practical handbook for the women of the day who aspired to the management of a first-class household.

Hannah Glasse published *The Art of Cookery, Made Plain and Easy . . .* in London "and most Market-Towns in England" in 1747, saying modestly on the title page only that it was "By a Lady."

Susannah Carter of Clerkenwell, London, wrote *The Frugal Housewife, or Complete Woman Cook,* "wherein The Art of Dressing all sorts of Viands, with Cleanliness, Decency, and Elegance, Is explained in Five Hundred Receipts." It was published in Boston in 1772, with illustrations by Paul Revere.

Amelia Simmons, "An American Orphan," penned the first American cookbook. *American Cookery, or The Art of Dressing Viands, Fish, Poultry and Vegetables . . . Adapted to this country and all grades of life* was published in Hartford, Connecticut, in 1796. Although most of Simmons's recipes were traditionally English, she also included such native American specialties as Indian pudding, johnnycake, hoecake, and Indian flapjacks.

Mary Randolph included regional native specialties such as okra and gumbo, of African origin, as well as Spanish dishes in *The Virginia Housewife,* which appeared in 1824.

Eliza Acton hoped to publish a volume of her verses, until her publisher told her no one would buy poems by maiden ladies and to write a sensible cookbook. *Modern Cookery in all its Branches; Reduced to A System of Easy Practice, For the Use of Private Families* (1845) was the result.

Catharine Beecher,[9] in *Miss Beecher's Domestic Receipt Book* (1846), described basic cookery techniques—a first—and gave specific recipes as well.

Mrs. Horace Mann, with the publication of *Christianity in the Kitchen* (1861), brought morality and the Puritan ethic to cookery in the United States.

Isabella Beeton was a journalist whose huge *Book of Household Management* (1861) made her the last word on running a proper home among Victorian women.

Mary Lincoln founded a cooking school in Boston in the 1880s for recently arrived Irish immigrants eager to work as cooks. Her recipes were so good that the society women who employed her students were soon asking for copies. To meet the demand, Lincoln wrote the first *Boston Cooking School Cookbook,* published in 1883.

Fannie Merritt Farmer ♀ produced, in 1896, one of the most popular cookbooks ever. Her *Boston Cooking School Cook Book* went through twenty-one editions before her death and soon became known as ***The Fannie Farmer Cookbook.*** Farmer was the first to offer the precise measurements now common in American cookbooks, and she even instructed her readers in the correct way to measure: "Dip the spoon in the ingredient, fill, lift, and level with a knife, the sharp edge of the knife being toward the tip of the spoon."

Sarah Tyson Rorer was thirty years old, had never cooked a meal in her life, and was severely depressed over the death of one of her children when a relative insisted she go to cooking lessons being given at the New Century Club in Philadelphia. Rorer found herself immediately, learned all she could about cookery, opened her Philadelphia Cooking School in 1883, and three years later published *Mrs. Rorer's Philadelphia Cook Book.*

Juliet Corson founded the first successful cooking school in New York and wrote various small cookbooks such as *Fifteen Cent Dinners for Workingmen's Families* (1877).

Agnes Catherine Maitland published *Rudiments of Cookery* and the *Afternoon Tea Book* in the 1880s in England, while she was examiner to the National Union Schools of Domestic Economy. Maitland had an unusual career progression, to say the least, having earlier been secretary to the Egypt Exploration Fund and subsequently principal of Somerville College, Oxford University, in 1889.

Lizzie Black Kander, who founded a settlement house in Milwaukee for recently arrived immigrants in the late 1880s, wrote the classic *Settlement Cook Book,* which is still going strong. With the proceeds from her sales, Kander was able to extend the social services offered by her settlement house.

PERFECT ATTENDANTS—THE FIRST EIGHT AIRLINE STEWARDESSES

──────────────── ✹ ────────────────

When the San Francisco district manager for Boeing Air Transport (forerunner of United Airlines) met registered nurse and student pilot Ellen Church in 1930, he wondered how her skills could be applied to the fast-growing commercial aviation industry. He thought of the stewards who served passengers on steamship lines and talked Boeing into allowing him to hire eight women to perform similar services in the air for a three-month trial.

The eight new employees, dubbed stewardesses, were hired at $125 a month with a $5 bonus for stormy weather and delays. "Stews" had to be unmarried, female, registered nurses, under twenty-five, under 5 feet 4, and weigh less than 115 pounds. Poundage was important, because both passengers and stewardesses could find themselves off-loaded in favor of the all-important U.S. mail. Their duties included carrying all luggage on board, helping to fuel the planes, and helping pilots push the planes into hangars, as well as serving box lunches, pouring coffee from thermos containers, and comforting the airsick.

Today there are more than 125,000 male and female flight attendants caring for jet-age passengers, but fifty years ago there were only these eight:

Margaret Arnott
Jessie Carter
Ellen Church
Ellis Crawford
Harriet Fry
Alva Johnson
Inez Keller
Cornelia Peterman

COME FLY WITH ME

There are now more than 100 women among the 33,000 commercial pilots flying for the nation's major airlines. A few of them are:

Emily Warner, Frontier Airlines, the country's first female commercial airline pilot and the only one so far to achieve the rank of captain.
Claudia Jones, Continental Airlines. A former Las Vegas entertainer, she took up flying to get from one nightclub engagement to the next, became an instructor, then went on to commercial flying.
Lynn Rhoades, Western Airlines. Scarcely a soul in her family is *not* connected with flying. Her father is an air traffic controller in Alaska, her grandmother an aircraft sheet-metal mechanic; her husband flies for Hughes Airwest; her brother-in-law is an engineer for United; her sister-in-law is a flight attendant; her father-in-law is a retired vice-president of engineering for United; and her mother-in-law was an American Airlines flight attendant.
Terry London Rinehart, Western Airlines. Both of her parents were pilots, her mother having flown with the WASPs during World War II. Her husband is also a pilot.
Jill E. Brown, Texas International Airlines. She is so far the only black woman pilot; her husband is a pilot, too.
Gail Gorski, United Airlines, the 1972 Queen of the Kentucky Derby and a former Federal Aviation Administration flight inspection pilot.
Mary Hirsch, Continental Airlines. She drove past an airfield one day on her way to a hairdresser's appointment, spent the money on a plane ride instead, and has been involved with flying ever since.
Mary Busch-Lowman, Hughes Airwest. She is married to her copilot, John Lowman.

Bonnie Tiburzi, American Airlines. Her father and brother, also pilots, are with other airlines.

Cheryl Ritchie, Piedmont Airlines. When she emerges from the cockpit, pilot Ritchie reports, she sometimes gets requests from passengers for soft drinks, pillows, and blankets.

Lennie Mettick Sorenson, Continental Airlines. Sorenson gave up dual careers as a marine biologist and a diving instructor to become a commercial pilot.

Valerie Walker, Western Airlines. Walker pursued a flying career because "I don't want to look back when I'm in my nineties and see I didn't do what I loved."

LATE STARTS AND SECOND CAREERS

Kate Waller Barrett was nearly thirty and the mother of seven children in 1886 when she decided to go to medical school. For years she had helped her minister husband in his work with prostitutes. When she got her medical degree, Barrett opened homes for unwed mothers, often in the face of hostility from neighbors.

Ruth Benedict didn't begin her distinguished career in anthropology until she was thirty-four years old. Before that she had been a poet, teacher, and social worker. Her best-known works are *Patterns of Culture* and *The Chrysanthemum and the Sword,* both pioneering studies in cultural psychology.

Rachel Carson,♀ a marine biologist, turned to her second career, writing, when she was thirty-four. Her award-winning book, *Silent Spring,* describing the dangers of pesticides to the environment, was completed shortly before her death at fifty-five.

Phyllis Diller was a homemaker until she made her professional debut as a comic at San Francisco's Purple Onion at the age of thirty-seven.

Isak Dinesen published her first book, *Seven Gothic Tales,* in 1934, when she was forty-nine.

Mary Baker Eddy♀ was fifty-seven in 1879 when she and her husband, Asa G. Eddy, founded the Christian Science Association, later the Church of Christ Scientist.

George Eliot (Mary Ann Evans)♀ tore herself away from a background of country piety to come to London at the age of thirty-two and look for a job as an editor. Her first novel, *Adam Bede,* appeared in 1859 when she was forty.

Katherine Gibbs was forty-three when she founded her first school for secretaries bearing her name, in Providence, Rhode Island. She was a widow with two sons to support.

Texas Guinan became the queen of New York night life when she was middle-aged, welcoming customers to her roaring twenties speakeasy with a booming, "Hello, sucker!" Before that she had had several careers: circus rider, chorus girl, vaudeville trouper, and movie actress.

Phoebe A. Hanaford♀ was nearly forty when she became a Universalist minister, the first woman ordained in New England.

Barbara Jordan,♀ the former congresswoman from Houston, declared herself at forty-three to be in a state of mid-life transition. She now teaches graduate seminars in political science at the University of Texas's Lyndon B. Johnson School of Public Affairs and says she has no intention of returning to politics.

Alice Lakey led a prosaic life until she was forty-six. Then she became the leader of the campaign for passage of the Pure Food and Drug Act, mobilizing thousands of women's club members across the country on its behalf. The law was passed in 1906.

Amy Lowell♀ was, until she was thirty-five, just another Boston Brahmin who dabbled in poetry. In 1913 she traveled to England, where she met poet Ezra Pound, who strongly influenced her work. Her first acclaimed poetry appeared in 1915, when she was forty-one.

Grandma Moses (Anna Mary Robertson Moses)♀ had embroidered all her life, but when she was seventy-eight, her fingers became too stiff to manage a needle. So she began to paint in oils and soon won fame for her primitive or "naïve" paintings. In 1960, when she was one hundred, she illustrated an edition of *'Twas the Night Before Christmas.*

Carry Nation was fifty when heaven directed her to the temperance cause and she began her saloon-smashing career.

Bethenia Owens took in washing and ironing in frontier Oregon to earn enough money to open a millinery shop. In mid-life she decided to attend medical school, and after years of struggle, she became an eye and ear specialist at the age of forty-one. She later supported her son and the daughter of a friend who had died while they attended medical school.

Beatrix Potter,♀ the creator of *Peter Rabbit,* had an ambition stronger than writing: to be a sheep farmer. At the age of forty-seven, she married, took up farming with her husband, and never wrote again.

Anne Newport Royall, who was to become America's first female journalist, was left penniless at age fifty-four when her husband died. In 1830 she began publishing *Paul Pry,* a weekly gossip sheet that was immediately successful. It is said that she once spotted President John Quincy Adams swimming *au naturel* in the Potomac. She parked herself on his clothing, refusing to budge until he granted her an exclusive interview.

WHY RETIRE? THIRTEEN WHO DIDN'T

Rose Brasch began studying for her bachelor's degree in 1918, but marriage, a family, and a job as an insurance agent interrupted her studies. Finally in 1978, at the age of eighty-seven, she received her sheepskin from the University of Missouri, St. Louis.

Jennie F. Cave was seventy-one when she was elected mayor of Norwalk, Connecticut.

Isabella Cannon became the mayor of Raleigh, North Carolina, when she was seventy-three. Her unconventional style of campaigning included wearing tennis shoes and a T-shirt with her special emblem, a cannon with daisies growing out of the barrel.

Sonia Delauney first received recognition, in the form of exhibitions of her work, in 1953, when she was sixty-five. Until then the artist had directed her efforts to promoting the work of her husband, Robert, who died in 1941. She continued evolving her own distinctive style of painting well into her ninth decade; her designs have appeared on fabrics, wallpaper, and other decorative items, as well as on canvas.

Louise Dingwall, a grandmother who had trained many winning race horses, was seventy-nine when she applied for a license to ride in women's races in England. Two mounts trained by her won the first and second races on the first day of the 1975–76 English National Hunt season, when she was eighty-two.

Ardath Evitt holds the record as the oldest woman ever to parachute. She was seventy-four when she jumped from a small plane, 3,000 feet over Mooresville, Indiana. Her landing was perfect. Says Evitt, "I think anyone, even as old as I am, who can walk and talk and act foolish, might as well have fun."

Mrs. Caleb Fox was a sixty-year-old grandmother when she won a golf championship from Glenna Collett♀ in 1923.

Lillian Fuller, a seventy-one-year-old grandmother, is the head of the auto-crime section of the Nashville, Tennessee, Police Department. In 1943 she became the city's first policewoman and in the course of her career has carried out almost every kind of assignment. She carries a small .38-caliber pistol in her purse along with her detective's badge.

Dale King, a seventy-two-year-old widow, is the queen of southern California prospectors, with seventy-eight mining claims in the Granite Mountains registered in her name.

Maggie Kuhn, a vibrant activist, organized the Gray Panthers in 1970, when she was sixty-four. The network of older people dedicated to fighting ageism in the United States has influenced legislation and the daily lives of millions of people.

Louise MacLeod, ninety-four, has been a Red Cross worker in San Francisco for eighty years. Her first assignment was to serve coffee and doughnuts to the boys leaving to fight in the Spanish-American War in 1898.

Mary Fairfax Somerville,♀ the great mathematician, continued her work until the day of her death at ninety-two. She was eighty-nine when her book *Molecular and Microscopic Science* was published in 1869.

Florence Sperbeck, sixty-five, is a private investigator in San Francisco.

Ida Eisenhower shows off a picture of her son, the general. *Dwight D. Eisenhower Library, Abilene, Kansas.* (PAEANS TO MOM)

Supporters surround Margaret Sanger during her trial for disseminating birth control information. *Library of Congress.* (FOUNDERS OF THE FIRST BIRTH CONTROL CLINICS)

Betty Crocker's appearance has changed to keep up with the times. Here she is in 1936, 1955, 1965, and 1972. *General Mills, Inc.* (FIVE COMMERCIAL FEMALES WHO NEVER WERE)

Ad for Lydia E. Pinkham's Vegetable Compound, 18 percent alcohol—a nineteenth-century cure-all for ailing women. *The Schlesinger Library, Radcliffe College.* (TAKING OVER FOR THEIR HUSBANDS)

MARION DAVIES in "TILLIE, THE TOILER"

YOU'VE seen Tillie in
HER inimitable, rib-bending
COMIC strip of the newspapers.
NOW she's on the screen
WITH all her jolly pals,
COME and see Mac, Simpkins
AND Bubbles and the rest!
MARION Davies, as Tillie, plays a
RHAPSODIE of blue-sky romance.
TILLIE tingles a dozen
THROBBING heart-strings in this
COMEDY—you'll scream—of complications!

Metro-Goldwyn-Mayer

"More stars than there are in Heaven"

"Tillie, The Toiler" was one of the first strips to celebrate the working woma was played in the movies by Marion I (WORKING WOMEN OF THE COMICS THEIR VERY OWN STRIPS)

A nineteenth-century cooking school. (THEY ASKED WHAT'S COOKING)

Female clerks leave work at the Treasury Department in Washington, D.C. in 1865. The Treasury was the first governmental bureau to employ women. *Library of Congress.* (UNCLE SAM'S FIRST FEMALE EMPLOYEES)

Captain Emily Warner (left) and pilot Cindy Morgan of Frontier Airlines. Warner was the first female pilot to fly for a major U.S. passenger airline. *Frontier Airlines, Denver, Colorado.* (COME FLY WITH ME)

VIII ❧ *THIRSTING FOR KNOWLEDGE*

THOMAS JEFFERSON'S CURRICULUM FOR HIS DAUGHTER MARTHA

❧

"From 8 to 10, practice music;
from 10 to 1, dance one day and draw another;
from 1 to 2, draw on the day you dance and write a letter next day;
from 3 to 4, read French;
from 4 to 5, exercise yourself in music;
from 5 till bedtime, read English, write, etc. . . . It produces great praise to a lady to spell well."

A DILLER, A DOLLAR—SOME VERY EARLY SCHOLARS

❧

Theano taught and wrote about mathematics, physics, medicine, and child psychology at the school founded by her husband, Pythagoras, the Greek mathematician, in about 539 B.C. After his death, Theano and two of her daughters took over administration of the school.

Aspasia,♀ the mistress of Pericles and a well-known mathematical scholar, persuaded that ruler by argument and example that women should be given educational opportunity. Socrates named her as one of his teachers.

Beruryah was the daughter of one noted rabbi and the wife of another. As a child in the second century, she listened while her father and other scholars discussed the meanings of the Bible—and grew up to become the only female Talmudic scholar whose opinions on matters of the law are respected by other scholars today.

Hypatia♀ was highly admired for her mind and her beauty, in that order, in the fourth century. Trained by her father in mathematics, astronomy, and religion, Hypatia became, like him, a professor at the University of Alexandria, wrote several books on mathematics, and may have invented an astrolabe and a planesphere for studying astronomy. At the height of her powers, however, she came under attack by Christian groups, was seized by a mob of fanatics, and was tortured to death.

Anna Comnena, the daughter of Emperor Alexius I Comnenus, was one of the great chroniclers of the eleventh century and one of the few women historians of premodern times.

Hildegard of Bingen,♀ sage and prophet, wrote on science, theology, and philosophy in the twelfth century. She also proclaimed that the sun was the center of our firmament and that it "holds in place the stars around it, much as the earth attracts the creatures which inhabit it," four centuries before Copernicus.

Margaret More Roper, one of the daughters of Sir Thomas More, studied at the school run by her father (as did her sisters and several other female relatives) and not only translated into English a Latin work by Erasmus, but suggested to Erasmus a change in the text of another of his works. She taught her own daughters, one of whom, *Mary Bassett,* also translated Latin scholarly works into English.

Jane Seymour,♀ one of the three daughters of the Duke of Somerset, carried on an extensive correspondence in Latin with religious reformers in Europe. The three Seymour girls were noted for their ability to read, write, and even speak in Latin and Greek, and together they composed a hundred Latin couplets in honor of Margaret of Navarre after her death in 1549. (The better-known aspect of Seymour's life, as one of the queens of Henry VIII, owed little to her scholarly skills.)

Anne Cooke Bacon, whose son was Sir Francis Bacon, possessed a fluent command of Latin, Greek, and Italian. In 1570 she translated Bishop Jewel's Latin *Apology in Defense of the Church of England* (a key document that helped establish the validity of Anglicanism) into English so that it could be read by the people most affected by it.

Elena Cornaro Piscopia was the first woman in the world to receive a university degree. Born into a noble Venetian family in the seventeenth century, she studied several languages, as well as math, philosophy, astronomy, and theology, and at the University of Padua her disputations attracted scholars from all over Europe. Because of Church objections, she could not receive a doctorate in theology but was asked to accept one in philosophy instead. Her examination drew such a crowd of onlookers that it had to be moved from the university to the Cathedral of Padua.

NINE DEDICATED TEACHERS

Sarah Kemble Knight (1666–1727) founded a school in early-eighteenth-century Boston which placed particular emphasis on writing skills. The best known of her writings: a *Private Journal of a Journey from Boston to New York in the Year 1704.* Her most illustrious pupil: Benjamin Franklin.

Susannah Brittano (d. 1764) taught summer sessions in Dedham, Massachusetts, at a time when it was still unusual for a woman to teach both male and female children. When she died, Brittano left her entire fortune—$100, a substantial sum for a working woman in those days—to endow a school that would be taught by a woman. At least fifteen successive schoolmistresses in Dedham owed their employment to Brittano's bequest.

Maria Cosway (1759–1838), an English friend and sometime traveling companion of Thomas Jefferson, founded the Collegio delle Dame Inglesi (College for English Women) in Italy and taught there in the last years of her life.

Rosa Philippine Duchesne, a French nun, came to New Orleans in 1818 with four colleagues and in the next few years opened three girls' boarding schools in frontier towns. She also founded several day schools, one of them the first free school west of the Mississippi. Duchesne also established classes for Indian and black girls in the southern frontier region.

Charlotte Forten, a black schoolteacher, followed the Union army so that as slaves were freed, she could teach them the survival skills of reading and writing. Forten's articles about her experiences were published in the *Atlantic Monthly.*

Anna Leonowens left her native Wales to teach the sixty-seven children in the court of King Mongkut (reigned 1851–1868) of Siam (now Thailand). Culture-shocked with a vengeance, Leonowens survived the experience and published a journal on which the best-selling book *Anna and the King of Siam* and the musical comedy *The King and I* were based. Her best pupil was Prince Chulalongkorn, who succeeded his father and reigned from 1868 to 1910.

Elizabeth Gray Vining was chosen to be tutor to Crown Prince Akihito of Japan after the Second World War, a position she held from 1946 to 1950, when she returned to the United States after receiving Japan's Third Order of the Sacred Crown for her services. She was succeeded by her friend . . .

Esther Biddle Rhoads, a native of Philadelphia. A few months before Rhoads died in 1979, both teachers had a reunion in Philadelphia with their former student, who was touring the United States with his wife.

Welthy Honsinger Fisher began her career as principal of a girls' school in China in 1906. In 1947, shortly before his assassination, Mohandas K. Gandhi told her to teach in the villages of India. She did just that, establishing Literacy House in Lucknow and developing new teaching techniques since put to use in dozens of developing countries. Fisher celebrated her one-hundredth birthday in November 1979, at New York's St. Regis Hotel, along with several hundred friends.

BLIMEY! THE FIRST WOMEN'S COLLEGES IN ENGLAND

❧

Queen's College, established in 1848, grew out of a series of evening classes known as Lectures for Ladies, begun the preceding year in an effort to make governesses more knowledgeable so that they could teach more to their charges.

Bedford College, founded in 1849, began as a series of classes held at a private home in Bedford Square, London.

North London Collegiate School, headed by ***Frances Mary Bass,*** was founded in 1850, the ***Cheltenham College for Young Ladies*** in 1854, and ***Holloway College,*** patterned after the American Vassar College, in 1886.

Three at Cambridge University

Girton, an outgrowth of the London Schoolmistresses' Association, was founded in 1869 as Hitchin College but renamed in 1873 after being moved to Girton Village, two miles northwest of Cambridge.

Newnham College grew out of the North of England Council for the Higher Education of Women; in the 1860s the council successfully petitioned Cambridge University for a special women's examination. More than eighty girls, accompanied by chaperones, presented themselves for examination—after barely six weeks' notice in which to prepare.

New Hall was founded in 1954.

And Five at Oxford

Somerville Hall, named in honor of mathematician *Mary Fairfax Somerville,*♀ was founded in October 1879.

Lady Margaret Hall, named in honor of *Lady Margaret Beaufort,*♀ mother of Henry VII, was chartered in October 1879.

St. Hugh's College was founded in 1886 by *Elizabeth Wordsworth* for female students of limited means. (Because an adequate endowment for a full scholarship program could not be raised, Wordsworth's noble goal had to be forfeited; the college, however, remained.)

St. Hilda's Hall, named for *St. Hilda of Whitby,* England's first great female educator, was founded in 1893 by *Dorothea Beale,* head of the Cheltenham Ladies' College, to provide an Oxford-quality education for her best students.

St. Anne's College, formally established in the 1850s, which grew out of a group known as the Oxford Home Students—women who attended classes at Oxford schools but lived in nearby homes—was founded in 1879.

Women attended these colleges, and the lecture series that preceded them, from the 1860s, but it was not until 1920 that any women received Oxford degrees, and none were admitted to full university status until 1959. The first honorary degree conferred by Oxford on a woman, a Doctorate of Civil Law, was presented to *Queen Mary* in 1921.

THE FIRST COLLEGE-EDUCATED AMERICAN WOMEN

Oberlin College in Ohio was founded in 1833 to provide equal educational opportunity for women and men of all races. Four women students entered in 1837:

Mary Hosford, Elizabeth Smith Prall, Caroline Mary Rudd, Mary Fletcher Kellogg

Kellogg became a dropout; Hosford, Prall, and Rudd earned their B.A. degrees in 1841.

Other early women graduates of Oberlin were:

Lucy Stone ♀ (entered 1843), suffragist.
Sallie Holley, abolitionist, 1851.

Emeline Cleveland, surgeon, 1853.
Fanny Jackson Coppin, black educator, 1865.
Margaret Maltby, physicist, 1882.
Mary Church Terrell,♀ black social reformer, 1884.

ELEVEN FIRST WOMEN OF AMERICAN
HIGHER EDUCATION

— ☙ —

Emma H. Willard,♀ founder of the first academically oriented secondary school for women in 1814, the Middlebury Female Seminary in Middlebury, Vermont. In 1821 Willard moved to Troy, New York, where she established the Troy Female Seminary, known today as the Emma Willard School.

Mary Mason Lyon,♀ founder of the first college for women, Mount Holyoke Female Seminary, later College, in Massachusetts in 1837; she served as its principal until her death twelve years later.

Rebecca Mann Pennell, a professor at Antioch College when it opened in 1853 and the first female college professor at a coeducational institution to be given privileges equal to those of male professors—such as being allowed to attend faculty meetings.

Sarah Parke Morrison, the first woman to receive a degree (1869) from the first *state* university to grant equality in higher education: Indiana University, Bloomington, Indiana.

Frances Elizabeth Willard,♀ the first to be termed a president of a women's college when she became head of Evanston College for Ladies in Illinois in 1871. All the school's faculty and trustees were women.

Helen Magill, recipient of the first Doctor of Philosophy degree awarded to a woman in the United States, from Boston University in 1877.

Kate Eugenia Morris, recipient of the first Doctor of Philosophy degree bestowed upon a woman by a women's college, from Smith College in 1882.

Florence Rena Sabin,♀ in 1917 the first female professor at a highly ranked medical school, Johns Hopkins University, in Baltimore, Maryland. She had earlier been the school's first female graduate.

Caroline Willard Baldwin, in 1924, the recipient of the first Doctor of Science degree awarded to a woman, from the School of Social Science Administration at the University of Chicago.

Frieda Wunderlich, the first woman to be dean of a graduate school when she was elected dean of the Graduate Faculty of Political and Social Science at the New School for Social Research, New York City, 1939.

Helen Hadassah Levinthal,♀ recipient of the first Master of Hebrew Literature degree given to a woman by the Jewish Institute of Religion in New York, 1939—and the first Jewish woman to graduate from a recognized theological college.

FOUNDING THE SEVEN SISTERS

❧

Mary Mason Lyon. There were no colleges for women when the New England teacher became obsessed with the idea of starting one. "My heart has so yearned over the adult female youth in the common walks of life, that it has sometimes seemed as if there were a fire shut up in my bones." For years she trudged from sewing circle to missionary society to town meeting, collecting funds, largely from women contributors. Lyon's dream was realized in 1837 when Mount Holyoke opened its doors in South Hadley, Massachusetts.

Matthew Vassar. What should a childless business executive do with his fortune? Schoolmaster Milo P. Jewett persuaded Vassar, a Poughkeepsie brewer, that immortality lay in starting a women's college, and Vassar gave his total funds, $400,000, to the cause. The school opened in 1865.

Sophia Smith. For years the shy woman was ruled by her miserly brother, Austin. When he died she broke loose, built herself the grandest mansion in Hatfield, Massachusetts, and cast about for other ways to spend the family's money. When the Reverend John M. Greene suggested she build a college for women, Smith insisted on only two conditions: that no professor from nearby Amherst ever be consulted about anything, and that all the students must live in a one-story building, since climbing stairs could be damaging to the female reproductive system. (This last stipulation was later rescinded.) Smith College, in Northampton, Massachusetts, the first women's school to have entrance requirements as stringent as those of the best men's schools, began taking students in 1875.

Henry Durant. The death of his only son persuaded Durant to abandon a legal career that bordered on the shady. Vowing that he would henceforth love only God, he became a revivalist, then made even more money manufacturing items for the Union army. After the war he decided to use his wealth to found a seminary in Massachusetts to train women teachers upon "sound Christian principles." Wellesley opened in 1875.

Elizabeth Cabot Cary Agassiz. The widow of naturalist Louis Agassiz persuaded a few Harvard professors to give private instruction to a group of knowledge-hungry young women in Cambridge, Massachusetts. Her organization, the Society for the Collegiate Instruction of Women, admitted its first students in 1879 after draping the windows with muslin so that professors would not be seen teaching women. A thirteen-year-old boy was hired to carry books to and from the university library, because women were barred from that institution. For years Harvard resisted acknowledging any connection to the "Annex," as Agassiz's Society came to be called, but in 1894 finally agreed to charter it as Radcliffe College, honoring Ann Radcliffe, who in 1642 had been the first woman to donate money to Harvard.

Annie Nathan Meyer. Agreeing with Columbia University librarian Melvil Dewey that a separate college for women would be a good idea, the twenty-year-old student bicycled from philanthropist to philanthropist to raise funds. Barnard College, named after Frederick A. P. Barnard, the first president of Columbia University, who endorsed higher education for women, opened in 1889 in a rented brownstone.

Joseph Taylor. A physician who had made a fortune as the owner of a tannery, Dr. Taylor was shocked when a friend, Dr. James Thomas of Baltimore, told him how difficult it was for his precocious daughter, Martha Carey Thomas,♀ to get the advanced education she needed. Taylor concluded that a proper Quaker college for women would solve such problems. He founded and donated the land for Bryn Mawr College in 1879; it accepted its first students in 1885. Martha Carey Thomas later became president of the school.

ELEVEN SUPER SCHOLARS

❧

Mercy Otis Warren ♀ (1728–1815) had achieved a respectable reputation for her poems, dramas, and satirical writings when, in 1805 at the age of seventy-seven, she published her *History of the Rise, Progress and Termination of the American Revolution, Interspersed with Biographical, Political, and Moral Reflections,* in three volumes, in Boston; it remains a key source of information on that period.

Hannah Adams (1755–1831) was the first American woman to be a scholar by profession, although she had little if any formal schooling, learning Latin and Greek in childhood from the theological students who boarded with her father. During the Revolutionary War and afterward she tutored young men about to enter Harvard, and her writings included such vast projects as *An Alphabetical Compendium of the Various Sects which have appeared in the World from the beginning of the World to the present day* (1784) and a *Dictionary of all Religions and Religious Denominations* (1817).

Margaret (Sarah) Fuller ♀ (1810–1850) was teacher, writer, poet, critic, translator, and more. For two years, starting in 1840, she was editor of the *Dial,* the literary publication of the Transcendentalists, and in the same years conducted academic classes, disguised as "conversations," for women in Boston. Her best-known publication was *Woman in the Nineteenth Century* (1845), a plea for political equality and intellectual fulfillment. Other writings included literary criticism, an analysis of frontier life, and letters from England, France, and Italy, where she traveled as correspondent for Horace Greeley's *New York Tribune.* She died in a shipwreck just off the coast of New York when returning from Italy with her husband and child.

Julie Victoire Daubié of France was the first woman to present herself for the rigorous examination leading to the *baccalauréat*—the degree required for university admission. Her most noted publication was *La femme pauvre au XIX siècle* (*The Poor Woman in the 19th Century*) (1866).

Janet Hogarth (Mrs. W. L.) Courtney was a student at one of the women's schools of Oxford in the nineteenth century, but wanted to study philosophy—deemed a fit subject for male inquiry only. Hogarth successfully petitioned to be allowed to attend the lectures held at the men's colleges—but was required to sit apart from the men. She went on to publish widely and in 1910 became head of the indexing staff of the *Encyclopaedia Britannica.*

Mary Lynda Dorothy Grier of England was acting professor of economics at Leeds University from 1915 to 1919, before becoming principal of Lady Margaret Hall at Oxford in 1920, the same year her trailblazing study, *Industry and Finance,* was published.

Hannah Arendt (1906–1975) received her Ph.D. from the University of Heidelberg in 1928. Her most controversial work, *Eichmann in Jerusalem* (1964), called attention to the "banality of evil." Her other major works included *The Human Condition* and the philosophical summation *The Life of the Mind.*

Joan Evans, an English archaeologist, has written more than thirty works on archaeology and literature, served as president of the Royal Archaeological Institute, and in 1954 became the first woman to be director of the Society of Antiquaries.

Bibi Palvanova of Ashkhabad, Turkmen Republic, U.S.S.R., born to illiterate parents, learned rug weaving as a child and was expected to follow in the traditions of her Islamic family, but after joining the Communist party and attending a prestigious school in Moscow, Palvanova became the first woman in the Turkmen Republic to receive a doctoral degree. Her dissertation dealt with the liberation of women in Soviet Central Asia. She became rector of the Turkmen State University, is a member of the Turkmen Academy of Sciences, and for more than eighteen years has been the minister of public education for the Turkmen Republic; in that position she has seen women become nearly half of the student body in institutions of higher education.

Barbara W. Tuchman ♀ has twice won the Pulitzer Prize in history, although she has no doctoral degree in that field, and is the first woman to be president of the American Academy and Institute of Arts and Letters. Tuchman calls herself "a late developer": her first noted work, *The Guns of August,* was not published until she was fifty years old. Since then, in rapid succession, she has produced *The Proud Tower, Stilwell and the American Experience in China,* and *A Distant Mirror*—best sellers all.

Marina von Neumann Whitman, daughter of a renowned mathematician, is herself an economist, a former member of the President's Council of Economic Advisers, the Distinguished Public Service Professor of Economics at the University of Pittsburgh, and a member of the boards of directors of several corporations. In 1979, at the age of forty-four, she was named vice-president and chief economist of the General Motors Corporation.

TOP NUMBERS IN HIGHER EDUCATION

- In 1977 alone, women accounted for 93 percent of the enrollment growth in U.S. colleges.
- Young women undergraduates now outnumber men. They make up 52 percent of students in the under-twenty-two age group.

- Women aged twenty-five to thirty-four are the fastest-growing group of post-secondary students. Their college enrollment increased 187 percent to 1.2 million between 1970 and 1978.
- Women in the over-thirty-five age group are close behind. Their enrollment went up from 418,000 to more than 700,000, or 68 percent, between 1972 and 1976.
- The Council of Graduate Schools reports that 52 percent of master's degree students are now female.
- Forty percent of doctoral students are women.
- Women in the entering classes of the nation's medical schools rose from 9 percent in 1970 to 25 percent in 1977. At some schools women make up 40 to 50 percent of the first-year class.
- In 1976 thirteen American women and eleven women of other nations received Rhodes Scholarships to study at Oxford University, the first women to participate in this prestigious program.
- In 1978 nearly 27 percent of doctoral degrees in all academic fields combined went to women, up from 18 percent in 1973, according to the National Research Council.

GOING HIGHER IN MATHEMATICS

Emilie de Breteuil (Marquise du Châtelet) (1706–1749) performed astounding feats of mental arithmetic as a small child. Beautiful as well as brilliant, she abandoned her husband for Voltaire and, while living with him, worked night and day on mathematics, sleeping only two or three hours a day. In 1740 she published *Institutions du physique,* a comprehensive analysis of the physical sciences of her day; later she translated Newton's *Principia.*

Maria Gaetana Agnesi ♀ (1718–1799), daughter of a mathematics professor, took part in his seminars while still in her teens. She spent ten years preparing two volumes on differential and integral calculus, published as *Analytical Institutions* in 1748. Despite its acclaim for her accomplishment, the French Academy of Sciences refused to admit her because she was female.

Sophie Germain (1776–1831). Her family tried to deter her from the unfeminine pursuit of mathematics by hiding her candles so that she couldn't study at night. Germain persisted, taught herself with borrowed lecture notes, and used the pseudonym "M. le Blanc" to correspond with the noted mathematician Karl Gauss, who encouraged his unknown friend. Her real identity remained undiscovered for several years. In 1816 Germain, now remembered for her work in number theory, won the *grand prix* in a competition sponsored by the French Academy of Sciences.

Mary Fairfax Somerville ♀ (1780–1872) as a teen-ager chanced upon some algebraic symbols in a fashion magazine and became forever hooked on math. Her mother, "appalled and shamed by such aberrant behavior," sent her off to schools for sewing, painting, and dancing. She studied secretly by sewing during her brother's lessons with a tutor. Later, she produced several important mathematical works, was honored by the British Royal Society, and had her name given to one of the five women's colleges at Oxford. Somerville, eighty-nine when her last book, a summary of the scientific knowledge of her day, was published, was working on others when she died at ninety-two.

Sonya Corvin-Krukovsky Kovalevsky (1850–1891) arranged a platonic marriage to escape from her family in Russia and study mathematics in Berlin, only to find herself refused entry to the all-male university. She convinced the great mathematician Karl Weierstrass to tutor her on his own and, in 1888, received the Prix Bordin of the French Academy of Sciences for a new solution to a key problem. The following year she became the first woman corresponding member of the Russian Academy of Sciences and a professor at the University of Stockholm.

Charlotte Angas Scott introduced both undergraduate and graduate-level mathematics courses at Bryn Mawr College after earning her doctorate in science at the University of London in 1885. In her forty years at Bryn Mawr she produced a geometry textbook and numerous papers.

Emmy (Amalie) Noether,♀ the daughter of a mathematician, was brought up to be a proper fräulein, but her ability was such that by 1907 she was substitute-teaching for her father and others while continuing her own research. Only in 1922 was she herself granted professorial rank—but no salary. Noether's Theorem ("To every symmetry there is a conservation law") has long been a household word in theoretical physics.

Mary Gray founded the Association for Women in Mathematics in the early 1970s.

Sophie Picard held a chair in higher geometry and probability theory at the University of Neuchâtel and has been influential in the development of modern statistical theory.

Paulette Liberman, professor at the University of Rennes in France, is an authority on algebraic topology.

Mina Spiegel Rees, dean of graduate studies and president of the graduate division at the City University of New York, is a researcher whose mathematical knowledge is in demand by government and industry. In 1971 she became the first woman president of the American Association for the Advancement of Science.

WOMEN IN SCIENCE

❧

- The first International Conference of Women Engineers and Scientists, sponsored by the American Society of Women Engineers, was held in New York City in 1964.
- With its twelfth edition, the reference volume *American Men of Science* was renamed *American Men and Women of Science* in 1973.
- In 1974 only 9 percent of American scientists were women. But in 1977 the National Research Council reported that the number of female scientists in faculty and advisory positions had increased three times faster than total faculty growth since 1973.
- Women scientists earn from 15 to 50 percent less than men working in the same fields, as the following figures indicate:

Field	Income	As percentage of men's income
Chemistry	$10,500	51.4
Earth and marine sciences	10,500	57.1
Atmospheric and space sciences	13,000	83.1
Physics	12,000	66.7
Mathematics	10,000	50.0
Computer sciences	13,200	72.0
Agricultural sciences	9,400	63.8
Biological sciences	11,000	59.1
Psychology	13,000	80.8
Statistics	14,000	77.9
Economics	13,400	76.9
Sociology	11,000	77.2
Anthropology	12,300	78.0
Political science	11,000	77.3
Linguistics	11,300	85.0

From the National Science Foundation, 1970

SEEING STARS

Maria Cunitz won renown in 1630 for her simplification of Kepler's tables of planetary motion.

Jeanne Dumée wrote in the seventeenth century about the theories of Copernicus. Of woman's capacity for science she had no doubt; women "are not incapable of study, if they wish to make the effort, because between the brain of a woman and that of man there is no difference."

Madame de la Sablière (Marguerite Hessein) studied mathematics before turning to astronomy. The notion that a woman could spend hours studying celestial objects was so ludicrous to Molière that he satirized her, and intellectual women generally, in *Les Femmes Savants.*

Madame du Pierry, the first woman to be a professor of astronomy in Paris, composed astronomical tables in the eighteenth century.

Madame Hortense Lepaute was an associate of Alexis Clairaut in studies to establish the influence of Jupiter and Saturn on Halley's Comet; Clairaut is usually given all the credit for their discoveries.

Caroline Herschel, the first woman to detect a comet, discovered eight between 1789 and 1797. Herschel assisted her brother William, court astronomer to George III, at a salary of 50 pounds annually and was the first woman appointed to government service in England. After her brother died, she completed cataloging the 1,500 nebulae and star clusters they had discovered together.

Maria Mitchell♀ catapulted to fame before she was thirty with her discovery of a comet in 1847. She was honored with membership in the newly formed American Association for the Advancement of Science and became a member of Vassar's faculty. In 1873 she founded the Association for the Advancement of Women.

Winnifred Edgerton became, in 1886, the first woman to earn a doctorate in astronomy and also the first woman to receive a degree from Columbia University. In agreeing to accept her for advanced training, the university emphasized that its acceptance "established no precedent for others."

Williamina Fleming started in 1900 as an assistant to Edward Pickering, director of the Harvard College Observatory, who hired women to record astronomical data because they accepted lower salaries than men; his staff was known as "Pickering's harem." Her contributions became so valuable that she received the first appointment ever given to a woman by the Harvard Corporation, "Curator of Astronomical Photographs."

Annie Jump Cannon identified, classified, and cataloged the spectra of more stars than anyone else in the world—nearly 400,000. In 1925 Oxford awarded the American astronomer the Doctorate of Science, the first honorary degree in science ever given to a woman; Cannon also received the first gold medal ever presented to a woman by the National Academy of Sciences.

Ida Barney did all the calculations for the thirteen-volume *Yale Photographic Zone Catalogue* of star positions. In that precomputer era, the job entailed a half-million measurements and twenty-three years of work.

Cecilia Payne-Gaposchkin was the first person to receive a doctorate from Harvard in astronomy, but although her dissertation was described as "undoubtedly the most brilliant Ph.D. thesis ever written in astronomy," she was a member of the Harvard Astronomy Department for thirty years before attaining the rank of full professor and, in 1956, chair of the department. She is known for cataloging variable stars.

Helen Sawyer Hogg, a full professor at the University of Toronto, published her *Second Catalogue of Variable Stars in Globular Clusters* in 1955. Of the 329 variables, Hogg had discovered 99.

Vera Rubin of the Department of Terrestial Magnetism of the Carnegie Institution of Washington, D.C., was in 1965 the first female guest investigator at the Mount Palomar Astronomical Observatory.

Margaret Burbidge, coauthor of a classic paper in astrophysics, became a senior research fellow at the Mount Wilson Observatory in 1960, and a dozen years later the first woman director of the Royal Observatory at Greenwich in her native England. After a year she returned to the United States, where in the late 1970s she became the first woman president of the American Astronomical Society.

SIXTEEN ON THE FRONTIERS OF SCIENCE

---------------------------------- ❧ ----------------------------------

Marie Sklodowska Curie ♀ (1867–1934) received the Nobel Prize for physics in 1903 along with her husband, Pierre, and Henri Becquerel for the discovery of radioactivity. She was the first woman to win this award and, in 1911, the first to do it twice when she won for chemistry. Polish-born Curie attended lectures at the Sorbonne in Paris, taught herself physics and chemistry, and became that institution's first female teacher in 1906. At age sixty-four she was still working a twelve-hour day in her lab, but a few years later she succumbed to leukemia caused by constant exposure to radium.

Irène Joliot-Curie,♀ her daughter, followed in her parents' path when she and her husband, Frédéric, won the Nobel Prize for chemistry in 1935. Their discovery, that radioactivity could be artificially produced, was an essential step that made possible the development of the atomic bomb.

Florence Rena Sabin ♀ (1871–1953) was a collector of "firsts": first woman to be admitted to the Johns Hopkins Medical School, first woman to become a full professor and head of a department there, first woman and department head of New York's prestigious Rockefeller Institute for Medical Research (1925), first woman elected to membership in the National Academy of Sciences (1925). Sabin was, to Dr. Simon Flexner, head of medical research at Rockefeller, "one of the foremost scientists of all time."

Edith Hinkley Quimby helped to create radiation physics. In 1919 she and Gioacchino Failu began to study the use of X-rays and radium on human beings. For decades Quimby patiently measured the results of various forms of radiation, making it possible to determine the exact dosages to be used in radiology.

Grace Murray Hopper earned a Ph.D. in mathematics from Yale, joined the U.S. Navy in 1943, and was assigned to the team developing the world's first electronic computer at Harvard. This was the Mark I, for which she worked out a "compiling system," ancestor of what are now known as programs; later she devised the first program to translate human-readable symbols into a machine-readable language. Hopper's fascination with machinery began in childhood when she took apart her mother's alarm clocks: "You bring any gadget around, and I've simply got to find out how it works."

Gerty Theresa Radnitz Cori ♀ (1896–1957) shared the Nobel Prize for physiology or medicine in 1947 with her husband, Dr. Carl F. Cori. The Coris, both biochemists, were cited for their work on carbohydrate metabolism and the discovery of a new enzyme, phosphorylase.

Lise Meitner ♀ (1878–1968), a physicist whose work on alpha and gamma radiation with her nephew, Otto Hahn, led to the first explanation of nuclear fission, was the first woman to receive the Atomic Energy Commission's Fermi Award. An escapee from the Nazis in 1938, after the start of the atomic age she acknowledged that "we were unaware what kind of powerful genie we were releasing from a bottle."

Mary Lyon first suspected that only one of the two X chromosomes in the cells of a female embryo is genetically activated in early development. The Lyon hypothesis has helped to explain the mechanism by which certain genetic disorders come about.

Rosalind Elsie Franklin, a biophysicist, was working at Kings College, London, in the early 1950s on X-ray diffraction analysis of crystalline DNA. Her description of the probable structure of the DNA molecule led to the successful construction of a model of DNA by J. D. Watson and F. H. Crick in 1953.

Chien-Shiung Wu,♀ a nuclear physicist, received in 1958 the first honorary doctorate in science ever given to a woman by Princeton University. Along with two male scientists who later became Nobel Prize winners, Wu performed experiments that demonstrated that, contrary to long-held belief, parity was not conserved. Wu, now at Columbia University, was elected to the National Academy of Sciences in 1958 and became president of the American Physical Society in 1975.

Wanda Kirkbridge Farr (b. 1895), a cytologist, took special interest in plant physiology. Her studies of plant cell membranes clarified the structure of cellulose. She also pioneered the use of X-ray diffraction and other techniques for analyzing natural fibers.

Libbie Henrietta Hyman♀ (1888–1969), a zoologist, received her Ph.D. from the University of Chicago in 1915. The daughter of an immigrant family, she would not have attended college without the encouragement of a high school teacher. Hyman was the first woman to receive the Elliot Medal from the National Academy of Sciences and was president of the Society of Systematic Zoologists in 1959. Hyman's ambition was to produce a ten-volume definitive work on the invertebrates; she had finished volume six by the time of her death.

Maria Goeppert Mayer♀ (1906–1972) received the Nobel Prize for physics in 1963, along with J. Hans D. Jensen and Eugene P. Wigner, for their research on the structure of atomic nuclei. Mayer, who had received her Ph.D. from the University of Göttingen in 1930, was working on separation of uranium isotopes at Columbia University by 1939 and in 1945 went to the Institute for Nuclear Studies at the University of Chicago.

Dorothy Mary Crowfoot Hodgkin♀ (b. 1910), a chemist, discovered the biochemical structures of penicillin and vitamin B-12, and received the 1964 Nobel Prize for chemistry. In 1969 she capped years of effort by deciphering the three-dimensional molecular structure of insulin.

Ruth Patrick♀ (b. 1907) is a limnologist, a scientist who studies ponds, streams, and other fresh-water environments. In 1975 she received the $150,000 John and Alice Tyler Ecology Prize in recognition of her discoveries, which have been applied in environmental projects worldwide.

Rosalyn S. Yalow,♀ with Roger C. L. Guillemin and Andrew V. Schally, received the 1977 Nobel Prize in medicine for development of radioimmunoassay, a test of body tissues which uses radioactive isotopes to measure the concentrations of hormones, viruses, vitamins, enzymes, and drugs. Yalow, a graduate of New York's Hunter College, was that school's first physics major—but was advised to take a job as a secretary.

EXPLORING FOR SCIENCE

❦

Evelyn Cheeseman traveled alone among cannibals in search of tropical insects for the British Museum. An entomologist, she spent much of her long life (1881–1969) hunting for species in the South Pacific and New Guinea, collecting more than 42,000 insects plus parasitic worms, moths, mollusks, spiders, and reptiles.

Marianne North, a nineteenth-century botanist and naturalist, looked throughout the world for new species of plants, eventually gathering enough to open her own museum in Kew, England. It contains 800 oil paintings by North of her botanical finds in Canada, the United States, Brazil, Sarawak, Java, India, Australia, and Africa.

Isobel Hutchinson, also a botanist, went to the Arctic for specimens. She traveled via dog sled through the sea ice and tundra, collecting plants and purchasing examples of crafts from the Eskimos.

Delia Akeley accompanied her husband, Carl E. Akeley, on numerous scientific expeditions to Africa between 1905 and 1911, and later undertook two on her own for the Brooklyn Museum in the 1920s, bringing back previously unknown species of antelopes and birds.

Mary Hastings Bradley, a Fellow of the Royal Geographical Society, explored the gorilla country of the Congo.

Mary D. Nicol Leakey, with her husband, Louis Leakey, proved that humans and their immediate ancestors have been on this earth for much longer than had previously been supposed. In 1959 she found the skull and teeth of an early hominid form, *Australopithecus,* determined to be about 1.75 million years old, in the Olduvai Gorge, Tanzania. After the death of her husband in 1972, she continued their work alone and with her son, Richard. In 1975, on an expedition at Laetolil, Tanzania, she found remains that pushed the date of the first ancestral human forms back to 3.6 million years ago.

FIGURING OUT WHAT'S GOOD FOR US

Madame Lavoisier recorded the experiments conducted by her husband, Antoine Lavoisier, in the eighteenth century measuring the absorption of oxygen—the first experiments providing accurate information about energy metabolism.

Ellen Henrietta Swallow Richards, after much badgering, became the first woman to study at the Massachusetts Institute of Technology, in 1901 earned her B.S. in chemistry, and set up a "Woman's Laboratory" to analyze household products and drinking water and to teach chemistry to women. The result of all her analyses of foods and fabrics was the formation of a new field called home economics, and in 1908 Richards became the first president of the American Home Economics Association.

Mary Engle Pennington knew more than anyone else in the United States about the refrigeration of perishable foods in the early 1900s. When the Department of Agriculture offered the young Ph.D. a job as a bacteriological chemist, she was advised to conceal her sex by signing the application "M. E. Pennington." Pennington produced the research support for the Food and Drug Act of 1906, and her pioneering research later contributed to the development of frozen foods.

May Mellanby noticed in 1917 that changes in the diets of puppies affected the structure of their teeth. Her observation led to trailblazing research on rickets and vitamin D deficiency.

Anna E. Boller Beach in 1918, years before insulin was available, established the first clinic for diabetics at the Central Free Dispensary of Rush Medical College in Chicago.

Mary Swartz Rose became the first professor of nutrition in the United States in 1921, at Teachers College, Columbia University. Rose was also the first to use serving and recipe amounts of foods in tables of food composition. In *Feeding the Family* (1916) she explained nutrition in terms of meal plans that could be understood and used by homemakers.

Marguerite Davis, an associate of Elmer V. McCollum, developed techniques for using animals in vitamin research and with him wrote the reports announcing their discoveries of vitamins A and B-1 (riboflavin) in the 1920s.

Katherine S. Bishop of the University of California at Berkeley was an associate of Herbert M. Evans in the research that led to their announcement in 1923 of the discovery of an "antisterility factor," later known as vitamin E.

Ida Smedley-Maclean, of the Lister Institute in London, in 1926 pinpointed acetyl coenzyme A, subsequently identified as a key substance in human metabolism.

Margaret Boas conducted the research that led to identification of the B-complex vitamin Biotin (vitamin H) at the Lister Institute in the late 1920s.

Lucy Wills, a physician working with pregnant women in India, discovered a form of anemia in her patients in 1931 that she thought might be a vitamin-deficiency-related disease. She fed them a form of yeast containing folic acid, a B-complex vitamin, and they recovered. The anti-anemia substance became known as Wills factor, and was later identified as a B vitamin.

Cicely D. Williams, a pediatrician working in Ghana, identified and described the severe protein deficiency disease *kwashiorkor,* for which she was cited in 1967 by the American Medical Association: "Perhaps more than any other person in the world, this great woman is responsible for the improvement of child and maternal health in developing nations."

Arda Alden Green was associated with ***Gerty Cori*** ♀ in the laboratory work that led to the isolation of the enzyme phosphorylase. Her 1926 publication assessing the nutritional health of children, a first of its kind, had enormous impact on nutrition education.

Lydia Roberts was the scientist chosen to head the committee that first established Recommended Daily Allowances in 1943, the well-known nutrient guide for meal planning.

WOMEN IN MEDICINE TODAY

❧

- The percentage of women in first-year medical classes in the United States increased from 8.4 to 22 between 1965 and 1975. Nearly 3,000 women graduated from American medical schools in 1979, four times as many as in 1970.

- The ratio of women to men entering medical schools has increased in Belgium, Czechoslovakia, Denmark, Finland, Great Britain, Portugal, Sweden, and elsewhere in recent years.
- By the time they receive their M.D.'s, 71 percent of women are married.
- Medical school faculties are 9 percent female; but only about one-sixth of these faculty women have tenure.
- Pediatrics has traditionally been the specialty selected by women; it is followed in popularity by psychiatry, obstetrics-gynecology, internal medicine, and anesthesiology, in that order. Some 22 percent of United States pediatricians are women, as are about one-fourth of child psychiatrists.
- The average income of women physicians in the United States is 54 percent that of men. This discrepancy is often ascribed to part-time or split-time schedules and maternity leaves, but it may be because few women have chosen the high-fee specialties that are dominated by men.
- Twelve percent of the physicians in the United States today are female, compared with about 20 percent in Italy and West Germany, 25 percent in the Philippines, more than 30 percent in Poland, and nearly 75 percent in the Soviet Union.

From "Women in Medicine," *MD Magazine,* June 1975, and other sources

THE FIRST LICENSED PHYSICIANS

❦

Dorothea Leporin-Erxleben,♀ Germany, University of Halle, 1754.
Anna Morandi Manzolini, Italy (elected professor of anatomy at University of Bologna), 1760.
Elizabeth Blackwell,♀ United States, Geneva Medical College, 1849.
Varvara Kashevarova-Rudneva,♀ Russia, St. Petersburg Academy of Medicine, 1868.
Shih Mai-yu, China, University of Michigan, 1876.
Sophia Jex Blake, Great Britain, University of Bern, 1877.
Rosina Heikel, Finland, University of Helsinki, 1878.
G. Ogino, Japan (licensed to practice in Tokyo), 1884.
Nielsine Mathilde Nielsen, Denmark, University of Copenhagen, 1885.
Anandibai Joshee, India, Woman's Medical College of Pennsylvania, 1886.
Constance Stone, Australia, Woman's Medical College of Pennsylvania, 1887.
Rita Lobato Velho Lopez, Brazil, University of Bahia, 1887.
Emily Jennings Stowe, Canada, New York Medical College and Hospital for Women, 1887.
Eloiza Díaz (Inunza), Chile, University of Chile, 1887.
Ernestine Pérez (Barahona), Chile, University of Chile, 1887.
Matilde Montoya, Mexico, University of Mexico, 1887.
Karolina Widerstrom, Sweden, Karolinska Institute, 1888.

Laura Martínez de Carvajales y Camino, Cuba, Havana Medical School, 1889.

Cecilia Grierson, Argentina, University of Buenos Aires, 1889.

Manuela Solís, Spain, University of Valencia, 1889.

Clemence Evrard (Demoor), Belgium, University of Brussels, 1892.

Gabrielle Possaner-Ehrenthal, Austria, University of Zurich, 1893.

Angelique Panayotatou, Greece, University of Athens, 1896.

Alexandra Panayotatou, Greece, University of Athens, 1896.

Marie Spangberg-Holth, Norway, University of Norway, 1893.

Esther Kim Pak, Korea, Woman's Medical College, Baltimore, 1900.

Laura Esther Rodríguez-Dulanto, Peru, University of San Marcos at Lima, 1900.

From *MD Magazine,* June 1975, and other sources

NINE ON CALL

☙

Merit Ptah. The earliest known woman doctor was an Egyptian who lived about 2700 B.C. Her picture was discovered on a tomb in the Valley of the Kings.

Agnodice. In 300 B.C. Athenian law forbade slaves and freeborn women to practice medicine, but Agnodice disguised herself as a man to study in Alexandria, then returned to Athens to practice. The new doctor was so good that envious physicians accused him of seducing his patients. To dispute these charges, Agnodice was forced to reveal her sex. Placed on trial, she argued so persuasively on behalf of the capability of women to be physicians that the law was changed.

Aspasia. The best obstetrical specialist in second-century Rome should not be confused with the scholarly hetaira of the same name who lived several centuries earlier.

Trotula Platearius. A leading gynecologist and obstetrician of the eleventh century, and the *magistra medicinae* at the medical school in Salerno, her book *De Mulierum Passionibus (On the Suffering of Women)* was the first compilation on women's health care and one of the earliest books to be set in type, in 1544. Physicians used it for the next one hundred years.

Jacoba Felicie. In a catch-22-type trial held in Paris in 1322, Felicie was prosecuted for practicing medicine without training at the university— but of course the university did not admit women. Although Felicie claimed that she and the other women defendants used the same procedures as male doctors, she was still fined. Not until 1868 did the Medical School of the University of Paris admit women.

Constanza Calenda. When she became a Doctor of Medicine in Salerno in 1430, she was the first woman anywhere to be awarded that degree.

Salomea Rusiecka. At the age of fourteen she married an elderly physician and learned from him how to be an oculist. After the failure of her marriage, Rusiecka traveled through Eastern Europe performing cataract operations. Her financial security was assured in the middle of the eighteenth century when she became medical adviser to the sultan's harem in Istanbul.

Dorothea Leporin-Erxleben.♀ She gained admittance to Halle University in 1741 by appealing personally to Frederick the Great and received her degree in 1754. The only woman to gain a medical degree in the eighteenth century, Leporin-Erxleben waited until after the death of her husband to begin her own practice.

Varvara Kashevarova-Rudneva.♀ She was a midwifery student when she was invited by a Bashkir chief to treat the women of his tribe, who were afflicted with venereal diseases, because as Muslims they would not allow male physicians to touch them. In return, the chief paid for Kashevarova's medical education—and thus secured her admission to the medical academy in St. Petersburg. Although she was not granted the official title, she became de facto the first woman physician in Russia in 1868.

MS. M.D.: FIRSTS AND FOUNDERS

※

Harriot K. Hunt ♀ practiced medicine in Boston without a diploma from 1835 until her death forty years later, after being trained by an English practitioner for whom she worked as a secretary. She tried twice to get into Harvard Medical School, but left after other students forced her to withdraw. Hunt was later awarded an honorary M.D. from the Female Medical College of Pennsylvania.♀

Elizabeth Blackwell♀ (1821–1910), after many rejections, was finally accepted by Geneva Medical College in upstate New York and graduated in 1847, becoming the first woman to obtain a medical degree in the United States in 1849. Barred from practicing in most medical facilities, she opened the New York Infirmary for Women and Children in 1857 and in 1868 added the Women's Medical College. The following year she returned to her native England and helped to found the London School of Medicine for Women.

Marie Zackrzewska (1829–1902), a German-born doctor, was associated with Blackwell in founding the New York Infirmary and later established the New England Hospital for Women and Children with a training school for nurses in 1863.

Lydia Folger Fowler was the second woman to earn an M.D. in the United States in 1850 and the first woman to be a professor in an authorized medical school when she was appointed professor of midwifery and diseases of women and children at Rochester College.

Anna Lukens, called "Doctoress," was the first woman physician in the United States to be elected to a county medical society (Montgomery County, Pennsylvania, 1870).

Ellis Shipp, trained at the Female Medical College of Pennsylvania in Philadelphia, founded a school of obstetrics in 1879.

Elsie Maud Inglis founded a maternity hospice staffed entirely by women in Edinburgh in 1901.

Dorothy Brown, the first black woman to practice general surgery in the South, was also the first black woman to serve in the Tennessee State Legislature. Brown was raised in an orphanage and attended college on a scholarship. She is now chief of surgery at Riverside Hospital, Nashville, Tennessee.

Olga Jonasson received her M.D. from the University of Illinois in 1958 and became chief of surgery at Cook County Hospital in Chicago in 1977. Firsts to Jonasson's credit include first female transplant surgeon in the United States, first woman to perform a kidney transplant, first woman to head a surgical department at a major U.S. hospital, and first woman member of the Society of Clinical Surgery.

Bette Stephenson Pengelly, a family physician in Ontario province and mother of six children, became in 1974 the first woman president of the 107-year-old Canadian Medical Association.

ELEVEN PIONEER WOMEN'S REMEDIES

Until recently, and especially in rural areas and the days of westward expansion in the United States, women had to do their own doctoring. Families relied upon traditional folk wisdom and the expertise of pioneer women in concocting medical remedies. Here are some standard procedures:

- For rattlesnake bite: Swallow a teaspoonful of ammonia diluted in a glass of water.
- For ordinary snakebite: Try a compress of raw chicken meat or a slug of whiskey.
- To cure gangrene: Apply toasted onion skins and plug tobacco wrapped in a warm cloth.
- To soothe earache: Insert a wedge of salt pork or puff pipe smoke into the ear.
- For sore throat: Swallow a teaspoonful of sugar moistened with turpentine.
- To prevent snow blindness: Smudge the skin below the eyes with burned pitch pine.
- To thaw a frostbitten ear: Apply drops of warm glycerine to it with a turkey feather.
- For open cuts: Use turpentine.
- To cure warts: Apply gunpowder.
- To keep teeth clean: Use ordinary salt.
- To relieve rheumatism: Drink whiskey laced with pokeroot.

TEN PHYSICIANS WITH A MISSION

Catharine MacFarlane, research professor of gynecology at the Woman's Medical College of Pennsylvania, where she earned her M.D. in 1898, pioneered in the establishment of cancer detection clinics for women.

Sara Josephine Baker, an expert on child care and health, went into the immigrant ghettos in the early twentieth century to teach mothers techniques that sharply reduced infant mortality in New York City and led to the establishment of the city's Division of Child Hygiene with Baker as its director. In addition to her medical degree, she earned a Doctorate of Public Health from New York University in 1917, the first woman to do so.

Virginia Apgar, an anesthesiologist, invented the test for newborns now known as the Apgar score (a physiological checklist that can rapidly identify life- and health-threatening problems) after observing that infants in the delivery room were often put aside to be examined later—but "later" was sometimes too late.

Helen Brooke Taussig♀ had a hunch that an operation on a blood vessel near the heart could save the lives of "blue babies" born with heart defects. One of the first operations to be performed successfully on the human heart, it was the forerunner of modern cardiac surgery.

Mary Steichen Calderone, a gynecologist and mother of three, began her career as medical director of the Planned Parenthood Foundation in 1953, then left to found the Sex Information and Education Council of the United States in 1964. Upon the coincidental observance of her seventy-fifth birthday and the fifteenth anniversary of SIECUS, Calderone noted, "We're still a sexophobic society, afraid of the wrong things for the wrong reasons."

Frances Kelsey, a physician and pharmacologist employed by the Food and Drug Administration, refused to approve a new drug for sale to the public in 1960 despite pressure from the manufacturer. The drug was thalidomide; it proved to be responsible for causing severe physical defects in thousands of infants born to women who had taken it in the early months of pregnancy.

Margaret Ann Krikker, a family physician in upstate New York, learned that the Food and Drug Administration was about to allow a threefold increase in the amount of iron used to enrich flour and bread. Krikker, who knew that an excess of iron could be dangerous for some individuals, alerted hematologists and joined in a protest to the FDA. Superenrichment was tabled.

Mary Ellen Avery (b. 1927), a noted authority on pulmonary physiology of newborns, pioneered in research on the causes of hyaline membrane disease, resulting in significant saving of infant lives. In 1974 Avery became physician in chief of the Children's Hospital Medical Center in Boston and chair of the Department of Pediatrics at Harvard Medical School, both firsts for a woman.

Rowine Hayes Brown, a pediatrician, became the first woman medical director of Cook County Hospital in Chicago in 1973. Brown was largely responsible for passage of a state law requiring physicians and other professionals to report all suspicions or confirmed cases of child abuse.

Ruth W. Tichauer left her native Germany with her husband in 1940, came to Bolivia, and set up her medical practice in a *barrio* in the capital city, La Paz, six years later. Now sixty-nine years old, the grandmother of six regularly leaves the city at dawn to drive to an outlying village where she starts to examine the mountain Indians gathered there, some of whom have walked all night to consult the "Doctora."

NINE WOMEN UROLOGISTS

❧

Although male gynecologists have long cared for the female reproductive organs, urology, which concerns male sexual organs, has always been a "males only" preserve. Today even that is changing. There are now nine practicing female urologists in the United States, and at least eight others are in training. Practicing are:

Dr. Barbara O. Black, Bethesda, Maryland.
Dr. Jean L. Fourcroy, Bethesda, Maryland.
Dr. Muriel Friedman, Oakland, California.
Dr. Catherine M. Galvin, Berwyn, Illinois.
Dr. Mary Louise Gannon, Spencer, Iowa.
Dr. Larrian Gillespie, Brentwood, California.
Dr. Occo E. Goodwin, San Francisco, California.
Dr. Kathleen I. Hagen, Boston, Massachusetts.
Dr. Elizabeth P. Pickett, Newburgh, New York.

Contributed by Dr. Jean L. Fourcroy Behr

SEVEN DAUGHTERS OF PSYCHE

❧

Mary Whiton Calkins (1863–1930) was welcomed into their Harvard Seminars by William James and Josiah Royce in 1890—but the university would not permit her to become a student. Even when the entire department approved Calkins's thesis, gave her an unauthorized examination, and informed university officials that she had earned a Ph.D., the Harvard administration stood firm: Calkins simply did not meet the biological requirements! She could, however, have a degree from Radcliffe. Calkins refused and went to Wellesley, where she headed the Department of Mental Philosophy and founded one of the first psychological laboratories in the United States. Calkins became fourteenth president of the American Psychological Association in 1905, the first woman to hold that post.

Maud Merrill James (1888–1978) earned her Ph.D. from Stanford University in 1923, established a small psychological clinic for children, and became a regular consultant to the juvenile court in San Jose. Later, she worked with Lewis M. Terman on a major revision of his IQ test, which revision, in those precomputer days, took eleven years.

Margaret Floy Washburn♀ (1871–1939), a graduate of Vassar, was the first woman psychologist to receive a Ph.D. at Cornell University (1894) and in 1921 the second woman to be president of the American Psychological Association. Washburn wrote the first comprehensive textbook in comparative psychology, *The Animal Mind* (1908), and was the first woman psychologist elected to the National Academy of Sciences in 1932. She returned to Vassar as a faculty member in 1903, established a psychological laboratory, and also somehow had time to be coeditor of the *American Journal of Psychology* from 1903 on.

Anna Freud♀ (b. 1895), the youngest of the six children born to the founder of psychoanalysis, was a schoolteacher when she decided to apply her knowledge of psychoanalytic therapy to children. In subsequent years she published important papers outlining child psychoanalysis and contributing ideas on the development of the ego and defense mechanisms. Emigrating to England with her father on the eve of World War II, she established residences for children orphaned or made homeless by the war and later published her studies of them and of children who survived the Holocaust. Anna Freud has directed the Child Therapy Course, a London clinic which she founded, since 1952.

Helene Rosenbach Deutsch (b. 1884), after a brief period as a socialist activist organizing strikes of working women, graduated from the University of Vienna Medical School in 1912; six years later she became the first woman analyst to be analyzed by Sigmund Freud. Later she helped found and was the first director of the Vienna Training Institute. Deutsch came to the United States in the 1930s; her two-volume landmark *The Psychology of Women* was published in 1944. Deutsch defines narcissism, passivity, and masochism as the essential traits of femininity and believes that the way these traits are combined in any woman leads her to accept or challenge male authority. Her theories are controversial, to say the least.

Karen Horney♀ (1885–1952) earned her M.D. at the University of Berlin in 1913, came to the United States from her native Germany, and lost no time in publishing her differences with Freud. In *New Ways in Psychoanalysis* (1939) and other publications she criticized his "penis envy" explanation for neurosis in women, asserting that the psychological problems experienced by women were a response to the mores of the male-oriented culture in which women had to live. So adamant was she that the New York Psychoanalytic Society expelled her from membership, which gave her the impetus for founding the Association for the Advancement of Psychoanalysis in 1941.

Clara Mabel Thompson (1893–1958), who earned her M.D. at Johns Hopkins University, is another of the "revisionist" analysts who challenged Freud's libido theory. The author of *Psychoanalysis: Its Evolution and Development,* Thompson, as much as Horney, is responsible for today's understanding of the psychology of women. "It seems clear that envy of the male exists in most women in this culture. . . . The attitude of the women in this situation is not qualitatively different from that found in any minority group in a competitive culture."

IX ❧ ARMS AND THE WOMAN

FABLED WOMEN WARRIORS

❧

Camilla. Camilla's father had consecrated her to Diana and taught her to use a bow, slingshot, and javelin. She could run over a field of grain without bending a single blade and race over the sea without getting her feet wet. Then Aeneas and the Trojan remnant arrived in what is now Italy, and Camilla, dressed in a tiger skin, led male and female troops into battle. With darts and battle-ax she slew many Trojans before being fatally wounded. Camilla died in the arms of her women.

Penthesilea. No other woman warrior has had the strength of this Queen of the Amazons. Nevertheless, as she led her army against the Greeks, she was killed by Achilles. It is said that when he bent over her slain body he was so touched by her beauty, youth, and valor that he wept. Penthesilea's name is used today to describe any woman, military or not, who is strong and commanding.

Hippolyta. Juno, jealous of Hercules, set him to twelve labors, the sixth of which was to acquire the girdle of the Amazon queen Hippolyta. The queen received him hospitably and even presented him with the garment, but Juno took the form of an Amazon to persuade members of the community that their queen was being carried off. Dressed for battle, the angry women approached Hercules' ship, and he, thinking Hippolyta had sent them, slew her and sailed for home, taking the girdle with him.

Antiope, the next Queen of the Amazons, had but a brief reign. While the women were still recovering from Hercules' attack, Theseus came and carried off their queen. The Amazons invaded Athens in return, penetrating into the city itself, but were repulsed—and Antiope remained with Theseus until her death.

Deborah. The Israelites were oppressed by the Canaanites, so the prophet Deborah summoned the general Barak and told him to gather 10,000 men and attack from a strategic location. Barak refused to fight unless Deborah accompanied him, and true to her words, the enemy was routed. Deborah also prophesied that a woman would be the one to slay Sisera, the captain of the Canaanites. This too came to pass when . . .

143

Jael invited the fleeing soldier in, gave him milk to drink and covered him with a mantle. While he slept, she hammered a nail into his forehead.

Semiramis, the wife of an Assyrian royal army officer, devised a plan to defeat the Bactrians, and King Ninus, impressed with her abilities and beauty, demanded that his officer relinquish her. He did, then committed suicide, and Semiramis became the wife of the king—who died shortly afterward, leaving her to rule. She is said to have founded Babylon and to have led her 3½ million troops as far as India, where she lost two-thirds of her army and was herself wounded in battle. The legend of Semiramis is based on the life of Sammuramat, who ruled Assyria from 810 to 805 B.C. after the death of her husband.

Boadicea (Boudicca). In the first century the Romans plundered the kingdom of the widowed British queen, flogged her, and ravaged the two daughters who were her husband's heirs. Incensed, Boadicea rallied the Britons against them and slaughtered a Roman legion and more than 70,000 sympathizers before the tide turned against her in a cataclysmic battle in A.D. 61. As her supporters fell around her, the defeated queen took poison rather than let herself be captured.

Zenobia. After her husband died in A.D. 266, she became Queen of Palmyra, but her ambitions were greater than that. Styling herself the "Queen of the East," Zenobia and her troops conquered Syria, Egypt, part of Mesopotamia, and much of Asia Minor before being captured, brought to Rome, and paraded through the streets. She was later pensioned and spent the rest of her life in a quiet villa near Rome.

Ethelfleda. The daughter of King Alfred the Great was married to Earl Ethelred of Mercia. Upon his death in 911, Ethelfleda became ruler, and she and her brother Edward led their armies against the Danes who had overrun the land. She had conquered Leicester and was about to receive the surrender of York when she died in 918. Her people offered the throne to Edward, who became the first king of the unified nation.

Sichelgaita, a Lombard princess, married Robert Guiscard, a leading eleventh-century soldier of fortune. Their togetherness was so great that she accompanied him into battle, usually in full military regalia. An impressed Byzantine historian wrote that "when dressed in full armor the woman was a fearsome sight."

Tomoe was a fair-skinned Japanese samurai of the thirteenth century, a period that boasted many women military chiefs. She was said to be "a match for a thousand warriors and fit to meet either God or devil."

Trung-Trac and *Trung-Nhi,* sisters, in Vietnamese legend went to war against China at the side of commander Than Hung Duo in the thirteenth century.

FOURTEEN IN THE THICK OF BATTLE

Women have always participated in wars. In the days before physical examinations, it was possible for a determined woman to cast off her skirts and emerge in uniform as a male soldier. Some followed their lovers, but many followed only their own inclinations for glory and the military pay that was higher than anything else a woman could earn. Historian Gerda Lerner estimates that there were probably 400 such women masquerading as men in the American Civil War alone. Some fighting women whose names are known to us:

Catherine de Segurane. One day in the early fifteenth century a fleet of Turkish ships appeared in the Mediterranean and landed a Muslim army in what is now Nice. As the surprised defenders of the town ran about in confusion, Catherine, a peasant woman, held high a dagger and shouted to the men, "If you are not afraid, follow me!" A reinspired force drove the invaders to their ships, and the Muslims never did get a foothold in southern France.

Joan of Arc.♀ As a young French peasant girl, Joan heard heavenly voices telling her to help the dauphin press his claim for the throne of France against the English. Joan's conviction was so strong she persuaded the dauphin to give her command of his army. Her military victories led her soldiers to believe that she was invincible. But after the dauphin was crowned king, Joan was captured by the English and, unaided by her friends, brought to trial as a heretic. The Maid of Orleans was burned at the stake on May 30, 1431.

Margaret of Valois.♀ The Queen of France and Navarre was estranged from her husband, Henry IV, and her brother when she took up arms against them in the battle of Agen. She was taken prisoner in 1586, but became mistress of the castle in which she was being held.

Ch'in Liang-Yu. Raised to fight by her soldier father, she and her chieftain husband put down a rebellion against the Ming dynasty in 1600. As a widow she suppressed another uprising, was made a general, and successfully defended Peking against the Manchus. The emperor presented her with four poems praising her prowess.

Shen Yunying. The daughter of a seventeenth-century army captain took over his command when he was killed, saving the city from marauding bandits. By special decree, she was made a second captain, so that she could legitimately succeed her father.

Chen Li.♀ China's first female major general was one of the thirty women to survive the famous Long March to Shensi in the 1930s. She later led Communist troops against the Nationalist forces.

Augusta Krüger, a German woman, was a subaltern in the Nineteenth Prussian Regiment. For her heroic services, Krüger received both the Iron Cross and the Russian Order of St. George. After she retired from the army, she married a former officer. In 1869 her grandson was given a commission in his grandmother's old regiment.

Thérèse Figuer. As a French dragoon from 1798 to 1812, she had four horses killed under her but managed to die a civilian at the age of eighty-seven.

Louisa Scanagatti. In two armies, the Austrian and the Sardinian, she had the rank of lieutenant during the Napoleonic Wars.

Angélique Brulon, a *sous-lieutenant* in the French infantry, received the Legion of Honor and died in the Hôtel des Invalides in 1859.

Marietta Guiliani and *Herminia Manelli* both fought in Garibaldi's ranks for Italian independence.

Flora Sandes, an English woman, served in the trenches with the Serbian army in 1915. Sandes fought so well that she was promoted from the ranks and was later wounded in hand-to-hand combat.

And finally, in memory of all the unknown women who fell in battle:

A young Russian officer was reported dead in action at Kacelyevo by the London *Times* in September 1877. The officer was revealed "to be a woman, after displaying a most brilliant gallantry in rallying the men against the Turks."

FIVE WHO FOUGHT FOR ENGLAND
—————————————————— ✹ ——————————————————

Hannah Snell. James Grey was the name this English woman used when she joined Frazer's Marines. In 1748 she received eleven wounds in her legs and one in the groin. To avoid having to be examined by surgeons, Snell kept quiet about the latter wound and removed the ball herself. Later she served aboard a British man-of-war without, as she later stated, "the least discovery of her sex."
Ann Mills. The hot-tempered Mills served on board the British frigate *Maidstone* in 1714. A contemporary print shows her in sailor's uniform holding a sword in one hand and a Frenchman's head in the other.
Mary Dixon. Dixon fought at Waterloo and was in the British army for sixteen years. She survived her army career to live to a ripe old age, meriting the description of a "strong powerful older woman" in 1865.
Kit Cavanagh. Disguised as a man, Cavanagh joined the British army in 1693 to search for her soldier husband and saw action during the War of the Spanish Succession. When she was seriously wounded, surgeons discovered her sex and she was demoted to cook, but the rebellious Cavanagh continued to go into battle dressed as a woman. She died of natural causes and was buried with full military honors.
Mary Anne Talbot. The British footboy and drummer was actually a teenage girl who sneaked into the army to be with her lover. She fought at Santo Domingo in the Caribbean and in France. When her paramour was killed, Talbot left the army and emerged as a sailor, enduring many wounds and imprisonments. She was captured by the French and recaptured by the British, maintaining her male identity through all of it. Her fighting career came to an end when her secret finally surfaced in 1796.

EIGHT WHO FOUGHT IN THE REVOLUTIONARY WAR
—————————————————— ✹ ——————————————————

Mrs. Wright and *Mrs. Shattuck* of Groton, Massachusetts, organized a female militia and dispersed a British detachment.
Nancy Van Alstyne of the Mohawk Valley, New York, was a renowned In-

dian fighter as well as the mother of fifteen children. She became known as "Patriot Mother."

A Massachusetts woman who enlisted as Samuel Gay became a sergeant, but was later discovered to be a woman and was discharged.

Sally St. Clair, a young Creole woman, passed as a man to enlist and was killed in action.

Margaret Corbin (1751–ca.1800) may have been the prototype for the Molly Pitcher ♀ legend. She accompanied her husband, John Corbin, an artillery private, to the battlefield, and when, in 1776, he was killed while operating a cannon in the defense of Fort Washington, Manhattan, New York, Margaret took his place, firing the cannon until she, too, was hit, receiving wounds in one arm and breast. After the war, she received a small congressional pension and was known as "Captain Molly." A colorful, ill-tempered woman, she was buried in an unmarked grave, but in 1926 was reburied at West Point with full honors.

Mary Hays may also have been the prototype for the Molly Pitcher♀ legend. She accompanied her husband, William Hays of the Pennsylvania artillery, and fired alongside him. An observer recorded that while she was assisting her husband, a cannonball passed directly between her legs, carrying off a piece of her petticoat. "She observed that it was lucky it did not pass a little higher, for in that case it might have carried away something else, and continued her occupation." In 1822 she received a small pension from the Pennsylvania legislature; in 1876 a special marker was placed on her grave.

Deborah Sampson Gannett enlisted at the age of twenty in 1781 as Robert Shurtleff. She was wounded at the battle of Tarrytown, New York, and, suffering a fever, was discovered by a surgeon and discharged in October 1783. She received pensions from Massachusetts and Congress and, after her death, her husband was given a congressional pension as the widower of a Revolutionary War soldier.

THEY ALSO SERVED ...

❦

Elizabeth King of Edenton, North Carolina, in October 1774 opened her home to a meeting of fifty-one women, who there resolved not to drink tea or wear any garments manufactured in England for the duration. This was one example of the phenomenon that spread through the colonies—whether organized as the Daughters of Liberty or Association of Ladies, or some more informal title.

Esther de Berdt Reed, wife of Pennsylvania governor Joseph Reed, founded The Association, a women's group, to raise money for Continental troops. The Association was coordinated in each state by the wife of the governor, and Martha Washington♀ was coordinator of the receipts. With the funds they raised, the women bought fine linen fabric and sewed 2,200 shirts for soldiers.

Mary Slocumb, whose husband was in the militia in North Carolina, rode sixty-five miles through desolate woodland at night to aid her husband and the others wounded in the Battle of Moore's Creek, February 27, 1776.

Emily Geiger, a farmer's daughter, volunteered to travel through a hundred miles of Tory-held South Carolina to carry a message from General Nathanael Greene to General Thomas Sumter. When stopped by Redcoat scouts, Geiger secretly read the message she was carrying and swallowed the paper. She was released—and delivered the message that helped coordinate the battle plans of the two generals.

Phoebe Fraunces, the daughter of a New York innkeeper, was housekeeper in Washington's headquarters. One June day in 1776, as she was serving peas to General Washington, she bent down to whisper something in his ear. The general got out of his chair and hurled the peas into the chicken yard below. A few hours later the yard was strewn with dead chickens. One of Fraunces's suitors had confided in her his plot to poison the general.

Lydia Darragh, a Quaker, overheard everything the British said in their Philadelphia headquarters, just across a narrow road from her home. Her husband transcribed the information on tiny scraps of paper, which she sewed into the cloth buttons on her fourteen-year-old son's jacket; then her son walked north to where his older brother was encamped with Washington's forces. In December 1777 the Redcoats asked to use Darragh's parlor for a meeting, and, hiding in a closet, she heard their plans for a surprise attack. Under pretext of getting her flour sack filled at a mill on the outskirts of town, she left early the next morning, met a lieutenant, delivered her warning, and went back to town, stopping to fill the twenty-five-pound flour sack, which she carried the remaining five miles to her home.

Sybil Ludington ⁹ was still in her teens in 1777 when her father, a colonel in the militia, received word that 2,000 British soldiers were raiding a supply depot in Danbury, Connecticut, just over the state line. Sybil rode forty miles through the countryside to alert the members of the militia. Her father's troops were not able to prevent the disaster at Danbury, but they later joined with other Continental troops and engaged the British at the Battle of Ridgefield.

Kate (Margaret Catherine) Moore Barry, the young wife of Captain Andrew Barry of the Continental Army, rode through the South Carolina countryside to alert the troops when a British attack was imminent; the success of her mission can be seen in the victory of the Continentals at the Battle of Cowpens.

Nancy Hart, ⁹ of Georgia, a tall, rawboned, resourceful woman, was a skilled hunter. When a band of Redcoats burst into her frontier cabin in 1779 with a dead turkey and insisted that she roast it for their dinner, Hart obliged. Meanwhile she sent her daughter for help. When the men fell to, Hart took one of their rifles, killed one of her guests, and held the others off until reinforcements arrived.

Susanna Bolling was the teen-age daughter of a family in whose Virginia mansion Cornwallis dined one evening in 1781. Bolling heard the British general boast of his plans to trap Lafayette. When the household was asleep, she silently left her bed, crossed the Appomattox River, and delivered a timely warning to Lafayette.

Sally Townsend was one of the three daughters of a Long Island man whose home was commandeered to be headquarters of a British contingent in the winter of 1778. Fearful that their father, an outspoken patriot, would be arrested, the daughters pretended to be Loyalists and entertained the British officers. Sally Townsend thus overheard a conversation between the local commander and Major John André about plans for a takeover of West Point and found an opportunity to pass the information on to her brother, a secret agent for the Continental army. Her information was put to good use.

Betty Zane, a young West Virginia woman, was in Fort Henry when it was under attack in 1782. As the supply of gunpowder ran low, Zane volunteered to run across an open field to the cabin where the supply was stored. She scooped up the powder in a tablecloth tied around her waist and raced back to the defenders, enabling them to return the enemy's fire and hold the fort.

I SPY—EIGHT UNDERCOVER AGENTS OF THE CIVIL WAR

For the South

Emmeline Piggott. It didn't seem possible that this elegant daughter of the South had her mind on anything but fashion, but pinned to the voluminous petticoats under her skirts were Confederate documents she was transporting. When Union troops detained her, Piggott disposed of the important papers by swallowing them. She was released and continued her work as a spy.

Belle Boyd♀ used feminine wiles to wheedle secrets out of Union soldiers. Her greatest coup came when she informed Stonewall Jackson that the Union army was retreating and destroying its bridges. The bridges were saved, and Jackson was able to advance to within a short distance of Washington, D.C. Boyd was imprisoned three times. She traveled to England, supposedly for her health, but actually to deliver secret Confederate documents. She also organized a spy ring in Virginia composed entirely of teen-age girls. After the war, the flamboyant spy went on the stage.

Rose O'Neal Greenhow. A leading Washington hostess, Greenhow was acquainted with most of the important men in the capital—who proved to be valuable sources of information for the Confederacy. The South's first significant victory, Bull Run, was credited to her knowledge of advance plans. She directed a ring of fifty spies, forty-eight of them women; it continued to operate even after the authorities uncovered her activities. Imprisoned for a year, Greenhow was released and sent back to Virginia. She later traveled to England to gain support for the Confederacy and was drowned in a storm as her ship neared home.

Nancy Hart. This West Virginia woman charmed the Union troops with her southern accent and flirtatious ways, hung around their encampments—and kept her eyes open. Finally, she was apprehended and confined to prison, but she charmed the young soldier who guarded her until he gave her his gun to hold; then she shot him and dashed off on the best horse in the compound. One week later Hart returned, leading 200 mounted Confederate troops, who recaptured their town.

For the North

Elizabeth Van Lew. When the war broke out, Van Lew began to spy for the Union in Richmond, avoiding discovery by posing as a harmless eccentric given to muttering to herself in the streets. "Crazy Bet" was sane enough; she had her own network of Union spies, including servants who sometimes carried messages in their shoes. She supplied Grant with a steady stream of military information that made possible his successful attack on the city. When Grant became president, he rewarded her with an appointment as postmistress.

Mary Bowser. No one in Jefferson Davis's household suspected the black servant of being a Union spy. Because it was assumed that she was illiterate, there could be no harm in allowing her to dust his study. Thus the well-educated Bowser was able to read Davis's dispatches: she was the manumitted slave of Elizabeth Van Lew and the source of much of the information about troop strength and location that Van Lew transmitted to Grant.

Pauline Cushman. Even as she toasted Jefferson Davis from the stage, the New Orleans actress was working as a spy for the Union, stealing plans of fortifications. Eventually she was discovered, jailed, and sentenced to be hanged—but, in a scene as dramatic as any she ever enacted, her pretty neck was saved by the last-minute arrival of Union troops. She was later given an honorary commission as a major. When she died many years later, she was buried with military honors in the San Francisco National Cemetery.

Emma E. Edmonds. This Union nurse turned spy had a variety of disguises which she used to move back and forth between the lines. She worked in a Confederate camp as a black boy and also used the cover of an Irish immigrant peddler. When she wasn't spying, Edmonds carried on as an army nurse. She continued spying for two years, longer than any other female agent of the war.

FOUR WHO WORE WAR PAINT

Because intertribal conflict between Plains Indian groups on the upper Missouri was unusually heavy in the third quarter of the nineteenth century, women warriors often went into battle beside their men.

Woman Chief was the greatest of the woman warriors, an adopted Crow who had always preferred men's work. As a hunter, she was the equal of any man and led many war parties against the Blackfeet. Her bravery won her a place in the council of the chiefs of the tribe and the name of Woman Chief, a position and title never before given to a woman by the Crow.

Running Eagle led Blackfeet warriors against the Flatheads. She was the bride of a young brave killed in a battle with the Crows. Contrary to tradition, she refused to remarry but became a warrior instead. Her battle attire was unique: men's leggings, an improvised loincloth, and a woman's dress. To the sun she prayed, "Sun, I am not a man. But you gave me this power to do what I desired."

Elk Hollering was another Blackfoot woman warrior about whom little else is known.

The Other Magpie, a Crow woman, fought with General Crook against the Sioux and Cheyenne at the Battle of the Rosebud in June 1876. Her ferocity may have stemmed from the recent loss of a brother to the Sioux. In the battle, which took place one week before the better-known Battle of Little Big Horn, she took a scalp and performed other heroic deeds; later she would count coup, reciting her exploits with the Crow men.

TOP BRASS: ACHIEVEMENTS OF AMERICAN MILITARY WOMEN

Women make up about 12 percent of "Today's Army." Of the 2 million members of all the armed forces, 5.5 percent are women. Some of the trailblazers have been;

Colonel Julia C. Stimson, chief of the American Red Cross nursing services in France during World War I. Stimson was the first woman of officer's rank in the Army Nurse Corps and received the Distinguished Service Medal from General John Pershing.

Colonel Oveta Culp Hobby, a lawyer and newspaper editor in Texas, who was asked, early in the Second World War, to organize the Women's Army Auxiliary Corps, later known as the Women's Army Corps or WACs. More than 140,000 women joined. Other military women contributed to the war effort: 18,000 SPARs (Coast Guard), 22,000 WAMs (marines), and 86,000 WAVES (navy). The WACs and other women's services were phased out by the 1970s as women became full partners in the regular services.

Jacqueline Cochran led the thousand WASPs (Women's Air Force Service Pilots) who transported planes, men, and materials to their destinations during World War II. The WASPs totaled about 60 million noncombat flying miles, and thirty-six of these women lost their lives.

Brigadier General Mary E. Clark, director of the WACs and commandant at Fort McClellan, Alabama, the first woman to command an army base.

General Margaret Brewer was director of women marines, the first woman general in the history of the Marine Corps and is also the first woman to serve as the marines' director of information.

Lieutenant Colonel Pamela Sylvester, the first woman to be executive assistant to a four-star general when she served on the staff of Alexander M. Haig, Jr., former supreme commander of the North Atlantic Treaty Organization.

Sally D. Woolfolk, who became, in 1974, the first woman in United States history to be an army aviator.

Deborah B. Doane, the first woman deck officer in the U.S. Merchant Marine. She graduated third in her class from the Maine Maritime Academy and is currently third mate on a cargo vessel. Her ambition: to become a ship's captain.

Rear Admiral Fran McKee, director of naval educational development, who became in 1976 the only woman among the navy's more than 230 line admirals. There were at the time two other female rear admirals, both with the Navy Nurse Corps.

Barbara Allen Rainey, who became the navy's first female pilot but resigned her lieutenant's commission in 1977 because she was barred from combat roles. Rainey stated that she faced "severe career limitations as a woman."

Lieutenant Colonel Jacquelin J. Kelly, the first woman army officer to be assigned as a full professor of military science. She is on the faculty at West Virginia University, where a staff of twelve army personnel reports to her. In 1967 Kelly was also the first woman officer to be chosen to participate in the foreign area officer specialty program in Chinese language and Asian studies, and she later attended the National War College in Washington, D.C.

Admiral Arlene B. Duerk, who became the first woman admiral in the U.S. Navy in 1972. Duerk's navy career had started nearly thirty years earlier when, as a twenty-two-year-old, she joined the Navy Nurse Corps, of which she later became head.

FIRST WOMEN IN THE WHITE HOUSE HONOR GUARD

꽃

The first women to serve in the previously all-male White House Honor Guard stood at attention at the entrance to the East Room at arrival ceremonies for Zambia's President Kenneth Kaunda on May 17, 1978. The five women, one from each branch of the service, were:

Navy Seaman (sic) *Apprentice Catherine Behnke,* twenty years old, of Reedley, California.

Army Specialist 4 Christine L. Crews, twenty years old, of Granite City, Illinois.

Marine Pfc. Myrna Jepsen, nineteen years old, of Manhattan, Kansas.

Coast Guard Apprentice Edna Dunham, nineteen years old, of Morencin, Arizona.

Air Force Sergeant Elizabeth Foreman of Medford, Oregon.

NINE POLICY MAKERS AT THE PENTAGON IN 1979

— ❧ —

Kathleen Carpenter, Deputy Assistant Secretary of Defense for Equal Opportunity.
Antonia H. Chayes, Assistant Secretary of the Air Force (Manpower and Reserve Affairs).
Lynn E. Davis, Deputy Assistant Secretary of Defense for Policy Planning and National Security Council Affairs.
Ruth M. Davis, Deputy Director of Defense Research and Engineering.
Sara Lister, Deputy Special Assistant to the Special Assistant, Office of the Secretary of Defense.
Deanne C. Siemer, General Counsel of the Defense Department.
Mary Snavely, Deputy Assistant Secretary of the Navy (Manpower).
Jill Wine Volner, General Counsel for the Department of the Army.
Mitzi Wertheim, Deputy Under Secretary of the Navy.

There was no Pentagon in the 1860s, but there was a woman military strategist. *Anna Ella Carroll* of Maryland knew the terrain, railroad lines, and supply routes, and she sketched them for President Abraham Lincoln, along with her recommendations for Union troop movements. *Godey's* magazine would report, several years after the Civil War, that Lincoln had had to conceal the fact that he was consulting Carroll because his generals would not take advice from a woman. The result was that her contributions went unrecognized and unrewarded. As she grew old and became ill, attempts were made to get her a military pension, but to no avail.

SOME LADY HELL CATS

— ❧ —

Advancement for women has often been born of male desperation. In World War I the military services needed women. With so many men overseas, who was to handle the paper work at home? Despite trepidation it was decided to try women, even though many doubted that they could adjust to military discipline. The Marine Corps inducted only 400 women out of more than 2,000 hopefuls. Based in Washington, D.C., the women, dubbed "Lady Hell Cats," caused some controversy. Said one young marine, "This is a fallen outfit when they start enlisting skirts." But enlisted they were. World War I marked the beginning of real career opportunities for women in the military service. Several of the "Marinettes" remained in the corps, and some inspired their children to become leathernecks.

Opha Johnson enrolled in the Marine Corps on August 13, 1918, becoming America's first woman marine. By the end of the war she was Sergeant Johnson, the corps's highest-ranking woman.
Alma Swope remained in the Marine Corps after the war, serving in the Supply Department for more than forty-four years.
Martrese Thek Ferguson, in the years after World War I, rose to the rank of lieutenant colonel; during the Second World War she commanded more than 2,000 women based in Arlington, Virginia.

Lillian O'Malley Daly, a former Lady Hell Cat, returned to service in 1943. At Camp Pendleton, California, she served as the West Coast liaison officer for the new women's organization of the Marine Corps.

Jane Von Edsinga Blakesy became head of the Decorations and Medals Branch at Marine Corps headquarters, serving three commandants in that capacity.

Edith Macias also saw four of her sons and one stepson join the marines, as well as her sister Sarah. Sarah's daughter *Major Anne Lenox* joined the Marine Corps Reserve.

EIGHT ENSIGNS

In December 1978 eight young women ensigns were assigned to duty aboard ships in the Atlantic and the Pacific; they were given staterooms with private baths, separate from the men. Fifty-three more women officers and 375 enlisted women were also scheduled to report for duty in 1979 on twenty-one noncombat ships. The eight pioneers:

Ensign Mary Carrol, twenty-three, of Roanoke, Virginia. Stepping aboard the 530-foot U.S.S. *Vulcan,* a repair vessel, made her the first woman in the navy's 203-year history to report for sea duty on other than a hospital or transport ship. Her skipper, Captain Harry Spencer, expected the change to benefit the navy. "Men will work hard not to be outdone by women, and women will work hard to prove themselves."

Ensign Jo Anne Carlton, twenty-three, of Lynchburg, Virginia, also assigned to the *Vulcan.*

Ensign Elizabeth Bres, twenty-two, of Alexandria, Louisiana, serving on board the U.S.S. *Puget Sound,* a 643-foot destroyer.

Ensign Linda Crockett, twenty-three, of Patterson, New Jersey, assigned to the submarine tender U.S.S. *Spear.*

Ensign Linda Day, twenty-three, of Gallipolis, Ohio, also on board the U.S.S. *Spear.*

Ensign Charlene Albright, twenty-six, of Easton, Maryland, on board the guided-missile ship U.S.S. *Norton Sound.* Albright is an electronics materials officer in charge of a small division of nine men. Says this ensign, "Just because this hasn't been done before doesn't mean it can't be done."

Ensign Roberta McIntyre, twenty-three, of Charlotte, North Carolina, the assistant navigator of submarine tender U.S.S. *Dixon.* Asked if she would ever like to be captain of a ship, McIntyre replied, "Sure, I'll go for it."

Ensign Macushla McCormick, twenty-three, of Selah, Washington, also assigned to the U.S.S. *Dixon.*

FIRST WOMEN IN SERVICE

❧

In 1980, 227 women became the first female graduates of the four military service academies.

At the U.S. Military Academy at West Point, sixty-one women cadets were graduated, along with 809 men. Half of the women would get married within a few days of the May 28 ceremony, mostly to West Point men. First woman to graduate from West Point:

Andrea Hollen of Altoona, Pennsylvania, a Rhodes Scholar, who ranked 10th in her class.

The U.S. Naval Academy at Annapolis graduated 55 female midshipmen (*sic*). First to receive her diploma:

Elizabeth Belzer of Westminster, Maryland.

At the Coast Guard Academy in New London, Connecticut, fourteen women became ensigns, with 142 men. Among the first women to graduate:

Jean Marie Butler of Hershey, Pennsylvania.
Linda Johansen of North Dartmouth, Massachusetts, ranked fifth in the class.
Karen J. Tweed of Bethesda, Maryland, received an award for being most proficient navigator.
Susan K. Donner of Longmeadow, Massachusetts, received an award for being most proficient in boatsmanship (*sic*).

At the United States Air Force Academy at Colorado Springs, ninety-seven women and 970 men graduated. About a third of the women got married shortly afterward. First woman to graduate:

Kathleen Conley of Long Beach, California, who ranked eighth in her class. Her father is Air Force Major General Philip Conley.

FOUR RUSSIAN FIGHTER PILOTS

❧

The military services of most countries assign their women's units to non-combat duties, but in the Soviet Union women have long fought beside men. During the Second World War there were three all-female flying units in the Soviet air force. Combat pilots in one of them, the 586th Fighter Air Regiment, took part in 4,419 sorties, fought in 125 air battles, and shot down 38 enemy aircraft. Thirty Russian airwomen have been decorated with the Gold Star of a Hero of the Soviet Union.

Princess Eugenie Shakhovskaya, the first female military pilot, was on active duty during the First World War. Trained to fly in Germany, she persuaded the czar to allow her to fly reconnaissance missions to the front in 1914. Shakhovskaya survived not only these missions but the Russian Revolution as well, impressing the Bolsheviks with her loyalty and becoming a member of their secret police.
Lilya Litvyak, who served in a mixed (male and female) unit in World War II, shot down twelve planes before she was killed.

Major Tamara Aleksandrovna commanded the 586th Fighter Air Regiment. *Polina Gelman,* a pilot in Aleksandrovna's unit, was decorated five times.

WEAPONS WITH FEMININE NICKNAMES

Brown Bess was the bronzed flintlock musket used in the British army (and by many American revolutionary soldiers) in the eighteenth century.

Mons Meg is a huge fifteenth-century piece of ordnance at Edinburgh Castle. Made at Mons in France, it was much renowned among the Scots.

Sweet Lips is the very familiar name of an ordnance employed at the siege of Newark by the British.

Big Bertha, a World War I German gun, was used to shell Paris from a range of seventy-five miles. The French named it after Frau Bertha Krupp, of the armament family that made the weapon.

Mother was a popular name for the English Mark I tanks used in World War I.

Moaning Minnie was a six-barreled German mortar of the Second World War. When fired, it sounded like a rising shriek. The name was also applied to an air-raid warning siren.

Old Mother Covington and her daughter were the two patriot cannons—a small fieldpiece and a swivel gun—that helped defeat a force of Scots Loyalists in the first Revolutionary War engagement in North Carolina, the Battle of Moore's Creek Bridge, on February 27, 1776.

X ❧ *THE SEARCH FOR ADVENTURE*

THE WILD WEST AND THE BIG TOP
❧

Madame Saqui, a French artist, performed a spectacular circus act in 1813, in which she slid down a sixty-foot rope totally enveloped in fireworks. Once, she pirouetted across a tightrope strung between the towers of Nôtre Dame Cathedral. Napoleon was so taken with her act that he let her follow the encampments of the Imperial Guard. But in her final years Saqui lost her popularity, earned only a pittance at outdoor carnivals, and died in poverty.

Annie Oakley. What couldn't she do with a gun? Her tricks included splitting a playing card balanced on its edge from thirty paces; demolishing glass balls while lying on the back of a cantering horse; knocking the ashes off cigarettes held by her husband, sharpshooter Frank Butler; and shooting the flames from revolving candles.

Lillian Leitzel's aerial act was the circus show-stopper of the early 1900s. Working fifty feet above ground without a net, Leitzel executed a series of one-arm somersaults on the high wire; with each turn she dislocated her shoulder, but her muscles were so superbly trained she immediately snapped it back into place. The thrice-married star was noted for her quick temper as well: in the heat of one marital argument she chopped off her husband's finger with a butcher knife.

Mabel Stark was a trained nurse on vacation when she first entered a tiger's cage on a dare. She liked the excitement so much that she never returned to nursing, becoming the first woman tiger tamer. Stark worked with as many as sixteen animals at a time and finished her act by putting her blond head into a Bengal tiger's mouth. She continued her act until she was well into her seventies.

Lucille Mulhall, the star of her father's Wild West show in the late 1800s, could rope four horses and riders at a time. Mulhall learned her craft on her family's Oklahoma ranch where, as a teen-ager, she often competed with the male ranchers—and usually won.

Bird Millman, whose specialties were dancing and turning somersaults on the high wire, crossed lower Broadway in 1924 on a wire twenty-five stories above the ground.

Cindy Dodge, a contemporary rodeo rider, won a broad belt buckle as women's champion team roper. She also excels at individual roping and bull riding. "I wanted to show men that women could compete just as well," says Dodge of her accomplishments on horseback, "and get off and still be a lady." Dodge is among the more than 3,000 members of the Girls' Rodeo Association.

FIVE SISTERS OF THE ROAD

In art, song, and film, the tramp has traditionally been male, but women, too, have been hobos. During the depression it was estimated that there were 6,800 "transient" women. Among the most colorful:

"Boxcar" Bertha Thompson♀ spent most of her life—from the early 1900s to the 1930s—on the road. Bertha was born into hobohemia, the daughter of "Mother" Thompson, widely known for her hospitality to radicals and hobos. She told her daughter, "Don't be afraid of life and love and nature. Anything you want to do is all right with me." Following Mama's advice, Boxcar Bertha traveled across the country, supporting herself as a shoplifter, prostitute, and social service worker. In the 1930s she published her autobiography, *Sisters of the Road,* in the hope of improving conditions for all migrant women.

Lena Wilson, tall and red-headed, was a well-known boxcar propagandist. Riding the rails, she argued the cause of socialism in every state in the Union without paying a cent in fare. "The railroads rob the workers," she said. "Why shouldn't we rob the railroads?"

Martha Biegler ("Red Martha") was among the most popular of the female hobos; anarchists and hobo literati hung out at the Chicago boarding-house she ran between her times on the road. Down-and-outers and suspicious characters were also welcome.

Lizzie Davis, who styled herself "Queen of the Hobos," claimed to know every kind of social outcast on the police blotter. She supported herself as a rather clumsy shoplifter. Whenever she met a ragged man or woman, she'd take them "shopping" and provide the very best. Davis once told Boxcar Bertha, "Anybody with a skirt can hitchhike. I go down between New York and Chicago just like a businessman. It never takes me more than three days and I always end up with more money than when I started. . . ."

Eileen O'Connor founded an organization of women hobos familiarly known as the "Women Itinerants' Hobo Union" and "Sisters of the Road." It held women's hobo conventions and in 1932 participated in the Bonus March in Washington, D.C. To improve the living conditions for "road women," O'Connor lobbied for collective feeding places, changing and repair rooms, places for writing and receiving mail, libraries, health centers, birth control clinics, and recreation centers.

LIVING DANGEROUSLY

❦

Maria Speltarini crossed Niagara Falls in July 1876 on a tightrope with a thirty-pound weight attached to each of her ankles.

Annie Edson Taylor celebrated her forty-third birthday on October 24, 1901, by going over Niagara Falls in a barrel. She was the first person, and remains the only woman, to have done so. The trip lasted a bumpy thirty-five minutes. For the occasion Taylor wore a long, full-skirted gown and a wide-brimmed feathered hat. After all, it *was* her birthday.

Tiny Broadwick became the first woman to parachute from an airplane on June 21,1913, near Griffith Field in California; she had frequently performed the same feat from balloons. Interviewed by Groucho Marx on "You Bet Your Life," Broadwick claimed to have more parachute jumps to her credit than any other woman in history.

Lillian Ward, the most sought-after stunt woman of silent films, was called "the girl without fear." It was nothing for Ward to ride horses over cliffs, crash cars and locomotives, and tumble down stairs. She doubled for almost all the top stars of the period, including a few men, and earned $150 a day. She was the woman tied to the railroad tracks by the diabolical villain in the *Perils of Pauline.* Today, at ninety-five, confined to a wheelchair, Ward lives in a nursing home.

Lorena Caven was the first to dive into the ocean while riding a Steel Pier High Diving Horse in Atlantic City, New Jersey. She was trained by her father, Dr. D. W. Caven, who invented the stunt for her in the 1930s. In later years the Steel Pier's horses dove into a tank of water fifteen feet deep and thirty feet in diameter. Riders have always been young women.

Carol Jackson and *Sandra Wilson* are the first women to be "powder monkeys," professionals at blowing things up. Both are recent graduates of the Institute of Explosives Specialists in Issaquah, Washington.

Kitty O'Neil,♀ racing-car driver and Hollywood stunt woman, became the world's fastest woman on December 6, 1976, when she set a new women's speed record of 512.70 miles per hour in a three-wheeled rocket car at Alvord Desert, Oregon.

Rita Egleston, Beth Nufer, and *Peaches Jones* are all TV and movie stunt women. Egleston was the Bionic Woman's action-ego, and Nufer did the same for Wonder Woman. A few years ago Nufer cracked her spine and suffered a concussion while leaping off a forty-foot building, but returned to her career soon after she recovered. Jones learned how to make her lively living from members of the Black Stunt Man's Association who were friends of her father.

Debbie Lawler,♀ the first woman motorcycle jumper, takes off at eighty miles per hour at the Houston Astrodome, hurtling over sixteen cars at a time. It all began on Lawler's tenth birthday, when she received a cycle as a present from her father, a professional motorcycle racer. Although she broke her back in three places in 1974, she intends never to give up jumping.

Pat Derby trains wild animals for their professional appearances in commercials. "I love seeing something wild and free. To have an animal that's huge and powerful, and a potential danger, accept me is wonderful."

LONG-DISTANCE ENDURANCE

❧

Mary Richardson Walker, like many other pioneer women, walked most of the way from the eastern seaboard to Oregon with her husband in 1836.

Mary Callinach was eighty-five years old in 1851 when her name became a household word in England because she walked 300 miles from her native village to visit the Great Exhibition in London. Callinach walked back, too.

Zoe Gayton, having heard about a professor who had gone from coast to coast on horseback, declared that she could do the same thing on foot. She set out on a successful cross-country trek on August 27, 1890, accompanied by two male companions and two poodles. Because she followed the railroad tracks across the country, railroad men dubbed her the "Sunset Special."

Mrs. Anderson, an English woman, walked 2,700 quarter miles from December 16, 1878, to January 13, 1879. The occasion was a marathon walking contest held at the Mozart Beer Garden in Brooklyn, New York, where a small track had been set up (seven times around it was exactly a quarter of a mile). Anderson huffed around the track for four weeks while a crowd of 2,000 people jammed into the hall to witness the feat.

Annie Londonderry, a young American, circled the globe by bicycle in 1894, traveling 28,000 miles.

Nelly Bly (Elizabeth Seaman), a hard-driving late-nineteenth-century journalist, specialized in sensational reporting. Her most notable exploit was a journey around the world in 72 days, 6 hours, 11 minutes, and 14 seconds. Bly succeeded in her goal of besting the 80-day record set by Jules Verne's fictional hero Phileas Fogg in *Around the World in Eighty Days.* More than one million people placed bets on the exact time her well-publicized trip would take.

Emma Gatewood, the first woman to walk the 2,000-mile Appalachian Trail alone, was also the oldest person to do so more than once. Gatewood, a grandmother, made the hike in the 1970s at ages sixty-five and sixty-eight.

Nan Jane Aspinall, the first woman horseback rider to journey across the continent solo, left San Francisco on September 1, 1910, with a letter from Mayor Patrick Henry McCarthy of that city to New York's Mayor William Jay Gaynor. Aspinall arrived in New York on July 8, 1911, having covered 4,500 miles in 301 days, 108 of them spent traveling.

Alice Hyler Ramsey drove across the country in 1909, covering the 3,800 miles from Hellgate in New York City to the Golden Gate in San Francisco in four days. She was the tenth driver and the first woman to make the trip, which was sponsored by the Maxwell-Brisco auto company. Ramsey, a veteran of more than thirty cross-country ventures, is still driving today.

Adeline Van Buren and her twenty-four-year-old sister *Augusta* were the first women to cross the continent by motorcycle. Setting out from Brooklyn, New York, on July 4, 1916, they arrived in San Francisco 5,500 miles and 60 days later. The purpose was to show that women could be counted on for physical fitness during World War I. "Woman can, if she will" was their motto. After the trip, Adeline volunteered for service in the army but was turned down, her point apparently unproven. Augusta next turned to flying and was a pilot well into her sixties.

Naomi James grew up on a dairy farm in the interior of New Zealand and neither swam nor saw a sizable body of water until she was twenty-one years old. A casual invitation to take a coffee break aboard a yacht introduced her to both sailing and her future husband, and in 1977–78, at the age of twenty-eight, she sailed alone 30,000 miles around the world in a fifty-three-foot sloop. The trip took 272 days—4 days better than the record set by Sir Francis Chichester. Said James, "Courage is only needed to do something you can't do and have to do; I knew I could do it."

TEN EXPLORERS

᙭

Isabella Bird Bishop was plagued by mysterious illnesses. Her doctor suggested travel as a cure and so, in the 1870s, at the age of forty, Bishop took off. She was never sick again. Alone, she traversed the Rocky Mountains, Japan, Malaya, India, the Kashmir, Tibet, and Korea, writing about the sights she witnessed. To pay her way, she worked as a cowgirl, cook, and missionary. Bishop became the first woman to be elected a Fellow of the Royal Geographical Society. In her fifties when she married, she announced that she would love to visit New Guinea but it was hardly the kind of place to which one could take a man!

May French Sheldon set out to prove that where a man could go, a woman could, too. In 1891 Sheldon journeyed through the Masai country north of Mount Kilimanjaro in Africa, carrying a pennant marked *Noli me tangere* and demonstrating that a woman could manage an expedition as well as a man. The Africans called her "Bébé Bwana"—Swahili for "Lady Boss."

Florence Baker was seventeen years old when her former nurse sold her to a Turk. Her fortune changed when explorer Samuel Baker purchased her; he made her his wife and partner in adventure. They explored Africa together, and in 1864 they jubilantly announced that they had found Lake Albert, one of the long-sought sources of the Nile. In 1869 Samuel Baker effectively suppressed the slave trade that had given him his wife.

Fanny Bullock Workman and her husband were fanatic bicyclers. For ten years, from 1890 to 1900, the pair cycled through most of Europe and a good part of Asia, crossing 14,000 miles of the Indian subcontinent, their longest run being 86 miles in one day. For relaxation they climbed mountains, ascending the Karakoram range in the Himalayas eight times between 1898 and 1912, and Fanny's name was given to Mount Bullock Workman, 19,450 feet high. In 1906 she set a new altitude record for a woman, ascending 23,350 feet to the summit of Pinnacle Peak in the Nunkun massif.

Mary Kingsley explored the interior of Africa between 1893 and 1895, totally on her own and always impeccably dressed. She lived off the land, learned how to paddle her own African canoe, and fulfilled her early ambition to become an expert on "all things West African." In 1900 Kingsley volunteered for service in South Africa and died while nursing Boer prisoners. She was buried at sea.

*Kate Marsden,*⁹ a trained nurse with as much determination as her model, Florence Nightingale,⁹ went to Russia in the 1890s to aid the lepers in the distant Siberian colony of Yakut. Doggedly she traveled through the uncharted frozen wastes to find them—and for her explorations was elected to the Royal Geographical Society in 1892.

Isabel Burton married the renowned explorer of Arabia Sir Richard Burton in 1861 and with him explored the Middle East, writing extensively about what she saw. As a devout Catholic, however, she never approved of her husband's successful sixteen-volume translation of *The Thousand and One Nights* (too erotic), and when he died in 1890, she destroyed his manuscript for another such volume, claiming his ghost had instructed her to do so. Her tombstone reads simply "Isabel, his wife."

Annie Taylor, one of the few Europeans to penetrate inner Tibet, was a committed missionary who dreamed of bringing the Gospel there. With the help of a native convert she covered 1,300 roadless miles in seven months in the late 1800s, enduring frequent attacks by bandits and other hardships. She later recruited nine volunteer missionaries to help her in her work—turning down all female applicants for the job.

Gertrude Benham spent more than thirty years walking around the world, covering the entire globe seven times. In the course of her career she climbed more than 300 peaks of 10,000 feet or taller, becoming in 1909 the first woman to climb 19,700-foot-high Mount Kilimanjaro. In 1908 she literally walked across South America, and five years later she performed the same feat in Africa. Usually alone, Benham never carried a gun, but always had with her a Bible, a pocket edition of Shakespeare, Kipling's *Kim, Lorna Doone,* and her knitting.

Mary L. Jobe, an educator and mountaineer, led six expeditions to the Canadian Northwest, was the first to map the headwaters of the Fraser River and the glaciers of Mount Sir Alexander, made several first ascents, and had Mount Jobe in the Rockies named in her honor by the Canadian government. In 1924 she married explorer Carl Akeley and two years later went with him on a collecting and photographing trip to West Africa. Akeley died during the expedition and Jobe took charge, working for five more weeks despite torrential rains. Jobe continued explorations in Africa and Canada until the last years of her long life; she died at age eighty in 1966.

CLIMB EVERY MOUNTAIN

――――――――――――――――― ❦ ―――――――――――――――――

Lucy Walker was the first woman to reach the summit of the Matterhorn—July 22, 1871.

Fay Fuller became the first woman to conquer 14,000-foot Mount Rainier in 1890. Her climbing outfit was considered scandalous at the time: heavy boy's shoes, ankle-length bloomers, and a blanket roll tied around her waist.

Annie Smith Peck, a Smith College classics professor, was in 1897 the first woman to climb Mount Orizaba, an extinct volcano in Mexico and at 18,700 feet one of the loftiest peaks in North America.

Dora Keen in 1912 was the first person to climb the 16,390-foot-high Mount Blackburn in Alaska, surviving snowstorms, avalanches, and temperatures as extreme as 90 degrees Fahrenheit in the daytime and −60 degrees at night. Only one of the seven men who set out with Keen was still with her when she reached the peak, four weeks later.

Junko Tabei was one of the fifteen Japanese women mountaineers, selected from hundreds of climbing clubs, who made an assault on Mount Everest. Only she reached the top, becoming, on May 16, 1975, the first woman to conquer the 29,028-foot mountain. The trek took a month, during which ten of the women were injured in an avalanche.

Beverly Johnson became, at thirty-one, the first woman to climb alone to the top of 3,600-foot-high El Capitan, a gigantic granite mass in the Yosemite Valley. It took ten days in 1978. Johnson carried about a hundred pounds of gear with her up the sheer rock, sleeping in slings she hung from the granite face of the mountain.

Arlene Blum lead a team of nine female climbers in a successful assault on 26,504-foot Annapurna in September 1978. When *Irene Miller,* a physicist from California, and *Vera Komarkova,* a Czech-born ecologist, reached the peak, they planted banners reading "A woman's place is on top." But *Alison Chadwick,* thirty-six years old, of Leeds, England, and *Vera Watson,* forty-six years old, of Stanford, California, were both killed in a fall in the final stage of the climb.

EIGHT FLOATING UPWARD

❧

Elisabeth Thible cried, "I'll go with him to heaven and to glory!" when she learned that the painter Fleurant was having trouble finding a male companion for his proposed balloon flight. On June 4, 1784, she became the first female aeronaut when the couple ascended from Lyons, France, in the presence of the French royal family and the King of Sweden. Thible felt such euphoria that she burst into song, treating Fleurant to the aria "I am victorious, I am Queen," from *La Belle Arsène.*

Letitia Sage was the first English woman to soar in a balloon. Sage set out with two male companions on June 29, 1785, but her excessive weight (200 pounds) required one member of the crew to withdraw before lift-off. When the balloon landed in a field in Middlesex, an irate farmer threatened to destroy it because of damage to his crops.

"Citoyenne Henri" is the only known name of the young woman who accompanied noted aeronaut Jacques Garnerin on a 1798 flight. When Garnerin announced that he would have a female partner, the Paris

police issued an injunction against the flight. Had he, the director of police inquired, "foreseen the accident which might result by the pressure of the air upon organs so delicate as those of a young woman?" Garnerin appealed to a higher tribunal and the flight was cleared for lift-off.

Marie Madeleine Sophie Blanchard, the widow of ballooning pioneer Jean-Pierre Blanchard, was the first woman to make repeated trips on her own. On July 6, 1819, horrified spectators watched as her balloon burst into flames and crashed onto the rooftops of Paris. The fatal flight was the aeronaut's sixty-seventh.

Elisa Garnerin, the niece of Jacques Garnerin, was the first woman parachutist, that being her customary manner of exiting from a balloon.

Madame Johnson, America's first female aeronaut, went up in a balloon from New York's Castle Garden on October 18, 1825. Johnson sailed across the East River and Brooklyn before touching down in a New Jersey marsh "without the least injury except getting wet."

Jeannette Piccard♀ set the altitude record for a woman balloonist—57,579 feet—on October 23, 1934. She and her husband, Jean Piccard, were conducting a study of cosmic rays.

Vera Simons, an artist, is one of five women in the United States today who are licensed to fly helium balloons. Her ten-story craft is called the *Da-Vinci TransAmerica.*

SIX WHO'LL JOURNEY INTO SPACE

In the summer of 1978 six women were selected from among the 1,500 who applied for the astronaut training program. They could be assigned to orbital missions in the space shuttle program in the early 1980s. Requirements for applicants included a bachelor's degree with a major in mathematics, engineering, biological or physical science; excellent health; a height of 60 to 76 inches; and vision corrected to 20/20. The first half-dozen women to join the U.S. space corps as astronauts were:

Sally Ride, an astrophysicist.
Anna L. Fisher, a physician and expert in X-ray crystallography.
Shannon W. Lucid, a Ph.D. in biochemistry and the only mother in the group.
Margaret Rhea Seddon, a surgeon.
Kathryn D. Sullivan, a geophysicist.
Judith Resnik, an electrical engineer. Says Resnik, "Astronauts don't have to be either very feminine or very masculine women, or very superhuman males, or any color or anything. It's about people in space."

THIRTEEN WHO WON'T

It wasn't always just "about people in space." In the early 1960s twenty-six women pilots were also tested for the space program to see if women could qualify. Although thirteen of them passed the tests, none were accepted, and no reason was ever given. As a group, the women pilots who passed the tests averaged 4,500 flying hours; the male astronauts who were selected averaged 2,500. Some of the women had more than 10,000 flying hours—three times the amount required by NASA. Nevertheless, the navy stopped testing women. As they go into orbit, the women astronauts of the 1980s may recall:

Jerrie Cobb, a licensed pilot since the age of sixteen who had logged more than 7,000 pilot hours and set three speed and altitude records.

Jane Hart, wife of Senator Philip Hart, mother of eight children, and an accomplished airplane and helicopter pilot.

Rhea Hurrle Allison
Myrtle T. Cagle
Jan Dietrich
Marion Dietrich
Mary Wallace Funk
Sara Lee Gorelick
Jean F. Hixson
Irene Leverton
Jerry Sloan
Bernice Trimble Steadman
Gene Nora Stumbough

AND TWO FEMALES WHO HAVE ALREADY BEEN IN ORBIT

Valentina Tereshkova, a Soviet cosmonaut, whose preorbital training was as a parachute jumper, is the only woman to have been in space thus far. In a three-day mission in June 1963, Tereshkova made forty-eight orbits totaling 1,225,000 miles. But neither Tereshkova nor any other female cosmonaut has been in space since.

Stryelka, the other female Soviet space traveler, was a mongrel dog. In August 1960 she and a canine companion became the first living creatures to return successfully to earth after being in space. Stryelka made seventeen circuits of the globe. Nikita Khrushchev gave one of her puppies to Caroline Kennedy as a gift.

Astronomer Maria Mitchell (seated), a member of Vassar's first faculty, at work in her observatory. *Vassar College Library.* (SEEING STARS)

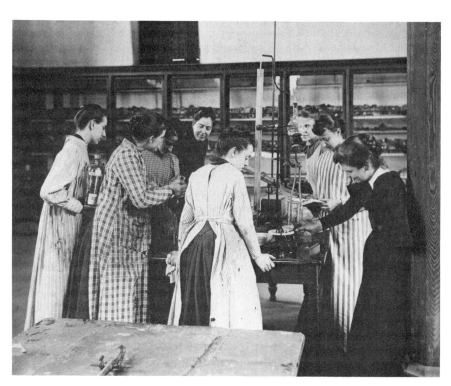

Women prepare to invade the sciences. The chemistry laboratory at Wellesley College, circa 1890. *Wellesley College Archives.* (FOUNDING THE SEVEN SISTERS)

elighted to be a Marine—seven "lady hell cats" are sworn in for World War 1 duty. *ational Archives.* (SOME LADY HELL CATS)

ˡah Sampson Gannett delivers a message to ˡe Washington. She served as a soldier in the ˡican Revolution under the name of Robert ˡeff. (EIGHT WHO FOUGHT IN THE REVOLU-ˡRY WAR)

Sharpshooter Annie Oakley could, while perched on the back of a moving horse, demolish a glass. *Library of Congress.* (THE WILD WEST AND THE BIG TOP)

Explorer May French Sheldon in the evening gown she wore for a state visit to an African chief. (TEN EXPLORERS)

In a photographer's studio, Fay Fuller recreates her ascent of 14,000-foot Mount Rainier in 1890. *Washington State Historical Society*. (CLIMB EVERY MOUNTAIN)

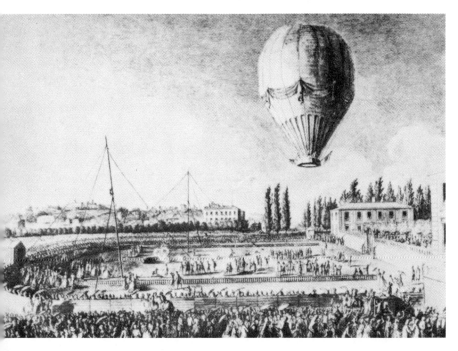

Madame Thible, the first female aeronaut, ascends in a balloon: Lyons, France, 1784.
(EIGHT FLOATING UPWARD)

The first women to be named by NASA as astronaut candidates. Left to right, Margaret Rhea Seddon, Anna L. Fisher, Judith Resnik, Shannon W. Lucid, Sally Ride, and Kathryn D. Sullivan. *National Aeronautics and Space Administration.* (SIX WHO'LL JOURNEY INTO SPACE)

XI ⚘ *THAT'S ENTERTAINMENT*

THE FIRST ACTRESSES

⚘

For most of history, dramatic performance has been a male prerogative. It wasn't until some 400 years ago that women began to be allowed on stage.

O-Kuni was a young woman who learned simple religious dances at the shrine at Izumo, Japan, and came to Kyoto in 1586. She soon began to improvise on her demure dances, adding broad comedic touches and erotic meanings. O-Kuni was a hit.

The Onna Kabuki, or Women's Kabuki, were troupes of dancing girls inspired by O-Kuni. But because many of the performers continued to work after the show in another role, organized brothel keepers objected to the competition and the government abolished their troupe "to preserve public morality." Young men took over and, as James Michener has put it, "gross immorality of a different type flourished until the young men also were driven off the stage." Only then did Kabuki go "straight"—in drag. Meanwhile, in Europe, female performers were just starting to put their toes through the stage door.

Isabella Andreini (1562–1604) was among the first, and was the most famous, of the prima donnas of the Commedia dell'Arte, the popular theater of Italy. Andreini was also a writer: her pastoral play *Mirtilla* was published in 1588, and her collected letters appeared posthumously in 1607.

Adrienne Lecouvreur (1692–1730) made her Comédie Française debut in 1717. Her life was shadowed by a love and tragedy as poignant as any she performed, and the story of her ill-fated romance and probable poisoning by a jealous rival lives on in the opera *Adriana Lecouvreur* by Francesco Cilèa.

Women did not appear on the stage in England until the Restoration, in 1660. By then, in fact, no one had appeared on an English stage in twenty years. Among the first English actresses were:

Mrs. Hughes, who performed the role of Desdemona beginning in October 1660.

Mary Sanderson,♀ who appeared as Juliet in 1662 (a male actor, however, played the nurse). Later known as *Mrs. Betterton,* she and her husband, Thomas, brought to dramatic performance a naturalistic style and interpretation, establishing a new stylistic tradition that continues to the present.

170

PLAYING THE WOMAN

━━━━━━━━━━━━━━━━ ❦ ━━━━━━━━━━━━━━━━

Ray Bolger cavorted as *Charley's Aunt* and Tony Curtis transformed himself into Marilyn Monroe's ♀ girlish chum in *Some Like It Hot,* but other actors have spent their entire onstage lives in women's skirts. ***Phylades of Cilicia*** and ***Bathyllus of Alexandria*** performed women's parts in the second-century Roman theater, and women have always been played by men in the classic theater of China. ***Onnagata*** (literally, "women actors") are the men in the Kabuki theater of Japan who specialize in the performance of women's roles, usually courtesans. Because women were forbidden on the stages of Europe until the 1660s, men played all female parts. The "boy actresses" of Elizabethan England were the first to speak the lines of Shakespeare's women. Sir Laurence Olivier, continuing this tradition, made his acting debut in 1922 as Katherine in *The Taming of the Shrew.* Among the actors who almost always played female roles:

Richard Robinson began playing women's parts at Shakespeare's Globe Theatre while still a youngster in 1613. As his voice changed, so did his roles, and by 1621 he had graduated to male leads. Robinson died defending the cause of King Charles I.

Alexander Cooke grew wealthy enough as an onstage woman to leave 50 pounds to each of his children when he died in 1614, quite a fortune at that time.

Robert Goughe first played female parts with Burbage's troupe (where Shakespeare got his start). ***Alexander Goughe,*** his son, followed in his father's footsteps and played a succession of Elizabethan heroines.

Edward Kynaston, described as "the handsomest of men, likewise the most beautiful of women," was the last and best-known of the Shakespearean "boy actresses." King Charles II, wondering why the curtain was late at a performance of *Hamlet,* was informed that the queen had "not yet shaved." "Odds fish," quipped the king. "Then we'll wait till her barber has done with her." Apparently the actor/actress was worth waiting for. "The loveliest lady I ever saw," said Alexander Pope.

Waldon was the name used by a French man who toured the United States in the early nineteenth century and, according to a contemporary account, "proved himself to be one of the best Spanish dancers in women's dress this country has ever seen."

Julian Eltinge, whose stage debut took place in 1904, was the first actor of female roles to achieve a sustained success in modern times. His tight-corseted beauty was said to rival that of most of the leading actresses of the day. Lillian Russell♀ designed his make-up.

Mei Lanfang of the Original Municipal Peking Opera Troupe was the most famous portrayer of *tan* or female roles in China in the first half of the nineteenth century. His son ***Mei Baojiu*** continues as a leading female impersonator with the Peking Opera today.

HAND ME MY DOUBLET AND HOSE:
Actresses Who Portrayed Shakespeare's Heroes

There have been at least fifty female Hamlets and thirty female Romeos—in fact, scarcely a Shakespearean hero has not been played by a woman. This switch-around was particularly popular in the nineteenth century, when several mother-daughter combinations and pairs of sisters appeared as the lovers in *Romeo and Juliet.* Among the most noteworthy "male" performers:

Kitty Clive, the first woman to portray a Shakespearean male, appeared as Shylock in the eighteenth century.

Sarah Siddons,♀ the noted actress, played Hamlet in 1775, 1786, and, for the last time, in Dublin in 1802.

Mrs. Webb, renowned for playing old women, was an old man instead when she acted Falstaff in 1786. Critics considered this idea to be in execrable taste. One *Mrs. Glover* fared no better with the same role in 1833, even though she boasted one of the widest girths on the English stage.

Charlotte Cushman,♀ the most respected nineteenth-century female interpreter of male parts, was able to make spectators totally oblivious to her gender. A fine fencer, Cushman played Romeo to her sister *Susan*'s Juliet in her own production of the play—the first faithful-to-Shakespeare version in more than two centuries. Cushman was the first female Hotspur on record; she excelled as Hamlet and also in such female Shakespearean roles as Lady Macbeth.

Charlotte Crampton managed to play Hamlet, Iago, Romeo, Shylock, and Richard III along with three female parts during one busy week in the mid-nineteenth century.

Malinda Jones was Romeo to her daughter *Avonia*'s Juliet in Albany, New York, in 1857. *Mrs. Freeman* played Romeo to the Juliet of her daughter *Maria Foote* in 1810; and *Emma Feist* was Romeo to her sister *Ellen*'s Juliet. *Esme Beringer* and her sister were the star-crossed couple at the Prince of Wales Theatre in 1896.

Sarah Bernhardt♀ was a novel Hamlet in Paris and London in 1899. Her interpretation included kicking Polonius in the shins and knocking the heads of Rosencrantz and Guildenstern together.

Sybil Ward alternated between the title role and every other part in *Hamlet.*

Emily Burke was Iago to her uncle, Henry Talbot's, Othello. She played Petruchio, too.

Dorothea Baird played Petruchio in an all-female version of *The Taming of the Shrew* at Oxford, England, in 1893.

Eva Le Gallienne♀ appeared as Hamlet before World War II. Despite women's liberation, no more recent female interpreters of the melancholy Dane have stepped forward.

THE FAMILY THAT ACTS TOGETHER
The Béjarts of France

※

Madeleine Béjart (1618–1672) was a member of a family of actors with their own company, Les Enfants de Famille, which included her brothers and sisters as well. Madeleine, an excellent actress, virtually managed the company, which failed on its debut in Paris in 1643. They went back to the provinces to perfect their act and triumphed on their return to Paris in 1658. Another member of the company was sister *Geneviève Béjart* (1624–1675). Madeleine became the mistress of Molière, who had joined the company as a teen-ager; but her younger sister *Armande Grésinde Béjart* (ca. 1640–1700) married him in 1662. Armande was trained by Molière, playing the roles he wrote for her. After his death, she arranged for what was by then called the King's Troupe to merge with another company and, after some further rearrangements, the combined dramatic forces emerged as the Comédie Française.

The Kemble Dynasty

※

Sarah Wood, an English actress, married actor Roger Kemble in 1753. They had twelve children, the most famous of whom was . . .

Sarah (Kemble) Siddons ♀ (1755–1831), who married actor William Siddons. She started acting in her father's company while still a child and was outstanding in every role she undertook throughout her career. Her portrayal of Lady Macbeth is legendary. Her younger sister . . .

Elizabeth (Kemble) Whitlock (1761–1836) was married to actor Charles Whitlock and received great acclaim in England and on a United States tour. Their younger brother Charles Kemble had two performing daughters. One was . . .

Fanny (Frances Anne) Kemble ♀ (1809–1893), whose debut at Covent Garden as Juliet under her father's management in 1829 was a triumph. Fanny was married for a while to an American and lived in the South before the Civil War, an experience she described in *Journal of a Residence on a Georgian Plantation in 1838-1839,* a widely read indictment of slavery. Her sister . . .

Adelaide Kemble (1814–1879) followed the family trade with a difference and became an opera singer.

The American Barrymores

※

Louisa Lane Drew was for thirty years manager of Philadelphia's Arch Street Theatre. Married to actor John Drew, she became the matriarch of what would long be regarded as the First Family of the American theater. Her three children and two of her grandchildren began their training with her company.

Georgiana Drew (1856–1893) began performing with her parents' Philadelphia company; after marrying Maurice Barrymore she acted with him in Helena Modjeska's♀ company and elsewhere. Her son John set out to have a career as an artist, but the family tradition caught up with him a little later. But Lionel and . . .

Ethel Barrymore ♀ (1879–1959) were sent to grandmother Louisa to learn their craft. Ethel made her stage debut at the age of fourteen in her grandmother's Montreal production of *The School for Scandal,* then built her reputation in London (and turned down a marriage proposal from Winston Churchill). In 1928 Ethel Barrymore directed and starred in the first production at the Broadway theater named for her. She also appeared in silent films and first spoke onscreen in 1932 in *Rasputin and the Empress,* her only appearance with both her brothers.

Diana Barrymore, John's daughter, had a brief career as an actress before she died at the age of thirty-eight, soon after publication of her shocking and best-selling autobiography, *Too Much, Too Soon.* The title tells all.

CROWD PLEASERS

※

Peg Woffington (1714–1760) was a creature of gaiety and wit who sparkled off the London stage as well as on. As Sir Harry Wildair, a rakish gentleman in *The Constant Couple,* Peg was so convincing that, reportedly, she received an insistent marriage proposal from a lady who refused to believe that she was not what she seemed to be. Woffington lived with her leading man, actor David Garrick, but although they often talked of marriage, she had numerous other attachments.

Sarah Siddons ♀ (1755–1831), a willowy figure with dark, burning eyes and a melodic voice, conveyed such deep emotion that members of her audience were prone to fainting, and she was said to have greatly raised the price of "salts and hartshorn," two commodities used to revive consciousness. At her farewell appearance on July 29, 1812, as Lady Macbeth, the audience refused to let the play continue after Siddons's last scene. Her brother led her offstage as the curtain descended.

Charlotte Cushman ♀ (1816–1876), the first great American actress, was affectionately known as "our Charlotte," especially after she also became the first American player of either sex to conquer English audiences. A tall, commanding woman with a firm, square jaw, she was proud of her assertiveness. "I was born a tomboy; my earliest recollections are of dolls' heads ruthlessly cracked open to see what they were thinking about."

Ellen Terry ♀ (1857–1928), the eternal child-woman, youthful for more than half a century, was an outstanding Shakespearean performer. She was Sir Henry Irving's leading lady for twenty years and with George Bernard Shaw carried on a "paper courtship" for eight years until they finally met in 1900. At fifty-eight Terry fell in love with an American actor four years younger than her son and made him her third husband. The marriage lasted, as her daughter had predicted, for two years.

Helena Modjeska ♀ (1844–1909), a Polish dramatic actress, practiced English by performing in America until she was fluent enough to realize her lifelong ambition of acting the Bard in his native tongue. She became renowned as an interpreter of Shakespeare.

Eleanora Duse (1858–1924) refused to wear make-up on stage ("I don't paint myself; I make myself up morally"). Although she usually spoke in subdued tones, audiences hung on her every word, especially when she appeared as Camille. One of her most passionate attachments was to Italian poet Gabriele D'Annunzio, whom she so adored that she would stand outside his studio for hours, simply listening to the scratching of his pen.

Sarah Bernhardt ♀ (1844–1923) first attracted attention while performing with the Comédie Française in the 1870s. Oscar Wilde hailed her as "the divine Sarah"—and audiences on two continents agreed. She ran her own theater in Paris, wrote plays in which she acted, penned poetry, and was also a sculptor and painter. She delighted in traveling with her rosewood coffin, always ready for the ultimate event; spent profligately; and acted continuously, even after her leg was amputated in 1915. She made four "farewell tours" of America: in 1905, 1910, 1912, and 1916.

Maude Adams (1872–1953) was beloved for her performances in James Barrie's *Peter Pan,* a role for which her diminutive voice and frame were ideally suited. Adams became the highest-paid performer of her time, earning more than $1 million a year until she retired in 1918. She continued to work behind the scenes and was noted as an inventor of lighting devices and a professor of theater arts.

Minnie Maddern Fiske (1865–1932) popularized Ibsen in the United States and became a crowd pleaser despite her refusal to appear in popular entertainments for "tired businessmen." Each opening night Mrs. Fiske, always unsure of her talent, suffered from nervousness. "I never said I could act," she remarked to critic Alexander Woollcott after a particularly bravura performance.

Ethel Barrymore ♀ (1879–1959) had her first success in *Captain Jinks of the Horse Marines* on February 4, 1901, and forty years later was still going strong on Broadway in Emlyn Williams's *The Corn Is Green.* Barrymore's bearing was so regal that, try as he would, Clifford Odets could not find an appropriately shabby hat for her to wear as a lowly charwoman in his film *None but the Lonely Heart.* "It's no use!" he moaned as he tossed the hats aside. "You still look like a queen."

HELEN HAYES'S ♀ LIST OF "ROLES I WOULD HAVE LIKED TO PLAY BUT NEVER DID"

❧

Mrs. Wiggs of the Cabbage Patch
L'Aiglon by Rostand, in French, because I studied the role once for a whole year with a student of Bernhardt's.♀

Hecuba in *The Trojan Women.*
Becky Sharp in Langdon Mitchell's *Vanity Fair.*

The two I wanted most to play, I have done: Shaw's *Cleopatra* and *Mary Tyrone* in Eugene O'Neill's *Long Day's Journey into Night.* I played both far from Broadway.

Exclusively for *Womanlist*

BEHIND THE SCENES

✌

Mary Sanderson Betterton,♀ an actress, was one of the first women to manage a theatrical company. With her actor husband, Thomas Betterton, she ran the Duke's Company at the Dorset Garden Theatre in seventeenth-century London. Her most taxing job was looking after unruly actresses who often stole costumes and had a tendency to disappear after receiving an attractive offer from a gentleman.

Madame Lucia Elizabeth Vestris took over the management of the small Olympia Theatre in London in 1831 and, with a topnotch acting company, turned it into the first successful "intimate" theater. Two Vestris innovations are still with us: actors wearing contemporary costumes on stage, and performances that end by eleven o'clock (a boon to theater goers who had straggled home in the wee hours of the morning). Vestris later managed the Covent Garden Theatre.

Laura Keene opened her own theater in Baltimore in 1856, becoming the first American female manager. She wrote, directed, stitched costumes, and acted in her own productions. It was under her direction that Tom Taylor's *Our American Cousin* was performed for Abraham Lincoln at Ford's Theatre on the fateful evening of April 14, 1865.

Emma Cons thought that the dilapidated Old Vic Theatre in London could be revitalized to bring high-quality entertainment to the poor. Well-to-do, middle-aged, and proper, she abolished the sale of liquor in the theater and in the early 1900s began a program of lectures, recitals, and music-hall entertainment. She was succeeded by . . .

Lillian Bayliss, her niece, in 1912, who two years later inaugurated the magnificent productions of Shakespeare for which the company is justly famous.

Eva Le Gallienne♀ started the Civic Repertory Theater, the first professional repertory theater in the United States, in 1926 on the theory that mass audiences could be attracted to good European drama. She was right, but her enterprise was unable to weather the depression, and it folded in 1932.

Cheryl Crawford, with Lee Strasberg and Harold Clurman, founded the Group Theatre in 1931, which became famous for its plays of social consciousness by young American playwrights, and its actors trained in naturalistic acting based on the Stanislavski system, later dubbed "The Method."

Hallie Flanagan, a professor of drama at Vassar, headed the Federal Theatre Project, a depression-era government project designed to give jobs to theater folk. Flanagan organized countless productions, presenting them in hundreds of towns, often in places where live theater had never been seen before.

Antoinette Perry, for whom the theater's annual Tony awards are named, was a producer and manager as well as an actress, and a founder of the American Theater Wing. She gave many young and inexperienced performers their first encouragement and opportunity.

Zelda Fichlander turned a decrepit old movie house in Washington, D.C., into the Arena Stage Theater in 1950, one of America's most successful regional theaters.

Judith Malina, with her husband, Julian Beck, founded the Living Theatre in 1947 to showcase the plays of unknown American playwrights. One of their successes was Jack Gelber's *The Connection* (1959), a play about a group of junkies waiting for a fix that drew the audience into unexpected dialogue with the actors.

Ellen Stewart founded the La Mama Experimental Theatre Club in New York City in the early 1960s and has presided over its growth as an important dramatic institution presenting innovative acting, writing, and directing talent.

"GLORIFYING THE AMERICAN GIRL":
Six Ziegfeld Follies Beauties and What Became of Them

———————————————— ❧ ————————————————

Lillian Lorraine, who sparkled in the Follies of 1910, was the first Follies girl to become the darling of the Great White Way and was one of Ziggy's personal darlings, but fast living and hard drinking made her the "Girl of Lost Chances." Erratic and unstable, she once set fire to her boardinghouse with a cigarette; her second husband was imprisoned for an attempt on Ziegfeld's life; and in 1921 she slipped on the ice and seriously injured her spine. Lorraine died in 1955 at the age of sixty-three, broke and drunk. When asked if she would do anything differently if she could, she replied, "I don't think I would have bobbed my hair."

Jessica Reed came a long way from slinging hash in Texas to the Follies of 1919, and the titian-haired knockout rapidly became the highest-paid chorus girl in the world. Reed chalked up five husbands, among them the eighteen-year-old scion of a wealthy Cleveland family, who met her on a train and proposed that night, completely forgetting his debutante fiancée. Reed went through several fortunes, wound up as a buy-me-a-drink hostess in a Chicago café, and was on welfare before dying penniless at age forty-three.

Olive Thomas left the Follies for Hollywood and a $2,500-a-week salary in 1917; married Jack Pickford, Mary's[?] brother; and soon rivaled her sister-in-law as the virginal darling of films. That illusion dissolved in 1920, when she was found dead in Paris of bichloride poisoning. Suicide or accident? The case remains unsolved—but it was rumored that Olive the innocent had frequented the worst dives in the city, possibly in search of heroin for her husband.

Dolores, the most spectacular beauty ever to grace the Follies (she made her

debut in 1917), was known as the "Girl Who Never Smiled." She didn't
have to when, over six feet tall, she simply stood there or paraded lan-
guidly across the stage decked out in peacock feathers. She had been ordinary Kathleen Rose before being discovered by fashion designer
Lady Duff-Gordon,♀ who taught her to walk, move, and talk in low,
well-bred tones. After six years Dolores left the Follies to marry multimillionaire Tudor Wilkinson, ignoring Ziegfeld's prediction: "You will
come back someday. They always do." She never did—the marriage
was a happy one.

Justine Johnson, a natural blond with blue eyes and a pink-and-white complexion, was New York's favorite photographic model before she appeared in the 1916 Follies as Columbia wrapped in an American flag.
She left the Follies to work as a dramatic actress and married film producer William Wanger, then in mid-life was seized by a new ambition:
to become a pathologist. She began working at New York's College of
Physicians and Surgeons and, although she never received a medical
degree, became highly respected in the field. On April 14, 1940, Justine
Wanger was part of the scientific team that announced a five-day cure
for syphilis.

Hilda Ferguson, a blond flapper with a rosebud mouth and turned-up nose,
palled around with an assortment of politicians, financiers, and gang-
sters. As a result she was involved in several interesting court cases, including the one that sought to determine how "Tough Willie" McCabe,
bodyguard of mobster Arnold Rothstein, was slugged and stabbed at
the 61 Club. Ferguson claimed to know nothing. "My dear," she
breathed to the judge, "I was in the ladies' room at the time." True to a
Hollywood scenario, she fell in love with an ordinary "nice" guy, tried
to break her gin habit for him, but couldn't make it and died at age
thirty of peritonitis.

Some other Ziegfeld beauties and stars: *Louise Andrews* (who married
boxer Bugs Baer), *Adele Astaire, Nora Bayes, Fanny Brice,*♀ *Jessica Brown,*
Betty Compton (who married New York's dapper mayor Jimmy Walker),
Marion Davies,♀ *Bessie McCoy Davis* (the "Yama Yama Girl"), the *Dolly*
Sisters,♀ *Billie Dove, Irene Dunne, Peggy Fears* (who became a producer in
her own right), *Susan Fleming* (who married Harpo Marx), *Gladys Glad*
(who married journalist Mark Hellinger), *Paulette Goddard,*♀ *Anna Held*♀
(Ziegfeld's first wife), *Peggy Hopkins Joyce* ♀ (who married better and more
often than any other Ziegfeld girl), *Ruby Keeler, Gypsy Rose Lee,*♀ *Marilyn*
Miller,♀ *Mae Murray, Nita Naldi,*♀ *Barbara Stanwyck,*♀ *Lilyan Tashman,* and
Sophie Tucker.

SEVEN RULES OF THE HONKY-TONKS

"Life upon the wicked stage" could turn out to be more regimented than a
woman could imagine. Here are some of the rules composed by music-hall
managers to create order out of the backstage chaos of vaudeville life:

- Ladies must be dressed and in the boxes by 7:30.
- Ladies must turn down the gas every time they leave the dressing rooms.
- All lady performers must wear tights.
- Ladies are not allowed to smoke during the show.
- Ladies must settle up before dressing.
- Ladies are allowed only two packages of cigarettes nightly.
- Ladies are not allowed to run each other down to the customers in the boxes.

From Joe Laurie, Jr., *Vaudeville: From the Honky-Tonks to the Palace* (New York: Henry Holt, 1953)

FOURTEEN STARS WHO STARTED IN THE CHORUS

❦

June Allyson
Joan Crawford
Marie Dressler ♀ (she organized Chorus Equity in 1919)
Jeanne Eagels
Lena Horne ♀
Tina Louise
Myrna Loy
Shirley MacLaine
Julie Newmar ♀
Ginger Rogers
Barbara Stanwyck ♀
Ethel Waters ♀
Peggy Wood
Gretchen Wyler

SIX WHO GOT A BREAK AT THE COTTON CLUB

❦

In the 1920s and 1930s, Harlem's Cotton Club was *the* place for hearing the latest jazz, doing the latest dance steps, and admiring a chorus line renowned for its beauty. Harlem residents themselves were not welcome customers, however—although the entertainers were black, the audience was white only. Over the years many talented women got a break of one kind or another at the Cotton Club:

Lena Horne ♀ was less than sixteen years old and shaking with stage fright when she was hired for the chorus in 1933. Two years later, angered when her stepfather was refused admission to the club, Horne said she was quitting. At that news the club's gangster bosses beat up her stepfather, pushed his head into a toilet bowl, and threw him out. The terrified chorus girl was forced to finish the night's shows, then left the building huddled among the other women, never to return.

Dorothy Fields,♀ twenty-three, got her first break at the Cotton Club collaborating with Jimmy McHugh on the music for the December 1927 show and invited her father, comedian Lew Fields of Weber and Fields, to opening night. In mid-show Dorothy realized that the lyrics to one song had been altered to make them more risqué. Father Fields told the gangster owner "that if he didn't announce that his daughter did not write those lyrics he would knock his block off. The gangster obliged." Fields and McHugh later went on to Broadway shows and such songs as "On the Sunny Side of the Street" and "I'm in the Mood for Love."

Ethel Waters ♀ had been performing in a basement dive for three years when she was hired by the Cotton Club. One night in 1933, her audience heard "Stormy Weather" sung for the first time, as Waters leaned against a lamppost in a deep blue spotlight. Within days the singer and the song were the talk of New York, and she was signed by Irving Berlin for his new revue, *As Thousands Cheer.*

Mildred Dixon, a short, lively partner in a dancing duo, got a romantic break when she opened at the Cotton Club on December 4, 1927. She was spotted by Duke Ellington, also making his first club appearance, who was reportedly so preoccupied with her that his band gave one of its rare poor performances. Dixon soon became the second Mrs. Ellington.

Lucille Watson succeeded in 1932 in breaking the club's rule that no female performer could be "darker than a light olive tint" by displaying so much talent that the management simply couldn't turn her down. Fears that audiences would be turned off by a dark-skinned woman did not materialize, and Watson remained with the club for eight years, later becoming Mrs. Louis Armstrong.

Dorothy Dandridge,♀ as part of the singing Dandridge Sisters act, appeared at the club in 1938 when she was fourteen. There she fell madly in love with dancer Harold Nicholas, his big car, and his generosity, even though she was warned that he had been around far too much. A few years later Nicholas became her first husband in a union that proved to be brief. Dorothy was the only one of the sister act to achieve stardom, but happiness eluded her. She died in 1965 at age forty-two of "acute drug intoxication."

Other Cotton Club women include: *Juanita Boisseau, Hyacinth Curtis, Peggy Griffiths, Carolyn Rich Henderson, Edna Mae Holly* (who married Sugar Ray Robinson), *Vivian Jackson, Mae Johnson, Winnie Johnson, Evelyn Sheppard, Maudine Simmons, Ethel Sissle* (wife of bandleader Noble Sissle), and *Isabel Washington* (who met Adam Clayton Powell while she was performing at the club and became his first wife).

STRICTLY FEMALE?

Karyl Norman, billed as the "Creole Fashion Plate," was described as the best female impersonator on the stage in 1928.

Candy Darling became a transvestite superstar with a cameo appearance in the 1971 Andy Warhol production *Flesh.* Darling, who wore female garb both onstage and off, refused chemotherapy treatment when he was dying of cancer because it might cause his nails and hair to fall out.

Craig Russell, after the release of the movie *Outrageous,* became the best-known of today's female impersonators, vying for that title with the other leading Judy Garland impersonator, *Jim Bailey.*

Divine, 300-plus pounds, blazing orange wig, and all, was an unmistakable standout in the cult film *Pink Flamingos.*

Arthur Blake, sixtyish, has had a thirty-five-year career as an onstage woman, mostly at the Blue Angel in San Francisco. He has entertained at deb parties, cotillions, London's Palladium, and twice at the White House when Franklin Roosevelt was in residence. "FDR would say, 'Do me. Now do Eleanor. Now do both of us.' "

Holly Woodlawn, born Harold Eisenberg and described as a cross between Marilyn Monroe ♀ and Jerry Lewis, achieved renown in Andy Warhol's *Trash* (1970). Woodlawn's stage act features a chatty alter ego named Chi-Chi Castenets.

Charles Pierce, a six-footer from upstate New York, had his own show for twelve years in San Francisco before he brought it to Manhattan. His impersonations include a haggard Auntie Mame.

Danny La Rue performs in London's West End wearing glittering gowns, blond hair, and red nail polish.

J. C. Gaynor impersonates Diana Ross ♀ and Shirley Bassey.

Charles Ludlam founded the Ridiculous Theatrical Company in New York to present transvestite drama.

SEVEN "DIZZY DAMES" OF RADIO

❧

Gracie Allen, whose husband, George Burns, happily played straight man to her scatterbrained malapropisms, was on the air from 1932 to 1950, before moving to TV. In 1940 Gracie announced her candidacy for president on the Surprise Party ticket and wrote an article, "America's Next President Should Be a Woman," for a national magazine.

Jane Ace was the Mrs. Malaprop *par excellence* for her husband, Goodman Ace, and their show, "Easy Aces," from 1931 to 1945, with such lines as "Time wounds all heels" and "I didn't do it of my own violation."

Minerva Pious was Mrs. Nussbaum, one of the neighbors in "Allen's Alley" in the 1940s, who effectively misunderstood everything she heard.

Shirley Mitchell played Alice Darling, the young man-chasing woman who worked in a war plant and rented a room from Fibber and Molly McGee. The character lasted from 1943 only until the regular male character actor returned from a stint in the navy in early 1946.

Judy Canova played the "Queen of the Hillbillies," wide-eyed and innocent, on "The Judy Canova Show" from 1943 to 1953.

Lulu McConnell was the woman panelist on "It Pays to Be Ignorant," a spoof of quiz shows that ran from 1942 to 1949, whose panelists managed never to answer such erudite questions as "What color was George Washington's white horse?"

Marie Wilson was "My Friend Irma" on a show that premiered in 1947.

Irma's wonderfully illogical logic followed all her notions to the ultimately wrong conclusion—and yet everything always worked out for the best until the end of the run in 1954.

Contributed by Norman Weiser

... AND SOME SMART ONES

ॐ

Mary Livingstone ♀ was Sadie Marks and a clerk at the May Company department store in Los Angeles when she met vaudeville star Jack Benny. She joined his radio show two years after it started in 1932 and continued to appear until the 1950s. Her main task was to attempt to bring Benny, in real life her husband, back to reality.

Marian Jordan was the long-suffering, good-humored Molly McGee, wife of the perpetually blundering but lovable Fibber (her husband, Jim Jordan), from 1935 to 1957.

The panelists on "Leave It to the Girls," who solved listeners' problems, included at one time or another between 1945 and 1949 *Dorothy Kilgallen, Robin Chandler, Eloise McElhone, Ilka Chase, Lucille Ball,* ♀ *Sylvia Sidney* ♀ *Constance Bennett,* and *Edith Gwynn,* with moderator *Paula Stone.*

Natalie Masters was "Candy Matson," a sharp detective who always got the murderer in the end, from 1949 to 1951. In the last script, the police officer whom she loved finally proposed to Candy, who announced she had worked on her last case.

Alice Frost and her successor, *Barbara Britton,* were Pam North, of the crime-fighting team of "Mr. and Mrs. North," whose logical thought processes and "female intuition" usually solved the crime—or at least uncovered the motive for it. The show started as a sitcom in 1941, but quickly found murder and mystery, a format that lasted into the midfifties and briefly moved to TV.

Gertrude Berg was Molly, the wise matriarch of "The Goldbergs," of which she was creator, chief writer, producer, and director as well as star performer from 1929 to 1945. As *Molly and Me,* the show resurfaced on Broadway in 1948 and was revived in 1980.

Lassie, the collie, had her own show following her successful screen portrayal in *Lassie Come Home,* from 1947 to 1950.

Contributed by Norman Weiser

THE THREE LONGEST-PLAYING SOAP OPERA ACTRESSES ON RADIO

ॐ

Because most radio soaps were on the air for so long, their heroines were played by a succession of actresses. Only three actresses kept the same role for the complete—or nearly complete—run of the series.

Virginia Payne played Oxydol's own "Ma Perkins" for the entire twenty-seven years the program was on the air, a total of 7,065 broadcasts. Ma offered succor and security to the inhabitants of Rushville Center, a small town where she ran a lumberyard.

Anne Elstner was "Stella Dallas" for eighteen and a half years. She commuted to New York five days a week from Stockton, New Jersey, and missed only two broadcasts in all that time. Based on a popular novel, the serial was "the true-to-life story of mother love and sacrifice, in which Stella Dallas saw her own beloved daughter Laurel marry into wealth and society and, realizing the difference in their tastes and worlds, went out of Laurel's life." Well, almost.

Mary Jane Higby appeared as Joan Field Davis in the popular show "When a Girl Marries" from shortly after its inception on CBS in 1939 until it ended in 1958. "This tender, human story of young married life . . . is dedicated to everyone who has ever been in love."

FIFTEEN WHO SANG ON "YOUR HIT PARADE"

That weekly program, featuring the most popular songs of the week, was heard on radio from 1935 through the 1940s and continued on television until 1959.

Joan Edwards
Fredda Gibbson (later "her nibs, Miss Georgia Gibbs")
Eileen Wilson
Doris Day ?
Kay Lorraine
Kay Thompson
Margaret McCrea
Bonnie Baker (known as "Wee Bonnie Baker"; her hit song was "Oh Johnny")
Dinah Shore
Bea Wain
Dorothy Collins
Gogo De Lys
Ginny Simms
Martha Tilton ("Liltin' Martha Tilton")
Giselle MacKenzie

The accompanying organist was *Ethel Smith.*

FIVE UNIQUE NOISEMAKERS

Sarah Fussell, Leone Ledoux, and *Madeleine Pierce* provided the sounds of crying babies when they were needed on radio. Sobbing into a pillow sometimes produced the desired effect. Fussell specialized in playing little boys' roles as well. Ledoux was the first "Baby Dumpling" Alexander and the first Cookie, the son and daughter of Blondie and Dagwood Bumstead. She also played the triplets Abigail, Deborah, and Constance Barbour, born into "One Man's Family" on January 1, 1949.

Nancy Kelly was much in demand as a radio "screamer" when she was seventeen years old. Hers were the shrieks of the terrified females heard on "Gangbusters," "Front Page Farrell," and "The March of Time," among other shows.

Ora Nichols was the only sound-effects woman to work in radio.

UNSEEN VOICES

Lucille Laverne was the voice of the wicked witch in Walt Disney's *Snow White and the Seven Dwarfs*. A galaxy of stars have performed offscreen in Disney pictures, including *Judy Garland,*♀ *Peggy Lee, Angela Lansbury, Eartha Kitt,* and *Pearl Bailey.*

Grace Lantz was the voice of Woody Woodpecker in her husband Walter Lantz's cartoons.

Mercedes McCambridge was the voice of the demon in *The Exorcist.*

Beverly Sills ♀ was the voice of the "Rinso White" bird call on radio.

Marnie Nixon supplied the singing voices of any number of actresses in film musicals, from Deborah Kerr in *The King and I* to Audrey Hepburn♀ in *My Fair Lady.*

NINE WOMEN OF "TODAY"

The "Today Show" debuted at 7:00 A.M. on Monday, January 14, 1952, with Dave Garroway as host. A few months later the "Today Girl" was introduced to chat amiably about fashion, food, homemaking and other "feminine" concerns. Among the occupants of the position, famous, later to be famous, and resolutely obscure:

Estelle Parsons, the first "Today Girl," who began as a $75-a-week production assistant and ended up interviewing such guests as Eleanor Roosevelt,♀ who dozed off in the middle of the conversation. Parsons was up to $1,000 a week when she left to become an actress.

Helen O'Connell, the big-band singer.

Betsy Palmer, who reportedly couldn't abide the high-strung Garroway early in the morning and quit the show at the urging of her husband.

Florence Henderson, who, unawed by Garroway, once smacked him in the face on the air with her seat cushion in response to what she thought was a nasty remark.

Beryl Pfizer, whom Dave Garroway spotted on a New York bus but who disappeared before he could make contact. Pleasantly astonished when she showed up as the new "Today Girl," he pursued her avidly off-camera, but to no avail.

Louise King, the "Today Girl" in 1961, who was less fond of host John Chancellor than he was of her. Miffed by her off-camera coldness, he began to make on-camera fun of her. The conflict was resolved with the arrival of Hugh Downs as host.

Maureen O'Sullivan, the film star, who suffered an immediate attack of bad chemistry with Hugh Downs, which ripened as both developed psychosomatic complaints. After six months O'Sullivan was given the ax. Her successor was ...

Barbara Walters,♀ a "Today" writer who proceeded to startle celebrities with questions that *Newsweek* was to call "dum-dum bullets swaddled in angora." She asked Mamie Eisenhower if she was familiar with rumors about her drinking and Lady Bird Johnson if she knew about her husband's reputation as a skirt chaser. On April 22, 1976, after twelve years as queen of "Today," she signed a five-year contract with ABC for $1 million a year, making her the world's highest-salaried newscaster.

Jane Pauley. One day during her tryout period, Pauley woke from a nap to discover with horror that it was past six. Dressing in a fever of anxiety, she demolished a pair of panty hose and raced to the studio—only to discover that the time was 6:00 P.M., not 6:00 A.M.

WHEN WOMEN RULED THE SILVER SCREEN

Film historian Anthony Slide asserts that "during the silent era, women may be said to have virtually controlled the film industry." In the early years of film, job opportunities for women were unlimited. Herewith some of those behind-the-scenes operatives:

- Camerawomen: *Dorothy Dunn, Grace Davison,* and *Margaret Ordway.*
- Scenario writers (in 1918 alone, forty-four women were employed as writers): *Beulah Marie Dix, Frances Marion*♀ (described in a *New York Times* obituary as the dean of Hollywood screenwriters), *Beth Meredyth,* and *Anita Loos*♀ (of whom much more would later be heard).
- Publicists: *Beulah Livingston* (the screen's first publicist, responsible for rocketing Norma Talmadge to stardom) and *Billie Bristoe* (who handled publicity for all the major silent stars of England).
- Studio managers: *Alexia Durant, Nellie Grant, Lillian Greenberger,* and *Annie Marchant.*
- Film editor: *Margaret Booth* headed the MGM editorial department for many years and is still active in the film industry. She received credit as supervising editor on *The Sunshine Boys.*
- Fan magazine writers; *Adela Rogers St. John, Ruth Waterbury, Hazel Simpson Naylor, Gladys Hall,* and *Adele Whitely Fletcher,* among many others.

And in the slightly more obscure department:

- *Marion E. Wong,* headed the Mandarin Film Company in Oakland, California, in 1917 and is known to have produced only one feature, *The Curse of Quon Qwon.*

TEN SILENT DIRECTORS
— ﹡ —

In the silent era, at least thirty women were directors. Among them:

Alice Guy Blaché was the first woman to become prominent. She began directing in her native Paris and later made most of her movies in her own studio in Fort Lee, New Jersey, from 1910 to 1920. Among her films are *The Tigress* (1914) and *The Heart of a Painted Woman* (1915). "There is nothing connected with the staging of a motion picture that a woman cannot do as easily as a man," said Blaché. She stopped making films in 1922 after refusing a bid to direct *Tarzan of the Apes,* tried unsuccessfully to make a comeback in the late twenties, and died in New Jersey in 1968.

Lois Weber made movies with a message. *Where Are My Children?* (1916) opposed abortion and supported birth control; *The Jew's Christmas* (1913) criticized anti-Semitism; and *Hypocrites* (1915), controversial because it featured a nude girl symbolizing "The Naked Truth," exposed the foibles of society. Working with her husband, Phillips Smalley, Weber turned out two two-reelers a month from 1913 to 1924 and died penniless in Hollywood in 1939.

Cleo Madison, an actress for Universal and a militant suffragist, began directing in 1915. Among her films with a feminist bent were *A Soul Enslaved* (1916) and *Her Bitter Cup* (1916). She retired from acting in 1931 and died alone and forgotten in Burbank in 1964.

Lulu Warrenton, a buxom, middle-aged actress known for "mother roles," formed her own company in 1917 to direct movies for children. Her one film, *A Bit O' Heaven* (1917), was well received by critics, but two future projects never went into production. Warrenton retired in the 1920s and founded the Hollywood Girls' Club.

Jeanie MacPherson wrote the scenario for Universal's *The Tarantula* (1916), then, when the original negative was destroyed, was asked to direct the remake. Her experience brought on a nervous breakdown. While recovering, MacPherson met Cecil B. DeMille, who persuaded her to become his scenarist, a post to which she devoted the rest of her life.

Ida May Park and her husband, Joseph De Grasse, were a directing team. In eleven months of 1916 and 1917 they made twelve features, but in 1920 Park dropped out of directing for reasons that were never made public.

Margery Wilson claimed to be the first director to make a film on location, "without a studio, without a single set." The movie, *Insinuation,* was shot in Vermont in the 1920s; no prints survive. The versatile Wilson had two other careers: she started as an actress for D. W. Griffith; and, after her marriage forced her to retire from directing, she wrote bestselling nonfiction. Among her books: *How to Live Beyond Your Means* (1945).

Mrs. Wallace Reid. Even professionally, Dorothy Davenport preferred to use the name of her screen idol husband, who died of a drug overdose. To save others from his fate, she produced and starred in *Human Wreckage,* an antidrug film dedicated to Reid's memory. In 1925 she formed her own production company, continuing to direct films well into the 1930s. "I believe it takes a woman to believe in a woman's notions," she said. She lives today in semiretirement in North Hollywood.

Frances Marion,♀ a screenwriter, directed three films in the 1920s: *The Love Light, Just Around the Corner,* and *The Song of Love.*

Dorothy Arzner, the only woman director to make the transition from silents to sound successfully, was virtually the only woman directing American sound films until Ida Lupino ♀ began to direct in the late 1940s. Arzner started out as a script typist, graduated to film cutter, and in 1922 directed *Blood and Sand,* starring Rudolph Valentino. Arzner directed her last sound film in 1943. She has since taught film at UCLA and made a series of TV commercials for Pepsi-Cola. Some of her films: *Fashions for Women* (Paramount, 1927), *Ten Modern Commandments* (Paramount, 1927), *Anybody's Woman* (Paramount, 1930), *Working Girls* (Paramount, 1931), *Christopher Strong* (RKO, 1933), *Nana* (Universal Studios, 1934), *Craig's Wife* (Columbia, 1936), *The Bride Wore Red* (MGM, 1937), *First Comes Courage* (Columbia, 1943).

ALL ABOUT EVE

Ladies Must Live (1921)
Ladies Must Dress (1927)
Ladies Beware (1927)
Ladies Love Brutes (1930)
Ladies Must Play (1930)
Ladies Should Listen (1934)
She Couldn't Help It (1920)
She Couldn't Say No (1930)
She Got What She Wanted (1930)
She Wanted a Millionaire (1932)
She Had to Say Yes (1933)
She Had to Choose (1934)
She Learned About Sailors (1934)
She Made Her Bed (1934)
She Was a Lady (1934)
She Gets Her Man (1935)

From Ted Sennett, ed., *The Movie Buff's Book* (New York: Pyramid, 1975)

A TRIBE OF INDIAN HEROINES WHO WEREN'T

The unlikeliest actresses have portrayed noble Indian maidens or half-breeds, but rarely has a true Indian played the part. In fact, as of 1971, only six "American Indian–speaking females" were listed by the Screen Actors Guild. Among the Caucasians who have painted themselves:

Mary Pickford,♀ Ramona (1910), *A Pueblo Legend* (1912).
Lupe Velez, The Squaw Man (1931).

Sylvia Sidney,♀ *Behold My Wife* (1935).
Loretta Young, Ramona (1936).
Linda Darnell, Buffalo Bill (1944).
Jennifer Jones, Duel in the Sun (1947).
Virginia Mayo, Colorado Territory (1949).
Debra Paget, Broken Arrow (1950).
Audrey Hepburn,♀ *The Unforgiven* (1960).
Julie Newmar,♀ *Mackenna's Gold* (1969).
Katharine Ross, Tell Them Willie Boy Is Here (1969).
Judith Anderson, A Man Called Horse (1970).

Also among their number: *Anne Bancroft,*♀ *Clara Bow, Cyd Charisse,*♀ *Yvonne De Carlo, Ann Dvorak, Rhonda Fleming, Paulette Goddard,*♀ *Rita Moreno, Jean Peters, Donna Reed,* and *Barbara Rush.*

DIVAS ON THE SILVER SCREEN

꙰

Grace Moore, soprano, made eight films from 1930 to 1938, including *The New Moon* (1930), *One Night of Love* (1934), *Love Me Forever* (1935), and *Louise* (1938).
Lily Pons,♀ soprano, was in *I Dream Too Much* (1935), *That Girl from Paris* (1936), *Hitting a New High* (1938), and *Carnegie Hall* (1947).
Gladys Swarthout, mezzo-soprano, appeared in *Rose of the Rancho* (1936), *Give Us This Night* (1936), *Champagne Waltz* (1937), *Romance in the Dark* (1938), and *Ambush* (1939).
Kirsten Flagstad,♀ soprano, was in *The Big Broadcast of 1938.*
Patrice Munsel, soprano, was in *Melba* (1953).
Risë Stevens,♀ mezzo-soprano, appeared in *The Chocolate Soldier* (1941), *Going My Way* (1944), and *Carnegie Hall* (1947).
Miliza Korjus, soprano, was in *The Great Waltz.*
Jarmila Novotna, soprano, was in *The Search* (1947).
Nina Koshetz, soprano, was in *Algiers* (1938).
Helen Traubel, soprano, was in *Deep in My Heart* (1954) and *Gunn* (1967).

And Two Who Made Silents

꙰

Mary Garden,♀ soprano, played *Thaïs* (1912) and *The Splendid Singer* (1918).
Geraldine Farrar, soprano, made fourteen silent films, among them *Carmen,* (1915), *Joan the Woman* and *The Woman God Forgot* (1917), *The Turn of the Wheel* (1918), and *Flame of the Desert* (1920).

Contributed by Norman Weiser

TWENTY-ONE DIRECTORS TODAY

—————————————— ❦ ——————————————

Perry Miller Adato, whose documentary on artist Georgia O'Keeffe ♀ (1977) earned her the first award ever given to a woman by the Directors Guild of America.

Anne Bancroft,♀ the actress who directed *Fatso* (1980).

Yannick Bellon, French director of *La Femme de Jean* (1974), *Somewhere Someone* (1972), and *Never More, Always* (1976).

Dyan Cannon, the actress who directed *Number One* (1973), a short film.

Vera Chytilova, Czech director of *Something Different* (1963) and *The Apple Game* (1978).

Joan Darling directed *First Love* (1977).

Barbara Koppel directed *Harlan County, U.S.A.* (1976), the first feature-length documentary to win an Oscar.

Diane Kurys directed *Peppermint Soda* (1979).

Barbara Loden, who started as a model and Copacabana showgirl, directed *Wanda* (1971) and is also a serious dramatic actress.

Ida Lupino,♀ a popular film actress from the middle 1930s to the early 1970s, directed *Never Fear* (1949), *Outrage* (1950), *On Dangerous Ground* (1951), *Beware, My Lovely* (1952), *The Hitchhiker* (1953), *The Bigamist* (1953), *The Young Lovers* (1965), and *The Trouble with Angels* (1966). Lupino also directs for television.

Elaine May, a comic actress, wrote, starred in, and directed *A New Leaf* (1971) and directed *The Heartbreak Kid* (1972).

Jeanne Moreau, stage and screen actress, wrote the screenplay for and directed *Lumière* (1975).

Leni Riefenstahl first came to public attention when her documentary *Triumph of the Will* (1935), commissioned by Hitler, glorified the achievements of the Nazi party. *Olympiad* (1938), filmed at the Berlin Olympics of 1936, delivered the same message. Twice cleared by de-Nazification courts, Riefenstahl has in recent years won acclaim for her photographs of and her documentary about the Nuba, a native people of the Sudan.

Joan Rivers directed *Rabbit Test* (1978).

Coline Serreau, French director of *Why Not!* (*Pourquoi Pas!*) (1979).

Joan Micklin Silver financed *Hester Street* (1975) with $400,000 raised by her husband and has since directed *Between the Lines* (1977) and *Head over Heels* (1979).

Joan Tewkesbury♀ directed *Old Boyfriends* (1979).

Agnes Varda. Her *La Point Courte* initiated the New Wave of French film making in 1954. A recent work is *One Sings, the Other Doesn't* (1976).

Jane Wagner, the writer as well as director of *Moment by Moment* (1978), has said of her craft, "I had no idea it was such a vast operation. . . . Nobody makes a move until you tell them to. I think the hardest thing in the world for a woman is to get used to having a position of power."

Claudia Weill directed *It's My Turn* (1980), *Girl Friends* (1978) and *The Other Half of the Sky: A China Memoir* (1975). She was also codirector of the documentary *Joyce at 34* (1973) and is a camerawoman.

Lina Wertmüller, the screenwriter and director, has been called the "female Fellini," and indeed a stint as assistant to the Italian film maker inspired her to direct her first film, *The Lizards,* in 1963. Her oeuvre in recent years: *The Seduction of Mimi* (1972), *Love and Anarchy* (1973), *All Screwed Up* (1974), *Swept Away by An Unusual Destiny in the Blue Sea of August* (1975), *Seven Beauties* (1976), and her first film in English, *The End of the World in Our Usual Bed in a Night Full of Rain* (1978).

SONGS BY WOMEN LYRICISTS NOMINATED FOR ACADEMY AWARDS

"The Way You Look Tonight" (winner)—lyrics by *Dorothy Fields.*♀ From *Swing Time* (1936).

"Linda"—music and lyrics by *Ann Ronnell.* From *G.I. Joe* (1945).

"The Moon Is Blue"—lyrics by *Sylvia Fine.* From the film of the same name (1953).

"The Five Pennies"—music and lyrics by *Sylvia Fine.* From the film of the same name (1959).

"Far Away Part of Town"—lyrics by *Dory Langdon* (later to become Dory Previn). From *Pepe* (1960).

Song for "Two for the Seesaw"—lyrics by *Dory Langdon.* From the film of the same name (1962).

"The Windmills of Your Mind" (winner)—lyrics by *Marilyn* and Alan *Bergman.* From *The Thomas Crown Affair* (1968).

"Come Saturday Morning"—lyrics by *Dory Previn.* From *The Sterile Cuckoo* (1969).

"Pieces of Dreams"—lyrics by *Marilyn* and Alan *Bergman.* From the film of the same name (1970).

"All His Children"—lyrics by *Marilyn* and Alan *Bergman.* From *Sometimes a Great Notion* (1971).

"Come Follow, Follow Me"—lyrics by *Marsha Karlin.* From *The Little Ark* (1972).

"Marmalade, Molasses, and Honey"—lyrics by *Marilyn* and Alan *Bergman.* From *The Life and Times of Judge Roy Bean* (1972).

"Live and Let Die"—music and lyrics by *Linda* and Paul *McCartney.* From the film of the same name (1973).

"The Way We Were" (winner)—lyrics by *Marilyn* and Alan *Bergman.* From the film of the same name (1973).

"Nobody Does It Better"—lyrics by *Carole Bayer Sager.* From *The Spy Who Loved Me* (1977).

"Someone's Waiting for You"—lyrics by *Carol Conners* and *Ayn Robbins.* From *The Rescuers* (1977).

"The Last Time I Felt Like This"—lyrics by *Marilyn* and Alan *Bergman.* From *Same Time, Next Year* (1978).

"Theme from 'Ice Castles' (Through the Eyes of Love)"—lyrics by *Carole Bayer Sager* (1979).

"Theme from 'The Promise' (I'll Never Say Goodbye)"—lyrics by *Marilyn* and Alan *Bergman* (1979).

TWO-TIME ACADEMY AWARD WINNERS

❧

Bette Davis,♀ for *Dangerous* (1935) and *Jezebel* (1938).
Olivia De Havilland, for *To Each His Own* (1946) and *The Heiress* (1949).
Jane Fonda, for *Klute* (1971) and *Coming Home* (1979).
Glenda Jackson, for *Women in Love* (1970) and *A Touch of Class* (1973).
Vivien Leigh for *Gone With the Wind* (1939) and *A Streetcar Named Desire* (1951).
Luise Rainer, for *The Great Ziegfeld* (1936) and *The Good Earth* (1937).
Elizabeth Taylor,♀ for *Butterfield 8* (1960) and *Who's Afraid of Virginia Woolf?* (1966).
Helen Hayes,♀ for *The Sin of Madelon Claudet* (1931–32) and *Airport* (1970), supporting actress.
Shelley Winters, for *The Diary of Anne Frank* (1959), supporting actress; and *A Patch of Blue* (1965), supporting actress.

A THREE-TIME WINNER

❧

Ingrid Bergman,♀ for *Gaslight* (1944), *Anastasia* (1956) and *Murder on the Orient Express,* (1974), supporting actress.

AND THE THREE-TIME WINNER WITH THE MOST OSCAR NOMINATIONS

❧

Katharine Hepburn,♀ for *Morning Glory* (1932–33), *Guess Who's Coming to Dinner* (1967), and *The Lion in Winter* (1968). She was also nominated for *Alice Adams* (1935), *The Philadelphia Story* (1940), *Woman of the Year* (1942), *The African Queen* (1951), *Summertime* (1955), *The Rainmaker* (1956), *Suddenly, Last Summer* (1959), and *Long Day's Journey into Night* (1962).

ELEVEN MODERN SCREENWRITERS AND THEIR FILMS

❧

Jay Presson Allen: Marnie (1964), *The Prime of Miss Jean Brodie* (1969), *Cabaret* (1972), *Travels with My Aunt* (1972), *Funny Lady* (1975), and *Just Tell Me What You Want* (1979), from her own novel.
Leigh Brackett: The Big Sleep (1946), *Rio Bravo* (1959), *Hatari!* (1962), *El Dorado* (1967), *Rio Lobos* (1970), and *The Long Good-bye* (1973). Brackett was a free-lance writer for science-fiction and Western magazines when Howard Hawks hired her to work on *The Big Sleep.*
Joan Didion:♀ *Panic in Needle Park* (1971), and *Play It as It Lays* (1972), from her best-selling novel. Didion was a *Vogue* movie reviewer and a columnist for *Life* and the *Saturday Evening Post* before becoming a novelist.

Nancy Dowd: *Slap Shot* (1977). Critics were shocked that a woman had written what *Newsweek* called "the most foul-mouthed movie of all time," but Dowd countered that for her script about professional ice hockey she "used the exact same language that the players do so I really don't understand the fuss."

Carole Eastman: *Five Easy Pieces* (1970), *Puzzle of a Downfall Child* (1970), and *The Fortune* (1975).

Penelope Gilliatt: *Sunday, Bloody Sunday* (1971). A former movie reviewer for the *New Yorker* magazine, Gilliatt also writes novels and short stories.

Gloria Katz: *American Graffiti* (1973), *Lucky Lady* (1973), and *French Postcards* (1979).

Gail Parent: *Sheila Levine Is Dead and Living in New York* (1975), from her novel. She has written TV comedy for Lily Tomlin, Mary Tyler Moore, and Carol Burnett.

Eleanor Perry: *David and Lisa* (1962), *Ladybug, Ladybug* (1963), *The Swimmer* (1968), *Last Summer* (1969), *Diary of a Mad Housewife* (1970), and *The Man Who Loved Cat Dancing* (1973). She has also written two Emmy Award–winning TV specials.

Renee Taylor: *Lovers and Other Strangers* (1970) and *Made for Each Other* (1971).

Joan Tewkesbury: ♀ *Thieves like Us* (1974) and *Nashville* (1975). Tewkesbury started out as a script girl for director Robert Altman on *McCabe and Mrs. Miller* (1971).

EIGHT MOVIE MOGULS

Karla Davidson, associate general counsel and a corporate officer of Metro-Goldwyn-Mayer, was hired as a young lawyer in the 1950s at a lower salary than the elevator operator. She now drafts the studio's most important contracts.

Lucy Fisher, thirty, vice-president of production at Twentieth Century-Fox, thinks that women movie executives work twice as hard because they want to prove themselves. She began as a script reader.

Willy Hunt, thirty-eight, vice-president of motion picture development at MGM, spent "eight or nine years as a secretary at Warner Brothers before I got a break."

Willette Klausner, vice-president of marketing at Universal, had a ten-year career in market research before joining the studio.

Sherry Lansing became president of Twentieth Century-Fox Productions on January 2, 1980, at an annual salary of $300,000. Lansing, the highest-ranking woman in the movie business, was formerly vice-president of Columbia Pictures.

Marcia Nasatir became vice-president of production at United Artists in 1974, paving the way for other women. Nasatir is now an independent producer.

Claire Townsend, twenty-seven-year-old vice-president of production at

Twentieth Century-Fox, spent fifteen months in a similar post at United Artists.

Paula Weinstein, former senior vice-president at Twentieth Century-Fox, is now a member of the Ladd Company.

THEIR WORLD OF DANCE

———————————— ⚸ ————————————

Marie Rambert (b. 1888) became interested in ballet as a medical student in Paris, returned to her native England, and founded the Ballet Rambert in 1926. Her students include Sir Frederick Ashton and Anthony Tudor.

Dame Ninette de Valois (b. 1898) founded the Sadler's Wells Ballet, now the Royal Ballet Company of Great Britain, in 1931. Until 1963 she was its director and is still creating new productions for the company. At sixteen, as Edris Stannus, she debuted in London, then changed her name; later she appeared with the Diaghilev Ballet, choreographed *Job* to the music of Ralph Vaughan Williams in 1931, and continues to be a leading figure in British dance at the age of eighty-one.

Dame Alicia Markova (b. 1910) danced with Diaghilev from the time she was fourteen years old, was prima ballerina with the Sadler's Wells Company, and was the first English ballerina to dance the traditionally Russian roles in *Giselle* and *Swan Lake.* In 1935 she founded the Markova-Dolin Company with Anton Dolin, reactivated and transformed it into the London Festival Ballet in 1949, and was its prima ballerina until 1952. Markova retired from dancing in 1962, the following year became director of the Metropolitan Opera Ballet, and has been governor of the Royal Ballet since 1973.

Amalia Hernández founded the Ballet Folklórico de México in 1952 to preserve her nation's ethnic dance traditions. The state-subsidized group performs throughout Mexico and abroad.

Sara Levi-Tanai in 1949 founded the Inbal Dance Company of Israel, which has brought folk dance traditions to a high art.

Bronislava Nijinska (1891–1972) danced with her brother Vaslav Nijinsky for Diaghilev from 1909 and as a choreographer experimented with new idioms, including jazz. In 1932 Nijinska founded her own Théâtre de Danse in Paris.

Lucia Chase did not begin to study ballet seriously until she was twenty-six yeas old, then became a founding patron of the American Ballet Theatre, danced with ABT for many years, and was from 1945 to 1980 artistic director of the company, transforming its classical style into a more American idiom.

Alicia Alonso (b. 1901), a native of Cuba, after dancing with the New Ballet Theatre of New York and the Ballet Russe de Monte Carlo, returned to Havana in 1948 to found her own company and, after the Cuban Revolution, founded and directed the Ballet Nacional de Cuba. Alonso was in 1957 the first Western-trained dancer to perform by invitation in the Soviet Union; she returned to New York in 1977 at the age of fifty-five to dance in *Giselle.*

Iolani ("Heavenly Bird") Luahine (1915–1978) was the last great exponent of the sacred hula ceremony of Hawaii. The daughter of a dancer and chanter at the court of the last king, she was by birth a *kapu,* or consecrated dancer. Luahine, who never let audiences forget that the hula was a sacred dance honoring gods and rulers, was named a "living national treasure" of the state and awarded the first State of Hawaii Order of Distinction for Cultural Leadership in 1970. She last performed on the mainland at the American Dance Festival in 1975.

May Gadd (1890–1979), born in England, came to the United States in 1927 to teach traditional English dances and founded and was national director of the Country Dance and Song Society of America. She had a repertoire of more than a thousand dances from the Anglo-American tradition and an encyclopedic knowledge of steps, routines, and dance history. Agnes de Mille ♀ called on her for assistance in choreographing *Oklahoma!* and other works; of Gadd, de Mille once said, "I've seen her get 700 people moving in correct circles in an armory in three minutes."

Violette Verdy, born Nelly Guillerm in France, debuted when she was twelve with Roland Petit's Ballets des Champs-Elysées and was a leading ballerina with the New York City Ballet company for many years. New York's loss was, in 1977, Paris's gain, as Verdy became the first woman to direct the Paris Opera Ballet.

Rosemary Dunleavy is assistant ballet master (*sic*) to George Balanchine at the New York City Ballet. She danced with the company for ten years from 1961, then began to "help out" at rehearsals. She carries in her head the choreography for nearly all Balanchine's ballets, coaches the lead dancers, teaches the corps de ballet, organizes schedules, and coordinates all facets of production.

Sophia Golovkina directs the Bolshoi Ballet School in Moscow.

Tai Ai-lien is director of the Peking Ballet, which was established in 1963. When it was closed for almost twelve years during and after the Cultural Revolution, Tai lived on a farm and in a mental hospital. Born in Trinidad and educated in England, she first went to her ancestral land in the late 1940s as a returning overseas Chinese. She taught ballet and built the Peking company, and is now rebuilding it in the cultural thaw of post-Mao China.

ELEVEN MAKERS OF MODERN DANCE

Mary Wigman (1886–1973), influenced by the expressionist movement in painting, created a "New German Dance" in the 1920s, using only percussive music from instruments of Africa and the Far East; costumes were kept simple to emphasize the body's forms and movements. Her school in Dresden was forced to close during the Nazi period, but after the Second World War, Wigman was again a major choreographer and honored cultural figure in Germany.

Loie (Marie Louise) Fuller (1862–1928) made her acting debut at the age of four, touring in burlesque and Buffalo Bill's Wild West Show. While rehearsing for a play in 1889, she was given an enormous skirt of diaphanous silk and, draping it about her, was inspired to create what she called the "serpentine dance." Her dance career blossomed, and she became noted for her use of lighting to create dramatic and sensuous illusions, in 1923 staging and designing the lighting at the Paris Opera for the inferno scene of Hector Berlioz's *Damnation of Faust.*

Isadora Duncan (1878–1927) danced and choreographed according to her own theories, glorifying the emotions and the human body at a time when women were still under Victorian constraints. Her improvisational style, free movement, and wildly unconventional life were unlike anything her contemporaries had seen. In 1978 one of her original "Duncan Dancers," eighty-four-year-old Maria-Theresa Duncan, founded the Isadora Duncan Heritage Group with one of *her* disciples, Kay Bardsley.

Ruth St. Denis (b. 1880?) founded the Denishawn School in 1915 with her husband, Ted Shawn. Inspired by the art nouveau movement in painting and design, and by the dances of India, the Far East, Egypt, and the American Indians, St. Denis was responsible for an entire era of dance in which even the suggestion of the exotic was prized. One of her most noted students was . . .

Martha Graham ♀ (b. 1894), who studied at Denishawn but developed her own starker approach to movement and choreography, and started her own dance company in New York in 1927. Her distinctive angular style has been imparted to several generations of dancers, and she was still dancing in her eighties.

Doris Humphrey ♀ (1895–1958), another alumna of Denishawn, developed a personal style using exaggerated movement and experimental musical backgrounds. She formed her own school and performing company in New York in 1928 in association with Charles Weidman, trained a generation of American dancers, was a founder of the Juilliard Dance Theater in 1935, and, after arthritis forced her to stop performing, continued her work as artistic director in the dance company of José Limón, one of her most outstanding students.

Agnes de Mille (b. 1908) did not begin to study dance until she was fourteen because her parents did not approve. Her *Rodeo,* choreographed for the Ballet Russe de Monte Carlo, first presented American folk idioms within a ballet context in 1942. The following year she created the dances for the musical play *Oklahoma!* and succeeded in integrating them into the story line—a theatrical first. De Mille has continued to choreograph for theater and films and has founded the Heritage Dance Theater to present dance that incorporates traditional American folk materials.

Hanya Holm (b. ca. 1900), a student of Wigman's in her native Germany, opened the Mary Wigman School in New York in 1931 and her own school five years later. Her choreography received critical acclaim with the 1937 *Trend* to the music of avant-garde composer Edgar Varèse; she was the first choreographer to get a copyright for her work (for *Kiss Me Kate*), and she was a founding director of the New York City Dance Company.

Pearl Primus (b. 1919), born in Trinidad, came to New York as a child and was planning to be a doctor when "the dance claimed me." She was sent to study with Graham, Holm, and Humphrey, and two years later, in 1943, she gave her first professional performance to critical raves. Performing in nightclubs and the theater, she developed a repertoire of modern dances of social protest, then explored African culture and dance, incorporating elements from African dance into her own work. Later she returned to school and received a Ph.D. in anthropology shortly before her sixtieth birthday.

Pauline Koner (b. 1912), a disciple of Wigman's, also studied with dancers of Spanish, Japanese, and other ethnic traditions, and has choreographed for the stage and danced with José Limón in the original cast of *The Moor's Pavane* in 1949. Koner last performed alone at a memorial tribute to Doris Humphrey in 1972. In her fiftieth year in dance in 1978, she founded her own company, the Pauline Koner Dance Consort.

Twyla Tharp ♀ founded her own company in 1965 when she was twenty-three years old and quickly set the dance world spinning with her stark early works of pure movement, performed on bare stages with the sparsest of costumes and no music. Her "pop" ballets incorporating popular dance movements have brought her a wide following among audiences that have never seen a classical ballet.

XII ❧ *MUSIC IN THE AIR*

EARLY TO PLAY
❧

Maria Anna Mozart (Nannerl), Wolfgang's older sister, born in 1751, composed and played her own music on the harpsichord before she was seven.

Blanche Hermine Barbot was an accomplished pianist at the age of seven, when she gave her first concert in 1851.

Birdie Blye, born in 1887, was feted as a "wonder child" who played Mendelssohn, Beethoven, Schumann, Liszt, Schubert, and Chopin from memory before the age of ten. In three years Blye appeared in more than 200 concerts.

Amy Marcy Cheney Beach ♀ (later known as Mrs. H. H. A. Beach) began composing at the age of four and played in concerts at age seven. Born in 1867, she was sixteen when she appeared for the first time on a Boston concert stage.

Hazel Scott, the pianist, was improvising at the age of five. At thirteen, described as "little Miss Hazel Scott, child wonder pianist," she performed classical music in a concert in Harlem.

Beverly Sills ♀ at three performed on a weekly radio show, "Uncle Bob's Rainbow Hour," in 1932. By age seventeen she could sing twenty-three opera arias.

Sarah Caldwell, ♀ conductor of the Boston Opera Company, was both a mathematical and musical prodigy by the age of fourteen.

Lilit Gampel, who lives in Los Angeles, had already been a violin soloist with the Vienna Symphony, the New York Philharmonic, the Boston Pops, the Los Angeles Philharmonic, and the Cincinnati Symphony by the time she was sixteen.

INSPIRATIONS
❧

Countess Giulietta Guicciardi was the woman to whom Beethoven dedicated the *Moonlight Sonata* (*Sonata quasi una Fantasia,* in C-sharp minor). It is said that the composer, walking on a moonlit night, heard music coming from the Guicciardi home and stopped to listen. The countess, seeing him through the window, invited him to join her guests. Sitting down at the piano, Beethoven improvised the *Moonlight Sonata* and raced home to copy it down.

Countess Caroline Esterhazy, a pupil with whom Schubert was hopelessly in love, may have inspired his *Serenade.* Once, when she accused him of never having written anything for her, Schubert is said to have replied, "Why should I? Everything I ever did is dedicated to you."

Clara Wieck ♀ was the young woman for whom Schumann wrote *Warum* (*Why?*) after her father had broken off their engagement and sent Clara to Dresden. Robert and Clara did not see each other for more than a year, during which time Schumann composed and dedicated his piano sonata in F-sharp minor to her. Clara also inspired his *Fantasie* before the lovers were finally reunited and married.

Maria Wodzinska ♀ was affianced to Chopin, who wrote *La Valse de l'Adieu* (op. 69 no. 1) for her in 1835. She broke the engagement and he wrote the Ballade in G minor in a frenzy of disillusionment.

George Sand ♀ commanded her lover Chopin to write the *Waltz of the Little Dog* (Valse in D-flat, op. 64 no. 1) after the pair had watched her little dog chasing itself around in circles, a sight that Sand thought deserved to be immortalized.

Fanny Mendelssohn's ♀ brother Felix dedicated his popular *Songs Without Words* to his devoted sister.

Jenny Pachta inspired the first opera, *Die Hochzeit* (*The Wedding*), by Richard Wagner. The composer had met Pachta in Prague, and his unrequited passion for her was reflected in the plot of his opera: a bride who pushes her lover out the window and then collapses at his funeral. Thus purged, Wagner recovered.

Mathilde Wesendonck, whose husband was responsible for financing the Zurich festival at which Wagner's operas were performed, inspired all the heroines of the *Ring* cycle, particularly Brunhilde. "I laid the whole festival at the feet of one beautiful woman," Wagner wrote later.

Countess d'Agoult (Marie Sophie de Flarigny), the mother of Liszt's three children, may have been the inspiration for his *Liebestraum* (*Dream of Love*). Another possibility is that Liszt composed it for **Princess Wittgenstein,** a later influence in his life.

Nadejda Von Meck, to whom Tchaikovsky dedicated his Fourth Symphony, supported the composer from 1877 to 1890. He wrote to his patron, "I believe that you will find in it echoes of your deepest thoughts and feelings." They never met, although they corresponded for fourteen years.

THE WOMEN OF CHOPIN'S MUSIC

On the screen, Cornel Wilde as Chopin had Merle Oberon as George Sand, but the real Chopin was involved with many other women—romantically and otherwise—during his short life (1810–1849). Some were pupils, some were friends, some were wives of friends, and one was another student at the Warsaw Conservatory. Here are some of the women to whom he dedicated his works, or who inspired them:

Madame Camille Pleyel, three Nocturnes of op. 9.

Mademoiselle Jane Wilhelmina Stirling, two Nocturnes of op. 55.

Mademoiselle R. de Könneritz, two Nocturnes of op. 62.

Madame la Comtesse d'Apponyi, two Nocturnes of op. 27.

Baroness Billing, two Nocturnes of op. 32.

Mademoiselle Laure Duperre, two Nocturnes of op. 48.

Delfina Potocka, Waltz no. 6 in D-Flat, op. 64 no. 1, *Minute Waltz.*

Madame la Baronne Charlotte de Rothschild, Waltz no. 7 in C-sharp minor, op. 64 no. 2.

Countess Catherine de Bronicka, Waltz no. 8 in A-flat, op. 64 no. 3.

Catherine Erskine, Waltz in B, unpublished.

Laura Horsford, Waltz no. 1 in E-flat, op. 18, *Grande Valse Brillante.*

Mademoiselle de Thun-Hohenstein, Waltz no. 2 in A-flat, op. 34 no. 1, *Valse Brillante.*

Madame la Baronne C. d'Ivri, Waltz no. 3 in A minor, op. 34 no. 2.

Mademoiselle A. d'Eichtal, Waltz no. 4 in F, op. 34 no. 3.

Mademoiselle Marie de Krudner, Madame Oury, and *Mademoiselle Elise Gavard,* Waltz no. 12 in F minor, op. 70 no. 2.

Konstancja Gladkowska, the other student, Waltz no. 13 in D-flat, op. 70 no. 3; Concerto no. 2 in F minor.

Maria Wodzinska,♀ Ballade no. 1 in G minor, op. 23; Waltz no. 9 in A-flat, op. 69 no. 1, *L'Adieu.*

Contributed by Norman Weiser

COMPOSING THEMSELVES

------------------------------ ❧ ------------------------------

Hildegard of Bingen,♀ a twelfth-century abbess, mystic, and scholar, later canonized, wrote more than eighty religious compositions. She corresponded frequently with the . . .

Countess de Dia, one of a group of active women troubadours. Only one of her *chansons* survives today.

Isabella Leonarda (1620–1700) wrote music for sixty of her eighty years, heard all of it played, and saw all of it published.

Elisabeth Jacquet de la Guerre (1651–1729), a court composer to Louis XIV, was one of the most highly regarded and performed composers of her time and a renowned harpsichordist as well.

Louise Farrenc was a nineteenth-century composer of works for piano as well as of chamber music and symphonic works praised by Berlioz and Schumann and often performed in her native France. Also a musicologist, Farrenc taught at the Paris Conservatoire and, with her husband, compiled a twenty-volume anthology of piano works from the sixteenth to nineteenth centuries.

Clara Wieck Schumann♀ was a noted pianist who composed selections for her own concerts. After her husband's death, she supported their family of seven children by performing, writing, and teaching.

Pauline Viardot-Garcia (1821–1910) wrote more than one hundred songs, three operettas (to librettos by her close friend Ivan Turgenev), and other music. Her only opera, *La Dernière Sorcière,* premiered in 1869.

She came from a family of musicians, studied singing with her parents and piano with Liszt, and married a music critic and impresario. An outstanding opera singer, she was noted for her expressive acting.

Fanny Mendelssohn Hensel ♀ was, like her brother Felix, a child prodigy. Her family was proud of her—but discouraged her from serious composition because, they said, a woman's primary responsibility was to her home. Consequently, when she died in 1847 at the age of forty-one, the body of work she left was not extensive.

Cécile Louise Stéphanie Chaminade (1861–1944) was a popular concert pianist and composer of romantic songs, piano pieces, and other works. In one year (1888) she wrote both a lyric symphony, *Les Amazones,* and a ballet, *Callirhoë,* whose "Scarf Dance" is a staple of the orchestral encore repertoire.

Dame Ethel Mary Smyth (1858–1944) was first recognized for her Mass in D performed in 1893 in London; wider acclaim greeted her one-act opera *Der Wald* (she also wrote the libretto) performed in Dresden in 1901 and at the Metropolitan Opera in 1903. Among her several operas, choral, chamber, and other works, most popular was her comic opera *The Boatswain's Mate* of 1916. She was also the composer of "The March of the Women" for the Women's Social and Political Union (WSPU).

Lili Boulanger ♀ (1893–1918) was in 1913 the first woman musician (although not the first woman) to receive the Prix de Rome of the French Académie for her cantata *Faust et Helène,* called "one of the masterpieces of modern music" by Walter Damrosch, who gave it its first United States performance at Carnegie Hall a few months after the death of its composer. She had completed fifty works by the time she died at the age of twenty-four.

Ruth Crawford Seeger ♀ (1901–1953) composed almost all her innovative works in a five-year period in the late 1920s–early 1930s.

Germaine Tailleferre (b. 1892) was the only female member of "Les Six," a group of early-twentieth-century French composers who reacted against the romanticism of the previous century, finding their inspiration in jazz, music-hall, and popular music.

Thea Musgrave ♀ (b. 1928), born in Scotland, studied under Nadia Boulanger♀ and was the first Briton to win the Lili Boulanger Prize. She has written orchestral, instrumental, and dramatic works; a full-length ballet, *Beauty and the Beast;* and several operas. Her 1974 opera, *The Voice of Ariadne,* based on a Henry James story, was followed in 1977 by *Mary, Queen of Scots.*

SEVEN LIBRETTISTS

❧

Helmine von Chézy's *Euryanthe,* music by Carl Maria von Weber, premiered in Vienna in 1823 and was not a success; nevertheless, it was presented in New York at the Metropolitan Opera in 1888. Her *Rosamunde of Cyprus,* with a score by Franz Schubert, was also a disaster.

Kathleen de Jaffa's *The Emperor Jones,* based on the Eugene O'Neill play, score by Louis Gruenberg, was performed at the Metropolitan Opera, New York, January 7, 1933.

Edna St. Vincent Millay's ♀ *The King's Henchman,* score by Deems Taylor, was performed by the Metropolitan Opera Company more than a dozen times following its February 17, 1927, premiere.

Constance Collier collaborated with Deems Taylor on the libretto of his opera *Peter Ibbetson.* It premiered at the Metropolitan Opera February 7, 1931.

Gertrude Stein ♀ wrote libretti for two operas by Virgil Thomson. *Four Saints in Three Acts* premiered at the Wadsworth Atheneum in Hartford, Connecticut, February 8, 1934; *The Mother of Us All* premiered at Columbia University May 7, 1947.

Dorothea Carroll Claflin wrote *Hester Prynne,* with a score by her husband, Avery Claflin. It was given a partial premiere—scene 2 of act 2—in Hartford, December 15, 1934.

Sylvia Regan, an actress and playwright, wrote the libretto for *The Golem,* an opera by her husband, Abraham Ellstein. The first performance was at the New York City Opera, March 22, 1962.

PANTS ROLES

❧

In several operas, female performers traditionally portray certain male characters. Among them are:

Cherubino, the young lad in love with love in *The Marriage of Figaro,* a mezzo-soprano role.

Count Orlofsky, the sardonic and elegant party giver of *Die Fledermaus,* sometimes interpreted as a transvestite female, a mezzo-soprano.

Romeo, in Bellini's version, *I Capuletti e i Montecchi,* a mezzo.

Prince Charming in Massenet's *Cendrillon,* intended for Falcon soprano, a voice between soprano and mezzo.

Jean, who is beatified for offering his only treasure, his skill as a juggler, to the Virgin Mary, in Massenet's *Le Jongleur de Nôtre-Dame.* Although written for a tenor, the part has traditionally been taken by a soprano since the legendary Mary Garden ♀ played it in an early performance.

Xerxes and *Arsamene* in the Handel opera *Xerxes,* originally played by castrati and now performed—albeit rarely—by female sopranos.

Aeneas, and all the other male parts, in Purcell's *Dido and Aeneas,* an opera for an all-female cast composed for production by a girls' school in London in 1689.

Octavian, a young gentleman of noble family in *Der Rosenkavalier,* mezzo-soprano.

A young shepherd in *Tannhäuser,* soprano.

Siebel, a student in *Faust,* soprano.

Nicklaus, the friend of the hero in *The Tales of Hoffmann,* written for tenor but usually performed by a contralto or mezzo-soprano.

Orpheus in Glück's *Orfeo ed Eurydice* was written for contralto, although usually performed by a tenor.

Holofernes and his servant *Vagans* in Vivaldi's *Juditha Triumphans,* a dramatic oratorio written for five female soloists.

BEVERLY SILLS'S♀ LIST OF THE MOST CHALLENGING ROLES FOR A SOPRANO

※

The Queen of the Night in *The Magic Flute.*
Isolde in *Tristan und Isolde.*
Elizabeth I in *Roberto Devereux.*
Salomé
Norma
Tosca
Carmen
Cleopatra in *Julius Caesar.*
Elektra

Exclusively for *Womanlist*

TEN ON THE PODIUM

※

Charlotte Bergen has conducted a symphony orchestra in New York's Carnegie Hall for more than ten years, paying the musicians' and rental fees herself, inviting the public free of charge, and presenting such ambitious programs as Beethoven's *Missa Solemnis* to critical acclaim.

Victoria Bond was the first woman to receive a doctor's degree in conducting from the Juilliard School of Music. In May 1978 she made her most important debut to date, conducting the Pittsburgh Symphony.

Nadia Boulanger ♀ was guest conductor of the Boston Symphony in 1938 and of the New York Philharmonic in 1939. She was appointed professor of composition at the Paris Conservatoire in 1945 and director of the American Conservatory, Fontainebleau, in 1950. A list of her students is a veritable *Who's Who* of today's most outstanding musicians. When she died in 1979 at the age of ninety-two, Aaron Copland, a pupil and friend, said, "She knew everything there was to know about music."

Antonia Brico ♀ was unable to gain a position with an orchestra at the beginning of her career and so organized her own all-female orchestra in 1935. She conducted the Philharmonic-Symphony Orchestra of New York at Lewisohn Stadium in 1938, has headed the Denver Symphony for more than thirty years, and has conducted orchestras again in New York since 1975.

Sarah Caldwell, ♀ founder and director of the Opera Company of Boston, established the Music Department of Boston University and in 1975 was only the second woman (after Boulanger) to conduct the New York Philharmonic, in a program devoted to works composed by women. In 1976 Caldwell was the first woman to conduct at New York's Metropolitan Opera and has since appeared on its podium several times.

Margaret Hillis founded and directed the American Choral Foundation, has conducted the Santa Fe Opera, and directs the Chicago Symphony Orchestra Chorus—a job that includes conducting their annual "Do-It-Yourself *Messiah.*"

Imogen Holst, the daughter of the late composer and conductor Gustav Holst, is an English conductor and musicologist with a special interest in the music of England past and present.

Dorothy Klotzman has conducted the Goldman Band in New York City.

Alberta Masiello is an assistant conductor of the Metropolitan Opera.

Judith Somogi, at thirty-three the first woman to conduct the New York City Opera, has also conducted at the San Francisco Opera, the Hollywood Bowl, Tanglewood, Spoleto, and elsewhere. The first time she conducted *La Traviata* the audience murmured upon seeing a conductor in an evening gown instead of white tie and tails, then gave her an ovation after the performance.

CALDWELL IN CONCERT

On November 10, 1975, Sarah Caldwell ♀ conducted the New York Philharmonic in "A Celebration of Women Composers" as a benefit for the orchestra's pension fund, in collaboration with *Ms.* magazine. On the program:

Overture for Orchestra by *Grazyna Bacewicz* (Polish, 1913–1969).

Andante for String Orchestra by *Ruth Crawford Seeger* ♀ (American, 1901–1953).

Faust et Hélène by *Lili Boulanger* ♀ (French, 1893–1918).

Sands . . . by *Pozzi Escot* (Peruvian American, b. 1933).

Clarinet Concerto by *Thea Musgrave* ♀ (Scottish American, b. 1928).

Profiles of these composers and a discography of music by women can be found in the November 1975 issue of *Ms.* magazine.

HEADING THE OPERA

Mary Garden, ♀ the Scottish-American soprano, directed a Chicago opera company in 1921–1922; she chose to be called the "directa." Among offerings in that season was the world premiere of Sergei Prokofiev's *Love for Three Oranges.*

Cosima Wagner managed the Bayreuth Festival performances from the death of her husband, Richard Wagner, in 1883 until 1908.

Winifred Williams Wagner codirected the Bayreuth Festival with her husband, Siegfried, son of Cosima and Richard Wagner, after the retirement of her mother-in-law and continued to direct the festival after Siegfried's death.

Carol Fox was a founder of the Chicago Lyric Opera in 1954 and celebrated the company's twenty-fifth anniversary in 1979. As its head, said critic Harold Schonberg, "she has made the Lyric Opera a company of the highest international standards."

Rosa Ponselle, upon retiring as a singer, became artistic director of the Baltimore Civic Opera in 1950.

Sarah Caldwell ♀ founded the Opera Company of Boston in 1957, for which she has created productions of more than forty-five operas. She also established the American National Opera touring company.

Mary Cardwell Dawson, founder of the National Negro Opera Company in 1941, was a singer, teacher, conductor, impresario, and the first woman president of the National Association of Negro Musicians. She decided to found an opera company after staging *Aïda* for the association's 1941 convention; her troupe performed in Pittsburgh and Chicago, and in 1956 was the first guest company to stage an opera at the Metropolitan Opera in New York. Dawson kept her company going until her death in 1962; by then her singers were performing at the Metropolitan Opera, the New York City Opera, and the Hamburg State Opera.

Kirsten Flagstad ♀ was head of the Norwegian National Opera for the 1959–1960 season, following her retirement as a performer.

Eve Queler, also a French horn player and pianist, founded the Opera Orchestra of New York in 1967 to produce concert versions of rarely performed works. Since 1975 Queler has also guest-conducted such orchestras as the Philadelphia and the Cleveland.

Risë Stevens ♀ was comanager of the Metropolitan Opera's National Company from 1964 to 1967.

Beverly Sills ♀ became general director of the New York City Opera in 1979.

AND THEN I WROTE . . .

Fourteen Popular Favorites by Women

———————— ❧ ————————

"The Blue Bells of Scotland," lyrics by *Mrs. James Grant (Annie McVicar)* to an old Scottish or English tune, in 1815.

"Charlie Is My Darling," lyrics by *Baroness Carolina Nairne* around 1820, inspired by Bonnie Prince Charlie's struggle to restore the Stuart monarchy to the throne of England. Among Nairne's most treasured possessions were the prince's spurs and a lock of his hair.

"Annie Laurie," music by *Lady John Scott (Alicia Anne Spottiswoode),* in 1835. A staunch Scottish nationalist, she was amazed when "Annie Laurie" became a favorite with British troops.

"Swing Low, Sweet Chariot." In 1847 the slave *Sarah Hannah Sheppard* was about to be sold away from her baby. She was preparing to throw herself and her child into the Cumberland River when an old black woman cried, "Wait! Let the chariot of the Lord swing low. Listen! I will read one of the Lord's scrolls to you." She told Sheppard that there was great work for her baby to do and that they would one day be reunited. As a slave in Mississippi, the bereft mother wrote "Swing Low, Sweet Chariot." The prophecy came true twenty-five years later when her daughter, a Fisk University student, searched for and found her mother.

"Come Back to Erin." *Charlotte Alington Barnard* composed this song in 1866 using the pseudonym "Claribel." She is credited with being the first song composer to receive royalties on sales.

"Happy Birthday to You." First published in 1893 and in an authorized edition in 1934, it was composed by *Mildred J. Hill,* a church organist and an authority on black spirituals; its lyricist was *Patty Smith Hill,* a professor of education.

"Rock-a-Bye Baby." Effie I. Crockett put the Mother Goose rhyme to music in 1872 when she was baby-sitting for a restless infant. She was fifteen years old at the time.

"In the Gloaming," composed by *Annie Fortescue Harrison* in 1877, the year of her marriage to Lord Arthur Hill, comptroller of Queen Victoria's ♀ household.

"Twinkle, Twinkle Little Star." Two English sisters, *Jane* ♀ and *Ann Taylor,* writers of children's verse, wrote this popular poem in 1806.

"America the Beautiful." The glorious scenery of the American West inspired Wellesley professor *Katherine Lee Bates* to write her poem in 1895; the present lyrics appeared in 1904. In 1926 the National Federation of Music Clubs conducted a contest for the best musical setting for the Bates poem. A hymn, "Materna," was selected out of 900 entries.

"I Love You Truly." The "must" song for weddings was written by *Carrie Jacobs Bond* ♀ in 1901. Bond later sang the song at the White House for Presidents Theodore Roosevelt, Warren G. Harding, and Calvin Coolidge.

"Aloha Oe" (Farewell to Thee"). Both words and music were written by *Liliuokalani,* later Queen of the Hawaiian Islands from 1891 to 1893, when she was imprisoned in 1878 by the republican government.

"Shine On, Harvest Moon," written by musical-comedy star *Nora Bayes,* "assisted and admired by Jack Norworth" (her husband), in 1908.

"Sweet Rosie O'Grady," composed at the turn of the century by actress *Maude Nugent.* Unable to find a publisher, she finally introduced it herself from the stage of Tony Pastor's in New York.

SEVEN SONGS AND THE WOMEN
THEY WERE WRITTEN FOR

❧

"I'll Take You Home Again, Kathleen." As the story goes, composer Tom Westendorf's wife, *Jennie Morrow Westendorf,* mourning the death of their son, was on the verge of a breakdown. Doctors suggested a trip to her home in New York State, but the struggling Westendorf didn't have the funds to get there from Indiana. To cheer his wife, he told her he was preparing for the trip and would take her home again. The phrase inspired the song, which became an instant hit in 1875.

"Sweet Adeline" was written by Henry Armstrong and Richard Gerard, inspired by posters for popular opera singer *Adelina Patti.* ♀ It was sung for the first time in New York City on December 27, 1903.

"Jeanie with the Light Brown Hair" was composer Stephen C. Foster's wife, *Jane McDowell.* The song was copyrighted in 1854.

"Lili Marlene" was inspired by German lyricist Hans Leip's girl friend, *Lili,* and his buddy's sweetheart, *Marlene.* Leip wrote the words in 1915 on his way to the Russian front, but they weren't set to music until 1940, when they immediately became an unofficial anthem in World War II Germany.

"Little Annie Rooney" was inspired by composer Michael Nolan's three-year-old cousin, *Annie Rooney.*

"Wait 'till the Sun Shines Nellie." Composer Harry Von Tilzer thought of this song in 1905 when he heard a honeymooning bride being consoled by her husband because the rain had spoiled their trip to Coney Island.

"Ain't She Sweet." The "she" in this song is writer and TV personality **Shana Alexander,** whose father, composer Milton Ager, wrote the song in the mid-1920s with his newborn first child in mind.

WOMEN'S MUSICAL GROUPS

Agnes Woodward and Her Whistling Chorus. By listening, Woodward learned literally to sing like the birds—and founded the School of Artistic Whistling in Los Angeles in the early 1900s to teach her skill to other women. Her chorus concertized widely, bringing fame to Los Angeles, and in 1912 the city presented her with its gold medal.

Phil Spitalny and His All-Girl Orchestra. Spitalny auditioned more than a thousand women to find twenty-two (later expanded to thirty-five and more) musicians for a radio orchestra. Evelyn Kaye Klein, the first violinist and concertmistress, soon became famous as "Evelyn and Her Magic Violin." The women used only their first names on the air and essentially ran the orchestra themselves, owning stock in the operation and deciding on all matters—personal as well as professional. They even had to submit prospective dates to committee approval, to dress alike, and to wear similar hair styles. Evelyn married Spitalny in 1946, after they had worked together for more than ten years, and the orchestra was disbanded in 1948.

The New York Women's Symphony Orchestra was founded by Antonia Brico ♀ in 1935 and later became the mixed female-and-male *Brico Symphony Orchestra* in 1938.

The Woman's Symphony of Chicago consisted of what one critic called "seasoned and well-trained musicians" when Isker Solomon became its conductor in 1939, developing the group into an ensemble that performed on a weekly coast-to-coast radio program called "Design for Happiness."

The Hip Chicks were a jazz septet of the 1940s.

International Sweethearts of Rhythm ♀ were a sixteen-member jazz group of the 1940s and 1950s.

The Womenfolk performed Eastern European folk material, with an emphasis on songs relating to women's lives, in the 1950s and 1960s.

The Sweet Adelines, probably the largest women's singing organization in the world, specialize in "barbershop"-style four-part harmony. Nearly 700 chapters, with more than 29,000 members, give public performances in their communities and hold an annual international competition and convention.

The All-Girl Reel World String Band are five young women from Kentucky who play old-time Appalachian music on banjo, guitar, and fiddle. "If you heard our tapes," says Sue Massek, "you wouldn't know we're women."

The Lyric String Quartet was in 1979 the only all-female string quartet in New York City.

The All-Girl Orchestra of Miss Faun consists solely of Faun Tracy, who plays the cello wearing musician's basic black—slit to the thigh, showing her "well-turned leg, cradling the cello," as one observer put it—while she accompanies two vocalists in nostalgia-*cum*-camp renditions of 1930s favorites.

NINE WHO SANG THE BLUES

Gertrude "Ma" Rainey, the first of the blues singers, was born in Columbus, Georgia, in 1886. At fifteen she married Will ("Pa") Rainey and joined his Rabbit Foot Minstrels, playing tent shows and the Negro vaudeville circuit. Ma Rainey sang for almost forty years, making about fifty recordings (one hundred songs), most by the old acoustic process without a microphone or electronic engineering. She died at the age of fifty-three in December 1939. Among her songs: "Levee Camp Moan," "Moonshine Blues," "Shave 'em Dry," "Slow-Drivin' Moon," and "Jelly Bean Blues."

Bessie Smith was already singing in 1907 when she was twelve years old. She was discovered by Ma Rainey and would later be known as "Empress of the Blues," making as much as $1,000 a week playing for black audiences. She recorded almost 200 sides before she died tragically after an auto accident in 1937 in Mississippi, when the "whites only" hospital to which she was taken refused to treat her. Her best-known songs: "Jazzbow Brown," "Careless Love," "Put It Right Here," "Spider Man Blues," "Empty Bed Blues," "Hard Drivin' Papa," "Black Water Blues."

Hociel Thomas, another early singer, performed churchlike blues and was known for her distinctive recitative style backed up with a horn obbligato. Thomas often worked with Louis Armstrong. Her best-known song: "Gambler's Dream."

Bertha "Chippie" Hill, known for her powerful and deep voice, was in her heyday in the 1920s and still recording in the 1940s. "How Long Blues" and "Trouble in Mind" were among her best-known numbers.

Sippie Wallace, whose voice was an odd mixture of shouting and quavering, was known in the 1920s and 1930s for "Trouble Everywhere I Roam," "There's No Hidin' Place," "Baby I Can't Use You No More," and "Section-Hand Blues."

Billie Holiday ("Lady Day") began singing with bands—Benny Goodman, Teddy Wilson, Artie Shaw, Count Basie—in 1930 when she was fifteen and ten years later was a soloist at nightclubs and theaters. A dynamic performer, she projected elegance along with her highly individual, strongly emotional style. Among her best: "Strange Fruit," "Night and Day," and "The Man I Love." Diana Ross ♀ played her in the film *Lady Sings the Blues.*

Victoria Spivey, who died in early 1980, was one of the original blues mamas. She began singing for OKeh Records while still a teen-ager in the 1920s and is best known for her double-entendre records with Lonnie Johnson and Spencer Williams, such as "Don't Wear It Out." She later founded her own Spivey Records.

Willie Mae ("Big Mama") Thornton went on the road in 1939, at the age of fourteen, after winning a talent contest in Atlanta, and she's been traveling since. Her biggest hit: "Hound Dog" in 1953, which became an even bigger hit for a fellow named Elvis Presley three years later. About her early life and hard times on the road: "I couldn't *express* what I went through. It don't make no sense to people today."

Aretha Franklin ♀ began performing with her father's gospel troupe when she was twelve; in 1960, when she was eighteen, she switched to pop, but it wasn't until seven years later, with "Respect," that she became "Lady Soul." With such songs as "Chain of Fools" and "A Natural Woman," she has become one of the best-selling female recording artists of all time.

TWENTY JAZZWOMEN

March 1978: The first Women's Jazz Festival is held in Kansas City, Missouri. June 1978: A four-night Salute to Women in Jazz takes place in New York City. In 1979: Three discs entitled *Women in Jazz,* collections of recordings made by jazzwomen in the years 1926–1961, are issued. June 1979: The second annual Salute to Women in Jazz, six days long, is held in New York as part of the Newport Jazz Festival. March 1980: The third Women's Jazz Festival is held in Kansas City, Missouri. It's impossible to list all the women who have made it in jazz. Following is a selection from the many greats:

Toshiko Akiyoshi, pianist and conductor from Japan, who first formed her own combo in 1952, now conducts a sixteen-piece all-male jazz band with her husband, Lew Tabackin. "Yellow Is Mellow" is among her best-known compositions; her "Minamata Suite" commemorates the small fishing village whose water supply and local fish were contaminated with mercury from industrial wastes.

Ivie Anderson started singing in her teens, signed with Duke Ellington in 1931, and stayed with his orchestra until 1943. Her hits include "It Don't Mean a Thing (If It Ain't Got That Swing)" (1932) and "Alabamy Home" (1937).

Lovie Austin started as an accompanist for her husband's variety act. In Chicago in the 1920s she founded a small group with Tommy Ladnier and Jimmy O'Bryant. Playing in New Orleans style, they provided the background for many blues singers. Among their hits: "Travelin' Blues," "Steppin' on the Blues" (1924); "Heebie Jeebies," "Mojo Blues," and "Peepin' Blues" (1925).

Valerie Capers, a composer, conductor, and music teacher, is experienced in the classics as well as in jazz, despite being blind since an illness at age six.

Lillian Hardin first played piano in a music store for $3 a week, then became the only woman in Joe Oliver's band. When the young Louis Armstrong joined the group five years later, Lil took him under her wing and became the second Mrs. Armstrong. Soon Lil's Dreamland Syncopators, her own group, starred "Louis Armstrong, World's Greatest Jazz Cornetist," and the rest is jazz history.

Helen Humes, best known as the vocalist with Count Basie's band from 1938 to 1941, sang the hit "Be-baba-leba," later switched her style to rhythm-and-blues, and was part of the jazz revival that began in the mid-1970s.

Alberta Hunter ran away from home at the age of eleven, began her career as a jazz singer by the time she was fifteen, and is said to have introduced blues singing to European audiences in the 1920s. Bessie Smith ♀ recorded her composition "Downhearted Blues" in 1923. In 1956 Hunter retired—but couldn't stay away. Today, in her eighties, she is still packing them into the clubs in which she appears.

Margie Hyams played vibes in Woody Herman's band in the 1940s and in George Shearing's first quartet.

Evelyn McGee sang with the original International Sweethearts of Rhythm ♀ in the 1930s and 1940s. The all-female group was formed originally to raise funds for a school for black students in Piney Woods, Mississippi.

Marian McPartland, pianist, born in England into a family of classical musicians, met and married U.S. soldier Jimmy McPartland during the Second World War. They started their own combo and later expanded it to a trio. She is known for her warm interaction with the audience and her cool elegance and energy as a performer.

Anita O'Day of the husky voice was heard with Gene Krupa in 1941 and later featured with Stan Kenton's band. She enjoyed a revival of popularity in the 1950s and again in the 1970s.

Mary Fettig Park, a saxophonist who also plays the flute, played in Stan Kenton's band.

Keely Smith, singer, widow of the late Louis Prima, performed with him and others.

Maxine Sullivan, a trombonist and vocalist, was a protégée of Claude Thornhill and performed with his band. Her biggest 1940s hit: a swing version of "Loch Lomond."

Mary Lou Williams, composer and pianist, started in vaudeville and by 1942 had her own band with her husband. Williams wrote "Trumpets No End" ("Blue Skies") for Duke Ellington, "The Zodiac Suite" (played by the New York Philharmonic in 1946), "Pretty-Eyed Baby," and "In the Land of Oo-Bla-Dee." Williams has, she says, "played through all eras of jazz" and, in her late sixties, became a member of the music faculty at Duke University.

Sylvia Syms, Nina Simone, Sarah Vaughan, Ella Fitzgerald, and *Helen Merrill*—five vocalists about whom nothing more need be said.

"GIRL GROUPS" OF THE FIFTIES AND SIXTIES

The Original Supremes: Diana Ross,♀ Florence Ballard, and *Mary Wilson:* "Baby Love," "Stop! In the Name of Love," and "I Hear a Symphony."
The Shirelles:♀ Addie Harris, Shirley Owens, Doris Kenner, and *Beverly Lee:* "Will You Still Love Me Tomorrow?" and "Soldier Boy."

The Shangri-Las: Mary Ann Ganser, Margie Ganser, Betty Weiss, and *Mary Weiss* (two sets of sisters)—"Leader of the Pack" and "Remember (Walking in the Sand)."

The Marvelettes: Gladys Horton, Katherine Anderson, Georgeanna Tillman, Juanita Cowart, and *Wanda Young:* "Please, Mr. Postman" and "Beechwood 4–5789."

Martha and the Vandellas: Martha Reeves, Betty Kelly, and *Rosalind Ashford* (the original group): "Jimmy Mack," "Heat Wave," and "Dancing in the Streets."

The Crystals: Barbara Alston, Pat Thomas, Deedee Wright, and *Lala Brooks:* "He's a Rebel" and "Da Doo Ron Ron."

The Ronettes: Estelle and *Veronica Bennett* (sisters), and their cousin *Nedra Talley:* "Be My Baby" and "Walking in the Rain."

The Chiffons: Barbara Lee, Patricia Bennett, Sylvia Peterson, and *Judy Craig:* "He's So Fine" and "One Fine Day."

And not to be forgotten: *The Chantels, Patti LaBelle and the Blue Belles, The Angels, The Jaynettes, Reparata and the Delrons, Rosie and the Originals,* and *The Dixie Cups.*

THE BRILL BUILDING SOUND

In the late 1950s and early 1960s, the "Brill Building Sound" was the most dominant force in rock music, notable for songs that possessed not only a genuine empathy with teen-agers, but a new professionalism—a polish and romanticism that gave rock-and-roll a whole new sound and texture. Located at 1619 Broadway in New York City, the Brill Building boasted the songwriting teams of Sedaka and Greenfield, Lieber and Stoller, Pomus and Shuman, and the talents of:

Carole King and Gerry Goffin, responsible for such songs as "Will You Love Me Tomorrow?" "Up on the Roof" and "Some Kind of Wonderful." King went on to an enormously successful solo career in the 1970s as both a singer and songwriter.

Cynthia Weil and Barry Mann, who wrote "Walking in the Rain," "You've Lost that Lovin' Feeling," and "Saturday Night at the Movies."

Ellie Greenwich and Jeff Barry, writers of "Da Doo Ron Ron," "Be My Baby," and "River Deep-Mountain High."

TWENTY WITH TWO OR MORE GOLD SINGLES

Aretha Franklin,[9] a remarkable fourteen, from 1967's "Respect" to 1974's "Until You Come Back to Me."
Donna Summer, eight.
Olivia Newton-John, eight.
The Carpenters, seven.

Roberta Flack, alone and with Donny Hathaway, five.
Cher,♀ alone and with Sonny, five.
Gladys Knight and the Pips, four.
The Captain and *(Toni) Tennille,* four.
Nancy Sinatra, alone and with her father, Frank, three.
Dionne Warwick,♀ three.
Helen Reddy, three.
Carly Simon, alone and with her husband, James Taylor, three.
Barbra Streisand, alone and with Neil Diamond, three.
The Mamas and the Papas, two.
Freda Payne, two.
Honey Cone, two.
Donna Fargo, two.
Rita Coolidge,♀ two.
ABBA, two.
Anne Murray, two.

From Ronald Zalkind, *Contemporary Music Almanac 1980/81* (New York: Schirmer Books, 1980)

TALKING HEADS: ROCK WOMEN SPEAK

—————————————————— ✹ ——————————————————

In 1974 Katherine Orloff published a book called *Rock 'n Roll Woman,* in which prominent rock women talked about their music and their roles as women in that music. Some of those interviewed by Orloff:

Nicoel ("Nickey") Barclay, an early member of Fanny, an all-female group: "I think at first most people thought we were 'pretty good for girls,' because they had never seen anything like us. They had no reference point. Now Fanny *is* the reference point. No matter what we do from now on, we were the first women's group to get international notice. . . . For the first year or so, we went through the phase of saying, 'We're musicians, and then we're girls.' It amounted to us apologizing for being women, shying away from any kind of glamour or attractiveness on stage. . . ."

Toni Brown, with *Terry Garthwaite,* founders of the Joy of Cooking: "Being women seemed to be secondary to the music. Finally, the press picked up on the fact that there were two women on stage who were playing instruments and singing songs and sort of doing the whole thing, and wasn't that extraordinary? Then Terry and I stopped and took a look at it. . . . I knew it was new, but I didn't realize how odd it was. . . ."

Rita Coolidge, whose first album was released in 1971: "It's hard for any person to make the decisions in the band. I imagine it's harder for a woman. But if the respect is there, they're going to listen to you. There is a certain kind of male ego thing. If I ever have to call down one of the guys in the band, even if I'm right, I think he's going to get defensive because it's a chick calling him down. There's no way to get around it. . . . At the same time, it was like having a bunch of big brothers who constantly looked out for me. . . ."

Maria Muldaur: "I have not run into any discrimination because I'm a woman trying to sing music. . . . Most of the guys I play with just straight on enjoy hearing me sing and want to help me out, and the guys who have been in my band have gently helped me to be their leader. . . . I think men have it much tougher, I really do. They've got so many other pressures that they grow up with, like having to make it. . . ."

*Grace Slick,*⁹ formerly of Jefferson Airplane: "I like to look sexy. Sometimes I like to look peculiar, too . . . to put on costumes and act like a jerk. . . . I've worked since I was eighteen and I have a kind of, well, violent personality. Before, people thought, well, that's just Grace. Now guys are inclined to think, oh, she's being women's lib at me, you know, being mad at men. I'm not ever mad at any men. . . ."

Bonnie Raitt: "A club will have its token female folkie, then its token angry young man, its token blues act, etc. Since there was already Joni Mitchell, Judy Collins, Laura Nyro, Janis Joplin, the only openings were for girls who played something different. I have a relatively sweet and small voice, but I played different songs, a bit more macho guitar and, 'yeah, that bottleneck—that's a great gimmick, honey—don't lose that.' . . . Some clubs are owned or run by women. There are a lot of successful women in the music business . . . a lot of whom got their jobs because they were women. But the business is as sexist as any other; you must be an *attractive* woman, with all the qualities that befit the mode of the day. . . ."

From Katherine Orloff, *Rock 'n Roll Woman* (Los Angeles: Nash Publishing, 1974)

QUEENS OF COUNTRY

❧

Sara Carter Bayes had been a performer for six decades when she died on January 8, 1979. Her first husband, A. P. Carter, organized the Carter Family in 1927, and by 1941 the small group, with Sara on guitar, autoharp, and vocals, had recorded nearly 300 songs. Although amicable, the breakup of their marriage in 1943 precipitated the breakup of the group. But Sara's sister-in-law . . .

Mother Maybelle Carter formed her own group, the Carter Sisters, with her three daughters and continued performing until her death at the age of sixty-nine on October 23, 1978. Her "Carter Lick" made the guitar a lead instead of a background instrument, while her rich alto voice sang harmony. Her daughters were *Anita Carter Wooten, Helen Carter Jones,* and *June Carter Cash,* who married top country singer Johnny Cash.

Lily Mae Ledford (vocalist, banjo, and fiddle) began her career as a fiddler on "The National Barn Dance" in 1936, then formed her own group, the Coon Creek Girls. Working with her until her death in 1976 were her sisters *Rosie Ledford* (vocal and guitar) and *Black-Eyed Susan Ledford* (bass). In its early years the group also featured *Violet Koehler* and *Daisy Lange.* Their best-known song is "You're a Flower That Is Blooming There for Me."

Kitty Wells (Muriel Deason), born in Nashville in 1918, took her performing name from a folk song. With a group called Johnny and Jack, backed by the Tennessee Mountain Boys, Wells developed a following in the late 1930s, joined the Grand Ole Opry in 1947, and was *Billboard* magazine's number-one country music female artist in the 1950s. Some songs: "It Wasn't God Who Made Honky Tonk Angels," "Paying for That Back Street Affair," "Mommy for a Day," and "Heartbreak U.S.A."

Dottie West, born in 1932 on a Tennessee farm, one of ten children, worked in cotton and sugar cane fields while putting herself through college, was spotted by recording executives during a visit to Nashville relatives in the early 1960s, and became an Opry familiar by 1964. She has written more than 400 songs and commercials, including "Let Me Off at the Corner" and "Here Comes My Baby."

Loretta Lynn, several times named female vocalist of the year by the Country Music Association, was born in Kentucky in 1935, married before she was fourteen, later formed her own group, and had her first hit, "Honky Tonk Girl," in 1960. Lynn is also part owner of a talent agency and owns a rodeo production company and the entire town in which she lives, Hurricane Mills, Tennessee. Her 1976 autobiography was a nationwide best seller. Lynn, who has six children and was a grandmother by the time she was thirty-two, uses material of her life in such songs as "One's on the Way," "Coal Miner's Daughter," and "Don't Come Home a Drinkin'."

Crystal Gayle (Brenda Gayle Webb) was part of her older sister Loretta Lynn's show at sixteen, but three years later her first single, "Don't It Make My Brown Eyes Blue," hit the charts.

Bobbie Gentry (Roberta Streeter) was born in Chickasaw County, Mississippi, in 1944. She took her stage name from the Jennifer Jones–Charlton Heston movie *Ruby Gentry.* She majored in philosophy at UCLA, studied theory at the Los Angeles Conservatory of Music, and was an overnight star after her first record, "Ode to Billy Joe," was released in 1967.

Connie Smith won an amateur talent contest in 1963 and has since had some thirty Top Ten hits. Born in 1941 and one of sixteen children in an Indiana family, Smith is deeply religious, will not work where alcoholic beverages are served, and goes on the road only five days a month. "The rest of the time is for Christianity and my family," she has said. Her hits: "Once a Day" and "Tiny Blue Transistor Radio."

Patsy Cline was only thirty-one years old when she died in an airplane crash while returning from a benefit concert in 1963, but her musical impact was such that even today her records—including "Imagine That" and "Leavin' on Your Mind"—are played, and she is a member of the Country Music Hall of Fame.

Brenda Lee,[♀] at four feet eleven inches the "Little Girl with the Big Voice," grew up in Nashville, where she won a talent contest at the age of six. By her mid-teens she already had her first hit, "Jambalaya"; the following year she hit the country and pop charts with "One Step at a Time" and has toed the boundary between pop and country ever since.

Tammy Wynette,[♀] the Country Music Association's female vocalist of the year for three years in a row (1968–1970), made country music history when her "Stand by Your Man" became the biggest-selling single by a woman. Married at seventeen, Wynette had three children and was single again by the time she was twenty, when she turned to music for added income to support her family. Another marriage and divorce were grist for the mill, as Tammy and her crying voice went on to score with such numbers as "I Don't Wanna Play House," "D-I-V-O-R-C-E" and "Another Lonely Song."

Dolly Parton, ♀ born in 1946, was the fourth of twelve children in a mountain family. At ten she was doing radio and TV guest shots, at thirteen cutting her first album and appearing at the Opry. Success doubled in 1967 with "Dumb Blonde" and "Something Fishy"; later that year "Last Thing on My Mind" started climbing through the Top Ten. Her 1970 "Joshua" was a number-one hit, and through the decade that followed Dolly was, too, with her own television show and that most valued of music business attributes, "cross-over" appeal.

XIII ❧ *IN THEIR OWN WRITE*

LITERARY FIRSTS

❧

- First woman poet (probable): *Enheduanna,* in Sumer in the nineteenth century B.C.
- First collection of biographies of women: *Biographies of Famous Women* by the Chinese civil servant and author Liu Hsiang, who lived from 80 to 9 B.C.
- First novelist of any gender and language: *Lady Murasaki (Murasaki Shikibu)* of Japan, whose great novel of court life, romance, and adventure in eleventh-century Japan, *The Tale of Genji,* was narrated with a frankness that would not appear in English-language novels by women for more than 900 years. Murasaki was one (and to today's critics, the best) of many Japanese women writers of the period.
- First autobiography in English: *The Book of Margery Kempe,* the life story of the fourteenth-century mystic who was ridiculed and imprisoned under the accusation of being a prostitute as well as a heretic. Written in Kempe's old age, the book was lost for nearly 500 years until a copy was discovered in 1934.
- First book by a woman to be published in English: *Le Livre des fais d'armes et de chevalerie* by *Christine de Pisan*♀ was translated and published by William Caxton in 1489 as *The Book of Fayttes [Feats] of Armes and of Chivalrye.*
- First woman to have more than one book published in English: *Christine de Pisan,*♀ whose work *Le Livre du duc des vrais amans* was published in 1521 in England as *The Book of the Duke of True Lovers.*
- First poetry by a woman to be published: *Centones,* a book of poems by *Proba* of Rome, fifth century, was published in 1513.
- First European collection of biographies of women: *De Claris Mulieribus (About Illustrious Women)* by Giovanni Boccaccio, ca. 1370, written in Latin. A French translation appeared in 1493, and the first Italian edition followed in 1506.
- First professional female writer in English: *Aphra Behn,*♀ (1640–1689). Forced by circumstances to earn her own living, she was first a secret agent in Holland. When this proved unremunerative, Behn turned to writing; between 1670 and 1687 she produced nineteen plays and from 1683 to 1688, eleven prose works.
- First American female poet: *Anne Bradstreet*♀ (1612–1672), whose

brother-in-law, without her knowledge, published a collection of her poems in London in 1650 under the title *The Tenth Muse, Lately sprung up in America.*

- First daily newspaper in the world: the *Daily Courant,* founded and edited by **Elizabeth Mallet** in London in March 1702. Mallet said it was her intention to "spare the public at least half the impertinences which the ordinary papers contain."
- First women's magazine edited by a woman: the *Female Tatler,* begun in England in July 1709 by "Mrs. Crackenthorpe," actually the notorious **Mary de la Rivière Manley** who, in October 1709, was arrested for libel for her no-holds-barred book *Secret Memoirs and Manners of Several Persons of Quality.* Stories in her magazine were equally scandalous: The *Female Tatler,* indicted by a grand jury, soon told no more.
- The first non-European to win the Prix Goncourt: **Antonine Maillet,** a French Canadian novelist and playwright, who won the top French literary award in 1979 for her novel *Pelagie-la-Charrette,* a celebration of the history of the Acadians, the French-speaking people of Canada's New Brunswick province.
- First female editor in chief of the nation's oldest daily college newspaper: **Andy (Anne) Perkins,** a twenty-year-old junior, chosen to head the *Yale Daily News* for 1979–1980. When she was a sophomore, her investigative reporting resulted in a series of articles detailing the misuse of $67,000 by a school official, leading to a Yale scandal and the official's resignation.
- First woman "Immortal": **Marguerite Yourcenar** (b. 1903), elected to the French Academy in March 1980. Novelist, classicist, historian, and translator, she triumphed in a secret ballot despite opposition expressed by one member: "The Académie has survived over 300 years without women, and it could survive another 300 without them." Yourcenar was born in Brussels and lives on Mount Desert Island in Maine. The male Immortals clearly preferred to choose a woman who could be expected to keep at a discreet distance.

SIX WRITERS OF LONG AGO

Sappho ♀ (ca. 610–580 B.C.) was called the "Tenth Muse" by Plato. She wrote passionate romantic poetry about and probably for women. Her poems were preserved because, unlike most writings of the day, they were inscribed on long-lasting papyrus.

Al-Khansa (ca. A.D. 645) wrote elegiac verses in Arabic, as did her daughter *Amra.* But that was before Islam conquered the Arab world and silenced its women until the twentieth century.

Marie de France, whose short narrative poems have been issued as *The Lais [Lays] of Marie de France,* may have been the Mother Abbess of Shaftesbury and was a half sister of Henry of Aragon (Henry II). The twelfth-century writer claimed that her poems were translations into English of lays composed by the minstrels of Brittany. Numerous manuscript copies exist, but the *Lays* were not published in book form until 1819.

Catherine Benincasa (1347-1380), the daughter of a Siena dyer, had visions from early childhood on and in 1370 was directed by one to become involved in political affairs. Although she had never learned to write, she dictated hundreds of letters to influential men of the day and also dictated a noted mystic work, *A Treatise on Divine Providence* (later known as *The Dialogue of Saint Catherine of Siena*).

Christine de Pisan ♀ (1364-ca. 1430) wrote *Cité des dames* in about 1405, a book in dialogue form recounting the achievements of specific women. Many women of her era are known to us only because de Pisan recorded their accomplishments. She also employed women artisans.

THREE PROSE WRITERS OF EARLY AMERICA

Mary White Rowlandson became the first narrative writer in the colonies in about 1675 with her account of her capture by the Indians, called *Captivity and Restoration*.

Hannah Webster Foster's *The Coquette* (1797) was a fictionalized version of the story of Elizabeth Whitman, a cousin; in it, a girl of good family is taken advantage of, suffers, and finally dies—although family and friends are ready to forgive.

Susannah Rowson (b. 1762) wrote *Charlotte, a Tale of Truth,* later known as *Charlotte Temple,* in 1791. It was also based on a local scandal, in which a woman, seduced and abandoned, dies in childbirth, and was first published in England before its 1794 appearance in the United States. A sequel, *Charlotte's Daughter,* soon followed. After launching her career as a novelist, Rowson joined her husband's acting troupe, adapting plays and performing in at least eighty-eight roles before leaving the theater in the late 1790s, when she established a school in Boston.

ELEVEN COLONIAL POETS

Anne Dudley Bradstreet ♀ (1612-1672), the first poet in the colonies, had eight children and a difficult life. A couplet from one of her poems: "If what I did prove well, it won't advance; / They'll say it's stolen, or else it was by chance."

Mercy Otis Warren ♀ (1728-1814), born in Plymouth Colony, is more noted as a historian.

Phillis Wheatley ♀ (ca. 1755-1784) was born in Africa and sold as a slave in Boston in 1761. Her mistress, Mrs. Wheatley, educated her; her *Poems on Various Subjects* were published in London in 1773; her poem honoring George Washington was published in the April 1776 *Pennsylvania Magazine*.

Jane Coleman Turrell (1708-1735) was born in Boston. After her premature death, her biography, including her poems, was published by her husband, Ebenezer Turrell.

Sarah Wentworth Morton (1759–1846) lived in Braintree, Massachusetts. Among her many verse efforts: *Beacon Hill* and *The Virtues of Society*, two parts of an unfinished rhymed history of the American Revolution.

Elizabeth Graeme Ferguson (1739–1801) and *Susanna Wright* both lived and wrote in Pennsylvania.

Deborah Norris Logan (1761–1839) was a social and intellectual leader as well as a poet.

Annis Boudinot Stockton? (1736–1801) of Pennsylvania wrote patriotic verses on liberty published during the Revolutionary War.

Anne Eliza Schuyler Bleecker (1752–1783) of New York had her poems appear in the *New York Magazine*; they were published in book form after her premature death, brought on by hardships suffered fleeing from the British during the Revolutionary War and her successful rescue of her captured husband.

Lucy Terry was a slave in Deerfield, Massachusetts. Her 1746 verses recounted an Indian raid on that town.

SEVEN ORIGINALS:
The Women Behind the Tales

———————————————— ❧ ————————————————

Camille. Alphonsine Marie Duplessis inspired the character of the doomed Marguerite Gautier in *The Lady of the Camellias* by Alexandre Dumas fils. Duplessis had done laundry at thirteen, was a street prostitute at sixteen, and by twenty was the most successful courtesan in Paris. Her charm was such that she was said to be able to make any vice dignified. She and Dumas had a turbulent affair in 1844, and, like his heroine, she was at the mercy of her own emotions. "It's wrong to have a heart when you're a courtesan," she cried; "you can die of it." And by the age of twenty-three she was indeed dead—of consumption. Five months later Dumas began working on his novel. Ironically, in his old age the author became obsessed with the wickedness of prostitutes, petitioning the government to deport all women of the streets to the colonies.

Marie Roget. In Edgar Allan Poe's *The Mystery of Marie Roget*, the detective hero Dupin attempts to solve a murder by following newspaper accounts of the investigation. The real Marie Roget was *Mary Cecilia Rogers*, a New York girl who worked in a tobacconist's shop in the 1840s. Pretty girls were hired as salesclerks to entice male customers into the shop; apparently Rogers was too attractive. In July 1841 her body was found in the Hudson River; she had been raped and strangled. For months the city talked of the murder, one of the first crimes to be sensationalized in the press. In his version, Poe transposed the story to Paris.

Madame Bovary. Delphine Delamare, the original of Gustave Flaubert's bored provincial housewife, lived in the same small town as the author's father. Married at the age of seventeen to an older man, she dreamed of a more romantic existence, spent money recklessly, and indulged in several affairs. By the ninth year of her marriage she had lost her looks, and her husband was losing his credit. When Madame Delamare died at the age of twenty-seven, perhaps a suicide, her husband learned of his wife's infidelities for the first time and ended his own existence. *Madame Bovary* took Flaubert fifty-five months to write, at the rate of only six pages per week.

Alice in Wonderland. The stories that mathematician Charles Dodgson (Lewis Carroll) used to spin for, and about, young *Alice Liddell*, the daughter of his Oxford colleague Dean Liddell, became the basis for this novel and its successor, *Through the Looking Glass.*

The Unsinkable Mrs. Brown. Her biography by Caroline Bancroft became a musical play by Meredith Wilson; the original: shanty-born *Maggie Tobin.* She married mine foreman James J. Brown and, when his mine paid off, the Browns were wealthy beyond their wildest dreams. They moved from the Colorado hills to Denver and there the rough-hewn Maggie set about becoming refined. She changed her name to Molly and bought her way into society, built a couple of mansions, including one back east in Newport, Rhode Island, and established a salon in Paris. She was labeled "unsinkable" after she helped to evacuate women and children—and herself—from the *Titanic.* Later in life she dropped her parvenu ambitions and became a welfare worker and philanthropist.

Frankie and Johnny. In 1899 mulatto prostitute *Frankie Baker* shot her faithless lover at 212 Targee Street in St. Louis. The song this incident inspired was originally called "Frankie and Albert," after the lover she had actually killed, but was soon transformed into "Frankie and Johnny." Baker, who was never convicted of the crime, eventually managed a shoeshine parlor in Portland, Oregon, and received an award for good citizenship. When Helen Morgan sang the song in the 1938 film *Frankie and Johnny,* Baker sued unsuccessfully for invasion of privacy.

Diamond Lil. Mae West♀ based her long-running play on the career of *Evelyn Hildegard,* a honky-tonk singer and yodeler who had a small diamond set in one of her front teeth. Although she styled herself the "Toast of the Barbary Coast" and the "Belle of New York," Hildegard never achieved great popularity as a performer. She was past forty-five when she settled down in Boise, Idaho, and became "Miss Lil," owner of a select type of rooming house. By the 1940s she was running a motel on the outskirts of the city.

REDISCOVERED FICTION

In 1977 Arno Press began reissuing long-forgotten novels by women, as selected by novelist and critic Elizabeth Hardwick. The first eighteen titles:

Dead Lovers Are Faithful Lovers by *Frances Newman,* originally published in 1928.
The Hard-Boiled Virgin by *Frances Newman,* 1926.
Black Is My Truelove's Hair by *Elizabeth Madox Roberts,* 1938.
The Narrow House by *Evelyn Scott,* 1921.

Narcissus by *Evelyn Scott,* 1922.
Country People by *Ruth Suckow,* 1924.
Iowa Interiors by *Ruth Suckow,* 1926.
The Story of Avis by *Elizabeth S. P. Ward,* 1879.
Anne by *Constance Fenimore Woolson,* 1882.
Work: A Story of Experience by *Louisa May Alcott,* ♀ 1873.
A Woman of Genius by *Mary Austin,* 1912.
The Shoulders of Atlas by *Mary E. Wilkins Freeman,* 1908.
The Man of the Hour by *Alice French,* 1905.
The Descendant by *Ellen Glasgow,* 1897.
The Romantic Comedians by *Ellen Glasgow,* 1926.
The Anglomaniacs by *Constance Cary Harrison,* 1890.
Nothing Is Sacred by *Josephine Herbst,* 1928.
Money for Love by *Josephine Herbst,* 1929.

EIGHT BEST-SELLING NOVELISTS

Anne Radcliffe ♀ became the most popular and best-paid English novelist of
the eighteenth century by scaring her readers to death—and fulfilling
their romantic fantasies at the same time. Books by the "Mother of the
Gothic" were full of ghostly screams, mysterious keys, creepy castles,
and twisted villains the reader might just find attractive. Her biggest
best sellers were *The Romance of the Forest* (1791) and *The Mysteries of
Udolpho* (1794). In contrast to the blood and thunder of her books, Mrs.
Radcliffe was a shy woman who kept her personal life private.

Harriet Beecher Stowe, ♀ as the wife of a struggling schoolteacher and the
mother of five young children, needed money. With her husband's encouragement, she wrote and, in 1852, published *Uncle Tom's Cabin,* the
powerful antislavery novel that, in Abraham Lincoln's words, "started
our great war." Within a year, 300,000 copies of the book in twenty
editions were sold, making it an unprecedented best seller for its time,
and it was translated into nineteen languages, including Armenian,
Portuguese, and Welsh.

Elinor Glyn ♀ styled herself as the "high priestess of love" and wrote the purple prose her readers imagined typified the torrid affairs of the well-to-
do during the roaring twenties. Her first novel, *Three Weeks,* sold
5,000 copies in one month, to be followed by *It*—the term she had
coined for sex appeal. *It* was equally successful, and Glyn moved to
Hollywood, where she was lionized as an expert on the ways of passion
and where, she later claimed, she showed Rudolph Valentino and
Gloria Swanson ♀ how to make love in front of the camera.

Margaret Mitchell ♀ grew up in Atlanta with the Civil War on her mind, her
childhood filled with tales of "the cause." Forced by an injury to give
up her job as a reporter, she began a novel, writing the last chapter first
and working backward. It took nine years. In 1935 a friend casually
mentioned it to a visiting New York editor—and in June 1936 the
1,037-page *Gone With the Wind* went on sale. Mitchell, ever modest,
hoped for a sale of 5,000, but on one day alone during the summer the

book sold 50,000 copies. By 1949, 8 million copies had been sold in thirty languages in forty countries.

Kathleen Winsor would later recall that at eighteen she had written "a list of things I was going to do with my life. One of them was that I was going to write a best seller." When her student husband had to write a term paper on Charles II, Winsor became fascinated by Restoration England; while he was overseas during World War II she read 356 books about the period. Then she produced six drafts of a book about a sexy and ambitious woman's rise to the top of seventeenth-century society. The book was published in 1944 as *Forever Amber* and became a scandal and sensation. Twentieth Century-Fox bought the film rights for $200,000—four times what had been paid for *Gone With the Wind.*

Grace Metalious never much cared for life in the small town of Gilmanton, New Hampshire, where she was the wife of the school principal and the mother of three children. In 1956 she blew the lid off the town with the publication of *Peyton Place,* which sold 300,000 hardcover copies and more than 8 million in paperback. A sequel, *Return to Peyton Place,* published in 1959, sold more than 4 million copies in paperback, and a third, *The Tight White Collar* (1965), 2 million. Metalious divorced her husband in 1958, briefly married a disc jockey, divorced him, and remarried her first husband. The pair separated again shortly before her death in 1964.

Barbara Cartland♀ at seventy-six is the author of 235 best-selling romances, all love stories, called "virgins" because they include none of the sexual specifics expected in fiction today. In 1978 alone Cartland produced 24 of them. Once she has the full plot in her mind, she dictates the book to her secretarial staff. The English author has written a number of nonfiction books as well and is a qualified historian.

Jacqueline Susann♀ was the top-selling novelist of all time. Her first best seller, *The Valley of the Dolls* (1966), sold more than 17 million copies, and successive volumes such as *The Love Machine* (1969) and *Once Is Not Enough* (1974) quickly rose to number one. Susann, who started as an actress, once described herself as a "book machine," and to literary criticism of the sex and sensationalism that reigned in her novels she retorted, "A good writer is one who produces books that people read. . . . So if I'm selling millions, I'm good."

THE LURE OF LURID ROMANCE

There's gold in them thar fantasies, as these best sellers, directed at women, show.

Title	*Copies in Print*
Wicked Loving Lies by **Rosemary Rogers** (Avon, 1976)	3,100,000
Dark Fires by **Rosemary Rogers** (Avon, 1975)	2,882,000
Sweet Savage Love by **Rosemary Rogers** (Avon, 1974)	2,729,000
The Flame and the Fury by **Kathleen Woodiwiss** (Avon, 1972)	2,655,500

Title	Copies in Print
Love's Tender Fury by *Jennifer Wilde* ♀ (Warner, 1976)	2,500,000
The Wolf and the Dove, by *Kathleen Woodiwiss* (Avon, 1974)	2,290,000
Shanna by *Kathleen Woodiwiss* (Avon, 1977)	1,840,000
Moonstruck Madness by *Laurie McBain* (Avon, 1977)	1,800,000
This Loving Torrent by *Valerie Sherwood* (Warner, 1977)	1,512,000
Dawn of Desire by *Joyce Verrette* (Avon, 1976)	1,500,000
Mavreen by *Claire Lorrimer* (Bantam, 1977)	1,500,000
Love's Wildest Promise by *Patricia Matthews* (Pinnacle, 1977)	1,320,000
Savage Surrender by *Natasha Peters* (Ace, 1977)	1,300,000
Dare to Love by *Jennifer Wilde* ♀ (Warner, 1978)	1,300,000
Love's Wildest Fires by *Christina Savage* (Dell, 1977)	1,300,000
Liliane by *Annabel Erwin* (Warner, 1976)	1,229,000

From Alice K. Turner, "The Tempestuous, Tumultuous, Turbulent, Torrid, and Terribly Profitable World of Paperback Passion," *New York* magazine, February 13, 1978

GETTING THE TOP DOLLAR

Helen Van Slyke received more than $1 million as an advance against royalties from Bantam Books for English-language rights to four unwritten novels. (Van Slyke, who died in 1979, reportedly left a large slice of that money to her editor and her agent in her will, setting other publishers' eyes aglow with dreams.)

Dorothy Uhnak, a former New York City police officer, received $1,595,000 for the reprint rights to *The Investigation.*

Colleen McCullough's *The Thorn Birds* was bought by Avon Books for $1.9 million.

Barbara Taylor Bradford's *A Woman of Substance* (Doubleday) was auctioned for publication in England for $110,000, the highest amount to be paid in Great Britain for a work of fiction by an unknown author.

Linda Goodman saw *Linda Goodman's Sun Signs* (1969) become the first astrology book ever to appear on the *New York Times* Best-Seller List; nearly ten years later a renewal of the paperback rights brought her $500,000. At the same time the reprint rights for *Linda Goodman's Love Signs* were sold to Fawcett Books for $2.25 million, the highest paperback price to that date for a nonfiction book.

Erma Bombeck, author of several comic volumes on domestic life, was guaranteed $1.9 million in 1979 for reprint rights to *Aunt Erma's Cope Book.*

Judith Krantz's novel *Scruples* sold more than 3¼ million copies in 1978–1979. In a fourteen-and-a-half-hour auction conducted by telephone in New York City in September 1979, Bantam Books acquired reprint rights for Krantz's second novel, *Princess Daisy,* for $3,208,875, setting two new records: the highest sum ever paid for a single title, and paid in a single transaction.

BELOVED BY GENERATIONS OF CHILDREN

❧

Louisa May Alcott,♀ for *Little Women, Little Men, Jo's Boys,* and a dozen other titles that began appearing in 1868.

Frances Hodgson Burnett, for *The Secret Garden,* the 1910 mystery tale that gently explored the psychology of an unpleasant, unloved, unwanted child.

Wanda Gag, for *Millions of Cats* (1928) and other storybooks for the very young.

Lucretia P. Hale, for *The Complete Peterkin Papers,* an 1880 compilation of previously published stories of a family whose members keep getting into improbable—and avoidable—scrapes.

Carolyn Keene♀ (*Harriet S. Adams*), for the fifty-nine Nancy Drew mystery tales she has completed in the last fifty of her eighty-seven years.

Selma Lagerlof, for *The Wonderful Adventures of Nils,* a 1907 fantasy about a small boy who could fly on the back of a wild goose.

Astrid Lindgren, for *Pippi Longstocking,* whose several adventures since 1950 have made it acceptable for girls everywhere to be unconventional in some ways.

Lucy M. (*Maude*) *Montgomery,* for turning Canada's Prince Edward Island into a familiar neighborhood in *Anne of Green Gables* and its sequels.

E. Nesbit (*Edith Nesbit Bland*), for her Victorian-era Barnstable Books, stories of magic and turn-of-the-century tales of *The Wouldbegoods.*

Beatrix Potter,♀ for *The Tale of Peter Rabbit* and her numerous other animal stories, featuring such unforgettable characters as Mrs. Tiggy-Winkle, Jemima Puddle-Duck, and Squirrel Nutkin.

Marjorie Kinnan Rawlings,♀ for *The Yearling,* a 1938 novel about a boy, his father, and the deer he tries to protect.

Anna Sewall, for *Black Beauty,* the all-time classic horse story, published in 1911.

Johanna Spyri, for her 1880 adventures of an energetic Swiss child, *Heidi.*

P. L. (*Pamela*) *Travers,* for *Mary Poppins,* the 1934 tale of a most fantastic nanny.

Laura Ingalls Wilder, for all the *Little House* books from 1932 on, based on the experiences of the pioneer Wilder family in Wisconsin.

TWENTY-ONE BLACK WOMEN WHO WRITE
ABOUT BLACK WOMEN

❧

Marian Anderson,♀ *My Lord, What a Morning,* autobiography (1956).

Maya Angelou, I Know Why the Caged Bird Sings, autobiography (1969).

Roseann P. Bell, Bettye J. Parker, and *Beverly Guy Shaftall,* eds., *Sturdy Black Bridges: Visions of Black Women in Literature* (1979).

Toni Cade, The Black Woman, an anthology of writings (1970).

Nikki Giovanni,♀ *Black Feeling, Black Talk—Black Judgment* (1970), *Gemini* (1971), and other works in poetry and prose.

Charlotte Forten Grimké,♀ *Journal,* a record of her life, begun in the 1850s when she was in her teens and first published in abridged form in 1953.

Lorraine Hansberry,♀ *To Be Young, Gifted, and Black,* autobiography of the playwright and poet (1969).
Frances Watkins Harper, *Poems on Miscellaneous Subjects,* generally the abuses of slavery (1854); and *Iola LeRoy,* a novel (1892).
Zora Neale Hurston, *Their Eyes Were Watching God,* novel (1937); *Dust Tracks on a Road,* autobiography (1942); and numerous poems, plays, stories, and novels that made her a leader of the Harlem Renaissance of the 1920s and 1930s.
June Jordan, *Who Look at Me* (1969), *Some Changes* (1971), and other collections of her poetry.
Elizabeth Keckley, *Behind the Scenes; or Thirty Years a Slave, and Four Years in the White House,* an autobiography featuring details of First Family life as she observed them while dressmaker to Mary Todd Lincoln, an 1868 sensation.
Coretta King, *My Life with Martin Luther King, Jr.* (1969).
Joyce Ladner, *Tomorrow's Tomorrow: The Black Woman* (1971).
Audre Lorde, *The First Cities* (1968), *Cables to Rage* (1970), and other books of poetry and essays.
Paule Marshall, *Brown Girl, Brownstones,* autobiography (1959).
Anne Moody, *Coming of Age in Mississippi,* autobiography (1959).
Toni Morrison,♀ *The Bluest Eye* (1970), *Sula* (1973), and *Song of Solomon* (1977), novels.
Ann Petry, *Harriet Tubman, Conductor on the Underground Railroad* (1955) and *Tituba of Salem Village* (1964), biographies for younger readers, as well as novels for adults.
Ntozake Shange,♀ *For Colored Girls Who Have Considered Suicide/When the Rainbow Is Enuf* (1977) and other plays.
Inez Smith Reid, *"Together" Black Women* (1975).
Michele Wallace, *Black Macho and the Myth of the Superwoman* (1978).

ALL ABOUT MEN

A few brave women have undertaken the risky task of interpreting male psyches—and in one case physique.

Genevieve Antoine-Darioux, *The Men in Your Life* (1968).
Phyllis Chesler, *About Men* (1978).
Rachel Copelan, *The Sexually Fulfilled Man* (1972).
Nancy Friday, *Men in Love: Men's Sexual Fantasies, The Triumph of Love over Rage* (1980).
Natalie Gittelson, *Dominus: A Woman Looks at Men's Lives* (1973).
Florence King, *He: An Irreverent Look at the American Male* (1978).
Gerarda Maria Kooiman-Van Middendorp, *The Hero in the Feminine Novel* (1966).
Nancy Mayer, *The Male Mid-life Crisis* (1978).
Joan Mellen, *Big Bad Wolves* (1977), about men in films.
Karen Shanor, *The Sexual Sensitivity of the American Male* (1978).
Jacqueline Simmenauer, with Anthony Pietropinto, *Beyond the Male Myth* (1977).

Anne Steinman, with David Fox, *The Male Dilemma: How to Survive the Sexual Revolution* (1974).
Margaret Walters, The Nude Male: A New Perspective (1978).

QUEENS OF CRIME

❧

Margery Allingham (1904–1966), creator of detective Albert Campion, made her first serious literary attempt at age seven. After her marriage to artist and editor Philip Youngman Carter in 1927, he became her literary adviser and unofficial collaborator and, after she died, completed the last of her two dozen books, *Cargo of Eagles* (1968). Allingham briefly abandoned mysteries for the war effort during World War II and also produced two works of English social history.

Charlotte Armstrong (1905–1969), a fashion reporter, turned to mystery writing while raising three children in a suburb of New York City. Her fourth mystery, *The Unsuspected* (1946), brought both book and film success and a permanent move to southern California. The film *Don't Bother to Knock* (1952), which starred Marilyn Monroe ♀ as a deranged baby-sitter, was based on a 1950 Armstrong work, *Mischief.*

Christianna Brand (Mary Christianna Milne Lewis) (b. 1907), forced to leave school at age seventeen when her father lost all his money, was a governess, dress packer, nightclub hostess, ballroom dancer, secretary, model, interior decorator, and salesclerk. She wrote *Death in High Heels* (1941) to take revenge in fantasy on another worker who irritated her. With the book's success Brand's hungry days were over; she wrote detective novels for fourteen years before switching to shorter mystery fiction.

Renee Buse (1914–1979) was editor in chief of *True Detective* and *Master Detective* magazines in the 1950s and wrote several detective stories as well as a true crime thriller, *The Deadly Silence* (1965). Because the market for her stories was in men's magazines, Buse used pen names, including "Robert Benton" and "Michael King." Her later career included stints as a children's book editor and as vice-president of an international health organization.

Dame Agatha Christie ♀ (1891–1976), foremost mystery writer of the century, wrote eighty-five mystery novels, more than one hundred short stories, seventeen plays, and an autobiography before her death in 1976. It has been estimated that nearly 400 million copies of her works have been sold throughout the world.

P. D. James (b. 1920) was a civil servant in the British Hospital Service for nearly twenty years before she began writing mysteries in 1961 to support her family during her husband's illness. She has written eight books so far featuring Adam Dalgliesh, the poetizing detective from Scotland Yard, as well as the best-selling non-Dalgliesh novel, *Innocent Blood.* James, who is really *Phyllis Dorothy White,* is regularly employed in the criminal law department of the Home Office.

Emma Lathen is the pen name of *Mary J. Latsis,* an attorney, and *Martha Henissart,* an economic analyst, who met while graduate students at

Harvard, discovered a mutual addiction to mysteries, and decided to write one for the fun of it. Like his creators, the amateur sleuth John Putnam Thatcher, senior vice-president of the Sloan Guaranty Trust Company, moves in the world of high finance; in seventeen mysteries he has solved murders that threaten his bank's investments.

Ngaio Marsh (b. 1899), a native of New Zealand and a theatrical director and producer as well as mystery writer, limits the number of investigations undertaken by her urbane detective, Superintendent Roderick Alleyn, so that she can devote at least half of each year to the theater. Working part-time, she has produced twenty-nine titles. Marsh was made a Dame of the British Empire in 1966.

Mary Roberts Rinehart ♀ (1876–1958), a graduate nurse, saw her reputation established with her first mystery, *The Circular Staircase* (1908), which, with Avery Hopwood, she later dramatized as *The Bat.* Her nineteen other whodunits also include *The Man in Lower Ten* and *The Yellow Room.*

Dorothy L. Sayers ♀ (1893–1957), secretly gave birth to a son in 1924, one year after she published her first mystery novel featuring Lord Peter Wimsey. Proceeds from the popular Wimsey books were used to support the boy, who was raised by a cousin after Sayers's subsequent marriage. In 1947 the author, a medieval scholar and one of the first women to receive an Oxford degree, lowered the curtain on her mystery-writing career ("I wrote the Peter Wimsey books when I was young and had no money") and devoted the last decade of her life to translating Dante.

Josephine Tey (*Elizabeth Mackintosh*) (1896–1952) worked briefly as a teacher of physical education and turned to her imagination for companionship during the last twenty-eight years of her life, which she spent nursing her ailing parents in a remote corner of Scotland. The first of her eight mysteries, *A Shilling for Candles*, appeared in 1936. In her best-known work, *The Daughter of Time* (1951), detective Alan Grant, confined to bed, decides to clear Richard III of the charges of having murdered his nephews in the Tower of London.

Dilys Winn, founder of the Manhattan bookstore called Murder Ink, received an Edgar from the Mystery Writers of America for a book of the same name about detective fiction and in 1979 compiled *Murderess Ink,* a companion volume of more than one hundred articles about women and whodunits.

"CHERCHEZ LA FEMME"—TO CATCH THE MURDERER

Among the scores of fictional female sleuths, let us celebrate these in particular:

Jane Brown, created by Delano Ames: the wife of amateur detective Dagobert Brown and the author of mystery novels.

Emily Bryce, created by Margaret Scherf: the scatterbrained spouse of amateur detective Henry Bryce.

Nora Charles, created by Dashiell Hammett: half of the "Thin Man" team with her socialite husband, Nick Charles.

Bertha Cool, created by A. A. Fair (Erle Stanley Gardner): weighs 200 pounds and is a partner in a private detective agency with Donald Lam.

Susan Dare, created by Mignon G. Eberhart: a female mystery writer with a penchant for stumbling onto real-life mysteries.

Theodolinda ("Dol") Bonner, created by Rex Stout: runs her own detective agency and is generally hostile to men.

Irish Duluth, created by Patrick Quentin: met her husband while both were patients in a mental hospital—now they solve mysteries from a psychological point of view.

Kate Fansler, created by Amanda Cross (pseudonym of Carolyn Heilbrun): an English professor who debuted in *In the Last Analysis* (1964), clearing a friend who was accused of murder, and has since appeared in four other Cross books.

Dr. Mary Finney, created by Matthew Head (pseudonym of John Canaday): a medical missionary in Africa who easily runs into cases in need of solution.

Miss Jane Marple, created by Agatha Christie ♀: a frail, aged inhabitant of St. Mary Mead, England, and one of the cleverest—and most durable—detectives ever.

Mom, created by James Yaffe: Mom never has to leave her dining-room chair to help her police officer son solve crimes; she dispenses chicken soup along with her advice.

Norah Mulcahaney, created by Lillian O'Donnell: a New York City homicide detective, married to a police lieutenant, who fought her way up in the department. O'Donnell conceived of Norah the night of the first New York City blackout (1965), and her career parallels that of many "real" women now rising in the law enforcement world.

Rachel Murdock, created by D. B. Olsen (pseudonym of Dolores Hitchens): a spinsterish cat fancier who loves to interfere in the lives of others; she's good at solving mysteries, too.

Pamela North, created by Frances and Richard Lockridge: a trouble-prone housewife who, with her husband, Jerry, constitutes one of the most popular husband-wife detective teams of all time.

Christie Opara, created by Dorothy Uhnak ♀: the widow of a slain New York City cop, Christie is a police officer herself.

Miss Marion Phipps, created by Phyllis Bentley: with her "chubby pink face and untidy white hair," Miss Phipps drives through the English countryside and solves murders wherever she goes.

Miss Pinkerton, created by Mary Roberts Rinehart ♀: the name given to Nurse Adams by the police who ask her to do a great deal of their crime solving.

Mrs. Jane Pollifax, created by Dorothy Gilman: a detective who works for the CIA.

Mrs. Pym, created by Nigel Morland: the assistant commissioner of the Criminal Investigation Department and the highest-ranking woman in the history of Scotland Yard.

Miss Emily Seeton, created by Heron Carvic: an elderly art teacher who frequently runs into crime while strolling the streets of London.

Jemima Shore, created by biographer Antonia Fraser ♀: a television star who also finds time for amateur sleuthing, Shore is bright, beautiful—and invariably right.

Miss Maud Silver, created by Patricia Wentworth (pseudonym of Dora Amy Dillon Turnbull): a former governess who turned to detective work to supplement her meager income.

Harriet Vane, created by Dorothy L. Sayers ♀: she was on trial for murdering her lover—when detective Lord Peter Wimsey lost his own heart to her. In *Gaudy Night* (1935) the independent and intellectual Harriet is the dominant detective and solves a mystery at a women's college at Oxford similar to the one Sayers attended.

Honey West, created by G. G. Fickling (pseudonym of Gloria and Forest E. Fickling): a beautiful blond private eye in her late twenties.

Persis Willum, created by Clarissa Watson: an artist and amateur sleuth inhabitant of "Gull Harbor," Long Island, who solves art-related crimes—including murder.

Hildegard Withers, created by Stuart Palmer: a lean spinster with an irritable disposition—but a romantic heart.

BY WOMEN PUBLISHED:

Sixteen Feminist Publishing Houses in the United States

━━━━━━━━━━━━━━━━━━━ ✹ ━━━━━━━━━━━━━━━━━━━

Alicejamesbooks, Cambridge, Massachusetts.
Daughters Publishing, Houston, Texas.
Diana Press, Oakland, California.
Dustbooks, Paradise, California.
Feminist Press, Old Westbury, New York.
Lollipop Power, Chapel Hill, North Carolina.
Moon Books, Berkeley, California.
Naiad Press, Weatherby Lake, Missouri.
New Seed Press, Palo Alto, California.
Out & Out Books, Brooklyn, New York.
Rainbow Books, Carlstadt, New Jersey.
Shameless Hussy Press, Berkeley, California.
Times Change Press, Albion, California.
Valkyrie Press, St. Petersburg, Florida.
Vanilla Press, Minneapolis, Minnesota.
Vanity Press, Atlanta, Georgia.

MAGAZINE WOMEN OF THE NINETEENTH CENTURY

━━━━━━━━━━━━━━━━━━━ ✹ ━━━━━━━━━━━━━━━━━━━

The first women's column in an American magazine was the "Occasional Letter on the Female Sex" in Thomas Paine's 1775 *Pennsylvania Magazine.* The first magazine exclusively for women was published in 1792 in Philadelphia by one William Gibbons. Appropriately named *Lady's Magazine,* this venture was not notably successful and folded the following year. Since then, however, this has proved a fertile field. Some early titles and dates: *Ladies Museum,* Philadelphia (1800); *The Ladies' Magazine and Musical Repository,* Philadelphia (1801–1802); *Lady's Weekly Miscellany,* New York (1805–1808); *The Ladies Afternoon Visitor,* Boston (1806–1807); and *Ladies' Garland,* Harpers Ferry, West Virginia (1824). More notable:

The Ladies Magazine, published in Boston from 1828 to 1837, by **Sarah Josepha Hale**♀, also a writer of poems and stories. Its most memorable feature was probably the 1830 publication of "Mary Had a Little Lamb," written, in part or in whole, by Hale herself (there is a dispute about the authorship).

Godey's Lady's Book, Philadelphia (1830–1898). In 1837 founder William Godey asked Hale to come aboard as editor, and with her at the helm, *Godey's* became an American institution, publishing nonfiction, fiction, fashion news, and crafts and stitchery instruction. Hand-colored fashion prints were a staple—and are today collectors' items.

Ladies Companion was published in New York from 1834 to 1844 by **Lydia Huntley Sigourney.**♀ She was born in 1791, and her first book, *Moral Pieces, in Prose and Verse,* was issued when she was twenty. In 1849 her collected poems were issued in a volume uniform with the collected poems of William Cullen Bryant and Henry Wadsworth Longfellow, and by the time she died in 1865, Sigourney's poems had been issued in no less than forty-eight volumes, and she had written 2,000 articles for her magazine and others.

Peterson's Ladies' National Magazine, published in Philadelphia from 1842 to 1898 by Charles J. Peterson and **Ann Stephans,** was *Godey's* chief competition in fashion and timely articles.

Union Magazine of Literature and Art was published from 1847 to 1852 by the novelist **Caroline M. (Stansbury) Kirkland.**

Mrs. Whittelsey's Magazine for Mothers, an idea perhaps ahead of its time, was a New York publication of 1850 to 1852, from **Mrs. A. G. Whittelsey.**

Genius of Liberty was a Cincinnati entry from **Mrs. E. A. Aldrich,** lasting only from 1852 to 1854.

Pioneer and Woman's Advocate appeared for a few months in 1852, the product of **Anna W. Spencer** of Providence.

Frank Leslie's Lady's Magazine, later to be known as **Leslie's Weekly,** was started in 1857. Leslie was the fourth husband of **Miriam ("Minnie") Leslie**♀; when he died in 1880, she spent a year in proper seclusion, then announced that just before he died, her husband had instructed her to manage the business and pay off the creditors. She turned the magazine around and made herself a fortune, as well as becoming the most successful businesswoman and most glamorous woman of her day before her retirement twenty years later.

FOURTEEN MAGAZINE WOMEN TODAY

Harriet Monroe founded *Poetry* magazine in 1912 and before it was a dozen years old had published the most important poets of the early twentieth century, including Ezra Pound, Wallace Stevens, T. S. Eliot, William Carlos Williams, and Conrad Aiken. According to critic Irving Howe, Monroe "was a poor poet, indifferent critic, gifted fund-raiser. . . . She also had a touch of cultural genius."

Margaret Anderson founded the *Little Review,* "A Magazine of the Arts, Making No Compromise with the Public Taste," in 1914 on an impulse and over the next fifteen years published such great writers and artists as William Butler Yeats, Ezra Pound, T. S. Eliot, and Pablo Picasso. She enthusiastically excerpted James Joyce's *Ulysses* over three years, during which time the magazine was burned four times for alleged obscenity by order of the U.S. Post Office. When Anderson got bored with her magazine, she turned it over to an associate, who kept it going until 1929. Virtually penniless, Anderson spent most of the rest of her long life in France, where she died in 1973 at the age of eighty-six.

Lila Acheson Wallace and her husband, DeWitt Wallace, founded the *Reader's Digest* in 1922 and ran it for fifty years; they continue as directors of the phenomenon today. The profits have subsidized such generous—and imaginative—philanthropies as the Bronx Zoo's fabulous birds exhibit and the lavish fresh flower arrangements in the lobby of the Metropolitan Museum of Art, among many others.

Lu Esther Mertz in 1962 founded *Choice Magazine Listening,* an aural magazine for the blind that offers eight hours of listening every other month, composed of articles selected from fifty current periodicals. *Marion Loeb* is executive editor.

Helen Gurley Brown ♀ revitalized the ailing *Cosmopolitan* in 1965 with a combination of sex and pizzazz directed at "that *Cosmopolitan* girl," the multifaceted, smart, sex-kittenish single working woman who can pick and choose her man.

Pat Carbine, Liz Harris, and *Gloria Steinem* ♀ established *Ms.* magazine in 1972 to bring the word of liberation to women (and men) everywhere.

Leda Giovannetti Sanford has been president, publisher, and editor in chief of *American Home* magazine and president and publisher of *Chief Executive* magazine; is now publisher and editor in chief of *Attenzione,* a magazine for Italian-Americans.

Cathleen Black, thirty-five, is copublisher of *New York* magazine and formerly the associate publisher of *Ms.*

Gray Davis Boone, publisher of *Antiques Monthly* and several spin-offs, became editor and publisher of a revived version of an in-the-red *Horizon* magazine in September 1978; by April of the following year was able to boast that every issue was being published at a profit.

Zelfa Draz, a twenty-eight-year-old Syrian-born Turkish woman, started *Sheba,* a fashion magazine in Arabic for women in the families of Arab oil millionaires, in 1979. To an audience that the publisher describes as having little to do but "sit around, change dresses, and flip through magazines" *Sheba* brings news of fashion, art, architecture, literature, interior decoration, travel, and entertaining.

Ava Stern started *Enterprising Women* as a newsletter and after four years was ready to turn it into a full-fledged magazine, with a 50,000-copy preview issue in January 1980. Her target audience is her own list of 2 million self-employed women and 1 million businesses owned and operated by women. Among the latter: her own Artemis Enterprises.

MS. PUBLISHER

❧

Helen Rogers Reid and her husband, Ogden M. Reid, became publishers of the *New York Tribune* in 1912, then purchased another noted New York journal a dozen years later to found the *New York Herald-Tribune,* with Helen Reid as its boss. After her husband died in 1947, Reid's two sons assumed management positions under their mother's leadership. The Reids' control came to an end in 1958, when financial difficulties and an accumulation of labor and financial problems resulted in the sale of the paper. It ceased publication less than a decade later.

Eleanor ("Cissy") Medill Patterson,♀ granddaughter of Joseph Medill, founder of the *Chicago Tribune,* persuaded William Randolph Hearst to let her edit his *Washington Herald* in 1930 when she was forty-six. Seven years later she added his evening *Washington Times* and in 1939 purchased both papers and merged them. At the *Herald* she created the women's page as well as the first gossip and scandal-mongering page, was the first person to cable fashion news from Paris to the States, and personally interviewed Chicago gangster Al Capone. After her death in 1948, her paper was purchased by and merged with the *Washington Post.*

Alicia Patterson (1906–1963) Cissy's niece, in 1940 founded and was editor and publisher of Long Island's *Newsday* until her death. Patterson had learned the business from her father, Joseph Medill Patterson, founder and publisher of the *New York Daily News,* and as a cub reporter for other family publications.

Agnes E. Meyer became de facto copublisher of the *Washington Post* when her husband purchased it in 1933. After her husband became president of the International Bank in 1946, she continued her active involvement with the paper, although the Meyers' son-in-law Philip L. Graham became publisher.

Katharine ("Kay") Meyer Graham took over as publisher of the *Washington Post* upon the death of her husband in 1964 and established it as one of America's major newspapers. In 1979 she handed the *Post, Newsweek,* and other media-related properties over to her son, but continued as chairwoman of the parent Washington Post Company. Graham was the only woman heading a "Fortune 500" company; in 1980 she was named chairwoman and president of the American Newspaper Publishers Association.

Dorothy ("Dolly") Schiff was associated with her family's newspaper, the *New York Post* (the oldest newspaper in the United States, published since 1801), as its major stockholder from 1939 and as its publisher from 1943 to 1976. She then sold the *Post* to Australian press magnate Rupert Murdoch. A leading supporter of liberal causes and the Democratic party, Schiff revealed in a 1976 authorized biography that she had had a clandestine relationship with President Franklin Roosevelt.

Dorothy ("Buffy") Buffum Chandler and her son Otis began to redesign and revitalize the *Los Angeles Times* in 1958, two years before her husband, Norman Chandler, publisher, resigned, and they jointly assumed full publication control. Although she has relinquished day-to-day control to her son, she still continues as a director of the Los Angeles Times–Mirror Company.

Helen Kinney Copley inherited the *San Diego Union and Evening Tribune* from her husband in 1973, became chairwoman of the board of the Copley News Service, and still presides over both.

BY THE SCRIPT:
Twenty-Five Women Playwrights

Hundreds of women have contributed their playwriting talents to the stages of the world. A few of the most notable:

Hrotswitha, a nun and the niece of the German emperor Otto I, wrote six religious dramas in Latin verse in the tenth century. Her works, based on the style of the Roman playwright Terence, were about mental and moral conflict and were intended for performance in her convent.

Aphra Behn's ♀ first play was produced in 1670; her fame was assured by *The Rover* in 1677. Her bawdy humor was a hit in Restoration London—and her unconventional life-style did not hurt at the box office.

Catharine Cockburn's first tragedy, *Agnes de Castro,* was produced at the Theatre Royal in London in 1695 when its author was sixteen years old and published (anonymously) the following year.

Joanna Baillie was a prolific writer of plays in verse; her *Plays on the Passions* (by which she meant "the stronger passions of the mind") in three volumes, issued from 1798 to 1812, brought her contemporary fame; she is remembered today for her verses set to traditional Scottish and Irish tunes and for her friendship with Sir Walter Scott.

Fanny Burney, the novelist and diarist, wrote *The Witlings,* called by critic Ellen Moers "very funny and quite stageworthy." It was, however, never produced because Burney's father, alarmed at the liberties she had taken in satirizing her influential intellectual female friends, interfered. Burney's blank-verse tragedy, *Edwy and Elvina,* lasted one performance in 1795.

Isabella Augusta, Lady Gregory, author of a series of plays based on Irish legends and history for the Abbey players in the early twentieth century, was a founder and director of Dublin's Abbey Theatre and the leading patron of the great twentieth-century flowering of Irish drama.

Rachel Crothers, called the "Neil Simon of her day," saw close to thirty of her plays open on Broadway between 1906 and 1937, mostly urbane comedies such as *Let Us Be Gay* (1929) and *When Ladies Meet* (1932); but some, such as the 1920s *He and She,* dealt with more thoughtful social issues as well. She continued to write plays almost until her death in 1958; from 1918 on she not only wrote, but directed and produced—and sometimes acted in—her plays as well. Among the stars of Crothers's plays: Ethel Barrymore,♀ Katharine Cornell, Tallulah Bankhead,♀ and Gertrude Lawrence.

Susan Glaspell's ♀ play *Alison's House* (1930), based on the life of Emily Dickinson,♀ won the Pulitzer Prize. She was also a novelist, actress, and cofounder, with her husband, of the Provincetown Players.

Clare Boothe Luce ♀ wrote *The Women* in 1939, a lethal portrait of the idle lives of wealthy women, drawn by a wealthy woman who worked hard as a journalist, politician, and diplomat.

Daphne du Maurier wrote the stage adaptation of her novel *Rebecca* (London, 1940; New York, 1945), as well as two other plays.

Bella Spewack and her husband, Sam, have collaborated on numerous plays, more than twenty films, and several television scripts. Best known are their book for the musical *Kiss Me Kate* (1958) and the play *My Three Angels* (1953).

Lillian Hellman wrote *The Little Foxes, The Children's Hour,* and more, and is considered by many the foremost woman playwright in the United States.

Carson McCullers adapted *A Member of the Wedding* from her own 1946 novel.

Lorraine Hansberry's ♀ best-known plays are *A Raisin in the Sun* (1959) and *The Sign in Sidney Brustein's Window.*

Cornelia Otis Skinner, born into an acting family in 1901, performed, from 1925 on, one-woman shows of her own short character sketches. Her first full-length play was *Captain Fury* (1925); more than a quarter of a century later she appeared in another of her plays, *The Pleasure of His Company* (1958), meanwhile continuing to create and tour in her character sketches.

Betty Comden has collaborated with one man, not her husband, all her professional life. She has written, with Adolph Green, lyrics, book, or both for such shows as *On the Town* (1944), *Wonderful Town* (1953), *Peter Pan* (1954), *Bells Are Ringing* (1956), *Subways Are for Sleeping* (1961), *Applause* (1970), and more, as well as screenplays.

Mary Orr has written many plays and more than forty television scripts with her husband, but is best known for the film and musical play based on her short story "The Wisdom of Eve," which became *All About Eve* (1950) and *Applause* (1970).

Ann Jellicoe, a leader in the experimental theater movement in England, has adapted and written numerous plays, the best known being *The Knack* (London, 1962).

Rochelle Owens wrote *The String Game, Istanboul, Futz, Beclch,* and other noted experimental theater pieces in the 1960s and 1970s.

Ntozake Shange's ♀ best-known works of the 1970s are *For Colored Girls Who Have Considered Suicide/When the Rainbow Is Enuf* and *Spell # 7.*

Gretchen Cryer and ***Nancy Ford,*** the only team of women writing musicals in the American theater, are the creators of, among other shows, *The Last Sweet Days of Isaac* and *I'm Getting My Act Together and Taking It on the Road.*

Micki Grant has written the music, lyrics, or book—or all three—for the Obie-winning *Don't Bother Me, I Can't Cope* (1971), *Your Arms Too Short to Box with God* (1978), and *It's So Nice to Be Civilized* (1980).

Eve Merriam, poet, teacher, and author of more than thirty books, spoofed male chauvinism in the Obie-winning *The Club* (1976)—a play that featured women in tuxedos playing members of a turn-of-the-century men's club.

Elizabeth Swados first came to critical attention in the early 1970s at the La

Mama Experimental Theatre Club, where she collaborated with Andrei Serban on startling new adaptations of *Medea, Electra,* and *The Trojan Women.* In 1978 she wrote, composed, choreographed, and directed *Runaways,* a collage of monologues and songs about adolescents estranged from their parents, which earned her a remarkable five Tony award nominations in one year.

Helen Hayes, with Vincent Price, in one of her best-known roles, *Victoria Regina* (1936). But there were others she longed to play. *Billy Rose Theatre Collection, New York Public Library at Lincoln Center.* (HELEN HAYES'S LIST OF "ROLES I WOULD HAVE LIKED TO PLAY BUT NEVER DID")

Ethel Waters was signed for her role in *As Thousands Cheer* (1933), after her smashing success at Harlem's Cotton Club. *Billy Rose Theatre Collection, New York Public Library at Lincoln Center.* (SIX WHO GOT A BREAK AT THE COTTON CLUB)

Virginia Payne, made up for her role as *Ma Perkins,* played the lead in the radio soap opera for 27 years. (THE THREE LONGEST-PLAYING SOAP OPERA ACTRESSES ON RADIO)

Harriet Beecher Stowe, author of *Uncle Tom's Cabin,* took up writing because she needed money. She's pictured here with her father, Lyman Beecher. *Sophia Smith Collection, Smith College.* (EIGHT BEST-SELLING NOVELISTS)

Shanty-born Margaret Tobin Brown rose to riches and fame as "The Unsinkable Mrs. Brown." *Denver Public Library, Western History Department.* (SEVEN ORIGINALS: THE WOMEN BEHIND THE TALES)

Simonetta Catteneo, Botticelli's model for the *Birth of Venus,* was idolized by the artist. *The Uffizi Gallery, Florence, Italy.* (FOURTEEN MODEL WOMEN)

(*Below left*): Grace G. Drayton, America's first female cartoonist, created these cherubs for a comic strip. Later they became the Campbell Kids. (DRAWING THE LINE)

(*Below right*): Rosa Bonheur, famed for her accurate paintings of animals, was the first woman artist to receive the Cross of the Legion of Honor. *Library of Congress.* (AT EASEL)

Frances Benjamin Johnston, the only woman prominent as a photo-journalist in the 1890s, in self-portrait. *Library of Congress.* (FRANCES BENJAMIN JOHNSTON AND HER FEMININE COLLEAGUES)

XIV ❧ FOR ART'S SAKE

THREE PAINTERS OF ANTIQUITY
❧

In *De Claris Mulieribus* (1370), Boccaccio combined brief biographies of 104 women of ancient times with moralizing commentaries. His sources for all were the writings of Pliny the Younger. Three artists were on his list:

Thamyris (whom Pliny had called Timarete), the daughter of the painter Micon, was known for her painting of Diana kept at the Temple of Ephesus. Boccaccio said Thamyris "scorned the duties of women and practiced her father's art."

Irene, also the daughter of a painter, did a picture of a girl that was at Eleusis; Boccaccio commented "that these achievements were worthy of some praise, for art is very much alien to the mind of woman, and these things cannot be accomplished without a great deal of talent, which in women is usually very scarce."

Marcia disavowed "womanly occupations, she gave herself up completely to the study of painting and sculpture so that she would not languish in idleness." Boccaccio claimed she surpassed Sopolis and Dionysius, the most famous painters of the day, worked harder and more rapidly than they did, and commanded higher prices. She carved and painted ivory, painted her self-portrait using a mirror, and remained unmarried.

KNOWN FOR THEIR NEEDLEWORK
❧

Until the end of the Middle Ages needlework was women's work, and large projects were collectively executed by teams of women, often under the aegis of a specific queen or abbess. After the fourteenth century the textile industry became "professionalized" as men in guilds took over most of the higher-paid work, although women continued to fill the workshops and do piecework. Some needlewomen of the Middle Ages whose work and names are known:

Harlinde and ***Relinde*** were eighth-century sisters who founded a settlement at Maaseik, now in Belgium, which many young women joined. The sisters created many embroidered wall hangings lavished with gold and jewels, and were also noted scribes and illuminators of manuscripts.

Queen Aelfflaed, the wife of Edward the Elder, is believed to have supervised production of the stole and maniple of St. Cuthbert in the tenth century; these works are now in the cathedral in Durham, England.

Queen Aelgiva, wife of Edward the Confessor, embroidered an altar cover in 1016 that was said to resemble a golden mosaic, worked in golden thread and studded with precious gems and pearls.

Kunigunde of Luxembourg, wife of Holy Roman Emperor Henry II, made vestments used in Bamberg Cathedral in the early eleventh century. Henry and his queen were both noted for their piety and have both been canonized. Henry's sister . . .

Gisela was married to Stephen I, first King of Hungary; she made the gold and purple chasuble that became his coronation robe and later presented it to the Church of St. Mary in Civita Alba. Her husband is the patron saint of Hungary.

Queen Mathilda, the wife of King William I, and the ladies of her court have long been credited with working the Bayeux Tapestry. The coarse linen strip, 330 feet long and 20 inches wide, which is worked in couching and stem stitch in eight colors of worsted, tells the story of William's conquest of England in 1066. In his history of England, Winston Churchill asserted that the tapestry was actually designed by English artists working under the supervision of William's half brother Odo, Bishop of Bayeux.

Christina of Mergate, in about 1155, was the artisan who created three miters and several pairs of sandals as a peace offering for Pope Hadrian IV from the Abbott of St. Albans.

Abbess Kunigunde's name is embroidered five times on the Goss Vestments, made in about 1275.

SEVEN PRECOCIOUS PAINTERS

Most women artists of the fifteenth through the nineteenth centuries had fathers who were painters or artisans; it was the only way women could get into a studio early enough, play with the materials of art, and get the notion that painting could be a career and not merely an accomplishment.

Susan Horenbout (Susanna Hornebolt) (1503–1545) was eighteen when Albrecht Dürer purchased a miniature from her and commented, "It is very wonderful that a woman can do so much."

Giovanna Garzoni is known for a signed painting of the Madonna done when she was sixteen.

Fede Galizia (1578–1630) received public acclaim for her paintings at the age of twelve and had established an international reputation as a portraitist before she was out of her teens. Her father, a miniaturist, was her teacher. She also did still lifes and work on commission from various churches; an altarpiece done by Galizia in 1616 is in Santa Maria Maddalene in Milan.

Artemisia Gentileschi♀ (1593–1652) was seventeen when she executed *Su-*

sanna and the Elders; by then she had been painting in her father's studio for several years.

Clara Peeters (1594–after 1657) dated and signed her first painting at the age of fourteen, although she had done others even earlier. Six more dated works done before she was eighteen are known, as well as more than two dozen later works, all delicate still lifes.

Elisabetta Sirani (1638–1665) started to keep a detailed list of her works in 1655; it included two paintings done at the age of seventeen. By the time of her premature death, there were 150 works on the list.

Louise Moillon (1610–1696) had already demonstrated talent by the time her artist father died in 1620; by the time her mother died ten years later, thirteen finished works by Moillon were listed in an inventory of her possessions. Most of Moillon's noted still lifes, primarily of fruits, were done before 1642.

ACADÉMIE WOMEN

All women members of the Académie Royale were elected to full membership and did not have to participate in the apprenticeship period required of men. This was less a tribute to their excellence than to the fact that they were forbidden to attend life drawing classes and consequently were not allowed to paint the historical paintings then in vogue.

In seventeenth-century France, four women still-life painters were admitted to membership in the Académie Royale:

Catherine Duchemin (1630–1698) was the first, when she submitted *Basket of Flowers on a Table* in 1663. When she was accepted, Louis XIV stated that he would "extend his support to all those who are excellent in the arts of Painting and Sculpture and to include all worthy of judgment without regard to the difference of sex." Nothing by Duchemin is now known, and it was said she stopped painting after her marriage to the sculptor François F. Girardon.

Geneviève (1645–1708) and ***Madeleine*** (1646–1710) ***de Boulogne,*** sisters from a large family of artists, were both admitted to the Académie on December 7, 1669. Nothing by Geneviève is known today, but there are a few surviving works by Madeleine.

Catherine Perrot was admitted to the Académie in 1682. Although she illustrated two art instruction books, none of her paintings is known today.

After these women were accepted, there was a hiatus of nearly forty years; in 1706 the Académie even declared that no women would be considered. Then along came a woman whom they could not refuse:

Rosalba Carriera ♀ of Venice, who was made a member during her triumphal visit to Paris in 1720, during which time she had more visitors and commissions than she could find time for. Unable to work amid all the hubbub about her, however, Carriera returned to her native city the following year and did not visit Paris again.

Margareta Haverman (1693–after 1750) was admitted in 1722; a year later the academicians decided that her painting had been done by her teacher, Jan van Huysum, and she was expelled.

Marie Thérèse Reboul (1729–1805), a miniaturist, was admitted in 1757, probably because she was the wife of Joseph Marie Vien, a leading member of the Académie. She was the first French woman so honored in seventy-five years.

Anna Dorothea Lisiewska-Therbusch (1721–1782), a successful portraitist in her native Germany who had painted Frederick the Great, decided to seek greater opportunities in Paris. After two years her genre painting of a man, *The Drinker,* won her admittance to the Académie in 1767. The critic Denis Diderot pronounced it "not . . . without merit for a woman, and three-quarters of the artists in the Académie could not have done this much."

Anne Vallayer-Coster (1744–1818) was admitted in 1770 for a pair of works, *Allegory of the Visual Arts* and *Allegory of Music,* both now in the Louvre. Vallayer-Coster was trained by her goldsmith father, a virtuoso artisan who also worked in the Gobelins tapestry factory.

Marie Suzanne Giroust (1734–1772), the wife of Académie member Alexandre Roslin, was next admitted. At this point the male academicians established that four was the maximum number of female members, and not until after the death of Giroust and Lisiewska-Therbusch were two other women elected; they would be the last for almost a century.

Elizabeth Vigée-Lebrun ♀ (1755–1842) was elected on May 31, 1783. Her father, a pastel portraitist and art teacher, encouraged her talent when she was a child and died before she was fifteen; after that Vigée-Lebrun supported her mother and younger brother with her painting. She was soon sought by the aristocracy and painted the royal family, including Marie Antoinette.♀ She left about 700 paintings in a remarkable and long career.

Adelaïde Labille-Guiard (1749–1803) was admitted to the Académie on the same day in 1783 as Vigée-Lebrun. Because she wanted to avoid charges that her work had been assisted by a man, she asked each of the male members of the Académie to sit for her so that he could watch her work; she received twenty-nine votes out of thirty-five. A noted teacher, Labille-Guiard was especially encouraging to her women students. For this reason she was refused an apartment-studio in the Louvre, then an artists' residence. The management felt that the presence of so many young women would distract male painters and their male students, and inevitably lead to scandal.

Matters were not any better in England. The Royal Academy was founded in 1768 and two women were among the founding members:

Angelica Kauffman ♀ (1741–1807) was born in Switzerland and trained by her father, who later became her manager. Kauffman painted historical scenes and portraits, and traveled widely through Europe with her father, meeting critics and artists; when she was invited to England, she left her father for the first time at the age of twenty-five. Two years later she was a founding member of the Royal Academy of Art and exhibited with the Academy annually for many years.

Mary Moser (1744–1819) was also the daughter of an artist, George Michael Moser, as well as an intimate of the royal family. Flower paintings and other works by Moser are in the Victoria and Albert Museum, the British Museum, and other collections in England.

The next woman full member was not elected until well into the twentieth century, although ...

Annie Louisa Swynnerton was elected associate member in 1922, as were three other women.

Dame Laura Knight became the third woman elected a full member, in 1936. Not until thirty-one years later, however, was she allowed to attend the annual members' banquet.

And in Germany:

Käthe Kollwitz (1867–1945) was the first woman to be elected to the Prussian Academy of Arts in 1919; she resigned in 1933 for political reasons, and three years later the Nazis banned her work. Kollwitz is today best known for her stark drawings and prints, but she was an important sculptor as well. Her 1933 war monument, now at a Belgian military cemetery, commemorating her son who was killed during the First World War, depicts grieving parents—herself and her husband.

UNCOVERED AT LAST

The names of some women painters have literally been covered over with paint. Modern research and recent techniques of restoration have brought the names of three such artists before our eyes:

Constance-Marie Charpentier was recently revealed to have painted the *Portrait of Charlotte du Val d'Ognes* that hangs in the Metropolitan Museum of Art; for a century and a half it had been attributed to Charpentier's teacher Jacques Louis David.

Marietta Tintoretto has been shown to have been the painter of the *Portrait of Marco dei Vescovi,* long attributed to her father and teacher. Marietta, the eldest and preferred child of the Renaissance painter, worked on the backgrounds of paintings in her father's studio. Her portraits were apparently sought after, and it is believed that her father insisted that she marry and settle down in Venice to keep her near him. Most of her work, apparently, was done with and/or for her father, and little by her hand is known. She died in her early thirties.

Judith Leyster (1609–1660) was unknown until 1893, when a Frans Hals painting acquired by the Louvre was shown to have been painted by his female friend and rival. There is still confusion over the attribution of many works, since Leyster's copies of Hals's paintings were a lucrative portion of her practice, and she also depicted similar subjects.

DRAWING FROM LIFE

————————————————————— ✹ —————————————————————

The road to art has not been easy. A major hurdle has been the prudery that kept women out of classes studying and drawing from the human body. It is barely more than a century since the first steps toward overcoming that hurdle were taken:

Eliza Bridell-Fox in the mid-nineteenth century opened an evening class in London in which women were able to draw from an undraped female model. One of her students . . .

Laura Herford gained admission to classes in the Royal Academy's "Antique Schools" by submitting her work signed only with her initials. Britain's male artists were gentlemen, and when they discovered the gender of their new student they did not renege. Rather, they permitted four other women students to join Herford in classes. But the Victorian double standard still prevailed: women had to make do with a "draped living model," rather than a nude. By 1893 an "almost nude" living male model was allowed for an all-female class—draped in a diaperlike affair nine feet long and three feet wide!

Things were more progressive in the United States. At the Pennsylvania Academy of Fine Arts, the Ladies' Life Class was drawing female nudes by 1868; men covered with togalike wrappings were allowed to model beginning in 1877. But when the drapery covering one male model was removed by teacher-artist Thomas Eakins, a scandal erupted and Eakins was forced to resign.

AT THEIR SIDE

————————————————————— ✹ —————————————————————

The wife of Gerardus Mercator assisted his early mapmaking efforts.

Mayken Verhulst, a painter of miniature portraits, was the first teacher of her grandson Jan Breughel. Although none of her works is known at present, she was a noted painter in her day.

Marie-Anne Collot (1748–1821) worked on the equestrian statue of Peter the Great in Leningrad as assistant to her teacher Etienne Falconet. The couple stayed in Russia for sixteen years, during which time Collot executed several portrait busts of members of the court of Catherine II.♀ She married not Falconet but his son, a painter, and later joined him in England.

Anna Cornelia Carbentus, the daughter of a bookbinder, was a fine draftswoman whose drawings were considered better than competent; her son was Vincent van Gogh. His nephew and biographer has related that the artist's first paintings were copies of his mother's work.

Suzanne Valadon♀ was the teacher and mentor of her son Maurice Utrillo.

Sophie Tauber-Arp, who began her career as a textile designer, urged her husband, Jean Arp, to use weaving and embroidery as media for his designs, which they then executed together. Tauber was among the earliest abstract expressionists and was the key influence on her husband's development in this direction.

AT EASEL

※

Art by women is not the same as women's art. In the past few years four exhibits have focused on the work of women:

"Women Artists 1550–1950," the Los Angeles County Museum of Art, 1976. The first international exhibit of art by women, it consisted of the work of eighty-four painters chronologically arranged, selected by art historians Ann Sutherland Harris and Linda Nochlin. Their catalog for the show is an outstanding reference work on the subject.

"Contemporary Issues: Works by Women on Paper" (1977) was the first exhibit sponsored by the National Women's Caucus for Art, founded in 1972. It was followed by . . .

"Fiber, Clay and Metal" (1978) and . . .

"Women Artists in Washington Collections," held in conjunction with the University of Maryland Art Gallery (1979); the catalog of this show, by Josephine Withers, is also an excellent source, especially for twentieth-century artists.

Of the women artists and their works in the above exhibits some are familiar, some unknown, and almost all of great aesthetic and human interest. In the following list are a few important women painters of the past:

Lavinia Terling (or *Teerlinck*), born in Belgium, came to London with her painter husband in 1545. The following year she received her first commission from Lady Herbert, sister to the queen, Catherine Parr; ♀ in 1559 Queen Elizabeth ♀ gave Terling a "grant for life for her service to Henry VIII, Edward VI, Queen Mary, and the present queen . . . of an annuity of £40." No works by Terling are known today, although some documents of her time refer to specific works; some paintings earlier thought to be by her have been reattributed.

Marie Guillemine Benoist (1768–1826) studied with Vigée-Lebrun; ♀ she painted historic scenes as well as portraits and genre works. Her *Portrait of a Negress,* considered an antislavery statement, was shown in the Salon of 1800. When her husband was given a high government post after the fall of Napoleon, Madame Benoist was required to forgo all public exhibitions of her work.

Rosa Bonheur (1822–1899) was, in 1865, the first woman artist to receive the Cross of the Legion of Honor. Trained by her father, a landscape painter, she spent her time as a young woman sketching animals in the Bois de Boulogne, later got parts of animal bodies from a butcher, and dissected them at home to study anatomy. Before she was seventeen her copies of the Old Master paintings in the Louvre were finding a ready market. She regularly visited slaughterhouses, horse fairs, and cattle markets, wearing men's clothing to do so unobtrusively, but she was first required to obtain an official permit from the police "for reasons of health."

Berthe Morisot (1841–1895), one of two women impressionist painters, showed talent for drawing in childhood and was encouraged by her (nonartist) parents. She was interested in painting directly from nature, then a revolutionary concept. She showed two landscapes at the Salon of 1864 and exhibited for the next ten years. She developed a close friendship with impressionist leader Edouard Manet; each was an important influence on the other. Morisot married Manet's younger brother, also a painter; from 1874 exhibited with the impressionists; and had her first one-woman show in 1892. Although not a commercial success in her own day, Morisot is regarded as a focal figure in the development of modern art.

Mary Cassatt ♀ (1844–1926), a native of Pennsylvania, studied art in Philadelphia before traveling to Europe. She developed a close friendship with Edgar Degas in the 1870s, and after being rejected by the official Salon, exhibited with the impressionists from 1879. In 1893 she did a mural, *The Modern Woman,* for the Woman's Building at the World's Columbian Exposition in Chicago; in the same year she had a one-woman show in Paris. When her eyesight failed, twelve years before her death, she had to stop painting.

Lady Elizabeth (Thompson) Butler (1850–1933) was the only woman painter of military subjects; her battle scenes are exceptional. She studied her subject thoroughly, questioning veterans, observing military maneuvers, and acquiring detailed knowledge of uniforms, firearms, and battle formations. She exhibited at Royal Academy shows from 1873 on, but her application for Academy membership was rejected by two votes in 1879.

Florine Stettheimer (1871–1944) took New York City, its streets and people, and the upper-class social life into which she had been born as her subjects; her sparkling, witty portrayals combined a sophisticated interpretation of events with a naïve arrangement of figures on a canvas. In the 1930s she created the sets and costumes for the Gertrude Stein ♀–Virgil Thomson opera *Four Saints in Three Acts.*

Marie Laurencin (1885–1956) was an intimate member of the circle of cubist artists and the *maîtresse* of the poet Guillaume Apollinaire. Her brightly stylized portraits of her friends show the influences of their innovations. She also wrote poems, illustrated books and other writings, and designed wallpaper, textiles, sets, and costumes for the Ballet Russe, and fabrics for couturier Paul Poiret.

SIX REVOLUTIONARY ARTISTS OF RUSSIA

―――――――――――――――――――――― ❧ ――――――――――――――――――――――

"Extraordinary women," said Hilton Kramer, art critic of the *New York Times,* of these painters whose work in the second and third decades of the twentieth century anticipated American canvases of forty or fifty years later.

Natalia Goncharova (1881–1962), with her friend Mikhail Larionov, organized the Donkey's Tail, the first Moscow exhibit of work by dissident artists in 1912; completed some 700 canvases for a one-woman show in 1913; and left Russia with Larionov the following year, never to return. Goncharova designed for Diaghilev's ballets; even as an expatriate she worked to bring Russian art into the twentieth century without Westernization. On her seventy-fourth birthday, after fifty-five years of living and working together, she and Larionov were married.

Alexandra Exter (1882–1949) exhibited with Goncharova and others in the first Russian avant-garde group show. After visiting Paris, she brought Fernand Léger's interpretations of industrial themes back to Moscow and by 1916 was painting pure nonobjective abstractions. In the early 1920s she designed innovative costumes and scenery for the avant-garde and antirealist Russian theater, but in 1924 settled permanently in France, where she taught with Léger at his Académie d'Art Moderne.

Olga Vladimirovna Rozanova (1886–1918) illustrated the poetry of the Russian futurists and exhibited at various avant-garde and futurist shows. Shortly before her death, Rozanova was selected as co-head of an official art and industry committee; her work was shown posthumously at the First State Exhibition in Moscow in 1919 and in an exhibit of new Russian art in Berlin in 1922.

Liubov Sergeevna Popova (1889–1924) studied painting in Moscow in 1907 and later in Paris, then returned to Russia in 1913. She exhibited with various avant-garde groups and was an important influence on other artists of her period, from 1920 until her death working in theatrical and textile design. Of her postrevolutionary work she said, "No artistic success has given me such satisfaction as the sight of a peasant or worker buying a length of cloth designed by me."

Varvara Stepanova (1894–1958) worked with Popova in industrial, clothing, and textile design in the early 1920s. Both were the first women professional textile designers in Russia, responsible for creating functional, comfortable clothing suited to job specifications.

Nadezhda Andreevna Udaltsova (1885–1961) met Popova in Paris in 1912 and through her other members of the Russian avant-garde, exhibited with them in 1914 and after, and continued to work in postrevolutionary Russia. Her works were purchased for exhibit in the Museum of Artistic Culture in Moscow.

PERSONAL PREFERENCE

Had we only enough space on our walls and money in the bank, these are the women of our own time whose works we would collect:

Georgia O'Keeffe ♀ (b. 1887), the *doyenne* of American painters, decided to be an artist when she was ten and has been fulfilling that vision for seven decades. She first exhibited in 1916 at the New York gallery of Alfred Stieglitz (who later became her husband). Her subjects are drawn largely from the scenes near her Taos, New Mexico, home. Her paintings—flowers in which her brush has caressed and magnified every petal, luminous desert landscapes, and bleached animal skulls—have been interpreted as an organic female iconography, although she denies this content.

Anne Ryan (1889–1954) did not begin to paint until she was forty-nine. Ten years later, after seeing an exhibit of the work of Dadaist/collagist Kurt Schwitters in 1948, she began the series of collages for which she is best known today, in eight years producing some 400 works. In her precise, gemlike arrangements of delicate materials—gold foil, Chinese tea papers, handmade papers, and scraps of fabric—texture is played against texture, and rectangles develop a rhythm of their own. A notable retrospective of her works was held at the Brooklyn Museum of Art in 1974.

Betye Saar is a black artist from South Carolina to whose work we first were introduced at the Wadsworth Atheneum, Hartford, in 1977 and who had had a one-woman show the previous year at the Whitney Museum of American Art. Saar creates miniature worlds of black female autobiography from such remnants as old photographs, dance programs, fans, buttons, bits of lace, and fragments of a plantation account book. Her boxed assemblages offer exquisite half-glimpses of a bittersweet life experience.

Bridget Riley (b. 1931) of London was a leader of the "op art" movement of the 1960s; her oil paintings in black and white or a few dazzlingly jarring colors create sensations of vibration and movement and explore the limits of visual perception and illusion. Riley, who won the International Prize for Painting at the Thirty-fourth Venice Biennale in 1968, found her distinctive style after seeing a black-and-white marble plaza in Italy through a sheet of rain. In her canvases the breakup and reconstitution of forms becomes a metaphor for the ups and downs of human emotion.

Catherine Murphy (b. 1946) paints realistic still lifes, interiors, and cityscapes, usually of the Jersey City rooftops and parking lots seen from her window. Her rooms, populated with ordinary people alone in time and the city, often include her own self-portrait in a mirror or a photo on a tabletop. Murphy was given a one-woman show by the Phillips Collection in 1976.

A SCATTERING OF SCULPTORS

꙾

Sabina von Steinbach was a stonecutter in the early fourteenth century. Upon the death of the master builder constructing the Strasbourg Cathedral, von Steinbach was given the contract to complete the job. Her work was damaged by a rival during the night—but the angels of the Lord, it was said, repaired the damaged sculptures before the morning.

Luisa Roldan (1656–1704) worked in Seville and Madrid.

Properzia de'Rossi is the only known Italian woman sculptor prior to the nineteenth century.

Patience Lovell Wright (1725–1786) was an American who, after financial reverses afflicted her family, moved to England and embarked upon a new, late, and successful career: sculpting portraits in wax.

Harriet Hosmer ♀ (1830–1908) was born in Watertown, Massachusetts; as a child she modeled with clay from the banks of the nearby Charles River. Hosmer studied art in Rome, where she was known for dressing in masculine garb and riding on horseback through the city in the middle of the night, as well as for her work which, unlike her unconventional life-style, suited the romanticized taste of the period. Her first success, a small marble *Puck,* provided a comfortable income through the sale of replicas.

Edmonia Lewis ♀ (b. 1843) was six years old when her Chippewa Indian mother and black father were killed by fugitive slave hunters. Lewis decided at seventeen to be a sculptor. Her medal honoring the leader of a black Civil War regiment sold enough copies to finance a trip to Rome, where she was the first black American expatriate artist, and she often used ethnic and political themes, such as Hagar in the wilderness, in her work. Lewis's work was shown in the Philadelphia Exposition of 1876; her figure of Hygeia marks the grave of Harriot K. Hunt.♀

Malvina Hoffman (1887–1966) was born in New York and studied with Auguste Rodin in Paris. She is particularly noted for a series of one hundred life-size bronzes representing the variety of human races, commissioned by the Field Museum of Natural History in Chicago.

Gertrude Vanderbilt Whitney ♀ (1875–1942), one of the few artists born to both money and social position, sponsored informal exhibitions of her contemporaries' work in her own Greenwich Village studios. After the Metropolitan Museum of Art rejected her collection of twentieth-century works in 1929, Whitney founded her own museum as a showcase for contemporary American talent with her secretary and long-time friend *Juliana Force* ♀ as director. Meanwhile she continued to sculpt; her Titanic Memorial and memorial sculpture of the founders of the Daughters of the American Revolution are in Washington, D.C.

Anna Hyatt Huntington (1876–1973) developed a reputation for her animal sculptures even as a student. While working on her most famous work, the bronze equestrian statue of Joan of Arc ♀ in New York City in 1910, she locked all men out of her Paris studio so that none could say, as they had of Hosmer's work, that it had been done with male assistance. Many works by Huntington are at the Mariners Museum of Newport News, Virginia, founded by her husband, Archer Huntington.

Elizabeth Catlett (b. 1915) was a painter and printmaker for much of her career; she is presently professor of sculpture at the University of Mexico. An early advocate of the black aesthetic in her work, Catlett's paintings stress social realism, but her sculptures are more abstract in form.

Louise Nevelson (b. 1899) was born in Russia and grew up in Maine. She always wanted to sculpt and literally found her medium when she came across discarded wooden cases in which rolls of carpeting had been packed. Using odds and ends of wood, she constructed rhythmic, collage-influenced works in three dimensions. Her sculptures, now cast in metal, are monumental in scale—and Nevelson, batting her real fur eyelashes and swathed in dramatic fabrics, has become a national institution.

Barbara Hepworth (1903–1975) described her studio as "a jumble of children, rocks, sculptures, trees, importunate flowers, and washing," and viewed her medium as a "primitive force." Somehow she combined art and mothering several children. Among her works: the Dag Hammarskjöld Memorial at the United Nations in New York.

Marisol (b. 1930) grew up in Paris, Venezuela, and California, and shows influences of pre-Columbian and Mexican stone carving in her witty, brightly painted rectangular wooden forms into which her self-portrait is nearly always incorporated.

Jackie Winsor is a relative newcomer whose large-scale sculptures of plywood, twine, trees, and bricks were shown at New York's Museum of Modern Art in 1978.

Ray Shaw sculpts hands, obsessively. She has sculpted the hands of violinist Mischa Elman, writer Fannie Hurst, actress Helen Hayes,? and President Franklin Roosevelt, among others. When she wanted to capture the hands of Albert Einstein, she was unable to arrange an appointment, so she took a chance and visited his home, to find the scientist just entering. He was so intrigued by the idea of posing that he allowed Shaw to spend three hours measuring and sketching his hands.

FOURTEEN MODEL WOMEN

Simonetta Catteneo. Her ethereal beauty shines in Botticelli's *Birth of Venus* and *Primavera,* but when Botticelli became a follower of Savonarola, he condemned many of his paintings of Catteneo as lewd, burning them in the Piazza della Signoria.

Lucrezia del Fede. After the "perfect painter" Andrea del Sarto set eyes on her, he vowed not to paint any other woman—and he never did. Her face became a symbol of purity and devotion, although she had been accused of poisoning her first husband and had a mean temper. The captivated del Sarto insisted on marrying her, and, according to art chronicler Giorgio Vasari, she made his life miserable. But del Sarto's devotion was unfailing.

Mona Lisa Gioconda. Her face and smile have tantalized the world for centuries. In 1503 her husband, Florentine noble Francesco di Bartolomeo di Zenobi del Gioconda, commissioned her portrait from Leonardo da Vinci. Leonardo was so slow in finishing his projects that he kept Lady Lisa posing for four years. Perhaps the enigmatic smile is the result of pure exhaustion.

Cecilia. She became the favorite model of Titian, who painted only red-haired women. So that his daughter would qualify, a hairdresser created the tint "Titian red," which later became a craze among Venetian women. "Paint women only when they are ripe and ready to conceive," Titian advised. To comply with this agenda, Cecilia had five children by him in five years. Eventually they wed, but Cecilia died a few weeks after the event, in childbirth, of course. Her eldest daughter, *Lavinia,* also posed for her father and was the model for some of his finest nudes.

Elizabeth of York. The wife of Henry VII and Queen of England was probably the most-viewed model of all time: all the queens in a standard deck of playing cards bear her features.

Helena Fourment. She posed for most of Peter Paul Rubens's ample nudes and appears in nineteen portraits and some 9,000 of his canvases. She also became his wife. Being in her husband's artistic productions was not easy. As Andromeda, Fourment had to spend days clinging stolidly to a rock, ignoring the bustle in the studio around her. The other hazards of her occupation can be estimated by observation of Rubens's works such as *The Rape of the Sabine Women.*

Hendrickje Stoffels. After the death of Rembrandt's wife, Saskia, Stoffels became his housekeeper, mistress, and model (*A Woman Bathing, Girl at the Window, Bathsheba*). A woman of simple background, Stoffels's sharp business head kept the debt-ridden artist afloat. Once when creditors were pressing him, she appointed herself his manager and employed him as a laborer; his paintings thus became her property and his creditors were legally unable to claim them.

Louise O'Murphy (La Morphise). This plump, dimpled nymphet posed for all the figures in François Boucher's decorations of the palace at Versailles. The painter introduced the knowledgeable teen-ager to his employer, Louis XV, and wasn't surprised when she became a royal mistress.

Pilar Teresa Cayetana, Duchess of Alba. The duchess dominates some of Francisco Goya's finest canvases as she is said to have dominated his heart. A dabbler in witchcraft, she regarded herself as a *maja,* a beauty of the lower orders whose attractions might be supernatural. Goya painted her twice in this guise, nude in one version, clothed in the other. It was rumored that Alba poisoned her noble husband when he tried to break up her tempestuous affair with the painter. Some art historians doubt the romantic side of this story.

Elizabeth Siddal. Painter Dante Gabriel Rossetti made her his exclusive model, mistress, pupil, and romantic ideal for ten years. Her flowing red-gold hair and sensuous mouth were the look expected of a Pre-Raphaelite beauty. After nine years as his model, Siddal and Rossetti married, but their union was not a happy one. She took an overdose of laudanum when it seemed that younger women were taking over her place in his heart.

Victorine Meurend. She is the nude seated complacently among clothed male companions in Edouard Manet's *Déjeuner sur l'herbe.* The painting created a *scandale,* and Meurend achieved the dubious distinction of being the most insulted model in modern art. She had met Manet after he literally bumped into her in the Louvre; soon she was his mistress. In his paintings her face can be found on matadors, schoolboys, sailors, gypsies, and angels.

Jeanne-Emilie Bheux du Pusieux. Hers is a familiar body: she posed for her lover, sculptor Frédéric Auguste Bartholdi, when he was modeling his best-known work, the Statue of Liberty—but the face of the lady with the torch is that of the artist's mother.

Fernande Olivier. The first of Pablo Picasso's model-mistresses or mistress-models, Olivier froze and starved with him in Montmartre and is immortalized in his *Nude in Green, Study in Charcoal,* and numerous other paintings.

FIVE "VIRGINS" WHO DEFINITELY WEREN'T

───────────────────── ✹ ─────────────────────

Agnes Sorel,♀ the stylish mistress of King Charles VII of France, appears
with her bastard son by the king in Jean Fouquet's painting of the Virgin and Child.

Lucrezia Buti and *Spinetta Buti,* two high-spirited nuns, fled their convent to
live with Renaissance painter Filippo Lippi and to pose for his pictures
of the Virgin. They had met the defrocked friar when their order hired
him—not too prudently—to work at the convent. His *ménage à trois*
with the look-alike sisters provided Lippi with two models, and he
painted day and night. Spinetta eventually returned to the convent, but
Lucrezia remained with the artist, bearing him a son, Filippino. As an
adult he practiced his father's art and, like the friar, painted his mother
into every picture of a woman.

Nell Gwynne,♀ Charles II's witty mistress, was painted with her son as the
Virgin Mary nursing an infant Christ Child by Sir Peter Lely.

La Fornarina was painted by Raphael as the Sistine Madonna, but the lady
was hardly virginal. Many thought her a witch, and she certainly had
Raphael under her spell. Her refusal to marry him so depressed the
painter that he was unable to complete an important papal commission.
To speed things up, Pope Leo had La Fornarina smuggled out of the
artist's studio and finally had to bribe her to disappear altogether.

FIVE EARLY COLLECTORS OF AVANT-GARDE ART

───────────────────── ✹ ─────────────────────

In the early twentieth century it took a thirst for adventure, a shrewd eye,
infinite faith, a moderate amount of money, and plain *chutzpah* to buy and
collect the paintings of young experimental artists of Paris. These five
American women shared those qualities, and the results of their collecting
now hang in many American museums.

Gertrude Stein,♀ a young American living in Paris, was introduced to Picasso
in 1905 by her devoted brother Leo. Gertrude bought works by Picasso,
Henri Matisse, and other twentieth-century artists, as well as Renoirs
and Cézannes, until paintings hung three deep on her walls, and she
introduced scores of young artists to other collectors. After her death in
1946 the paintings remained in the apartment she had shared with her
long-time companion, Alice B. Toklas ♀; most were sold at auction several years after Alice's death in 1967.

Dr. Claribel Cone and *Miss Etta Cone,* two sisters from Baltimore, met Picasso at one of Gertrude Stein's salons in 1905 and began buying works
by him and Matisse. Visiting Picasso in his studio, they literally picked
up sketches from the floor and gave him a few dollars for them. After
her sister's death in 1929, Miss Etta continued to build their collection,
which included textiles and decorative arts of all periods. When she
died at the age of seventy-eight in 1949, she bequeathed Matisse's *Blue
Nude,* a version of Cézanne's *The Bathers,* and much more to the Baltimore Museum of Art.

Saidie A. May, also of Baltimore, intentionally supplemented the Cones' collecting efforts, adding twentieth-century works by such artists as Fernand Léger, Piet Mondrian, and Jackson Pollock to the collection she gave to the Baltimore Museum of Art.

Sarah (Mrs. Michael) Stein, Gertrude's sister-in-law, was called by Matisse the "really intelligent, sensitive member of the family." She and her husband were his most important patrons from 1905 to 1907; they gave architect Le Corbusier his first commission and introduced him to Matisse. Sarah, the last surviving Stein of her generation, in her old age sold her Matisses for a pittance to support the whims of the grandchildren to whom she was devoted. Fortunately some of her friends rescued—at a fair price—a few of the best paintings and started a Sarah and Michael Stein Memorial Collection at the San Francisco Museum of Art.

THIRTEEN WHO FOUNDED MUSEUMS

Isabella Stewart Gardner: the Boston museum that bears her name, in 1902.

Marjorie Phillips, with her husband, Duncan Phillips: the Phillips Collection, Washington, D.C., 1921.

Sarah H. Joslyn: the Joslyn Art Museum of Omaha, Nebraska, in memory of her husband, 1929.

Lillie P. Bliss, Mrs. Cornelius J. (Mary Quinn) Sullivan, and *Mrs. John D. (Abby Aldrich) Rockefeller, Jr.:* the Museum of Modern Art, New York, 1929.

Gertrude Vanderbilt Whitney♀ and *Juliana Force*♀: the Whitney Museum of American Art, New York, 1931.

Mrs. Eugene Fuller and her son Richard Eugene Fuller: the Seattle Art Museum, 1933.

Alice Bemis Taylor: the Taylor Museum of the Colorado Springs Fine Arts Center, 1936, in honor of her husband.

Electra Havemeyer (Mrs. J. Watson) Webb: the Shelburne Museum, Vermont, 1947.

Aileen Osborn Webb: the Museum of Contemporary Crafts, New York City, 1956.

Jean Flagler Matthews: the Flagler Museum of Palm Beach, Florida, 1960, in honor of her grandfather Henry Morrison Flagler, a founder of the Standard Oil Company.

ON TOP AT THE MUSEUM

The museum world has long been a male bastion, but gradually, in the twentieth century, women began to make their mark.

Mrs. Mogridge may have been the first woman to be employed professionally by a museum. She executed the first habitat group for the American Museum of Natural History in New York, consisting of two robins hovering over eggs in a nest built on apple-tree boughs.

Anna Billings Gallup, the first woman to direct a museum, was a Brooklyn schoolteacher who decided in 1899 that children would actually learn something if they could examine artifacts and art at close range; she established a "please touch" atmosphere at the new Brooklyn Children's Museum.

Cornelia Bentley Sage Quinton became director of the Buffalo, New York, Albright Art Gallery (later the Albright-Knox) in 1910.

Belle da Costa Greene, who had been J. P. Morgan's librarian, confidante, and adviser in the purchase of paintings, *objets,* and rare books, helped his son found the Morgan Library in New York in 1924 and was its director until her death in 1950.

Grace McCann Morley was director of the San Francisco Museum of Art from 1935 to 1960.

Adelyn Breeskin became director of the Baltimore Museum of Art in 1947 after five years as acting director. Her career began in 1918, when she became an assistant in the Print Department of the Metropolitan Museum of Art, and has continued past "retirement" with curatorial positions with the Smithsonian Institution.

Linda L. Cathcart became director of the Contemporary Art Museum of Houston in September 1979 at the age of thirty-one, not only one of the few women museum directors in the country, but one of the youngest of either sex. She had previously been a curator at the Albright-Knox Gallery in Buffalo, New York.

Jean Sutherland Boggs became director of the Philadelphia Museum of Art in July 1978. Boggs had previously been director of the National Gallery in Ottawa for ten years; at the time of her appointment to Philadelphia, she was a full professor of art history at Harvard.

Hsio-yen Shih succeeded Boggs as director of the National Gallery of Canada.

Lowery Sims, an assistant curator at New York's Metropolitan Museum, was put in charge of the Department of Twentieth-Century Art in 1978 when she was twenty-nine years old. Her department contains more than 700 paintings, 2,000 drawings and watercolors, and 300 pieces of sculpture. The young black woman travels around the world representing the museum, sees young artists and their portfolios, supervises packing and shipping of works of art, plans exhibits, and writes catalogs—among her other responsibilities.

Anna Cohen directs the Philip B. Klutznick Museum of B'nai Brith in Washington, D.C.; its collections and exhibitions are devoted to Jewish history and culture.

Rosa Maria Subirana has directed the Picasso Museum in Barcelona, Spain, since 1977, and is a member of the International Contemporary Art Museums Committee. Subirana, who joined the museum in 1968 as a curator and rides a motor bike to work every day, is mounting a major exhibit in honor of the 1981 centenary of the birth of the Spanish artist.

DRAWING THE LINE

━━━━━━━━━━━━━━━━ ❊ ━━━━━━━━━━━━━━━━

Grace G. Drayton, the first American female cartoonist, originated a roly-poly group of youngsters for her comic strip "Dolly Dimples" (1914); these cherubs later developed into the Campbell Kids. Drayton, the daughter of an art publisher, also drew "The Pussycat Princess" and "Toodles and Pussy Pumpkins."

Nell Brinkley penned a panel dubbed "Nell Brinkley's Cartoon" around 1915.

Fanny Young Cory drew strips called "Little Miss Muffit" and "Sonnysayings" during the World War I years.

Edwina Frances Dumm, the first woman editorial cartoonist to work for a newspaper, also drew "Captain Stubbs and Tippie."

Cecilia May Gibbs, an Australian, called her strip "Gumnut Babies."

Helen (Elna) Hokinson drew more than 1,700 cartoons of bumbling but well-meaning club women for the *New Yorker.* She sold the first to editor Harold Ross in the first year of the magazine's existence, 1925.

Eva Herrman drew playful, oversimplified caricature portraits that paradoxically illuminated the complex personalities of her subjects; a book of her collected work, *On Parade,* was published in 1929.

Martha Orr, niece of a political cartoonist, invented "Apple Mary," a dowdy but well-meaning busybody, in 1932. Seven years later she relinquished the strip to her young assistant Dale Conner. He collaborated with writer Allen Saunders and, as Dale Allen, they transformed "Apple Mary" into "Mary Worth," a stylish, middle-class widow—but still a busybody.

Peggy Bacon, an illustrator, turned her fine-arts training and judgment of character to portrait caricatures; her work was collected in *Off With Their Heads,* published in 1934.

Mary Petty produced gently lethal pictures of rich dowagers and Wall Street brokers for the *New Yorker* from 1927 until 1966. She illustrated thirty-eight covers for the prestigious magazine.

Marjorie Henderson ("Marge") created *Little Lulu* in 1935 as a feature for the *Saturday Evening Post.*

*Dale (Dalia) Messick,*² creator of red-headed reporter "Brenda Starr" in 1940, took the name Dale because she wasn't able to sell her ideas as Dalia. "It was always the same story. They couldn't believe I could draw because I was a woman. They would just put my samples away and say, 'C'mon, honey, let's go out and talk things over.' "

Tarpe Mills first penned the adventure strip "Miss Fury" in 1941.

Hilda Terry originated "Teena" in 1941, a strip detailing the ups and downs of adolescence. Terry was discovered by Cleveland Amory, then cartoon editor of the *Saturday Evening Post,* in which her character first appeared.

Claire Bretécher at thirty-eight is Europe's most outstanding satirical cartoonist. Her weekly strip, "Les Frustrés," celebrates the difficulties of modern life and mores from a feminist point of view.

Cathy Guisewite is a young draftswoman who puts herself into every frame of her strip "Cathy," whose bemused title character keeps trying to organize her life, but finds her best intentions foiled by the distractions of being young and single.

SIXTEEN MASTER BUILDERS

❧

Lady Deborah Moody, known as the "first city planner," designed villages in early-seventeenth-century England.

Plautilla Bricci, sister of the Italian architect Basilio, helped him design a villa near Porta San Pancrazio for Abbate Elpidio Benedetti in the 1660s; she also designed a chapel in San Luigi dei Francesi, Rome.

Jaquette de Mombron was responsible for most of the architectural design of her family's château and executed most of the painting and sculpture that adorned it.

Baroness Micaela Almonester Pontalba in 1849 designed two block-long apartment buildings on Jackson Square in New Orleans; her monogram, AP, is worked into the design of the cast-iron grillwork of these buildings. A woman of independent spirit, she divorced her first husband after twenty-five years of marriage (the marriage had been prearranged and she had not met the gentleman until her wedding day), and her enraged father-in-law retaliated by shooting off one of her fingers.

Julia Morgan was the architect for 800 to 1,000 buildings, her greatest triumph being William Randolph Hearst's castle, San Simeon, in California. Morgan studied structural engineering at the University of California at Berkeley and was the first woman to attend the Ecole des Beaux Arts in Paris. She made a point of hiring other women to work for her.

Sophia Hayden,[9] the first female graduate of the Massachusetts Institute of Technology's four-year architectural program, built her first and last building in 1891. At twenty-two she won the $1,000 national competition to design the Woman's Building for the World's Columbian Exposition in Chicago; the job was so overwhelming to Hayden that she developed brain fever and never worked at her profession again.

Theodate Pope Riddle got her architectural training from Princeton University in an unorthodox way. Since women were not admitted to the school, she hired male faculty members as her tutors. In 1909 Riddle's design for the Westover School in Middlebury, Connecticut, won her critical acclaim.

Marion Mahony Griffin, an 1894 graduate of M.I.T., made drawings for Frank Lloyd Wright and designed a Unitarian church in 1904. At the age of forty she married another architect, Walter Burley Griffin, and became the anonymous partner in their professional collaboration.

Alice Constance Austin, a self-taught architect, in 1914 designed a communal building conforming to feminist principles of her day for the California community of Llano del Rio. A central kitchen-commissary was at the heart of Austin's building, and residents' quarters were along the outer walls. A network of underground tunnels led from the kitchen to the living area so that the women residents would be able to pursue their chosen activities free from food-preparation chores.

Eileen Gray became an architect and designer after the First World War, pioneered in the use of new building materials—metal tubing, glass, plastic, plywood—for furnishings and structures, and was a leader in the art deco movement. She was rediscovered by the high-tech generation in 1972, when she was ninety, and saw her furniture designs reissued and her original works set auction records. She died at ninety-seven in spring 1980.

Elinor Raymond designed a house that used solar energy in 1948.

Natalie de Blois designed several of the glass skyscrapers that mark the Manhattan skyline today, among them the Pepsi-Cola building of 1959, now the Olivetti building.

Gae Aulenti, a contemporary Italian design architect and industrial designer, has produced showrooms for Olivetti, Fiat, and other corporations in ten major cities and is widely known for her innovative furnishings and accessories for home and office.

Florence Holmes Gerke was official landscape architect of Portland, Oregon; she died in 1964.

Lauretta Vinciarelli has had her work exhibited at the Institute for Architecture and Urban Studies in New York (1978). Vinciarelli practices in New York and Texas, and teaches at Pratt Institute in New York.

Sylvia Crowe is a British landscape architect who protested against the spread of the BBC's antennas by asking the rhetorical question "Do we really want a hatpin sticking out of every hilltop?"

FRANCES BENJAMIN JOHNSTON AND HER FEMININE COLLEAGUES

On July 6, 1900, the *Washington Evening Star* reported: "Miss Frances Benjamin Johnston of this city, one of the most widely known of women photographers, has succeeded in securing a collection of pictures of incomparable beauty from her feminine colleagues, which she is taking to Paris, to be exhibited at the international photographic congress in the French capital as a feature of the great exposition now in progress." Johnston took with her 142 works by twenty-eight women, the first to receive national and international recognition, and from there an admirer took the exhibit to St. Petersburg and Moscow. It was never shown in the United States, however, until partially re-created by New York's International Center of Photography in 1979. A few of these notable photographers:

Frances Benjamin Johnston herself was active as a portraitist as well as a documentary and architectural photographer from 1890 in Washington, D.C. She was the only woman prominent as a photojournalist in the 1890s, an outspoken advocate for women in photography, and the author of a series "The Foremost Women Photographers of America" for *Ladies' Home Journal* in 1901.

Frances Stebbins Allen and *Mary Electa Allen* worked together in Deerfield, Massachusetts, from 1890. They specialized in book and magazine illustration.

Alice Austin studied with Gertrude Kasebier and was a professional portraitist in Boston for about twenty years from 1897 on. She spent most of her life on Staten Island in New York where, after her family's fortune was lost during the depression, she lived in poverty, forgotten until shortly before her death in a nursing home in 1952 at the age of 86.

Mary Bartlett of Chicago was active from about 1887. An amateur photographer, she exhibited in the Vienna Salon of 1891 and was a book illustrator.

Zaida Ben-Yusuf was a professional portraitist and pictorialist from 1897 in New York City and a member of the circle of artists around Alfred Stieglitz.

Emma Justine Farnsworth was called by Stieglitz "the strongest woman amateur photographer in the United States" in 1893; she had started working in Albany only three years earlier. "I know of nothing that requires more energy and patience than to try to realize one's ideas in an artistic attempt with a camera."

Gertrude Kasebier was New York City's leading portrait photographer from 1897 and a member of the Photo-Secession group of avant-garde photographers founded by Stieglitz in 1902. Not until after raising a family did she start photographing; she made at least 100,000 negatives before her death in 1934, when she was past eighty. Known for her soft-focus portraits of women and children, and for her interpretive portraits of Plains Indians, Kasebier taught herself lighting and composition by studying Old Master paintings. Probably the most important photographer in Johnston's show, Kasebier would not be given a solo exhibit until 1979.

Mary F. C. Paschall worked in Doylestown, Pennsylvania, from 1893. An amateur with no formal training, she began photographing "as a pastime" while recovering from a severe illness.

Mary F. S. Schäffer worked in Philadelphia; her photographs include detailed close-ups of wild plants.

Alta Belle Sniff was professionally active as a portraitist and employed female assistants in Columbus, Ohio, from 1899. "I am thoroughly in love with my work and think it is a woman's vocation in every sense."

Amelia C. Van Buren, a friend and student of Thomas Eakins at the Pennsylvania Academy of Fine Arts, worked in Detroit from 1895. After an attempt at commercialism, she resolved "to use photography solely as a medium through which to express artistic ideas."

Eva Lawrence Watson-Schütze, a close friend of Van Buren's who like her had studied with Eakins, was photographing in Philadelphia before 1899. She concentrated on portraits and writing about photography.

Mathilde Weil, a painter, became a professional portraitist in Philadelphia in 1896, "three months after I got my first camera."

Mabel Osgood Wright worked in Fairfield, Connecticut, from 1891 and was an author and book illustrator. Her greatest interest was in nature and recording "a life very largely spent out of doors."

FOURTEEN PHOTOGRAPHERS

———————————————— ❧ ————————————————

Clementina, Lady Hawarden (1822–1865) was one of the earliest photographers. Her tableaulike groupings of costumed subjects in affected or pensive poses are today considered suggestive of the repressed sexuality of the Victorian era. In her own day, however, her work and its innovative details of light and shadow made her part of the prestigious "high art" scene.

Julia Margaret Cameron (1815–1879), like Clementina a member of the "high art" in group, was noted for her portraits, many of which were published as *Victorian Photographs of Famous Men and Fair Women*, including such subjects as Alfred Lord Tennyson, Henry Wadsworth Longfellow, and Ellen Terry.♀

Imogen Cunningham (b. 1883) began taking pictures at eighteen, studied abroad, opened her own studio in Seattle in 1910—and received a Guggenheim fellowship when she was eighty-seven. At various periods she has specialized in portraiture, plant photographs, views of San Francisco, and darkroom manipulation of the recorded image.

Dorothea Lange (1895–1965) is best known for her compassionate recording of thousands of impoverished victims of the depression, as well as for her pictures of Japanese-American internment camps and her photo essays on the Mormons, Irish, and other ethnic groups. She died of cancer shortly before the opening of a major retrospective of her work at the Museum of Modern Art.

Louise Dahl-Wolfe (b. 1895) took her first photographs with a Brownie box camera, then made her own enlarger from a camera, an apple box, and a candy tin. From 1936 on, her still lifes and later fashion illustrations and portraits appeared in *Harper's Bazaar* and other magazines.

Nell Dorr (b. 1893) learned in the darkroom of her father, a portrait photographer, received her first pinhole camera when she was seven, and later used a Brownie box camera to photograph her childhood friend Lillian Gish.♀ As a portraitist, Dorr is known for her sensitive pictures of mothers and children; she has written, designed, and illustrated four books and produced three films.

Margaret Bourke-White♀ (1904–1971) virtually defined photojournalism. She started as an industrial photographer using a secondhand camera, and as a staff photographer for *Fortune* and *Time*, and then *Life*, she produced some of the most indelible images of our time, including farmers of the rural South during the depression—later published (1937) as a book, *You Have Seen Their Faces*, with text by her husband, novelist Erskine Caldwell. She also did portraits of Stalin in 1941, the liberation of Büchenwald in 1945, life in the mines of South Africa, and guerrilla warfare in Korea. The onset of Parkinson's disease in the late 1950s brought her career to a halt.

Berenice Abbott (b. 1898) learned photography in the 1920s as assistant to Man Ray in Paris, where she had gone to study sculpture. In the 1930s she recorded the changing face of New York City for the Works Progress Administration–Federal Art Project and more recently has worked with physicists at M.I.T. to explore the uses of photography in scientific education.

Toni Frissell (b. 1907) made fashion and photographic history as the first photographer to take models out of the studio and on location, and by photographing the first bikini (for *Vogue* in Jamaica in 1946). Frissell was the official photographer for the Red Cross in England and Scotland, and for the Women's Auxiliary Corps during the Second World War. In the 1950s she was among the first women sports photographers.

Laura Gilpin (1891–1979) started to study photography seriously in 1916 when encouraged by Gertrude Kasebier and is most noted for recording the faces and lives of the Indians of the Southwest; fifteen years of preparation went into her 1968 book *The Enduring Navaho.*

Lotte Jacobi (b. 1896), born in West Prussia, now lives and works in New Hampshire. In her sixty-year career, which was inspired by a pinhole camera in 1908, she has specialized in portraits, especially of Berlin theater and art personalities of 1927–1935 and later of New York, where she had a studio for twenty years. At eighty-three, while being interviewed for a magazine, she wore a black leather jacket and said, "I am opinionated, I am a born rebel and troublemaker."

Barbara Morgan (b. 1900) turned from painting to photography at thirty-five and began a five-year collaboration with Martha Graham,♀ during which she recorded a substantial part of the dancer's choreography and produced the first of several books of her own design. Later she photographed other modern dance figures—Doris Humphrey,♀ Erich Hawkins, Merce Cunningham—and their repertoires.

Diane Arbus (1923–1971) spent twenty years as a fashion photographer before deciding to seek out subjects who would give her a feeling of "awe and shame," a discomfort her photos of dwarves, transvestites, prostitutes, and other "freaks" transmit with eerie clarity to the viewer. Through her lens even ordinary people in ordinary settings—twins, sunbathers, old folks at home—look as strange as her more marginal subjects.

Marie Cosindas has been a pioneer in the use of the Polaroid camera in fine color photography in our time, and is noted for portraits and still lifes composed as carefully as paintings. Widely hailed as a colorist, Cosindas had a one-woman show at the Museum of Modern Art in 1968.

XV ❧ IN THE MONEY

DOLLAR PRINCESSES

❧

Americans have always been attracted to titles, and during the late-nineteenth-century Gilded Age ambitious American millionaires satisfied this craving by marrying their daughters off to European nobility (who were in turn fascinated by the prospect of American funds). As one commentator put it, "the more numerous the millions, the worthier she."

Elizabeth ("Eliza") Astor, daughter of fur merchant Jacob Astor, was forced by her father to marry Count Vincent Rumpff in 1824, thus becoming one of the first American-born countesses. After eight loveless years, Eliza died.

Jennie Jerome, daughter of millionaire sportsman Leonard Jerome, married Lord Randolph Churchill in 1874, quickly becoming a political asset to her husband—and the mother of Winston Churchill.

Lilian Price ("Lily") Hammersley, a wealthy American widow, became the second wife of the eighth Duke of Marlborough, Randolph Churchill's brother, in the early 1890s. The Hammersley millions were reputed to be the most stimulating part of this union.

Consuelo Vanderbilt wed the ninth Duke of Marlborough in 1895 at the insistence of her mother. The bride loved another, but Mama had the last word: "You do as you are told." The price of making the unhappy girl the Duchess of Marlborough was $2.5 million in railroad stock, plus. Ultimately the upkeep of the ducal estate totaled $10 million. The couple separated after eleven unhappy years, but both partners went on to happier second marriages.

Helena Zimmerman, the daughter of a Cincinnati iron and oil millionaire, eloped with the Duke of Manchester in 1900. Her father immediately paid the duke's debts, amounting to $135,000, and also footed the $150,000 bill when King Edward VII visited the ducal couple for four days in 1904.

Mary Leiter and *Marguerite ("Daisy") Leiter* were two sisters who did quite well. The daughters of Marshall Field's partner, Levi Leiter, in 1895 Mary married Lord Curzon, later to become Viceroy of India, and Marguerite allied both herself and her fortune with the impoverished Earl of Suffolk.

Anna Gould, daughter of railroad magnate Jay Gould, captured two titled

261

husbands. The first was Count Boni de Castellane, a free-spending French nobleman whose entertainments cost the Gould family at least $5.5 million between Anna's 1895 marriage and 1906 divorce. Two years later, Gould married the count's cousin, Helie de Talleyrand-Périgord, Prince de Sagan, later to be the Duc de Talleyrand.

May Goelet, heiress to a fortune built on midtown New York City real estate, married the Duke of Roxburghe in 1903. Police had to be summoned to the wedding when thousands of spectators and souvenir hunters grappled with one another on the street outside the church.

Vivien Gould, Anna Gould's niece, married the fifth Baron Decies in 1911. Armies of dressmakers were employed to create the wedding ensembles, and the couple received thousands of gifts. Gould went to live on her husband's country estate, which he later lost as a result of gambling debts.

Alice Cornelia Thaw, heiress to a Pittsburgh railroad fortune, was to marry the Earl of Yarmouth on April 27, 1903. He was, however, arrested that morning on a writ from London for a debt of £317/5s/2d. Not until negotiations with the bride's brother Harry K. Thaw raised the marriage settlement to $1 million did the groom depart for the church. His bride and guests had waited forty-five minutes for him. When they left for their honeymoon the newlyweds were pursued by a marshal seeking to attach the earl's luggage in lieu of bad debts.

Anita Stewart Morris, from an old New York family, was wed in 1909 to Prince Miguel de Braganza, pretender to the Portuguese throne. Since the prince tended to accumulate debts at an impressive rate, Morris's mother supported the couple and their children until they were separated; then the prince was on his own.

Nancy Langhorne married William Waldorf Astor in 1906. After the death of his father in 1919 William became Lord Astor, and Nancy, as Lady Astor,♀ became one of the more outspoken members of the British aristocracy. In 1919 she was elected to Commons as M.P. from Plymouth, the first woman, and an American-born one at that, to serve in Parliament.

TRAVELING IN STYLE

Between 1890 and the Second World War no status symbol was more impressive than a private railroad car. In 1915 such a luxury cost $75,000; by the late 1920s the tab had risen to $300,000. Some women who traveled on their own timetables were:

Jenny Lind,♀ in the first private railroad car in the United States, designed specifically for her use.

Lillie Langtry♀ in the "Lalee," the gift of playboy Freddy Gebhard.

Adelina Patti,♀ in the "Adelina Patti"; the opera star was not burdened by modesty.

Helen Gould, in the "Stanrear" (her father was Jay Gould).

Eleanor Medill ("Cissy") Patterson♀ in the "Ranger."

Helen Whitney, in the "Adios," a gift from her husband, Payne Whitney.

EIGHT BIG SPENDERS

☙

Gloria Swanson ♀ earned $900,000 a year from Paramount Pictures for acting in silent films; in 1926 alone her clothing bill totaled $125,000.

Sarah Bernhardt ♀ always spent more money than she took in. Her furs came from Russia, her velvets from Italy, and her silks were woven to order in Lyons, France. When Bernhardt earned 20,000 francs a year, she spent 50,000. She earned $6 million from her American tours alone, but at the age of seventy-nine had to appear in a silent movie because her coffers were low.

Mrs. S. Stanwood Menken was famous for wearing fabulous outfits to the Beaux Arts balls in the 1920s and early 1930s. One year publicity releases put the cost of her ensemble at $25,000; another, Mrs. Menken appeared as a peacock—when she pressed a button, the entire outfit lit up with electric lights.

Mrs. Loel Guinness was estimated to have spent $200,000 a year in the 1960s to maintain her position on the list of best-dressed women.

Mrs. Electra Waggoner Wharton, the wife of a Texas oil millionaire, was a Neiman-Marcus habitué and its first regular account holder. She even bought a house in Dallas so that she could be near the fabulous emporium. A new pair of shoes went to her almost daily until she had 350 pairs. Because their prized customer refused to try on a dress that anyone else had tried on, the department store shipped her eight or ten dresses, in their original Paris wrappings, at a time.

Evalyn Walsh McLean ♀ bought three important diamonds: the Star of the East ($120,000), the Star of the South ($135,000), and the infamous Hope Diamond, purchased from Pierre Cartier ($154,000). To celebrate buying the Hope, McLean gave a dinner party that cost $1,000 per guest. She considered the $4,000 she spent for a pair of sheets a bargain because "as any woman knows, forgetful, restful sleep will take out the wrinkles." Not surprisingly, by the time she died, her estate of millions had dwindled to $606,110.80. But she still had the diamonds.

Mrs. Richard Cadwalader, a Philadelphia matron, had a 408-foot-long private vessel, the *Savarona,* constructed for her. She was outraged when she found out that the big boat, which had cost about $5 million, lacked elevators. Consultation with the shipbuilders revealed that to put in elevators the entire boat would have to be reconstructed; the cost was estimated at $1 million. This was done.

Jacqueline Kennedy Onassis ♀ has an annual clothing bill that Jackie watchers estimate as at least $30,000.

LIFE OF THE PARTY

☙

Alva Smith (Mrs. William K.) Vanderbilt. Her new Fifth Avenue mansion, a $3-million French château, was launched at a fancy-dress ball in 1883. Perfectly trained servants served a huge dinner from gold plates. The hostess wore an exact replica of an outfit originally worn by a Venetian

Renaissance princess, with a brocade underskirt covered with gold embroidery and transparent sleeves woven of gold threads. Her cap was covered with jewels, some forming a magnificent full-feathered peacock. When Mrs. Vanderbilt posed for photographers, a small flock of doves was set loose to flutter auspiciously around her head.

Cornelia Sherman (Mrs. Bradley) Martin. The Bradley-Martins (as they styled themselves) of upstate New York were eager to break into New York City society. So Mrs. Bradley-Martin threw a lavish costume ball, ordering a Versailles ballroom, garlanded with roses and 6,000 orchids, to be re-created at the Waldorf in 1897. Guests were brought to the hotel by 400 rented two-horse carriages; the hostess was dressed as Mary, Queen of Scots,♀ wearing $100,000 worth of diamonds and—an anachronism—a ruby necklace once worn by Marie Antoinette.♀ The total bill for the evening came to $369,200, and the ostentation so outraged both press and public that the Bradley-Martins, their social hopes dashed, fled to England. They found time before leaving, however, to give a small farewell dinner for eighty-six people at a cost of $116.28 per plate.

Elsa Maxwell,♀ a leader of "café society" in the 1930s and 1940s and one of the world's best-known party givers, was noted for her originality. At one bash, champagne was served from an artificial cow, and guests had to "milk" the creature to fill their glasses. Exotic scavenger hunts were a Maxwell hallmark. At a legendary Halloween party in 1933, ninety-nine couples searched for Marilyn Miller's ♀ underpants, a live goat, and a hair from Kermit Roosevelt's mustache, among other items. There were no winners, but second prize went to the audacious soul who managed to acquire Fanny Brice's ♀ brassiere.

Elsie de Wolfe (Lady Mendl).♀ A superorganizer, de Wolfe gave extravagant parties and invented a cross-filing system so that she would never offer a guest the same menu or dinner partner at two events. In 1938 she produced a huge circus party in Paris featuring fashion designer Mainbocher as ringmaster, with acrobats, ponies, and a chorus. Three planeloads of roses were flown from London, and three different orchestras played, while dancers cavorted on a specially built dance floor with millions of tiny springs underneath so that it would move gently up and down as they danced.

Barbara Hutton.♀ At the Woolworth heiress's eighteenth birthday party in 1930, four orchestras played through the night. Imported from California to New York for the affair were eucalyptus trees and singer Rudy Vallee. Later in the decade Hutton would celebrate another birthday by flying an orchestra from London to Paris at a cost of $10,000.

Brenda Frazier.♀ For the 1938 coming-out party of the leading debutante of the deb-conscious 1930s, the Ritz-Carlton Hotel was festooned with flowers, gold-branched trees, and gilded fruit. One thousand guests danced all night to the music of two orchestras.

Marion Davies.♀ The actress-mistress of newspaper magnate William Randolph Hearst gave a costume ball at the Ambassador Ballroom in Hollywood in 1926 that was attended by most of the notables of the silent screen. For the evening the room was transformed into a lush Hawaiian paradise. Mary Pickford ♀ appeared as Lillian Gish ♀ in *La Bohème*, Douglas Fairbanks came as Don Q, son of Zorro, Charlie Chaplin was

Napoleon, John Barrymore a tramp, and Bebe Daniels an unusual Joan of Arc ♀ draped in silver lamé.

Perle Mesta gained fame as the nation's "hostess with the mostess' " during the administration of her friend Harry Truman, which skills gained her an ambassadorial assignment to Luxembourg in 1949. Ambassador Mesta used her penchant for entertaining to solve a knotty diplomatic challenge. U.S. soldiers on leave in Europe viewed the tiny country as the ideal place to go on a bender, creating ill feeling among the local population. Mesta invited the troops to stay at her home when on leave, providing entertainment and refreshments until it was time for them to return to their units.

A LIST FROM ONE OF ELSA MAXWELL'S ♀ SCAVENGER HUNT PARTIES
(*Paris, 1930s*)

❧

- One red bicycle lamp
- One cooled sausage
- One live animal other than a dog
- One swan from the Bois de Boulogne
- One slipper worn by Mistinguette that night
- One handkerchief belonging to the Baron Maurice de Rothschild
- One hat from Mrs. Reginald Fellowes
- One live duchess
- One autographed photograph of royalty signed that night
- One red stocking
- One Métro ticket
- One mauve comb
- Three red hairs
- One pompon from a sailor's hat
- The cleverest man in Paris

From Georgina Howell, *In Vogue: Six Decades of Fashion* (London: Allen Lane, 1975)

CURSED BY THE HOPE DIAMOND

❧

Little is known about the fabulous gem before Jean Baptiste Tavernier, the great French jeweler and traveler, brought it back from the East to Paris and sold it to Louis XIV in 1668. From that time on, it is said, its female owners have met sad fates:

Marie Antoinette ♀ considered the gem one of her favorite possessions and wore it often. Her dear friend . . .

Princesse de Lambelle frequently borrowed the stone. Both these noble ladies were decapitated during the French Revolution.

Lorena LaDuc, an actress at the Folies Bergère, was given the Hope by her lover, Prince Kanitovsky. She wore the diamond on stage on the opening night of her new show. Kanitovsky, momentarily insane, shot her dead from his box, using the diamond as his target.

Salma Zubata, the French favorite of former sultan Abdul-Hamid, was given the diamond as a token of his affection. Soon afterward a party of Young Turks attacked his palace. Abdul-Hamid shot his beloved to death, wishing to save her from a worse fate.

Evalyn Walsh McLean,♀ the wealthy American, was the diamond's last owner. McLean's son, styled by the press as the "hundred-million-dollar baby," was killed by a car outside his parents' home. By this time the diamond had gathered so much unfavorable publicity that its owners were unable to sell it. Eventually the McLean family presented it to the Smithsonian Institution in Washington, D.C., where it is on view today in the gem collection.

NINE GIFTED WOMEN

Lina Cavalieri, an opera singer of the 1890s, was presented with $3 million worth of jewelry by the Czar of Russia and the Prince of Monaco.

Lillie Langtry,♀ the "Jersey Lily," was the mistress of King Edward VII of England and others, and by the time the actress died at the age of seventy-six, she had been given jewels said to be worth 40,000 pounds, including one of the largest rubies in existence.

Jenny Dolly,♀ half of the popular vaudeville team of the Dolly Sisters, was loved by the English department store magnate Gordon Selfridge. He is alleged to have spent 2 million pounds on her between 1924 and 1931. When Jenny lost 80,000 pounds in one night at a casino, her lover sent her a diamond bracelet (with a rope of pearls thrown in for sister Rosie ♀), along with a note reading, "I hope this will make up for your losses last night, darling!"

Florence ("Peaches") Browning ♀ received a $10,000 check as a sixteenth birthday present from her husband, Edward "Daddy" Browning. Peaches was a few months past fifteen when she wed the fifty-one-year-old realtor in 1926.

Marion Davies ♀ received countless gifts from her lover William Randolph Hearst, including the financing of her films, most of which fared poorly at the box office. When an uninformed financial adviser suggested to Hearst that there was money in films he snapped, "Yes, mine."

Baby Lake reigned in the chorus of the Latin Quarter nightclub during the 1950s. In the course of her career as a top New York showgirl she accumulated two mink coats, eight mink stoles, one otter sports coat, six diamond bracelets, two diamond-and-ruby necklaces, scores of diamond rings including one of seven carats, two watches encrusted with diamonds, one Cadillac convertible, twenty evening dresses, twenty-five daytime dresses, six tailored suits, and forty pairs of shoes.

Linda Christian,♀ a glamour girl of the 1950s, was given a $140,000 solitaire diamond by playboy Francisco ("Baby") Pignatari in 1958. There were hidden strings attached to the big rock, however, and when Christian refused to run off with Pignatari, he hired thirty pickets to surround her hotel.

Elizabeth Taylor ♀ was given one of the world's largest and most perfect diamonds, a flawless 69.24-carat gift by her husband at the time, Richard Burton. He purchased the gem at auction in 1969. It was recently sold for $3 million.

Patricia Nixon ♀ received fabulous emeralds and diamonds from Prince Fahd of Iran in 1969 and kept them for four years despite the Foreign Gifts and Decorations Act that forbids government employees and their families to accept substantial gifts from a foreign leader. Only after attendant newspaper publicity were the jewels deposited in the Gifts Unit in the Executive Office Building. Nixon lawyers held that because the law had never been tested in court, there was no way of knowing whether it covered presidential families.

CHARLES HAMILTON'S LIST OF MOST VALUABLE WOMEN'S AUTOGRAPHS
(as of July 12, 1980)

St. Joan of Arc ♀	$250,000
St. Theresa ♀	85,000
Anne Boleyn ♀	40,000
Charlotte Corday ♀	35,000
Betsy Ross ♀	25,000
Mary, Queen of Scots ♀	20,000
Martha Jefferson ♀ (wife of Thomas)	15,000
Margaret Taylor (wife of Zachary)	9,000
Nell Gwynne ♀	8,000
Martha Washington ♀	6,000
Lucrezia Borgia ♀	6,000

AND NINETEEN OTHERS
(as of July 12, 1980)

Emily Dickinson ♀	$3,000
Mary Baker Eddy ♀	3,000
Madame de Pompadour ♀	1,700
Eva Braun (Hitler's wife)	1,600
Belle Boyd ♀ (Confederate spy)	1,500
Greta Garbo ♀	1,500
Marie Antoinette ♀	1,400
Madame du Barry	1,300
Abigail Adams ♀	1,200
Mata Hari ♀	1,200
Mary Lincoln ♀	1,200

Marie Curie ♀	1,000
Dolley Madison ♀	1,000
Marilyn Monroe ♀	400
Florence Nightingale ♀	400
Susan B. Anthony ♀	350
Jacqueline Kennedy Onassis ♀	300 (see below)
Helen Keller ♀	250
Barbra Streisand	25

A letter of Jacqueline Kennedy Onassis was sold for $3,000 in 1965 at the Hamilton Galleries in New York and for many years held the world's record as the top price for any autograph ever fetched by a living person. This price, not really representative of Jackie O's value, is recorded in *The Guinness Book of World Records.*

LUCKY OR NOT? SIX WIDOWS WHO WON THE LOTTERY

※

Doris Turner won $1 million just ten months after her husband died. She bought a $118,000 home in a remote wooded area and left her job because "they started giving me funny flak. You know, like 'Here comes Miss Money Bags.' " Generally satisfied with her good fortune, but sad that her husband wasn't able to enjoy it, Turner planned to open a shop of her own.

Helga Fischer, a seventy-four-year-old widow, became a lottery millionaire just ten months after her husband died of a long illness. "I wish I could have shared it all with him," she said. The couple had no children. The money has helped Fischer keep her small house, but it hasn't brought her happiness. She is harassed by constant appeals for funds. "You can't imagine the problems I had. All the troubles it caused. It wasn't worth it."

Rita Fortunato won $200,000 in the lottery. The same night her husband fell ill; he died two months later. "We were hoping to go on a cruise but he never got better." At fifty-nine she continues to run the couple's Italian restaurant. After being followed and receiving unwanted calls, she had to get an unlisted telephone number.

Alice Bowers was a waitress in her late forties when she became a millionaire. She wanted to continue working, but "the other waitresses got jealous. There was too much pressure, so I had to quit." Some of her in-laws no longer speak to her because she didn't give them as much money as they expected.

Minnie Petraglia, a fifty-eight-year-old widow, was in poor health and working part-time in a supermarket when she won $1 million. The money has ended her financial worries but brought her some different ones. She had to give up playing bingo, her favorite recreation, because the other players resented her presence. And she quit her job at the supermarket because so many curiosity seekers came to stare. "I was heartbroken," she said.

Angela D'Antonio, after years of counting other people's money, got a windfall of her own. She had just retired from a job as a tax examiner for the Internal Revenue Service when she won $250,000 in the lottery. "I had a four-leaf clover for twenty years under my blotter, and that morning I was going through my papers and that fell right at my feet. I won that money in a supermarket across the street from where my husband is buried. I went to visit him in the morning. It was like an omen."

From H. Roy Kaplan, *Lottery Winners: How They Won and How Winning Changed Their Lives* (New York: Harper & Row, 1978)

SETTLED AT LAST

❦

Cristina Ford was awarded property with a value of $10 million to $15 million in 1980, after two years of litigation following the breakup of her marriage to Henry Ford II. Three weeks after the settlement was reached, it was announced that part of his art collection would be sold at auction to raise funds. A sale of his French furnishings and other *objets* in 1972 netted $2,051,700 for his first "ex," ***Anne McDonnell Ford.***

Barbara ("Bobo") Sears Rockefeller, a coal miner's daughter, received $6,393,000 when she divorced Winthrop Rockefeller in 1954, in one of the largest matrimonial settlements up to that time; the marriage had lasted two years.

Peggy Hopkins Joyce,♀ a former showgirl, accumulated $3 million in settlements from five ex-husbands.

Khalilah Tolona, Muhammad Ali's ex-wife, settled for $2 million.

Linda Christian,♀ upon her divorce from Tyrone Power in 1955, received a settlement of more than $1 million, a percentage of his earnings for the next two years, plus a hefty share of two of his current films.

Susan Glassman Bellow, ex-wife of Nobel Prize–winning novelist Saul Bellow, was granted a lump-sum alimony award of $500,000 plus $800 a month for support of their son. Bellow was also ordered to pay her $200,000 for legal fees.

Barbara Cooke saw her marriage to sports promoter Jack Kent Cooke end in Los Angeles in 1979 with what may have been the largest divorce settlement in the United States to date: under California's Equal Property Law, the couple split a $200-million fortune fifty-fifty. The Cookes' romance had begun forty-two years earlier in Canada, when he sold encyclopedias door-to-door.

Margaret Cheatham may well be, as she claims, "the only person in the entire United States" who ever paid alimony to a man. She had supported her husband for twenty years while he chose not to work. After their 1974 divorce she agreed to pay him $125 a week because, as he put it, out of long habit he was unable to work and she therefore had a duty to continue to support him. After six months Mrs. Cheatham learned that New York State law forbade payment of alimony by an ex-wife and stopped payments. Mr. Cheatham brought suit, and New York's highest court decided in his favor because Mrs. Cheatham had agreed to make the payments. Ultimately, she gave him a lump-sum settlement in an amount she refuses to divulge.

Billie Jean Campbell, former wife of country singer Glen Campbell, received more than $500,000 in cash, 10,000 shares of stock in eight companies, 50 percent interest in eleven partnerships, 50 percent of all his record royalties through September 1, 1975, and 50 percent of his deferred earnings. The former Mrs. Campbell also wound up with the couple's Los Angeles home, half the land they owned in Tennessee and Texas, two cars, and a $500,000 life insurance policy.

Not yet settled is the suit filed by:

Soraya Khashoggi in California, probably the largest personal suit ever made in a marital case. She is demanding $2.54 billion from her banker husband, Adnan M. Khashoggi, described as an Arab financier and arms agent and head of Triad Financial Establishment, for business services she performed while they were married. The English-born Mrs. Khashoggi (originally Sandra Jarvis-Daley) married at the age of seventeen, took the veil and a new name, and became a Muslim. Five children and thirteen years later, the Khashoggis were divorced by proxy in a Beirut court—but Mrs. K. was not told of the action until some time later.

XVI ❧ *FADS AND FASHIONS*

ARTIFICE ON THE NILE

❧

The art of applying make-up was highly developed in ancient Egypt; upper-class women spent a great deal of time with their cosmetics. Here is a list of the contents of a make-up box belonging to Thuthu, the wife of Ani. The box is now in the British Museum.

Slippers to wear while putting on the make-up; the process was a long one.
Elbow cushions, for the same reason.
Pumice stone, used to remove body hair and make the skin smooth.
A tube of eye pencils, made of ivory and wood.
An ointment of liquid color, put on the eyes to protect them from the strong sun.
A bronze dish for mixing make-up colors.
Three cosmetic pots, which held face creams and ointments. Even today they still have a scent. The cosmetics consisted of one part perfumed resin to nine parts animal fat.

WHAT THEY DID FOR BEAUTY

❧

Isabeau of Bavaria, Queen of France, kept her complexion by bathing in asses' milk. To make herself thin, she would stay for hours in sweating rooms, after which cupping glasses were applied to her body. Her fourteenth-century skin lotion was concocted of crocodile glands, wolves' blood, and boars' brains.
Diane de Poitiers,[2] the mistress of Henry II of France, was the fifteenth century's most celebrated beauty. One of her secrets was to use only rain water for the complexion.
Maria Gunning, Lady Coventry, vain and dedicated to beauty, was a sixteenth-century noblewoman who fell victim to her own passion for cosmetics. To achieve the white complexion that was the ideal of the period, she painted her face with white lead—and eventually died of lead poisoning.
Pauline Bonaparte, Napoleon's sister, gloried in self-indulgence. She bathed

daily in twenty liters of milk mixed with hot water. On her deathbed Bonaparte had make-up applied and her hair arranged. Her last request was that her face be covered with a cloth after death so that her distorted features would not be visible. She died with a mirror in her hand.

Anne, Empress of Russia, an eighteenth-century monarch, never washed or bathed. Her beauty technique was to dab molten butter on her face and hands. It was not particularly wise to stand downwind of the empress.

Anna Held,♀ the actress, went to extraordinary lengths to achieve a tiny waist: she had her two lower ribs surgically removed so that she could bind herself even more tightly into her corset.

Lillie Langtry's♀ method of keeping her skin fresh was to roll naked in the early-morning dew.

Germaine Gallois, a nineteenth-century actress, would never accept a role in which she had to sit down. The reason? She wore a corset that went from just beneath her bosom to below her knees. It had two heavy steel bars all the way down the back along with six meters of lacing. It's a wonder that Gallois could manage even a walk-on appearance in this contraption.

SEVEN UNDERGARMENTS THAT CHANGED
THE FEMALE FORM

※

The farthingale and the bum-roll worked together to alter the bottom half of a woman's body. Queen Elizabeth I of England is frequently pictured wearing both. The farthingale, which appeared about 1545, was a stiff, conical petticoat held in shape by a graduated series of hoops of wire, whalebone, or cane. With a farthingale one wore a bum-roll or cylindrical bustle just below the waist. The general effect of this double-barreled underwear was to make the wearer look wide on the bottom and enticingly narrow in the waist. Queen Anne ♀ of England is said to have worn a farthingale that was four feet wide at the hips.

Pannier is French for "bread basket," and that's what this shaper, made of wire, whalebone, or wicker, made a woman's hips resemble. One was worn on each side. Panniers were introduced in the 1700s and caught on immediately. By the 1740s the width of some panniers was so enormous that wearers had to turn sideways to go through doors.

The bustle had been around since the Middle Ages but reached the peak of its popularity in the late nineteenth century. The idea was to enhance the derriere and make certain that its attractions would not go unnoticed. Originally the bustle was a large fabric roll, padded with cork or some other kind of filling, tapered at the ends and tied around the waist. At the height of their popularity, Victorian bustles were constructed of wire frames. How their wearers managed to sit down is anybody's guess.

Bust improvers. Ingenious women have always known ways to enhance bosom size without anyone's being the wiser but this idea did not become commercial until the 1840s, when the first manufactured falsies appeared. One advertisement touted, "The registered bust improver, of air-proof material, an improvement on the pads of wool and cotton hitherto used."

Crinolines were superwide petticoats, designed to set off a small waist and display the female ankle, since it was impossible for a woman to move in the contraption without revealing the latter. Often the crinoline was a wire cage with material over it. When the garment was introduced in 1856 it was actually called "the cage." This name proved apt: many wearers burned to death because they could not judge their distance from the fireplace, remaining unaware of the fact that their skirts were aflame until it was too late.

Brassieres first appeared under that name in 1916. They were advertised as "the new undergarment which takes the place of the old-fashioned camisole."

TEN BEAUTY AIDS THAT PROBABLY WON'T COME BACK

White lead was a popular facial cosmetic during the Renaissance. Users often applied one coat right on top of another. The effects could be lethal.

Ceruse, a seventeenth-century facial paint, came in white, flesh color, or pink tones. It made the skin look like enamel and could become so hard that it was difficult to move the muscles of the face. Like white lead, ceruse was frequently too troublesome to remove; one simply kept applying additional coats.

The plumper. Tooth extraction was the most common remedy for dental complaints in the eighteenth century. The plumper was a tiny cork ball used to fill the cavities left when a tooth was removed and restore attractiveness to the lower part of the face.

Homemade breath sweeteners were popular before the age of toothpaste. One eighteenth-century version consisted of "wine, bramble leaves, cinnamon, cloves, orange peel, burnt alum, gum lague, and honey mixed with burnt ashes." Extensive users wound up with fresh breath and rotted gums.

The bosom friend was an eighteenth-century falsie, designed to make its wearer appear both fuller and more nubile.

Homemade freckle removers. Freckles were considered a major menace to beauty in the eighteenth and nineteenth centuries, and their owners went to extraordinary lengths to remove them. The active ingredient of one homemade "freckle wash" was lead sulfate; which surely removed some epidermis along with the pigmentation.

Wax bosoms appeared in the early nineteenth century. They were, of course, intended to expand the owner's own.

Breast piercing became fashionable in the 1890s, along with gowns of deep décolletage. The nipples were lacerated so that gold or jeweled pins could be inserted.

Tattooing was a method of gaining a permanently pink complexion in the late 1880s. When Edward VII was crowned in 1902, "coronation tattoos" (on other parts of the anatomy) became popular, usually displaying a patriotic motto or the royal coat of arms.

Papiers poudrés were small books of colored paper, an early version of rouge, used during the Edwardian era. The papers were rubbed against the cheeks to give them a touch of color.

PATCHING IT UP

※

Patches, or beauty spots, became popular in England during the reign of Queen Anne ♀ in the late 1600s. Originally used to cover blemishes, they soon became part of every well-dressed woman's ensemble. Like fans, patches developed a language of their own. At the court of Louis XV, one's intentions for the evening were revealed by where one placed a patch:

On the eye: feeling passionate.
On the center of the cheek: in a gay mood.
On the nose: sauciness.
On the dimple: feeling playful.
On the upper lip: an invitation to kisses.
On the forehead: in a majestic mood.
On the breast: seduction is the goal!

ON A NINETEENTH-CENTURY DRESSING TABLE

※

"A box of *Fumigating Pastilles.*
"A *Lucifer Box.*
"A Bottle either of *Ede's Highly Concentrated Aromatic Spirits of Vinegar, Preston's Smelling Salts, Spirits of Hartshorn,* or of *Spirit of Sal-volatile.*
"A *Dressing Case,* with Scissors.
"A *Pincushion* and *Pins.*
"A Paper of *Royal Court Plaster.*
"A Paper of *Prepared Gold-beater's skin.*
"Half-pint bottle of *Rose Water.*
"Half-pint bottle of *Ede's Royal Extract of Lavender* or any of his other Perfumes, viz: *The Hedyosmia;* or *Persian Essence,* . . . a powerful and colourless *Esprit* for the handkerchief and Toilet.
"The *Odoriferous Compound;* or *Persian Sweet Bags,* . . . a very agreeable perfume for scenting clothes, drawers, writing desks, &c., and an effectual preventive against moth. . . .
"*Reece's Walnut Oil Soap.*
"*Tooth Powder* in a box and *Brushes.*
"*Soft Curl Paper.*
"Some *Hair Oil* or *Pomatum, Brushes* and *Combs,* &c.
"A pot of *Cold Cream.*
"A box of *Lip-salve.*"

From *The Toilet—A Dressing-Table Companion,* 1839

DO-IT-YOURSELF COSMETICS

Looking for some new beauty tricks? Try these:

Queen Elizabeth I's ♀ *"Cosmeticle Water":* "Take the whites of two new layd eggs, beat the shells of them to powder and put them in a quarter bottle with the whites and let them be beaten together for three hours; then put into it four ounces of burnt Allum in fine powder, beat it two hours longer; then put into it three ounces of white Sugar candy in powder, beat it also for two hours, then put in it four ounces of Borax also in powder and beat it also; then take a pynte of water that runs from under the wheel of a mill, and put into it four ounces of white Poppy seeds well beaten, mix them well together, so that it be like milk, then pour that into the quart bottle with the other things . . . then strain it through a fine white linnon cloath; and having put it into the bottle again let it be beaten for two or three hours longer. And to know when it is well made and well beaten is when it froths the breadth of three fingers above it. It will keep twelve months, it is a very good cosmetick, it whitens, smooths, and softens the skin, use it only three times a week."

From Hartman, *The True Preserver,* sixteenth century

Queen Isabella of Hungary's Hungary Water: "Take what Quantity you please of the Flowers of Rosemary, put them in a Glass Retort, and pour in as much Spirit of Wine as the Flowers can imbibe—Close the Retort well, and let the Flowers macerate for six Days; then distil in a Sand-Heat."

From the queen's *Book of Hours,* October 12, 1652

According to the queen, she first used this formula at the age of seventy-two; it cured her gout and restored her youthful beauty so completely that the young King of Poland begged her to marry him. She did. It's no wonder that Hungary water became a very popular beauty aid, used by hopeful women for centuries.

A seventeenth-century wrinkle remover: "To take the wrinkles away from the Face: Take a Fire-shovel and heat it; and cast thereon the Powder of Myrrh; putting the Face over it, to receive the Fume, having a course Cloth about the Head, the better to receive the Fume; do this thrice, then heating the Fire-shovel again, take some White-wine in your mouth and besprinkle the Shovel therewith, receiving the Fume that rises, doing this like wise thrice, continuing it morning and evening, as long as you will and you will see wonders."

From Nicolas Lémery, *Curiosities of Art and Nature,* 1685

Lola Montez's ♀ *formula for "Elasticity of Form":* "To achieve 'elasticity of form'—rub yourself with the following preparation before retiring to bed: Fat of the stag, or deer 8 oz., Florence oil (or olive oil) 6 oz., Virgin wax 3 oz., Musk 1 grain, White brandy 1/2 pint, Rose water 1/2 oz. Put the fat, oil, and wax into a well glazed earthen vessel, and let them simmer over a slow fire until they are assimilated; then pour in the other ingredients, and let the whole gradually cool, when it will be fit for use. There is no doubt that this mixture, frequently and thoroughly rubbed upon the body on going to bed, will impart a remarkable degree of elasticity to the muscles. In the morning, after this preparation had been used, the body should be thoroughly wiped with a sponge, dampened with cold water."

From Lola Montez, *The Arts and Secrets of Beauty with Hints to Gentlemen on the Art of Fascinating*, 1853

Sarah Bernhardt's ♀ ***Beauty Bath:*** Two pounds of barley, a pound of rice, six pounds of bran, two pounds of oatmeal, and a half-pound of lavender. Boil the ingredients in two quarts of water for an hour, then strain them. Add the liquid, along with an ounce each of bicarbonate of soda and borax, to the bath water.

From Richard Corson, *Fashions in Makeup.* (New York: University Books, 1972)

SEVEN RULES FOR PUTTING ON LEG MAKE-UP

Nylon stockings were in short supply during World War II, so leg make-up was invented to cover the gap. Applying the gooey stuff took some practice, however.

"1. Before you begin, rub your fingernails over a cake of soap so that the tops of the nails won't be filled with brown.

"2. To avoid splashing makeup around the bathroom, stand on a newspaper and put one foot on the tub.

"3. Cup your hand, pour out enough to cover the entire leg, and press hands together. Starting at the foot, spread the color with a round-and-round motion of both hands . . .

"4. Work fast, concentrating on covering the surface before the makeup dries. Use a light touch; heavy pressure makes streaks.

"5. When the leg is covered, lightly pat it with the fingertips of both hands, paying special attention to spots where color is uneven. When the makeup seems to stick to the fingers stop patting.

"6. Never try to patch spots after the makeup is dry. The results will be streaky.

"7. If you dress before the leg is dry, pin up your skirt with pinch clothespins to keep it from rubbing off the color."

"Leg Makeup: How to Put It On and Take It Off Nicely," *Good Housekeeping*, July 1943

THREE MAKE-UP MAVENS

Estée Lauder started out selling her Viennese uncle's face cream to friends and neighbors. The magic cream gave birth to an empire. Some of Lauder's good ideas include a line of cosmetics for men (Aramis), a hypoallergenic line (Clinique), and a scented bath oil (Youth Dew).

Elizabeth Arden started producing cosmetics in 1910, successfully developing a luxury line for a luxury-loving clientele. Then she decided that a short getaway vacation could be combined with a beauty regimen and established the first beauty spa at her farm in Maine. In 1946 Arden also opened a beauty spa in Arizona, named Maine Chance (West), where a week-long workout costs upward of $1,000; a day behind Elizabeth Arden's well-known Red Door on Fifth Avenue in New York is a less costly luxury. She died in 1966 at the age of eighty-eight.

Helena Rubinstein left medical school in her native Krakow, Poland, to go to Australia in 1902, taking with her twelve jars of face cream. Begged by friends for the secret substance that kept her skin from drying out, she sent home for the formula, then started manufacturing the cream herself, took courses in chemistry and dermatology, and created other products. Leaving two of her sisters in charge of the Melbourne office, Rubinstein took her beauty secrets around the world and in ten years had opened salons in London, Paris, and New York. She died in New York in 1965 at the age of eighty-two.

TREND SETTERS

※

Agnes Sorel,♀ the beautiful and audacious mistress of Charles VII of France, was responsible for two fashion trends of the fifteenth century: a high, round forehead (to get one, the hair had to be plucked), and a one-sided plunging neckline that left one breast entirely exposed.

Anne of Bohemia, the wife of England's Richard II, had an anatomical deformity that made it uncomfortable for her to ride on the saddles then in use by both sexes. She adjusted by riding sidesaddle, setting a trend for fourteenth-century women.

Mary of Burgundy was the first woman to receive a diamond engagement ring from her betrothed, Maximilian I of Austria, in 1477. Soon diamond rings became a familiar sign that a woman was on her way to the altar.

Anne of Brittany put on black clothing as a sign of mourning when her husband, Charles VIII of France, died in 1498. She was the first woman to do so since ancient times. As a result, black became the proper color for expressing sorrow at the death of a loved one.

Princess Charlotte was one of the first women to wear "drawers" or underpants. The year was 1806. Her innovation was considered quite shocking in England at the time. Until then it was customary for women to wear no underpants at all.

Ellen Demorest ♀ democratized high fashion in the late 1800s. She introduced mass-produced patterns in standard sizes for the home dressmaker, making it possible for women to create the latest styles at home.

Madame Gaches-Sarraute invented, unintentionally, the S-shaped corset in 1900. The French woman intended to design a foundation garment that would free women from the tight-laced cages they had been wearing and constructed what she thought was a comfortable garment that followed the body's natural contours. But her customers laced their new corsets too tightly, pushing the bosom far forward and thrusting the derriere sharply to the rear—producing the elongated "S" line popular during the Edwardian era.

Caresse Crosby (Mary Phelps Jacobs) took out the first patent on a brassiere in 1914 (although many others also claimed to have created this undergarment). Crosby and her maid constructed their version from two handkerchiefs and some pink ribbon. Warner Corset Company bought the patent for $15,000.

Irene Castle, the popular dancer, cut her hair, and a million American women followed suit. By the 1920s bobbed hair was one of the symbols of the live-it-up freedom of the Jazz Age.

Marlene Dietrich ♀ first wore a trouser suit in a 1933 movie. After that, pants were *de rigueur* for the fashionable woman.

Brenda Frazier, ♀ the leading 1930s debutante, showed her womanly figure to good advantage in strapless evening gowns. Her picture appeared in all the newspapers and magazines, and soon strapless gowns were the only thing to wear to a prom or ball, a fashion that persisted for more than twenty years.

Jane Russell made bra size important when Howard Hughes starred her in *The Outlaw* in the early 1950s. Her ample bust inspired a decade during which the big bosom became a sex symbol. Both outer and undergarments were styled to produce a well-endowed appearance.

SHOWING OFF FASHION—SOME SUPERMODELS
In the 1950s

Suzy Parker, the top-paid model of the decade.
Fiona Campbell-Walter, Vogue's star British model.
Jean Patchett
Alla, a beautiful Eurasian model for the House of Dior.
Bronwen Pugh, a model for Balmain.

In the 1960s

Jean Shrimpton, whose ingenuelike expression typified the look of the sixties. She was the first fashion model also to become a pinup.
Twiggy (Leslie Hornby), ♀ five feet six inches and only 92 pounds; the reason for her nickname is obvious.
Verushka
Penelope Tree

In the 1970s

Lauren Hutton, who received $200,000 a year for personifying Revlon's Ultima beauty products.

Naomi Sims, the first black model to become a superstar in the high-fashion world.

Farrah Fawcett-Majors

Cheryl Tiegs, the highest-paid model of 1978, earning $2,000 per day.

Inman, who first captured the eye of a photographer in her native Somalia. She came to New York, where she rose to supermodeldom and married basketball player Spencer Haywood.

Patti Hansen, discovered at the age of sixteen selling hot dogs on Staten Island.

Shelley Smith, who earned the most money of any model in 1978. Her discoverer was fashion *doyenne* Diana Vreeland.

HERE SHE COMES—THERE SHE GOES:
What Happened to Thirteen Miss Americas

❧

Margaret Gorman (1921), the first Miss America, had measurements that would not merit a second glance today. She was 5 feet 1 inch, weighed 108 pounds, and had a 30-inch bust and 32-inch hips. Gorman, who never traded on her title, married Victor Cahill, a Washington real estate dealer.

Ruth Malcolmson (1924), thrilled by her victory, wired President Coolidge, "To be worthy of the honor, I will endeavor to live the principles and traditions of a real American life." Presumably she did so as a Broomall, Pennsylvania, homemaker. Her niece, Lorna Ringler, Miss Pennsylvania 1956, became the first relative of a former contestant also to enter the pageant.

Bette Cooper (1937) immediately found that the crown lay heavy upon her head. She fled home to New Jersey, disconnected her phone, and the next day announced that she didn't want to be Miss America. Pageant officials never heard from her again. "This work is too strenuous for Bette," her father told reporters.

Jean Bartel (1943) became the vice-president of a documentary film company, owned a travel agency, appeared in opera, and chaired the Hollywood chapter of the Television Academy of Arts and Sciences.

Venus Ramey (1944) ran unsuccessfully for Congress.

Bess Myerson (1945), the only Jewish Miss America, became a television performer, consumer affairs official, and New York political figure. In 1980 she ran for nomination to the U.S. Senate.

Marilyn Buferd (1946) married, successively, an Italian count and two commoners; all three unions ended in divorce.

Jacque Mercer (1949), got married during her reign, which displeased the organizers of the contest. As a result, every Miss America has had to sign a contract stipulating that she will not marry during her year in office. Mercer later wrote a book called *How to Win a Beauty Contest.*

Lee Ann Meriwether (1955), got her first TV job on the Dave Garroway "Today Show" and later costarred in "Barnaby Jones."

Marian McKnight (1957) made guest appearances on such TV shows as "77 Sunset Strip" and the "Bob Cummings Show," and was most visible as the girl in the Clairol commercials in the mid-1960s.

Mary Ann Mobley (1959) made her first TV appearance on the CBS variety show "Be Our Guest" and also performed in films, including several beach party sagas.

Maria Fletcher (1962) became a Rockette.

Phyllis George (1971) became a sports reporter for CBS, then married Kentucky Fried Chicken tycoon John Y. Brown, Jr., and helped him run for—and win—the governorship of Kentucky.

IT HAPPENED AT THE MISS AMERICA PAGEANT

- In 1939 Miss Michigan sang "Old Man Moses Is Dead" and played the bass fiddle. She won.
- In 1949 Miss Montana and her palomino horse almost tumbled into the orchestra pit. From then on animals were barred from taking part in the pageant. Miss Montana was not a winner.
- In 1961 Miss Oklahoma recited the Lord's Prayer in Indian sign language. She did not win.
- In 1962 Miss Nebraska accidentally tossed a flaming baton into the judges' box. She didn't win either.

INTERIORS BY

Elsie de Wolfe, Lady Mendl,♀ was in 1905 the first woman in the United States to become an interior decorator; she is said to have named that occupation. A one-time actress and the wife of a British official, de Wolfe brought flair, extravagance, taste, enthusiasm, and daring to her enterprise. Zebra skin rugs, upholstery in white, yellow, and other pale shades, and outrageous accessories were her innovations, creating an effect that was quite unlike anything the Edwardians on either side of the Atlantic had ever seen. She was followed, but couldn't be imitated.

Syrie Maugham, the wife of W. Somerset Maugham, designed all-white rooms and other elegances for European and American clients.

Dorothy Draper, some twenty years after de Wolfe, wrote and lectured widely to encourage every woman to bring a decorator's eye to her own individual home furnishing. Draper urged her public to follow its own taste and not adhere slavishly to rules. She designed hotel interiors; her commission to do the Hampshire House on New York's Central Park South was the largest hotel design contract ever awarded to a woman. In the 1930s and 1940s she popularized the new concept of color-coordinated rooms, and introduced strong colors—rose, greens, blues—concepts influential even today.

Rose Cumming could get away with such outrages as burning black candles at a formal dinner, or wearing a sheer chiffon gown over—her bare self. In her New York shop she held court for generations of decorators until her death in 1960 at the age of eighty-one.

Ruby Ross Wood brought perfectionism to bear on interior design, and trained the women and men who became the leading designers of the 1960s and 1970s.

Sister Parish started in the late 1920s the company that would become Parish-Hadley, Inc., when she added a younger male partner some years ago. Self-taught, Parish has a sense of style that has kept her successfully in business for more than fifty years.

Eleanor McMillen Brown is at eighty-eight the chairwoman of McMillen, Inc., which she founded in 1924. Brown has been looking, unsuccessfully, for a man to take over the business when she retires, because for a woman, "her profession is only her *second* duty," while for a man it comes first.

Elizabeth Draper (who married the former husband of her competitor Dorothy Draper) started her company in 1929 and is now seventy-eight and still designing.

EIGHT DESIGNING WOMEN

Madame Paquin was the first woman in *haute couture*. The designer opened her establishment in Paris in 1891 and, later, branches in London, Buenos Aires, and Madrid.

Madeleine Vionnet, a designer of elegance, overturned the billowing fashions of the *fin de siècle* by introducing soft, bias-cut, clinging garments of satin and crêpe de chine that moved sensuously along with their wearers. Vionnet was the first couturier to design for individuals. She also claimed to be the first to have her models abandon their corsets.

Lucille, Lady Duff-Gordon,[?] was the first English woman to achieve an international reputation as a designer and introduced the use of a parade of models to show off her new creations at fashion shows. It proved such a crowd pleaser that Ziegfeld adopted it for his Follies—and stole several of Lucille's models, too.

Gabrielle ("Coco") Chanel brought beautiful simplicity to high fashion, transforming black from the color of mourning into the height of elegance. In addition to the "little black dress," she introduced the easy-fitting cardigan jacket, the pleated skirt, the use of knit jersey as a fashion fabric, triangular scarves, and cut-glass bead and fake-pearl necklaces. Chanel achieved her intention—to put an end to fashions that restricted their wearers' movements.

Elsa Schiaparelli designed dresses and suits with squared, padded shoulders in the early 1930s and originated a style that would last a decade. The squared shoulders were picked up by Hollywood and then by women all over the world. All Schiaparelli's ideas were bold ones; she adorned her garments with exotic motifs based on oriental, African, cubist, and surrealist art (one hat was in the shape of a shoe), worked in lavish embroidery, and sometimes painted onto exquisite fabrics. Her favorite color, shocking pink, became her trademark and was even named for her.

Ann Fogarty's name became synonymous with the shirtwaist dress, a fresh, young, American interpretation of Christian Dior's "New Look," in the 1950s. Her full-skirted fashions, poufed out with rustling petticoats from a cinched-in waist, and made in chambrays or taffetas, sold for about $35 each. After *Life* magazine carried a feature article on Fogarty's clothes, sales at New York's Lord & Taylor jumped from $5,000 to $25,000 a day. The foresighted women who have kept their Ann Fogarty's—and their waistlines—are wearing them still.

Mary Quant turned fashion upside-down when she created the miniskirt and with it the "youth revolution" of the early 1960s. In 1966, when Quant was awarded the Order of the British Empire for her services to fashion, she went to Buckingham Palace wearing her own mini.

Hanae Mori brought the Western fashion industry into the Japanese industrial miracle. As Japan's first female tycoon, Mori presides over fifteen companies and 1,200 employees producing her gowns, dresses, bath towels, and bed sheets—and a restaurant—with total annual sales of $100 million. Although her styles are strictly Western, Japanese traditional design comes through in the flowing cut of a sleeve, the flattering drape of a neckline, and the delicate, subtly tinted prints of her fabrics.

IN THE RAG GAME

Following are a few women who have made truly innovative contributions in design and merchandising:

Nell Quinlan Donnelly, a former stenographer, thought that women should wear something comfortable when doing household chores, so she designed a housecoat and started producing it at home. Her husband backed her with an investment of $1,270 from his savings, and, adding other styles to the line, they formed the Donnelly Garment Company, manufacturers of "Nelly Don" dresses. In 1954 Nell Donnelly sold her stock in the company for $1 million.

Lena Himmelstein Bryant, a young immigrant who supported her infant son by dressmaking, was one day given a problem assignment by a regular customer. The woman was pregnant and did not want to go into homebound seclusion for half a year, as had been the custom. Bryant designed something comfortable and attractive that would expand with a woman's growing body—and soon pregnant customers were flocking to order her simple dresses with the elasticized waists or loose-fitting overblouses. Her Lane Bryant department store, founded in 1909 and still on Fifth Avenue in New York, specializes in clothing for the tall and the plump as well as the pregnant.

Ida Rosenthal ♀ took a look at the slim straight fashions of the 1920s and saw a need for an undergarment that would slim and straighten female contours to match. Working at home, Rosenthal experimented with a simple two-section band to contain the breasts. Her husband was so enthusiastic about her idea that he gave up his dress business to help her produce the new brassieres, and Maidenform, Inc., was born in 1924.

Frieda Loehmann gave 1920s dress manufacturers a way to dispose of extra stock without taking a loss while providing women of modest means with the ability to acquire high-fashion bargains. She opened the first discount dress store, expanded it into a chain, and saw her idea copied successfully by others. Loehmann, wearing plain clothes, visited manufacturers, always accompanied by her son Charlie, who would carry off the bargains. When asked once why she wasn't wearing her new mink coat, Loehmann answered, "I wouldn't be able to look for bargains if I got all dressed up."

Armi Ratia found herself the owner, with her husband, of a company in her native Finland whose merchandise—oilcloth—was unsalable. She started to design textiles herself—big, colorful, splashy prints with a handwrought appearance. Then she designed a garment to be made up in them—a loose-fitting, practical, dress-coverall—and gave it a simple, unpretentious name: "a little dress for Mary" or, in Finnish, Marimekko. The company had 6 employees in 1951 when Ratia took over, and by 1978 had 375 workers and was worth $15 million.

Leah Gottlieb and her husband, who had manufactured raincoats in Hungary, arrived in Israel after the Second World War. There isn't too much rain in the Middle East, and anyway the large amount of fabric needed for raincoats was not available. But there was plenty of sunshine. Gottlieb thought of a garment that did not require very much fabric, designed and sewed a few bathing suits, and found herself in business. Her firm, Gottex, now employs some 800 workers, 80 percent of them women, and produces over a million swimsuits a year.

NINE FASHIONS NAMED FOR WOMEN

Mother Hubbard: a loose dress, usually fitted only through the shoulders, customarily worn while doing chores, named for the nursery-rhyme character whose cupboard was bare.

Pompadour: a hairdo, rolled high and back from the forehead, named for Madame de Pompadour.? Sometimes pads or "rats" are used to produce the desired effect, but skillful back-combing can do the trick as well.

Palatine: a small cape of lace or fur, just circling the shoulders, named for Princess Palatine, who brought the garment to France from Germany in 1676.

Bertha: a long, capelike collar, often of lace, falling loosely from the neckline to cover the shoulders. The source of this name is not known.

Juliet cap: a small, close-fitting cap, usually of openwork set with pearls, named for Shakespeare's heroine and today usually worn as part of a bridal or other formal ensemble.

Tawdry: cheap, gaudy, tasteless ornaments and accessories, named for St. Audrey. The seventh-century Anglian princess Aethelthreda, after fleeing from an undesired marriage, established a convent. She later died as a result of a tumor in her throat, allegedly a punishment for an early fondness for gold necklaces. Her convent expanded, the neighboring town prospered, and she was canonized as St. Audrey. At the annual fair held in the town, the most popular objects for sale were remembrances of the saint—"gold" chains or bands of lace to be worn about the throat. Peddlers hawked their wares in rapid country dialect, and "St. Audrey's lace" soon became "tawdry lace"; by association with the quality of the merchandise, the word came to have its present meaning.

Bloomers: billowy pantaloons, held by elastic just above or below the knees and at the waist, named for Amelia Jenks Bloomer. Bloomer did not invent them, wasn't the first to wear them, and objected strenuously to their being called by her name. The garment was designed and worn by Elizabeth Smith Miller, a cousin of Elizabeth Cady Stanton.♀ Consisting originally of a short skirt worn over loose trousers that were gathered at the ankles, it was a practical alternative to the many-petticoated, street-sweeping skirts that were the dress of the day. Bloomer publicized and advocated this "sanitary attire" in the February 1851 issue of her publication, *The Lily.* Unfortunately, her advocacy of this liberating garment has obscured her other activities on behalf of women's suffrage.

Mary Janes: Every little girl—and big girl, too—knows these black patent-leather shoes with the cross straps, but nobody knows how they got their name.

Mae Wests: bulky lifesaving vests, standard gear on boats of every size, named for the amply-bosomed, bluntly sexy actress.♀

ARBITER OF BEAUTY:
Florenz Ziegfeld's Standards for Choosing a Ziegfeld Girl

The Ziegfeld showgirls represented the pinnacle of feminine beauty in the early 1900s. The standards, of course, were man-made, set by Ziegfeld himself. The first of his follies productions appeared in 1907; they continued successfully into the 1930s. Ziegfeld paid most of his beauties $75 a week, although a single costume could cost as much as $20,000. Over the years the master showman turned down 200,000 and selected 3,000 applicants who met these exacting criteria:

Bust: 36 inches.
Waist: 26 inches.
Hips: 38 inches. Hips, Ziegfeld believed, were the most important feature.
Arms: "Ideal arms must reach two-thirds of the distance between hip and knee with finger-tips extended."
Feet: "The foot should be about one-third as long as the leg is high from knee to ankle. And when the applicant stands erect the feet must touch at the inner sides while the legs must taper evenly down to the ankles. I never diverge from these two rules."
Face: "If the contour of all features is perfect, the face need not fear the footlights."

HEARTTHROBS

There are fashions, too, in the men over whom women swoon. Here are the males who have made the hearts of women beat faster for more than a century:

John Wilkes Booth was the swashbuckling hero of thousands of dramas before he killed Abraham Lincoln. He received a hundred love letters a week and was the first actor to have the clothes ripped off his back by overwrought fans. After he was shot, portraits of five beautiful fans who had sent him their pictures were found on his body. In a touch of official gallantry, their names were never revealed.

Harry Montague was the first actor to be called a "matinée idol." It was 1878, matinées were just coming into vogue, and women were able to attend unescorted. Without male companions, female fantasies were concentrated on the man on stage. Hundreds of fans congregated at the stage door for Montague. When he died, gigantic altars of flowers were built in his memory. One woman even built a shrine to him in her closet.

Kyrle Bellew, a Shakespearean actor of the 1880s, was the first to have fan clubs organized in his honor. When he sailed from America, two girls tried to stow away on his ship, and one jumped into the water after it.

James J. Corbett, the prize fighter, was a nonthespian heartthrob. So many women would sneak in to watch him train that his manager began to charge extravagant rates for the experience.

William Faversham held the world's record for playing afternoon performances by the time he died in 1940. Thus Faversham, a turn-of-the-century favorite, is remembered as the "Hero of a Thousand Matinées."

Francis X. Bushman, the superrugged hero of early silent movies, was one of the first male film stars to attract "movie fans" before his popularity plummeted following a scandalous divorce. The more than $6 million, tax-free, he had earned was all gone by 1930. During the depression the former idol publicly offered to marry any woman who would have him—but there were no takers.

Rudolph Valentino, star of epics like *The Sheik* (1921) and *Blood and Sand* (1922), made millions of women wish they were being carried off to the Latin lover's tent. A former gigolo, the sloe-eyed actor gave the screen its heaviest dose of sex to date and embedded himself so firmly in the psyche of his fans that 200 mothers claimed to have good reason to name their children after him. When he died in New York, rioting broke out as 125,000 people, mainly women, lined up to bid him farewell.

John Barrymore enjoyed a reputation as one of Hollywood's greatest lovers, both on and off the screen. The height of his film fame came in the 1920s, but the actor had earlier won female hearts as a stage matinée idol. During a performance of George du Maurier's *Peter Ibbetson* the curtain had to be rung down because the sound of sobs was drowning out the dialogue; another performance was canceled altogether when a woman was taken from the theater with what was termed "an unaccountable weeping hysteria." She was hospitalized for two weeks.

Clark Gable was a new kind of he-man idol produced by talking pictures, one who was as quick with a quip as he was good with his muscles. Gable, a former oil well driller, reached stardom with *It Happened One Night* (1934). When he failed to wear an undershirt in a key scene, sales of that garment plummeted.

Cary Grant was discovered by Mae West ♀ on a movie set, and she picked the "tall, dark, and handsome" newcomer for her next film, *She Done Him Wrong* (1933). After that, it was stardom all the way for Grant, who reigned for three decades as the epitome of all that is smooth and charming.

Marlon Brando, almost the antithesis of Grant, brought a new kind of animal magnetism to the "idol" category with his screen debut in *A Streetcar Named Desire* (1951). The slouch and the mumble were something new, but his sex appeal was something very, very old.

Robert Redford is probably the first since Francis X. Bushman to make hearts throb by playing all-American heroes. An outdoor type as well as an actor, he crusades offscreen for the preservation of the environment.

John Travolta, the latest matinée idol, hails from a theatrical New Jersey family. He first attracted attention as the soft-hearted hood Vinnie Barberino in the "Welcome Back, Kotter" television series, and film fame came with *Saturday Night Fever* (1977) and *Grease* (1978).

NO LIFE WITHOUT RUDY

Four women killed themselves when they learned of the death of Rudolph Valentino (1926):

Agatha Hearn, a New York mother, shot herself. When her body was found, a sheaf of Valentino photographs was clutched in her hand.

Peggy Scott, a twenty-six-year-old dancer, killed herself in London. Her suicide note read, "It is heartbreaking to live in the past when the future is hopeless—please look after Rudolph's pictures."

Two Japanese girls, their names unknown, clasping hands, leaped into a live volcano.

XVII ❧ *INSIDE AND OUTSIDE THE LAW*

FIRSTS AT THE BAR
❧

The first female lawyer? A Babylonian clay tablet in the British Museum, dating from 550 B.C., tells of a lawsuit brought by a woman against her brother-in-law, "a man of Babylon." She pleaded her own case and won.

Bettisia Gozzadini, one of the first female lawyers, occupied the Juridical Chair at the University of Bologna between 1239 and 1249.

Margaret Brent♀ was the first woman lawyer in colonial America and one of the largest landowners in Maryland. Active in politics, she was involved in more lawsuits than any other citizen, serving as attorney for relatives and friends. Her name appears 124 times in the court records from 1642 to 1650.

Arabella Mansfield was the first woman in the United States to be admitted to practice law, in Iowa, June 1869, but she never actually practiced.

Myra Colby Bradwell was one of the first American women to attempt to have a legal career. In 1870 her application was turned down by the Illinois Supreme Court because "this step . . . would mean . . . that it is in harmony with the Constitution and laws that women should be made governors, judges, and sheriffs." Bradwell lost her appeal to the U.S. Supreme Court, but the uproar over the issue caused the Illinois legislature to pass a law in 1872 forbidding sex discrimination in employment. In 1890 Bradwell was at last admitted to the bar but did not practice, devoting herself instead to working for women's civil rights.

Ada H. Kepley was the first American woman to receive a law degree, from Union College, Chicago, 1870.

Charlotte Ray became, in 1872, the first black woman authorized to practice law. Because of prejudice against her, however, she never did so.

Belva Ann Bennett Lockwood♀ was the first woman to plead before the U.S. Supreme Court. Graduated from the National University Law School in 1869, she was refused her law degree and obtained her diploma only by petitioning President Ulysses S. Grant, the school's ex officio president. In 1873 she was admitted to the District of Columbia bar, but was not permitted to plead in the federal courts. She overcame that obstacle by securing a congressional bill to allow women lawyers in the federal courts and became, in 1879, the first woman admitted to the bar of the Supreme Court. In her most famous case she won a $5-million reimbursement for the Cherokee Indians from the U.S. government for land that had been bought but not paid for.

Ivy Williams was the first woman called to the bar in England, in the early years of the twentieth century. As an Oxford home student in the 1890s, she had developed her skills in the Women's Intercollegiate Debating Society.

Laura de Force Gordon and *Clara Shortridge Foltz,* admitted to the bar in 1879, were the first women lawyers in California. Gordon also organized the first suffrage group in Nevada and gave the first speech for women's rights in California. Foltz ran for governor of that state in 1930, when she was eighty-one years old.

Ella Louise Knowles Haskell was the first woman admitted to the Montana bar, in 1889, when she was twenty-nine years old. Three years later Haskell was a deputy attorney general for the state.

Sadie Tanner Alexander was the first woman president of Philadelphia's bar association and the first black woman to earn a Ph.D. in the United States. In 1979, at the age of seventy-nine, she was still practicing law as she had been for fifty-two years.

Susan Estrich was in 1976 the first woman elected president of the *Harvard Law Review.*

Rose Elizabeth Bird, chief justice of the California Supreme Court and the first woman to serve on that seven-judge court, was appointed by Governor Edmund G. Brown, Jr., in 1977. Other firsts in her career: first female law clerk in the Nevada Supreme Court, first woman to work in the Santa Clara County public defender's office, and first woman to serve in the California state cabinet.

There are now more than 45,000 women practicing law in the United States, about 10 percent of the total number of lawyers. In 1978 there were nearly 33,000 women law students, about 28 percent of the total. This was more than ten times the number of women in law school ten years earlier and about as many as all law students a quarter of a century earlier.

When in 1978 Harvard Law School celebrated the twenty-fifth anniversary of the first graduating class to include women, the school boasted a thousand female graduates—and only one female professor.

MAKING LEGAL HISTORY

❧

Mahlah, Noah, Hoglah, Milcah, and *Tirzah,* five sisters, brought the first recorded suit to redress inequality after the death of their father. "Why should the name of our father be done away from among his family, because he hath no son? Give unto us therefore a possession among the brethren of our father." The Lord spoke through Moses and ruled in their favor: "The inheritance of their father [was] to pass unto them. . . . If a man die, and have no son, then ye shall cause his inheritance to pass unto his daughter" (Numbers 27:1–8).

Elizabeth Freeman, a slave known as Mumbet, successfully sued for her freedom in a Massachusetts court in 1781, basing her case on the state bill of rights according to which all Americans were born free and equal.

Virginia L. Minor of St. Louis wanted to vote in 1872. Believing that the Fourteenth Amendment gave her that right, she pursued her case to the Supreme Court—which ruled against her. A new constitutional amendment would be required, they said. Minor promptly joined the fight for one, which finally came about forty-eight years later.

Ida Johnson Carter, an elementary-school teacher in Jersey City, was told after her marriage to a World War I lieutenant that, as a married woman, she could no longer teach in the school system. Carter found a teaching position in another New Jersey city and brought suit to establish her right to retain her former position regardless of marital status. In a 1921 decision that set a precedent for the nation, she was reinstated.

Linda Brown was nine years old in 1952 when her father tried to enroll her in a school near his Topeka, Kansas, home. No black child had ever attended that school; Kansas was one of twenty-one states that, along with Washington, D.C., permitted or required segregation of students by race and school. Ultimately thirteen adults and nineteen children would be involved in *Brown* v. *Board of Education of Topeka,* which reached the Supreme Court in 1954 and resulted in nationwide desegregation of all schools.

Lori Paton, a fifteen-year-old high school student who needed some information for a social studies project, by mistake wrote to the Socialist Workers party instead of the Socialist Labor party. In 1973 Paton found herself the subject of an FBI investigation and mail cover in which all her mail was intercepted. She brought suit, and five years later a federal district court, ruling in her favor, held that the FBI had violated her First Amendment rights and that interception of a citizen's mail in the name of "national security" was unconstitutional.

IN JUSTICE

In 1979 one hundred women judges attended a four-day meeting and founded the National Association of Women Judges. As president they elected ***Joan Dempsey Klein,*** of the California State Courts of Appeal. In that year only 28 of the 605 federal judges in the United States were women.

According to a 1978 study by University of Wisconsin–Milwaukee political scientist Beverly B. Cook, 38 percent of all female trial judges do all or most of their own housework. Cook also found that, of 500 female judges, 22 percent had never met a female judge from another state; except in metropolitan areas, female judges were likely to be the only female judges in their courthouses; and two-thirds of those queried felt that they were not accepted by their male colleagues.

Following, a few judicial notables:

Anna Moscowitz Kross, who graduated from New York University's School of Law in 1910 and was municipal judge in New York City for two decades, was the first woman to be commissioner of corrections in that city, a post she held from 1953 to 1966. Eleven years later she was honored by the dedication of the Anna M. Kross Center at the city's Rikers Island correctional facility.

Jane M. Bolin was appointed to the Domestic Relations Court of New York City in 1939 by Mayor Fiorello La Guardia; she served on that court and others until her retirement in 1978. In a legal career of firsts, she was also the first black woman to graduate from Yale Law School, the first black woman admitted to the Bar Association of the City of New York, and the first black woman judge in the United States.

Charlotte Murphy became the first woman appointed a trial judge of the U.S. Court of Claims in 1973.

Amalya Lyle Kearse became the first woman and the second black appointed to the federal appeals bench in Manhattan in 1979. At forty-two, she was also one of the youngest judges ever appointed to the court. Chief Judge Irving R. Kaufman, referring to his new colleague as "our sisterly scholar," decided that "no longer may I say brethren." A long-time trial lawyer, Kearse was also the first black female partner in a major Wall Street firm.

Patricia McGowan Wald was assistant attorney general of the United States, heading the Office of Legislative Affairs of the Justice Department, when she was nominated to become the first woman on the United States Court of Appeals for the District of Columbia in 1979. Wald, who resumed her legal career after a ten-year absence to raise her five children, became known as an advocate of the rights of the poor, handicapped, and children.

Jean Everhart Dubofsky became the first female supreme court justice in Colorado in 1979 at the age of thirty-seven. The governor said he had appointed her as the most qualified candidate, and not because he wanted a woman to join the six male members of the court. Said Dubofsky, "I think any woman who has benefited from our society in the last couple of years has to consider herself a feminist."

DECISIONS, DECISIONS

The first jury to include women was impaneled in Laramie, Wyoming, in 1870, only three months after women first voted in that town. Five women sat on a grand jury there. In most states, however, women were not generally seen on juries until the 1970s, and all states had laws excluding women from jury service unless they specifically asked to be registered as prospective jurors.

In recent years a wide range of inequities have come up for decision. Some you win, some you lose.

- In 1972 the Equal Employment Opportunity Commission issued guidelines holding that pregnancy should be treated as any other temporary disability in employment-related situations. However, in June

1974 the Supreme Court held that exclusion from a state's income protection program for disabled mothers was not a denial of equal protection to pregnant women (or to institutionalized drug addicts.)
- In 1973 the U.S. Supreme Court upheld a Pittsburgh, Pennsylvania, law by ruling that newspaper employment ads specifying that "female" or "male" help was wanted were unconstitutional. The five-to-four decision held that such ads encouraged discriminatory employment practices.
- In December 1973 a federal district court in Trenton, New Jersey, ruled that a man whose wife had died is entitled to the same Social Security survivor's benefits that would automatically be granted to a woman whose husband had died. In the case in question, the wife had supported the husband while he struggled to start up his own business, then died in childbirth, leaving him to support their infant. The court stated that the customary practice of the Social Security Administration violated the Fifth Amendment by discriminating "against women such as *Paula Wiesenfeld* who had successfully gained employment, as well as against men and children who have lost their wives and mothers."
- In January 1974 the Supreme Court held that a female schoolteacher could not be denied the right to work while pregnant if her physician thought her health would not be impaired.
- In September 1978 a U.S. district court in Manhattan ruled that women sportswriters must be allowed into team locker rooms. In a thirty-four-page decision, *Judge Constance Baker Motley*♀ ruled in favor of *Melissa Ludtke Lincoln*♀, a reporter for *Sports Illustrated,* that exclusion from the New York Yankees locker room after the 1977 World Series had violated Ludtke's constitutional rights to due process and equal protection. Ironically, the ruling came during a newspaper strike in New York City, so on the first day of open locker rooms only the television press was there to cover the big uncover event. Ludtke missed the opening, too; it was a Tuesday, day off at *Sports Illustrated.*
- In late 1978, thirteen men arrested in Lansing, Michigan, by policewomen posing as prostitutes pleaded guilty to soliciting and were fined about $200 each and ordered to write essays on how the arrest had affected their lives.
- In March 1979 the Supreme Court ruled unconstitutional state laws requiring husbands but not wives to pay alimony. Eleven states had such laws. Fears that men would no longer be required to pay alimony or that previous alimony requirements would now be unenforceable were dismissed by lawyers, who generally felt that the ruling would make little difference in reality.
- In March 1980 the Iowa Civil Rights Commission awarded $2,000 in damages, $26,400 for legal fees, and $145 for two days' lost pay to *Linda Eaton,* a fire fighter from Iowa City who had been suspended for breast-feeding her infant son in a women's locker room during unassigned work time. Her boss had cited an unwritten policy forbidding "regularly scheduled family visits." In the same month in a similar case in New York, a Long Island village agreed to pay $7,500 damages to *Barbara Demon,* who was evicted from a community wading pool area

while breast-feeding her infant son. In a settlement reached in a federal court, the village also agreed to build a special canopied area for the use of nursing mothers.

- In March 1980 the city of Chicago agreed to settle a civil rights suit by paying $69,500 in damages to 191 women who had been subjected to body searches by police officers after being arrested for such minor offenses as traffic violations and smoking on the subway. The suit was brought by the American Civil Liberties Union, with the U.S. Department of Justice, against the Chicago Police Department. The Justice Department particularly protested "body cavity searches" conducted by police matrons "without medical training . . . under offensive and unhygienic conditions . . . [sometimes] in the view of male personnel."

IT'S LEGAL—TWELVE LAWS, STATUTES, AND ORDINANCES

- 1641: The Massachusetts Bay Colony forbade husbands to inflict bodily harm on their wives—unless the wife had physically attacked the husband, who then, of course, had to defend himself.
- 1839: Mississippi enacted the first Married Women's Property Act, according to which "any married woman may become seized or possessed of any property, real or personal . . . in her own name, and as of her own property. . . ." For many years, however, legal decisions in that state and elsewhere held that the law did not cover a wife's *earnings,* or property purchased with such earnings. By 1875 most state legislatures had passed laws explicitly giving women control of their earnings.
- 1851: The Massachusetts legislature passed the first state law giving adopted children all the legal rights possessed by natural children; sixteen states followed in the next quarter century.
- 1870: Parliament allowed English women to own property and retain any wages they might earn.
- 1908: New York City's Sullivan Ordinance forbade women to smoke in public; infraction was punishable by fine, imprisonment, or both.
- 1963: Congress enacted the Equal Pay Act, which became effective on June 11, 1964. It forbade discrimination "between employees on the basis of sex" and required equal pay "for equal work on jobs the performance of which requires equal skill, effort, and responsibility, and which are performed under similar working conditions. . . ."
- 1964: The Civil Rights Act included Title VII forbidding discrimination in employment on the basis of race, religion, national origin, and sex.
- 1965: The Supreme Court declared unconstitutional a Connecticut law that made it illegal for any person to use contraceptives, holding that such a law invaded a "right of privacy older than the Bill of Rights," that is, privacy in marriage.
- 1969: California became the first state to have a no-fault divorce law. The bill limited the possible grounds for divorce to irreconcilable differences and incurable insanity, and eliminated the traditional as-

sumption that a wronged spouse, as determined by the court, should be granted the major portion of the couple's assets. On the assumption that both partners to a marriage contribute equally to the accumulation of assets as well as to the failure of the marriage, the law divided community property as equally as possible. Ten years later, all but three states had instituted some form of no-fault divorce.

- 1972: In Title IX of the Education Amendments, Congress banned financial aid to educational institutions that discriminate on the basis of sex.
- 1975: Congress passed the Equal Credit Opportunity Act to end discrimination against women by financial institutions.
- 1978: Congress voted to require employers with medical disability plans to provide disability payments for pregnancy on the same basis as other medical conditions. The bill went into effect the following year.

"LEGAL" HOLIDAYS

❦

Sarah Josepha Hale.♀ The idea of Thanksgiving as a national holiday originated in the mind of the influential *Godey's Lady's Book* editor. Of course, the event had been celebrated since the time of the Pilgrim mothers, but only on occasion. It was Hale who prevailed upon President Lincoln to declare the last Thursday in November an official day of rejoicing in the bounty of the harvest.

Mrs. John A. Logan. The wife of the Union army general noticed that schoolchildren in Petersburg, Virginia, were decorating the graves of Confederate army soldiers on the June 9 anniversary of the attack on that city. At her urging, her husband, an official in the Reconstructionist government, designated an official Memorial Day. It became a national holiday two years later, in 1868.

Anna M. Jarvis. Jarvis first suggested the idea of a national holiday honoring mothers after the death of her own mother in 1905; then she gave up her job as a schoolteacher to campaign, writing clergy, business leaders, members of Congress, and every other influential group she could think of. In 1914 Jarvis's perseverance resulted in a joint resolution of Congress establishing Mother's Day. But the founder hadn't counted on the commercialization that would follow. She died a recluse in 1948, reportedly regretting that she had thought of the whole thing.

Sondra Dodd. What about fathers? The thought came to sculptor Dodd, whose own devoted sire had raised six motherless children. She successfully promoted the idea in Spokane, Washington, where the first Father's Day was celebrated on June 19, 1910. By 1919 families throughout the nation were marking the holiday, and in 1922 President Calvin Coolidge made it official by proclaiming a national observance.

THREE PIRATES

—————————————————————— ❧ ——————————————————————

Maria Cobham met a smuggler in Plymouth, England, and joined him on his
    pirate ship; the crew, originally hostile, soon accepted her for her ability
    to get their punishments reduced or excused and for her eager partici-
    pation in their adventures. She stabbed the captain of a Liverpool brig
    in the heart with her own small hand knife; on another occasion she or-
    dered three prisoners tied to the windlass while she shot them with her
    pistol. Her last act at sea, before "retiring" with her husband to an es-
    tate on the French coast, was to poison the entire crew of a ship they
    had taken prisoner. But she had one more brief fling at piracy sometime
    later when, while out fishing, she and her husband encountered a mer-
    chant vessel, disposed of the captain and crew, and took the spoils.
    Some say Maria died of laudanum poisoning, self-administered, per-
    haps from remorse. Her husband became a magistrate and lived to a
    ripe old age.
Anne Bonny, the illegitimate daughter of an Irish attorney, was brought up
    on a South Carolina plantation. Said to have had "a fierce and coura-
    geous temper," she killed her English serving maid with a knife, then
    ran off with the notorious pirate "Calico Jack" Rackam. Prudently
    wearing sailor's garb, Bonny took part in whatever piratical business
    was at hand. One day their ship was boarded by a crew sent by the gov-
    ernor of Jamaica; in the fight that followed, the male pirates were soon
    driven below decks, while Bonny and Mary Read (see below) contin-
    ued to battle for their lives and their men. Eventually, in the fall of
    1720, all were brought to Jamaica and sentenced to be hanged, though
    Anne, pleading pregnancy, obtained postponement of her sentence.
    Her farewell to Rackam was characteristic; it is said that she told him,
    just before he was hanged, that "she was sorry to see him there, but if he
    had fought like a Man, he need not have been hang'd like a Dog."
Mary Read of London was, for some unknown reason, brought up as a boy
    and dressed in male garments for all but a few months of her life. After
    stints in the navy, infantry, and cavalry, and a short but happy marriage
    that ended when her husband died, Mary joined another regiment, then
    deserted and shipped aboard a merchant vessel bound for the West
    Indies. The ship had the good fortune to be captured by Rackam's pi-
    rates, and Mary joined his crew. She left for a while to ship aboard a
    government vessel, but when the crew mutinied and turned pirate,
    Mary joined Rackam again. Having fallen in love with one of the pris-
    oners they took, she came to his defense in a quarrel and promptly
    killed his opponent in a duel, using both sword and pistol. Not long
    after she married her pirate love, Read was taken prisoner with the rest
    of Rackam's crew. Pleading pregnancy, she obtained postponement of
    her sentence, but died of fever in prison in 1720.

SEVEN BANDITS OF THE OLD WEST

❧

Belle Starr. The "Bandit Queen" was hard-drinking, hard-driving, and hard-loving; she lived with a series of men, including outlaw Cole Younger, who probably fathered her daughter Pearl. Starr learned thievery from her first husband, James H. Reed. After he was gunned down, she married Samuel Starr and, disguised as a man, took part in his horse-stealing raids. The pair was arrested twice and jailed. After her spouse was killed in a gun fight, Belle took another "husband," Jim July, and forced him to change his name to Starr. For several years she evaded the law, sheltering outlaws like Jesse James in her hideout. The Bandit Queen was finally gunned down while out riding alone in 1889. Her killer was never found. Accusing fingers pointed at one of her former lovers; others suspected Starr's son, with whom she was supposedly having an incestuous relationship.

Ella Watson. "Cattle Kate" did no actual cattle rustling herself. This job was assigned to her cowboy lovers, who surrendered their bounty as the price of a night in her arms. Watson and her lover James Averill were lynched in 1889. This was a notable breach of chivalry, since few women were hung in the Old West, and indicated the strong revulsion felt for her deeds.

Flora Quick. Searching for a way to support herself after her husband died, Quick first ran a whorehouse and then traded horses, but she quickly realized that there was bigger money to be made by thievery and turned to horse stealing under the name of "Tom King." In this disguise, Quick met her death during a holdup in a small Arizona town.

Grace Newton led a cattle-rustling gang in New Mexico that included one of her sons. Finally brought to trial, Newton used language so abusive that the judge adjourned the proceedings "until such time as she can testify like a lady."

Etta Place. The loyal mistress portrayed in the film *Butch Cassidy and the Sundance Kid* was a real woman, a schoolteacher and homemaker before she gave up respectability to consort with "Sundance" Harry Longbaugh. At first she was a mere witness to his crimes, but later joined the gang, wearing men's clothes and sporting a revolver. In Argentina the trio stole about $30,000, but she was not present at the famous shoot-out in which Cassidy was said to have died. In 1907 Place and "Sundance" returned to the United States, and their relationship broke up soon afterward.

"Queen" Anne Richey was the only woman ever convicted of cattle rustling, in Wyoming in 1919. Before she could serve her sentence, though, Richey was poisoned, probably by a member of her own gang.

Pearl Hart held up an Arizona stagecoach in 1899, netting a total of $431. This act earned her a jail term and a place in history as the very last stagecoach bandit.

MURDER MOST FOUL

☙

Frankie Silver. Shortly before Christmas 1831, Silver hacked her sleeping husband to death, cut his body into pieces, burned what she could, and hid what was left in a hollow log behind their North Carolina cabin. The log was discovered and Silver convicted of murder, but though her father and uncle helped her escape from jail by cropping her hair and dressing her like a boy, she was caught. On July 12, 1833, she became the first white woman hanged in the state. Was Silver guilty? According to one account, her drunken husband had attacked her, and she was forced to defend herself with an ax. Because at the time married women were not allowed to testify in their own defense, no jury ever heard Frankie Silver's side of the story.

Marie Lafarge. The daughter of a French family with social pretensions, Marie was, by arrangement, wed in the 1840s to a widower from a small provincial town. Several months later, after eating a cake baked by his wife, her husband began complaining of stomach pains. Although Marie nursed him tenderly, dosing him with medicine, his condition continued to deteriorate. Her suspicious mother-in-law had the medicine analyzed—and traces of arsenic were found. But it was too late to save M. Lafarge. France talked of little else during Marie Lafarge's murder trial. She was found guilty and sentenced to life imprisonment, a fate that was for her, apparently, no worse than her marriage.

Madeleine Smith. At the age of nineteen, two years out of boarding school, Madeleine Smith entered into a tempestuous affair with a poor clerk in Edinburgh, then broke it off. Upon hearing of her plans to marry a prominent merchant, her lover threatened to divulge her torrid love letters—and shortly thereafter died of arsenic poisoning. An apothecary reported selling Smith a lot of the stuff for use in a face wash. In one of the most sensational trials of the nineteenth century, Smith was acquitted, her guilt "not proven." The psychological reasoning behind the acquittal? In the Victorian era, respectable unmarried women could not be considered at fault; the "seducer" was always to blame.

Lizzie Borden. Mr. and Mrs. Borden were found hacked to death in Fall River, Massachusetts, in 1892, their murder immortalized in the doggerel:

> Lizzie Borden took an ax
> Gave her mother forty whacks;
> When she saw what she had done
> She gave her father forty-one.

Lizzie, known to have hated her stepmother, was put on trial. Although much of the circumstantial evidence pointed in her direction, she maintained her innocence, and the jury could not believe that proper Miss Lizzie was a murderer. She was acquitted and spent the rest of her life in seclusion in the mansion she bought with her inheritance. Did she or didn't she?

Cordelia Botkin. When newspaper reporter John Dunning sailed off to cover the Spanish-American War, his lover feared that he would return to his spouse rather than to her. So Botkin sent Mrs. Dunning a box of arsenic-filled candy, which had its intended effect upon the recipient and her sister. At Botkin's trial, Dunning testified that the note accompanying the candy had been written by his paramour, and in 1898 she was found guilty and given a life sentence. She managed, however, to leave prison two days a week by granting sexual favors to her guards.

Belle Gunness. A jury ruled the death of the Indiana widow's first husband accidental, but the men who answered her newspaper ads for a new husband all disappeared after brief courtships. The remains of fourteen male bodies, chopped to bits, were found in the ruins of the Gunness house in April 1908, after it had been burned down by a jealous lover. The widow had apparently enticed each of the fourteen with promises of wedlock, relieved them of a total of $30,000, and killed every one. Her own three children perished in the fire. By the time this came out, Belle Gunness had disappeared and was never heard of again.

Ruth Brown Snyder went to the electric chair in January 1928 for the murder of her husband, Albert. Her accomplice was her lover, corset seller Henry Judd Gray. Snyder had tried to poison Albert several times and finally carried off the crime with Gray's assistance by bashing in his skull with a dumbbell. The lovers turned on each other almost immediately, and it took a jury only ninety-eight minutes to convict them. Their trial was one of the first "media events." As Snyder was being executed, a photographer with a camera strapped to his ankle sneaked a picture of her that was splashed over front pages the next morning.

Winnie Ruth Judd was a slightly built twenty-three-year-old when she shot and killed two friends in 1931, dismembered their bodies, and tried to ship them in two trunks and a suitcase from Arizona to Los Angeles. Red fluid oozing from the luggage aroused the suspicions of a baggage attendant. Judd was tried, convicted, and sentenced to be hanged, but at a special hearing held seventy-two hours before the scheduled execution, she was judged to be insane and sent to an Arizona mental hospital, from which she subsequently escaped several times. She was finally paroled in 1971.

Caril Ann Fugate. After her boyfriend, Charles Starkweather, murdered her mother, stepfather, and baby sister in 1958, the two fled the premises. Within forty-eight hours they had murdered seven complete strangers. Apprehended and tried, Starkweather was sentenced to death and the fourteen-year-old Fugate to life imprisonment. She was released in June 1976, after spending eighteen years behind bars.

Susan Atkins, Patricia Krenwinkel, and *Leslie Van Hooten* believed, with other members of Charles Manson's hippie "family" living at a ranch on the outskirts of Los Angeles, that Manson was Jesus Christ reincarnated. They performed in the sexual orgies that he orchestrated and totally submitted their wills to his whims. On August 9, 1969, at his orders, Atkins and Krenwinkel took part in the brutal murders of actress Sharon Tate, her unborn child, and four guests at her mansion in the canyons of Beverly Hills. On the following day Van Hooten was among the Mansonites who killed Leno and Rosemary LaBianca. Rosemary LaBianca was stabbed forty-one times, and Voyteck Frykowski, a Tate guest, fifty-one times. To Manson's mind, the murders signaled the onset of a "helter-skelter revolution." The women expressed no remorse for the crimes and on hearing the guilty verdicts against themselves and Manson showed no emotion. "You couldn't meet a nicer group of people," said Van Hooten of her "family."

THE STING

Constance Cassandra Chadwick, an attractive young woman, in 1866 journeyed to Cleveland, Ohio, where she passed herself off as the mistress of steel magnate Andrew Carnegie and the mother of his illegitimate child. She persuaded one banker that the millionaire had given her $12 million worth of "securities" which she deposited in his vault; using them as security, Chadwick borrowed $40 million, which she shrewdly invested in stocks. For nearly ten years she lived luxuriously on the proceeds, until the stock market crashed and the banker checked the documents, which turned out to be newspaper clippings of articles about Carnegie. When Chadwick was brought to trial in 1870, it was estimated that she had cost the country's banks at least $100 million and brought several of them to ruin. Two years later she died in prison.

Thérèse Humbert, while working as a lady's maid in Toulouse, France, announced that a rich old woman had left her a château and she would soon come into a fortune. Then Thérèse added another winning tale: she had saved the life of an elderly American millionaire when he'd become ill on a train by giving him an herbal potion, and in gratitude he had left $20 million to her and her sister. Frédéric Humbert, her employer's son, fell for the stories and the "heiress." Married, the young Humberts lived luxuriously on the basis of his (real) and her (anticipated) money. The "Crawford inheritance," consisting of bonds and securities, was to remain in a sealed safe until the sister came of age. Tales of continuing litigation involving the "inheritance" were enough to hold creditors off for years. In the meantime, the former servant girl amassed a fortune of 64 million francs, most of it in other people's money. But she could not hold off inquiry indefinitely. Articles in the press, some by Emile Zola, questioned the Humberts' financial wizardry, and finally the safe containing the "Crawford inheritance" was opened and its contents revealed: a single solid brick. Thérèse was tried, convicted, sentenced to five years of solitary confinement, and divorced by her husband. She was released from prison after three and a half years and disappeared without a trace.

Violet Blossom, the "Queen of the Female Pitch Doctors," sold patent medicines in the early 1900s. Dressed in a Mandarin gown, she pushed her best seller, Vital Sparks, an old "Chinese Remedy" that supposedly cured impotence; and when she sold "Pure Concentrate of Madame V. Pasteur's Herbs" she wore academic attire to give marks the impression that she was related to the great scientist. In thirty years she worked in at least two "Medical Institutes," ran a Museum of Anatomy, and toured country fairs posing as a famous dentist. She made it a rule never to treat women—they were, she said, much harder to fool than men.

Martha Hanau, a successful self-made businesswoman who published a financial newspaper, recommended shares of companies run by her associates and eventually created a whole network of journals touting her own business interests. Hanau's empire was a remarkably profitable one, but by 1928 the public prosecutor's office in Paris had so many charges against her that she was arrested. Tried in 1931, she was given a two-year sentence, but was freed at the end of one year. Dauntless, she acquired a new newspaper and a whole new set of swindles. Her next arrest was, however, her last. She died of an overdose of sleeping pills.

Alice Gerard traveled to Uruguay in 1977 to purchase a race horse, Cinzano, that her husband, Dr. Mark Gerard, had been commissioned to buy and, while there, also bought Lebon, a mediocre ringer. Two months later Alice switched halters on the two horses. The next day the horse wearing the "Cinzano" halter was killed in a freak accident. Lloyd's of London paid $150,000 to the owner of "Cinzano," and when "Lebon" won in a race at Belmont that year at fifty-seven-to-one odds, Dr. Gerard's bets pulled in $78,000. Before then, however, the Gerards had separated. Dr. Gerard was prosecuted for felony, but Alice testified that her husband had learned of the switch only after the race. The jury failed to reach a verdict. Alice, having been granted immunity for testifying before the grand jury, could not be prosecuted. She explained her horse switching as an attempt to embarrass the racing establishment because she felt they had a callous attitude toward horses.

SIX MOST WANTED BY THE FBI

Since the FBI's "most wanted" list was started in 1950, 365 fugitives have appeared on it. Of these, 6 have been women. FBI agents apprehended 3 of the 6, one was dropped from the list when state charges against her were dismissed, and one is still "wanted."

Ruth Eisemann-Schier (kidnapping, extortion, interstate transportation in aid of racketeering, aiding and abetting). The 293rd fugitive on the "top ten" list, she was the first woman to appear on it on December 28, 1968. Eisemann-Schier, wanted in connection with the kidnapping of Barbara Jane Mackle, was apprehended by the FBI on March 5, 1969, in Norman, Oklahoma.

Marie Dean Arrington (unlawful flight to avoid confinement, murder and manslaughter). Arrington was put on the list on May 29, 1969, after escaping from a Florida prison, where she was confined after being convicted for killing two people. The 301st fugitive and second woman to be "most wanted," Arrington was captured on December 22, 1971, by FBI agents in New Orleans.

Angela Yvonne Davis♀ (unlawful flight to avoid prosecution, murder and kidnapping). Wanted in connection with the Marin County Court House shoot-out on August 7, 1970, Davis was added to the "top ten" on August 18, 1970. She was captured by the FBI on October 13, 1970, in New York City and acquitted in California on June 4, 1972, after a much-publicized trial.

Bernardine Rae Dohrn (unlawful flight to avoid prosecution, mob action, riot, conspiracy). Dohrn was listed on October 14, 1970, in connection with a series of violent confrontations between the Weathermen, a violence-advocating faction of the Students for a Democratic Society, and Chicago police in October 1969. Dohrn was dropped from the list on December 7, 1973, after state charges were dismissed. However, she is still being sought as a federal fugitive.

Katherine Ann Power (unlawful flight to avoid prosecution, murder, theft of government property, bank robbery), and . . .

Susan Edith Saxe (unlawful flight to avoid prosecution, murder, theft of government property, bank robbery) were both added to the list on October 17, 1970. They were allegedly involved in the September 23, 1970, robbery of a Boston bank, in the course of which one of the bandits shot a Boston police officer to death. Saxe was apprehended by the Philadelphia Police Department on March 27, 1975. Power remains at large as the only woman currently on the list.

Also from the Federal Bureau of Investigation: In the five-year period ending in December 1978, there was an increase of 6.2 percent in the number of women arrested for crimes of all kinds: fraud was up 49.2 percent; embezzlement up 47.9 percent; forgery and counterfeiting up 27.7 percent. Says Professor Rita J. Simon, author of a Justice Department study of women and crime, "Women now have the kinds of opportunities men have always had and are taking advantage of those opportunities."

But increases in crimes of violence have not been as great for women. In 1975 women committed only 5.5 percent of all burglaries, up from 2 percent in 1953; 7.1 percent of robberies, up from 4.3 percent; and 15.6 percent of homicides, up from 14.1 percent two decades earlier, according to the F.B.I.'s annual crime reports.

FIVE "SOAP" MURDERS

The heroines of television's "soaps" seem constitutionally incapable of keeping their fingerprints *off* the murder weapon. Will they ever learn?

Leslie Norris. The wife of Stanley Norris on "The Guiding Light" was the prime suspect when he was found shot to death in his penthouse and Leslie's fingerprints were found on the gun. She was innocent, of course. It was the mother of Norris's secretary who pulled the trigger.

Tess Prentiss. Two underhanded males were trying to cheat Tess out of her inheritance on "Love of Life," and one of them dispatched his rival with a gun. Typically, Tess planted her fingerprints on the weapon and was brought to trial. All seemed lost when she was found guilty of second-degree murder, but Dr. Joe Corelli, who truly loved her, produced a witness who confessed to helping the real murderer invent a phony alibi.

Missy Palmer. Actually, it was a jealous old girl friend who stabbed Missy's con-man lover to death on "Another World," but the heroine unwittingly picked up the knife and was tried for murder.

Peggy Dillman. Losing consciousness during one of her many marital spats with husband, Marty, Peggy came to on "The Guiding Light" to find her spouse dead and herself charged with the deed. For a while even she was convinced of her guilt, but the real murderer turned out to be Flip Malone, an appropriately suspicious character.

Lisa Shea. On "As the World Turns," Dr. Michael Shea accused his wife, Lisa, of being an unfit mother and threatened to take away her young son. The very night that Lisa fled to Mexico with the child, Michael was found dead. In this case it was Lisa's older son Tom who wound up in the defendant's chair, having confessed to the crime to shield his mother. Fortunately, all ended well. The real murderer turned out to be a woman who was having an affair with the heartless physician.

THE AMBITIOUS MOTHER AND THE OBLIGING CLERGYMAN

Charles Dana Gibson comments on the epidemic of unions between
American heiresses and titled Europeans, 1902. (DOLLAR PRINCESSES)

Alva Smith Vanderbilt, wearing a
Venetian Renaissance gown, let loose
a small flock of doves when she
posed at her 1883 ball. (LIFE OF THE
PARTY)

With a little re-arranging here and there, the S-shaped corset produced the elegant line so popular during the Edwardian era. (TREND SETTERS)

Miss America 1956 poses with other contestants in a fairy-tale setting. *Miss America Pageant.* (HERE SHE COMES—THERE SHE GOES: WHAT HAPPENED TO THIRTEEN MISS AMERICAS)

Belle Starr, the hard-drinking and hard-loving "bandit queen," with one of her many husbands. *Oklahoma Historical Society.* (SEVEN BANDITS OF THE OLD WEST)

Belva Ann Bennett Lockwood, the first woman to argue before the United States Supreme Court. *Sophia Smith Collection, Smith College.* (FIRSTS AT THE BAR)

ale pirates Anne Bonny and Mary Read, who fought in male attire, were as formidable as any who d beneath the Jolly Roger. (THREE PIRATES)

XVIII ❦ *VICTIMS*

SACRIFICED

❦

Sacrifice is a recurrent motif in mythology and religion. Sometimes the most powerful deities could be appeased only by presentation of an un-blemished female; sometimes a sacrifice was politically motivated; and other times the victim was chosen more capriciously. A range of 4,000 years is covered in these examples from five cultural traditions.

The daughter of Jephthah. Jephthah led the ancient Israelites against the Ammonites, vowing that if his forces won he would sacrifice "whatsoever cometh forth of the doors of my house to meet me, when I return in peace." When he returned home triumphant, his only child "came out to meet him with timbrels and with dances." Heartbroken, he told her of his vow, and she agreed it must be fulfilled, begging only for a two-month delay, "that I may go up and down the mountains and bewail my virginity." After two months the girl, never named in the biblical account (Judges 11), was sacrificed. Every year the women of ancient Israel mourned her death for four days.

Iphigenia. Unfavorable winds halted the ships of her father Agamemnon, on his way to fight the Trojans. To change the winds, the goddess Artemis demanded the sacrifice of his daughter. His child or his country? The father chose the latter and, despite her mother's protestations, Iphigenia's throat was cut.

Lady Jane Grey.♀ To fulfill the political ambitions of her father and father-in-law, she was maneuvered onto the throne of England after the death of her cousin Edward VI, in place of the rightful heir, Mary Tudor.♀ Grey's unlawful reign came to an end after nine days, and her seventeen-year life ended soon after on the block (1554).

Victims of the Morning Star Ceremony. The Skidi Pawnee placated their most wrathful deity, the Morning Star, by sacrificing a virgin captive. Ignorant of her ultimate fate, the girl was treated as an honored guest by her captors for several months, then one day bathed in perfumed oils by attendants and dressed in a robe of fine white doeskin, elaborately decorated with quill work. The captors worked themselves into an ec-static state for four days, then the girl was dressed in black, with many beaded ornaments and a splendid feathered headdress, and made to climb a scaffold, where her finery was ripped from her and flaming torches were thrust at her nude body. Finally a chosen warrior would shoot a holy iron-tipped arrow into her heart, and a sacrificial knife would cut out her heart. Reports of the grisly ceremony came occasionally even into the 1860s.

The Women of Uttar Pradesh. In the summer of 1979 the farmers of the Indian state suffered the worst drought in forty years and resorted to ancient custom. In a symbolic sacrificial ritual to appease the rain god Varuma, the women were sent, nude, to till the soil in the fields at night. Rains came the following month—too little and too late. Did that prove the uselessness of the rite? Or did the women's nighttime labor bring what little rain did fall, saving 40 percent of the autumn crop? Only Varuma knows.

VICTIMS OF HENRY VIII

&

"King Henry the eighth to six wives was wedded— / One died, one survived, two divorced, two beheaded" goes the ditty. His wives were not the only victims of the king's lusts, jealousies, rages, and royal determination to get his own way. Sisters, daughters, female subjects, and relatives of his associates came to early ends.

Catharine of Aragon, the widow of Henry's brother Arthur, married Henry in 1509, six weeks after he became king. In more than twenty years of marriage, Katharine bore six children, but only one daughter survived. Henry, in need of a male heir and infatuated with a young woman, tried to divorce her, and when the pope refused to allow it, Henry confined her to a series of estates. She died three years later after a long illness. Meanwhile . . .

Mary,♀ their daughter, was forbidden to see her mother, forced to serve as lady-in-waiting to her younger half sister Elizabeth, and forced to assert her illegitimacy to demonstrate the invalidity of her parent's marriage and repudiate her church. (After the death of her father and half brother, she would succeed to the throne and become known as Bloody Mary for the religious persecutions that took nearly 300 lives.) Another Mary . . .

Mary of England, Henry's sister, was married off by him when she was only eighteen, forging an alliance with Louis XII of France. Her husband was fifty-two and ailing, and three months later the unhappy marriage ended when Mary was widowed. A third Mary . . .

Mary Boleyn, had been one of his sister Mary's attendants and was the wife of one of Henry's courtiers when she became his mistress. Soon, though, Mary B's younger sister . . .

Anne Boleyn♀ caught Henry's eye, and he married her even before his divorce from Katharine was officially validated. Anne was immediately crowned queen, and Parliament ruled that her children would inherit the throne. Henry ordered the execution of citizens who protested. One of them was **Elizabeth Barton,** also known as the Holy Maid of Kent. A one-time serving girl, she had gone into a trance to prophesy disaster if

Henry divorced Catharine to marry Anne Boleyn. Barton was arrested, forced to confess, and she and her alleged accomplices were hanged at Tyburn in 1534. Meanwhile, Anne gave birth to a daughter but no son, and Henry found a new infatuation. In 1536 Anne was convicted of adultery with several courtiers and of incest with her brother. She was beheaded, and ten days later Henry married . . .

Jane Seymour,♀ who bore a son, the sickly Edward VI, the following year, and died twelve days later. Probably the only wife Henry truly loved, Seymour had been lady-in-waiting to both his previous queens. Henry mourned for three years—an unaccustomed interval between wives.

Margaret, Countess of Salisbury, was in her eighties and the mother of a distant cousin, Reginald Pole, a cardinal who opposed Henry's divorce and marital arrangements, when Henry arrested her in 1538. The countess asserted that "my head never committed treason and if you want it, you shall seize it" and ran around the scaffold until the executioner caught up with her and was able to proceed with his job.

Anne of Cleves♀ was married to Henry in January 1540 and divorced by him in July of the same year. His advisers had urged the match to cement relations with Anne's royal German relatives, but when she reached England and Henry had a look at her, he decided not to consummate their union.

Catherine Howard, a cousin of the Boleyn sisters, married Henry the same busy year. The prettiest of his six wives, Catherine was more interested in a handsome cousin than in the aging king. Charges of adultery were brought against her and—possibly on trumped-up evidence—she was convicted and beheaded in 1542.

Catherine Parr,♀ twenty-one years old and already the veteran of two earlier marriages, married Henry the following year. The last Catherine survived Henry's 1547 death, married the brother of his third wife later the same year, and died in childbirth a year later. But before Henry's death, a week-old infant, later known as . . .

Mary, Queen of Scots,♀ succeeded to the throne of Scotland. Henry tried to marry her off to Edward, but her mother and Henry's niece *Mary of Guise* had other ideas. Henry sent his army to attack Scotland but, after causing extensive destruction, he was defeated. So the Marys were left to rule Scotland, and ultimately plague . . .

Elizabeth,♀ who succeeded to the throne of England after the death of her half sister Mary. Her reign is remembered as a golden age of English power and culture, but she could never forget that her father had beheaded her mother and banished her from his sight, and that she herself had narrowly escaped execution during her half sister's reign. The daughter, though, learned much from her father. She avoided marriage despite numerous suitors and ordered the execution of the one man she truly loved.

A COVEN OF WITCHES

A fifteenth-century volume on the activities of witches offered reasons why women were more likely than men to become servants of the devil:

"Women are more gullible, women are more impressionable, women are feebler in both mind and body, women are insatiable in their carnal lust and, of course, women have slippery tongues." A century later, England had both a legal definition of a witch—"a person who hath conference with the Devil, to consult with him or to do some act"—and a strict death penalty.

Dame Alice Kyteler was tried in Ireland in 1324 on charges that she met nightly with a familiar, and also that she was "wont to offer sacrifices to devils of live animals." Her accusers found in her closet some ointment which she used to grease a staff "upon which she ambolled and galloped through thicke and thin, when and what manner she listed."

Joan of Arc,[9] the "Maid of Orleans," heard voices commanding her to wear men's gear and lead the French army. When captured by the English, she was accused as a witch, convicted of heresy, and burned at the stake in Rouen, France, on May 31, 1431.

Elizabeth Francis, when brought to trial in Chelmsford, England, in 1556, testified that her familiar, a "whyte spotted Catte," had been given to her by her grandmother, who also "taughte her to cal it by the name of Sattan and to kepe it in a basket." When Francis wanted the "catte" to do something, she testified, "he required a drop of bloude, which she gave him by prycking herselfe."

Agnes Sampson, known as the "Wise Wife of Keith," was a Scots woman accused of plotting against King James VI (later James I of England) around 1590. After being tortured, she "confessed" to sorcery and was burned at the stake.

Alice Samuel lived in Warboys, England, where local children accused various townspeople of witchcraft. Samuel, a poverty-stricken old woman of seventy-six, was one of their special targets. At her trial she claimed to be pregnant—but the judges were not moved. She, her husband, and her daughter were all sentenced to the gallows; she died in 1593.

Alison Balfour, believed to be a "notorious witch" in Scotland, was burned at the stake around 1596. Her husband and daughter were also tortured, the seven-year-old with thumbscrews.

Perrenette Gaudillon terrified her fellow villagers, who believed that she was a werewolf. In 1598 a mob hunted her down and tore her to pieces. Then they seized three other members of her family, tried them, and burned them.

Elizabeth Southerne and **Anne Whittle,** two old women, did belong to a coven of witches in Lincolnshire, England, around 1612. Rumors about their activities multiplied until they were formally accused, tried, and hanged.

Elizabeth Demdike, it was alleged, headed a coven of thirteen like-minded souls and "brought up her owne Children [and] instructed her Graundchildren . . . to bring them to be Witches." Demdike, eighty years old and blind, died in prison; ten of her alleged followers were executed, after a trial that lasted two days in Lancashire, England, in 1612.

Helen Guthrie revealed in 1661 that, under instruction from the devil, she had collapsed a bridge at Cortaquhie, Scotland. In the same year, but in another town, Guthrie and four other witches exhumed the body of an unbaptized infant and cut "severall peices thereof . . . and they made a py thereof, that they might eat of it, that by this meanes they might never make a confession" of being witches.

Isobel Gowdrie in 1662 in Scotland voluntarily confessed to witchcraft charges that included child and adult murders. The devil, she said, made her do it. He appeared to her as a small black man and forced her to give her body to him and was "abler for us that way than any man can be." He was, moreover, generously endowed and had "a hudg nature." Then Gowdrie committed the crimes as he instructed.

Janet Breadheid, Gowdrie's sister, also confessed to having intercourse with the same devil. His genitals, she reported, were "exceeding great and long." Curiously, Breadheid's husband had induced her to consort with Satan.

The Accused of Salem. In Salem, Massachusetts, in 1692 the daughters of a certain Mr. Parris fell ill. The sickness spread among their friends, caused they said, by the evil machinations of witches in the community. Which witches? They began by accusing *Tituba,* the half-Indian, half-black family slave, and she was flogged until she "confessed" and implicated two neighbors. But the sickness continued to rage among the girls of Salem, who next accused several elderly women, some of whom had chastised them. By this time the town was in a frenzy. Who would be accused next? The girls named some of the most honorable and respected citizens, and apparently relished the attention being lavished on them. Twenty persons were executed before the hysteria ended, almost all of them women. Many "confessed." Still others died, or went mad, in jail. In later years some of the leaders of the Massachusetts colony came to believe that they had been tragically duped, and one of the accusers recanted. All the convictions were annulled, and relatives were indemnified. Among the accused were the following twelve: *Bridget Bishop, Martha Carrier, Sarah Cloyce, Martha Corey, Mary Esty, Sarah Good, Dorcas Good* (her five-year-old daughter), *Abigail Hobbs, Susanna Martin, Rebecca Nurse, Sarah Osburne,* and *Elizabeth Proctor.*

A FIELD HAND'S LIFE

꙰

Female field hands on southern plantations lived a life of anonymous toil. We know them mainly through the diaries and letters of their owners. *Fanny Kemble,*⁹ a popular British actress who married a Georgia plantation owner, was particularly attuned to the despairing lot of her female slaves. Of nine unhappy women who appear in her journal for March 1839 Kemble wrote: "There was hardly one of these who might not have been a candidate for a bed in a hospital, and they had come to me after working all day in the fields."

Fanny. "Has had six children: all dead but one. She came to beg to have her work in the field lightened."

Nanny. "Has had three children; two of them are dead. . . ."

Leah. "Has had six children; three are dead."

Sophy. "Came to beg for some old linen. She is suffering fearfully; has had ten children; five of them are dead."

Sally. "Has had two miscarriages and three children born, one of whom is dead. She came complaining of incessant pain and weakness in her back."

Charlotte. "Had had two miscarriages, and was with child again. She was crippled with rheumatism, and showed me a pair of swollen knees that made my heart ache. . . ."

Sarah. "Had had four miscarriages, had brought seven children into the world, five of whom are dead, and was again with child. She complained of dreadful pains in the back and an internal tumor which swells with the exertion of working in the fields. . . . She told me she had once been mad and run into the woods, where she contrived to elude discovery for some time. . . ."

Sukey. "Had had four miscarriages; had brought eleven children into the world, five of whom are dead."

Molly. "Hers was the best account I have yet received; she had had nine children and six of them were still alive."

EIGHT WHO WERE CAPTURED BY INDIANS

Esther Williams and *Eunice Williams,* two young sisters, were victims of an Indian and French raid of 1704 on Deerfield, Massachusetts. Luckier than the 49 who were slaughtered, they were among 112 captives forced to march through 300 miles of wilderness to Canada. Eventually survivors ransomed the captives. Esther returned home with her father, but Eunice, who had been seven years old when taken, married one of the Indians nine years later and did not return to Massachusetts for thirty-six years.

Olive and *Mary Ann Oatman* were teen-agers when most of their family was slaughtered and they were captured by the Yavapai Indians in 1851 and sold as slaves to the Mohaves. Their brother, refusing to give them up for lost, continued searching for five years. Meanwhile, Mary Ann died. At last he found Olive and secured her release, but his sister was almost unrecognizable. Her arms, jaw line, and chin were covered with the tattoos she would bear for the rest of her life.

Fanny Wiggins Kelly was a bride of nineteen when she was captured by the Oglala Sioux in 1864. The Indians named her Real Woman because of her capacity for hard work and wed her to their chief, Ottowa. Her small niece was scalped. In time Real Woman was returned to her people in exchange for three army horses and a load of food supplies. She wrote the history of her adventures in *My Captivity Among the Sioux Indians,* making the unlikely claim that in all those years she had never been violated.

Sarah Larimer was captured by the Sioux in the same raid as her friend Fanny Kelly. Resourceful in a different way, Larimer managed to escape two days later with her son. She too wrote a successful book about her experiences.

Maria Weichel and *Susannah Allerdice,* two German-born women who had emigrated to the United States, were taken from a ranch house by the Cheyenne chief Tall Bull in an 1869 raid to avenge a U.S. Cavalry attack on his people. The cavalry pursued them and located the Cheyenne camp later the same day. Taken by surprise, the chief, his family, some followers, and the two captives hid in the ravine. The warriors defending the ravine were killed, and it was overrun in an instant. Historian Dee Brown tells the rest of the story: "All the Cheyennes except Tall Bull's wife and child were dead. Both of the German women had been shot, but one was still alive. The white men said that Tall Bull had shot the white captives, but the Indians never believed that he would have wasted his bullets in such a foolish way."

FROM SWEATSHOP TO DEATH
❧

Even in the days of notorious sweatshops, the Triangle Waist Company was known as a poor place to work. The 500 young women on the eighth, ninth, and tenth floors were so crowded that they had to stand back to back. The bins beneath the sewing machines were filled with oil-soaked rags. The narrow fire doors were kept locked to prevent thievery. The building had no workable sprinkler system. In such a setting tragedy was inevitable, and it struck on April 20, 1911. Fire broke out and within minutes raged through the three floors, killing at least 146 trapped workers. Many women leaped to their deaths, looking to the horrified spectators like human torches against the gathering dusk. The owners of the Triangle Waist Company were indicted for manslaughter—and later acquitted.

Almost all the dead were extremely young. Most were Italian and Jewish, recent immigrants and the daughters of immigrants. Here are the names of a few of these voiceless victims, with what little is known about them:

Julia Aberstein

Gussie Bierman

Della Costello and *Sophie Salemi,* who leaped from the ninth floor, their arms around each other. Afterward, they shared a funeral as well. Sophie's mother was able to identify her daughter by means of a repair she had made in her stocking.

Celia Eisenberg

Jennie Franco, fifteen years old.

Sarah Kupla, sixteen years old.

Jennie Levin, nineteen years old.

Catherine Maltese, thirty-eight years old, and her daughters . . .

Lucia Maltese, twenty years old, and . . .

Rosalie Maltese, fourteen years old.

Sadie Nussbaum, eighteen years old. Her mother identified her body, then attempted suicide.

Julia Rosen—$852 was found in her stocking; she did not trust banks.

Freda Velakowsky

TEN WHO FELL FROM THE HEIGHTS

※

Emma Hamilton.♀ The adored mistress of Lord Nelson fell victim to wine and gambling after he was killed at Trafalgar. In 1813 she was arrested for debt and sentenced to a year in prison. She died in France, penniless.

Lola Montez.♀ Toward the end of her life the notorious dancer repented of her wicked ways and began speaking against sin. When she became ill in New York, an old school "friend" offered to care for her at home. Montez deeded all her belongings to the woman, who shortly dumped her in a Hell's Kitchen tenement, where she died in 1861, impoverished and alone.

Calamity Jane (Martha Jane Cannary).♀ Calamity's rip-roaring adventures were known throughout the country. Penny novels were written about her exploits, and she appeared in Wild West shows. But when she died in 1903, she was a destitute old woman in rags.

Elizabeth ("Baby") Doe.♀ When mining millionaire Horace Tabor, twice Doe's age, shed his first wife to marry her, everyone thought the young woman was seeing dollar signs. The Tabors' high style of living did little to dispel that impression. But to everyone's surprise, Baby Doe stuck by her man when his silver mines failed. At his death she was desperately poor but never requested charity. In 1935 she was found frozen to death in her Colorado shack.

Imogene ("Bubbles") Wilson. The one-time Ziegfeld Follies beauty landed in a Long Island sanitarium for drug treatment under her real name, May Noland.

Helen Lee Worthing. Another Ziegfeld showgirl, who once had "the most beautiful profile in America" according to the producer himself, also became a drug addict.

Mae Murray. The actress, once a millionaire, was found sleeping on a bench in Central Park and was arrested for vagrancy. In 1964 she was admitted to the Motion Picture County Home and died there the following year.

Barbara La Marr. The star of silent films was called the "too beautiful girl," and it turned out to be true. She tried every kind of drug, storing her cocaine in a gold casket on her grand piano. In 1926, at the age of twenty-six, she took a fatal overdose.

Kiki of Montparnasse. The Parisian model was the darling of poets and painters in the years between the wars. Her lover, Man Ray, immortalized her back by painting it as a violin. In 1953, distressed by the passing years, Kiki killed herself with a combination of absinthe and cocaine. Her still-beautiful body was discovered, stretched out on a bug-infested mattress.

Lillian Roth. A singer and former child star, Roth wrote the best-selling *I'll Cry Tomorrow* in 1954 about her battle with alcoholism. The book sold 7 million copies in twenty languages, but Roth was unable to hold on to her second round of good fortune. She wound up working as a bakery employee, hospital attendant, and package wrapper.

WOMEN: ADDICTION, SUICIDE, AND FAMILY VIOLENCE

ॐ

- One out of every three narcotics addicts in the United States is a woman.
- Women account for 43 percent of all drug-related deaths. Women over the age of forty are more likely than men to die of causes related to drugs.
- Women constitute about 25 percent of the 235,000 people in drug treatment programs; 86 percent of those women being treated are under the age of thirty.
- Women receive 80 percent of the prescriptions for amphetamines, 67 percent of those for tranquilizers, and 60 percent of those for barbiturates.
- Nearly one of every four girls of ages twelve to seventeen, and almost one of every five women eighteen and older, had used marijuana, according to a 1977 national survey.

- One out of three alcoholics is a woman.
- More than a third of all women in the United States—22.3 million— smoke cigarettes. Another 9.6 million are former smokers.

- In 1977, 11.4 women per 100,000 died in motor vehicle accidents, 15.7 in all other accidents.
- By age group, the leading causes of death among women in 1977 were: age fifteen to twenty-four, accidents; age twenty-five to forty-four, malignant neoplasms (cancer); age forty-five to sixty-four, also cancer; and sixty-five and over, heart diseases.
- In 1977, 7,572 women committed suicide. Of them, 3,147 chose poison and 2,743 used firearms.
- By age group, 5.3 of 100,000 fifteen-to-twenty-four-year-old women, 9.5 of 100,000 twenty-five-to-forty-four-year-old women, 11.6 of 100,-000 forty-five-to-sixty-four-year-old women, and 7.8 of 100,000 women age sixty-five and older committed suicide (1977).

- There are several categories of crimes that are chiefly perpetrated against women by men. In 1978, 19,700 men were arrested for forcible rape, 22,400 for prostitution and commercial vice, and 32,000 for offenses against family and children.
- Every year 1.8 million American women are beaten by their husband, or one every eighteen seconds.
- Every year about 250,000 American men are beaten by their wives.
- Of the 20,510 people murdered in the United States in 1975, one-fourth were killed by a family member, often a spouse.
- About one-fourth of all police officers killed in the line of duty were responding to calls involving family disputes when they were killed.

From *Statistical Abstract of the United States, 1979,* and other sources

A VARIETY OF VICTIMS

Victimization takes many forms . . .

Artemisia Gentileschi,[♀] a painter, was raped by Agostino Tassi, an artist whom her artist father had hired to teach her perspective drawing. Her father sued Tassi for the theft of several of his pictures as well as for raping his daughter. Tassi, who had previously been convicted of arranging the murder of his wife, then promised to marry Gentileschi. Artemisia had to testify and, to ensure her veracity, was tortured. As the thumbscrews were applied, she cried out to the accused, "Is this the ring you promised me?" But Tassi was acquitted. Apparently the trial did nothing to injure his reputation; in three years he was considered a noted painter—of female nudes.

Virginia Rappe. The hopeful starlet attended a weekend orgy given by popular comedian Fatty Arbuckle in 1921. Rappe left the party in an ambulance, her bladder ruptured "by violence," and died soon afterward of peritonitis. Arbuckle was charged with manslaughter, but testimony at three trials tended to concentrate on Rappe's checkered past rather than the violence that had been done to her. By the time the actor was finally acquitted of the charges, his movie career was in ashes.

Annette, Cecile, Emilie, Marie, and *Yvonne Dionne.*[♀] The circuslike atmosphere that surrounded their early years had a lasting effect on the quintuplets. They were removed from their parents and reared by nurses and nuns under the supervision of their own doctor, at the expense of the Canadian government, in a specially built hospital. When they finally were allowed to return home, their father forced them to work as servants in the house he had built with the money their fame had earned. All five of the quints, two of whom died as young adults, grew up to be shy and withdrawn.

Helen Gahagan Douglas.[♀] In 1950 the U.S. representative (and former film star) from California ran against fellow Representative Richard M. Nixon for the Senate. Although she had served three terms in the House, she lost badly after Nixon succeeded in painting her liberal politics "red," and she never again ran for public office.

Barbara Reed, a truck driver, was raped and beaten by three men after her employer sent her out on a rainy January 1979 night in a truck with a defective defroster, windshield wipers, and doors. While phoning for help she was attacked and woke up in the hospital in Long Beach, California. She returned to work four days later, only to be told that she was being fired "for her own good." Reed filed suit against her employer, alleging that male truck drivers who were crime victims were not dismissed. Her case is still in the courts.

Grace Pierce. The former research director of Ortho Pharmaceutical Corporation claims she was forced to resign because her conscience would not allow her to approve the testing on children of a new drug containing large amounts of saccharin. The case is now being heard in the courts.

Ronni Karpen Moffitt, in her early twenties and an associate at the Institute for Policy Studies in Washington, D.C., was on her way to the Institute with its director on September 21, 1976, when a remote-control bomb exploded under the front seat of the car in which they were driving. Moffitt was not the target—her companion, Orlando Letelier, leader in exile of the opposition to the military junta ruling Chile, was. Both were killed. Three years later, one man pleaded guilty, three others were convicted of related offenses, and three more, indicted in the United States for ordering Letelier assassinated, remain in Chile, which has refused extradition.

Princess Misha'al was nineteen years old in July 1977 when she and her twenty-year-old boyfriend were publicly executed in Saudi Arabia for adultery, a crime under Islamic law. Six months later a brief news items in England inspired a television "docudrama," *Death of a Princess,* widely shown in Europe and the United States in the spring of 1980 despite efforts by Saudi officials and others to keep it off the air. The controversial film was shown at the same time as Iranian public executions took place for the same offense.

Tatyana Mamonova, Tatyana Goritscheva, and **Natalya Nalachoskaya** were expelled from the Soviet Union on July 20, 1980, for publishing three issues of an underground magazine, *Women and Russia.* Critical of the male-dominated Soviet society, the July 1980 issue exhorted women to urge the men in their families to risk imprisonment rather than fight with Russian invading forces in Afghanistan.

UNLUCKY IN LOVE

There are many ways to be unlucky in love. The Elizabethan age was a particularly bad time for women who knew what they wanted when it came to men and marriage. Fathers provided no dowry for headstrong daughters who insisted on choosing their own spouses. One **Miss Paston,** who did not care for the man her widowed mother had chosen for her, was beaten "some time twice in one day, and her head broken in two or three places." *Elizabeth I*♀ punished the younger sisters of *Lady Jane Grey*♀ for marrying secretly and without her consent. And she sent . . .

Elizabeth Throckmorton, one of her maids of honor, to the Tower, along with her lover (or secret husband), Sir Walter Raleigh, when Throckmorton became noticeably pregnant. Then there was the queen's distant relative . . .

Arabella Stuart,♀ first cousin to Elizabeth's heir, James, and therefore second in line for the throne. The queen had Arabella arrested because of a rumor linking her to William Seymour, whose family claimed the right to the throne. When James acceded to the throne he released his cousin, then placed her under house arrest because he did not approve of her intended marriage. When the couple married secretly anyway, Arabella was placed in custody and her husband taken to the Tower. She escaped, wearing male garb, and set sail for France, only to be captured and brought back to the Tower. In 1615 she died there, still a prisoner.

Mrs. John Osborne. On January 3, 1815, her husband, a resident of Maidstone, Kent, England, sold her and her child to William Sergeant for one pound. Sergeant received a deed for the two.

Julia Pastrana. Covered from head to toe with hair, she was exhibited in circuses as "the ugliest woman in the world." Her husband was the manager. At the sight of her newborn daughter, who was also hideous, Pastrana declined and eventually died. Undaunted, the loving husband had her body mummified and continued to exhibit Julia. But eventually he found another ugly woman to love, renamed her *Leonora Pastrana,* and presented her to the world as Julia's sister. He married Leonora, too.

Imogene Remus. Her husband, George Remus, was a leading bootlegger of the 1920s. While he was in prison, she had an affair with the federal agent who had put him there. When Remus emerged, he shot her in the stomach. He was brought to trial, but quickly acquitted on the grounds of temporary insanity. He promptly repaired to the local jail, where he threw a party for an assortment of friends and the twelve jurors.

Linda Pugach. In 1960 her rejected boyfriend, Burton Pugach, hired thugs to throw lye in her face and blind her. After he served a prison term, she agreed to marry him. The couple have written a book about the bonds that forged their matrimony; they stop short of recommending the procedure to others.

Angela Diniz, a thirty-two-year-old millionaire, captivated a certain Doca Street, a forty-five-year-old business failure and playboy, who left his wealthy wife and children to live with her. But Diniz, whose romantic exploits had long been a leading gossip-column item in São Paulo, did not abandon her friendly ways. After she flirted with both a French man and a German woman on a beach in one day, Street shot her point-blank four times in the face with a revolver. In 1980 a jury acquitted him of murder on the grounds that he had defended his honor; but for using "excessive" means and for fleeing the scene of a crime, he was given a two-year sentence, suspended.

SEVEN VICTIMS VINDICATED

Jeanne of Portugal. Whenever she defeated her husband, Fernando, at chess, he took revenge with his fists. She finally got her chance to retaliate by refusing to ransom him when the Turks held him captive from 1213 to 1226.

Inés de Castro. Dom Pedro, heir to the throne of Portugal, fell madly in love with his wife's beautiful lady-in-waiting, who was banished, then ordered murdered by the king. When Dom Pedro succeeded to the throne in 1357 as Peter I, he had her murderers tortured and killed, and built a monument to the story of their devotion. It was said, too, that he disinterred her body, crowned the corpse, and demanded that her former enemies pay homage to his queen.

Sadie Sachs. When nurse Margaret Sanger ♀ first tended her in 1912 in her slum dwelling, Sachs, the mother of several young children, hovered near death from a botched abortion. A year before she had begged a doctor for birth control information, but his only advice had been "Tell Jake to sleep on the roof." Under the law Sanger couldn't give Sachs information either, and a few months later she was dead. Sanger spent the rest of her life challenging the law and fighting to make birth control available to women.

Carrie Buck. In the 1920s the Virginia teen-ager bore an illegitimate child as a result of a rape and was taken from her foster home to the State Colony for Epileptics and Feeble-Minded. In a case that went to the Supreme Court, Justice Oliver Wendell Holmes authorized the sterilization of Carrie, her sister Doris, and their mother, Emma, stating, "Three generations of imbeciles are enough." In 1979 the Bucks were traced: Emma had died in the hospital in the 1940s; Carrie's daughter had been considered a "bright child" by her schoolteachers, but had died of measles at seven; Doris had married and, believing her abdominal scar the result of an appendectomy, had wondered through thirty-nine years of marriage why she had not borne children; and Carrie, seventy-two, was living in poverty with her second husband. In response to the injustice done to the Bucks and tens of thousands of others like them, a concerted drive is on to repeal the old sterilization laws in Virginia and other states.

Camella Teoli went to work for a textile mill in Lawrence, Massachusetts, in 1911 when she was thirteen years old. Three weeks later she was scalped by a machine that twisted cotton into thread and was hospitalized for seven months. When a strike of mill workers led to congressional committee hearings, Teoli was among the witnesses called to testify. Her story became front-page news and helped spark a thorough investigation of working conditions in the United States. Teoli worked in the mills most of her life, was never promoted, and died in the 1970s. In 1980 Lawrence recognized her contribution to the history of labor in America and named a walkway across the city common for her.

Gloria Mendoza, one of the one million clients of New York City's welfare system, applied for welfare benefits for herself and her four children in the mid-1970s, but was assigned a caseworker who, because she did not understand the Spanish-speaking Mendoza, had her client apply for lower disability benefits instead. Mendoza filed a complaint that resulted in a federal directive to the city and other jurisdictions to hire enough bilingual personnel to serve the Hispanic community.

Margaret Hasselman was fired from her job as a lobby attendant in a Manhattan office building after refusing to wear a Bicentennial uniform chosen by her employer—a red, white, and blue poncho held together by two stitches at each side, worn over blue dancer's panties and with white high-heeled pumps. Hasselman said she experienced "repeated sexual harassment [which] greatly interfered with my ability to perform my job." A federal district court agreed, ruling that she could sue her employer for sex discrimination.

SEVEN HELD HOSTAGE

When Iranian militants stormed the United States Embassy in Teheran on November 4, 1979, seven American women were among those captured and held hostage. One was among three hostages released on November 19; four more were released the following day. Two women remained prisoner in the embassy compound, along with forty-eight men. The women hostages were:

Kathy Jean Gross, twenty-two, of Cambridge Springs, Pennsylvania, an embassy secretary, released November 19.

Elizabeth Montagne, forty-two, of Calumet City, Illinois, secretary to the chargé d'affaires, released November 20.

Terri Thetford, twenty-four, of South San Francisco, California, a secretary in the administrative section of the embassy, released November 20.

Joan Walsh, thirty-three, of Ogden, Utah, a secretary in the political section of the embassy, released November 20.

Lillian Johnson, thirty-two, of Elmont, Long Island, a secretary in the security office, released November 20.

Elizabeth Ann Swift, thirty-eight, of Washington, D.C., chief of the political section of the embassy and the senior career diplomat among the fifty hostages held for endless months in 1979 and 1980. Her assignment to Iran had begun only a year before, after a fifteen-year career in the Foreign Service. Swift is known as an outspoken advocate of human rights.

Kathryn Koob, forty-one, of Iowa, an officer of the United States International Communications Agency with which she had been associated for ten years. She was also director of the Iran-American Society in Teheran, which operated an educational and cultural exchange program between the two countries before the Iranian revolution of February 1979 brought its activities to a halt. She too remained among the fifty captives held for months in the embassy.

The women, guarded by matrons, were kept in the building apart from the men within the embassy compound. Those who were released reported being blindfolded some of the time, forced to sit for hours on end with their hands, and sometimes their legs, tied to their chairs. "We had to ask for everything," reported Montagne after her release. "If you wanted to go to the bathroom, you had to ask. You couldn't talk to each other." "I don't think I could have lasted another week," said Thetford, "not another day."

XIX ❧ *WHAT'S IN A NAME?*

A ROSE BY EVERY OTHER NAME

❧

New breeds of roses are often named for women. Here are just forty of the more than seventy so honored:

Eve Allen
Sarah Arnot
Madame Lauriol de Barny
Honorine de Brabant
Josephine Bruce
Maria Callas
Madame Alfred Carrière
Irene Churruca
Lucy Cramphorn
Anne Crocker
Lady Curzon
Wendy Cussons
Frau Karl Druschki
Elizabeth of Glamis
Queen Elizabeth
Kathleen Ferrier
Mrs. Oakley Fisher
Evelyn Fison
Elizabeth Harkness
Kathleen Harrop

Frau Dagmar Hartopp
Maryse Kriloff
Madame Louis Laperrière
Molly McGredy
Flora McIvor
Princess Margaret of England
Meg Merrilies
Princess Michiko
Jeanne de Montfort
Louise Odier
Esther Ofarim
Madame Pierre Oger
June Park
Dorothy Peach
Madame Isaac Pereire
Yvonne Rabier
Baroness Rothschild
Constance Spry
Lady Waterlow
Madame Zöetmans

THE SOUP COURSE

❧

Consommé Adelina Patti,♀ named for the nineteenth-century soprano, is garnished with small cubes of custard, carrots, or puréed chestnuts.

Potage Agnes Sorel♀ is dedicated to the mistress of Charles VII of France and is an appropriately rich but delicate liaison of chicken stock, puréed mushrooms, and heavy cream, garnished with cubes of ox tongue and chicken breast.

*Consommé George Sand,*⁰ named for the French novelist, is a fish stock garnished extravagantly with tiny fish quenelles, slices of morels (wild French mushrooms), shrimp butter, and croutons spread with carp roe.

*Consommé Jenny Lind*⁰ is a game stock garnished with strips of quail breast and slices of mushroom, named in honor of the opera star.

*Consommé Sarah Bernhardt*⁰ is an elaborate soup, befitting the actress whom it honors, made from chicken stock slightly thickened with tapioca and garnished with chicken quenelles, julienned truffles, asparagus tips, slices of poached beef marrow, and croutons spread with shrimp butter.

Soupe à la reine, a purée of spit-roasted breast of chicken with twelve sweet almonds, three bitter almonds, and the yolks of six hard-cooked eggs, blended into consommé with bread and a half pint of cream or rich milk, was served every Thursday at the court of **Queen Margaret of Valois.**⁰

SELECT DISHES

❦

Chicken Maintenon was named for the companion of Louis XIV, the **Marquise de Maintenon;** a quarter of a small chicken is brushed with lemon juice, broiled, and served on toast with sautéed chicken livers and a parsley-sherry sauce.

Bouchée à la reine, a puff pastry shell filled with creamed chicken and truffles, was created for **Marie Leszczynska,** daughter of King Stanislaus II of Poland and wife of Louis XV of France.

Chicken Tetrazzini, named for the coloratura soprano **Luisa Tetrazzini,** consists of pieces of poached chicken in a rich sherry sauce served over spaghetti.

Marie Stuart is a garniture served with roast meats, consisting of individual tart shells filled with purée of turnips or onions, topped with rounds of cooked marrow and *glace de viande* (meat gravy).

Rachel, a nineteenth-century French actress, is honored by a garnish of artichoke bottoms poached in butter, over which *tournedos* or *noisettes* (steaks or chops) are set.

Roast à l'Impératrice begins with an olive whose pit is replaced with an anchovy. The olive is put inside a lark, the lark in a quail, the quail in a partridge, the partridge in a pheasant, the pheasant in a turkey, and the turkey into a suckling pig. The whole is then spit roasted. According to Alexandre Dumas, one should not "make the mistake of serving it whole, just like that. The gourmand eats only the olive and the anchovy." L'impératrice was **Josephine,**⁰ of course.

Veau Sylvie (Veal Sylvia) is veal roasted with ham and cheese after being marinated in brandy, Madeira, and diced vegetables. But—who is Sylvia?

Anadama bread is a heavy corn meal and molasses loaf; when asked by fellow travelers who had baked the bread he shared with them, her husband replied, "Anna, damn her!"

SWEETS AND DESSERTS NAMED FOR WOMEN

❧

Peggy's Leg is a toffee or chewy sweet, popular in Ireland, made from brown sugar, molasses, syrup, butter, ginger, and vinegar. The name describes the shape of the confection; Peggy's name was undoubtedly added for alliteration.

Coupe Eugénie was named for the empress; it consists of vanilla ice cream blended with morsels of preserved chestnut (*marrons*) and topped with whipped cream and additional *marrons.*

Poirs Belle Hélène was named for the Offenbach operetta. It is a superb concoction of vanilla-poached pears filled with vanilla ice cream and covered with hot fudge sauce.

Peach Melba was created by the great chef Escoffier for the Australian soprano **Dame Nellie Melba.** To make this calorie-laden wonder, puréed fresh raspberries are poured over a ripe peach that has been poached in vanilla syrup and perched on a bed of vanilla ice cream.

Riz à l'Impératrice is a molded cream dessert containing rice and fruits; *l'impératrice* was, again, Napoleon's **Empress Josephine.**♀

Charlotte aux pommes or *Apple Charlotte,* a molded dessert filled with rum- and apricot-flavored apple purée and served with whipped cream or custard sauce, was named for **Princess Elizabeth-Charlotte of France,** daughter-in-law of Louis XIV, who was also called Liese-Lotte.

Brown Betty, an American cousin of Apple Charlotte, is a baked pudding made with sliced apples or other fruits and buttered bread crumbs, served with ice cream or hard sauce.

Crêpes Suzette were named for the woman who was with the Prince of Wales—later to be Edward VII—on the occasion when, dining out in Paris, a careless waiter accidentally burned the orange liqueur sauce before pouring it over the dessert pancakes. Since then it has become customary to ignite the sauce—flambé it—in a chafing dish before serving.

Sally Lunns are golden yeast tea cakes that were baked and sold by a young woman of that name in Bath, England, around 1800.

And *Ladyfingers* are named for the shape and delicate taste, of course.

OUR TOWN

❧

Thirty American communities named after women:

Alcott, South Carolina, named for **Louisa May Alcott.**♀

Allamore, Texas, named for **Alla Moore,** the wife of an early settler.

Ambler, Pennsylvania, named for **Mary Ambler.** Following a train collision in 1856, Ambler, a Quaker, heroically cared for the injured. The town was renamed in her honor a year after her death in 1868.

Amelia Island, Fernandina Beach, Florida, named for the sister of King George II by the British soldiers who founded it.

Annabella, Utah, named for **Ann Roberts** and **Isabella Dalton,** the first two women residents.

Ann Arbor, Michigan, named for *Ann Allen* and *Mary Ann Rumsey.* Rumsey provided the name when she called an arbor of wild grapes "Ann's Arbor."

Benarnold, Texas, named for *Bennie Arnold,* a three-year-old girl who was the mascot of the first wagon train to make its way to the community.

Carrabelle, Florida, named for *Carrie Hall,* the leading local belle in 1897.

Charlotte, North Carolina, named for *Queen Charlotte,*♀ wife of King George III. The city was founded in 1750. Other communities that honor the queen are *Charlottetown,* capital of Prince Edward Island, Canada, and *Charlottesville,* Virginia.

Christina River, Fort Christina, near Wilmington, Delaware, named for *Queen Christina* by Swedish settlers when they landed there in 1638. The queen had been crowned but later abdicated and often dressed in men's garb.

Cynthiana, Kentucky, named for *Cynthia* and *Anna,* daughters of the original landowners.

Elizabeth, New Jersey, named for *Elizabeth Carteret,* a member of the family of early colonial proprietors in 1665.

Elmira, New York, named for a child whose mother is alleged to have often called loudly for her in 1828.

Exira, Iowa, named for *Exira Eckman* around 1875. Her father agreed to buy a lot in the new town on the condition that it be named after his daughter.

Hartwell, Georgia, named for *Nancy Hart,*♀ a Revolutionary War heroine.

Helmetta, New Jersey, named for *Etta Helme,* daughter of a local factory owner.

Hisega, South Dakota, named for the first initials of *Helen, Ida, Sadie, Ethel, Grace,* and *Ada,* six young women who used the original campground there.

Italou, Texas, named for *Ida Bassett* and *Lou Bacon,* wives of the two founders.

Ladiesburg, Maryland, named for the seven women who constituted the vast majority of the town's population when it was founded in the early 1800s. Oh, yes, one man lived there also.

Langtry, Texas, named for *Lillie Langtry.*♀

LeMars, Iowa, named for *Lucy, Elizabeth, Mary, Anna, Rebecca,* and *Sarah*—six women who were visiting when the town was founded in 1869.

Lilypons, Maryland, named for singer *Lily Pons,*♀ and also for the area's specialty, raising pond lilies.

Marietta, Ohio, named for *Queen Marie Antoinette*♀ of France, and founded in 1788.

Medora, North Dakota, named for *Medora Hoffman,* a noted pianist, whose husband established a successful meat-packing business in the area in 1833.

Signourney, Iowa, named for nineteenth-century writer *Lydia Sigourney,*♀ who never visited the town but was the favorite author of an early settler.

Sisterville, West Virginia, named for *Sarah* and *Delilah Wells,* two sisters.

Vinita, Oklahoma, named for noted sculptor *Vinnie Ream* by an admirer, Colonel Elias C. Boudinot, who was promoting the settlement.

Wimauma, Florida, named for a combination of the names of three women, *Willie, Maude,* and *Mary,* in 1903.

HER MOCCASINS TROD HERE

※

Cateechee, South Carolina, named in honor of *Isaqueena,* a Choctaw woman who in 1750 unearthed a Cherokee plot against the English settlers and made a daring nighttime ride to warn them. The Cherokees later captured and enslaved her in retaliation; Cateechee was her name in the Cherokee language.

Montour Falls, New York, named for the Seneca Indian queen *Catharine Montour,* who was known for her courage and determination. She took over leadership of the tribe after her husband died in the mid-eighteenth century.

Waleska, Georgia, named around 1836 for a Cherokee girl whose name was probably *Warluskee.*

Watseka, Illinois, derived from the name of a Potawatomi woman around 1863.

Mount Wee-hun-ga, Wisconsin, named for the wife of the chief, Moo-na-pa-ga.

Wilmette, Illinois, named after *Archange Ouilmette,* the Potawatomi wife of a French trader who was granted lands in this area in 1829. The spelling of her name is anglicized.

IN HONOR OF THE QUEEN ♀

※

Victoria, Australia. The smallest and most densely populated state in the country was founded as a separate colony in 1851.

Victoria, British Columbia, Canada. The largest city on Vancouver Island, started out as Fort Camosun in 1843, and was later named *Fort Victoria.*

Victoria Falls, in the Zambezi River on what is now the Zambia-Zimbabwe border. It was discovered in 1855 by David Livingstone.

Victoria Island, off northern Canada, in the Arctic Ocean, is one of the largest islands in the area. Thomas Simpson discovered it between 1836 and 1839.

Lake Victoria, also known as *Victoria Nyanza,* the largest lake in Africa, on the Uganda-Tanzania-Kenya border. It was first seen by British explorer John Speke in 1858; Henry Stanley named it after the queen in 1875.

Victoria Land, Antarctica, is a desolate series of snow-covered mountains with a high plateau in the interior. It was discovered by Sir James Clark Ross during an expedition that lasted from 1839 to 1843.

Victoria Nile, a stretch of the White Nile in central Uganda.

Victoriaville, Quebec province, Canada; population 18,720.

NATURE ECHOES HER NAME

Mount Emily, 6,317 feet, La Grande, Oregon. Allegedly named by the husband of one *Emily Leasy* in honor of his 300-pound spouse.

Mount Florence, 12,507 feet, Yosemite National Park, California. Named for *Florence Hutchings,* the first white child born in Yosemite (1864). Reputed to have been a gutsy and active youngster, Florence was struck by a rock while hiking and died at the age of seventeen.

Lake Helen, Lassen Volcanic National Park, California. Named for *Helen Brodt,* the first woman to climb Lassen Peak, by her husband, who accompanied her.

Mount Hosmer, Missouri. Named for sculptor *Harriet Hosmer,*♀ who studied anatomy in nearby St. Louis and was an indefatigable mountain climber.

Mount Inez, Elizabethtown, New York. Formerly Mount Discovery, it was renamed in memory of suffragist *Inez Milholland Boissevain,* who died in 1916.

Kates Mountain, West Virginia. Named for *Kate Carpenter,* who hid in the woods on this mountain after Indians had killed her husband in October 1764.

Lake Louise, Banff National Park, Alberta, Canada. Discovered in 1882 and named for *Princess Louise.*

Lake Marie, near Laramie, Wyoming. Named by her husband in honor of *Mary Godot Bellamy,* the first woman elected to the state legislature (1910).

Marias River, Loma, Montana. Explorer Meriwether Lewis named the river after his cousin *Maria Wood.* He loved her but she spurned his offers of matrimony.

BRA-LESS

Breast Mountain, Arkansas.
Les Mamelles, Montana.
Nipple Mountain, Colorado.
Grand Tetons, Wyoming.
Maggie's Nipples, Wyoming, named by cowboys for a certain *Maggie Baggs,* about whom nothing else is known.

CHOOSING A NAME FOR BABY

Judy McCartney of Phoenix, Arizona, named her daughter *Era,* after the proposed constitutional amendment.

Joan Didion,♀ the novelist, called her daughter *Quintana Roo,* after a site on the Yucatan penisula.

Baby Doe Tabor,♀ the wife of a nineteenth-century mining magnate, called their young daughter *Silver Dollar.*

Boxcar Bertha Thompson,♀ the hobo queen of the 1930s, had little time to devote to naming her infant so she decided to call it simply *Baby Dear.*

Barbara Hershey named her child by David Carradine *Free.*

Grace Slick, the rock star, hailed the arrival of *God.*

Cher ♀ and Sonny, the singers, named their daughter *Chastity,* after the film failure Sonny wrote and produced.

NICKNAMES FOR HER AND HIM

Alex (Alexandra; Alexander)
Bernie (Bernadette, Bernadine; Bernard)
Bert, Bertie (Alberta, Bertha, Roberta; Albert, Robert, Berthold)
Cass (Cassandra; Casper)
Chris (Christina; Christopher)
Clem (Clementine; Clement)
Gus (Augusta; Gustave)
Jackie (Jacqueline; John)
Jan (Janet; John)
Jess (Jessica; Jesse)
Jody (Judith; Joseph)
Kit (Katherine; Christopher)
Lou (Louisa; Louis)
Nicky (Nicole; Nicholas)
Pat (Patricia; Patrick)
Ray (Rachel; Raymond)
Reggie (Regina; Reginald)
Sammie, -y (Samantha; Samuel)
Sandy (Sandra, Alexandra; Sanford, Alexander)
Stevie (Stephanie; Steven)
Terry (Theresa; Terrence)
Winnie (Winifred; Winston)

THE MOST POPULAR GIRLS' NAMES

Here are two lists of the ten girls' names that appeared most often on birth certificates in New York City in 1948 and 1979, in order of frequency used. These data are compiled at irregular intervals by the city's Bureau of Health Statistics and Analysis. The lists show that, when it comes to names, popularity can be fleeting.

1948:	*1979:*
Linda	*Jennifer*
Mary	*Jessica*

1948:	1979:
Barbara	*Nicole*
Patricia	*Melissa*
Susan	*Michelle*
Kathleen	*Lisa*
Carol	*Elizabeth*
Nancy	*Marie*
Margaret	*Christine*
Diane	*Danielle*

HOW THEY GOT THEIR NAMES

Theda Bara.♀ The insatiable vamp of the silents was born Theodosia Goodman in Cincinnati, Ohio. Fox studios converted the Jewish girl into an exotic Eastern sphinx by inventing the name Theda Bara—an anagram of the words *Arab death.*

Mata Hari.♀ Margaretha Zelle had her first taste of scandal when she was expelled from a convent school because of allegations that she had slept with a priest. To earn a living she worked in a brothel before turning to exotic dancing and then to a short-lived career as a double agent. Zelle first heard the name Mata Hari ("Eye of Dawn") while she was living in the Far East and decided to make it her own.

Mariel Hemingway. The young actress was named for the bay in Cuba where her parents picnicked in the 1950s.

Jackie ("Moms") Mabley. The comedian grew up as Louella May in the Blue Ridge Mountains of North Carolina. Her stage name was lifted from Jack Mabley, an ex-boyfriend. "He took a lot off me," said Moms, "and the least I could do was take his name."

Sally Rand. Her exotic fan dance, performed while attired only in ostrich feathers, was a hit of the 1933 Chicago World's Fair and of fairs and carnivals for thirty years afterward. Born Helen Beck in the Ozarks, she took her surname from a handy copy of a *Rand-McNally Atlas.*

Dixy Lee Ray.♀ Washington's governor was born to parents who wanted a boy so badly they had selected no name for a girl. "Baby Ray" was the entry on her birth certificate. The superactive child was soon known as "Little Dickens." This nickname was shortened to "Dick" and later to "Dixy." The "Lee" was for Robert E. Lee, a distant relative.

Anne Shirley. The child actress was Dawn O'Day until 1934, when she starred in *Anne of Green Gables* and appropriated the name of the title character.

Sally Stanford.♀ The noted San Francisco madame was born Marcia Busby on a farm in Oregon. Looking for a classy handle to suit her trade, she lifted a last name from the university in Palo Alto, California, and added an alliterative first to go with it.

Twyla Tharp.♀ The choreographer was named after a hog-calling champion named Twyla.

Sojourner Truth.♀ The abolitionist and mystic was born into slavery as Isabella Baumfree. Her new name was revealed to her in powerful visions that also drove her to become a traveler and preacher in the cause of freedom.

May Wynn. This actress also took the name of a character she played, in *The Caine Mutiny.*

Jiang Xing (Chiang Ching).♀ The powerful wife of the late Chairman Mao Zedong was given her name by her husband. It means "Green River." She was born Ch'ing Yun, which translates as "Blue Cloud."

A.K.A.

Julie Andrews—Julia Wells.
Eve Arden—Eunice Quedens.
Lucille Ball♀—Dianne Belmont.
Anne Bancroft♀—Annemarie Italiano.
Theda Bara♀—Theodosia Goodman.
Sarah Bernhardt♀—Rosine Bernard.
Ellen Burstyn—Edna Rae Gillooly.
Cyd Charisse♀—Tula Finklea.
Cher♀—Cherilyn LaPiere.
Doris Day♀—Doris von Kappelhoff.
Sandra Dee—Alexandra Zuck.
Marlene Dietrich♀—Maria Magdalena von Losch.
Diana Dors—Diana Fluck.
Barbara Eden—Barbara Huffman.
Greta Garbo♀—Greta Gustafsson.
Ava Gardner—Lucy Johnson.
Mitzi Gaynor—Francesca Mitzi Marlene de Czanyi von Gerber.
Paulette Goddard♀—Marion Levy.
Katherine Grayson—Zelma Hednick.
Rita Hayworth—Margarita Cansino.
Judy Holliday—Judith Tuvim.
Hedy Lamarr—Hedwig Kiesler.
Dorothy Lamour—Dorothy Kaumeyer.
Lillie Langtry♀—Emily Le Breton.
Carol Lawrence—Carol Maria Laraia.
Gypsy Rose Lee♀—Rose Louise Hovick.
Mary Livingstone♀—Sadie Marks.
Carole Lombard♀—Carol Jane Peters.
Nita Naldi♀—Anita Donna Dooley.
Kim Novak—Marilyn Novak.
Maureen O'Hara—Maureen FitzSimons.
Minnie Pearl—Sarah Ophelia Colley Cannon.
Martha Raye—Margie Yvonne Read.
Della Reese—Deloreese Patricia Early.
Ginger Rogers—Virginia McMath.
Lillian Russell♀—Helen Louise Leonard.
Ann Southern—Harriette Lake.
Tina Turner—Annie Mae Bullock.

Twiggy ♀—Leslie Hornby.
Natalie Wood—Natasha Gurdin.
Tammy Wynette ♀—Wynette Pugh.

MAD MONICKERS

In his book *First Names First,* Leslie Alan Dunkling lists these names carried by *real* women. Unbelievable as they sound, none is fictitious. The names were collected and authenticated by George F. Hubbard.

Susan Eatwell Burpitt	**Adeline Horsey De Horsey**
Mary Cutter Bottorff	**Ruth Pinches Finch**
Elizabeth Turner Downward	**Nancy Pigg Bacon**
Sweet Clover Goodrich	**Twinkle Starr Gibbs**
Mary Hatt Box	**Heidi Yum-Yum Gluck**
Zita Ann Apathy	**Victoria Regina Zarubin**
Albina Terrasina Rosina Beak	**Margaret Wears Black**
Juliet Seashell Moonbeam Gamba	**Della Short Speed**
Diana Brown Beard	**Shirley Foote Eye**
Mary Ada Berry	**Wava White Flagg**
Armenia Funk Goff	**Nancy Hertz Good**
Lil Lovey Dove	**Ima June Bugg**
Evie Ott Gott	**Mary Rhoda Duck**
Anna Dumpling Cheesecake	**Virginia Burns Feine**
Precious Darling Dare	**Daisy Etta Cock**
Hazel May Call	**Penelope Palm Tree Groves**

THEY GAVE THEIR NAMES

Quinine. In 1638 the **Countess Aña de Chinchón,** wife of the Spanish Viceroy of Peru, was cured of an attack of malarial fever by a preparation made from the bark of a local evergreen tree. When the countess returned to Europe, she took along a supply of the magic bark. Both the tree and the remedy were given the name of Chinchona (or Cinchona), which became *quina quina* to the Peruvian Indians—which became *quinine.* For many years the drug was known to European druggists as "countess's powder."

Aqua Toffana. In the seventeenth century a **Signora Toffana** of Italy put liquid arsenic into this cosmetic she created. Purchasers who wanted to use it for purposes other than beauty were given "private instructions" by the signora. It was not until more than 600 husbands had perished that the lady was arrested as the most prolific poisoner of the period.

The Molly Maguires. Molly Maguire, an elderly widow of Roscommon, Ireland, was alone at her spinning wheel when her landlord sent a gang of ruffians to evict her for nonpayment of rent; they tore the small cottage down around her, crushing her to death. Days later a secret organization was formed to avenge Molly's death by fighting against all landlords. In the 1860s and 1870s the Molly Maguires became famous in the Scranton, Pennsylvania, area by using violence to terrorize coal mine owners in their campaign to unionize mine workers.

Baby Ruth. The candy bars were named for the oldest daughter of President and Mrs. Grover Cleveland, the first child born in the White House and known to the nation as "Baby Ruth." Until that time the bar had been known, not too successfully, as Kandy Kake.

Maudgonning. The term for agitating for a cause in a headstrong and dramatic way bordering on recklessness comes from ***Maud Gonne*** (1865–1953), a rebel and patriot who devoted a good part of her life to the cause of Irish independence and who was not circumspect in her opinions or activities. She was beloved by the poet William Butler Yeats, who hoped in vain that she would eventually consent to marry him.

Granny Smith. One day in 1868 ***Mrs. Thomas Smith*** of New South Wales, Australia, found some rotting apples in a case of gin that had been brought from Tasmania. She dumped the fruit in her backyard—and presumably enjoyed the gin. Years passed, a tree grew, and its fruit was so tasty that Mrs. Smith saved the seeds and presented them to a grower. Granny Smiths are now grown far and wide.

Rolfing. This therapy involves manipulation of the soft tissues of the body. According to practitioners, the body should be aligned from the ear to the ankle to increase energy and enhance the sense of well-being. It was developed by biochemist ***Ida P. Rolf,*** who first applied her knowledge of physiology and yoga in the 1940s to restore the use of the hand and arm of a friend who was a piano teacher. She first called her method "structural integration" and demonstrated it not as a medical therapy, but as a way to enhance enjoyment of life. The name Rolfing caught on with those to whom she taught her method, and at the time of Rolf's death in 1979, at the age of eighty-two, there were 200 Rolfing practitioners.

Ada. The newest interactive computer language is named for ***Ada Augusta Byron, Lady Lovelace,***⁹ who has become known as the first programmer because of her mathematical contribution to the early mechanical calculators invented by Charles Babbage in the 1830s. The Department of Defense, which is sponsoring the new language, requested permission from the descendants in England of Lady Lovelace to use her name. Ada is expected to replace the several different programming languages now used in the armed services; the U.S. Army will be the first service to reprogram its computers.

GETTING AWAY FROM THE MAN

❧

In compound words, *man* and *men* are no less male than when they appear as words by themselves. These eight compounds (and others like them) should not be used to refer to individual women or to groups that include women and men:

Chairman. *Chairperson* has become a jest; *chair* is preferable.

Spokesman. A well-known dictionary defines *spokeswoman* as "a female spokesman"—a biolinguistic freak. *Spokesperson, advocate,* or *representative* is preferable.

Policeman. *Police officer.*

Fireman. *Fire fighter* is the job description.

Congressman. Incorrect, as well as sexist; the proper terms are *members of Congress* or *representatives.*

Businessman. *Business executives* come in two sexes, and some of them are *business leaders* or *entrepreneurs.*

Man-hours. *Work-hours* would be more accurate.

Manpower. The *work force, personnel,* or *staff* get the job done.

Note: Many words containing the letters m-a-n, m-e-n, or *h-i-s are unrelated* to the English words *man, men, and his* and have no sexist bias. Feminists (and nonfeminist punsters) are being overzealous when they play with such words as *manual, mandatory, talisman, mentality,* and *history.*

Contributed by Ruth Ulmyn

HIMMICANES

❧

Female names have been used by the World Meteorological Organization since 1953 to identify tropical storms; protests finally led in 1979 to the selection of both male and female names for storms. That year they were:

Atlantic storms	Eastern Pacific storms
Ana	*Andres*
Bob	*Blanca*
Claudette	*Carlos*
David	*Dolores*
Elena	*Enrique*
Frederic	*Fefa*
Gloria	*Guillermo*
Henri	*Hilda*
Isabel	*Ignacio*
Juan	*Jimena*
Kate	*Kevin*
Larry	*Linda*
Mindy	*Mary*
Nicolas	*Nora*
Odette	*Olaf*
Peter	*Pauline*
Rose	*Rick*
Sam	*Sandra*
Teresa	*Terry*
Victor	*Vivian*
Wanda	*Waldo*

UNDER A WOMAN'S NAME:
Female Pseudonyms Used by Men

Alice Hawthorne was the name used by Septimus Winner when he wrote the song "Listen to the Mocking Bird" in 1856. Hawthorne was his mother's birth name.

Fiona Macleod was the popular poet and writer William Sharp who, in the late 1800s, put Macleod's name on some of his best work. The woman he invented was reputed to be a talented but retiring Celtic lady. Only after Sharp's death did his wife reveal Macleod's true identity.

Carolyn Keene,♀ author of the Nancy Drew books; *Helen Louise Thorndyke,* author of the Honey Bunch books; *Laura Lee Hope,* author of the Bobbsey Twins books; *Alice B. Emerson,* author of the Ruth Fielding books; and *Gertrude W. Morrison,* author of the Girls of Central High books, were all originally Edward Stratemeyer. In addition to these "girls' " series, Stratemeyer also penned the Rover Boys, Hardy Boys, and Tom Swift books. All in all, he used 100 pseudonyms and, from 1894 to 1930, wrote or edited more than 750 books. Upon his death, his daughters Harriet and Edna took over the writing of the series of series.

Mary Earl was the name used by Robert A. King when he wrote the song "Beautiful Ohio" in 1918.

Penelope Ashe sold 20,000 copies of her searing novel *Naked Came the Stranger* within two weeks of publication in August 1969 before it was revealed that her suburban sex exposé was meant to be a parody of suburban sex exposés. "Penelope" and her libido-driven heroine Gillian Blake were the brainchild of a group of Long Island *Newsday* writers— twenty-three in all. *Billie Young,* the attractive sister-in-law of one of them, impersonated Penelope in advertisements and on talk shows. All shared in the profits.

Jennifer Wilde,♀ whose romances have sold millions of copies, is actually a six-foot tall Texas man, Tom Huff.

UNDER A MAN'S NAME
Male Pseudonyms Used by Women

Women who wanted to be taken seriously as writers often adopted men's names; that way their work would not be dismissed as mere "women's scribbling." George Sand, George Eliot, and the Brontë sisters are, perhaps, the best-known women to have used this stratagem, but they have had plenty of company.

George Sand♀ was *Amandine Aurore Lucie Dupin Dudevant.*

George Eliot♀ was *Mary Ann Evans.*

Acton, Ellis, and *Currer Bell* were *Anne,*♀ *Emily,*♀ and *Charlotte Brontë.* ♀

Leslie Ford and *David Frome* were *Mrs. Zenith Jones*, a popular writer of detective stories in the early 1900s.

Comte Paul Vasili was *Juliette Adam,* founder and editor of *La Nouvelle Revue.*

Michael Strange was *Blanche Marie Louise Barrymore,* wife of actor John Barrymore.

Ralph Iron was *Olive Schreiner,*♀ South African–born novelist and feminist, when she wrote her most successful book, *The Story of an African Farm* (1883).

Charles Egbert Craddock was *Mary Noailles Murfree,* frail and crippled, who wrote stories about her native Tennessee in the 1870s, using the name of a character in one of her early local-dialect tales as a pseudonym.

Henry Handel Richardson was *Ethel Henrietta Richardson,* a popular English novelist of the early 1900s. Among her books: *Maurice Guest* (1908) and *The Getting of Wisdom* (1910), recently a film.

"Frank" was *Frances Miriam Berry Witcher,* the first woman humorist in America.

Birch Arnold was *Alice Eloise Bartlett,* a late-nineteenth-century writer and journalist. Her publisher once told a friend that he intended to "adopt that promising young man."

Laurence Hope was *Adela Florence Cory,* respectably married to a middle-aged British army commander in India, who wrote passionate poems in the 1890s. One described the doomed love of a married English lady for an Indian rajah in the Kashmir. When Hope's real identity was unmasked, all London was abuzz: was she telling the truth?

NO MARRIED NAME

※

Lucy Stone ♀ is considered to have been the first modern woman to hold on to her own name after marriage, in 1855, in both public and private life. She may not actually have been the first, but she was certainly not the last. Herewith some particularly interesting examples:

Countess Ida von Hahn. The novelist thought that the custom of a woman's taking her husband's name was "barbarous." When she married her cousin, Count F. W. Adolf von Hahn, in 1826, she took the hyphenated surname of Hahn-Hahn. If she had simply kept her birth name, people might have thought she had assumed her husband's name.

Mary E. Walker.♀ Dr. Walker married Dr. Albert Miller in 1855 shortly after receiving her medical degree. The diminutive bride wore trousers and refused to surrender her surname. Why, asked she, if a wife must adopt the title "Mrs." ("Mistress"), shouldn't a husband call himself "Misterer"?

Elisabet Ney.♀ The Texas sculptor opposed marriage on principle but agreed in 1863 to marry Dr. Edmund Montgomery only on condition that she never have to relinquish her famous name. Dr. Montgomery respected his wife's wishes until her death in 1907, referring to her only as Fraülein, Mademoiselle, or Miss Ney. This led to complications when she was obviously pregnant and he introduced her as "Miss Ney, my sister." Only once did she agree to pass as Mrs. Montgomery; it was in Italy in the summer of 1866, when they were acting as spies for Garibaldi and did not wish to be conspicuous.

Victoria Woodhull♀ took the name of her first husband, Dr. Canning Woodhull, but did not follow the custom when she wed her second, Colonel James H. Blood. Both advocated what was known as "free love," and among their associates it may have been far more respectable to appear *not* to be married.

Ida Lewis,♀ the lighthouse keeper who had rescued several shipwrecked men, was a celebrity when she married a sailor, William Heard Wilson. Lewis used his name during the short time she lived with him, but after they separated she refused to be addressed as Mrs. Wilson, clinging instead to her famous premarriage name.

Olympia Brown,♀ minister and feminist, kept her own name when she wed John Henry Willis in 1873. Brown complained to Susan B. Anthony♀ that a great deal of her time was taken up in explaining why she had decided to be Mrs. Brown instead of Mrs. Willis.

Martha Strickland refused to take her husband's name when she married Leo Miller in 1875. She believed, she said, in "the individuality of women." The daughter of a lawyer, Strickland received her own law degree in 1883.

Aletta Jacobs,♀ a pioneer advocate of birth control, remained Jacobs after she became the wife of Cornelius Victor Gerritsen. She made it a practice to sign hotel registers "Mr. Gerritsen and Mrs. Jacobs." An American room clerk once refused to allow them to share accommodations, so Gerritsen signed in "Mr. and Mrs. Jacobs."

Elizabeth Oakes Smith. Edgar Allan Poe hailed her as one of the fine poets of the nineteenth century, and she wanted to pass her family name on to her son. Her husband, Seba Smith, approved, and she had the names of their sons legally changed to Oaksmith.

Alice Chenoweth. When she wed Charles Selden Smart in 1875 she took his name, but after becoming a feminist she sought a name of her own. In 1884 she published an iconoclastic book, *Men, Women, and Gods,* under the name of Helen Hamilton Gardener. The name became more than a pseudonym; she used it for the rest of her life, even during her second marriage. The only way for a woman to have her own name, Chenoweth believed, was to make it up completely. It was as Helen Hamilton Gardener that she was appointed to the United States Civil Service Commission in 1920.

Olive Logan, an actress turned writer, was fifty-three years old when she wed her third husband, James O'Neill, her secretary and twenty years her junior. After the marriage, he called himself James O'Neill Logan.

Olive Schreiner♀ was known as a writer when she married South African farmer Samuel Cron Cronwright. Her husband agreed to change his name, adopting the appellation Samuel C. Cronwright Schreiner. Although this decision led to much ridicule for him, he kept the name even after his wife's death. While making a speech once he was interrupted by a heckler who demanded that he talk under his "maiden" name.

Ellen Owens was the last in her family to bear the name of Owens and did not want it to die out. When she married Barry Beaver in 1977, he got a court order allowing him to change his name to hers. The judge called it "a beautiful expression of love."

Brenda Feigen. When she and Marc Fasteau married in 1968, they took as their married surname a combination of both names, by which both activist lawyers became well known in New York. When Brenda Feigen Fasteau became a candidate for the state senate ten years later, she encountered a new state election law stating that names on the ballot must contain no more than fifteen letters. For four letters—and an important principle—the candidate took her case to court. A federal judge ruled that full names must appear on ballots as requested by candidates. Feigen Fasteau won her case, but not that election.

XX ❧ THE BALLOT—AND BEYOND

TEN AMERICAN FOREMOTHERS

❧

Margaret Brent♀ came to Maryland from England in 1638 and became the owner of a sizable amount of property. In 1647 she asked for admittance to the legislature of the colony, demanding two votes because she was both a lawyer and a landowner. Her request denied, Brent devoted her considerable energies to proving beyond doubt the validity of both claims: she bought even more land and brought numerous cases to court, winning 124 of them in eight years. The legislature remained unmoved.

Abigail Adams♀ pleaded with her husband, John, to include a women's rights plank in the Declaration of Independence: "Remember all men would be tyrants if they could. If particular care and attention are not paid to the ladies we are determined to foment a rebellion, and will not hold ourselves bound to obey any laws in which we have no voice or representation."

Lucretia Coffin Mott♀ and *Elizabeth Cady Stanton*♀ arrived in London in 1840 as delegates to the World's Anti-Slavery Convention, only to find, to their dismay, that the credentials of women delegates were not being accepted and that they were allowed to sit only in the gallery. They determined to work for eradication of this form of injustice as well. Their raised consciousness led them to organize the convention at Seneca Falls, New York, on July 19, 1848, at which the movement for women's rights was formally born. The rest of Stanton's life was dedicated to the struggle for suffrage. In 1851 she gained an important recruit in . . .

Susan Brownell Anthony,♀ a strong-willed schoolteacher who worked for five decades organizing petitions, running conventions, lecturing, canvassing, and lobbying for the vote. "Men, their rights and nothing more; women, their rights and nothing less" was the motto on the masthead of the newspaper she published.

Lucy Stone♀ in 1855 married Henry Blackwell but insisted on keeping her maiden name. Women who followed in her footsteps were later called "Lucy Stoners." Stone founded the American Woman Suffrage Association, the less radical wing of the women's movement, in collaboration with . . .

Julia Ward Howe,♀ whose husband at first forbade her to speak at public meetings. But after she published the popular "Battle Hymn of the Republic," Ward grew bolder. She started the first women's clubs in New England and, in 1868, embarked on a crusade for woman suffrage.

Carrie Chapman Catt♀ worked with Susan B. Anthony and assumed the presidency of the National Woman Suffrage Association in 1900 when the great leader resigned. Catt stayed in the suffrage battle until it triumphed, taking time off only to care for her dying husband.

Anna Howard Shaw,♀ both a theologian and a medical doctor, succeeded Catt in 1904 as president of the NWSA.

Alice Paul,♀ acknowledged as the mother of the Equal Rights Amendment, first had the amendment introduced in Congress in 1923. The most militant of the "second generation" of suffragists, Paul led demonstrations in front of the White House until Wilson endorsed the suffrage amendment in 1919.

FOUR ON THE CONTINENT

Olympe de Gouges, playwright, believed that the French Revolution must bring freedom for women too, and in 1791 published *A Declaration of the Rights of Woman and of Women Citizens.* Just as outspoken in criticism of the excesses of the Revolution, she paid for her bluntness on the guillotine in 1793.

Luise Otto-Peters advocated women's rights during and after the 1848 Revolution and in 1865 founded the General Association of German Women, which advocated civil equality for women.

Clara Zetkin was in 1889 one of seven women attending the Paris International Workers' Congress, helped Engels develop a theory of women's emancipation, and advocated jobs for women both as an economic necessity and as the only way to liberate women from male domination. Her 1889 pamphlet *The Question of Women Workers and Women at the Present Time* became the framework for the Social Democratic and Socialist party positions on women's emancipation.

Wilhelmina Drucker (1847–1927), who had been born to an unmarried mother, founded the Dutch women's suffrage movement and edited a newspaper for women. The most outspoken members of the women's liberation movement in Holland today call themselves the *Dolle Minas* ("Wild Minas") in her honor.

AND EIGHT IN ENGLAND

Mary Wollstonecraft♀ wrote *A Vindication of the Rights of Woman* (1792) in response to Jean Jacques Rousseau's claim that women's major role was to please men. "Independence is the grand blessing of life," she argued. Her own life, though, could have used more blessings. Her father was a drunkard, her brother-in-law abused her sister, and her own lover, the father of her first child, abandoned Wollstonecraft and drove her to attempt suicide. She decried traditional marriage, but reluctantly agreed to marry William Godwin when she became pregnant for the second time. Wollstonecraft died of complications following the birth of her daughter Mary.

Barbara Leigh Smith (Bodichon) and ***Bessie Rayner Parkes (Belloc)*** founded the *Englishwoman's Journal* in the 1850s, the first magazine of the women's movement in England. In 1860 Smith and Parkes also founded the Society for the Promotion of Employment of Women, along with . . .

Emilia Jessie Boucherett, who organized the first petition to Parliament for voting rights for women in 1866. In the same year Boucherett founded the *Englishwoman's Review,* which she edited until 1871.

Millicent Garrett Fawcett joined the first women's suffrage committee in England in 1867 and started speaking out in public on the subject the following year. As president of the National Union of Women's Suffrage Societies from 1897 to 1918, she was leader of the moderate suffragists, retiring from that post only after passage of the Representation of the People bill which accorded women limited voting rights. Fawcett was named a Dame of the British Empire in 1925.

Emmeline Goulden Pankhurst ♀ (1858–1928), disappointed in the lack of progress toward suffrage in Britain, founded the Women's Social and Political Union in 1903. Its militant members were often arrested. Pankhurst herself was imprisoned in 1912, but released after a hunger strike, a sequence that was repeated thirteen times the following year. By the time she died, while campaigning for Parliament, she was a national hero—but she left a new generation to carry on. Her daughter . . .

Christabel Pankhurst ♀ (1880–1958), a leading militant in the WSPU, studied law but was refused entrance to the bar because of her sex. She ran for Parliament in 1918, when women were first allowed to do so, but lost. She later became an evangelist and in 1936 a Dame of the British Empire. Another daughter . . .

Sylvia Pankhurst ♀ (1882–1960) became involved with the social work aspects of the WSPU and wrote a history of *The Suffragette Movement* (1931) and a biography of her mother (1935). But she attracted more attention for her advocacy of free love and the life-style that went with it, and later with her political activities on behalf of Ethiopian independence. She left England to live in that African nation and died there.

ISSUERS OF THE CALL FOR THE SENECA FALLS CONVENTION OF 1848

———————————— ❧ ————————————

"WOMAN'S RIGHTS CONVENTION. A Convention to discuss the social, civil, and religious condition and rights of woman, will be held in the Wesleyan Chapel, at Seneca Falls, N.Y., on Wednesday and Thursday, the 19th and 20th of July, current; commencing at 10 o'clock A.M. During the first day the meeting will be exclusively for women, who are earnestly invited to attend. The public generally are invited to be present on the second day, when Lucretia Mott, of Philadelphia, and other ladies and gentlemen, will address the convention."

This announcement, in the semiweekly *Seneca County Courier,* July 14, 1848, was the beginning. It was issued, but not signed, by:

Lucretia Mott ♀
Martha C. Wright
Elizabeth Cady Stanton ♀
Mary Ann McClintock

As Stanton would later tell the story, "These four ladies, sitting round the tea-table of Richard Hunt, a prominent Friend near Waterloo, decided to put their long-talked-of resolution into action, and before the twilight deepened into night, the call was written, and sent to the *Seneca County Courier.* On Sunday morning they met in Mrs. McClintock's parlor to write their declaration, resolutions, and to consider subjects for speeches. As the convention was to assemble in three days, the time was short for such productions; but having no experience in the *modus operandi* of getting up conventions, nor in that kind of literature, they were quite innocent of the herculean labors they proposed. . . ."

Joining the others in composing resolutions and speeches was:

Elizabeth W. McClintock

WHY WOMEN SHOULD NOT BE ALLOWED TO VOTE

———————————— ❦ ————————————

In a 1917 pamphlet issued by the National Woman Suffrage Publishing Company, *Alice Stone Blackwell* ♀ answered frequently heard objections to woman suffrage. Among the reasons people were opposed to votes for women:

- Women are represented already by their husbands, fathers, and brothers.
- If laws are unjust, they can be corrected by women's indirect influence.
- It would double the ignorant vote.
- It would double the foreign vote.
- To the vote of every criminal man, you would add the vote of a criminal woman.
- The bad women would outvote the good ones.
- A municipality is a great business corporation. Men, by nature of their occupations, know more about business than women, and hence are better fitted to run a city or state.
- The growth of civilization is marked by an increasing specialization and division of labor. Woman suffrage would therefore be a step backward.
- Women would cease to be respected.
- Women would lose their influence.
- Women are already overburdened. A woman would not have time to perform her political duties without neglecting higher duties.
- It will lead to family quarrels and increase divorce.

- It will destroy chivalry.
- Women are too emotional and sentimental to be trusted with the ballot.
- It would only double the vote without changing the result.
- We have too many voters already.
- It will turn women into men.

JAILED FOR THE VOTE

More than 500 members of the Woman's party, the most militant wing of the suffrage movement, were arrested between 1917 and 1919 for demonstrating in Washington, D.C. For such offenses as "obstructing traffic" and "blocking sidewalks," nearly 170 women were sentenced to as much as seven months in jail, where some were kept incommunicado and subjected to physical and psychological abuse. No charges were ever brought against the mobs who attacked the demonstrating suffragists.

A few of those imprisoned in the cause of women's suffrage were:

Lucy Burns: "I was handcuffed all night and manacled to the bars part of the time for asking the others how they were. . . ."

Alice M. Cosu, who suffered a heart attack as a result of the experience.

Dorothy Day,♀ social worker.

Edna Dixon, a public-school teacher from Washington, D.C.

Lavinia Dock, a trained nurse and secretary of the American Federation of Nurses.

Margaret Fotheringham, a teacher of domestic science and dietetics.

Anna Gvinter, who wrote Congressman Meyer London, "I am suffering very much from hunger and nearly blind from bad nourishment."

Florence Bayard Hilles, the daughter of a former ambassador to Great Britain, who whispered in the courtroom, "Well, girls, I've never seen but one other court in my life and that was the Court of St. James's."

Mrs. Lawrence Lewis, who was force fed after leading a hunger strike with Lucy Burns.

Mary Nolan, the oldest picket, seventy-three years old when she was imprisoned.

Alice Paul,♀ the leader of the Woman's party, sentenced to six months in a Washington jail for "obstructing traffic," who went on a two-day hunger strike.

Mrs. John Rogers, Jr., a descendant of Declaration of Independence signer Roger Sherman.

Doris Stevens, who later wrote a book, *Jailed for Freedom,* about the experience.

CARRIE CHAPMAN CATT'S ♀ LIST OF WHAT IT TOOK TO WIN THE VOTE

❧

Catt fought for the cause most of her adult life. In 1920 the Nineteenth Amendment became a reality. The struggle had taken fifty-two years. Catt recalled that it included:

- 56 referenda voted on by male voters.
- 277 attempts to induce state party conventions to add women's suffrage planks to their platforms.
- 47 efforts to persuade state constitutional conventions to include women's suffrage in their state constitutions.
- 480 campaigns to talk state legislatures into introducing suffrage amendments.
- 30 concerted drives to get presidential party conventions to make women's suffrage planks a part of national party platforms.
- 19 lobbying assaults on 19 successive U.S. Congresses.

WHERE U.S. WOMEN FIRST VOTED

❧

New Jersey, 1797. The 1776 Constitution enfranchised all inhabitants of the colony who met age, residence, and property requirements, and a 1790 revision of the election law referred to voters as "he or she." But no woman voted in New Jersey until 1797, when supporters of one candidate in a close legislative contest in Elizabethtown, Essex County, brought some seventy-five women to vote just before the polls were to close. (Nevertheless, the opposition candidate won by a narrow margin.) Three years later women throughout the state voted in the presidential contest between Adams and Jefferson, and two years after that a few women's votes made the difference in electing a state legislator. But when every eligible woman voted "not only once, but as often as by change of dress or complicity of the inspectors, they might be able to repeat the process," in a local contest in Essex County, woman suffrage was repealed in 1807, not to reappear for more than a century.

Kentucky, 1838. Women were allowed to vote, but only in school elections—as they were in Kansas in 1861, Michigan and Minnesota in 1875, and eighteen other states by the turn of the century.

Wyoming, 1869. Violence was rampant throughout the turbulent territory, and *Esther Hobart Morris* ♀ persuaded the legislature that votes for women would strengthen the forces of law and order. The following year *Mrs. Luther Fillmore* and seventy-year-old *Louisa Ann Swain* were the first women to vote, in Laramie. In 1890, when Wyoming achieved statehood, it officially became the first state in which women had the franchise.

Utah, 1870. The Mormons allowed women to vote so that they could show their approval of polygamy. To put an end to polygamy in Utah, Congress first had to abolish woman suffrage in the territory (1887). But in

1896, when Utah was granted statehood, woman suffrage was included in its constitution.

Colorado, 1893. Supported by the Populist party, woman suffrage was adopted with a majority of 347 by referendum, which eight years later was incorporated in an amendment to the state constitution. After six years the state legislature urged all states and territories to do likewise, declaring that better candidates had been selected, election methods had been purified, the character of legislation improved, civic intelligence increased, and womanhood developed.

Idaho, 1896. A large Mormon population helped to win the ballot here; so did female activists such as *Rebecca Brown Mitchell,* who brought the suffrage message to men about to vote, and *May Arkwright Hutton,* who supported miners and their labor unions and was repaid by the working men who voted for woman suffrage.

SIXTEEN COUNTRIES WHERE WOMEN FIRST VOTED

American women got the vote in 1920. Before that, female citizens could vote in:

New Zealand, 1893.
Australia, 1902.
Finland, 1906.
Norway, 1913.
Denmark, 1915.
Iceland, 1915.
USSR, 1917.
Canada, 1917 (except the province of Quebec, where women could not vote until 1940).
Austria, 1918.
German Federal Republic, 1918 (thirty-six women were elected to the 421-seat National Assembly the following year).
Poland, 1918.
Belgium, 1919.
Great Britain, 1919.
Holland, 1919.
Ireland, 1919.
Sweden, 1919.

COUNTRIES THAT LAST GAVE WOMEN THE VOTE

France, Guatemala, and *Japan,* 1945.
Argentina, Belgium, and *Mexico,* 1946.
China (mainland), 1947.
Iran, 1963.

Switzerland, 1971 (in federal elections; women were earlier able to vote in canton and local elections).
Portugal, San Marino, and *Syria,* 1971 (limited suffrage and right to hold office).
Liechtenstein, 1972.

In 1980 there were still some nations whose women are not fully franchised citizens: *Jordan, Kuwait, Saudi Arabia,* and *Yemen.* Generally, in the new nations of Africa, women became enfranchised at the same time as men, when national constitutions were adopted.

In 1952 the United Nations General Assembly adopted the Convention on the Political Rights of Women. It was the first international legal statement dealing with women's rights.

THEY DIDN'T PROMISE TO OBEY

Mary Robinson, when she married social reformer Robert Dale Owen in 1832.
Angelina Grimké,♀ when she married Theodore Weld in 1838.
Lucy Stone,♀ when she married Henry Blackwell in 1855.
Catherine Mumford,♀ when she married William Booth in 1855. She refused to wed until he capitulated to her egalitarian principles.
Annie Cobden, when she married James Sanderson in August 1882. She had converted him to her feminist beliefs and they combined surnames, calling themselves Mr. and Mrs. Cobden-Sanderson.
Lillian Harman, when she married Edwin C. Walker in Kansas in 1886. Harman read a statement saying that she would make no immoral promise to obey her husband and retained "the right to act always as my conscience and best judgment shall dictate."
Lydia Kingsmill Commander, when she married Herbert Newton Casson on May 4, 1899. Casson repudiated the rights the law gave him over his wife, declaring, "I wish to marry a free-hearted woman, not a slave." He swore "never to let this marriage interfere with the life work she has chosen." Reporting on the unusual ceremony, the *St. Louis Post-Dispatch* headlined its story WIFE WHO RETAINS HER MAIDEN NAME AND WON'T OBEY.

STANDING BY THEIR WOMEN:
Eight Male Feminists of the Past

George Fox (1624–1691), founder of the Society of Friends, insisted on leadership roles for women within the Quaker group. When he married Margaret Fell♀ he refused to claim her large estate, Swarthmore Hall, as their joint property, to which he was entitled under English law. Fox and Fell were frequently apart and each made decisions independently in an "open" marriage of mutual respect and trust.

Robert Owen (1771–1858). The nineteenth-century reformer and socialist founded the Utopian community of New Harmony, Indiana, where women and men had equal status. When the Indiana constitution was revised in 1850, he secured in it the extension of property rights to women throughout the state.

Charles Brockden Brown (1771–1810), an American novelist, whose fiction advocated social reform at the turn of the nineteenth century. His first published book, *Alcuin: A Dialogue* (1798), was a treatise on the rights of women.

Theodore Weld (1803–1895). The abolitionist husband of suffragist and abolitionist Angelina Grimké ♀ predicted that "the devil of dominion over women will be one of the last that will be cast out [of men]."

John Stuart Mill (1806–1873). Before his wedding to Harriet Taylor, he repudiated the legal powers that Victorian marriage gave him over his wife. With the publication of *The Subjection of Women* in 1869, Mill became the source of modern consciousness raising about the status of women.

Frederick Douglass (1817–1895). The abolitionist and former slave was the only man asked to take part in the Seneca Falls Convention of 1848. The masthead of his weekly newspaper contained the legend "Right is of no sex."

Henry B. Blackwell (1825–1909). The brother of Dr. Elizabeth Blackwell ♀ became the husband of outspoken feminist Lucy Stone.♀ Antisuffragists were relieved at news of their engagement in 1855 for, at last, "a wedding kiss shuts up the mouth of Lucy Stone!" But far from silencing his wife, Blackwell became her ally.

Karl Johann Kautsky (1854–1938), husband of the leading German feminist Luise Kautsky. At a conference of the Social Democratic party he proposed laws making possible equal educational opportunities for women and the abolition of all laws that discriminated against women. But Germany would have a long wait before either became reality.

ALAN ALDA'S INCOMPLETE LIST OF TODAY'S MALE FEMINISTS

❦

Sey Chassler, editor of *Redbook.*
Phil Donahue, television talk-show host.
Jordan Miller, Chicago publisher.
Marc Feigen Fasteau, lawyer.
Warren Farrell, author of *The Liberated Man.*
Birch Bayh, senator.

These are just people who come to mind. I know there are others. . . . The list is damned short. Any conversation about male feminists can be accomplished without taking a second breath. I'd hate to discourage anyone by leaving them off a list—they're too hard to come by. Let's leave some blank spaces for write-in votes.

Editor's note: Contributor Alda also belongs on this list. An outspoken male feminist, he has worked for passage of the Equal Rights Amendment, was a member of the National Commission for the Observance of International Women's Year (cochair, ERA Committee). And as our write-ins we also nominate **William M. Agee** and **Coy C. Eklund,** named cochairmen of the National Business Council for the ERA in 1980. Agee is chairman of the Bendix Corporation and Eklund is president of the Equitable Life Assurance Society. Says Agee, "Some people say ERA will raise the cost of business, but I don't buy that. I think it will raise purchasing power and cut out some of the inequities that exist."

Exclusively for *Womanlist*

ASSERTING RIGHTS TODAY

After suffrage was won, the women's movement went into a lull, not to be revived until sometime after the Second World War. Although by then most women in the United States and Europe were used to voting and generally had access to equal education, fully equal status still eluded them. Numerous women have been effective leaders in the struggle for social, economic, and psychological equality—more than we can honor here. Among the most influential:

Simone de Beauvoir, whose analysis of women's social status, *The Second Sex,* appeared in France in 1949 and who has raised consciousnesses ever since. In late 1973 she began writing a column containing "all the insults, all the stupidities written about women," with the purpose of shaming men. By then she had also turned her attention to a new minority, the elderly, and published *The Coming of Age* in 1970. De Beauvoir has headed the League for the Rights of Women, and Choisir ("To Choose"), an organization advocating liberalized abortion laws in France.

Betty Friedan,♀ who exploded the myth of the happy homemaker in *The Feminine Mystique* in 1963, rekindling the quiescent feminist movement in the United States. Friedan, a suburban homemaker when she started the research for her book, was a founder of the National Organization for Women (NOW) and the National Women's Caucus.

Gloria Steinem,♀ a founder of *Ms.* magazine in 1972; journalist Steinem is the granddaughter of a president of the Ohio Women's Suffrage Association.

Ann Follis, who founded Housewives for ERA in the mid-1970s after research into actual women's rights revealed such findings as: under common law in most states unemployed wives could be left penniless if their husbands died without leaving a will; and the right to be supported during marriage was dependent on husbands' good will and had little legal foundation. "People say that the ERA is vague," Follis says. "What is vague is the Constitution without ERA."

AND SOME IN OTHER LANDS

※

Dr. Soad Abu El-Soud, former president of the Women's Organization of Egypt.

Anilu Elias and *Marta Acevedo,* leaders of the women's liberation movement in Mexico.

Mariana Bracetti and *Lola Rodriguez de Tio,* leaders of the women's movement in Puerto Rico.

Mahnaz Afkhami, former minister of state of women's affairs in Iran, now head of the Iranian Organization of Women.

Parivash Khajehnouri, Farzaeh Nouri, and *Kathe Vafardi,* leaders of the protest against the Iranian Revolutionary Council's edict ordering all women to wear the chador, or long veil, in public. "No man—not the Shah, not Khomeini, and not anyone else—will ever make me dress as he pleases," said Nouri. The edict was repealed when thousands of unveiled women took to the streets in March 1979.

Thekla Yeroyanni, secretary-general of the All-Greece Women's Association.

IS IT WORTH ALL THIS TROUBLE?
Keeping Women Down

※

- When Benjamin Franklin appointed *Mary Katherine Goddard* ♀ postmaster of Baltimore in 1775, no one else wanted the job. But by 1789 it had become a political plum and the first woman postmaster of the Republic was replaced by a man. When Goddard complained, she was told that a man was needed because the postmaster had to tour the area on horseback. Her appeal to the United States Senate was tabled, with no action taken.

- In the 1880s a female mathematician at the Treasury Department was so capable that she compiled all the department's statistical reports to Congress. The man "officially" assigned this responsibility was an alcoholic. When he was carted off to the Government Hospital for the Insane, she was accorded a great honor: she was officially assigned all his work—with no increase in salary.

- For the Columbian Exposition of 1891, a competition was held to choose the designer of the Women's Building. The female architect who won, *Sophia Hayden,* ♀ was granted half of the remuneration given to the male architects who designed the other buildings at the fair.

- When explorer *Kate Marsden* ♀ applied for a ticket to the annual dinner of the Royal Geographical Society in London in 1894, she was refused on the grounds that she would be "the only lady among 200, nearly all of them smoking." The discomfort would probably have been a small matter to Marsden, who had just returned from trekking through Siberia on her own.

- Although the first telephones were installed in the White House in 1878, it was not until 1933 that a woman, *Louise Hachmeister,* became a switchboard operator there. For more than half a century, men feared that women would not be able to keep top secrets.

- Early in the career of award-winning atomic physicist *Lise Meitner,*♀ scientist Emil Fischer allowed her to work with him only after making her promise that she would never enter the laboratories while men were working there.
- In 1953, when Fritz Reiner took over the conductorship of the Chicago Symphony, he fired all its women musicians sight unseen—and instruments unheard—including two first-desk players.
- It has been reported that journalist *Mary McGrory*♀ was once offered a job by the head of the *New York Times*'s Washington bureau—if she would agree to answer the switchboard part-time.
- *Jean Halloway,* who became the first woman to write for the "Wagon Train" TV series, later had a proposal for an "Emergency" episode rejected. The excuse offered was that writers for the show sometimes had to sleep at firehouses to absorb "real" material and, naturally, this would be impossible for her.
- In 1977 Judge Victor McEwan of Toronto dismissed the testimony of a forty-eight-year-old woman. Said His Honor, "There comes a certain stage in a woman's life . . . when the evidence is not too reliable."

WOMEN PRO STATUS QUO

Patt Barbour, national director of Happiness of Womanhood (HOW), an organization "dedicated to the . . . preservation of the masculine role as provider and preservation of the feminine role as wife, mother, and homemaker."

Betty J. Hoxsey, one of twenty-two members of the Illinois State Legislature who voted against the Equal Rights Amendment. "The vagueness of the proposed ERA would be a real Pandora's box, to be opened for decision upon decision in the courts for many years to come, causing endless problems for the institution of the family."

Marabel Morgan, author of *The Total Woman:* "If you can't adapt to a man, I advise you not to marry—it won't last. He'll find some gal who knows how to adapt."

Nancy Reagan, whose husband opposes ERA: "What I really wanted out of life was to be a wife to the man I loved and mother to our children. . . . We're for equal rights, equal pay, and equal opportunity. We just believe in doing it by statute."

Phyllis Schlafly, author of *The Power of the Positive Woman* and chairman (*sic*) of Stop ERA. "The defeat of the equal rights amendment [*sic*] is the greatest victory for women's rights since the women's suffrage amendment of 1920."

FIGHTING WORDS FROM WOMEN

"Marriage? I'd rather be a *free* spinster and paddle my own canoe." *Louisa May Alcott*♀

"Failure is impossible."   ***Susan B. Anthony*** ♀

"I married beneath me. All women do."   ***Nancy, Lady Astor*** ♀

"He who steals my purse may steal trash, but he who holds the purse strings controls my life."   ***Harriot Stanton Blatch*** ♀

"Women feel just as men feel; they need exercise for their faculties, and a field for their efforts as much as their brothers do. . . ."
Charlotte Brontë

"Women must try to do things as men have tried. When they fail, their failure must be but a challenge to others."   ***Amelia Earhart*** ♀

"No matter what your fight, don't be ladylike."   ***Mother Jones*** ♀

"If men could get pregnant, abortion would be a sacrament."
Florynce R. Kennedy

"Why should it be necessary for a mother to be there like a grindstone at the heart of everything?"   ***Doris Lessing***

" 'Mother, what is a Feminist?'
'A Feminist, my daughter,
Is any woman who cares to think about her own affairs
As men don't think she oughter.' "
Alice Duer Miller, 1915

"I desire to live before I die, not after."   ***Lola Montez*** ♀

"Marriage is a Great Social Lie."   ***Elizabet Ney*** ♀

" 'Woman writer' has no meaning . . . not intellectually, not morally, not historically . . . a writer is a writer."   ***Cynthia Ozick***

"While man enjoys all the rights, he preaches all the duties to a woman."   ***Elizabeth Cady Stanton*** ♀

"Do everything."   ***Frances Willard*** ♀

KAREN DECROW'S LIST OF NO PLACE TO GO

———————————————— ✹ ————————————————

We asked attorney DeCrow, a leading women's rights activist and former president of the National Organization for Women, for a list of the best and worst states in which to be a woman. After much pondering, she came up list-less. The reason: "The answer is that until we have the Equal Rights Amendment we live in an unratified country. Therefore, speaking legally, there is no state in this country where it is good (where one can expect justice) to be a woman."

Exclusively for *Womanlist*

Billed as "the ugliest woman in the world," Julia Pastrana was exhibited in circuses by her husband-manager. (UN-LUCKY IN LOVE)

This is one of a hundred murdered—is anyone to be punished for this?" *The New York Evening Jour-al* pleads for justice for the victims of the Triangle fire (1911). (FROM SWEATSHOP TO DEATH)

This nineteenth-century beauty was named $ Dollar by parents whose mining investments paid off. *Colorado Historical Society.* (CHOOSI NAME FOR BABY)

Dr. Mary Walker didn't surrender her maiden name when she married in 1855. And, in bot earlier and later years, she was proud of wearing the U.S. Medal of Honor she received for surgi cal services during the Civil War. *Library of Congress.* (NO MARRIED NAME *and* FIFTEEN ON AND ONLY ONES)

MISS LYDIA KINGSMILL COMMANDER.

(*Above left*): Lydia Kingsmill Commander made news when she refused to promise to obey the man she married. *St. Louis Post-Dispatch, May 14, 1899.* (THEY DIDN'T PROMISE TO OBEY)
(*Above right*): Mary Wollstonecraft wrote *A Vindication of the Rights of Woman* (1792), a declaration of independence for women. (AND EIGHT IN ENGLAND)
Below): A suffragist reply to one of the many arguments for withholding the vote from women. *Sophia Smith Collection, Smith College.* (WHY WOMEN SHOULD NOT BE ALLOWED TO VOTE)

MODERN REPRESENTATIVE GOVERNMENT
Question : If a man represents the women of his household how can he represent himself?

IT is a common notion that men represent women at the polls.

DID you ever know a man who asked his wife how she wanted him to vote?

IF a man votes as his wife wishes him to do, he doesn't represent himself.

OR, if a man votes to please himself, he doesn't represent his wife.

THE predicament of a man who attempts to represent a family consisting of a wife, mother and daughters who hold different opinions, is conclusive that it cannot be done.

IF there are sons, the idea of a family vote isn't applied; they vote for themselves.

CAN you see any sense in the argument that men represent women at the polls? Of course not; there isn't any sense to see.

VOTE FOR THE SUFFRAGE AMENDMENT IN 1915.

WOMEN SUFFRAGE PARTY

27 Lafayette Avenue   Brooklyn, N. Y.

REPORT

OF THE

WOMAN'S RIGHTS CONVENTION,

HELD AT

Seneca Falls, N. Y.,

JULY 19TH & 20TH, 1848.

ROCHESTER:
PRINTED BY JOHN DICK,
AT THE NORTH STAR OFFICE.
1848.

The feminist movement is born in America: the front page of the *Report of the Woman's Rights Convention* at Seneca Falls, N.Y. *Library of Congress.* (ISSUER OF THE CALL FOR THE SENECA FALLS CONVENTION OF 1848)

Three pioneers: Susan B. Anthony, Elizabeth Cady Stanton, Lucretia Mott. (TEN AMERICAN FOREMOTHERS)

XXI ❧ *IN AND AROUND POWER*

NINE LANDS THAT NEVER WERE AND THE WOMEN WHO RULED THEM

❧

Aeaea, the island ruled by *Circe,* who converted the crew of the Greek hero Odysseus into swine. He protected himself with a magic plant and later prevailed upon Circe to change his men back again.

Avalon, ruled by the fairy queen *Morgan le Fay.* When King Arthur was mortally wounded, three of her sisters carried him to Avalon, where she healed him. There he has lived ever since, waiting until England needs him.

Female Island. Marco Polo heard of but never actually saw this island inhabited only by women and children; its twin was inhabited solely by men. Each spring the men supposedly journeyed to Female Island, worked the soil and planted crops for the women, and returned to their all-male sanctuary three months later with all boys over twelve. Polo reported both islands to be peaceful and contented, possibly because of this unique arrangement.

Garden of the Hesperides, ruled by the beautiful nymphs of its name. On it was a magic tree that bore golden apples, a wedding gift to Hera from Zeus, guarded by a dragon with one hundred heads.

Island of Fair Women, featured in many ancient tales. Sailors stranded there died either of unrequited love for the beautiful women who ruled there, or of starvation, because there was no escape from the Island of Fair Women.

Kuen-Luen or *Kun-Lun,* a fabulous mountain located at the exact center of the earth's surface, ruled by the Lady Queen of the Western Heavens, *Great Mother Wang.*♀ She and her consort, the August Personage of Jade, lived in a nine-story palace on the top of Kuen-Luen surrounded by the most beautiful gardens imaginable. Only truly virtuous humans could reach this mountain where the gods would feed them the fruit of immortality from the peach trees of life that grew in their gardens.

Ogygia, an island ruled by *Calypso.* She held Odysseus prisoner there for seven years, trying to make him forget his home and beloved wife in Ithaca, until at last Zeus had pity on Odysseus and ordered Calypso to let him set sail.

Tir-Na-Mban, "Land of Women" of the Celts, where all was beautiful beyond belief. Every service received by a male guest was everything he could possibly wish for—but time was suspended in this magical place and, upon leaving it, the visitor could find himself suddenly grown old.

Wak Wak. According to Arabian legend, this land was inhabited by *Bird Maidens* able to remove their wings at will and appear as the fairest of women.

RULING THE HOLY LAND

The Queen of Sheba heard of the wisdom of King Solomon and came to visit, bearing gifts and many questions. She had lots of competition—the king already had 700 wives and princesses, and 300 concubines. He was particularly fond of foreign women, and his consorts included "the daughter of pharaoh, [and] women of the Moabites, Ammonites, Edomites, Sidonians, and Hittites." But the Queen of Sheba stayed, and stayed.

Jezebel, the daughter of Ethbaal, King of Sidon and Tyre, was married to King Ahab of Israel. When a landowner refused to sell property that Ahab coveted, Jezebel arranged his death so that her husband could possess his vineyard. For this and other evil acts, her son King Joram was killed, and Jezebel herself was thrown from a window and died. Her remains were consumed by the town dogs, as the prophet Elijah had foretold. But still alive was her daughter . . .

Athaliah, who married King Jehoram of Judah. Enemies killed all their sons except Ahaziah, the youngest. After Jehoram "died of sore diseases," Ahaziah became king, and Athaliah was his chief adviser. When Ahaziah was slain, Athaliah murdered his children (except for one) and "reigned over the land," the only ruling queen in the Bible. Finally the supporters of the hidden rightful king found the opportunity to rebel; the seven-year-old king was installed and Athaliah slain.

Vashti, the wife of King Ahasueros (Xerxes) of Persia, was giving a feast for the women of the royal household when she received a message from the king. He ordered her to come in her royal garb to be shown to the princes and other men he was entertaining. Vashti refused and was sent away in disgrace by the king, who set about finding a replacement.

Esther, a Jewish maiden, was chosen. When she learned (from her cousin Mordecai) that the king's chief adviser Haman was plotting to destroy the Jews, Esther did a little plotting of her own. As a result, Haman's evil intentions were unmasked, he and his sons were hanged, and Mordecai became chief adviser to the king. These events are celebrated every year at the holiday of Purim.

The first Crusaders captured Jerusalem from the Muslims in the last year of the eleventh century and founded the Crusader, or Latin, Kingdom of Jerusalem. Some women of the Jerusalem dynasties of the next two centuries were:

Mélisende, the daughter of the king, who became queen in 1143 after her husband died. But she was crowned at the same time as her twelve-year-old son Baudouin III, and he deposed her nine years later.

Sybylle, the daughter, wife, and mother of kings, had to wait until the death of her thirteen-year-old son for her turn on the throne. She ruled with her second husband, Guy de Lusignan; during their reign they lost Jerusalem to the sultan Saladin. They were deposed in 1192, when Sybylle's sister . . .

Isabelle I became queen, ruling first with her third husband, Henri de Troyès, until he was beheaded in September 1197, and a few months later with her fourth husband, Amalric II of Cyprus, from January 1198 until her own death in 1205. Then her daughter . . .

Marie de Montferrat, known as "La Marquise," became queen at the age of fourteen. Marie ruled with her uncle as regent for several years. She was finally crowned in 1210 and ruled with her husband, Jean de Brienne, until she died two years later after giving birth to a daughter . . .

Isabelle II (or *Yolande de Brienne*), still an infant when she succeeded to the throne. Her father acted as king until 1225, when Isabelle at the age of thirteen married Holy Roman Emperor Frederick II, twenty years her senior, and was crowned Empress and Queen of Jerusalem. Four years later her husband recaptured Jerusalem from the Muslims and was crowned there—but Isabelle had died the year before, a month after giving birth to a son.

Alix de Champagne, Isabelle II's great-aunt (daughter of Isabelle I and Henri de Troyès, if you're keeping track), became regent for Isabelle II's son, serving from 1243 to 1246.

Plaisance, Alix's daughter-in-law, was queen briefly a decade later, from January 1253 to May 1254; she then became regent for an infant male heir until 1262. The next regent was . . .

Isabelle of Cyprus, a sister of the king of Cyprus, who governed in 1263 and 1264. For some time the official rulers of the Latin Kingdom had preferred to remain in Europe, and by the end of the thirteenth century their lands were retaken by the Muslims.

AFRICAN QUEENS

More than a thousand years ago, in parts of what are now Ghana, Niger, Chad, Nigeria, and the Cameroons, women led migrations of people, founded cities, led conquering armies, and governed. In the tenth and eleventh centuries a succession of seventeen women, the Habe queens, ruled Daura in the Hausa States in what is now northern Nigeria. At the end of the eleventh century the last Daura queen, so says tradition, married the son of the King of Baghdad, Abayajidda, and he became the first Habe king. The Habe queens were:

Kufuru	*Daura*
Gino	*Gamata*
Yakumo	*Shata*
Yakunya	*Batatume*
Walzama	*Sandamata*

Yanbamu	*Jamata*
Gizirgizir	*Hamata*
Innagari	*Zama*
	Shawata

More recently the Lovedu and neighboring groups in the northeastern Transvaal (located in southeast Africa) have had a female royal succession. In the early nineteenth century the Lovedu king, Mugodo, named his daughter as his successor after a period of troubles and disasters. For religious and political reasons, Mugodo insisted that his daughter first commit incest with him to establish a spiritually as well as temporally powerful ruling line. That daughter was . . .

Mujaji I. When she died, her daughter . . .

Mujaji II inherited the throne. The Lovedu queens had strict ritual obligations, prerogatives—and prohibitions. They were forbidden to take a husband, although they might choose men from a "harem" to father their children. They took "wives" instead, young women from politically and economically important families. The children of these wives, who could marry men chosen for them by the queen, were thus regarded as belonging to the queen. When Mujaji II died in 1894 . . .

Mujaji III became ruler of the Lovedu. She was the daughter of the "principal spouse" of her predecessor.

The Lovedu queens were required—if they lived long enough—to commit ritual suicide at the end of a specific period; thus no one could rule for longer than (approximately) forty years. However, the ruling Mujaji in the early 1950s put an end to this practice—out of enlightened self-interest, no doubt.

WOMEN OF POWER IN THE SIXTEENTH CENTURY

In the sixteenth more than in any other century, women moved the European world. They amassed wealth; inspired love—and fear; arranged alliances, marriages, wars—and beheadings. Their exploits are recounted in numerous other volumes. Here we simply list them, letting their familiar names, titles, and dates suggest the intrigues they were involved in, and the power they possessed.

Mary I ♀ (Mary Tudor, or "Bloody Mary") (1516–1558), the daughter of Henry VIII and Catherine of Aragon,♀ Queen of England from 1553 to 1558.

Elizabeth I ♀ (1533–1603), daughter of Henry VIII and Anne Boleyn,♀ Queen of England from 1558 to 1603.

Mary Stuart, ♀ Queen of Scotland from 1542 to 1587.

Margaret of Valois ♀ (1533–1615), first wife of Henry IV of France, and Queen of France and Navarre.

Margaret, Duchess of Parma (1522–1586), the illegitimate daughter of Holy Roman Emperor Charles V. She was appointed Spanish governor of the Netherlands 1559–1567.

Catherine of Austria, the sister of Charles V and regent for her grandson King Sebastian of Portugal from 1557 (when he was three years old) to 1562.

Catherine de' Medici ♀ (1519–1589), the queen of Henry II of France, who reigned from 1547 to 1559; then regent for her son Charles IX, who reigned from 1560 to 1574.

MODERN MATRI-MONARCHS

Wilhelmina ♀ (1880–1962), Queen of the Netherlands for half a century from 1898 to 1948, was a dominating personality known for her impetuous temper, great will power, and total lack of any sense of humor. She was an important influence on foreign and domestic policy, in 1924 preventing the establishment of diplomatic relations with the Soviet Union, and twice almost abdicating to show her disapproval of the actions of the elected government. When Germany occupied Holland in 1940, she fled to England, where she served as a rallying point for her people, talking to them over the radio, entertaining all who escaped from occupied Holland, and becoming the symbol of freedom for her nation. In 1948 she abdicated, and her only daughter became queen.

Juliana ♀ (b. 1909), Queen of the Netherlands from 1948 to 1980, was not as popular as her mother. Juliana was particularly vulnerable to the inquisitiveness of the press which, in an age in which royalty is more exposed than ever before, did not hesitate to print all manner of gossip as well as fact. In particular Juliana was criticized sharply in 1956 for being influenced by Greet Hofmans, a faith healer and mystic to whom she resorted in hopes of restoring the failing eyesight of her daughter Christina, and more recently for the involvement of her husband, Prince Bernhard, in a corruption scandal. Nevertheless, she remained a well-liked mother figure up to her own abdication in favor of her daughter Beatrix.

Elizabeth II ♀ (b. 1926) became Queen of England after the death of her father in 1952; her coronation took place the following year. She is one of the world's wealthiest women, owner of a fabulous art collection and spectacular real estate, and is also a noted sportswoman whose fondness for horses has been transmitted to her daughter Anne. Although the royal family's private affairs, as recorded daily in the outspoken British press, are public entertainment, the queen is widely admired by her subjects. She has brought a high level of professionalism to a demanding occupation.

Margrethe II (b. 1940) became Queen of Denmark the day after her father, King Frederick IX, died, January 15, 1972. The first Margrethe had ruled as regent nearly 500 years earlier, but was not recognized as queen. The right of female succession was not established in Denmark until 1953, when it became apparent that the king would have no male heirs. The modern Margrethe was educated at Cambridge University in England, has contributed articles to archaeology journals, and has said that had she not been a princess, she would have been an archaeologist.

MODERN NATIONS HEADED BY WOMEN

Ceylon became, in 1960, the first modern nation to have a woman as head of government when **Sirimavo Bandaranaike** ran for office to replace her assassinated husband. Although her tears as a recent widow carried the electorate, she turned out to be a strong politician. Defeated in 1965, she rallied to lead a three-party coalition to landslide victories in 1970 and 1975. Among her accomplishments in office: changing the name of her nation to Sri Lanka; replacement of colonial English with native Singhalese as the official language; enactment of a new constitution; nationalization of foreign-owned industries; and initiation of broad medical and social welfare programs.

India, in 1966, added *Indira Gandhi* to the women prime ministers of Southeast Asia. Gandhi, daughter of Jawaharlal Nehru, founder of Indian independence, had been her father's adviser and, when the former prime minister died, was selected by leaders of the Congress party as titular head only. She soon asserted her own power, however, and was elected by a huge popular vote in 1967 and again in 1972, before being defeated in 1977 because of charges of corruption and abuses of power. The following year Gandhi rallied, formed a splinter political party, won election to Parliament, and in 1979 made a spectacular comeback when she was reelected prime minister.

Israel's fourth prime minister was *Golda Meir,* chosen in 1969 by the Mapai (Labor) party upon the death of the previous prime minister; she won in her own right in the general election later that year. Known throughout the world simply as Golda, she had grown up in Milwaukee, Wisconsin, emigrated to Palestine in 1921, and become active politically shortly afterward. On May 14, 1948, she was a signer of the Israeli Declaration of Independence; she then became the only female member of the provisional legislature, the first minister to the Soviet Union, a member of the first Knesset (Parliament), the first and only female cabinet member. She also headed her country's United Nations delegation and was secretary-general of her party. In 1974, unable to form a governing coalition, Meir resigned.

Argentina became the first Western Hemisphere nation to be headed by a woman on July 1, 1974, when vice-president *María Estela (Isabelita) Martínez de Perón* succeeded to the presidency upon the death of her husband, Juan Perón. A touring folk dancer with a sixth-grade education, she met the exiled former dictator in Panama City in 1956 and quickly moved to fill the gap in his life left by the death of his second wife, *María Eva ("Evita") Duarte de Perón* (1919–1952), a film and radio actress. Even more popular than her husband, Evita had made religious education compulsory in the public schools; organized women workers and worked for women's suffrage; and channeled government funds into programs that built her husband's power base among the *descamisados,* "shirtless ones." Army opposition forced withdrawal of her vice-presidential candidacy in 1951. No similar intervention was at hand in 1973, when Juan Perón, after a seventeen-year exile, introduced Isabelita as his running mate. When he died after nine months in office, she refused to step down and stubbornly presided over a deteriorating economy and increased social unrest. Her husband's former supporters called a two-day general strike, Isabelita's health failed along with her popularity, and in March 1976 a military junta removed the president from office. In 1978 she was convicted on several charges of misuse of funds and abuse of power.

Central African Republic's Elizabeth Domitien was appointed prime minister in December 1974 by President Jean Bokassa, who had set aside the national constitution. But Domitien, who had been politically active for a quarter of a century as a leading orator and nationalist, proved more independent than he had expected. When Bokassa declared himself emperor in 1976, Domitien, who opposed his monarchical tendencies, was removed from office and placed under house arrest.

Great Britain became the first European nation to have a female minister when Conservative *Margaret Thatcher* was elected in 1979. A lawyer and chemist who attended Somerville College, Oxford University, Thatcher first ran for Parliament when she was twenty-four years old. Elected on a second try in 1959, she became secretary for education early in the 1970s and was elected party leader in 1975. With the growing unpopularity of the ruling Labour party as years of inflation and labor unrest took their toll, it was only a matter of time before "Maggie" held the reins of power.

Portugal became the second European country to have a female minister when *Maria de Lurdes Pintassilgo* was appointed to head a caretaker government in July 1979. Pintassilgo functioned as a nonparty official with backing from both Communists and Socialists; her liberal positions on many questions sharply divided the Catholic church hierarchy, which is an important factor in Portugal's affairs. She handed in her resignation on December 27, 1979, after 149 days in office, to make way for the newly elected government.

Bolivia became the second Western Hemisphere nation to have a woman head in November 1979, when *Lidia Gueiler Tejada* was sworn in to replace a dictator and junta. Trained as an accountant, the fifty-one-year-old prime minister had been active in Bolivian politics for thirty years and a leader of Congress. Gueiler was appointed to hold office as caretaker until the installation of an elected government in August 1980—but was overthrown in a coup in July. Bolivia averages one coup a year.

FIFTEEN RULERS WHO REIGNED FOR MORE THAN THIRTY YEARS

❧

Empress Suiko Tenno	Japan	592–626
Empress Wu Chao ♀ (*Emperor*)	China	655–705
Queen Juana I	Spain	1274–1307
Queen Joanna I	Italy	1343–1381
Queen Elizabeth I ♀	England	1558–1603
Queen Maria Theresa	Hungary	1740–1780
Empress Catherine II (*the Great*) ♀	Russia	1762–1796

Queen Maria I	Portugal	1777–1816
Queen Ranavalona I	Madagascar	1828–1861
Queen Isabella II	Spain	1833–1868
Queen Victoria ♀	England	1837–1901
Dowager Empress Tz'u Hsi (Ci Xi) ♀	China	1861–1908
Queen Wilhelmina ♀	Netherlands	1890–1948
Queen Salote Tubou	Tonga	1918–1965
Queen Juliana ♀	Netherlands	1948–1980

FOUNDING MOTHERS:
Wives of the Signers of the Declaration of Independence

※

Lists of the signers of the Declaration of Independence are legion. Here we call the roll of those who have been forgotten—the women who waited at home.

Abigail Smith Adams ♀ (John Adams, Massachusetts). The correspondence between wife and husband has survived, showing the daily activities of Abigail, who managed the family farm, educated the children, tended the final illnesses of her mother and other relatives, reported on Boston's political intrigues, gave birth to a stillborn child, and only occasionally gave in to lamentation: "How many are the solitary hours I spend, ruminating upon the past, and anticipating the future, whilst you overwhelmed with the cares of State, have but few moments you can devote to any individual."

Elizabeth Welles Adams (Samuel Adams, Massachusetts). Samuel and John Adams were second cousins, and John asked Abigail to look after Elizabeth in the event of "Distress and Danger in Boston."

Mary Bartlett (Dr. Josiah Bartlett, New Hampshire)

Elizabeth Corbin Braxton (Carter Braxton, Virginia)

Mary ("Molly") Darnall Carroll (Charles Carroll, Carrollton, Maryland). Her husband, also her first cousin, was one of the richest men in the colonies.

Ann Baldwin Chase (Samuel Chase, Maryland)

Sarah Hatfield Clark (Abraham Clark, New Jersey)

Elizabeth Meredith Clymer (George Clymer, Pennsylvania)

Abigail Cary Ellery (William Ellery, Rhode Island)

Isabella Jones Floyd (William Floyd, New York)

Deborah Read Franklin (Benjamin Franklin, Pennsylvania). She became Franklin's common-law wife in 1730 because she was not legally divorced from a previous husband in England. A carpenter's daughter, she stayed home and managed his business affairs while Franklin traveled, and reveled, abroad. In his *Autobiography* he wrote that "she proved a good and faithful helpmate, assisted me much by attending to the shop. We throve together, and ever mutually endeavored to make each other happy."

Ann Bourne Gwinnett (Button Gwinnett, Georgia)

Abigail Burr Hall (Lyman Hall, Georgia)

Dorothy Quincy Hancock (John Hancock, Massachusetts). She had quite a reputation as a coquette and resisted Hancock's persistent proposals until she was twenty-eight. Perhaps the price the British put on his head made him more attractive to her and influenced her decision to give in at last. The couple honeymooned in Philadelphia while he was president of the Second Continental Congress.

Elizabeth Bassett Harrison (Benjamin Harrison, Virginia). Their son William Henry would be ninth president of the United States his father helped establish; their great-grandson Benjamin would be the twenty-third president, more than a century after independence was declared.

Deborah Scudder Hart (John Hart, New Jersey)

Elizabeth Matthewes Heyward (Thomas Heyward, Jr., South Carolina)

Ann Clark Hooper (William Hooper, North Carolina)

Ann Smith Hopkins (Stephen Hopkins, Rhode Island)

Ann Borden Hopkinson (Frances Hopkinson, New Jersey). She visited him in Philadelphia and had her portrait painted by Charles Willson Peale while the Continental Congress was in session.

Martha Devotion Huntington (Samuel Huntington, Massachusetts)

Martha Wayles Skelton Jefferson (Thomas Jefferson, Virginia). When they married in 1772 she was a twenty-three-year-old widow, and he was head over heels in love with her. The letters that passed between them do not survive, but it was widely known that Jefferson left the Philadelphia meeting to spend months in Monticello with her. She would die in 1782, in her early thirties.

Anne Pinckard Lee (Richard Henry Lee, Virginia)

Rebecca Tayloe Lee (Francis Lightfoot Lee, Virginia)

Elizabeth Annisley Lewis (Francis Lewis, New York)

Christina Ten Broeck Livingston (Philip Livingston, New York)

Hannah Motte Lynch (Thomas Lynch, Jr., South Carolina)

Sarah Armitage McKean (Thomas McKean, Delaware)

Mary Izard Middleton (Arthur Middleton, South Carolina). She and her children watched while British troops pillaged their plantation, Middleton Place, during the Revolution.

Mary Walton Morris (Lewis Morris, New York)

Mary White Morris (Robert Morris, Pennsylvania). She was the wealthiest woman in Philadelphia, and he the richest merchant. Their life-style glittered even in the midst of the Revolution, but the glitter stopped abruptly in the late 1790s when Morris lost his fortune and went to debtor's prison for more than three years. His wife, refusing to leave him alone in Philadelphia during the dreaded yellow fever epidemics, continued to visit him in prison, even when she had to walk past rows of coffins to reach his cell.

Anne Justice Morton (John Morton, Pennsylvania)

Lucy Grimes Nelson (Thomas Nelson, Jr., Virginia)

Mary Chew Paca (William Paca, Maryland)

Sally Cobb Paine (Robert Treat Paine, Massachusetts)

Susannah Lyme Penn (John Penn, North Carolina)

Gertrude Ross Till Read (George Read, Delaware)

Anne Lawler Ross (George Ross, Pennsylvania)

Julia Stockton Rush (Dr. Benjamin Rush, Pennsylvania). The daughter of signer Richard Stockton of New Jersey, she married another signer, the most famous physician and medical teacher of his generation.

Henrietta Middleton Rutledge (Edward Rutledge, Jr., South Carolina). The sister of Maryland delegate Arthur Middleton had married the South Carolina delegate on March 1, 1774.

Rebecca Prescott Sherman (Roger Sherman, Massachusetts). Sherman had fifteen children by this and an earlier marriage.

Eleanor Armor Smith (James Smith, Pennsylvania)

Annis Boudinot Stockton ♀ (Richard Stockton, New Jersey). She was a noted poet.

Margaret Brown Stone (Thomas Stone, Maryland)

Naomi Smith Taylor (George Taylor, Pennsylvania)

Hannah Jack Thornton (Matthew Thornton, New Hampshire)

Dorothy Camber Walton (George Walton, Georgia)

Catharine Moffatt Whipple (Captain William Whipple, New Hampshire)

Mary Trumbull Williams (William Williams, Massachusetts)

Rachel Bird Wilson (James Wilson, Pennsylvania)

Elizabeth Montgomery Witherspoon (Reverend John Witherspoon, New Jersey)

Laura Collins Wolcott (Oliver Wolcott, Connecticut). In 1776 a mob pulled down the statue of King George II in New York City, broke its 4,000 pounds of lead into pieces, and shipped them to Litchfield, Connecticut. The women of Litchfield melted the fragments into musket balls desperately needed by the Continental Army. Laura Wolcott is credited with making 4,250 of them.

Elizabeth Taliaferro Wythe (George Wythe, Virginia)

THE WORKING LIVES OF TEN PRESIDENTS' WIVES

❧

Before their White House days, in most cases before they met their future husbands, these ten First Ladies-to-be held paid employment:

Abigail Fillmore, schoolteacher and book lover, was horrified to find that there were no books, not even a Bible, in the White House, so she wheedled a modest appropriation of $250 out of Congress and started a presidential library. An invalid, she fell victim to the brutal Washington weather at President Pierce's inauguration in March 1853 and died a month later.

Lucretia Rudolph Garfield, schoolteacher, was a childhood playmate and then a pupil of her husband's at the small college he headed in Hiram, Ohio. She had been First Lady only four months when her husband was shot; a half a month later he was dead.

Ellen Herndon Arthur, a fine contralto, never got to live in the White House. While waiting for a cab in the rain after a performance she caught a cold which developed into pneumonia; she died soon afterward. Arthur installed a portrait of Ellen in the White House, in front of it setting a vase of fresh flowers that were changed daily.

Ida Saxton McKinley, cashier in her father's bank in Canton, Ohio. The local belle, she attracted many young male depositors, including McKinley. Throughout their long marriage his devotion to her was legendary, even though she became increasingly neurotic after the death of their two young daughters. One of her favorite occupations was making slippers—ultimately she produced 5,000 pairs that went to friends and charities.

Helen Herron Taft, schoolteacher, preferred her work at a girls' prep school to the bubbly life of a socialite that could have been hers as the daughter of a prominent Cincinnati attorney. She also ran a literary salon. Taft was attracted by her independence, praised her for wanting "to do something in life and not be a burden." After they wed in 1886 she successfully focused her considerable ambitions on his career.

Florence DeWolfe Harding, music teacher, gave lessons to support her young son after divorcing her first husband. One of her pupils was Harding's sister, and it was at the piano that she first met the editor of the Marion, Ohio, *Star,* five years younger than herself. Despite her family's objections, Florence sensed that both the newspaper and its handsome editor could go places. After they married, she was the *Star*'s circulation manager for fourteen years, reorganizing the paper's delivery system and putting it well in the black. Harding called her "Duchess" because of her imperial competence both in the newspaper business and in politics.

Grace Goodhue Coolidge, teacher of the deaf. Dignified and low-key, Grace Coolidge restored decorum to the White House after the scandal-ridden Harding administration. "Silent Cal," renowned for his refusal to chatter, once said of his wife that having taught the deaf to hear, she "might perhaps cause the mute to speak." But he remained taciturn throughout his term in office.

Lou Henry Hoover, geologist, met her husband-to-be while they were both geology majors at Stanford, where she became the first woman graduate in that field. She was working for a geologist in 1898 when Hoover cabled "Will you marry me?" from a field assignment in China. In the three years they spent in China she learned Chinese and toted a Mauser automatic .38-caliber pistol during the Boxer Rebellion of 1900. She later said she wouldn't have missed it for anything. In January 1933 she established a precedent by becoming the first outgoing First Lady to show her successor, Eleanor Roosevelt,♀ through the White House.

Jacqueline Bouvier Kennedy,♀ "Inquiring Camera Girl" for the *Washington Times-Herald* for a year and a half, didn't know how to take professional pictures when she landed the job in 1952, so she chose a photography school from the yellow pages and learned quickly. One day she went up to the Hill to do a picture/interview on the new members of Congress, among them the junior senator from Massachusetts. She was earning $56.75 per week when she left the job to marry John F. Kennedy.

Patricia Ryan Nixon,♀ schoolteacher, had lost both her parents before she was grown and worked in an Artesia, California, bank to earn enough money to finish high school and in a New York City hospital laboratory before attending the University of Southern California on a research fellowship. She was teaching typing and shorthand in Whittier, California, when she met eligible attorney Richard Nixon. A relatively unknown part of Pat Nixon's paid working life is a microscopic career as a movie actress: while a student at USC she made brief appearances in *Becky Sharp* and *Small Town Girl.*

POWERS BEHIND THE PRESIDENT

———————————————— ❧ ————————————————

Dolley Madison,♀ when the British approached Washington and her husband
was away at the front, supervised the loading of four cases of state
papers and other valuables onto a wagon, removed the portrait of
George Washington from the White House wall and entrusted it to
"two gentlemen of New York," and evacuated the executive mansion
and the city just in time.

Edith Wilson assumed a quasi-political function when Woodrow Wilson was
incapacitated by a stroke in October 1919. For more than two months
Mrs. Wilson and the president's doctor acted for him, determined
which visitors he could receive, what correspondence he would read,
and which documents he would sign. Mrs. Wilson also concealed the
president's true condition from the public, and she opposed and prevented the temporary transfer of power to the vice-president.

Eleanor Roosevelt,♀ in the words of historian Samuel Eliot Morison, was
"indispensable to [FDR's] well-being and success." In 1933 Mrs. Roosevelt held the first press conference by a president's wife and from
1935 wrote a widely syndicated column, "My Day." She traveled by
every conceivable means of transportation throughout the country and
around the world. In 1944 she led a White House Conference on How
Women May Share in Post-War Policy-Making, for some time served
as a go-between for scientists working on the atomic bomb and her
husband, and generally kept after FDR. Her competence was recognized with official assignments from President Truman to represent the
United States in the founding of, and later at, the United Nations.

Rosalynn Carter has been described as her husband's closest political adviser, actively consulted by him during regularly scheduled luncheon
meetings on matters ranging from policy to personnel, and officially
represented him on diplomatic trips to Latin America and Southeast
Asia. Mrs. Carter became the first president's wife in more than thirty-
five years to testify before a congressional committee in February 1979
when, as honorary chairwoman of the President's Council on Mental
Health, she advocated an increase in programs and funding for the
mentally ill.

EIGHT CANDIDATES FOR HIGHEST OFFICE

———————————————— ❧ ————————————————

Victoria Claflin Woodhull♀ was the first woman to be a candidate for president. She was nominated by the People's party in 1872.

Belva Ann Bennett Lockwood♀ was the presidential candidate of the National Equal Rights party in 1884 and 1888.

Senator Margaret Chase Smith♀ became the first woman to have her name
put in nomination as a presidential candidate of a major party, in 1964.
The Maine Republican announced her candidacy in January of that
year, at the age of sixty-six, at a Women's National Press Club

luncheon. She campaigned in the primaries and brought thirty delegates to the Republican National Convention. Sixteen years later Smith asserted that "a woman who was dedicated" could someday be elected; she didn't "think it will be too far in advance before we have such a woman. And certainly things couldn't be any worse."

Charlene Mitchell was the presidential candidate of the Communist party, U.S.A. in 1968; she got 1,075 votes in four states.

Frances T. ("Sissy") Farenthold, a Democrat, the first woman elected to the Texas legislature and a candidate for governor of that state, became the first woman whose name was placed in nomination for vice-president at a convention of a major political party, in 1972.

Angela Davis ♀ was unanimously made the vice-presidential candidate of the Communist party, U.S.A., in November 1979. It was the first campaign for public office of the black militant and teacher of philosophy. Her running mate was Gus Hall, who had also run in 1972 and 1976.

Deirdre Griswold was nominated for president by Workers World, a splinter leftist party, in late 1979. Griswold is the editor of the party's publication.

LaDonna Harris ♀ was nominated for vice-president by the Citizens party in April 1980; her running mate was Barry Commoner. The platform of the party called for dispersion of the largest food-producing corporations, public ownership of all corporations, and the phasing out of nuclear power plants.

LEGISLATIVE RECORD SETTERS

Martha Hughes Cannon, a physician who had established the first nursing school in Utah in 1886, became the first woman member of a state legislature when she was elected to the Utah Senate in 1896.

Minnie Craig, elected to the North Dakota legislature in 1923, and elected Speaker of the House ten years later, was the first woman to be a speaker of a state legislature.

Edith Nourse Rogers, Massachusetts Republican, served nineteen terms in the House of Representatives, from her election in June 1925 until her death in 1960—longer than any other woman, or most men. As member and chair of the Veterans Affairs Committee, Rogers sponsored legislation to establish the women's divisions of the armed services and veterans hospitals across the country.

Margaret Chase Smith, ♀ Maine Republican, served four terms as senator, from 1948 to 1972—longer than any other woman or most men. She had previously served four terms in the House of Representatives, from 1940 to 1948.

Lindy Boggs, Democrat of Louisiana, was, in 1976, the first woman to chair a national convention of a major political party in the United States. Boggs has been a congresswoman since 1973, when she was elected to fill her husband's term after his disappearance during a flight over Alaska the previous year.

Nancy Landon Kassebaum, Republican of Kansas, elected in 1978, was the only woman senator in the Ninety-sixth Congress. A radio executive whose only previous political position had been as a school board member in her town, Kassebaum is the daughter of Alfred M. Landon, Republican presidential candidate in 1936.

Marjorie S. Holt, Republican; *Gladys N. Spellman,* Democrat; and *Barbara Mikulski,* Democrat, were reelected to Congress; and *Beverly Byron,* Democrat, was elected as her late husband's successor to Congress, all from Maryland, in 1977. They made Maryland, with eight representatives, the only fully equal delegation with regard to sex—and the first ever.

TEN CONGRESSIONAL FIRSTS

Jeannette Rankin,♀ the first congresswoman, was elected as a Republican from Montana and served from 1917 to 1919 and from 1941 to 1943.

Rebecca Latimer Felton, the first woman to occupy a seat in the Senate, was appointed by the governor of Georgia to fill the vacancy caused by the death of Senator Thomas E. Watson. Her term lasted two days, November 21–22, 1922. Felton had a larger impact as a journalist for thirty years with the *Atlanta Journal,* championing penal reform, woman suffrage, and other liberal issues.

Mae Ella Nolan, the first congresswoman elected to complete her deceased husband's term, served from 1923 to 1925.

Alice Mary Robertson was the first woman to preside over the House—at a special session in 1921 the Oklahoma representative was asked to take the chair. Her function was merely to announce the vote.

Florence Prag Kahn was the first Jewish woman elected to Congress. The Republican representative from San Francisco was elected five times, beginning in 1925, before succumbing to the Roosevelt landslide of 1936.

Hattie Wyatt Caraway became the first woman elected to the United States Senate, in 1932. She had first been appointed to fill out the unexpired term of her husband, who died the year before. In 1943 Caraway became the first woman senator to preside over the Senate, opening the proceedings on October 19, 1943, in the absence of Vice-President Henry Wallace.

Caroline O'Day, the first woman to come to Congress with a broad political power base of her own in 1935, was also the first congresswoman elected from New York State. O'Day, a Democratic politician with ties to trade unionism, was a friend of Eleanor Roosevelt's.♀

Frances Payne Bolton, elected in November 1952 to the Eighty-third Congress, was the first woman to be elected to Congress simultaneously with her son. She and Oliver Payne Bolton were both Ohio Republicans.

Shirley Chisholm ♀ was the first black woman elected to Congress, in 1968. Chisholm represents a Brooklyn, New York, district.

Yvonne Brathwaite Burke ♀ was the first representative given maternity leave by the Speaker of the House—Burke gave birth to a daughter in 1973, one year after her election.

THREE ACTRESSES ELECTED TO CONGRESS

—————————————— ❧ ——————————————

Clare Boothe Luce,♀ Republican, Connecticut, 1943–1947.
Emily Taft Douglas, Democrat, Illinois, 1944–1946.
Helen Gahagan Douglas,♀ Democrat, California, 1945–1951.

UNREPRESENTATIVE REPRESENTATION

—————————————— ❧ ——————————————

	Percent men	*Percent women*
U.S. population	48.7	51.3
U.S. Senate	99	1
U.S. House	96	4
U.S. Supreme Court	100	0
Federal judges	99	1
Governors	96	4
State representatives	90	10
State senators	95	5
Statewide Elective/Appointive Offices	89	11
County governing boards	97	3
Mayors and councilors	92	8
School board members	75	25

Compiled by the National Women's Education Fund and the Center for the American Woman and Politics, 1979. Courtesy Women's Campaign Fund, Inc.

HER HONOR, THE MAYOR

—————————————— ❧ ——————————————

Mary Woolley Chamberlain Howard, mayor of the incorporated town of Kanab, Utah, from 1912 to 1914. Howard governed with an all-female city council.

Doña Felisa Rincon de Gautier, mayor of San Juan, Puerto Rico, for twenty-two years, from 1946 to 1968. Gautier was a founder of the Popular party in 1940 and ran for mayor over the objections of her father and husband—a most untraditional thing for a Puerto Rican woman to do.

Sally Stanford♀ (formerly Marcia Busby), elected mayor of Sausalito, California, in 1972 when she was seventy-two years old. Stanford's checkered career included stints as a bootlegger, speakeasy manager, brothel keeper, and restaurant owner, but for about twenty years before her remarkable political coup she had been an active participant at city council meetings and a contributor to the public good in numerous ways.

Janet Gray Hayes, elected mayor of San Jose, California, in 1974, the first woman to be mayor of a major city on the mainland United States. Hayes, the wife of a physician, became politically active after her PTA's attempts to get a school crossing guard took two years. She defeated six men in the primary and a runoff election, but the mayoral election itself was a close call.

Lila Cockrell, elected mayor of San Antonio, Texas, in 1975, despite the fact that her opponent spent three times as much on his campaign as she did on hers. Married and the mother of two, Cockrell had been a member of the city council for seven years, and mayor pro tem. Inspired by Hayes's success in San Jose, she decided to make the race.

Unita Blackwell, elected mayor of Mayersville, Mississippi, in 1976, one of ten black mayors in the state. Earlier in her career, Blackwell had been jailed in Jackson, the state capital, for demonstrating for black voting rights, had been an organizer of the Mississippi Democratic Freedom party, and had served on two presidential commissions.

Viola Leggett, also one of Mississippi's black mayors, of the town of Gunnenson, elected in 1976.

Dianne Feinstein, selected mayor of San Francisco in December 1978 following the tragic slaying of Mayor George B. Moscone; elected in her own right in November 1979. Feinstein had unsuccessfully attempted to become mayor twice before and had been three times elected president of the Board of Supervisors of the County and City of San Francisco, from 1969 on.

Jane M. Byrne, described as a "Democratic maverick," elected mayor of Chicago in February 1979 in an upset victory over the incumbent supported by the "machine." Byrne was, however, a protégée of the late Mayor Richard Daley, the political power in Chicago. As commissioner of sales, weights, and measures, she had done her best to enforce regulations, making herself unpopular with many politicians and commercial interests.

Sister Carolyn Farrell, a member of the Sisters of Charity of the Blessed Virgin Mary, elected mayor of Dubuque, Iowa, in January 1980, at a meeting of the five-member city council, defeating a male council member who had seniority. She is believed to be the first nun to head a city government.

WHERE THE MAYORS WERE

In 1974 there were a total of 566 women mayors in cities and towns throughout the United States. By state, they broke down like this:

Alabama—7	Georgia—10	Maine—0
Alaska—2	Hawaii—0	Maryland—5
Arizona—6	Idaho—7	Massachusetts—3
Arkansas—29	Illinois—19	Michigan—14
California—32	Indiana—0	Minnesota—23
Colorado—10	Iowa—29	Mississippi—8
Connecticut—13	Kansas—21	Missouri—28
Delaware—3	Kentucky—8	Montana—6
Florida—13	Louisiana—9	Nebraska—12

Nevada—0	Oklahoma—17	Utah—3
New Hampshire—5	Oregon—10	Vermont—0
New Jersey—15	Pennsylvania—22	Virginia—6
New Mexico—8	Rhode Island—2	Washington—4
New York—26	South Carolina—5	West Virginia—15
North Carolina—10	South Dakota—12	Wisconsin—10
North Dakota—4	Tennessee—2	Wyoming—8
Ohio—29	Texas—36	

From *Women in Public Office,* Center for the American Woman and Politics, Eagleton Institute of Politics, Rutgers, New Jersey (New York: R. R. Bowker, 1976).

FIVE GOVERNORS

❧

Nellie Tayloe Ross, the first woman to be inaugurated as a state governor, was elected in Wyoming in 1924 to fill the seat of her husband, who had died in office. She won without campaigning—but was defeated two years later when she tried for reelection. From 1933 to 1953 she served four terms as director of the U.S. Mint, the first of several women to hold that office.

Miriam ("Ma") Ferguson,♀ using the slogan "Two governors for the price of one," ran for governor of Texas in 1924 in place of her husband, James ("Pa") Ferguson, who had been impeached on charges of corruption. She was elected and won a second term in 1932.

Lurleen Wallace, elected governor of Alabama in 1966 because her husband, George Wallace, was not allowed by state law to succeed himself, loyally performed the duties of office even though suffering from a terminal illness. She died in 1968 before completing her term.

Ella Tambussi Grasso, the occupant of the Connecticut State House, is the first woman governor who, in her words, "was not previously a governor's lady." Grasso was first elected governor in 1974, reelected in 1978. A former state legislator and U.S. representative, she has not lost an election in a quarter century of political life.

Dixy Lee Ray,♀ the nonconformist former head of the Atomic Energy Commission (she lives in a twenty-eight-foot mobile home with her two dogs), was elected governor of Washington State in 1976 in her first political campaign. Before entering public life Ray was a professor of invertebrate zoology and marine biology. She was defeated for reelection in 1980.

AND SEVEN LIEUTENANT GOVERNORS

❧

Mary Anne Krupsak, Democrat, was elected in New York in 1974, after eight years in the state legislature and a primary triumph over two male opponents. Her slogan: "She's not just one of the boys." And she wasn't. In 1978 she set out to buck the incumbent governor, Hugh Carey, in the primary and went down to defeat.

Thelma L. Stovall, Democrat, was elected in Kentucky in 1975 after a twenty-five-year political career which included positions as state legislator, secretary of state, and state treasurer.

Evelyn Gandy, Democrat, was elected in Mississippi in 1976 after a political career studded with firsts: first woman president of the University of Mississippi Law School; first woman editor of its *Journal*; first woman elected to the state legislature from Forrest County; first woman attorney general of Mississippi; first woman commissioner of public welfare; and first woman elected to a state office (state treasurer, 1959). Those who watch these things in Mississippi expect her to rise even higher, despite the fact that in 1979 she lost a four-way gubernatorial primary contest.

Madeline Kunin, Democrat, was elected in Vermont in 1978, becoming the highest-ranking member of her party to hold statewide office.

Also elected lieutenant governors in 1978 were *Nancy Dick,* Democrat of Colorado, *Jean King,* Democrat of Hawaii, and *Nancy Stevenson,*♀ Democrat of South Carolina.

SIX CABINET SECRETARIES
(*as of July 1980*)

In the history of the United States, only six women have held cabinet posts, four of them in recent administrations.

Frances Perkins,♀ secretary of labor, 1933–1945, appointed by Franklin Delano Roosevelt.

Oveta Culp Hobby,♀ first secretary of health, education, and welfare, 1953–1955, appointed by Dwight David Eisenhower.

Carla Anderson Hills, secretary of housing and urban development, 1975–1977, appointed by Gerald Ford.

Patricia Roberts Harris,♀ secretary of housing and urban development, 1977–1979; secretary of health, education, and welfare, 1979–1980, appointed by Jimmy Carter. Harris thus became the first woman to hold two different portfolios.

Juanita Kreps, secretary of commerce, 1977–1979, appointed by Jimmy Carter.

Shirley Mount Hufstedler, secretary of education, appointed by Jimmy Carter in 1979.

FORTY-TWO IN THE HIGHEST COUNCILS

Only in the twentieth century have women been elected to national legislatures and served as cabinet ministers; their particular interests have included education, health, labor and women's rights, and foreign affairs. Some firsts and special achievements:

The British Commonwealth

Margaret Bondfield was the first minister of labor in Great Britain, 1929–1931. A trade union organizer, Bondfield was defeated in her stand for reelection to Commons by . . .

Irene Ward, who remained in Parliament until 1945 and again from 1950 to 1974, thus becoming the longest-sitting woman M.P. Ward, a Conservative who represented working-class districts, was known for her blunt speeches and outspoken heckling of other speakers, and was once suspended from the House of Commons for five days for charging that the Labour government was a dictatorship.

Barbara Anne Castle, elected to Commons in 1945, became Labour minister of transport in 1965–1968. She has held cabinet-level positions in Labour governments ever since.

Edith Summerskill was minister of insurance in the postwar 1940s. During the war Lady Summerskill had some success in getting women enrolled in the Home Guard. She chaired the Labour party in 1954–1955 and was for many years a member of its National Executive Committee. She caused a mild furor when she entered Commons under her birth name, fought for financial and property rights for married women, and was a key influence in the establishment of the National Health Service. In 1961 she was created a life peer and entered the House of Lords. Lady Summerskill died in 1980 at the age of seventy-eight. Her daughter . . .

Shirley (Samuel) Summerskill adopted her mother's name; became, like both her parents, a physician; and joined her mother in Parliament, where they were the first "mother-daughter" legislative team.

Shirley Williams,♀ a member of Parliament, was the highest-ranking woman in the Labour party in the late 1970s.

Bernadette Devlin,♀ a Socialist from Northern Ireland and the youngest woman to be a member of Britain's Parliament, was elected in 1969 when she was twenty-two. Devlin lost her seat in 1974.

Enid Muriel Burnell Lyons was the first woman member of Australia's House of Representatives, from 1943 to 1951. Born in 1897 in Duck River, Tasmania, she was the wife of a former prime minister and had been an active member of the Liberal party for many years.

Mary Ellen Smith was the first woman cabinet minister in the British Empire, when she served as minister without portfolio in British Columbia from 1921–1922.

Agnes Macphail was the first woman to be elected to Canada's Parliament in 1921.

Cairine Wilson was the first woman to be a senator in Canada in 1930.

Flora MacDonald was minister for external (foreign) affairs of Canada during the short-lived government of Prime Minister Joe Clark, 1979–1980. A high school dropout, MacDonald started in politics as a secretary at party headquarters, has been a Conservative member of Parliament since 1972, and became, at age fifty-three, the highest-ranking woman ever in Canadian politics. She achieved international prominence when Canadian embassy officials in Teheran protected and arranged the escape of six Americans in hiding there after the takeover of the American embassy in 1979.

Continental Europe

Nina Bang of Denmark, the first woman member of the Danish cabinet, was minister of education from 1924 to 1926. Bang, a schoolteacher, had been elected to Parliament in 1918. She died in 1928.

Eva Gredal was minister of social affairs in Denmark in 1979. Three of the nineteen cabinet officers of that country were women, also including *Lise Ostergaard,* minister without portfolio for foreign affairs, and *Ritt Bjerregaard,* education minister.

Baroness Alexandra Gripenberg, Hedvig Gebhard, Dagmar Neovius, and *Lucina Hagman* were among the nineteen women elected in 1907 to Finland's Parliament, the first in the world to have women members. Also elected then was . . .

Miina Sillanpää, who in 1926 became the first woman cabinet minister in Finland when she was named assistant minister for social affairs. Sillanpaa served four nonconsecutive terms in her nation's Parliament, the last ending in 1947 when she was eighty-one.

Pirkko Tyolajarvi, minister of social affairs and health, is the only current woman cabinet officer in Finland. In 1978, 44 of the 200 members of the Finnish Parliament were women.

Anna Rogstad, a teacher, became the first woman member of Norway's Parliament in 1909. Rogstad, elected as an alternate, took her seat to replace the male delegate. The Speaker of the House proclaimed the day one of the most important in the nation's history.

Gro Harlem Bruntland is the environment minister of Norway and was considered a serious contender for the premiership at the end of the 1970s. Of sixteen cabinet ministers in Norway, four are women: those for environment, justice, consumer affairs, and welfare.

Karin Söder has been a member of the Swedish Parliament since 1970 and foreign minister since 1976—the first woman foreign minister in Europe in twenty-five years.

Dr. Hertha Firnberg was appointed minister for science and research in Austria in 1970. She had been elected to the upper house of the Federal Parliament in 1959 and to the lower house in 1963.

Annemarie Renger was the first woman president of West Germany's Bundestag, from December 1972 to December 1976. She remains prominent in West German politics.

Genevieve Aubry was one of twenty-four women elected to the Swiss Parliament in October 1979. Since getting the vote in 1971, women have been increasingly represented in Switzerland's National Legislature. In that year they won 10 of 200 places in the lower house, four years later upped that to 15, and in 1979 to 21. In 1975 one woman was elected to the upper house, and two others joined her in 1979. "More Female Representatives in Switzerland than in the United States," crowed the *Tribune de Genève,* which noted that the women had "partly made up for time lost."

Elizabeth Blunschy-Steiner was the first woman to be elected president of the

Swiss National Council, the country's highest political office, in 1977.
Françoise Giroud became the first minister for women's affairs in France in
1974. Also in 1974, *Annie Lesur* became minister for education and *Helene Dorlhac* minister for penal affairs. In 1979 *Monique Pelletier* succeeded Giroud as minister for women's affairs.

Nilde Jotti was elected president of the Italian Chamber of Deputies in June
1979. Although she is a Communist party member, support of the majority Christian Democrats was responsible for her victory. Jotti, who
was vice-president of the Chamber for seven years, became its first
woman president.

Alexandra Kollontai, the only woman member of the Bolshevik Central
Committee following the Russian Revolution, was Soviet ambassador
to Norway, Mexico, and Sweden before she retired to a sometime literary career. She died in 1952 at eighty. In 1970, 30 percent of the Supreme Soviet were women—but they were not represented at the highest policy-making (that is, Communist party) levels. The highest-
ranking Soviet woman of recent note: *Yekaterina Furtseva,* minister of
culture.

Irene Kosmowska was vice-minister of social welfare for Poland for a short
time in 1918—the first female minister anywhere.

Ana Rabinsohn Pauker was foreign minister of Rumania from 1947 to 1952.
Born into an Orthodox Jewish family and once a Hebrew schoolteacher, she joined the Communist party in 1921 and was arrested and
imprisoned many times. Meanwhile she attracted the attention of Europe's leading Communists, among them Russia's Josef Stalin and Andrei Vishinsky, who installed her as their watchdog in the new Eastern
European satellite. She did not disappoint her sponsors, personally in-
stigating purges as soon as she was sworn into office. Pauker died of
cancer in 1960.

Middle East

Farrokhrou Parsa was the first female member of Parliament in Iran and
minister of education. She was executed on the night of May 8, 1980,
immediately after a secret trial.

Geula Cohen, a member of the Knesset (parliament) of Israel, has a reputation for repudiating the policies of the prime minister of her own party.
A member of the resistance and terrorist forces that battled the British
mandate occupation of Palestine in pre-Israel years, Cohen has been
ejected from the Knesset chamber for interrupting Menachem Begin's
speeches. "It's not that I can't control myself," she explains. "I don't
want to."

Asia and Latin America

Chen Muhua became a deputy prime minister of the People's Republic of
China in 1979.

Violeta Barrios de Chamorro became in June 1979 a member of the provisional junta that governed Nicaragua after the expulsion of dictatorial

President Anastasio Somoza. Her husband, a newspaper editor opposed to the Somoza regime, had been assassinated a year and a half earlier. Violeta de Chamorro was forty-nine years old and the mother of four when she was named to the junta.

SIXTEEN INTERNATIONAL WOMEN

———————————— ✹ ————————————

From its earliest days women have been involved in the work of the United Nations. Some of them are listed here, along with women who have taken prominent places in other international assemblies and conferences.

Eleanor Roosevelt,♀ appointed by President Harry Truman as a delegate to the San Francisco Conference of 1945 which drafted the United Nations Charter. Roosevelt also served as a U.S. delegate to the United Nations from 1946 to 1953 and was reappointed in 1961 by President John F. Kennedy. In 1946 she chaired the Commission on Human Rights.

Wanda G. Grabinska, a director of one of the UN's earliest activities, the operation of relocation camps for displaced persons in the U.S. zone of occupied Germany, as an official of the United Nations Relief and Rehabilitation Administration. A native of Poland, Grabinska had been the first woman judge in that country and a delegate to the League of Nations. After emigrating to the United States in 1947, she served as a consultant to the United Nations Economic and Social Council.

Alva Reiner Myrdal of Sweden, a noted sociologist and principal director of the United Nations Department of Social Affairs in 1949–1950; later her nation's ambassador to India; minister for disarmament and for church affairs; a member of the Swedish delegation to the United Nations; and head of her country's delegation to the Geneva disarmament talks.

Vijaya Lakshmi Pandit of India, head of her nation's delegations to the United Nations from 1946 to 1951 and, in September 1953, the first woman to be elected president of the United Nations General Assembly. Sister of Jawaharlal Nehru, Pandit had also served as the first woman member of the Indian cabinet (1937), as governor of Maharashtra province, and in ambassadorial capacities.

Angie Brooks of Liberia, the second woman president of the General Assembly, 1969–1970. Brooks was also the first woman in her country to become a lawyer, a founder of its first law school, and the first Liberian woman to become a cabinet member.

Jeanne Martin Cissé of Guinea, the first woman president of the UN Security Council, in 1972. Cissé also held many positions in her country, including first vice-president of the Guinea National Assembly.

Helvi Linnea Sipila of Finland, a member of her nation's delegation to the General Assembly from 1966 to 1971, assistant secretary-general for Social Development and Humanitarian Affairs in 1973, and secretary-general for the International Women's Year in 1974; she also chaired the UN Commission on the Status of Women.

Mary Lord, U.S. representative to the United Nations Commission on Human Rights from 1953 to 1961.

Marietta Tree, a United States representative to the United Nations Commission on Human Rights, 1961–1964; delegate to the UN's Trusteeship Council with the rank of ambassador, 1964–1965; and on the staff of the secretary-general, 1966–1967.

Rita F. Hauser, U.S. representative to the United Nations Commission on Human Rights, 1969–1972.

Elizabeth Duncan Koontz, U.S. representative to the Commission on the Status of Women since 1969. Koontz was also director of the Women's Bureau, U.S. Department of Labor, 1969–1973.

Princess Ashraf Pahlavi of Iran, several times head of her country's delegation to the United Nations, and chair of the Commission on the Status of Women and the Commission on Human Rights.

Gloria L. Scott, assistant undersecretary of the Ministry of Development in her native Jamaica before becoming a senior adviser in the Department of International Economic and Social Affairs of the United Nations.

Nguyen Thi Binh, minister of foreign affairs of the Provisional Revolutionary Government (the National Liberation Front) of the Republic (Communist) of South Vietnam, recipient of the International Lenin Prize in 1968, and representative of her government at the Paris Peace Conference in 1973. In 1976 Binh became Vietnam's minister of education.

Simone Veil, elected the leading delegate from France to the new European Assembly in 1979—the first elected Parliament of the nine Common Market nations—despite never having run for office before. She had, however, been France's health minister for five years and had often been voted France's most popular public official. When the Assembly met, Veil was chosen to be its president.

Louise Weiss, eighty-six years old, gave the principal address at the European Assembly's opening session on July 17, 1979. Weiss had been dean, or senior member, of the previous, appointed-membership, Parliament.

IN AND AROUND POWER IN CHINA

Although generally women were of low status in traditional China—and girl babies were unwanted—China's long history has repeatedly produced women who attained great power. Some have been mentioned elsewhere in this book. Perhaps the first was . . .

Fu Hao, a twelfth-century B.C. "royal consort and lady general," about whom we have known only since 1976. That is when her opulent tomb, measuring 35 by 50 meters (95 by 135 feet) was discovered at Anyang, in Henan province. The intact royal burial contained 44 brass food cauldrons, wine vessels, and other containers, all inscribed with her name; 590 jade pendants, brooches, and other ornaments; 560 bone objects; numerous stone, ivory, and shell carvings, pottery vessels; and nearly 7,000 cowrie shells (used as money). Fu Hao's husband, Wu Ding, had his own tomb.

Modern China's women of power are still the exception rather than the rule, but let no one underestimate the influence once wielded by:

Jiang Xing (Chiang Ching),♀ a Shanghai actress when she met Mao Zedong, whose fourth wife she became in 1939. As Chairman Mao aged, Jiang became increasingly influential, holding the position of deputy director of the Cultural Revolution of 1966, which made her virtually sole arbiter of all music, dance, and theater in the country. In 1969 Jiang became a member of the Politburo, ranking third in the party hierarchy, after her husband and Chou En-lai. After Mao's death in 1976, the Cultural Revolution was reviled and blamed for the nation's lack of economic development and intellectual stagnation. Jiang and several colleagues, now known as the Gang of Four, were imprisoned or placed under house arrest to await trial.

He Zizhen, Mao's third wife, was eighteen years old when they were married in 1928. She had already led a regiment of women in Nanching during the Communist uprising of 1927 and was one of the few women on the 6,000-mile Long March north to Yenan in 1934–1936. During the northern exile, Mao left He for Jiang, and little was heard of her for nearly four decades, although it was rumored that she and Mao had had five daughters and that she was in a mental institution. Then she was resurrected and in 1979 appointed a representative to the Chinese People's Political Consultative Conference.

Yeh Chun was the second of two women in the Politburo or ruling committee of the Communist party in the 1960s. Yeh, the wife of Defense Minister Lin Piao, presumed heir to Mao, is believed to have been killed with her husband in an airplane that crashed under mysterious circumstances in 1971.

Deng Yingquiao (Deng Ying Chao), the widow of former premier Chou En-lai, was, in her late seventies, the only woman member of the Politburo. Deng's revolutionary activities began while she was still in her teens, when she was a leader of a student movement that began in protest against international agreements unfavorable to China.

EVIL IN HIGH PLACES

❧

". . . When she was bad, she was horrid." Here, starting with three ancient Romans, are eight of the most infamous women in history:

Livia Drusilla (Julia Augusta) (58 B.C.–A.D. 29). The beautiful teen-ager was pregnant with her second son when the man who would soon be the emperor Augustus decided he wanted her and forced her to divorce her husband and marry him. She was known to be the power behind Augustus's throne, but in their long marriage they produced no children, leading Livia to push the fortunes of her favorite older son, Tiberius. As the many other males who stood in the way—including even her second son and eventually Augustus himself—literally fell by the wayside, it was whispered that Livia had a way with poisonous plants. No one ever dared to bring charges. Tiberius finally did become emperor, but the event did not meet Livia's expectations: he would not let her be the power behind his throne.

Valeria Messalina (A.D. 25–48). Her marriage to her distant cousin Claudius was arranged by the emperor Caligula as a joke: the bride was fifteen and very beautiful, Claudius fifty and a cripple. After Claudius became emperor, Messalina, seeing herself as a second Livia, assumed governmental powers. Official duties did not keep her sufficiently occupied, however, and her love affairs with men of all social classes were soon the talk of Rome. Men who refused to commit adultery with the wife of their emperor were accused of treason and executed. She finally went too far when she decided to marry another and kill Claudius, installing her new husband as emperor; the Imperial Guard stormed the wedding celebration and hunted her down. Refusing the suicide dagger her mother implored her to use, Messalina cowered in a corner as she was stabbed to death.

Agrippina the Younger♀ (A.D. 15–59), the sister of Caligula, seduced and married the emperor, her uncle Claudius—an incestuous arrangement that was, under some duress, ratified by the Roman Senate. As the emperor's wife she married off Claudius's daughter to her son Nero, only eleven at the time, then she forced Claudius to name Nero as his successor. Meanwhile, she was ordering executions of Claudius's advisers, as well as any women on whom he looked with favor. In A.D. 54 the emperor died, after eating a choice mushroom fed him by his wife. For three years the teen-age Nero ruled with his mother as regent, then struck for independence: he sent her out onto the Bay of Naples in a boat guaranteed to capsize. But after she escaped from the wreck and swam ashore, he found surer methods: he sent his troops to kill her at her country villa.

Wu Chao (Empress Wu)♀ (A.D. 625–705), the concubine of Tang emperor Kao-tsung, strangled her own baby daughter and blamed the emperor's wife, Wang, who was deposed and Wu installed in her place. But Kao-tsung continued to visit Wang, so Wu ordered her rival's hands and feet cut off. Wu became literally the power behind the throne, concealing herself behind a curtain during state audiences and telling Kao-tsung what to do. Officials who opposed her were assigned to distant posts, but usually did not reach their destinations. Any woman the emperor glanced at was invited to dine with the imperial couple—and became fatally ill afterward. Wu and the emperor had four sons, but she was not about to let them inherit the throne. She imprisoned one of her daughters-in-law and starved her to death; a son who protested tasted his parent's hospitality, another was exiled, and a third was forced to commit suicide. After Kao-tsung died in 684, Wu made the youngest son emperor in name only and kept him prisoner in a distant wing of the palace. Finally she became too ill to continue her palace intrigues and on her deathbed was forced to abdicate in favor of her exiled son—who was poisoned by his wife five years later.

Catherine de' Medici♀ (1519–1589). When her ten-year-old son became King Charles IX of France in 1560, Catherine ruled as regent, alternately goading both her militant Catholic kin and the Protestant (Huguenot) opposition to war. As Charles grew older he came under the influence of the Huguenot commander Gaspard de Coligny. On Sunday, August

24, 1572 at Catherine's direction, Coligny was attacked, and the Saint Bartholomew's Day massacre began. In week-long rioting, thousands were killed in Paris and throughout the country. Catherine's renewed power lasted barely two more years. Charles died of tuberculosis in 1574, and her more independent son Henry III was king. Out of power, Catherine continued plotting. She wanted her favorite grandson named heir so that she could be regent once more. The king found himself forced to kill the boy, and Catherine died two weeks later.

Countess Elisabeth Bathory of sixteenth-century Transylvania, desperate to retain her youthful beauty, had her women servants deliver 650 young virgins to her castle torture chamber, where she sank her teeth into their flesh and drank their blood. When four bloodless bodies were carelessly dumped on the ground outside her castle walls, neighboring villagers finally had evidence of what they had suspected all along and reported Bathory to the king. In 1611 her accomplices were tried, found guilty, and executed. But the countess's powerful family intervened, and she was never even tried. Instead, she was imprisoned in a small room whose door and windows were sealed, and died three years later.

Tz'u Hsi⁹ (1834–1908), Dowager Empress of China from 1861 until her death, had entered the palace as an eighteen-year-old concubine. Six years later she was regent, first for her young son and then for her infant nephew. A stern tyrant who went into homicidal rages and enjoyed puffing an opium pipe after work, she was called the "Old Buddha" behind her back. When the emperor tried to institute reforms in 1898, she had him seized and sent into exile, his favorite concubine thrown down a well, and his associates arrested and cut in half at the waist. Then she sent the secret anti-Western society known as the Boxers out to attack foreign embassies in Peking, thus setting off the unsuccessful Boxer Rebellion, but after defeat was forced by the Western powers and Japan to accept their terms.

Ilse Koch (1906–1967), a Berlin secretary, married SS Colonel Karl Koch, commandant of the concentration camp at Buchenwald, in 1937, and soon reports of torture and mass murders were filtering out. But it was disobedience to orders and expense account hanky-panky that concerned the SS in 1943. Colonel Koch was tried, convicted, and executed, but Frau Koch, already known as the Red Witch of Buchenwald, was acquitted. Relieved of her post, she sat out the war and hoped to survive unnoticed, but was brought to trial at Nuremberg in 1947. Pregnant at her trial, she was given a life sentence, later commuted to four years, but in 1950 she was charged in a German court with 45 murders and 135 attempted murders, and given a life sentence once again. Eventually, tiring of imprisonment, she committed suicide.

XXII ❧ *WOMEN OF FAITH*

IF GOD WERE A WOMAN ...

❧

Ishtar,♀ the great mother goddess of the Babylonians and Assyrians, is concerned particularly with fertility, healing, sexuality, and lust.

Isis,♀ the mother goddess of Egypt, was both the sister and wife of Osiris. She ruled the land while he traveled abroad disseminating knowledge of her deeds. Isis protects children, ensures fertility, cures the sick, brings the dead to life, and cares for and protects sailors.

Hsi Wang Mu, "Great Mother Wang,"♀ or the Lady of the Western Heavens, is the essence of Yin or the female principle. She had one son and more than twenty daughters, but their paternity is unknown. The peaches in her garden are female phallic symbols; to eat one is to become immortal. On their fiftieth birthday, Chinese women are particularly attentive to Hsi Wang Mu.

Sarasvati,♀ worshiped by the Aryans of ancient India (1500–500 B.C.), presides over art, music, wisdom, and learning. She invented the Sanskrit language and alphabet, and is "mother" of the Vedas, the ancient Indian scriptures. Sarasvati was immaculately conceived by Brahma, who grew four heads to look for her as she tried to avoid him. His offer to make her mother of all living things, with himself as father, could not be refused, and they lived together for a hundred years. She is always shown with her husband, sometimes seated on a lotus, and usually as a beautiful woman with four arms—her right hands hold out a flower to her husband and a book of palm leaves; her left hands hold a garland and a drum.

Freyja,♀ the Norse deity of youth, love, beauty, and the dead, loved spring, flowers, elves, music, and love songs. When she accompanied her husband, Odin, to the battlefield, she had the right to bring back half the fallen warriors, whom she entertained in the great banquet hall of her mansion in the sky. She was the first of the Valkyries and their supreme commander; her magic robe of falcon plumes enabled her to fly through the air. In ancient German mythology the attributes of Freya are sometimes combined with those of ...

Frigga (also *Frigg* and *Frija*), the Scandinavian deity whose special concern is marriage. She also protected warriors and was known for her wisdom and foresight.

Kali is the Hindu destructive mother goddess who devours the life she has produced. In her other nature she is **Parvati,** the life-giving, nurturing mother. (Kali/Parvati has about ten different personae, most of them assumed to fight off specific demons.) As Kali, she is usually shown spattered with blood, wearing a necklace of human skulls and corpses for earrings. As Parvati, she is usually depicted with four arms, sometimes holding a ladle and a bowl of food, sometimes holding the Indian symbols of death and of immortality to show the duality of life.

Amaterasu Omikami is the principal deity of Japan and the sun goddess as well. The ancestor of the imperial family, she is worshiped especially at the great Shinto shrine at Ise.

Gaea, the most ancient Greek deity, was the first being to develop out of Chaos. She gave birth to the first gods, Uranus (sky) and Pontus (sea), thus creating the universe. She then became the spouse of Uranus and gave birth to the Titans (elder gods), the Cyclopes, and finally to three monsters. From Gaea's offspring all things came, because her soil nourishes all life. She was the original sponsor of the Oracle at Delphi, before handing that chore over to her grandson Apollo. As the guardian of the sanctity of oaths, she is worshiped with the sacrifice of a black ewe. One of Gaea's daughters was . . .

Rhea,♀ also called **Ops.** As the spouse of her brother Cronus she became the mother of all the gods, including . . .

Hera, who in her turn became the wife of her own brother Zeus. Her Roman counterpart, **Juno,** is the special protector of women and marriage, and also the queen of heaven and the goddess of war. A very ancient deity of the Romans was . . .

Cybele, worshiped by the Phrygians as the Great Mother of the Gods (*Magna Deum Mater*). As the goddess of caverns, symbolizing the most primitive condition of earth, Cybele is worshiped on the tops of mountains. Wild beasts attend her, and she is shown on a throne flanked by or in a chariot drawn by two lions, sometimes holding a whip decorated with knucklebones, the symbol of her power. Such whips were carried by her priests, who, flailing shields and swords in a wild dance of worship, would whip themselves into a frenzy and mutilate their own bodies. These distinctive observances were initiated by Cybele's son King Midas (whose later misfortunes had nothing to do with his mother).

PATRON DEITIES OF CHINA

Sao Ch'ing Niang, as the "girl who sweeps the weather clear," is in charge of fine weather. She is sometimes called the "broom goddess" because she lives on the broom star. When there is too much rain, little girls cut paper representations of Sao to hang near the house gates; her help is also invoked to avert drought.

Fu Fei, daughter of the legendary emperor Fu Hsi (who established the institution of marriage), drowned herself in the river Lo and became the patron goddess of streams.

Kuan Yin, the goddess of mercy (whose Japanese counterpart is **Kwannon**), protects women, brings fertility to the barren, rescues shipwrecked sailors, and brings rain. Her image is found and worshiped in both Taoist and Buddhist temples.

T'ai Shan Mu, daughter of the God of the Sacred Mountain, is the patron deity of immortality. She is present at all births, accompanied by the *Lady of Posterity,* the *Lady of Fecundity,* the *Lady Who Brings On Birth,* and the *Lady Who Brings the Child.*

THE WOMEN IN JESUS' LIFE

Mary,? his mother.

Anna, an aging prophet, who blessed the infant Jesus when he was presented at the Temple.

Mary of Magdalene,? whom Jesus cured of her afflictions; she remained faithful to him to the end of his life and was instrumental in establishing belief in his resurrection.

"The other Mary," mother of the apostles James and Joses (Barnabas).

Mary, the wife of Cleophas, who stood by the cross.

Mary, the younger sister of Lazarus, who anointed Jesus' feet.

Martha, the older sister of Lazarus, who served Jesus at dinner.

Joanna, wife of Chuza, a steward of Herod's, a female disciple.

Susanna, one of the women who ministered to Jesus and followed him.

Salome, another follower, who witnessed the crucifixion from a distance.

Salome, mother of the disciples James and John, who was present at the death and burial of Jesus.

Veronica, a Jerusalem woman who allegedly wiped the blood from Jesus' face with her handkerchief while he was being taken to Calvary. It was said that the image of his face remained on the handkerchief, and Veronica was later canonized.

PROSTITUTES WHO BECAME SAINTS

St. Mary Magdalene.? Who was the Magdalene? The Gospels tell us little about the woman who, next to the Virgin Mary, is the most important female in Christian tradition. Before she met Jesus she could have been a high-class courtesan or a relatively unknown streetwalker. Perhaps prostitution was not her main trade after all: some scholars trace the Greek word *Magdalene* to *magdala,* "hairdresser."

St. Mary the Harlot. Raised in the desert by her uncle, a saintly holy man, she entered a brothel after being seduced by a young monk. Her distraught uncle searched for two years and finally found his niece in the lower depths of Alexandria. Disguising himself as a customer, he persuaded her to return to the desert. Mary's prayers of repentance proved miraculous; crowds flocked to her to be cured of illness.

St. Afra. As soon as she abandoned prostitution for Christianity, she became one of the victims of the Diocletian persecutions of the third century. To add insult to injury, her torturers commented repeatedly on her past trade, but Afra remained steadfast to her new-found faith until the end. Her nude exposed body was rescued by her mother and three former prostitutes who were put to death for their act of bravery.

St. Pelagia. The top-ranking courtesan in the city of Antioch was converted by Bishop Nonnus. After her baptism, Pelagia left the city wearing that cleric's clothing. She traveled to Jerusalem, where she presented herself as Pelagius, a eunuch monk who became much admired for his holiness. Her true sex was not revealed until her death, and she was made into a female, rather than a male, saint.

St. Thaïs. Determined to convert the courtesan, a holy abbot paid the rather substantial fee necessary to enter her quarters. He was successful, and Thaïs determined to do penance for her former career. She had herself walled up in a cell in a convent, which had only one small opening for bread and water to pass through. She endured these conditions for three years, at the end of which time she declared herself cleansed of sin.

St. Theodota. After being converted to Christianity, she was so committed to her new faith and life-style that she suffered the most severe tortures rather than recant and became a martyr.

EIGHT APPEARANCES OF THE VIRGIN MARY？

At Guadalupe, Mexico, Juan Diego, an Indian, saw the Virgin four times in 1531 on a hill outside Mexico City. Following instructions he received from her, he told the bishop to build a church there. Originally dedicated in 1709, the church stands today as the Basilica of Our Lady of Guadalupe.

In Paris, France, Mary appeared three times to **Catherine Laboure** in 1830 in the chapel of the motherhouse of the Daughters of Charity of St. Vincent de Paul, Our Lady of the Miraculous Medal.

At La Salette, France, a sorrowing and weeping Virgin appeared to two peasant children on September 19, 1846. She gave them the "secret" of La Salette, a message about world peace.

At Lourdes, France, the fourteen-year-old **Bernadette Soubirous** saw Mary eighteen times between February 11 and July 16, 1858, at the grotto of Massabielle. The Virgin requested that a church be built there. In 1958 the underground chapel of St. Pius X, the second-largest church in the world (capacity: 20,000 worshipers) was consecrated at the site.

At Knock, Ireland, on August 21, 1879, fifteen people saw an apparition of Mary, along with the figures of St. Joseph and St. John the Apostle, near the parish church.

At Fatima, Portugal, the Virgin was seen by three children six times between May 13 and October 13, 1917, in a field north of Lisbon. After a seven-year investigation by the Church, these apparitions were declared worthy of belief.

At Beauraing, Belgium, five children in the garden of a convent school saw

Mary; she appeared thirty-three times between November 29, 1932, and January 3, 1933.

At Banneux, Belgium, the Virgin appeared eight times between January 15 and March 2, 1933, to an eleven-year-old peasant girl, *Mariette Beco,* in a garden behind the family cottage.

From *Catholic Almanac*

WORSHIPED WOMEN

Queen Nefertiti, wife of King Akhnaten (Amenhotep IV) of Eighteenth-Dynasty Egypt, was worshiped as a guardian ancestor of New Kingdom royalty.

Fatima (606?–632), the daughter of Mohammed by his first wife Khadija, became the wife of Ali, the fourth Muslim caliph. One of the titles accorded her, "bright-blooming," implies that she never menstruated. Fatima, who was above all women "pure" (that is, virginal), nevertheless gave birth to three sons who, with her husband and grandsons, became the twelve holy ones who rule the hours of the day. She herself, as their wife/mother/grandmother, is revered in all branches of Islam.

Ayesha (or *Aisha*) ♀ (610?–678), the childless but beloved second wife of Mohammed, saw to the appointment of her father as the second caliph after the Prophet died in 632. When Ali became caliph in 656, Ayesha led a rebellion against him and was taken prisoner. She died at Medina and is revered by all Muslims as the Prophetess and the Mother of Believers.

Wilhelmina, in thirteenth-century Bohemia, declared herself to be an incarnation of the Third Person of the Blessed Trinity and was worshiped by crowds of fanatics.

Doujebamo, now thirty-nine years old, became a Living Buddha in Tibet when she was four. In 1959, when the Chinese forced the Dalai Lama to flee to India, she was carried off with his retinue. They rode until their horses died under them, then continued on foot. When she returned to Tibet four months later, she renounced her position, married, and became a delegate to the National People's Congress.

CHASED, CHASTE, AND SAINTED

Eugenia, daughter of the Duke of Alexandria, dressed as a monk and, concealing her true identity, was so pious that she was appointed abbot. One woman, cured by the "holy father," failed in an attempt to seduce "him." To get revenge, she accused the abbot of adultery, and Eugenia was brought before a judge—none other than her own father, who did not recognize her. She was imprisoned, but called the judge to her and converted him to Christianity. Then she tore open her robe, revealed her secret, and was saved. Her father became a bishop and died a martyr, and the woman who had accused Eugenia, with all her friends and relations, "burnt with fire of Hell." Eugenia, too, died a martyr.

Cecilia, a third-century Roman Christian betrothed to a pagan, had previously consecrated her body to God and refused to consummate the marriage. Her piety led her husband and his brother to convert, but they were martyred, and Cecilia herself sentenced to suffocation in her own bathroom. When this failed, a soldier was sent to behead her, but she survived three blows of the sword and lived on, half dead, for three days. Her house was dedicated as a church, and in 1599 her tomb was opened and the body found excellently preserved. She has become the patron saint of musicians because, it was said, at her wedding feast she sang in her heart to the Lord.

Catherine, of fourth-century Alexandria, refused to marry the emperor because she had promised herself to Christ. Fifty philosophers were called in to persuade her that Christianity was in error, but Catherine converted them all, and she was condemned to death by torture. Her body was strapped to a huge spiked wheel that kept turning, but the machine broke, injuring onlookers and giving us the term "Catherine wheel" as a synonym for a somersault. She was finally beheaded—but milk, not blood, flowed from her severed veins, and her body was transported by angels to Mount Sinai.

Winefride, a maiden living in seventh-century Wales, was seen and loved by a young prince who attempted to seduce her. When she rebuffed his advances, he flew into a rage, chased her through the town, and finally cut off her head. A fountain of fresh waters gushed forth where her head fell to the ground, and the town has been known as Holywell since that day. Her uncle, a saint, brought her back to life so that she could become a nun, and she became abbess of a Holywell nunnery. Winefride's fountain's waters were credited with curing the sick until they were diverted by mining construction in 1917. Pilgrims still visit what is now the best-preserved medieval pilgrimage center in Britain.

Wulfhilda was brought up in an English abbey near the end of the tenth century and was preparing to take her vows when she was seen by King Edgar. He would not take no for an answer and pursued her to another abbey, where she was forced to escape through the drainage system. When the king saw her among the altars and relics of the dead in the sanctuary of her own abbey, he at last gave in, made her an abbess, and took her willing cousin Wulftrudis to the royal bed instead. One day Edgar visited his lost love with a royal retinue; finding that she did not have enough refreshment, Wulfhilda performed a small miracle and there was plenty of wassail to go around.

Catherine of Genoa, in the fifteenth century, was married when only sixteen to a bad-tempered, spendthrift, and lustful man. Although he was seldom with her for the first five years of their marriage, she was so pious that she succeeded in converting him. They moved from their ostentatious home to a small house and agreed to live together chastely, devoting their energies and remaining fortune to the care of the sick in a local hospital.

Kateri Tekakwitha was born in 1656 in what is now Auriesville, New York, to a Mohawk chief and a captured Algonquin woman. While growing up, she met Roman Catholic missionaries and, despite fierce opposition, converted at the age of twenty, taking a vow of virginity. Drunken men were sent to molest her, braves threatened her with tomahawks, and children pelted her with stones. Finally she fled to a small settlement on the St. Lawrence River, where she died in 1680, "a model of prayer." According to reports, upon her death, the ravages of childhood smallpox disappeared and her face became "fresh, radiant, and incredibly beautiful." Three hundred years later, on June 22, 1980, she was beatified by the Church. If canonized, she would become the first "first American" to be so honored.

Cornelia Peacock Connelly, a native of Philadelphia, married Episcopalian minister Pierce Connelly but became interested in Catholicism and led her husband to convert in 1835. When he decided to enter the priesthood, he needed a deed of separation from his wife and her agreement to enter a convent, which, although she had three children, she granted. Cornelia Connelly entered a convent in Rome in 1844, Pierce Connelly was ordained in 1845; and two years later Cornelia took her vows. She established an order of teaching nuns in England and became the first superior of the Society of the Holy Child Jesus. But—Father Connelly changed his mind. First he tried to gain control of her order. Then he left the Church and brought suit for restoration of his conjugal rights. When the judgment went against him, he spent the rest of his life harassing Cornelia in public and private. She, however, managed to ignore him, devoted her energies to expanding her order, and died in 1879. In 1959 she was proposed for beatification.

ALL IN ORDER

Clara of Assisi ran away from an arranged marriage in 1212 to follow in the footsteps of St. Francis of Assisi. She founded the Poor Clares, an order dedicated to poverty and penitential prayer.

Colette Boillet, a former recluse, founded the Colettine Poor Clares in 1408 because she thought the original Poor Clares were not sufficiently unworldly.

Birgitta Persson started the Brigittine Order in Sweden in the fourteenth century.

Angela Merici began, in her late fifties, to organize a group of young women to do charitable works and teach. Her order, the Ursulines, founded in the early 1530s, was one of the first women's orders to leave the cloister for the outside world.

Virginia Bracelli founded the Daughters of Our Lady of Mount Calvary, later known as the Brignoline Order, in the late sixteenth century. Her order took its name from a convent where she housed orphaned girls and trained them to care for the sick. Her students showed so much skill during an epidemic that they were recognized as a nursing order, albeit one that cared only for female patients.

Mary Ward, a lay sister at a convent in England, founded the Roman Catholic Institute of the Blessed Virgin Mary to ensure the religious education of girls.

Louise de Marillac founded the Daughters of Charity, a congregation devoted mainly to nursing, in 1633. Its members alternated between their convent community in Paris and serving among the general populace.

Jeanne de Chantal, with St. Francis de Sales, initiated the Visitation Order in the first decade of the seventeenth century, which combined a cloistered life with the tending of the sick in the outside community.

Elizabeth Ann Seton was born in New York City in 1774 and widowed before she was thirty. Her conversion to Roman Catholicism estranged her from her Protestant family, and she had to open a school to support her five young children. A few years later, invited by Bishop John Carroll of Baltimore, she opened the first Catholic free school in Maryland, then founded St. Joseph's College for Women. Gradually a community of women grew around her, to become the first American congregation of Daughters (or Sisters) of Charity. With Seton as mother superior, the order grew to twenty communities before her death in 1821. She was beatified in 1963 and canonized in 1974, the first native-born American to become a saint.

Constance Cerioli, after her husband died, devoted herself and his fortune to the care of poor orphans. In 1857, three years after she was widowed, she took her vows as Sister Paula Elizabeth, a few months later founded the Sisters of the Holy Family, then founded the Brothers of the Holy Family to care for male orphans.

Francesca Cabrini, born in Italy, was sent to the United States with six other nuns by Pope Leo XIII to minister to Italian immigrants in the 1870s. "Mother" Cabrini founded the congregation of the Missionary Sisters of the Sacred Heart in America, established schools and hospitals in North and South America, and was granted American citizenship in recognition of her works. She died in 1917, was beatified in 1938, and in 1946 became the first American citizen to be canonized.

FRIENDLY PERSUADERS

The Quakers, with their insistence on the spiritual equality of men and women, were the first religious sect to defy the ancient edict against women speaking in church. In fact, the Quaker doctrine of the "inner light" encouraged women to share whatever divine inspiration was vouchsafed to them. Many early Quaker preachers and leaders were women; in the seventeenth century, to follow their calling took courage and perseverance.

Elizabeth Hooton, the first convert to Quakerism, was imprisoned repeatedly in England for speaking out against the evils of the day. In 1661 she and *Joan Broksopp* set sail, intending to preach in the Massachusetts Bay Colony. Authorities there, however, so feared the Quakers that ship captains were forbidden to deliver them to Boston; thus the two women were taken to Virginia. Although both were well past middle age, they set out on foot for New England. There Hooton, with royal authorization, tried to buy land in Boston, but was turned down and imprisoned. She was tied to the tail of a cart and forced to walk to the whipping posts of Cambridge, Watertown, and Dedham, in each place being stripped to the waist and lashed with a three-corded whip. Finally she was abandoned in the wilderness, but survived, to go on a mission to Jamaica, where she died peacefully of natural causes.

Mary Fisher and *Elizabeth Williams* in 1653 went to Cambridge, England, where they "discoursed about the things of God" with theological students. Their audacity so enraged the mayor that he had them publicly scourged at the Market Cross. Undaunted, Fisher sailed for the West Indies, then felt the call to preach to Sultan Mohammed IV of Turkey. She got as far as Smyrna when the British consul, fearing for her life, had her put on a ship bound for Venice. She persuaded the captain to deposit her on the coast of Greece and proceeded on foot through Macedonia and the mountains of Thrace to the potentate's camp. The sultan was impressed by Fisher but declined to convert. Refusing his offer of an armed escort, she returned to England as she had come—alone.

Barbara Blaugdone, a schoolteacher, was persecuted by the Bristol authorities for speaking out in church. Her pupils were taken away, and she was imprisoned for three months, beaten, and sent out of town with a band of gypsies. As soon as she could, Blaugdone ran away from the gypsy camp, returned to Bristol, and continued preaching.

Loveday Hambly refused to pay tithes despite pressure from local authorities. In 1662 she was imprisoned under such deplorable conditions that she fell ill; her livestock were confiscated; and she was forced, at age sixty, to ride on a "poore bad horse" which almost tossed her to her death. But she never did pay the tithes.

Margaret Fell♀ was the organizing mother of Quakerism. From her estate, Swarthmore Hall, she kept track of traveling Quaker missionaries, making sure their routes did not overlap; with her daughter Sarah she handled most of the sect's finances. Fearlessly she wrote letters to authorities condemning unjust laws. In 1666 she published *Women's Speaking, Justified, Proved and Allowed of by the Scriptures,* arguing for women's equal place in religious life.

Mary Coffin Starbuck was helping her husband in his general store in Nantucket, Massachusetts, in 1701, when she became attracted to the Society of Friends. Starbuck gained fame for her knowledge and interpretation of Scripture, and preached Quakerism until her death in 1717.

Jane Fenn Hoskins felt called to Pennsylvania from London by a 1719 vision; a second vision called the shy woman to preach Quakerism. Summoning up her courage, Hoskins traveled through the southern colonies and Barbados, and recorded her adventures in an autobiography, *A Life of the Faithful Servant of Christ* by "A Minister of the Gospel, among the People called Quakers."

FOUNDERS OF FAITH

❧

Selina Hastings, Countess of Huntingdon (1707–1791), founded a nonconformist Calvinist Methodist sect known as the Countess of Huntingdon's Connexion. The daughter of an earl, she married the Earl of Huntingdon when she was in her teens. After his death in 1746 she established chapels in fashionable resort towns throughout England and as a peeress of the realm appointed her own ministers. In 1768 she established a training college for ministers and in 1781 reluctantly agreed to the separation of the Connexion, which had great appeal to the upper classes, from the Church of England.

Barbara Ruckle Heck was the founder of Methodism in North America. She had been converted by John Wesley in 1753 and gathered her first congregation of four at the home of a reluctant cousin in New York. Her prayers were answered, and the cousin became a convert; the small group grew into the first Methodist church in the colonies. A Tory sympathizer, Heck went to Canada during the American Revolution and there founded the Canadian Methodist church.

Ann Lee ♀ (1736–1784) joined the "Shaking Quakers" in England, then had a vision in which she represented the second coming of Christ. After that she was hailed as the sect's leader, called "Ann the Word" or "Mother Ann." With eight followers she came to America in 1774 and two years later founded the first of her celibate, hard-working communities of Shakers near Albany, New York.

Omiki-san Nakayama (1798–1887), founder of Tenri Kyo, one of the major sects of Shinto, was married at twelve to a farmer, gave birth to six children while in her early twenties, and when she was thirty became convinced that the god Tenri had taken possession of her body. Despite opposition in her village on the island of Honshu, the sect grew, aided by reports of healing performed by "Grandmother Miki" and by her writings, which became the scriptures of the sect. Similar in concept to Christian Science, Tenri Kyo holds that "the root of suffering and sickness is in the mind" and that those who succeed in dispelling the "eight dusts" live to a ripe old age—as did Nakayama.

Mary Anne Girling (1827–1886) founded the English Shaker group known as Children of God. In 1864 she claimed to have received the stigmata, announced that God had been newly and finally reincarnated in her, and founded a religious community. Neighbors protested their "naked dancing," and the community died out after Girling died of cancer.

Helena Petrovna Blavatsky (1831–1891), born in Russia to a German family, claimed to have been inducted into occult mysteries during seven years in Tibet. She founded the Theosophical (divine wisdom) Society in the United States in 1875 and three years later left for India, where she established her headquarters near Madras. Convinced that she communicated with spirits, she persuaded numerous disciples as well. In a trance she wrote esoteric books that became scriptures for the faithful, who honor Blavatsky on White Lotus Day, the anniversary of her death on May 8. Believers strive to form a universal human brotherhood; encourage the study of comparative religions, philosophies, and sciences; and investigate the laws of nature and the latent powers of human beings. One of her followers was . . .

Annie Wood Besant (1847–1933), president of the Theosophical Society from 1907, who brought new life into the movement when she turned up in England in the winter of 1926–1927 with a young male protégé whom she announced to be the new messiah.

Mary Baker Eddy ♀ (1821–1910) was sickly as a child and often ill as an adult. In 1866, after a fall on the ice, she took to bed with the Scriptures. Three days later, free of pain, she arose, ready to spread the word of the healing power of faith and mental concentration. In 1875 she published her plan for a church, two years later married a disciple (her third husband), and in 1879 founded the Church of Christ Scientist. Eddy herself planned and supervised every aspect of the church's growth and in 1908 founded the *Christian Science Monitor,* a newspaper still highly respected for its journalistic quality. By the time she died there were 420 Science congregations.

Ellen Gould White (1827–1915) converted to Adventism, which preached the imminent coming of Christ, when she was fifteen, then had a vision in which she became a messenger of God. Two years later she married Adventist minister James White and with him founded an offshoot sect, the Seventh-Day Adventists, which rapidly surpassed the parent sect in appeal, advocating nonmedical health care, "correct" diet—no coffee, tea, alcohol, or drugs—observance of a Saturday sabbath, and belief in the literal meaning of the Old Testament.

Catherine Mumford Booth ♀ (1829–1890), wife of William Booth and with him, in 1878, a founder of the Salvation Army, was a popular leader of revival services. Thousands attended her meetings, attracted by the advertising slogan "Come and Hear a Woman Preach." Her belief that sacraments were not necessary for salvation was the basis of the Army's theology. The Booths started by preaching on east London street corners to idle men, whose attention they attracted with brass bands and dancing, and created a movement that spread throughout the world by the end of the century.

WHERE THE MINISTERS ARE

- Women make up 4 percent of the Christian clergy in those denominations that ordain women, according to the National Council of Churches.
- In 1976 women accounted for 40 percent of the enrollment at the nation's theological schools.
- The number of women studying for the ministry in 1978 was more than double that in 1970. And in 1978 there were 10,470 female clergy as compared to 6,314 in 1970.
- One of every three Reform rabbis ordained in 1979 was a woman, reports the Union of American Hebrew Congregations. By 1980 almost half of the rabbinic students at the Hebrew Union College–Jewish Institute of Religion in New York were women, and fifteen women cantors had been invested after completing studies at HUC–JIR's School of Sacred Music.
- There are about 150 women priests in the Episcopal (Anglican) churches of the United States, Canada, New Zealand, and Hong Kong.
- A recent Gallup poll found that 54 percent of Catholics under the age of thirty favored the ordination of women priests. Overall, the percentage of Catholics endorsing women's ordination rose from 30 percent in 1974 to 41 percent in 1977.

FIRSTS IN THE PULPIT

❧

Antoinette Brown Blackwell was the first American woman to be ordained. A graduate of Oberlin College, she became a Congregationalist minister in 1853 in South Butler, New York. Many years later she earned a Doctor of Divinity degree.

Olympia Brown,♀ ordained in Malone, New York, became the first woman Universalist minister in 1863.

Phoebe A. Hanaford♀ became a Universalist minister in 1868, the first woman ordained in New England. "Truth knows no sex, . . ." she argued. "The soul may be helped by truth, whether proclaimed by man or woman. . . ." Hanaford was also the first woman to act as chaplain for a state legislature (Connecticut).

Maggie Newton Van Cott in 1869 became the first woman licensed to preach in the Methodist Episcopal church.

Anna Howard Shaw♀ was the first woman ordained by the Methodist church, and also the first woman minister of any denomination to preach in England, Germany, Denmark, Holland, and Sweden. She was turned down when she asked permission to preach in Norway. Shaw went on to earn a medical degree as well and was a leader of the suffrage movement.

Sister Kathleen Cannon, the chaplain at Connecticut's Albertus Magnus College, became, in 1974, the first Catholic woman preacher.

Marjorie S. Matthews became, in July 1980, the first female bishop in the United States and the first woman named to the ruling hierarchy of an American church body. The Reverend Matthews, sixty-four years old, has a Ph.D. in humanities and was an auto-parts manufacturing executive in Michigan before entering her second career in the United Methodist church.

ALMOST A RABBI

❧

Ray Frank traveled up and down the Pacific coast in the 1890s preaching before Jewish groups and inspiring the founding of many congregations. Turning down several positions as "spiritual leader," she went to Cincinnati in 1893 to study at the Hebrew Union College and completed one semester. Newspapers erroneously reported that she had been ordained a Reform rabbi, but Frank needed no certification, she said, as long as she had proved that women were capable of doing the job.

Lily H. Montagu, one of the founders of the Jewish Religious Union (1902) in England and later a magistrate, scored a number of firsts for Jewish women in the pulpit. In 1918 she preached a sermon at London's Liberal Jewish Synagogue, becoming the first Jewish woman to be formally recognized as a "lay minister"; and, by speaking in 1928 at the Reform Synagogue in Berlin, she became the first woman to occupy a rabbinic pulpit in Germany.

Martha Neumark, a student at the Hebrew Union College in Cincinnati, petitioned the faculty in 1919 to be allowed to lead High Holy Day Services. Her request, eventually granted, raised the larger issue of whether women should be ordained. There was considerable feeling in favor of this, but the final decision of the board of the college was negative. Neumark, foiled in her ambition to become "America's first woman rabbi," was consoled by the first "Certificate of Sunday School Superintendentship" issued by the newly founded Hebrew Union College School of Teachers in New York.

Regina Jonas finished studies for the rabbinate at the Berlin Academy for the Science of Judaism in the late 1930s. When ordination was denied, Rabbi Max Dienemann of Offenbach privately gave her a Hebrew rabbinic diploma. She worked briefly at her profession before perishing at the Theresienstadt concentration camp in the early 1940s.

Helen Hadassah Levinthal completed the entire rabbinic course at the Jewish Institute of Religion, a progressive rabbinic seminary (later merged with Hebrew Union College), in 1939, but the faculty refused to ordain a woman. Instead she was awarded a Master of Hebrew Literature degree and a certificate stating that she had completed the curriculum. With the recent ordination of women by Reform Judaism, Levinthal's family requested that she be awarded the title posthumously, but no action has as yet been taken on their petition.

Paula Ackerman of Meridian, Mississippi, was the first woman spiritual leader of a Jewish congregation in the United States. Following the death of her rabbi husband in 1950, she succeeded him at Reform congregation Beth Israel from 1951 to 1954 until an ordained rabbi was found to replace her. Wrote Ackerman, "If I can just plant a seed for the Jewish woman's larger participation, if perhaps it will open a way for women students to train for congregational leadership, then my life would have some meaning."

MY DAUGHTER, THE RABBI

Sally J. Priesand, the first woman rabbi, ordained in 1972. She served as associate rabbi of the Stephen S. Wise Free Synagogue in New York City until resigning in 1979 and has cochaired a task force on women in the rabbinate. Priesand is now spiritual leader of Temple Beth-El, Elizabeth, New Jersey.

Sandy Sasso, the first woman rabbi ordained in Reconstructionist Judaism, 1974. She married a classmate, Dennis Sasso, and they became the first rabbinic couple. Her first congregation was the Manhattan Reconstructionist Havurah, for which she continued to officiate while pregnant and even while nursing her infant son. In 1977 the Sassos were chosen to share a pulpit at the large Indianapolis congregation Beth El Zedeck.

Laura J. Geller, ordained in 1976, director of the Hillel Foundation Center at the University of Southern California.

Karen L. Fox, ordained in 1978, director of the New Jersey–West Hudson Valley Council of the Union of American Hebrew Congregations.

Rosalind A. Gold, ordained in 1978, assistant rabbi of Temple B'rith Kedesh, Rochester, New York.

Deborah R. Prinz, ordained in 1978, assistant rabbi, Central Synagogue, New York City, and married to a rabbi.

Myra Soifer, ordained in 1978, assistant rabbi, Temple Sinai, New Orleans.

Linda Joy Holtzman, ordained in 1979 by the Reconstructionist Rabbinical College. She became the only woman presiding rabbi in the United States when she was chosen from thirty applicants by Beth Israel, Coatesville, Pennsylvania.

Debra R. Hachen, ordained in 1980 at Hebrew Union College–Jewish Institute of Religion. She may be the first rabbi's daughter to become a rabbi. Her great-grandfather was also a rabbi. They, too, were ordained at Hebrew Union College.

The ordination of women rabbis has grown rapidly. By 1980 more than twenty women had been ordained at the Reform movement's HUC–JIR in New York, and several more at the Reconstructionist Rabbinical College of Philadelphia and at the Leo Baeck College in London. Despite growing pressure, however, and notwithstanding that the two Reconstructionist women rabbis were serving Conservative congregations, the Conservative branch of Judaism has not ordained women as yet.

THREE CANTORS

Barbara Ostfeld, invested in 1975, was the first woman to become a cantor in the United States. A mezzo-soprano, she attended the School of Sacred Music of Hebrew Union College–Jewish Institute of Religion and now sings at Temple Beth-El, Great Neck, New York. She is secretary of the American Conference of Cantors and the only woman on its executive board.

Helene Reps, a brilliant mezzo-soprano, was invested in 1979 and is cantor at Temple Israel in New Rochelle, New York. Reps was in her mid-forties when she began studying at the School of Sacred Music.

Sarah Sager, a soprano, was invested in 1979. She is married to Rabbi Stuart Gertman, with whom she serves at Fairmount Temple in Cleveland, as the first husband-and-wife rabbi-cantor team anywhere.

Contributed by Cantor Jeff Klepper, Temple Beth-El, Chappaqua, New York

WHO BLEW THE SHOFAR?

The ritual production of buglelike notes from a ram's horn is a distinctive part of services for the Jewish High Holy Days. Several candidates for First Female Shofar Blower surfaced in the fall of 1978:

Mrs. Samuel Globe of Temple Israel, Columbus, Ohio, the only member of the congregation who could get a blast instead of a squeak out of the instrument, began blowing in 1977.

Judith Gruber had begun blowing the shofar for children's and adult services at New York's East End Temple twenty years earlier, but after a few years she was superseded by her sister **Barbara Gruber,** who continues the practice. The Gruber sisters are granddaughters of the famous cantor Jossele Rosenblatt, who taught their father, who taught them.

Judith Kopperman of Congregation Or Ami, Lafayette Hills, Pennsylvania, began blowing the shofar at adult services in 1977 when she was fifteen years old. Her career as a shofar blower began at children's services even before she was bat mitzvah.

Naomi Rabin is one of several young women who have been blowing the shofar at Temple Sinai in Chevy Chase, Maryland, for the past few years.

Z. Willard Finberg of St. Paul, Minnesota, had been blowing the shofar for fifty years by 1978. Finberg was the founder of the first shofar-blowing dynasty—two daughters and seven grandchildren. One of her daughters began blowing the shofar when she was only ten and now performs for an Aspen, Colorado, congregation.

GROUPING FOR CONVERTS

In a burst of religious fervor women became the driving force behind much of the missionary work launched from America in the late nineteenth century. By 1882 sixteen women's missionary societies had raised almost $6 million and sent 694 single women missionaries abroad. Eight years later the same groups were supporting 856 women missionaries and 96 doctors in numerous schools, hospitals, and orphanages in all corners of the globe.

The women's groups behind the missionary women were:

Woman's Board of Missions (Congregational), founded 1868.

Woman's Foreign Missionary Society (Methodist Episcopal), founded 1869.

Woman's Foreign Missionary Societies of the Presbyterian Church, U.S.A., founded 1870.

Woman's Auxiliary (Protestant Episcopal), founded 1871.

Woman's Baptist Foreign Missionary Society, founded 1873.

Woman's Parent Mite Missionary Society of the African Methodist Episcopal Church, founded 1874.

Christian Woman's Board of Missions (Disciples), founded 1874.

Woman's Board of Foreign Missions of the Reformed Church in America, founded 1875.

Woman's American Baptist Home Missionary Society, founded 1877.

Woman's Executive Committee for Home Missions (Presbyterian), founded 1878.

Woman's Board of Foreign Missions (Methodist Episcopal Church South), founded 1878.

Woman's Missionary Society of the Evangelical Lutheran Church, founded 1879.

Congregational Women's Home Missionary Association, founded 1880.
Woman's Home Missionary Society (Methodist Episcopal), founded 1884.
Woman's Missionary Union, auxiliary to the Southern Baptist Convention, founded 1888.
Woman's Auxiliary, Presbyterian Church in the U.S., founded 1912.

From Rosemary Reuther and Eleanor McLaughlin, *Women of Spirit: Female Leadership in the Jewish and Christian Tradition* (New York: Simon & Schuster, 1979)

SEVEN CHURCHES THAT ORDAIN WOMEN

United Methodist Church
United Presbyterian Church
United Church of Christ
The Episcopal Church
The Lutheran Church in America
The American Lutheran Church
The Southern Baptist Convention

IN PRIESTLY GARB

More than one hundred women have become priests since the U.S. Episcopal church approved female ordination in September 1976. Even earlier, though, several women—the so-called "Philadelphia eleven"—were ordained by liberation-minded bishops in July 1974:

Jeannette Piccard♀ was seventy-nine years old at the time of her ordination. She had wanted to be an Episcopal priest since she was eleven; when she entered Bryn Mawr in 1914, she was asked what she wanted to do after graduation and replied, "Something impossible . . . to be a priest of the Episcopal church." In the 1960s she wrote a church law allowing women to become lay readers on an equal basis with men. At seventy-seven she enrolled in a theological seminary. On the eve of her ordination as a priest, her bishop asked her not to go through with it, but she defied him.

Suzanne Hiatt had been the first woman ordained as a deacon, in 1971. Recently the Episcopal Diocese of Minnesota put her name in nomination for bishop.

Alla Bozarth-Campbell wrote about the experience in her autobiography, *Womanpriest* (1978).

Carter Heyward had wanted to be a priest since she was six years old. "The God I believe in is calling women to the full ministry right now. You don't respond to God by saying, 'Well, okay, but I'll wait until everybody's ready for it.' "

Merrill Bittner, Alison Cheek, Emily Hewitt, Marie Moorefield, Betty Bone Scheiss, Katrina Swanson, and *Nancy Constantine Hatch Wittig* were also ordained in Philadelphia in 1974.

Other notable ordinations:

Ellen Marie Barrett was ordained by Bishop Paul Moore, Jr., at the Church of the Holy Apostles in New York City in 1977, despite protests over her avowed lesbianism.

Jacqueline Means, the first woman priest to be officially recognized by the church, was ordained in Indianapolis in 1977 at the age of forty.

Beverly Messenger-Harris, the first female rector in the U.S. Episcopal church, was unanimously chosen by Gethsemane Episcopal Church in upstate New York. Her husband is a Presbyterian minister.

Pauli Murray,♀ a black lawyer and civil rights activist, was ordained in 1977.

Patricia Park, ordained in 1977, is married to a priest.

Daphne Parker Hawkes, ordained in January 1977, became the first female Episcopal priest in the diocese of New Jersey. Her four children, ages six through thirteen, assisted in the ceremony.

Carol Anderson, ordained in 1977 and the first female priest in the Episcopal Diocese of New York, was first associate rector at St. James Episcopal Church, then became the first female rector in New York with her appointment to All Angels Episcopal Church in 1979.

SIX FAITH HEALERS

❧

Aimee Semple McPherson,♀ founder of Los Angeles's International Church of the Four-square Gospel, combined religion with show biz in the 1920s and preached to the largest congregation in the world. Her brand of fundamentalism included divine healing, often dispensed in an atmosphere of theatrical effects, bright lights, and music. Followers of the glamorous Sister Aimee were so loyal that they tended to overlook her three marriages, numerous lawsuits, and other misadventures.

Linda Martel, probably the youngest faith healer on record, reportedly alleviated the sufferings of hundreds of residents of the Channel Islands before she died in 1961 at the age of five in her home on the Isle of Guernsey. Martel was a toddling two-year-old when she performed her first cure, relieving her father of a severe migraine headache with the touch of her hand.

Normita de la Cruz grew up in the small Mexican town of Agua Dulce, spent more time at religious devotions than in play with other children, and believed that St. Lazarus had given her the power to heal. When she cured a gypsy's two-year-old son of epilepsy, her fame began to spread. Prosperity came to the small town as crowds waiting to see Normita filled hotel rooms, created traffic jams, and gave residents the hope that they might soon dwell in another Lourdes. Normita held all-night sessions with the sick in her small home, sleeping only when overcome with exhaustion. Eventually the crowds created health problems, several people died while waiting to see the young healer, and there were fights among those waiting to gain entry to her house. In January 1970, when she was thirteen, she and her family, perhaps overwhelmed by controversy and confusion, mysteriously abandoned their home. But hucksters in Agua Dulce continue to sell bottles of Normita's "healing oil."

Kathryn Kuhlman, perhaps the most revered charismatic healer today, embarked on an evangelistic career as a school dropout at fourteen and soon realized that she had psychic healing power. Today thousands claim to have been made well by her. Kuhlman says she is in an altered state of consciousness when she heals and is not aware of what she says or whom she treats. Once in Los Angeles, fifty marines came to hear her preach. As Kuhlman laid her hand on the first, all fifty fell to the ground—a sign of her enormous power. Her ministry, now institutionalized in the humanitarian Kathryn Kuhlman Foundation, is heard on some 150 radio stations.

Ruth Stapleton Carter is a practitioner of "inner healing," a therapy-oriented form of faith cure. Carter believes that psychic pain can be helped by a combination of prayer and the reliving of troublesome past experiences. She has conducted healing and teaching missions all over the world—but became best known when her brother Jimmy was elected president in 1976.

Dzhuna Davitashvili, a former waitress from Soviet Georgia, charges 250 rubles—$350—for a healing seance. Aided by a "biological force field," she is said to have brought health to the ailing Leonid Brezhnev and other Soviet government officials, including the minister of public health. Davitashvili, who also treats film stars, writers, and dissidents, says, "For me, there are no good people and no bad people, only people who are well and people who are sick." Patients who have to wait for hours to be treated in public clinics gladly line up for hours in front of her apartment building.

ou Henry Hoover was the first woman to
aduate from Stanford University in ge-
ogy. *Library of Congress.* (THE WORKING
VES OF TEN PRESIDENTS' WIVES)

Jeannette Rankin, America's first congresswoman.
Sophia Smith Collection, Smith College. (TEN CON-
GRESSIONAL FIRSTS)

A bust in the state capitol honors
Miriam ("Ma") Ferguson, elected
governor of Texas in 1924. *Texas
Highways Magazine.* (FIVE GOVER-
NORS)

(*Above*): Catherine Mumford Booth, with her husband, William, founded the Salvation Army. (FOUNDERS OF FAITH)
(*Below*): Olympia Brown, one of the earliest women ministers in the United States. *Library of Congress.* (FIRSTS IN THE PULPIT)

(*Above left*): Charlotte (Lottie) Dod, the youngest winner ever at Wimbledon (1887). (RACQUET-BEARERS)
(*Above right*): Gertrude Ederle, first woman to swim the English Channel, in uncharacteristic attire—sans bathing suit. *Photo by Mitchell, N.Y., New York Public Library Picture Collection.* (SWIMMING THE DISTANCE)

(*Above left*): Under the name of Fanny Fern, Sarah Payson Willis Parton wrote one of the first etiquette columns for women. *Sophia Smith Collection, Smith College.* (AND WHAT THEY ADVISED)
(*Above right*): Master spy Mata Hari, some years before she faced a firing squad. *Dance Collection, New York Public Library at Lincoln Center.* (PARTING REMARKS: WHAT THEY SAID BEFORE THEY DIED)

Esther Hobart Morris, Wyoming suffragist, is one of four women honored in Statuary Hall of the U.S. Capitol. *Library of Congress.* (CAPITOL WOMEN)

The recipients of Radcliffe College's first honorary degrees (1978) pose with Radcliffe president Matina Horner (left, foreground). *Radcliffe College.* (OUTSTANDING—TEN WOMEN WHO RECEIVED RADCLIFFE COLLEGE'S FIRST HONORARY DEGREES)

XXIII ❧ GAMES WOMEN PLAY

SEVEN MYTHS ABOUT WOMEN ATHLETES
❧

- Women are less competitive and aggressive than men.
- Contact sports harm women's reproductive organs and breasts.
- Women cannot regain physical prowess after childbirth.
- Women cannot attain peak athletic performance during menstruation.
- Weight lifting builds large muscles in women.
- Competition in contact sports is not feminine.
- Men are inherently better athletes than women.

From Marc Leepson, "Women in Sports," *Editorial Research Reports,* May 6, 1977

FOUR DEMYTHOLOGIZERS: MEN WHO STUDIED WOMEN ATHLETES
❧

W. A. Pfeiffer in 1950 studied twenty-four Olympic women athletes and found that their athletic performances frequently were better after childbirth than before, and that they had easier deliveries than nonathletic women.

G. J. Erdelyi in 1962 surveyed 729 women athletes and found that none was prevented by menstruation from participating in her chosen sport.

Jack Wilmore, who chaired the Physical Education Department at the University of Arizona, compared leg strength of women and men in a ten-week weight-training program in the mid-1970s. He found that the women came within 25 percent of the men in leg strength; when the figures were adjusted in proportion to body weight, the male-female leg-strength difference was an insignificant 7 percent.

K. F. Dyer compared the performances of female and male track athletes of fifteen countries in the mid-1970s. He found that women performed best where women and men had equal athletic opportunities, often coming within 10 percent of the track achievements of their male counterparts. Female swimmers did even better, coming within 6 percent of the male performances.

HAVING AN IMPACT ON SPORT

❧

Skarda, a giant Scandinavian deity, is known as the goddess of ski in the northern countries of Europe and may be said to be responsible for that sport, since it is dedicated to her. Skarda's influence is ancient; the oldest pair of skis in the world, at the Djugarden Museum in Stockholm is at least 4,000, and perhaps as much as 5,000, years old.

Mary, Queen of Scots ♀ was the first woman golfer. Her enthusiasm for the Scotch game increased its popularity, and St. Andrew's golf course was founded during her reign (1552). Mary, who had lived in France, called the young men who chased her balls *"cadets,"* the French term at that time for students, and this evolved into the still-used *caddy.*

Queen Elizabeth I ♀ of England issued a proclamation in 1572 that "no foteball play be used or suffered within the city of London and the liberties thereof upon pain of imprisonment." Elizabeth, like other monarchs, was annoyed with the early version of soccer because it attracted crowds and hooliganism, and diverted the common people from the important business of learning archery. Elizabeth's edict had a dampening effect on soccer, but couldn't suppress it. Fans continued to take their chances against Queen Bess's law, and as late as 1779 one John Wonkell was sent to prison for a week and ordered to do penance in church for playing the game on Sunday.

Queen Anne ♀ of England, a horse-racing enthusiast, gets the credit for originating sweepstakes racing for a cash award. In 1703 Her Majesty put up a silver plate, worth about $20 at the time, as the prize in the big race at Doncaster. By 1710 she had donated a gold cup, valued at $300, and established rules for the competition. In 1714 the queen raised the prize money on her cup to $500 but required the owners of the starters to contribute 10 guineas ($50) each, winner take all—the beginning of cash prizes. Star, the queen's own horse, fittingly won history's first money race. Anne was also responsible for standardizing the breeding of horses, a hit-or-miss proposition until that time.

Mary Ewing Outerbridge of Staten Island, New York, was delighted with lawn tennis when she saw it played in Bermuda, and sailed home from her 1874 vacation with balls, racquets, rules, and a determination to introduce the game to this country. Customs officials confiscated the equipment for a week while considering what tax, if any, should be levied on the strange objects, but finally admitted them duty free. Outerbridge set up a tennis court on the edge of the cricket field at the Staten Island Cricket and Baseball Club, and there her brothers popularized the game among their friends. Some men held back because a woman had introduced the sport, but the thrill of the game overcame their misgivings and soon it was being played in the society centers of New York, Newport, Boston, and Philadelphia.

Constance M. K. Applebee of the British College of Physical Education came to the United States in 1901 to study anthropometry (measurement of the human body). While debating the merits of British versus American female athletes, she demonstrated one of her enthusiasms, women's field hockey, in a concrete courtyard outside the Harvard gymnasium.

The sport, then unknown in this country, appealed to ***Harriet I. Ballintine,*** director of physical education at Vassar. At her request, Applebee taught it there and later at Wellesley, Smith, Mount Holyoke, and Bryn Mawr. Soon field hockey was a staple at girls' prep schools and colleges, and in 1922 the U.S. Field Hockey Association was founded.

Katherine Peckett of New Hampshire introduced alpine skiing to the United States in the early 1930s, when she hired four Austrian ski instructors to work at her winter resort, according to newscaster Lowell Thomas. Thomas and his son were in the first group of students, and their public enthusiasm quickly contributed to the growth of the sport.

OH, BABE!

Mildred ("Babe") Didrikson Zaharias ♀ (1914–1956) belongs on so many women's sports lists that she deserves a list of her own. She set more records, won more medals, and dominated more tournaments than any other athlete of the twentieth century, male or female. She was, simply, a giant.

- While still in high school, she was named All-American forward for her contribution to the Golden Cyclones, an outstanding girls' basketball team (1930). Later in her career she would tour the country as the only woman on the Babe Didrikson All-American Basketball Team.
- In track and field she set eight records for the South, three for the nation as a whole, and captured nineteen medals and seventeen loving cups. She established the Southern Amateur Athletic Union record for every track and field event she entered in the early 1930s. In 1932, all by herself, she totaled 30 points to win the pre-Olympic National Women's Track and Field Championship; the entire twenty-two-member Illinois track team trailed her for second place.
- In the 1932 Summer Olympics she won two gold medals and one silver, and established three world records—for high jump, 5 feet 5¼ inches (tied with Jean Shiley); for the 80-meter hurdles, 11.7 seconds; and for the javelin throw, 143 feet 4 inches.
- Golf attracted Didrikson because she had "done everything else." She won every golf title from 1940 to 1950, including the world and national opens, won seventeen amateur victories in a row in 1946 and 1947, turned pro and suffered only one tournament defeat in seven years. After cancer surgery in 1953 she triumphed in the Women's National Open.
- She was unanimously named Woman Athlete of the Year in a poll of Associated Press sportswriters in 1945.
- There wasn't a sport she tried at which she didn't excel. She trained as a boxer before switching to golf. She was one of the country's best field place kickers. She could throw a baseball as far as many outfielders and set the women's record for a throw—296 feet. She was a top-flight diver and lacrosse player, although she never competed professionally in either of these sports. And she went on tour as a member of the National Exhibition Billiards Team.

TOPS AT MID-CENTURY

❧

In 1950 the Associated Press asked sports experts in the United States to choose the greatest athletes of the first half of the twentieth century. On their "woman's list," in order of rank, the greatest female athletes:

1. *Mildred ("Babe") Didrikson Zaharias*♀ (golf, track)
2. *Helen Wills Moody*♀ (tennis)
3. *Stella Walsh* (track and field)
4. *Fanny Blankers-Koen*♀ (track)
5. *Gertrude Ederle*♀ (swimming)
6. *Suzanne Lenglen*♀ (tennis)
7. *Alice Marble*♀ (tennis)
8. *Ann Curtis* (swimming)
9. *Sonja Henie*♀ (figure skating)
10. *Helen Stephens* (track and field)
11. *Eleanor Holm*♀ (swimming)
12. *Patty Berg*♀ (golf)
13. *Helene Madison* (swimming)
14. *Glenna Collett Vare*♀ (golf)
15. *Mary K. Browne* (golf, tennis)
16. *Eleonora Sears* (hiking, tennis, squash racquets)
17. *Helen Jacobs*♀ (tennis)
18. *Louise Suggs* (golf)
19. *Joyce Wethered* (golf)
20. *Zoe Ann Olsen* (swimming)
21. *Barbara Ann Scott* (figure skating)
22. *Mildred Burke* (wrestling)

RIDING IN THE MONEY

❧

Ever since "man" learned to ride, women have been enthusiastic about horses. But when it came to professional horse racing, they remained on the periphery. For young men, the route from stable hand to jockey was long established. But girls who worked around stables—and there were many—had no place to go until the late 1960s, when the first women were finally licensed as professional jockeys.

Alicia Meynell Thornton was a prominent rider in England at the beginning of the nineteenth century. On August 25, 1804, a match took place between her and Captain William Flint, with stakes of 1,000 pounds for a four-mile course and odds of six to four in her favor. Thornton was a sensation in a skin-tight dress of imitation leopard, and the crowd was outraged when Flint won, apparently as a result of unscrupulous tactics. Thornton's next match was with a Mr. Bromhead, for four hogsheads of Burgundy and 2,000 guineas forfeit. Bromhead failed to appear and Thornton won, cantering over the course alone. Her most triumphant race was with jockey Frank Buckle. Every inch of the five-

mile course was hotly contested, but she emerged triumphant by half a
neck. Her attire was again splendiferous, a "purple cap and waistcoat,
long nankeen, purple shoes and embroidered stockings."

Ada Evans Dean entered her horse in races at Liberty, New York, in 1906
and learned, at the last minute, that her jockey could not ride. Dean
rushed to Liberty and rode her own horse in the race. She won and,
flushed with success, competed again, winning the last event by the skin
of her mount's teeth. A jubilant Dean told incredulous reporters that
she had never participated in a horse race before.

Mary Money claimed to have won twenty-eight races and fourteen silver
cups in various American towns near the turn of the century.

Judy Johnson finished tenth of eleven in a steeplechase event at Pimlico,
Baltimore, Maryland, on Lone Gallant, April 27, 1943.

Kathy Kusner became the first licensed female jockey in the United States in
1968.

Barbara Jo Rubin won by a neck riding Cohesion at Charles Town, West
Virginia, on February 22, 1969, to become the first woman jockey to
ride a winner. She was also the first woman to win a major track race, at
Aqueduct on Brave Galaxy, a first-time starter. Rubin had her own
starting problems, as male jockeys boycotted the first race in which she
was scheduled; but they came around fast enough after being fined
$100 apiece.

Diane Crump became a professional jockey in 1969 and broke the sex barrier
at Hialeah on February 7, 1976.

Meriel Tufnell rode the winner in the first race to include women under English Jockey Club rules, in the Goya Stakes at Kempton Park, May
1972.

Anna-Marie la Ponche of France became the first woman to race against
male professional jockeys on the Continent in March 1974.

Robyn Smith, riding professionally since 1969, was the first woman to race at
a major track, Saratoga, in 1970, and the first to win a major stakes victory, March 1, 1973, winning $27,450 in the Paumanauk Handicap at
Aqueduct riding North Sea. Smith has placed in the money 44 percent
of her times up. Even so, she rides much less frequently than her male
counterparts, in 1976 competing in about 250 races while the top male
jockeys rode four times as often. But there is no question about her addiction: on June 24, 1980, the thirty-eight-year-old Smith was racing,
even though it was the day after her marriage to film star and racing enthusiast Fred Astaire.

Mary Bacon♀ became a professional jockey in 1969 and has ridden more
than 300 winners. The 5-foot-4-inch rider has broken her back twice,
raced with her collarbone taped, and been on the critical list three
times. In 1974 she was listed as one of the top ten jockeys at Aqueduct,
and the Sports Writers Association has honored her as the "Most
Courageous Athlete of the Year." One day Bacon rode in three consecutive races, then went to the hospital, where she gave birth to her
daughter.

Joan Phipps won the first all-female daily double in New York, with Mary
Bacon at Aqueduct.

Bea Farber is a harness driver who lives in Brighton, Michigan. At thirty-
seven, she has driven more than 3,000 races, broken four track records,

and won nearly $1.5 million in 1978 alone. In that year, too, she was th first woman to be listed in harness racing's top ten—for driving at leas 300 times in a year.

Marina Lezcano began riding in Argentina as a *jocketta* in 1976 and tw years later rode a chestnut colt named Telescopio to the winner's circl in four of the nation's racing classics. She became the first woman an second jockey to triumph in all four contests in one year. Lezcano, wh started racing professionally when she was seventeen years old, begar training when she was a child, cajoling her father into entering her ir local bareback races. "It was wrong," he recalls. "On the other hand she usually won and it was very profitable."

Karen Rogers, 5 feet 1 inch and 95 pounds, has been called "the female Steve Cauthen," but it seems likely that from now on young jockeys will be compared with Rogers, who has been riding since she was three and go her jockey's license at sixteen. On September 20, 1979, her seventeenth birthday, she rode three winners at the New Jersey Meadowlands, by the end of the season was the fourth leading jockey at that track, and had won ten races at Aqueduct to become the leading apprentice and the leading female rider in the United States, earning $584,769 for her horses' owners. On January 31, 1980, riding two long shots, she won the daily double at Aqueduct—the first woman to carry off this feat. A back injury felled her shortly afterward, but only temporarily.

FILLIES AT THE FINISH

Regret won the Kentucky Derby in a field of sixteen by two lengths, in 1915, the first filly to do so. She had won three races in fourteen days as a two-year-old the year before. Regret also won at Saratoga in her only other race that year, took one of two starts the following year and three of four starts at five years old before retiring. Her Derby purse was $11,450.

Ruffian, a three-year-old filly, had tied or broken records in eight of her ten starts, when a match race was proposed between her and Kentucky Derby winner Foolish Pleasure at Belmont on July 6, 1975. Ruffian was ahead, with Foolish Pleasure moving in close behind, when both leading jockeys heard a snapping noise; the bones in the filly's right foreleg had shattered as she ran. Veterinarians worked through the night to save her, but in vain; her pain was ended the following morning.

Davona Dale was the best three-year-old filly of 1979, in that year sweeping both the "old" and the "new" versions of the Triple Crown for fillies. (The "old" was Kentucky Oaks at Churchill Downs, the Black-Eyed Susan at Pimlico, and the Coaching Club at Belmont; the "new" was the Acorn, Mother Goose, and Oaks, all at Belmont.) She was only the fifth filly to take a triple and the first to take both old and new. Davona Dale is from Calumet Farm, owner also of *Our Mims,* the best filly of 1977, and *Twilight Tear,* the first filly to be named Horse of the Year in 1944.

Genuine Risk, by Exclusive Native out of Virtuous, won the Kentucky

Derby on May 3, 1980, beating out ten colts and two geldings, and paying $28.60 for $2, the first filly in 65 years to win. Only thirty fillies had ever run in the 103-year history of the classic for three-year-old thoroughbreds, and Genuine Risk was the first filly to enter the Derby since C. V. Whitney's *Silver Spoon* finished fifth in 1959. Her Derby purse was $250,550. She continued to make history as the only filly ever to enter all three races of the Triple Crown, coming in a close second to Codex in the Preakness and another close second to Temperence Hill in the Belmont Stakes.

Genuine Risk was the first filly to enter the Preakness since 1939, when *Ciencia* got mired in mud to finish sixth and last. Before then, forty-nine fillies had entered the race, and four had won: *Flocarline,* 1903; *Whimsical,* 1906; *Rhine Maiden,* 1915; and *Nellie Morse,* 1924.

UPLIFTING WOMEN

Josephine Schauer Blatt is credited in the *Guinness Book of Women's Sports Records* with the greatest lift ever made by a woman—3,564 pounds with a hip and harness. Blatt was twenty-six years old when she made the lift on April 15, 1875, at the Bijou Theatre in Hoboken, New Jersey.

Katie Brumbach Sandwina, a professional strong woman with the John Ringling's circuses in the early 1900s, was famous for carrying a 600-pound cannon on her back and executing the entire sequence of commands in the manual of arms using a 160-pound Maxim machine gun instead of a rifle. Sandwina was 6 feet 1 inch and weighed 210 pounds.

Jane de Vesley, according to the *Guinness Book of World Records,* lifted 392 pounds in a two-handed lift in Paris on October 14, 1926.

Florence Rogers, although she'd never trained, miraculously lifted one end of a 3,600-pound car, twenty-nine times her own weight of 132 pounds, in Tampa, Florida, in 1960. She had a good incentive—the car had fallen on her young son when a jack gave way.

Cindy Reinhoudt, of Fredonia, New York, holds the record for the bench press, 210.8 pounds. A track competitor, she took up lifting at the urging of her husband, Don, world superheavyweight power-lift champion. In February 1976, at a men's meet in Erie, Pennsylvania, Reinhoudt became the first woman to move into class 3 (an intermediate category) of the Amateur Athletic Union's power-lifting classification.

Jan Suffolk Todd, a Canadian farmer and high school teacher, is the strongest woman in the world today. In a power-lifting contest in Newfoundland in June 1976 she raised a total of 1,041.8 pounds: 424.4 pounds in a squat, 176.4 in the bench press, and 441 in the dead lift. This was 100 pounds more than any woman had ever lifted before, and two of the three lifts are world's records.

Shirley Patterson, the manager of a North Hollywood health club, is one of the strongest women in the United States. She can dead-lift 225 pounds from the floor, squat down and up again with 180 pounds on her shoulders, and bench-press 125 pounds over her head. Patterson's height of 5 feet 2 inches, weight of 112 pounds, and age, forty-plus years, prove that perseverance and training, rather than body build, determine success in weight lifting.

Rebecca Joubert, competing for the University of Tennessee at Chattanooga, won a men's 132-pound power lift at the Chattanooga open with a bench press of 135 pounds. She has set four American power-lifting records.

Kathy Schmidt, an Olympic javelin thrower, uses lifting to improve her muscle control but does not compete in weight-lifting contests. Schmidt, who is 6 feet 1 inch and weighs 175 pounds, can dead-lift 400 pounds. Like other uplifting women, she believes the sport expands her body's capabilities. "I love to lift. . . . It makes me feel good—healthier and stronger—and I can see my body taking a different shape."

COME OUT FIGHTING

In 1975 women were licensed to box by the athletic commissions of only six states. By 1978, forty-three states allowed women to fight professionally. Still, according to one estimate, only about a dozen women box professionally in the United States today. Some female practitioners of the fine art:

Elizabeth Wilkinson and *Hannah Hyfield* nearly participated in a boxing match for 3 guineas ($15) in England in June 1722; their contest would have been the first between women on record. Wilkinson publicly challenged Hyfield after having angry words with her, but the fight never came off because the police judged that it would violate public decency.

Caroline Svendsen and *Jean Lange* were the opponents in the first U.S. women's professional boxing bout, held in Virginia City, Nevada, in 1976. It took Svendsen, a thirty-four-year-old grandmother, fifty seconds to knock out Lange.

Marion Bermudez became, at the age of twenty-three, the first United States woman to take part in the formerly all-male Golden Gloves boxing tournament held in Mexico City in 1975. Bermudez was the winner in her first match even though she had had only seven practice rounds the week before. She has also competed successfully against men in karate.

Jackie ("Tonowanda") Garret claims to have knocked out thirteen opponents in the ring. She has also served as a bodyguard to Muhammad Ali.

Marian ("Tyger") Tremiar boxes wearing black velvet shorts and a bare midriff; her head is shaved. Tremiar, who claimed fifteen wins to two losses in 1978, would like to see more women enter the boxing lists. "Girls shouldn't be so passive," she says. "They should start getting strong and protecting themselves early."

Cathy Ann ("Cat") Davis, a blond drama student from New Orleans, unbeaten in sixteen fights with fifteen knockouts, claims to be the lightweight champion of women's boxing. In 1976 the New York State boxing commissioner ripped her application for a license to pieces. Cat sued the commission, and the New York State Supreme Court ruled in her favor. As a result, in September 1978, Tremiar, Garret, and Davis received licenses in the state. "I'm not a feminist," Cat Davis said. "I believe everybody should be liberated. It's just something I wanted to do. I wouldn't be a fighter if I gave up."

Gwen Hibbler is licensed to box in four states.

Pat Pineda was the first woman licensed to fight professionally in California.

Carol Polis was licensed in 1974 as the first woman boxing judge in the United States. She officiates primarily in New York.

Eva Shane was the first woman to judge a heavyweight championship fight. The fifteen-round bout was between Muhammad Ali and Earnie Shavers, the year was 1977, and the place was New York.

COURT STYLE

The first women tennis players appeared on the courts in garden party attire: flouncy floor-length dresses with high necks and cinched waists worn over corsets and petticoats. A large floppy hat completed the immobilizing costume. But as women became serious about their game, concessions to comfort were made. The first innovation was black, flat, rubber-soled shoes. Other changes followed:

May Sutton,♀ the first non-English Wimbledon champion, caused consternation in 1905 when she rolled up her shirt-sleeves because she was "too hot"—the first recorded instance of a woman player putting performance ahead of propriety. Corsets, however, continued to be *de rigueur. Elizabeth Ryan,*♀ a major Wimbledon title holder, recalls that in 1914 the ladies' dressing room there was equipped with a rail on which the garments could be hung to dry. "It was not a pretty sight," she notes, "as many of them were bloodstained from the wounds they had inflicted."

Suzanne Lenglen♀ appeared on the courts in 1919 in the one-piece calf-length short-sleeved tennis dress that became her uniform. Worn without corsets or petticoats, the outfit was described as "shocking"—but it matched the mood of the coming Jazz Age, and other tennis players quickly picked up the style. In that outfit Lenglen won fifteen Wimbledon titles, losing only six sets in ninety-four matches in the next eight years. In 1920 she introduced the "Lenglen Bandeau," two yards of brightly colored silk swathed around her bobbed hair. Like the one-piece dress, it caught on.

Helen Wills Moody♀ had always worn a white eyeshade while playing tennis. When she wore it at Wimbledon in the late 1920s, tennis players around the world aped the style.

Lili de Alvarez in 1929 introduced a "divided skirt," actually pagodalike culottes, that failed to be trend setting.

Billie Tapscott caused a wave of criticism in 1929 by playing at Wimbledon without stockings. Instead she wore socks, a sensible measure soon followed by most players.

Eileen Bennett and *Betty Nuthall* became the first to wear tennis dresses with plunging backs, in 1930.

Helen Hull Jacobs♀ was the first woman to wear shorts (on the longish side) in a major tournament at Forest Hills, New York, in 1933. She went on to become a commander in the navy and a writer of fiction and books about tennis.

Alice Marble♀ wore the shortest tennis shorts yet before an international audience at Wimbledon in 1933. The first reaction was shock; then practicality took over and everyone was soon wearing shorts or short skirts.

Gussie Moran created another Wimbledon fashion scandal in 1949 when her lace-edged panties were clearly visible under her brief tennis skirt. Moran herself did not invent the costume; that honor belonged to Ted Tinling, a dress designer and tennis fan who had been put in charge of "player liaison" by the Wimbledon committee. A yard of lace led to his dismissal.

Billie Jean King,♀ wanting to be a real standout at her Houston "male chauvinist" match with Bobby Riggs in 1973, wore a mint green polyester knit tennis dress with a sky blue collar decorated with a band of rhinestones and green sequins.

RACQUET BEARERS

Some of the following should probably be better remembered than they are:

Margot, a young French woman of the fifteenth century, was the first woman known to have played tennis—and she played it spectacularly. She apparently came to Paris from the region of Hainaut in 1427 when she was twenty-eight or thirty years old. A contemporary account records that she "played very strongly both forehanded and backhanded, very cunningly, very cleverly, as any man could, and there were very few men whom she did not beat, except the very best players."

May Langrishe in 1879 was the first women's tennis champion, winning the women's singles at the Irish Open Championship, the first open to include a women's competition. Wimbledon did not allow women to compete until 1884; Langrishe won the women's singles there in 1891.

Ellen Forde Hansell became the 1887 equivalent of the first U.S. national women's singles champion, despite having to play in the cumbersome full-length costume of the day. Hansell was also a musician.

Charlotte ("Lottie") Dod was fifteen years and nine months old in 1887 when she won at Wimbledon, the youngest ever or since. She repeated her triumph in the following year and again in 1891, 1892, and 1893. Dod also triumphed at ice skating, hockey, and tobogganing; was British ladies' golf champion in 1904; and won an Olympic silver medal for archery in 1908.

May Sutton,♀ who grew up in California, won the U.S. women's championship in 1904 at age sixteen, the youngest ever to do so. In 1905 she returned to her native England and became the first player from the United States to win at Wimbledon. In a match at Forest Hills in 1930, Sutton suffered a fracture of the left leg and dislocated her right elbow. She asked for a crutch and, holding her racquet in her left hand, went grandly down to defeat rather than default.

Hazel Hotchkiss Wightman, U.S. women's champion from 1909 to 1911 and again in 1919, and winner of forty-three tennis titles altogether, inaugurated the Wightman Cup competition with her husband, George, in 1923. The cup is the prize in an ongoing competition between teams of American and British women tennis players.

Elizabeth Ryan,♀ a top American player, ironically became the last women's singles champion of Imperial Russia in 1914. With the fires of war and revolution spreading, the game died out in that country even as it continued to grow in popularity everywhere else.

Anita Lizana of Chile was the first South American, male or female, to become one of the world's top ten tennis players, in 1938.

Simone Mathieu was the leading woman tennis player in France in the decade before the start of the Second World War, playing more than a thousand matches and debuting on the international scene in 1929 when she was twenty years old and the mother of two sons. She had another distinction as well: during the war she led the women's division of the Free French forces, was condemned to death but never executed by the government of occupied France, and later received the Legion of Honor and other awards from her grateful country. Mathieu died in early 1980.

Althea Gibson♀ (b. 1927) won the National Negro Girls Championships in the 1940s, went to Florida A & M on an athletic scholarship, and became in 1950 the first black to play in the U.S. nationals at Forest Hills. She debuted at Wimbledon the following year and in both 1957 and 1958 took the Wimbledon singles and doubles and the U.S. Tennis Association singles. She later played exhibition tennis on tour with the Harlem Globetrotters.

Kathleen Horvath of New York State became the youngest player in the United States National Tennis Open in 1979. She won three qualifying matches—the fourteen-, sixteen-, and twenty-one-and-under championships—in three days, one on her fourteenth birthday, before advancing to the championship matches. Horvath, who had started playing when she was eight years old, slipped up only on the eighteen-and-under championship, which was won that year by *Andrea Jaeger* of Lincolnshire, Illinois, another fourteen-year-old.

ALLISON DANZIG'S LIST OF ALL-TIME TOP-RANKING WOMEN TENNIS PLAYERS

Danzig, tennis reporter for the *New York Times* from 1923 to 1968, is a former president of the Lawn Tennis Writers' Association of America and a member of the U.S. National Lawn Tennis Hall of Fame. In the *Encyclopedia of Tennis* (1974) he selected his all-time top tennis women. Here they are, with our annotations:

Tied for number 1:

Suzanne Lenglen♀ (1899–1938), in eight years as an amateur (1919–1926), was beaten only once in singles and that because she was ill. In 1926 at Wimbledon, a scheduling mix-up caused her to keep Queen Mary♀ waiting in the royal box; Her Majesty's frosty response reduced the high-strung Lenglen to hysterics, caused her to withdraw from the tournament and, shortly thereafter, turn pro.

Helen Wills Moody ♀ (b. 1905) won the Wimbledon singles eight times out of nine and, in 1927–1932, did not lose a single set in singles competition anywhere.

3. *Maureen ("Little Mo") Connolly Brinker* (1934–1969) was the first woman to win the Grand Slam—four major championships in one year (Wimbledon, United States, France, and Australia)—in 1953. Only sixteen when she won her first U.S. championship, at seventeen she triumphed at Wimbledon in her first attempt there. Connolly was still under twenty when a horseback-riding accident caused a leg injury that ended her tennis career.

4. *Alice Marble* ♀ (b. 1913), triple champion (singles, doubles, and mixed doubles) at Wimbledon in 1939, adapted aggressive male playing techniques to women's tennis, including a ruthless serve-volley. Her innovations set a new pattern for women that was followed by the post–World War II champions.

5. *Helen Hull Jacobs* ♀ (b. 1908), among other accomplishments, won the U.S. championship four years in a row.

6. *Margaret Smith Court* (b. 1942) of Australia was the second woman to win the Grand Slam; she also won every other title of every important competition. From 1960 to the end of 1972, when she captured the Australian singles for the eleventh time, she scored eighty-five major tennis triumphs.

7. *Billie Jean King* ♀ (b. 1943) was the first woman since Connolly to win the women's Wimbledon title for three years in a row and has also chalked up the most Wimbledon titles ever: nineteen. Her demands for equal pay and recognition for women athletes brought women's tennis into the forefront of sports popularity.

8. *Maria Bueno* (b. 1939) was a legend in her native Brazil by the age of fourteen, even before her Wimbledon triumphs of 1959 and 1960, after which she was honored by a statue in her hometown of São Paulo and a postage stamp. She won 585 tournaments in a career that was halted, but only temporarily, by severe tendinitis in her right arm. Today Bueno is again on the tournament circuit.

9. *Molla Mallory* (1892–1959), among other accomplishments, won the U.S. championship seven times between 1915 and 1926.

10. *A. Louise Brough (Clapp)* (b. 1923), in the late 1940s and 1950s, won four Wimbledon singles and five doubles championships, was runner-up three times, and won the U.S. title once. She also won twelve U.S. doubles championships between 1942 and 1957.

AND SOME MORE RECENT ADDITIONS

Evonne Goolagong Cawley (b. 1951), the daughter of an Australian sheepherder, was discovered as a child and coached by tennis experts in her native Australia. She came to world notice by beating Margaret Court ♀ at Wimbledon when she was eighteen, and a year later won not only Wimbledon, but several other tournaments as well. Goolagong took a few months off to have a baby in 1977 and returned to the courts to win the Australian Open in 1978—and Wimbledon again in 1980.

Christine ("Chris") Evert Lloyd (b. 1954), with an unmatched record of 118 victories on clay courts, five U.S. Open championships, and two Wimbledon singles titles, has chalked up more wins than losses against every major woman tennis player today. Her earnings, $454,486 in 1978 alone, total in the millions. In 1976 *Sports Illustrated* named her "Sportsman [*sic*] of the Year," the first time a woman was so honored (Billie Jean King♀ had shared the title four years earlier).

Martina Navratilova (b. 1957) was born into a tennis-playing family in Czechoslovakia and in 1975 came to Forest Hills and defected; she now lives in Texas. In 1976 she and Chris Evert were doubles champions at Wimbledon. Navratilova then went on to win the Wimbledon singles championship in 1978 and again in 1979.

THREE UMPS

Bernice Gera was the first woman to umpire a professional baseball game, in 1972. After she changed her mind about a play during her first game, she got so much flak from managers, players, and fans that she decided to quit.

Christine Wren called 'em for four years in the late 1970s for the Class A Northwest League. Wren herself was playing for a Yakima, Washington, team, the Webcats, in 1970, when she disagreed with a call the ump made on her, figured she could do at least as well, and got accepted at a professional umpire school in California.

Pamela Postema is presently judging games in the Florida State League.

PLAY BALL!

Jackie Mitchell was the first woman pitcher in the history of professional baseball, in 1931. Playing for Chattanooga, she struck out Babe Ruth her second day on the team. No fooling—it was April 2.

Joan Whitney Payson was the long-time president of the New York Mets, presiding over the team's World Series win in 1969. After Payson died in 1975, her daughter . . .

Lorinda de Roulet took over until the club was sold in early 1980.

"Blazin' " Bertha Tickey has pitched for Amateur Softball Association teams for more than twenty-three years and is the only player to have taken part in eleven national championship contests. She pitched a record for strike-outs in a single game, twenty in seven innings in 1950. Tickey holds other records, too: most perfect games, three, in 1950, 1954, 1968; most national tournament wins, sixty-nine in nineteen national tournaments; most consecutive strike-outs, eleven in 1968.

Joan Joyce (b. 1940) was thirteen when she joined the Raybestos Brakettes, an amateur softball team, pitched the team to its first National Women's Major Fast Pitch Championship with a no-hitter in 1958, and won for them again in 1959, 1960, 1963, 1966, 1967, 1968, and

1971–1975. In 1975 Joyce was a founder, with Billie Jean King? and sports promoter Dennis Murphy, of the International Women's Professional Softball Association and helped win its first World Series the following year, pitching for the Connecticut Falcons. She can hit, too: her batting average with the Brakettes was .327. In 1961 she broke Tickey's strike-out record, pitching forty in an eighteen-inning game. Joyce holds world championship records for most strike-outs, seventy-six in 1974, and most perfect games in one year, two in 1974.

Lanny Moss became, in 1974, the first and only woman to manage a pro baseball team when she was signed by the minor league Portland Mavericks.

Crystal Fields, eleven years old, was, in July 1979, the first girl ever to win the Pitch, Hit, and Run championship in preliminary events to the Little League All-Star Game, coming in ahead of seven boys in the nine-to-twelve age group. "The boys kept laughing at me when I showed up for the Pitch, Hit, and Run competitions," said the all-star shortstop and outfielder from Cumberland, Maryland, who was five feet tall and weighed ninety pounds. She showed 'em. Girls were officially admitted to the Little League in 1974.

THROUGH THE HOOP

❧

Theresa Shank Grentz played for Immaculata College, Philadelphia, from 1972 to 1974. Known as the "Female Bill Walton," the 5-foot-11-inch Grentz was the leading player of her day and led her team to three national titles. She now coaches at Rutgers.

Ann Meyers was unsuccessful in a 1979 attempt to become the first woman to play in the National Basketball Association, but got $50,000 for a three-day tryout with the Indiana Pacers anyway. A four-time all-American from UCLA, Meyers signed a three-year $130,000 contract with the New Jersey Gems of the new Women's Professional Basketball League (WPBL) in November 1979.

Rita Easterling, 5 feet 7 inches tall, a guard for the Chicago Hustle, was named Most Valuable Player in the first (1979) season of the WPBL.

Althea Gwyn of the New York Stars was, at 6 feet 4 inches, the tallest player in the Women's Professional Basketball League's first all-star game in 1979. The league planned the game in only three weeks; the players' jerseys did not arrive until shortly before the game, and the playing floor had to be hastily borrowed from the United States Military Academy at West Point. Yet nearly 3,000 spectators applauded the players at New York's Felt Forum.

Janet Karvonen, a Minnesota high school senior with a perfect 4.0 grade average, National Honor Society member, class valedictorian, and homecoming queen, was the hottest recruit of 1980, averaging thirty-three points and eleven rebounds a game. Karvonen, 6 feet tall, decided to join the Lady Monarchs of Old Dominion University. One reason:

Nancy Lieberman, 5 feet 10 inches tall, who led the Old Dominion Lady Monarchs to a thirty-four and one record in 1979 and became the

WPBL's top draft choice in 1980. While contract negotiations with the Dallas-Diamonds hovered around $100,000, she became the first and only woman player ever to participate in the New York Pro Summer League, an informal league that boasts such NBA stars as Nate Archibald and Marvin Barnes. Lieberman held her own, scoring ten points in one game, seven points and five assists in another. Says Archibald, "She's not a woman out there, she's a player." Other Lieberman records: still in high school, she was the youngest person on the 1976 Olympic squad, and she was the first woman basketball player to have a basketball autographed with her name placed on the market, by Spaulding.

TEEING OFF

❧

Mrs. John G. Reid played the first golf mixed foursome in the United States with her golf promoter husband, Carrie Low, and John B. Upham on March 30, 1889. Mrs. Reid and Upham won the match by 1 1/2 holes.

Dorothy Campbell Hurd (1883–1945), the dominant figure in women's golf during the early years of the century, was the first to win both the British Women's Amateur (1909, 1911) and the United States Golf Association's Women's Amateur championships (1909, 1910, 1924).

Harriot Curtis (1881–1974) was the USGA women's champ in 1906, but lost the title in 1907 to her sister **Margaret Curtis** (1883–1965), who held on to it in 1911 and 1912 as well. In May 1932 the Curtis sisters presented the Curtis Cup for competitions between British and American golf teams, a hotly contested rivalry ever since.

Glenna Collett Vare ♀ (b. 1903), the greatest woman golfer of the 1920s and 1930s, won forty-nine amateur championships in eighteen years and was unrivaled until women began to play professionally after World War II. For all her silver trophies, Vare earned not a sou at her beloved game, of which she still gets in a few rounds every week.

Helen Hicks (1911–1974), a member of the first Curtis Cup team in 1932, defeated Vare for the USGA Women's Championship in 1931, then turned pro in the spring of 1934, the first woman golfer of note to do so.

Patricia Jane ("Patty") Berg (b. 1918) triumphed in more than eighty-three tournaments, forty-one of them as a member of the Ladies' Professional Golf Association, which she helped to found in 1946. Berg was the leading money winner on the women's pro golf tours of 1954, 1955, and 1957.

Elizabeth Earle ("Betsy") Rawls ♀ (b. 1928) won at least one golf tournament every year from 1954 to 1965 and, in 1959, swung her way to the top in ten tournaments, collecting $26,744, considered a lot of loot for a woman golfer at the time.

Mary Kathryn ("Mickey") Wright (b. 1935) won eighty-two tournaments in her golfing career and in 1963 earned thirteen titles—the most ever won in a single season. In that year and the next she was named Associated Press Woman Athlete of the Year. In 1964 she shot the lowest score ever recorded for a woman—sixty-two on an eighteen-hole course in Midland, Texas.

Susie Maxwell Berning (b. 1941) was the first girl to attend Oklahoma City University on a golf scholarship, where she played on the men's team. Berning, who turned pro in 1964, is one of three women golfers, with Wright and Rawls, to win the USGA Women's Open three times.

Kathrynne Ann ("Kathy") Whitworth (b. 1939), all-time top money winner among women golf pros ($745,359 as of January 1978), was the first female pro to earn over $300,000 at the game and has won more tournaments than any woman but Mickey Wright.

Carol B. Mann (b. 1941) is, at 6 feet 3 inches, as notable for her height as for her game. From 1961 to 1975 she won thirty-eight pro tournaments, collecting $413,301.91. An outspoken proponent of big money for golfing women, Mann believes that cash is the only real recognition.

Sandra B. Haynie (b. 1943) had racked up thirty-nine tournament triumphs by 1975, among the most for an active woman golf pro. From 1962 to 1975 there wasn't a year in which she didn't win at least once. Her lifetime earnings are second only to those of Whitworth.

Joanne Gunderson Carner (b. 1939) won the U.S. Amateur five times before she turned pro in 1970, promptly won the open in 1971, and had six major tournament victories in 1974 for official earnings of $86,000. Carner started off 1980 with "the hottest streak I ever had," winning four tournaments and $72,886 by mid-March.

Judy Rankin (b. 1945) won her first National Pee Wee Championship in 1953, when she was eight, turned pro at seventeen in 1962, and by 1976 was LPGA Player of the Year, the first woman to break the $100,000 annual earnings mark.

Nancy Lopez-Melton at age twenty-one captured five consecutive tournament wins and nine altogether, including the LPGA Championship in 1978, making her the all-time rookie money winner, male or female, in professional golf, with $189,813. Lopez-Melton topped her own record in 1979, with $197,488 for eight wins, and was named Player of the Year.

Hisako Higuchi Matsui, the most celebrated woman athlete in Japan and known there as the "Queen," has led women's golf in that country for a decade. Higuchi, with more than forty tournament wins to her credit, took both the Japanese title and the European Open in 1976, and the LPGA in 1977. According to Ray Volpe, commissioner of the Ladies' Professional Golf Association, there are 200 women playing tournament golf in Japan, more than the 175 on the U.S. tour. In 1979 five of Japan's golf women played on the LPGA tour, but only Higuchi qualified for the Winners Circle in Palm Springs.

AND OTHER GOLF WOMEN

Barrie Naismith of Georgia in 1978 had to bring suit against the Professional Golfers' Association of America (PGA) in order to get a job in a pro shop. The suit was settled out of court in her favor, and Naismith was employed as an assistant pro at a club near Atlanta. In retaliation, two male golfers applied (and were refused admission) to a qualifying program of the Ladies' Professional Golf Association (LPGA). Although the men-only PGA tour deleted the world *male* from its constitution, no woman attempted to qualify.

Patty Kamin, fifteen years old, and *Lori Hawkins,* sixteen, both of Michigan, became the first female caddies at a major golf championship when they worked at the PGA in August 1979.

Bronwin Russell became the first woman to caddy the U.S. Men's Open, in June 1980, for her husband, pro Arthur Russell. Liberated? Not exactly. Said Mr. Russell: "As long as she does what I tell her to, everything is fine and so far she has always done that. Besides, as long as she's caddying for me, I always know where she is, don't I?" A few hours later . . .

Pam Shuttleworth became the second female caddy in the eighty years of the Men's Open, for Jim Dent. Shuttleworth and Russell were issued the same mustard-colored jump suits worn by all Open caddies. And . . .

Betsy Rawls ♀ became the first woman to be named a rules official in a Men's Open, also in June 1980. Tournament director of the Ladies' Professional Golf Association and an outstanding pro herself, Rawls was chosen "for two reasons, neither one of which is because she is a woman," according to the chairman of the USGA rules committee. "First, she is a superb rules person . . . [and second] we want to get input from the LPGA Tour as we have been getting from the PGA Tour."

OVER TRACK AND FIELD

Shirley Strickland de la Hunty (b. 1925) of Australia holds the record for Olympic track and field medals. She was awarded seven in all—three gold, one silver, and three bronze—in 1948, 1952, and 1956. However, a recent examination of a photo finish of the 200 meters in 1948 showed that she came in third and not fourth—thus "earning" another bronze, but unofficially.

Irena Kirszenstein Szewinska (b. 1946) of Poland received three gold, two silver, and two bronze medals in track and field, a total of seven, the only woman to win medals in four successive Olympics—1964, 1968, 1972, and 1976. She set a record of 49.29 seconds for the 400 meters in 1976.

Francina ("Fanny") Blankers-Koen ♀ (b. 1918) of the Netherlands earned four gold track and field Olympic medals in 1948: for 100 and 200 meters, 80-meter hurdles, and 4 × 100-meter relay. Her record was equaled by . . .

Betty Cuthbert (b. 1938) of Australia, who took the 100 and 200 meters and the 4 × 100-meter relay in 1956, and the 400 meters in 1964.

Iolanda Balas ♀ of Rumania is the only woman to receive two Olympic gold medals for the high jump. Balas, who captured her golds in 1960 and 1964, was the first woman to jump over 6 feet, setting Olympic records of 6 feet 1/4 inch and 6 feet 2 7/8 inches respectively. But records are made to be broken, and . . .

Rosemary Ackermann of East Germany set a record of 6 feet 4 inches for the high jump at the 1976 Olympics, and . . .

Sara Simeoni of Italy went even higher, in 1978 setting a world record of 6 feet 7 inches at Brescia, Italy, and in 1980 an Olympic record of 6 feet 5 1/2 inches.

Ivanka Khristova of Bulgaria set the Olympic women's shot put record of 69 feet 5 1/4 inches in 1976.

Kathryn Joan Schmidt of the United States set a women's world javelin throw record of 227 feet 5 inches at Fürth, Germany, in 1977.

Evelyn Schlaak Jahl of Denmark set a world discus throw record of 232 feet at Dresden, East Germany, in 1978.

Vilma Bardauskiene of the USSR holds the world's women's long jump record, 23 feet 3 1/4 inches, set in 1978 in Prague, Czechoslovakia.

Nadezhda Tkacenko ♀ holds the world women's pentathlon record of 4,839 points, set at Lille, France, in 1977.

SPEEDSTERS

※

Shirley Muldowney, the first woman to win national titles in drag racing, won the National Hot Rod Association World Final race in 1976. Her 1,500-horsepower dragster achieved the second-fastest time ever recorded in that category—249.30 miles per hour.

Claudine Trautmann of France, a racing-car driver, captured the ladies' championship in her sport nine times and was the first woman works driver hired by Citroën.

Kitty O'Neil ♀ broke the women's land speed record in 1976 when she raced 512.710 mph in a three-wheeled rocket car on the Alvord Desert in Oregon. The world land speed record is 627.287 mph.

Denise Kelly, a twenty-five-year-old would-be speeder, was awarded $1,300 by a hearing examiner for the New Jersey Civil Rights Division in 1979 in a sex discrimination case that grew out of the East Windsor Speedway's refusal to permit her to race at that track.

Karen Stead was the first girl to win the All American Soap Box Derby in 1975, at age eleven. Like All Soap Box Derby entrants, Stead made her own racing car.

Tatiana Averina of the USSR holds the women's speed skating record of 1 minute 23.46 seconds for 1,000 meters and took two Olympic golds in 1976.

Lidia Skoblikova, also of the USSR, has chalked up more Olympic golds than any other speed skater. She won two in 1960 and four in 1964. The most-medaled male holds four.

Marcia Jones Smoke is the outstanding American canoe paddler, with a total of thirty-three national championships, including eleven won in the single kayak.

Sue Novara of the United States has been a top cyclist since 1972, when she took her first national title. In 1974 she won the national cycling championship and, in 1975 and 1977, the world titles.

Yvonne Reynders of Belgium holds seven women's cycling titles, earned from 1959 to 1966; she is tied with . . .

Beryl Burton of Great Britain, with seven titles earned from 1959 to 1967.

Wilma Rudolph♀ was a speedster on two feet. Stricken with crippling illnesses in early childhood, she had to relearn how to walk when she was eight, but by the time she was in high school she was a leading runner and became the first black American woman to earn Olympic medals: a bronze for the 400-meter in 1956, and three golds in 1960, for the 100-meter and 200-meter dashes and the 400-meter relay.

CUTTING A FINE FIGURE

※

Sonja Henie♀ (1912–1969) of Norway won ten world figure skating titles between 1927 and 1936, and also won the most Olympic gold medals in that sport, in 1928, 1932, and 1936. Henie then turned pro and accumulated a record $47.5 million in earnings, a record in professional sports that would be topped only by boxer Muhammad Ali. Henie began collecting titles when she was ten years old as the figure skating champion of Norway, held six Norwegian titles in all, and won the European title eight times. She also starred in eleven films and was the only woman to win the Grand Slam of figure skating titles—World, European, and Olympic in the same year—*twice*, in 1932 and 1936.

Marabell Vinson Owen won the women's U.S. National Figure Skating Championship a record nine consecutive times in the 1930s—and upon retirement became the *New York Times*'s first woman sports columnist.

Tenley Albright, United States: U.S. figure skating champion, 1952–1956; world, 1955; Olympic gold, 1956.

Carol Heiss, United States: U.S. figure skating champion, 1957–1960; world, 1956–1960; Olympic gold, 1960.

Peggy Fleming, United States: U.S. figure skating champion, 1964–1968; world, 1966–1968; Olympic gold, 1968.

Janet Lynn, United States: U.S. figure skating champion, 1969–1973.

Dorothy Hamill, United States: U.S. figure skating champion, 1974–1976; world, 1976; Olympic gold, 1976.

Linda Fratianne, United States: U.S. figure skating champion, 1977–1979; world, 1977, 1979; Olympic silver, 1980.

Irina Rodnina (b. 1949) of the USSR has won the most world championship titles in pairs competitions of anyone, man or woman. She won four times, from 1969 through 1972, with Alexei Ulanov, and seven times, from 1973 through 1978 and again in 1980, with her husband Aleksandr Zaitsev, before retiring to teach. She has also won gold medals at three successive Olympics—1972, 1976, and 1980—another record.

WATER SPORTS

※

Records in water sports are made, and broken, yearly. Herewith some of the lesser known, or by now forgotten, events—along with a few superlatives.

Martha Gerstung of Germany became the first woman to set an official swimming record in 1908, for a 100-meter freestyle competition.

Fanny Durack of Australia took the first gold medal in 1912 when women's swimming and diving were included in the Olympics for the first time; she swam the 100-meter freestyle in 1:22.2.

Elsie Jennings was an organizer in 1918 of the Women's Swimming Association of New York. Jennings, who later coached record breakers Gertrude Ederle? and Eleanor Holm,? died at the age of ninety in 1978.

Ragnild Hveger of Denmark holds more swimming world records than any swimmer: forty-two between 1936 and 1942. (The nearest male record is held by Arne Borg of Sweden, with thirty-two records set between 1921 and 1929.)

Dawn Fraser Ware, Australia, *Shirley Babashoff,* United States, and *Kornelia Ender,* East Germany, each hold eight Olympic medals for swimming. Ware's four gold and four silver came in 1956, 1960, and 1964; she is the only swimmer to win the same event—the 100-meter freestyle—in three successive Olympics. Babashoff's two gold and six silver came in 1972 and 1976; the golds were for successive victories in the 4 × 100-meter freestyle relay. Ender's four gold and four silver came in 1972 and 1976 as well, during which time she set three individual and one team record (some of those records were broken, by other East German swimmers, at the Moscow Olympics in 1980).

Marjorie Gestring of the United States was the youngest Olympic event winner ever, earning the springboard diving title in Berlin in 1936 when she was thirteen years and nine months old.

Joyce Hoffman of the United States is the only surfer to win two world championships since the sport became competitive on that level in 1964. Hoffman earned her titles in 1965 and 1966.

Irene Horton of California was the oldest water-ski competitor in a U.S. National in 1974 when she competed in the slalom. She had three grandchildren and two children entered in the same competition.

Linda Giddens of the United States holds the record for the longest water-ski jump by a woman, 128 feet, set in 1976.

Maria Victoria Carrasco of Venezuela holds the record number of points for water-ski tricks by a woman, 5,570 earned at Milan, Italy, in September 1977. Carrasco won the women's world championship in tricks for that year, and in 1973 and 1975 as well.

Donna Patterson Brice holds the women's water-ski speed record, 111 mph set in August 1977.

Ronnie De Luca was twenty-five years old and pregnant when boredom led her to begin sport fishing. Thirteen years and three children later, the 110-pound Long Island woman held five world fishing records and had hooked dozens of sharks, including a 143-pound mako and a 427-pound dusky, taken with an 80-pound test line off New York's Montauk Point in 1977. Weekdays, De Luca fishes from 4:30 to 8:00 A.M., returning in time to go to work selling real estate; on weekends she is first mate on a charter boat. She was once married to a man who got seasick.

Christine Scheiblich of East Germany has earned world championships in single-scull rowing since 1974, when the competition began, earning titles also in 1975, 1976 (the Olympic record, first for a woman), 1977, and 1978. She set a world record of 3:34.31 for a 1,000-meter course in 1977, with an average speed of 10.43 mph. Rowing is one of the last male sports bastions to be toppled, and there is still, so to speak, a long row to hoe. The sculling course is 1,000 meters for women, 2,000 meters for men.

Penny Chuter was the first woman to become a chief rowing coach in Great Britain. In late 1979 she hailed the falling of a major barrier when the Henley Royal Regatta management committee announced that a series of invitation races for women would begin in 1981, for the first time in its 140-year history.

SWIMMING THE DISTANCE

Gertrude Ederle ♀ of the United States was the first woman to swim across the English Channel. On August 6, 1926, she swam from France to England in 14 hours 39 minutes, surpassing the existing men's record. Ederle had been preparing for years: when she was twelve years and ten months old she broke the women's 880-yard freestyle swimming record, going 13 minutes 19 seconds on August 17, 1919, to become the youngest person ever to break a world sports record. Three weeks after Ederle's cross-Channel swim, *Mille Gade Corson* accomplished the same feat. The first such swim had been made in 1875; by 1980 more than 215 swimmers had crossed at least once.

Ivy Hawke swam from France to England on August 19, 1928, in 19 hours 16 minutes.

Martha Norelius won $10,000 in 1929 in a ten-mile race for women on Lake Ontario sponsored by Wrigley's Chewing Gum. Norelius had just turned professional when she entered the "Wrigley Swim."

Myrtle Huddleston of New York is the holder of the women's record for continuous swimming—87 hours 27 minutes—set in 1931. She swam in a salt-water tank in Coney Island, New York, and broke her own previous record of 86 hours 16 minutes.

Florence Chadwick of the United States was the first woman to conquer the English Channel via the more difficult England-to-France route, crossing in 16 hours 22 minutes on September 11, 1951. She did it again in 1953 and then on October 12, 1955, in 13 hours 33 minutes, the fastest time for a woman swimming in that direction.

Abla Adel Khairi of Egypt was thirteen years and ten months old on August 17, 1974, when she crossed the Channel from England to France in 12 hours 30 minutes—the youngest woman to make the crossing.

Stella Taylor of the United States, who made two crossings, was forty-five years and eleven months old and the oldest woman to swim the Channel on August 26, 1975; her time was 18 hours 15 minutes.

Rosemary George, who lives right on the Channel in Dover, was the only English woman to cross twice.

Diana Nyad became, in 1975, the first person to swim the 32 miles across Lake Ontario. She accomplished this nonstop in 20 hours. That same year Nyad broke the 1927 record for a swim around Manhattan Island, completing the circuit in 7 hours 57 minutes. A dedicated marathon swimmer, Nyad has swum in shark cages on all the challenging waterways of the world and in August 1979 was the first person to make the 60-mile swim against sharks, jellyfish, and the wicked Gulf Stream current from the Bahamas to Florida. She was in the water for 27 hours 38 minutes.

Wendy Brook swam across the Channel from France to England in September 1976 in 8 hours 56 minutes, the fastest time for anyone, male or female, on that crossing.

Penny Lee Dean of the United States set a record for the fastest Channel crossing, male or female, in July 1978—7 hours 40 minutes from Dover to Cap Gris-Nez.

Cynthia ("Cindy") Nicholas of Canada made the fastest two-way Channel crossing in 1979 when she was nineteen years old, swimming for 19 hours 12 minutes on August 4 and 5 and beating her own record of two years earlier. Then, on September 7 and 8, 1977, she became the first woman to complete a two-way crossing, making the round trip in 19 hours 55 minutes—10 hours faster than the previous double-crossing record. Nicholas has accumulated a women's record of eight Channel crossings altogether.

JAWS

❧

Record shark catches by women anglers:

- Blue shark, 410 pounds, caught by ***Martha C. Webster*** at Rockport, Massachusetts, August 17, 1967.
- Hammerhead shark, 460 pounds, caught by ***Pamela Hudspeth*** at Sydney, Australia, December 29, 1974.
- Porbeagle shark, 369 pounds, caught by ***Patricia W. Smith*** at Looe, Cornwall, England, July 20, 1970.
- Short fin mako shark, 911 pounds, 12 ounces, caught by ***Audrey Cohen*** at Palm Beach, Florida, April 9, 1962.
- Thresher shark, 729 pounds, caught by ***Mrs. V. Brown*** at Mayor Island, New Zealand, June 3, 1959.
- Tiger shark, 1,314 pounds, caught by ***Mrs. Bob Dyer*** at Cape Moreton, Australia, July 27, 1953.
- White shark, 1,052 pounds, caught by ***Mrs. Bob Dyer*** at Cape Moreton, Australia, June 27, 1954.

Information courtesy of International Game Fish Association, Fort Lauderdale, Florida, in Frank G. Menke, *The Encyclopedia of Sports,* 6th rev. ed. (Cranbury, N.J.: A. S. Barnes, 1977)

DOWN TO THE BARE ESSENTIALS

❧

Some women athletes have been so powerful that they have aroused suspicions as to their true sex, and in 1966 recurrent speculation finally caused the International Amateur Athletic Federation (IAAF) to take action. At the European track and field championships in Budapest in September of that year, 234 female contestants were required to parade nude before a panel of female gynecologists. Four athletes refused to have their sex authenticated in this manner; they were barred from the meet. They were:

Iolanda Balas,♀ Rumania's world record high jumper.
Tatyana Schelkanova, a Soviet long jumper who claimed to be injured and unable to appear for the exam.
Irina Press, Soviet Union, hurdler.
Tamara Press, Soviet Union, discus thrower. The sexual identity of the Press sisters was so cloudy that they were dubbed by the media the "Press brothers." Two years later, when a laboratory test using cells scraped from the lining of the mouth was instituted at the 1968 Olympics, Tamara Press refused to be examined. So did *Erike Shinegger* of Austria, world champion in downhill skiing.

In one form or another, the problem persisted. In 1978 the IAAF accused five athletes of taking steroid hormones. Disqualified and stripped of the medals they had won at the European track and field championship meet in Prague were two men and:

Elena Stojanova, Bulgaria, who had placed fifth in the women's shot put.
Nadezhda Tkacenko,♀ Soviet Union, first place, women's pentathlon.
Yekaterina Gordiyenko, Soviet Union, fifth place, women's pentathlon.

A year went by, and seven women from Eastern European nations failed drug tests at the 1979 track and field meets in Athens and Sofia:

Totka Petrova, Bulgaria, the Europa Cup and World Cup champion at 1,500 meters.
Natalia Marasescu, Rumania, holder of the women's world record in the mile.
Ileana Silai, Rumania, Europa Cup semifinalist in the 1,500 meters.
Daniela Teneva, Bulgaria, winner of the 100-meter hurdles.
Santa Vlad, Rumania, third place in the long jump.
Uelena Kovaleva, Soviet Union, discus thrower.
Nadezhda Kudruavtseva, Soviet Union, discus thrower.

Anabolic steroids, derived from the male hormone androgen, are banned by the International Olympic Committee as well as by the IAAF. Their use in training has been testified to by athletes who have left Eastern European nations. Taking these drugs can indeed make a difference in performance: Petrova, at twenty-two years of age, ran the fastest 1,500 meters on record in the summer of 1979, 3:57.4. Silai, at thirty-eight years of age, ran the 1,500 meters at 3:58.5 in 1979. And Marasescu's mile record, set when she was twenty-seven, was 4:22.1. In contrast, the fastest 1,500 meters run by an American woman in that year was *Mary Decker's* 4:05; the fastest time by champion *Grete Waitz* of Norway was 4:00.6.

RECORD BREAKERS

Some record-shattering happenings that may have been overlooked because of competition from more dramatic events:

Josie Morris of Utah won first prize in a calf-roping contest when she was eighty-plus, some years before her death in 1964.

Lyn Lemaire was the only woman to enter Hawaii's Iron Man Triathlon in August 1979. Swimming 2.4 miles, biking 112 miles, and running 26.2 miles, in one day, Lemaire placed fifth.

Kim Jin-Ho of Korea became the first archer to win five gold medals, competing in the thirtieth World Archery Championships in Berlin in July 1979. Kim's bow weighs thirty pounds.

Janina Spychajowa-Kurkowska of Poland captured seven world titles in archery between 1931 and 1947, the largest number ever accumulated by an archer of either sex.

Janou Tissot of France has twice won the women's world championship in equestrian sports, in 1970 and 1974.

Patty Costello of the United States has set two Professional Women's Bowling Association records: most career victories (sixteen) and most national championships (three). The PWBA named her Woman Bowler of the Year in 1976.

Annedore Haefker of West Germany holds the women's bowling world record, 4,615 pins in 24 games, knocked down in Surrey, England, in 1975. The women's world bowling championship was first played in 1963.

Ruth Hangen of Getzville, New York, is a horseshoe-pitching record setter, scoring a record 95 percent of ringers on one game, in 1973, and a women's consecutive ringer record of forty-two, set in 1974.

Vera Menchik-Stevenson (1906–1944) of Great Britain won most women's world chess championships, holding the title from 1927 until her death.

Nona Gaprindashvili of the USSR has held the women's world chess championship title since 1962.

Inna Ryskal of the USSR is the only woman to receive four Olympic medals for volleyball—a silver in 1964 and golds in 1968, 1972, and 1976.

Vicki Johnson won both the women's *kata* (a contest of form) and the women's *kumite* (sparring) at karate in 1979.

Maureen Braziel of the United States won her third straight AAU heavyweight judo championship in 1976 and was vanquished in only six matches during ten years of tournament competition.

Shari Melnick, twenty-one years old, 5 feet 4 inches tall, and 120 pounds, came in first in the women's lightweight division of the Empire State Wrist-Wrestling Championship contest, held in May 1980 on the observation deck of the Empire State Building. An art major at Brooklyn College, the right-handed Melnick had previously won seven trophies in her chosen sport.

Christel Cranz of Germany is the downhill skier with the greatest number of world titles: twelve (four slalom, three downhill, five combined). The record for a male skier is seven.

Galina Kulakova of the USSR, with nine golds, one silver, and two bronze

medals gained in Olympic and world competition, is history's most
decorated cross-country skiier.

Vera Caslavska-Odlozil (b. 1942) of Czechoslovakia holds the women's
record for individual gymnastics Olympic gold medals, seven. She
earned three in 1964 and four in 1968.

Larissa Semyonovna Latynina of the USSR holds the women's record for the
most gymnastics championships—ten individual and five team titles
between 1956 and 1964. She also earned an all-time record eighteen
Olympic medals—six individual and three team golds, five silvers, and
four bronzes. Latynina retired in 1966.

Ellen Müller-Preiss (b. 1912), a fencer from Austria, holds the women's
record for the longest span of Olympic consecutive competition:
Müller-Preiss competed in every Olympics for twenty-four years, from
1932 to 1956, and won the women's foil in 1932. She also earned world
championships in the non-Olympic years of 1947, 1949, and 1950.

WRITE IN THE LOCKER ROOM

Mary Garber of the *Winston-Salem Journal* is the dean of all women sportswriters. In wartime 1944 no male reporters were available, so society-
page journalist Garber was reassigned to the sports desk and has been
there ever since.

Lynn Rosellini of the *Washington Star* produced an award-winning 1975 series on homosexuals in sports, a subject rarely covered by male
sportwriters.

Le Anne Schreiber, who had covered the 1976 Olympics for *Time* magazine,
was in November 1978 appointed sports editor of the *New York Times,*
heading a staff of fifty-five, largely male, reporters, editors, and columnists. Before joining the *Times* as assistant sports editor earlier that
year, Schreiber had been editor in chief of a women's sports magazine.

Nancy Scannell of the *Washington Post* concentrates on the legal, legislative,
economic, and labor aspects of sports stories.

Melissa Ludtke Lincoln,♀ a reporter for *Sports Illustrated,* protested the publicity given to women sportswriters assigned to interview male players
in their locker rooms, editors who make such assignments merely for
their novelty value and not for the real story of the game. The journalists covering the event should not, asserts Lincoln, become the event itself.

Estelle M. Shanley of the *Lowell Sun,* of Lowell, Massachusetts, was assigned
to cover the Red Sox locker room. She found the male reporters hostile
and many players inhibited, while "others undress anyway, determined
not to change their habits because a female has invaded their turf."
Shanley states the issue succinctly: "The constitutional question focuses
on a woman's right to make a living. If she is a sportswriter, she has the
same rights to obtain the same stories as her male counterparts. If she is
a feature writer, she has a right to enter the clubhouse to collect data.
And, if she is assigned the story, she has little choice but to deliver."

XXIV ❧ *WORDS OF WISDOM —AND OTHERWISE*

SOME MEN'S OPINIONS

❧

"There are two days when a woman is a pleasure: the day one marries her and the day one buries her." **Hipponax (*ca. 570–520* B.C.)**

"Women are only children of a larger growth."

Lord Chesterfield

"A woman, a dog, and a walnut-tree,
The more you beat 'em the better they be."

Thomas Fuller

"It requires nothing less than a chivalric feeling to sustain a conversation with a lady." **Henry David Thoreau**

"Women and elephants never forget an injury."

Saki (*Hector Hugh Munro*)

"The woman is expressly formed to please the man."

Jean Jacques Rousseau

"A woman is only a woman, but a good cigar is a Smoke."

Rudyard Kipling

"The man's desire is for the woman: but the woman's desire is rarely other than for the desire of the man." **Samuel Taylor Coleridge**

"No man worth having is true to his wife, or can be true to his wife, or ever was or ever will be." **Sir John Vanbrugh**

"All the pursuits of men are the pursuits of women also, but in all of them a woman is inferior to a man." **Plato**

"Woman may be said to be an inferior man." **Aristotle**

"It is a good horse that never stumbles,
And a good wife that never grumbles."

English proverb

"The souls of women are so small
That some believe they've none at all."

Samuel Butler

"He seldom errs
Who thinks the worst he can of womankind."

John Home

"I should say that the majority of women (happily for society) are not much troubled with sexual feeling of any kind." ***Dr. William Acton, 1857***

"I will not affirm that women have no character, rather they have a new one every day." ***Heinrich Heine***

"Don't let any woman dazzle you with her decked-out rump; behind the twaddle, she's after your barn." ***Hesiod***

"To me women are no more than a pastime, a hobby. Nobody devotes too much time to a hobby." ***Henry Kissinger***

"A woman is nobody. A wife is everything."
Philadelphia Public Ledger and Daily Transcript, 1848

"Misogynist—a man who hates women as much as women hate one another." ***H. L. Mencken***

ADVICE FROM THE MEN

- *The Ménagier of Paris,* a fourteenth-century guide for homemakers, advocated extreme modesty: "If you are walking out go with your head turned straight forward, your eyelids low and fixed, and look straight before you down to the ground at twelve yards, without turning your eyes on man or woman, to the right or to the left, or staring upwards or moving your eyes from one place to another, or laughing, or stopping to talk with anyone in the streets."
- *The Book of the Knight of La Tour Landry,* written ca. 1371 and published by William Caxton in 1484, taught the qualities of "pure and perfect womanhood" to daughters of knights. If they were properly devout and had good manners, they would be rewarded by marriage to wealthy and influential knights, after which they should be affectionate and dutiful.
- *How the Good Wife Taught Her Daughter,* ca. 1420, advocated—in verse—diligence in housework, firm and physical discipline for children, piety, and submission to husbands. That many women had other ideas about how to spend their time is evident from the book's frequent admonitions against attending wrestling matches and cockfights, drinking in taverns, and accepting gifts from men.
- Cotton Mather offered luxurious advice to the Puritan women of New England in *Ornaments for the Daughters of Zion,* 1692: "Cloath your selves with the *Silk* of Piety, the *Satin* of Sanctity, the *Purple* of Modesty; So the Almighty God will be a Lover of you."
- Moses Mendelssohn, an eighteenth-century philosopher, held that "moderate learning becomes a lady, but not scholarship. A girl who has read her eyes red deserves to be laughed at."
- John Gregory put his advice into *A Father's Legacy to His Daughters,* which went into twenty-seven editions between 1775 and 1798. If a woman happened to be educated, she should "keep it a profound secret, especially from the men, who generally look with a jealous and malignant eye on a woman of great parts, and a cultivated understanding."

- Thomas Jefferson, traveling far and frequently on government business, kept in touch with his several children. To his daughter Maria he sent these late-eighteenth-century paternal cautions: "Be you, from the moment you rise till you go to bed, as cleanly and properly dressed as at the hours of dinner and tea. I hope, therefore, the moment you rise from bed, your first work will be to dress yourself in such style, as that you may be seen by any gentleman without his being able to discover a pin amiss, or any other circumstance of neatness wanting."
- The Reverend John Bennet put his recommendations in the form of *Letters to a Young Lady,* which went through six editions in the 1790s. A typical sample of the Reverend's advice: "Politics, philosophy, mathematics, or metaphysics are not *your* province. Machiavel, Newton, Euclid, Malebranche, or Locke, will lie with a very ill grace in your closet. Be content with what God and nature *intended* you."
- Doctors Daniel Brinton and George Napheys decreed, in their *Laws of Health in Relation to the Human Form* of 1870, that for women, "for cosmetic reasons, immoderate laughter is objectionable."
- Doctor Robert Tomes wrote *The Bazar Book of Decorum. The Care of the Person, Manners, Etiquette, and Ceremonials,* published in New York in 1870, but kept his name off the title page. He was strongly opposed to "ear-boring" and "hanging the ears with trinkets," and "dancing the German from midnight to four o'clock in the morning, six days out of the seven in each week." And he did "not pretend to give, as some have assumed to, formularies for making love or plighting troth, but we doubt not that many a person has been left to pine away in a single misery for want of knowledge of the proper procedure."

FROM THE LIPS OF MAE WEST ♀

"It's not the men in my life, it's the life in my men that counts."

"When women go wrong, men go right after them."

"Give a man a free hand, and he'll try to put it all over you."

"The wildest men make the best pets."

"A man in the house is worth two in the street."

"I always figured, never leave yourself down to one man or one dollar."

"Some men are all right in their place—if only they knew the right places!"

"Men are all alike—except the one you've met who's different."

"Never judge a man by the spots on his waistcoat. They may conceal a great big heart and a wallet full of gold."

"Most men like women when they look like women. You can get a handful of toothpicks in a restaurant, free of charge."

"I like a man who's good, but not too good—for the good die young, and I hate a dead one."

"Don't come crawlin' to a man for love—he likes to get a run for his money."

"Don't sacrifice too much for a man—he never enjoyed anything more than giving up a rib."

"Don't marry a man to reform him—that's what reform schools are for."

"Don't keep a man guessing too long—he's sure to find out the answer somewhere else."

"Men are my hobby. If I ever get married I'd have to give it up."

WOMAN TO WOMEN

Hester M. Chapone's Letters on the Improvement of the Mind (six editions, 1783–1797) was one of the first books in which a woman told women about proper behavior. Until then, giving advice was a man's game.

Fanny Fern (Sarah Payson Willis Parton)♀ wrote one of the first etiquette advice columns in Godey's Lady's Book.

Sarah Josepha Hale,♀ editor of Godey's, herself produced a popular etiquette book, Manners, or Happy Homes and Good Society, in 1866.

Eliza W. Farrar, the wife of a Harvard professor, told teen-agers what was what in The Young Lady's Friend, 1836.

Harriet Beecher Stowe,♀ the author of Uncle Tom's Cabin, wrote an advice book, House and Home, in 1864.

Ruth Ashmore (Isabel A. Mallon) started writing her column on social propriety, "Side Table Talks with Girls," for the Ladies' Home Journal in the 1890s. Ashmore received queries from 158,000 young women.

Beatrice Fairfax (Marie Manning) was a reporter on the New York Evening Journal who noticed a plethora of letters from heartsick readers. The result was the debut on July 28, 1898, of her advice column, "Letters from the Lovelorn." "Dry your eyes, roll up your sleeves, and *dig for a practical solution*" was her typical chin-up response. Her mail often contained as many as 1,400 letters a day.

Dorothy Dix (Elizabeth Meriwether Gilmer) wrote her first advice column for the New Orleans Picayune in 1896 and went on to do "Dorothy Dix Talks" for the New York Journal. The sob sister's own life was as full of troubles as any of the letters she received. Shortly after she married, her husband developed an incurable mental disease that progressively worsened until his death thirty-five years later. "I never once thought of divorce," she recalled. "I could not say to others 'Be strong' if I did not myself have strength to endure."

Mary E. W. Sherwood (Mrs. John Sherwood),♀ a Harper's Bazaar editor, produced a whole spate of etiquette aids, including Amenities of the Home (1881), Manners and Social Usages (1884), and The Art of Entertaining (1892).

Clara Sophia Jessup Bloomfield-Moore (Mrs. H. O. Ward) wrote Sensible Etiquette of the Best Society, which went through twenty editions in the 1860s and 1870s.

Florence Hartley published *The Ladies' Book of Etiquette* in 1873.

Florence Kingsland's *Book of Good Manners* was the last word on the subject in 1901.

Lillian Eichler ♀ was an eighteen-year-old cub copywriter when she thought of writing an etiquette book in 1921. She finished it in two months, working after office hours. By 1945 her *Book of Etiquette* was still in demand and had attracted one million buyers.

Emily Post, ♀ a divorced society matron, was asked in 1922 by a publisher to write a book on etiquette and proper behavior. *Etiquette, the Blue Book of Social Usage* was an immediate hit, going into ten editions and ninety printings in forty years. It also led to a newspaper advice column and a radio program for Post.

Ann Landers (Esther Pauline Friedman) ♀ and **Abigail Van Buren (Pauline Esther Friedman)** ♀ are twins who've enjoyed giving other people advice since they were preteens. Both write syndicated columns and are noted for their witty, no-holds-barred suggestions. Readers who thought that Landers knew all the answers were surprised when she and her husband went their separate ways in 1975. And readers who depended on Dear Abby were shocked to read her 1979 report on the failure of her long-time marriage.

AND WHAT THEY ADVISED

꙳

"Always keep callers waiting, till they have had time to notice the outlay of money in your parlours."
> *Fanny Fern (Sarah Payson Willis Parton),* ♀ in
> a tongue-in-cheek column in *Godey's Lady's Book,*
> early 1800s

"A dinner well performed occupies two or three hours, and if you are not warned to expect an evening party added to it, the sooner you depart the better, when all is ended."
> *Mrs. L. G. Abell, Woman in her Various Relations:*
> *containing Practical Rules for American Females,* 1851

"The fashion of wearing black silk mittens for breakfast is now obsolete."
> *Miss Leslie, Behavior Book* 1853

"A lady in society must, if she would not grow utterly wearing in company, know how to dance. . . . It is one of the most healthful and elegant amusements, and cannot be too highly recommended."
> *Florence Hartley, The Ladies' Book of Etiquette,* 1873

"Compromising positions are easily fallen into, and a woman should be constantly on her guard."
> *Anonymous female author, Manners That Win,* 1880

"[The chaperone] must accompany her young lady everywhere. . . . She must watch the characters of the men who approach her charge, and endeavor to save the inexperienced girl from the dangers of a bad marriage, if possible."
> *Mrs. John Sherwood,* ♀ *Manners and Social Usages,* 1884

"Proposals by women, while permissible, are not customary."
Harriet Beecher Stowe,♀ *Household Papers and Stories,* 1896

"Even if his kiss would be acceptable, let him make the first move. The reputation of being a 'hot number' is anything but complimentary."
Lillian Eichler,♀ *Book of Etiquette,* 1921

"No rule of etiquette is of less importance than which fork we use."
Emily Post,♀ *Etiquette, the Blue Book of Social Usage,* 1922

"When it comes to opening the door, the first one who gets there is responsible."
Letitia ("Tish") Baldridge, *The Amy Vanderbilt Complete Book of Etiquette,* rev. ed., 1978

EMILY POST'S WOMEN

Emily Post ♀ sprinkled "real-life" vignettes through her *Blue Book of Social Usage.* The characters inhabiting her pages included:

Mrs. Distinguished	*Mrs. Grundy*
Mrs. Worldly	*Gloria Gorgeous*
Muriel Manners	*Mrs. Highbrow*
Mrs. Toplofty	*Mrs. Oncewere*
Doris Debutante	*Her Grace the Duchess of Overthere*
Mrs. Oldname	*Mrs. Fastidious*
Mrs. Social Leader	*Mary Warmhart*
Miss Elizabeth Orphan	*Mary Neighbor*
Miss Marian Helen Smartlington	*Mrs. Richling*
Miss Madeleine Anne Fairplay	*Louise Lonely*

WOMEN QUOTED IN THE FIRST EDITION OF BARTLETT'S *FAMILIAR QUOTATIONS,* 1855

Out of 2,200 authors cited in today's edition of Bartlett's, only 164 are women. A hundred and twenty-five years ago, John Bartlett himself found only four women eligible for excerption. The four quotes (whose names are not exactly household words today), and the selections representing them, were:

"Man is the nobler growth our realms supply
And souls are ripened in our northern sky."
"The Invitation"

"This dead of midnight is the noon of thought
And wisdom mounts her zenith with the stars."
"A Summer's Evening Meditation"
Mrs. (Anna Letitia) Barbauld (1743–1825)

"Let this great maxim be my virtue's guide,—
In part she is to blame that has been tried;
He comes too near, that comes to be denied."

"The Lady's Resolve"

"And we meet, with champagne and a chicken, at last."
"The Lover"
Lady Mary Wortley Montagu ♀ (1690–1762)

"The last link is broken
That bound me to thee,
And the words thou hast spoken
Have rendered me free."

"Song"
Miss Fanny Steers

"The tree of deepest root is found
Least willing still to quit the ground;
'Twas therefore said, by ancient sages,
That love of life increased with years
So much, that in our latter stages,
When pains grow sharp, and sickness rages,
The greatest love of life appears."

"Three Warnings"
Mrs. (Hester L.) Thrale (1740–1822)

FAMILIAR WORDS FROM UNFAMILIAR NAMES

"Backward, turn backward, O Time, in your flight,
Make me a child again, just for tonight!"

Elizabeth Akers Allen, "Rock Me to Sleep"

"Nearer, my God, to Thee,
Nearer to Thee!"
Sarah Flower Adams, "Nearer, My God, to Thee"

"Little drops of water, little grains of sand,
Make the mighty ocean and the pleasant land."

Julia Carney, "Little Things"

"Twinkle, twinkle, little star,
How I wonder what you are!
Up above the world so high
Like a diamond in the sky."

Jane Taylor, ♀ "The Star"

"Let us question the thinkers and doers,
And hear what they honestly say;

And you'll find they believe, like bold wooers,
  In 'Where there's a will there's a way' "
            Eliza Cook, "Where There's a Will There's a Way"

"Kathleen Mavourneen! the grey dawn is breaking,
The horn of the hunter is heard on the hill;
The lark from her light wing the bright dew is shaking,—
Kathleen Mavourneen! what, slumbering still?"
       Louisa Macartney Crawford, "Kathleen Mavourneen"

    "The breaking waves dashed high
      On the stern and rock-bound coast;
    And the woods against a stormy sky
      Their giant branches tossed;
    And the heavy night hung dark
      The hills and waters o'er—
    When a band of exiles moored their bark
      On the wild New England shore."
  Felicia Dorothea Hemans, "The Landing of the Pilgrim Fathers"

    "When you come to the end of a perfect day,
    And sit alone with your thought,
    While the chimes ring out with a carol gay
    For the joy that the day has brought,
    Do you think what the end of a perfect day
    Can mean to a tired heart,
    When the sun goes down with its flaming ray
    And dear friends have to part?"
            Carrie Jacobs Bond, ♀ "A Perfect Day"

    "I know Thou wilt not slight my call,
      For Thou doest mark the sparrow's fall;
    And calm and peaceful is my sleep,
    Rocked in the cradle of the deep."
      Emma Willard, ♀ "Rocked in the Cradle of the Deep"

    "Seated one day at the Organ
    I was weary and ill at ease,
    And my fingers wandered idly
    Over the noisy keys.

    I knew not what I was playing
    Or what I was dreaming then;
    But I struck one chord of music
    Like the sound of a great Amen."
         Adelaide Anne Proctor, "The Lost Chord"

  " 'She's somebody's mother, boys, you know,
    For all she's aged and poor and slow.
    And I hope some fellow will lend a hand
    To help my mother, you understand,

If ever she's poor and old and gray
When her own dear boy is far away.' "
                    Mary Dow Brine, "Somebody's Mother"

"Laugh, and the world laughs with you,
Weep, and you weep alone.
For the brave old earth must borrow its mirth—
But has trouble enough of its own."
              Ella Wheeler Wilcox, "The Way of the World"

WOMANLY WISDOM

❧

"The hen also knows when day breaks, but she lets the rooster announce
      it."   Ashanti proverb

"Seek to be good but aim not be to great
A woman's noblest station is retreat
Her Fairest virtues fly from public sight
Domestic worth that shows too great a light."
            Sampler, 1818, by *Sarah Ann Flagg* (1807–1832),
        Collection Worcester, Massachusetts, Historical Society

"When I see the elaborate study and ingenuity displayed by women in the
      pursuit of trifles, I feel no doubt of their capacity for the most herculean
      undertakings."   *Julia Ward Howe* ♀

"I love men, not because they are men, but because they are not women."
                            Queen Christina of Sweden

"I'm not denyin' the women are foolish: God Almighty made 'em to match
      the men."   *George Eliot,*♀ *Adam Bede*

"A man must know how to defy opinion: a woman how to submit to it."
                        Madame de Staël,♀ *Delphine*

"Perhaps you have heard my theory that you can't appreciate the form of an
      object—its proportions or its volume—nor of a piece of furniture—until
      you have dusted it many times."
        Alice B. Toklas,♀ letter to Donald Sutherland, November 30, 1947

"In a moment of decision it is better to make the wrong move than to make
      no move at all."   *Anna Howard Shaw* ♀

"Fortunately, analysis is not the only way to resolve inner conflicts. Life it-
      self still remains a very effective therapist."
                    Karen Horney,♀ *Our Inner Conflicts*

"I'll match my flops with anybody's but I wouldn't have missed 'em. Flops
      are a part of life's menu and I've never been a girl to miss out on any of
      the courses."   *Rosalind Russell*

"Man thinks he knows, but a woman knows better."   Old Chinese proverb

EXCUSES, EXCUSES

❦

- In 1783, twelve-year-old *Lucinda Foote* was examined and found to be "fully qualified, except in her sex, to be received as a pupil of the freshman class of Yale University." It was unthinkable for her to be admitted, of course, so Foote never went to Yale, and the child prodigy was not heard of again.
- The Harvard Medical School considered letting *Harriot K. Hunt* ♀ work for a degree in 1850, but male students insisted that she leave, resolving that "no woman of true delicacy would be willing in the presence of men to listen to the discussions of the subjects that necessarily come under consideration of the student of medicine. . . . We object to having the company of any female forced upon us, who is disposed to unsex herself, and to sacrifice her modesty by appearing with men in the lecture room."
- John Ruskin, professor of art at Oxford University, refused in 1871 to allow women to attend his very popular lectures, explaining himself thus to an associate: "I cannot let the bonnets in, on any conditions this term. The three public lectures will be chiefly on angles, degrees of colour-prisms (without any prunes) and other such things of no use to the female mind, and they would occupy the seats in mere disappointed puzzlement."
- In the 1870s *Martha Carey Thomas,* ♀ later to become president of Bryn Mawr College, was at first thrilled to learn that she had been admitted to Johns Hopkins University as a postgraduate student under "special conditions." The "conditions" turned out to be that "student" Thomas could not attend classes, tutorials, or seminars at the university.
- Columbia University used a similar dodge a decade later. Under pressure to admit women, the university set up a "Collegiate Course for Women." Scholars could pursue their studies anywhere *but* at Columbia or its library; the only Columbia facilities offered were a desk and a chair for the final exams. Amazingly, one woman out of the thirty who tried managed to get a degree under these conditions. *Mary Parsons Hankey* became a "Bachelor of Literature." She died a few months later, unaware that this made-up degree was as meaningless as her acceptance by the university. Her early death was used to argue that women could not survive the rigors of higher education!
- *Erica Morini* was turned down when she wanted to study the violin at the Vienna Conservatory in 1914; women were allowed to study only voice or piano. Two years later Morini won a state-sponsored violin contest but was refused the prize money on the grounds that award rules presumed the winner could only be a male. It was clear, therefore, that she had not actually won.
- During World War I German mathematician *Emmy (Amalie) Noether* ♀ was refused an official appointment to the Göttingen University faculty. Grounds for the turn-down? "What will our soldiers think when they return to the university and find that they are expected to learn at the feet of a woman?" Later Albert Einstein would hail Noether as "the most significant creative mathematical genius thus far produced since the higher education of women began."

THE UN DECLARATION OF WOMEN'S RIGHTS

♛

On November 7, 1967, the General Assembly of the United Nations adopted Resolution 2263 (XXII), a declaration of the elimination of discrimination against women. Following are some excerpts:

"Article 1. Discrimination against women, denying or limiting as it does their equality of rights with men, is fundamentally unjust and constitutes an offense against human dignity.

"Article 2. All appropriate measures shall be taken to abolish existing laws, customs, regulations and practices which are discriminatory against women, and to establish adequate legal protection for equal rights of men and women. . . .

"Article 3. All appropriate measures shall be taken to educate public opinion and direct national aspirations toward the eradication of prejudice and the abolition of customary and all other practices which are based on the idea of the inferiority of women.

"Article 4. All appropriate measures shall be taken to ensure to women on equal terms with men without any discrimination: a) The right to vote in all elections. . . . b) The right to vote in all public referenda; c) The right to hold public office. . . .

"Article 5. Women shall have the same rights as men to acquire, change or retain their nationality. Marriage to an alien shall not automatically affect the nationality of the wife either by rendering her stateless or by forcing on her the nationality of her husband.

"Article 6. 1. Without prejudice to the safeguarding of the unity and the harmony of the family which remains the basic unit of any society, all appropriate measures, particularly legislative measures, shall be taken to insure to women, married or unmarried, equal rights with men in the field of civil law. . . . 2. All appropriate measures shall be taken to insure the principle of equality of status of the husband and wife. . . . 3. Child marriage and the betrothal of young girls before puberty shall be prohibited . . . (and all marriages shall be registered) in an official registry. . . .

"Article 7. All provisions of penal codes which constitute discrimination against women shall be repealed.

"Article 8. All appropriate measures, including legislation, shall be taken to combat all forms of traffic in women and exploitation of prostitution of women.

"Article 9. All appropriate measures shall be taken to insure to girls and women, married or unmarried, equal rights with men in education at all levels. . . .

"Article 10. 1. All appropriate measures shall be taken to insure to women, married or unmarried, equal rights with men in the field of economic and social life. . . . 2. In order to prevent discrimination against women on account of marriage or maternity and to insure their effective right to work, measures shall be taken to prevent their dismissal in the event of marriage or maternity . . . and to provide the necessary social services, including childcare facilities. 3. Measures taken to protect women

in certain types of work for reasons inherent in their physical nature shall not be regarded as discriminatory.

"*Article 11.* The principle of equality of rights of men and women demands implementation in all states in accordance with the principles of the United Nations' Charter and of the Universal Declaration of Human Rights. Governments, nongovernmental organizations and individuals are urged, therefore, to do all in their power to promote the implementation of the principles contained in this Declaration."

TOMBSTONE REPORTS

Thirteen Women's Epitaphs

❧

"Here lies a poor woman who always was tired
She lived in a house where help wasn't hired
The last words she said were:
'Dear friends, I am going
Where washing ain't wanted, nor sweeping nor sewing;
And everything there is exact to my wishes,
For when folks don't eat, there's no washing dishes,
In heaven loud anthems forever are ringing,
But having no voice I'll keep clear of singing.
Don't mourn for me now, don't mourn for me never;
I'm going to do nothing for ever and ever.' "

"Mary Randolph Keith Marshall
wife of Thomas Marshall, by whom she had
Fifteen Children,
was born in 1737 and died in 1807,
She was good but not brilliant
Useful but not great."
Tombstone of the mother of John Marshall, Chief Justice
of the Supreme Court of the United States (1801–1835)

"Here lie the bones of Elizabeth Charlotte
Born a virgin, died a harlot.
She was aye a virgin at seventeen,
a remarkable thing in Aberdeen."
From a churchyard, Aberdeen, Scotland

"Here lies the body of Joan Carthew,
Born at St. Columb; died at St. Cue:
Children she had five,
Three dead and two alive:
Those that are dead choosing rather
to die with their mother than live with their father."
St. Agnes's Churchyard, Cornwall

"Martha Blewitt
of the Swan, Baythorn End of this Parish.
Buried 7th May, 1681.

Was the wife of nine husbands
Successively, but the 9th outlived her.
The text to her Funeral Sermon was,
'Last of all Women died also.' "

"Mrs. Oldfield, Actress
This we must own in justice to her shade,
'Tis the first bad exit OLDFIELD ♀ ever made."

"Some have children, some have none:
Here lies the mother of twenty-one."
On a gravestone in Wolstanton, Staffordshire

"Sacred to the memory of Martha Gwynn,
Who was so very pure within,
She burst the outer shell of sin,
And hatched herself a cherubim."
The churchyard of St. Albans

"Here lies Ann Mann;
She lived an old Maid,
And she died an old Mann."

"Here lies in silent clay,
MISS ARABELLA YOUNG,
Who on the 21st of May,
Began to hold her tongue."

"In memory of JANE BENT,
Who kick'd her heels and way she went."
Rockville, Massachusetts

"Here lies Mary, the wife of John Ford
We hope her soul is gone to the Lord;
But if for Hell she has chang'd this life
She had better be there than be John Ford's wife."
Potterne, Wiltshire

"Poor Martha Snell! her's gone away,
Her would if she could, but her couldn't stay;
Her'd two sore legs and a baddish cough,
But her legs it was as carried her off."

From Raymond L. Brown, *The Book of Epitaphs* (New York: Taplinger, 1968)

PARTING REMARKS:
WHAT THEY SAID BEFORE THEY DIED

☿

Joan of Arc,♀ At the stake: "Jesus! Jesus! Blessed be God."
Anne Boleyn,♀ Henry VIII's second wife, who was beheaded: "The executioner is, I believe, very expert; and my neck is very slender."
Lady Jane Grey.♀ Used as a foil in a futile attempt to capture the British

throne, she "reigned" for nine days before facing the executioner: "Lord, into Thy hands I commend my spirit."

Elizabeth I♀*:* "All my possessions for a moment of time."

Ninon de Lenclos.♀ The seventeenth-century beauty, perhaps the greatest courtesan of all time, *must* have had more than a few minutes to compose these words: "I put your consolations by / And care not for the hopes you give: / Since I am old enough to die, / Why should I longer wish to live?"

Madame de Pompadour.♀ To the cleric who was attending her final hours: "Stay a little longer, M. le Curé, and we will go together."

Marie Antoinette,♀ on her way to the guillotine: "Farewell, my children, for ever. I am going to your father."

Manon Roland, in the tumbril, headed toward the same fate: "Oh, Liberty! Oh, Liberty! What crimes are committed in your name!"

Marie Walewska.♀ The emperor's twenty-eight-year-old mistress's last thoughts were of her lover: "Napoleon."

Lady Mary Wortley Montagu. ♀ "It has all been very interesting."

Harriet Martineau. The nineteenth-century political writer viewed her end philosophically: "I see no reason why the existence of Harriet Martineau should be perpetuated."

Queen Victoria ♀ addressed her oldest son who was to succeed her as Edward VII: "Bertie."

Calamity Jane (Martha Jane Cannary),♀ referring to her lover, Wild Bill Hickok: "Bury me next to Wild Bill." Her last wish was honored, and a distance of only twenty feet separates their graves.

Katharine Elisabeth Goethe.♀ The mother of the poet was a realist to the end: "Say that Frau Goethe is unable to come, she is busy dying at the moment."

Edith Cavell,♀ the heroic English nurse, condemned to die before a German firing squad in 1915 for helping allied soldiers escape from Belgium: "Patriotism is not enough. I must have no hatred or bitterness toward anyone."

Mata Hari (Margaretha Zelle).♀ Before facing a French firing squad in 1917, the notorious spy left three sealed letters, one addressed to her daughter and the others to two lovers. Her last request: "Don't mix up the addresses; that would be fatal."

Mabelle Hollenbeck.♀ The mother of actor Clifton Webb devoted her life totally to her son. As she lay dying at the age of ninety, her final maternal query was: "How is Clifton? Has he had his luncheon?"

Gertrude Stein. ♀ "What is the answer . . . what is the question?"

XXV ❧ HONORS

PRESERVED IN CEMENT

❧

According to Hollywood legend, silent star *Norma Talmadge* stepped out of her limousine one day in 1927 in front of Grauman's Chinese Theatre and found herself mired in wet cement. Sid Grauman, who was with her at the time and knew a good gimmick when he stumbled into it, had her sign her name in the goo. *Mary Pickford,*♀ another member of the party, followed suit. After that, the courtyard became a repository for cement impressions—and not just footprints. Also enshrined among the 150 so honored:

Sonja Henie's♀ left skate print.
Eleanor Powell's tap shoes.
Betty Grable's leg.
Susan Hayward's hand prints.
Sophia Loren's hand prints.
Ali MacGraw's hand prints.
And the posterior of an unidentified female star.

The entire forecourt pavement was dedicated to *Rosa Grauman* in 1940. Gary Cooper, who was scheduled to be footprinted, failed to show up, and owner Sid Grauman, not wanting the press to go away empty-handed—and sensing another gimmick—seized the opportunity to honor his mother.

THE MOST HONORED WOMAN

❧

Sacajawea♀ is the most honored woman in American history, as the following list of monuments and memorials amply demonstrates:

Salmon, Idaho. Here, in a Shoshoni village, now marked by a boulder on Route 28, Sacajawea was born ca. 1786.
Three Forks, Montana. The Missouri Headwaters State Monument marks the place where Sacajawea as a young girl was captured by the Hidatsa, to which she later returned during her travels with the exploring party of Lewis and Clark. The Sacajawea Hotel and a small park also commemorate the Indian woman who served as a guide to the explorers.
Washburn, North Dakota. Fort Mandan is a replica of the fort in which the

pregnant sixteen-year-old girl was living with Toussaint Charbonneau,
when in April 1805, the explorers met and engaged her to be their guide
on their westward journey.

Bismarck, North Dakota. A statue of Sacajawea, with her baby carried in a
sling on her back, stands in the state capital.

Pasco, Washington. Sacajawea State Park is near an 1805 campsite of the
exploring party.

Salem, Oregon. A statue outside the state capitol shows Sacajawea, on foot,
pointing the way to the explorers on horseback. Inside the capitol the
guide is depicted in a mural.

Mobridge, South Dakota. A monument in Dakota Memorial Park commemorates the alleged burial place of Sacajawea at the age of twenty-five,
on December 1812, at Fort Manuel near here. There is some dispute
over the place and age at death of the heroine.

Fort Washakie, Wyoming, claims also to be the site of the death of Sacajawea. According to this version of her story, the remaining years of her
life were spent wandering from tribe to tribe, until she died at a very
advanced age among her Shoshoni people in Wyoming in April 1884.
The cemetery at the Wind River Reservation honors her with its largest
monument, next to which are small markers for her son and nephew.

Charlottesville, Virginia. Sacajawea never visited Virginia, but both Lewis
and Clark were natives of the state; a monument honoring them shows
her also.

Anadarko, Oklahoma. A bronze bust of Sacajawea is one of more than
twenty sculptures honoring American Indian leaders in an outdoor pavilion of the Indian Village here.

Portland, Oregon. A statue of Sacajawea, sculpted by Alice Cooper Hubbard, was dedicated by Susan B. Anthony♀ and Abigail Scott Duniway
during the national suffragist convention held here in 1905.

From Lynn Sherr and Jurate Kazickas, *The American Woman's Gazetteer* (New York:
Bantam Books, 1976)

THIRTY FIRSTS FOR BLACK WOMEN

Phillis Wheatley,♀ first slave and second woman to publish a book of poetry
in America, 1775. One poem was titled "On Being Brought from Africa
to America."

Lucy Sessions, first black woman to earn a degree from an American college,
Oberlin, 1850.

Frances Ellen Watkins Harper, first black woman to publish a novel, *Iola
LeRoy, the Shadows Uplifted.*

Elizabeth Greenfield, first black opera star, known in the 1850s as the "Black
Swan."

Mary Ann Shadd Cary, first black newspaper editor in North America. She
founded the *Provincial Freeman* in Canada in the 1850s.

Rebecca Lee, first black woman to receive a medical degree, from the New
England Female Medical College in 1864.

Mary Elizabeth Mahoney, first black graduate nurse, 1879.

Edmonia Lewis,♀ first black woman sculptor, 1870s.

Susan McKinney Steward, first black woman doctor to practice medicine in New York City, 1870.

Maggie Lena Walker,♀ first black to organize and act as president of a United States bank.

Sarah Breedlove Walker,♀ first black woman millionaire.

Lillian Evanti, first black woman to sing with a European opera company, 1890.

Lucy Diggs Slowe, founder of the first sorority for black college women, Alpha Kappa Alpha, 1908.

Augusta Savage, first black woman member of the National Association of Women Painters and Sculptors and a leading sculptor of the Harlem Renaissance of the 1920s.

Bessie Coleman, first black woman to receive a pilot's license. Turned down by aviation schools in this country, she earned the license in Europe in the 1920s.

Jane Matilda Bolin,♀ first black woman judge in America, appointed to the Domestic Relations Court in New York City in 1939.

Hattie McDaniel, first black to win an Oscar, for her role as Mammy in *Gone With the Wind,* 1939.

Alice Coachman, first American black woman to win an Olympic gold medal, for high jumping, 1948.

Gwendolyn Brooks,♀ first black woman to receive a Pulitzer Prize, for poetry, for *Annie Allen,* 1950.

Frances Wills, first black officer in the Women's Reserve of the United States Navy.

Althea Gibson,♀ first black woman to win the U.S. National Women's Grass Court title at Forest Hills, 1957.

Lorraine Hansberry,♀ first black woman playwright to have her work produced on Broadway, *A Raisin in the Sun,* 1959.

Diahann Carroll, first black actress to star in a long-running television series, "Julia," 1962.

Constance Baker Motley,♀ first black woman appointed a federal judge, 1966.

Jeanne Craig Sinkford, first black woman dean of a dental school, Howard University.

Shirley Chisholm,♀ first black congresswoman, Brooklyn, New York, 1969.

Yvonne Brathwaite Burke,♀ first black congresswoman from California, 1972.

Barbara Jordan,♀ first black congresswoman from Texas, 1972.

Linda Gainer, first woman to help ready a space vehicle for launch. She was a member of the Chrysler Corporation *Saturn IB* launch crew in 1973.

Patricia Harris,♀ first black woman to be a cabinet member, appointed secretary of the United States Department of Housing and Urban Development (HUD), 1977.

From Smithsonian Institution Traveling Exhibition Service, *Black Women: Achievements Against the Odds, Calendar 1978–80* (Washington, D.C.: 1978)

AWARDED THE IRON CROSS

━━━━━━━━━━━━━━━━ ❧ ━━━━━━━━━━━━━━━━

The Iron Cross, Germany's top military honor, has been awarded to several women for bravery under fire. The following list covers World War II only; records of previous wars are not available.

First-class medal

Flightcaptain Hanna Reitsch received the medal twice, in August 1941 and November 1942. Reitsch was the first woman to receive the highest grade of the Iron Cross.

Flightcaptain Countess Schenk Von Stauffenberg a test pilot, was honored in February 1943.

Marga Droste, a nurse, was decorated in November 1942 for hiding the badly wounded during an air attack.

Second-class medal

Elfrieda Wunk, September 1942.

Magda Darchinger, March 1943.

Lieselotte Maaseen, December 1943.

Therese H., representing all nurses or nurse's aides in field hospitals on the Eastern Front, in January 1945.

Grete Fock and *Ilse Schulz,* nurses in a field hospital in Africa, April 1943.

Maria Stolle, aide at a field command post, November 1944.

Alice Bendig and *Hildegard Bellgardt,* with the commandant's office at Elling, January 1945.

Leni S., a volunteer on the Eastern Front, March 1945.

From The Bundesarchiv, Federal Republic of Germany

OUTSTANDING—TEN WOMEN WHO RECEIVED RADCLIFFE COLLEGE'S FIRST HONORARY DEGREES

━━━━━━━━━━━━━━━━ ❧ ━━━━━━━━━━━━━━━━

In celebration of its centennial in 1978, Radcliffe College presented its first honorary degrees to ten women distinguished in the sciences, humanities, arts, and religion. The outstanding ten were:

Mary Ellen Avery, pediatrician and professor at the Harvard Medical School, noted for her studies of the diseases of the newborn, particularly lung disorders; Doctor of Science.

Jessie Bernard, sociologist, who has written extensively about the changing role of the American woman and its effect on family life; Doctor of Humane Letters.

Mildred Cohn,[♀] educator, biophysicist, and biochemist, the recipient of a lifetime grant from the American Heart Association in 1964; Doctor of Science.

Bernice Brown Cronkhite, educator and scholar, the first dean of the Radcliffe Graduate School and holder of that position for twenty-five years; Doctor of Humane Letters.

Helen Frankenthaler, artist, a leading abstract expressionist painter; Doctor of Arts.

Nancy Hanks, art consultant, chair of the National Endowment for the Arts from 1968 to 1977, a period in which federal funding for the arts increased fourteenfold; Doctor of Humane Letters.

Ada Louise Huxtable,♀ Pulitzer Prize–winning journalist and architecture critic of the *New York Times,* crusader for the preservation of the nation's architectural treasures; Doctor of Humane Letters.

Pauli Murray,♀ lawyer, author, and civil rights leader, also the first black woman to be ordained by the Episcopal church; Doctor of Humane Letters.

Helen Brooke Taussig,♀ physician, the discoverer of the cause of death in newborn "blue babies"; Doctor of Science.

Shirley Williams,♀ member of Parliament in Great Britain; Doctor of Humane Letters.

RECIPIENTS OF THE AMERICAN PSYCHOLOGICAL ASSOCIATION'S DISTINGUISHED SCIENTIFIC AWARDS

❧

Nancy Bayley, 1966, "For the enterprise, pertinacity, and insight with which she has studied human growth over long segments of the life cycle. . . . Her studies have enriched psychology with enduring contributions to the measurement and meaning of intelligence. . . ." Born in The Dalles, Oregon, 1899; Ph.D., State University of Iowa, 1926; president of the Society for Research in Child Development, 1961–1963.

Eleanor Jack Gibson,♀ 1968, "For distinguished studies of perceptual learning and perceptual development. . . . She has imaginatively shown how to bridge the gap from laboratory to classroom." Born in Peoria, Illinois, 1910; Ph.D., Yale University, 1938. Fellow of the Institute for Advanced Study, Princeton University, 1958–1959; of the Center of Advanced Study in the Behavioral Sciences, Stanford University, 1963–1964.

Dorothea Jameson♀ (with Leo M. Hurvich), 1972, "For [studies] of color vision through a broadly based program of conceptually sophisticated and rigorously conducted experiments. . . . Their very unusual scholarship, technical skill, untiring motivation, and contagious enthusiasm for scientific discovery have set new standards of excellence against which future experimenters and theorists will be judged." Born in Newton, Massachusetts, 1920; A.B., Wellesley College, 1942; married Hurvich, 1948.

Brenda (Langford) Milner, 1973, "For outstanding psychological study of the human brain. . . ." Born in Manchester, England, 1918; B.A., Cambridge University, 1939; Ph.D., McGill University, 1952; Sc.D., University of Cambridge, 1972.

Beatrice C. Lacey (with John T. Lacey), 1976, "For conceptions of autonomic nervous system activity that have had an explosive impact on research in psychophysiology. . . . Few areas of psychology remain unaffected by the implications of their work." Born in New York City, 1919; married Lacey, 1938; B.A. "with distinction," Cornell University, 1940; did not resume education and professional career until their two children were school age; M.A., Antioch College, 1958.

Marie Jahoda, 1979, "Through [her] work, we know more about psychological aspects of unemployment, prejudice and race relations, work satisfaction, mental health, and social forecasting." Born in Vienna, Austria, 1907; Ph.D., University of Vienna, 1933; professor of social psychology, University of Sussex, England, retired 1973.

From *American Psychologist,* the journal of the American Psychological Association

ELECTED TO THE NATIONAL ACADEMY OF SCIENCES

The academy, a private organization, has elected a total of 1,284 members since it was incorporated in 1863 to honor original research.

Florence Rena Sabin,♀ 1925 (anatomist).
Margaret Floy Washburn,♀ 1931 (psychologist).
Barbara McClintock, 1944 (botanist).
Gerty T. Cori,♀ 1948 (pathologist, biochemist).
Maria Goeppert-Mayer,♀ 1956 (physicist).
Katherine Esau, 1957 (plant morphologist).
Chien-Shiung Wu,♀ 1958 (physicist).
Libbie Henrietta Hyman,♀ 1961 (zoologist).
Berta Vogel Scharrer, 1967 (anatomist).
Rita Levi-Montalcini, 1968 (neurobiologist).
Ruth Patrick,♀ 1970 (biologist, ecologist).
Rebecca Craighill Lancefield, 1970 (bacteriologist).
Mildred Cohn,♀ 1971 (chemist).
Eleanor Jack Gibson,♀ 1971 (psychologist).
Gertrude Scharff Goldhaber, 1972 (physicist).
Elizabeth Shull Russell, 1972 (geneticist).
Beatrice Mintz, 1973 (medical geneticist).
Helen M. Ranney, 1973 (hemoglobin biologist).
Helen Brooke Taussig,♀ 1973 (pediatric cardiologist).
Estella Bergere Leopold, 1974 (research botanist).
Sarah Ratner, 1974 (biochemist).
Gertrude Mary Cox, 1975 (statistician).
Frederica Annis De Laguna, 1975 (anthropologist).
Dorothea Jameson,♀ 1975 (psychologist).
Margaret Mead,♀ 1975 (cultural anthropologist).
Rosalyn S. Yalow,♀ 1975 (medical physicist).
Dorothy Millicent Horstmann, 1975 (epidemiologist, pathologist).
Charlotte Friend, 1976 (oncologist).
Julia Robinson, 1976 (mathematician).
Elizabeth Florence Colson, 1977 (anthropologist).

Elizabeth Fondal Neufeld, 1977 (biochemist).
Ruth Sager, 1977 (geneticist).
Evelyn Maisel Witkin, 1977 (geneticist).
E. Margaret Burbidge, 1978 (physicist).
Mary Rosamond Haas, 1978 (linguist, anthropologist).
Isabella Lugoski Karle, 1978 (physical chemist).
Elizabeth Cavert Miller, 1978 (oncologist).
Mary Jane Osborn, 1978 (biochemist).
Salome Gluecksohn-Waelsch, 1979 (geneticist).
Gertrude Henle,♀ 1979 (pediatrician).
Maxine F. Singer, 1979 (biochemist/oncologist).
Eloise R. Giblett, 1980 (medical researcher).

From the National Academy of Sciences, Washington, D.C.

COMMEMORATED ON U.S. POSTAGE STAMPS

※

Fifty years ago, only four women had appeared on U.S. stamps. In 1980 alone, six women were added (on five stamps). Here is the roster to date:

Jane Addams,♀ 1940, 5 cents.
Louisa May Alcott,♀ 1940, 5 cents.
American Homemakers, 1964, 5 cents.
The American Woman (a mother and daughter), 1960, 4 cents.
Susan B. Anthony,♀ 1936, 3 cents; and 1954–1961, 50 cents.
Clara Barton,♀ 1948, 3 cents.
Emily Bissell ("Christmas Seal Lady," pioneer in the fight against tuberculosis and other lung diseases), 1980, 15 cents.
Elizabeth Blackwell,♀ 1974, 18 cents.
Camp Fire Girls, 1960, 4 cents.
Mary Cassatt,♀ 1966, 5 cents.
Willa Cather,♀ 1973, 8 cents.
Virginia Dare (with her parents), 1937, 5 cents.
Emily Dickinson,♀ 1971, 8 cents.
Amelia Earhart♀ (appropriately, an air mail stamp), 1963, 8 cents.
General Federation of Women's Clubs, 1966, 5 cents.
Girl Scouts Fiftieth Anniversary, 1962, 4 cents.
Gold Star Mothers, 1948, 3 cents.
Queen Isabella of Spain (with Columbus), 1893, $4.
Helen Keller♀ and *Anne Sullivan*♀ (together), 1980, 15 cents.
Juliette Gordon Low, 1948, 3 cents.
Sybil Ludington,♀ 1975, 8 cents.
Clara Maass,♀ 1976, 13 cents.
Dolley Madison♀ (the third First Lady to appear on a stamp), 1980, 15 cents.
Moina Michael ("Founder of Memorial Poppy," symbol of Memorial Day), 1948, 3 cents.
Grandma Moses,♀ 1969, 6 cents.
Frances Perkins,♀ 1980, 15 cents.
Pocahontas,♀ 1907, 5 cents.

Molly Pitcher,♀ 1928, 2 cents.
Eleanor Roosevelt,♀ 1963, 5 cents.
Betsy Ross,♀ 1952, 3 cents.
Elizabeth Cady Stanton, ♀ *Carrie Chapman Catt,* ♀ *Lucretia Mott* ♀ (all on one
    stamp honoring "100 Years of Progress of Women"), 1948, 3 cents.
Lucy Stone,♀ 1965–1968, 50 cents.
Harriet Tubman,♀ 1978, 13 cents.
Martha Washington,♀ 1901, 8 cents; 1918, 2 cents prepaid postal card; 1920, 4
    cents; and 1938, 1½ cents.
Edith Wharton,♀ 1980, 15 cents.
"Whistler's Mother,"♀ for Mother's Day, 1934, 3 cents.
Frances Elizabeth Willard,♀ 1940, 5 cents.
Women of the Armed Forces, 1952, 3 cents.
Women Marines, 1968, 5 cents.
Women's Suffrage—Fiftieth Anniversary, 1970, 6 cents.
and the *Statue of Liberty,* many times, most recently in 1978, 16 cents.

Can you think of a woman you'd like to see honored on a stamp? Suggestions can be sent to Postmaster General, U.S. Postal Service, Washington, D.C. 20260. Remember that no living person is eligible. The post office receives some 4,000 stamp suggestions each year.

PULITZER PRIZE WINNERS

❧

Journalism

Minna Lewinson, Meritorious Public Service, special award, 1918.
Anne O'Hare McCormick, New York Times, Foreign Correspondence, 1937.
Mrs. William Allen White, special citation honoring her husband, 1944.
Marguerite Higgins, New York Herald Tribune, International Reporting,
    1951.
Mrs. Walter M. Schau, News Photography, 1954.
Mrs. Caro Brown, Alice (Texas) *Daily Echo,* General Reporting, 1955.
Mary Lou Werner, Washington (D.C.) *Evening Star,* Special or Investigative
    Reporting, 1960.
Hazel Brannon Smith, Lexington (Mississippi) *Advertiser,* Editorial Writing,
    1964.
Ada Louise Huxtable,♀ *New York Times,* Criticism, 1970.
Lucinda Franks, United Press International, National Reporting, 1971.
Ann DeSantis, Boston Globe, Special Local Reporting, 1972.
Emily Genauer, Newsday, Criticism, 1974.
Slava Veder, Associated Press, Feature Photography, 1974.
Mary McGrory,♀ *Washington* (D.C.) *Star,* Commentary, 1975.
Margo Huston, Milwaukee Journal, General Reporting, 1977.
Meg Greenfield, Washington Post, Editorial Writing, 1978.
Catharine Mitchell (with her husband, David Mitchell), *Point Reyes* (California) *Light,* Public Service, 1979.
Madeleine Blais, Miami Herald, Feature Writing, 1980.
Ellen H. Goodman, Boston Globe, Commentary, 1980.

Bette Swenson Orsini, St. Petersburg Times, National Reporting, 1980.
Joan Vennochi, Boston Globe, Special Local Reporting, 1980.
Anne C. Wyman (a runner-up), *Boston Globe,* Editorial Writing, 1980.

Fiction

Edith Wharton,♀ for *The Age of Innocence,* 1921.
Willa Cather,♀ for *One of Ours,* 1923.
Margaret Wilson, for *The Able McLaughlins,* 1924.
Edna Ferber,♀ for *So Big,* 1925.
Julia M. Peterkin, for *Scarlet Sister Mary,* 1929.
Margaret Ayer Barnes, for *Years of Grace,* 1931.
Pearl S. Buck,♀ for *The Good Earth,* 1932.
Caroline Miller, for *Lamb in His Bosom,* 1934.
Josephine W. Johnson, for *Now in November,* 1935.
Margaret Mitchell,♀ for *Gone With the Wind,* 1937.
Marjorie Kinnan Rawlings,♀ for *The Yearling,* 1939.
Ellen Glasgow, for *In This Our Life,* 1942.
Harper Lee, for *To Kill a Mockingbird,* 1961.
Shirley Ann Grau, for *The Keepers of the House,* 1965.
Katherine Anne Porter, for *Collected Stories of Katherine Anne Porter,* 1966.
Jean Stafford, for *Collected Stories,* 1970.
Eudora Welty, for *The Optimist's Daughter,* 1973.

Drama

Zona Gale, for *Miss Lulu Bett,* 1921.
Susan Glaspell,♀ for *Alison's House,* 1931.
Zoë Akins, for *The Old Maid,* 1935.
Mary Chase, for *Harvey,* 1945.
Frances Goodrich (with coauthor Albert Hackett), for *The Diary of Anne Frank,* 1956.
Ketti Frings, for *Look Homeward, Angel,* 1958.

U.S. History

Margaret Leech, for *Reveille in Washington,* 1942.
Esther Forbes, for *Paul Revere and the World He Lived In,* 1943.
Margaret Leech, for *In the Days of McKinley,* 1960.
Constance McLaughlin Green, for *Washington: Village and Capital, 1800–1878,* 1963.

Biography

Laura E. Richards and *Maude Howe Elliott,* assisted by *Florence Howe Hall,* for *Julia Ward Howe,* 1917.
Ola Elizabeth Winslow, for *Jonathan Edwards,* 1941.
Margaret Clapp, for *Forgotten First Citizen, John Bigelow,* 1948.
Margaret Louise Coit, for *John C. Calhoun: American Portrait,* 1951.
Mary Wells Ashworth (with coauthor John Alexander Carroll), for volume seven of *George Washington,* 1958.

Poetry

Sara Teasdale, for *Love Songs,* 1918.
Margaret Widdemer, for *Old Road to Paradise,* 1919 (shared prize with Carl Sandburg).
Edna St. Vincent Millay,♀ for *The Ballad of the Harp-Weaver, A Few Figs from Thistles,* eight sonnets in *American Poetry, 1922, A Miscellany,* 1923.
Amy Lowell,♀ for *What's O'Clock,* 1926.
Leonora Speyer, for *Fiddler's Farewell,* 1927.
Audrey Wurdemann, for *Bright Ambush,* 1935.
Marya Zaturenska, for *Cold Morning Sky,* 1938.
Gwendolyn Brooks,♀ for *Annie Allen,* 1950.
Marianne Moore, for *Collected Poems,* 1952.
Elizabeth Bishop, for *Poems—North & South,* 1956.
Phyllis McGinley, for *Times Three: Selected Verse from Three Decades,* 1961.
Anne Sexton, for *Live or Die,* 1967.
Maxine Winokur Kumin, for *Up Country,* 1973.

General Nonfiction

Barbara W. Tuchman,♀ for *The Guns of August,* 1963.
Ariel Durant (shared with her husband, Will Durant) for *Rousseau and Revolution,* 1968.
Barbara W. Tuchman,♀ for *Stilwell and the American Experience in China, 1911-1945,* 1972.
Frances Fitzgerald for *Fire in the Lake: The Vietnamese and the Americans in Vietnam,* 1973 (shared with Robert M. Coles).
Annie Dillard, for *Pilgrim at Tinker Creek,* 1975.

NOBEL PRIZE WINNERS

Literature

Selma Lagerlöf, Sweden, 1909.
Grazia Deledda, Italy, 1926.
Sigrid Undset, Norway, 1928.
Pearl S. Buck,♀ United States, 1938.
Gabriela Mistral, Chile, 1945.
Nelly Sachs, Sweden, 1966 (shared with S. Y. Agnon, Israel).

Peace

Bertha von Suttner, Austria, 1905.
Jane Addams,♀ United States, 1931 (shared with Nicholas Murray Butler, United States).
Emily G. Balch, United States, 1946 (shared with John R. Mott, United States).
Mairead Corrigan♀ and **Betty Williams,**♀ Northern Ireland, 1976.
Mother Teresa of Calcutta, India, 1979.

Physics

Marie S. Curie,♀ France, 1903 (shared with her husband, Pierre Curie, and Henri Becquerel, both of France).

Maria Goeppert Mayer,♀ United States, 1963 (shared with J. Hans D. Jensen, Germany, and Eugene P. Wigner, United States).

Chemistry

Marie S. Curie,♀ France, 1911.

Irène Joliot-Curie,♀ France, 1935 (shared with her husband, Frédéric Joliot-Curie).

Dorothy Mary Crowfoot Hodgkin,♀ England, 1964.

Medicine

Gerty T. Cori,♀ United States, 1947 (shared with her husband, Carl F. Cori, and Bernardo A. Houssay of Argentina).

Rosalyn S. Yalow,♀ United States, 1977 (shared with Roger C. L. Guillemin and Andrew V. Schally, both of the United States).

TIME'S "MAN" OF THE YEAR

Every year since 1927, *Time* magazine has chosen a person or persons who have had the most impact on events in the course of that year, the first being Charles A. Lindbergh in 1927. Women who have been "Men of the Year" have been few and far between. They are:

Wallis Warfield Simpson, 1936.
Madam Chiang Kai-shek,♀ who shared honors with her husband in 1937.
Queen Elizabeth II,♀ 1952.

In 1966 the "Man of the Year" was "The 25 and Under Generation" (*sic*), and the cover illustration showed the face of a young man in the foreground, hiding most (but not quite all) of the face of a young woman. In 1969 *Time* gave us a "Man and Woman of the Year" in the Middle Americans; this time the cover illustration featured a woman's face in profile positioned to cover partly the profile of a man. At last, in 1975, *Time* hailed "Women of the Year," with photographs of twelve not particularly well-known women whose lives, described in the accompanying story, typified many of the issues and situations facing women today.

WOMEN OF THE 1970s

The following women were chosen as the most important in that decade by readers of the *Ladies' Home Journal:*

Margaret Mead,♀ anthropologist.
Katharine Hepburn,♀ actress.

Beverly Sills,♀ opera singer.
Marian Anderson,♀ singer.
Betty Ford, president's wife.
Helen Hayes,♀ actress.
Barbara Walters,♀ television journalist.
Joan Ganz Cooney, television producer.
Barbara Jordan,♀ former U.S. representative.
Elisabeth Kübler-Ross, psychiatrist and writer.
Sylvia Porter, financial writer/journalist.

MS. MAGAZINE'S WOMEN TO WATCH IN THE 1980s

♀

Women to watch in the 1980s were those capable of taking over "existing feminist tasks and organizations" and who had not previously received national attention, according to *Ms.* editor Gloria Steinem.♀

Polly Baca-Barragan, state senator, Colorado.
Marianne Bruesehoff, poultry farmer, Minnesota.
Jan Zimmerman, consultant, telecommunications and aerospace industry, California.
Maxine Waters, state assemblywoman, Colorado.
Dudley Dudley, member of the state executive council, New Hampshire.
Nancy Stevenson,♀ lieutenant governor, South Carolina.
Mary E. Hunt, theologian and theorist in lesbian feminism, California.
Carolyn Forrest, administrative assistant to the president, United Automobile Workers Union, Detroit.
Fran P. Hosken, journalist and urban planner, Massachusetts.

"BUSTED" IN THE HALL OF FAME

♀

The Hall of Fame, dedicated in 1901 at New York University's University Heights campus, has 102 niches for busts of the famous lining a colonnade overlooking the Harlem River. All these spaces have now been filled, 10 of them by women. The last election was held in 1976. Candidates must have been dead for at least twenty-five years before election to the Hall of Fame. University Heights is now home to Bronx Community College, which is maintaining the Hall of Fame as well as three landmark buildings on the campus. The women in the Hall of Fame are:

Jane Addams,♀ social worker and reformer.
Susan B. Anthony,♀ suffragist leader.
Clara Barton,♀ founder of American Red Cross.
Charlotte Saunders Cushman,♀ actress.
Mary Lyon,♀ educator.
Maria Mitchell,♀ astronomer.
Alice Freeman Palmer, educator.

Harriet Beecher Stowe,♀ author.
Emma Willard,♀ educator.
Frances Elizabeth Willard,♀ reformer.

THE WOMEN'S HALL OF FAME
♀

A Women's Hall of Fame was a feature of the New York World's Fair of 1965. Honoring "Twenty Outstanding Women of the Twentieth Century," it was the idea of Charlotte C. Klein. The nominating committee chaired by Margaret Truman Daniel submitted one hundred names to women's editors of newspapers and magazines, who were to vote for ten living and ten deceased women from among those on the list. The winners were:

Living (in 1965)

Marian Anderson ♀
Pearl Buck ♀
Margaret Bourke-White ♀
Edna Ferber ♀
Helen Hayes ♀
Helen Keller ♀
Dr. Frances O. Kelsey ♀
Margaret Mead ♀
Margaret Sanger ♀
Senator Margaret Chase Smith ♀

Deceased:

Jane Addams ♀
Ethel Barrymore ♀
Evangeline Booth
Rachel Carson ♀
Amelia Earhart ♀
Edna St. Vincent Millay ♀
Grandma (Anna Robertson) Moses ♀
Eleanor Roosevelt ♀
Dr. Florence Sabin ♀
Babe Didrikson Zaharias ♀

In 1979 the Women's Hall of Fame found a permanent—and highly suitable—home at last, in Seneca Falls, New York. Honorees, now selected by a National Honors Committee, are "those women, citizens of the United States of America, whose contributions to the arts, athletics, business, education, government, the humanities, philanthropy and science, have been of greatest value for the development of their country."

WESTMINSTER WOMEN

꙳

Buried in Westminster Abbey:

Katherine of Valois (d. 1437) was first buried in the old Lady Chapel, but her body was removed when Henry VII tore the chapel down. For 200 years Katherine's remains rested above ground in an open coffin near Henry V's tomb. In 1776 she went underground again, this time in the Chapel of St. Nicholas. And in 1878 she was finally set to rest under the altar slab in the Chantry Chapel of Henry V.

Elizabeth of York (d. 1503) wife of Henry VII, first buried in a side chapel, later reburied in 1519 at the side of her husband when his Lady Chapel was completed.

Margaret Beaufort♀ (d. 1509), mother of Henry VII, also buried in Henry's new chapel.

Anne of Cleves♀ (d. 1557), buried in an unfinished tomb in the sanctuary.

"A female giantess" who lived at the time of Henry VIII, long supposed to lie under a large blue stone known as "Long Meg." It is now believed that the stone covers twenty-six monks who died of the plague.

Mary, Queen of Scots♀ (d. 1587), first buried at Peterborough Cathedral, then reburied in the Abbey in 1612.

Lady Elizabeth Russell, called the "Child of Westminster" because she was not only born in the vicinity, but christened and buried in the Chapel of St. Edmund at the age of twenty-six. Her monument depicts her pointing to a skull, an image that led to a legend that she had pricked herself while sewing and bled to death; this story first appeared eighty-two years after her death of consumption in 1601 and resurfaced as late as the mid-nineteenth century when retold by Dickens.

Aphra Behn,♀ buried in the East Walk of the Cloister, the only "feminine imaginative writer" in the Abbey.

Baroness Burdett-Coutts, the last body buried in Westminster Abbey (except for the Unknown Warrior) in 1907. Since then, cremation has been required first.

Beatrice Webb. Her ashes and those of her husband were brought to the nave for reburial in 1948.

And *Aveline of Lancaster* (d. 1273), *Queen Eleanor*♀ (1290), *Queen Philippa* (1369), *Anne of Bohemia*♀ (1394), *Mary I*♀ (1558), *Queen Elizabeth I*♀ (1603), *Frances Grey, Duchess of Suffolk* and mother of Lady Jane Grey♀ (1559), *Lady Arabella Stuart*♀ (1615), *Anne of Denmark* (1619), *Elizabeth, Queen of Bohemia,* daughter of James I (1662), *Anne Hyde,* first wife of James II (1671), *Sarah, Duchess of Somerset* (1692), *Queen Mary II* (1694), *Queen Anne*♀ (1714), *Queen Caroline* (1737), and *Ann Oldfield*♀ (1730) and *Hannah Pritchard* (1768), actresses.

Commemorated by monuments in Westminster Abbey:

Charlotte,♀ *Emily,*♀ and *Anne Brontë,*♀ a tablet erected in the Poets' Corner in 1939.

Sarah Siddons♀ (d. 1831), actress.

Carola (d. 1674) and *Ann* (d. 1680), the two wives of Sir Samuel Morland. Their monument, located in the nave in the south aisle, bears an inscription in English, Hebrew, Greek, and Ethiopic.

Lady Elizabeth Nightingale (d. 1731). Her father and husband are both buried in the north aisle. Her son erected a white marble monument to her in 1761.

George Eliot ♀ (d. 1880), added to those honored in the Poets' Corner a hundred years later. Eliot's request to be buried in the Abbey had been denied because of objections to her long-term (1854 to 1878) cohabitation with George Henry Lewes, who was legally unable to divorce his first wife, and also because she had rejected sectarian Christianity in favor of a more universalist concept of religion.

CAPITOL WOMEN

☙

Every state may place a commemorative sculpture in Statuary Hall in the Capitol. In 1905 the first figure of a woman was added to the line-up of males when . . .

Frances Willard, ♀ the temperance leader and suffragist, sculpted by Helen Farnsworth Mears, was presented to the nation by the state of Illinois.

Maria Sanford, the Minnesota educator and feminist, sculpted by Evelyn Raymond, became the second figure of a woman in Statuary Hall in 1958.

Florence Rena Sabin, ♀ the Colorado-born medical researcher, was sculpted by Joy Buba and added in 1959.

Esther Hobart Morris, ♀ Wyoming suffragist and coauthor of the statute that made women of that state the first to vote in the nation, by Avard Fairbanks, dedicated in 1960. Hers is the only one of the four figures of women in Statuary Hall not sculpted by a woman.

VENUSIANS

☙

The first contour map of Venus, prepared from data collected by radar aboard the Pioneer *Venus I* which went into orbit around the planet on December 4, 1978, was released in May 1980 by the National Aeronautics and Space Administration. It showed almost every plateau and crater, mountain and valley on the planet. Scientists, under some pressure from the women's movement, have named every feature of the planet for women—goddesses of many cultures and famous women who are no longer living—subject to approval by a committee of the International Astronomical Union. Among the women whose names are to be perpetuated on earth's nearest neighbor are:

Aphrodite, Greek goddess of love and beauty.
Freyja, ♀ Norse goddess of love, beauty, and fertility.
Eve, ♀ the first woman of the Judaeo-Christian tradition.
Hathor, Egyptian goddess of love, beauty, fertility, and marriage.
Ishtar, ♀ Babylonian goddess of love and fertility.

Lakshmi, Hindu goddess of agriculture and wealth and mother of all life in the universe.
Lise Meitner,♀ physicist.
Rhea,♀ Greek Titan, mother of all the gods.
Sappho,♀ Greek poet.
Theia, Greek Titan, mother of Helius, Eos, and Selene.

NATIONAL PARKS

※

In May 1980 the House of Representatives approved legislation appropriating $74.2 billion for the establishment of seven new units, and the expansion of existing units, in the National Park System. Three of the proposed new units were historical sites honoring women's achievements:

Women's Rights National Historical Park, Seneca Falls, New York.
Georgia O'Keeffe♀ *National Historical Site,* Abiquiu, New Mexico.
Mary McLeod Bethune♀ *National Historical Site,* Daytona Beach, Florida.

RECENT WINNERS: A MISCELLANY

※

Some lesser-known awards of recent years:

Ela Bhatt of Ahmadabad, India, received the $20,000 Ramon Magsaysay Award for humanitarian work in 1978 for organizing the Self-Employed Women's Association, a cooperative labor union of subsistence women workers. Bhatt, an English teacher, was moved to action after meeting three women who earned less than half a penny delivering groceries carried on their heads from wholesalers to retail markets. She donated her prize money to establish a maternity and infant care program for the union's members.

Begum Ra'Ana Liaquat Ali Khan, Pakistani women's rights activist, and *Helen Suzman,* civil rights activist and member of Parliament in South Africa, received human rights awards from the United Nations in December 1979.

Marlo Thomas, an actress, was given the Tom Paine Award of the National Emergency Civil Liberties Union for her advocacy of the Equal Rights Amendment in December 1979.

Elizabeth Brosby, a University of Michigan at Ann Arbor researcher in comparative human neuroanatomy, was the only woman to receive, along with nineteen men, a national Medal of Science, the highest honor given by the federal government to U.S. scientists and engineers, in December 1979.

Philomena De Sopo became a Cavaliera of the Order of Merit of the Italian government in March 1980 for tutoring and counseling immigrants at the Italian Catholic Center in Paterson, New Jersey. De Sopo, who emigrated from Italy twenty-five years earlier, received a gold medallion.

Jo Ann Burch of Indianapolis was awarded $100 in 1980 for her barbecued pork chops, but was not allowed to advance to the national finals of the "national cookout king" sponsored by the National Pork Council. A special board including three women was appointed to consider a rules change. Said Burch, "I knew the rules before I entered the contest. I think anything we can do to encourage the men to help with the cooking is fine."

Ozcan Tekgul was awarded a certificate of honor in June 1980 by the National Turkish Cinema Council. Or was she? Challenged by the fundamentalist Islamic opposition party, the minister of culture was quick to deny that any award was being given to the belly dancer. Said Tekgul, "I win this prize not for my belly dancing . . . but because of my contributions to the Turkish Oriental dance."

Pauline Frederick was the first woman to be given the Paul White Award of the Radio-Television News Directors' Association, in 1980. Frederick's career began with newspaper reporting, and from 1954 to 1974 she served as United Nations correspondent for NBC News. As the international affairs analyst for National Public Radio, she moderated the second 1976 presidential campaign debate between Gerald Ford and Jimmy Carter.

Molly Picon was guest of honor on July 10, 1980, when proprietor Abe Lebewohl of New York's Second Avenue Deli dedicated the new Molly Picon Room in his restaurant. Its decor features a brass plaque and posters reflecting the sixty-five-year career of the eighty-two-year-old Yiddish-American actress.

❧　❧　❧

BIBLIOGRAPHY

It is impossible to list all the works we consulted; by now they are, literally, countless. We have, therefore, chosen to cite those we feel would be most rewarding to other readers. We are grouping them in three lists: *Classics* are the books that made, and continue to make, a difference—to women in living their lives, to men and women in pointing out the possible. *Basics* are the reference works, both well-known and highly specialized, that make the researcher's task a little easier, pointing out what exists, where to find it, and most of all, the gaps that remain to be filled. And under the heading *Recommendations* we list a too-brief selection of works that shed particularly useful light on a topic or period.

Classics

de Beauvoir, Simone. *The Second Sex.* New York: Alfred A. Knopf, 1953.

Flexner, Eleanor. *Century of Struggle: The Women's Rights Movement in the United States.* Rev. ed. New York: Atheneum, 1975.

Friedan, Betty. *The Feminine Mystique.* New York: W. W. Norton, 1963.

Fuller, Margaret. *Women in the Nineteenth Century.* 1874. Reprint. New York: W. W. Norton, 1971.

Gilman, Charlotte Perkins. *Women and Economics, The Economic Relation Between Men and Women as a Factor in Social Evolution.* 1898. Reprint. New York: Harper & Row, 1970.

——————————, *The Man-made World.* 1911. Reprint. New York: Hacker, 1970.

Greer, Germaine. *The Female Eunuch.* New York: McGraw-Hill, 1971.

James, Edward T., et al., eds. *Notable American Women, 1607-1950. A Biographical Dictionary.* Cambridge, Mass.: Harvard University Press, 1971.

Janeway, Elizabeth. *Man's World, Woman's Place.* New York: Morrow, 1971.

Lerner, Gerda. *The Woman in American History.* Menlo Park, Calif.: Addison-Wesley Publishing, 1971.

Maccoby, Eleanor Emmons, and Jacklin, Carol Nagy. *The Psychology of Sex Differences.* Stanford, Calif.: Stanford University Press, 1974.

Mead, Margaret. *Male and Female.* New York: Morrow, 1949.

Miller, Casey, and Swift, Kate. *Words and Women.* New York: Doubleday & Co., 1976.

Millett, Kate. *Sexual Politics.* New York: Avon Books, 1971.

Ms., Vol. 1, No. 1 (January 1972), *et seq.*

Stanton, Elizabeth Cady; Anthony, Susan B.; and Gage, Matilda Joslyn. *History of Woman Suffrage.* 2 vols. New York: Fowler & Wells, 1881. Reprint (6 vols). New York: Hacker, 1971.

Woolf, Virginia. *A Room of One's Own.* 1929. Reprint. New York: Harcourt Brace Jovanovich, 1963.

Wollstonecraft, Mary. *A Vindication of the Rights of Woman.* 2nd ed. London: J. Johnson, 1792. Reprint. New York: W. W. Norton, 1967.

Basics

Agonito, Rosemary. *History of Ideas on Woman: A Source Book.* New York: G. P. Putnam's Sons/Capricorn Books, 1977.

"The American Woman," *Time,* Special Issue (March 29, 1972).

The Good Housekeeping Woman's Almanac. New York: Newspaper Enterprise Association, 1977.

Ireland, Norma Olin. *Index to Women of the World from Ancient to Modern Times: Biographies and Portraits.* Westwood, Mass.: F. W. Faxon, 1970.

Kostman, Samuel. *Twentieth Century Women of Achievement.* New York: Rosen Press, 1976.

Leonard, Eugenie Andruss; Drinker, Sophie Hutchinson; and Holden, Miriam Young. *The American Woman in Colonial and Revolutionary Times, 1565-1800, A Syllabus with Bibliography.* Philadelphia: University of Pennsylvania Press, 1962. Reprint. Westport, Conn.: Greenwood Press, 1975.

O'Neill, Lois Decker, ed. *The Women's Book of World Records and Achievements.* New York: Doubleday/Anchor, 1979.

Sherr, Lynn, and Kazickas, Jurate. *The American Woman's Gazetteer.* New York: Bantam Books, 1976.

Who's Who of American Women with World Notables. Chicago: Marquis. Biennial publication.

Yost, Edna. *American Women of Science.* Rev. ed. New York: Lippincott, 1955.

————, *Women of Modern Science.* New York: Dodd, Mead & Co., 1959.

Recommendations

Adoff, Arnold, ed. *The Poetry of Black America. Anthology of the Twentieth Century.* New York: Harper & Row, 1973.

Angelouglou, Maggie. *A History of Make-up.* New York: Macmillan, 1970.

Barksdale, Richard, and Kinnamon, Keneth. *Black Writers of America.* New York: Macmillan, 1972.

Barnstone, Willis, and Barnstone, Aliki, eds. *A Book of Women Poets from Antiquity to Now.* New York: Schocken Books, 1979.

Baum, Charlotte; Hyman, Paula; and Michel, Sonya. *The Jewish Woman in America.* New York: The Dial Press, 1976.

Bernard, Jessie. *Academic Women.* Philadelphia: University of Pennsylvania Press, 1964.

Bird, Caroline. *Enterprising Women: Their Contribution to the American Economy, 1776-1976.* New York: W. W. Norton, 1976.

Black Women: Achievements Against the Odds, Calendar 1978-1980. Washington, D.C.: Smithsonian Institution Traveling Exhibition Service, 1978.

Blanch, Leslie. *The Wilder Shores of Love.* New York: Simon & Schuster, 1954.

Brasch, R. *How Did Sex Begin?* New York: David McKay, 1973.

Brittain, Vera. *The Women at Oxford.* New York: Macmillan, 1960.

Brownlee, W. Elliot, and Brownlee, Mary H. *Women in the American Economy: A Documentary History.* New Haven: Yale University Press, 1976.

Bryant, Barbara Everitt. *American Women Today & Tomorrow.* National Commission on the Observance of International Women's Year. Washington, D.C.: U.S. Government Printing Office, 1977.

Bullough, Vern L., and Bullough, Bonnie L. *Prostitution—An Illustrated Social History.* New York: Crown Publishers, 1978.

Burford, E. J. *Bawds and Lodgings, A History of the London Bankside Brothels, c. 100-1675.* London: Peter Owen, 1976.

Center for the American Woman and Politics, Eagleton Institute of Politics, Rutgers, The State University of New Jersey. *Women in Public Office.* New York: R. R. Bowker, 1976.

Chamberlin, Hope. *A Minority of Members: Women in the U.S. Congress.* New York: Praeger, 1973.

Corson, Richard. *Fashions in Makeup.* New York: University Books, 1972.

Dexter, Elisabeth Anthony. *Career Women of America, 1776–1840.* Francestown, N.H.: M. Jones, 1950. Reissued, Clifton, New Jersey: Augustus M. Kelley, 1972.

———————, *Colonial Women of Affairs: Women in Business and The Professions in America before 1776.* Clifton, N.J.: Augustus M. Kelley, 1972.

Drago, Harry Sinclair. *Notorious Ladies of the Frontier.* New York: Dodd, Mead & Co., 1969.

Edmondson, Madeleine, and Rounds, David. *From Mary Noble to Mary Hartman.* New York: Stein & Day, 1976.

Emrich, Duncan, ed., *The Folklore of Wedding and Marriage.* New York: American Heritage Press, 1970.

Ewing, Elizabeth. *History of Twentieth-Century Fashion.* New York: Charles Scribner's Sons, 1975.

Faber, Doris. *The Presidents' Mothers.* New York: St. Martin's Press, 1978.

Fiedler, Leslie. *Freaks: Myths and Images of the Secret Self.* New York: Simon & Schuster, 1978.

Friar, Ralph E., and Friar, Natasha A. *The Only Good Indian . . . The Hollywood Gospel.* New York: Drama Book Specialists, 1972.

Hargreaves, Reginald. *Women at Arms.* London: Hutchinson and Company, Ltd., 1930.

Harris, Ann Sutherland, and Nochlin, Linda. *Women Artists 1550–1950. An Exhibit at the Los Angeles County Museum of Art.* New York: Alfred A. Knopf, 1977.

Hartman, Mary S. *Victorian Murderesses.* New York: Schocken Books, 1976.

Henry, Alice. *Women and the Labor Movement.* New York: George H. Doran Company, 1923. Reissued New York: Arno/The New York Times, 1971.

Hewitt, Linda L. *Women Marines in World War I.* Washington, D.C.: History and Museums Division, Headquarters, U.S. Marine Corps, 1974.

Hogrefe, Pearl. *Tudor Women: Commoners and Queens.* Ames, Iowa: Iowa State University Press, 1975.

Howell, Georgina. *In Vogue: Six Decades of Fashion.* London: Allen Lane, 1975.

Kendall, Elaine. *Peculiar Institutions.* New York: G. P. Putnam's Sons, 1975.

Marinacci, Barbara. *Leading Ladies.* New York: Dodd, Mead & Co., 1961.

Marks, Geoffrey, and Beatty, William K. *Women In White.* New York: Charles Scribner's Sons, 1972.

Massachusetts Institute of Technology, *Symposium on American Women in Science and Engineering, 1964.* Cambridge, Mass.: M.I.T. Press, 1965. Reprint. Greenwood Press, 1976.

McDonald, Kathryn. "Women in Higher Education: A New Renaissance?" *The College Board Review,* Spring 1979.

McWhirter, Norris. *Guinness Book of Women's Sports Records.* New York: Bantam Books, 1980.

Middleton, Dorothy. *Victorian Lady Travellers.* New York: E. P. Dutton, 1965.

Moers, Ellen. *Literary Women.* Garden City, New York: Doubleday/Anchor, 1976.

Mohr, James C. *Abortion in America.* New York: Oxford University Press, 1978.

Morton, Carol A. "Black Women in Corporate America," *Ebony,* November 1975.

Mozans, H. J. *Women in Science.* New York: D. Appleton & Co., 1913. Reprint. Cambridge, Mass.: M.I.T. Press, 1974.

Osen, Lynn M. *Women in Mathematics.* Cambridge, Mass.: M.I.T. Press, 1974.

O'Sullivan, Judith, and Gallick, Rosemary. *Workers and Allies: Female Participation in the American Trade Union Movement, 1824–1976.* Washington, D.C.: Smithsonian Institution Press, 1975.

Paxton, Annabel. *Women in Congress.* New York: The Dietz Press, 1945.

Pearson, Hesketh. *The Marrying Americans.* New York: Coward McCann, 1961.

H.R.H. Peter, Prince of Greece and Denmark. *A Study of Polyandry.* The Hague: Mouton and Company, 1963.

Petersen, Karen, and Wilson, J. J. *Women Artists.* New York: Harper & Row, 1976.

Post, Robert C., ed. *A Centennial Exhibition.* Washington, D.C.: The National Museum of History and Technology, Smithsonian Institution, 1976.

Prindiville, Kathleen. *First Ladies.* New York: Macmillan, 1964.

Ray, Grace Ernestine. *Wily Women of the West.* San Antonio, Texas: The Naylor Company, 1972.

Reuther, Rosemary, and McLaughlin, Eleanor. *Women of Spirit.* New York: Simon & Schuster, 1979.

Segal, Muriel. *Painted Ladies.* New York: Stein & Day, 1972.

——————, *Virgins: Reluctant, Dubious and Avowed.* New York: Macmillan, 1977.

Simon, Rita James. *The Contemporary Woman and Crime.* Rockville, Maryland: National Institute of Mental Health, Center for Studies of Crime and Delinquency, 1975.

Skinner, Cornelia Otis. *Elegant Wits and Grand Horizontals.* New York: Houghton Mifflin Co., 1962.

Slide, Anthony. *Early Women Directors.* South Brunswick, New Jersey: A. S. Barnes Co., 1977.

Smith, Liz. *The Mother Book.* Garden City, New York: Doubleday & Co., 1978.

Smith, Ralph E., ed. *The Subtle Revolution: Women At Work.* New York: The Urban Institute, 1979.

Stannard, Una. *Mrs. Man.* San Francisco: Germainbooks, 1977.

Stein, Leon. *The Triangle Fire.* Philadelphia: J. B. Lippincott Co., 1962.

Stevens, Doris. *Jailed for Freedom.* Originally published 1920. New York: Schocken Books, 1976.

Stites, Richard. *The Women's Liberation Movement in Russia.* Princeton, New Jersey: Princeton University Press, 1978.

Swerdloff, Peter. *Men and Women.* New York: Time-Life Books, 1975.

Thorndike, Joseph J., Jr., *The Very Rich: A History of Wealth.* New York: Crown Publishers, 1976.

Time-Life Books Editors, *The Old West: The Women.* New York: Time-Life Books, 1978.

Torre, Susana, ed. *Women in American Architecture.* New York: Watson-Guptill/Whitney Library of Design, 1977.

U.S. Department of Commerce, Bureau of the Census, *A Statistical Portrait of Women in the U.S.* Current Population Reports, Special Studies, Series P-23, No. 58. Washington, D.C.: U.S. Government Printing Office, April 1976.

U.S. Department of Labor, *The Earnings Gap Between Women and Men.* Washington, D.C.: Employment Standards Administration; Women's Bureau, 1976.

——————, *Women Workers Today.* Washington, D.C.: Employment Standards Administration; Women's Bureau, Rev. Ed. October 1976.

Warner, Deborah Jean. "Women Astronomers," *Natural History.* May, 1979.

Wertheimer, Barbara Mayer. *We Were There: The Story of Working Women in America.* New York: Pantheon, 1977.

"Why So Few Women Have Made It to the Top," *Business Week,* June 5, 1978.

Willett, C., and Cunnington, Phillis. *The History of Underclothes.* London: Michael Joseph, 1951.

Winn, Dilys. *Murderess Ink.* New York: Workman Publishing, 1979.

Withers, Josephine. *Women Artists in Washington Collections;* with Toby Quitslund, *Her Feminine Colleagues, Photographs and Letters Collected by Frances Benjamin Johnston in 1900.* Catalogue of an exhibit. College Park, Md.: University of Maryland Art Gallery and Women's Caucus for Art, 1979.

INDEX

ABBA, 211
Abbott, Berenice, 259
Abdul-Hamid, Sultan, 266
Abell, Mrs. L. G., 430
Abelard, Peter, 36
Aberstein, Julia, 312
Abishag, 49
Abolitionists, 31, 75, 123, 327–328, 336
Abortionists, 72, 345, 348
Académie Française, 128, 129, 200, 216
Académie Goncourt, 77, 216
Académie Royale, 241–242
Academy Awards, 5, 189, 190, 191
Accident statistics, 314
Ace, Jane, 181
Acevedo, Marta, 346
Ackerman, Paula, 391
Ackermann, Rosemary, 417
Acton, Eliza, 110
Acton, William, 427
Actors: American Film Institute honorees, 8; in female roles, 171, 180–181; women's idols, 285–286
Actresses, 172–176, 232, 233; assumed and real names, 327, 328–329; black, 34, 442; child, 5, 6; in Congress, 367; earliest, 170; "fallen," 313; Indian-speaking, 187–188; in male roles, 172, 174; mother-daughter combinations, 78, 172; movie, 187–188, 191; multiple Oscar winners, 191; sister combinations, 76, 172, 173; Wild West, 103
Ada computer language, 330
Adam, Juliette, 332
Adams, Abigail Smith, 69, 336, 360
Adams, Elizabeth Welles, 360
Adams, Hannah, 126

Adams, Harriet S. (Carolyn Keene), 223, 332
Adams, John, 336, 360
Adams, John Quincy, 69, 114
Adams, Maude, 175
Adams, Samuel, 360
Adams, Sarah Flower, 432
Adamson, Joy, 73
Adato, Perry Miller, 189
Addams, Jane, 30, 446, 449, 451, 452
Addicts, 313, 314
Akins, Zoë, 448
Adler, Dr. Karl, 40
Adultery, executions for, 308, 316
Advertising, women in, 81, 82, 86
Aeaea (mythical island), 353
Aelfflaed, Queen, 240
Aelgiva, Queen, 240
Aethelthreda, Princess, 283–284
Afkhami, Mahnaz, 346
African queens, 355–356
Agarwal, Bella, 63
Agarwal, Durga, 63
Agassiz, Elizabeth Cabot Cary, 125
Age records, 4
Agee, William M., 345
Ager, Milton, 206
Aglaia (Grace), 74
Agnesi, Maria Gaetana, 5, 128
Agnodice, 137
Agnon, S. Y., 449
Agrippina II, Roman Empress, 68, 377
Ah Toy, 91
Aiken, Conrad, 230
Ainsworth, Macie Marie ("Sunny," Mrs. Manville), 56
Airline stewardesses, 26, 111–112
Airport operations workers, 100
Akeley, Carl E., 134, 162

Akeley, Delia, 134
Akihito, Crown Prince of Japan, 122
Akiyoshi, Toshiko, 208
Alba, Duchess of (Pilar Teresa Cayetana), 251
Albright, Charlene, 154
Albright, Tenley, 419
Alcoholics, 313, 314
Alcott, Abigail May, 69
Alcott, Louisa May, 69, 220, 223, 322, 347, 446
Alda, Alan, 344, 345
Alden, John, 65
Aldrich, E. A., 229
Aleksandrovna, Tamara, 156
Alençon, Emilienne d', 44
Alexander the Great, 44
Alexander VI, Pope, 7, 45, 68
Alexander, Sadie Tanner, 288
Alexander, Shana, 206
Alexandra, Czarina, 66
Alexius I Comnenus, Eastern Roman Emperor, 121
Alfred the Great, King, 144
Ali, caliph, 383
Ali, Muhammad, 269, 408, 409, 419
Alice in Wonderland (Carroll), 219
Alicejames books, 228
Al-Khansa (poet), 216
Alimony, 269, 291
Alix de Champagne, 355
All-Girl Orchestra of Miss Faun, 207
All-Girl Orchestra of Phil Spitalny, 206
All-Girl Reel World String Band, 206
All-Greece Women's Association, 346
Alla (fashion model), 278
Allen, Ann, 323
Allen, Elizabeth Akers, 432
Allen, Eve, 320

461

Allen, Frances Stebbins, 257
Allen, Gracie, 181
Allen, Helen Greenwood, 86
Allen, Jay Presson, 191
Allen, Mary Electa, 257
Allen, Sandy, 4
Allerdice, Susannah, 311–312
Allingham, Margery, 225
Allison, Emma, 104
Allison, Mrs. Hudson J., 28
Allison, Lorraine, 28
Allison, Rhea Hurrle, 165
Allyson, June, 179
Alonso, Alicia, 193
Alston, Barbara, 210
Althea, 68
Altman, Robert, 192
Alvarez, Lili de, 409
Amaterasu Omikami (goddess), 380
Amazon Valley Indians, 48
Amazons, 143
Ambler, Mary, 322
Amelia, Princess of England, 322
American Academy and Institute of Arts and Letters, 127
American Association for the Advancement of Science, 129, 130
American Association of Retired Persons, 27
American Astronomical Society, 131
American Ballet Theatre, 193
American Civil Liberties Union, 292
American Film Institute Lifetime Achievement Award, 8
American Home Economics Association, 134
American Home magazine, 230
American Journal of Psychology, 141
American Men and Women of Science, 129
American Museum of Natural History, 254
American National Opera, 204
American Newspaper Publishers Association, 231
American Physical Society, 133
American Psychological Association, 141, 444, 445
American Society of Women Engineers, 129
American Stock Exchange, first woman governor, 83
American Theater Wing, 177
Americans for Indian Opportunity, 33

Ames, Delano, 227
Amich, Frances, 101
Amory, Cleveland, 255
Amphetamine users, 314
Ampthill, Lady and Lord, 51
Amra (poet), 216
Amuhia, Queen, 8
Anadama bread, 321
Anastasia, Princess of Russia, 9
Anatomy, 88, 136, 445
Ancker-Johnson, Betsey, 81
Anderson, Mrs. (marathon walker), 160
Anderson, Carol, 395
Anderson, Ivie, 208
Anderson, Judith, 188
Anderson, Katherine, 210
Anderson, Liz, 78
Anderson, Lynn, 78
Anderson, Margaret, 230
Anderson, Marian, 34, 223, 451, 452
Anderson, Mrs. Sherwood, 57
André, Major John, 149
Andreini, Isabella, 170
Andrews, Julie, 328
Andrews, Louise, 178
Andrews, Nelma J., 80
Andrews Sisters, the, 74
Andrus, Ethel Percy, 27
Anesthesiology, 136, 140
Angelou, Maya, 223
Angels, The, 210
Anglicus, Johannes, 21
Animal mothers, 73
Animal trainers, 157, 159–160
Anna (prophet), 381
Anna and the King of Siam (Leonowens), 122
Anna Comnena, 121
Anne, Czarina, 272
Anne, Queen of England, 272, 274, 402, 453
Anne Boleyn, Queen of England, 267, 307–308, 356, 438
Anne of Bohemia, Queen of England, 277, 453
Anne of Brittany, Queen of France, 277
Anne of Cleves, Queen of England, 308, 453
Anne of Denmark, Queen of England, 453
Annis, Francesca, 71
Anorexia nervosa, 19
"Another World" (TV show), 300
Anthony, Daniel, 77
Anthony, Susan B., 7, 77, 268, 334, 336, 337, 348, 441, 446, 451
Anthropology, 113, 134, 196, 445, 446; pay, 130
Antioch College, 124

Antiope, Amazon Queen, 143
Antiques Monthly, 230
Anti-slavery fighters, 26, 31, 75, 161, 245, 288–289, 336
Antoine-Darioux, Genevieve, 224
Apathy, Zita Ann, 329
Apgar, Virginia, 140
Aphrodite (goddess), 454
Apollinaire, Guillaume, 246
Applebee, Constance, M. K., 402–403
Apponyi, Comtesse d', 199
Arbuckle, Fatty, 315
Archaeology, 127
Archery, 424
Architecture, 256–257, 346
Arden, Elizabeth, 277
Arden, Eve, 328
Arden, Jane (comic-strip character), 108
Arena Stage, Washington, D.C., 177
Arendt, Hannah, 127
Argentina: woman suffrage, 342; women in government, 358–359
Aristotle, 426
Armed forces. *See* Military forces; *and see individual services*
Armstrong, Charlotte, 225
Armstrong, Henry, 205
Armstrong, Louis, 180, 207, 208–209
Army Nurse Corps, 151
Arno Press, 219
Arnold, Bennie, 323
Arnold, Birch (pseudonym), 333
Arnold, Dorothy Harriet Camille, 11
Arnot, Sarah, 320
Arnott, Margaret, 112
Aron, Ernest. *See* Eden, Elizabeth
Around-the-world journeys, 160, 161, 162
Arp, Jean, 244
Arrington, Marie Dean, 299
Art collectors, 252–253
Art museum founders, 249, 253
Arthur, Chester A., 362
Arthur, Ellen Herndon, 362
Arthur, King, 353
Artists, 239–250, 255–260; of antiquity, 239; black, 249, 254, 442; cartoonists, 255–256; early academy members, 241–243; exhibits, 245; handicapped, 28–29; photographers, 257–260; precocious, 6, 240–241; various media, 239–240, 247–248. *See also* Painters; Sculptors
Artists' model, 43, 44, 45, 250–252

Arzner, Dorothy, 187
"As the World Turns" (TV show), 301
Ashe, Penelope (pseudonym), 332
Ashford, Daisy, 5
Ashford, Rosalind, 210
Ashmore, Ruth (Isabel A. Mallon), 429
Ashton, Sir Frederick, 193
Ashworth, Mary Wells, 448
Aspasia (*hetaira*), 43, 120
Aspasia (obstetrician), 137
Aspinall, Nan Jane, 160
Associated Press, Woman Athletes of the Year, 403, 415
Association for the Advancement of Psychoanalysis, 142
Association for the Advancement of Women, 131
Association for Women in Mathematics, 129
Association of Ladies, 147
Astaire, Adele, 178
Astaire, Fred, 405
Astor, Jacob, 261
Astor, Elizabeth ("Eliza," Countess Rumpff), 261
Astor, Nancy, Lady, 262, 348
Astor, Lord William Waldorf, 262
Astronauts, 164, 165
Astronomy, 77, 120, 121, 130–131
Athaliah, Queen, 354
Athletics. *See* Sports
Atkins, Susan, 297
Atropos (Fate), 74
Attenzione magazine, 230
Aubry, Genevieve, 372
Auctioneers, 100
Augustus, Roman Emperor, 376
Aulenti, Gae, 257
Austin, Alice, 257–258
Austin, Alice Constance, 256
Austin, Lovie, 208
Austin, Mary, 220
Austin, Tracy, 5
Australia: woman suffrage, 342; women in government, 371
Austria: woman suffrage, 342; women in government, 372
Auto racing, 7, 30, 159, 418
Autobiographers, 215, 223–224
Autographs, famous women's 267–268
Automobile accidents, 314
Automobile dealers, 100
Automotive engineering, 100

Avalon (mythical island), 353
Aveline of Lancaster, 453
Averill, James, 295
Averina, Tatiana, 418
Avery, Mary Ellen, 140, 443
Aviation, women in, 4, 12, 112–113; WASPs, 151. *See also* Pilots
Ayer, Harriet Hubbard, 92
Ayesha (Aisha), 67, 383

Babashoff, Shirley, 420
Babbage, Charles, 330
Babbit, Sister Tabitha, 106
Baca-Barragan, Polly, 451
Bacewicz, Grazyna, 203
Bacharach, Burt, 87
Bacon, Anne Cooke, 121
Bacon, Sir Francis, 121
Bacon, Lou, 323
Bacon, Mary, 63, 405
Bacon, Nancy Pigg, 329
Bacon, Peggy, 255
Bacteriology, 445
Baer, Bugs, 178
Baganda people, Africa, 48
Baggs, Maggie, 325
Bailey, Elizabeth, 88
Bailey, Ellene Alice, 106
Bailey, James, 88
Bailey, Jim, 181
Bailey, Pearl, 184
Baillie, Joanna, 232
Baird, Dorothea, 172
Baker, Bonnie, 183
Baker, Florence, 161
Baker, Frankie, 219
Baker, Mary (Princess Caraboo of Javasu), 8
Baker, Samuel, 161
Baker, Sara Josephine, 139–140
Balanchine, George, 194
Balas, Iolanda, 417, 423
Balch, Edith G., 449
Baldridge, Letitia ("Tish"), 431
Baldwin, Caroline Willard, 124
Balfour, Alison, 309
Ball, Ernest R., 67
Ball, Lucille, 182, 328
Ballard, Florence, 209
Ballerinas, 193–194
Ballet Folklórico de México, 193
Ballet Nacional de Cuba, 193
Ballet Rambert, 193
Ballet Russe, 193, 246; de Monte Carlo, 193, 195
Ballintine, Harriet I., 403
Balloon flights, 163–164
Baltimore Museum of Art, 252, 253, 254
Bancroft, Anne, 188, 189, 328
Bancroft, Caroline, 219

Bandaranaike, Sirimavo, 358
Bandits, Old West, 295
Bang, Nina, 372
Bankhead, Tallulah, 10, 232
Banking: women in, 82–83, 84, 442; women as customers, 82
Baptist Church: missionary groups, 393, 394; ordination of women, 394
Bara, Theda, 15, 327, 328
Barbauld, Anna Letitia, 430
Barbie Doll, 86
Barbiturate users, 314
Barbot, Blanche Hermine, 197
Barbour, Patt, 347
Barclay, Nicoel ("Nickey"), 211
Bardaum, Grete, 63
Bardauskiene, Vilma, 418
Bardens, Dennis, 13
Bardsley, Kay, 195
Barker, Ma, 66
Barnard, Charlotte Alington, 204
Barnard, Frederick A. P., 125–126
Barnard College, 125–126
Barnell, Jane (Lady Olga), 6
Barnes, Margaret Ayer, 448
Barnett, Joni E., 100
Barney, Ida, 131
Barnum, P. T., 6, 9, 88, 93
Barnum and Bailey, 6, 88
Barny, Mme. Lauriol de, 320
Barrett, Ellen Marie, 394
Barrett, Kate Waller, 113
Barrett, Monte, 108
Barrie, Sir James M., 5, 175
Barry, Captain Andrew, 148
Barry, Dr. James (Miranda Stuart), 21
Barry, Jeff, 210
Barry, Kate (Margaret Catherine) Moore, 148
Barrymore, Blanche Marie Louise, 333
Barrymore, Diana, 174
Barrymore, Ethel, 174, 175, 232, 452
Barrymore, John, 174, 265, 285, 333
Barrymore, Lionel, 174
Barrymore, Maurice, 174
Bartel, Jean, 279
Bartholdi, Frédéric Auguste, 251
Bartlett, Alice Eloise, 333
Bartlett, John, 431
Bartlett, Mary (Mrs. Josiah Bartlett), 360
Bartlett, Mary (photographer), 258
Bartlett's Familiar Quotations, women in, 431–432
Barton, Clara, 4, 102, 446, 451

Barton, Elizabeth, 307–308
Baseball, 413–414
Basie, Count, 207, 209
Basketball, 403, 414–415
Bass, Frances Mary, 122
Bassett, Ann, 81
Bassett, Ida, 323
Bassett, Mary, 121
Bassin, Amelia, 84
Batatume, Habe queen, 355
Bateman, Mary, 83
Bates, Daisy, 34
Bates, Katherine Lee, 205
Bates, Mercedes A., 82
Bathory, Countess Elisabeth, 378
Bathyllus of Alexandria, 171
Bauer, Madame, 103
Bayes, Nora, 178, 205
Bayes, Sara Carter, 212
Bayeux Tapestry, 240
Bayh, Birch, 344
Bayley, Nancy, 444
Bayliss, Lillian, 176
Bayreuth Festival, 203
Beach, Amy Marcy Cheney (Mrs. H. H. A. Beach), 78, 197
Beach, Anna E. Boller, 135
Beak, Albina Terrasina Rosina, 329
Beales, Hannah, 90
Beard, Diana Brown, 329
Bearded ladies, 6, 317
Beatrix, Queen of the Netherlands, 357
Beaufort, Lady Margaret, 123, 453
Beauty secrets, 271–272, 273–274; do-it-yourself, 275–276
Beauty spots, 274
Beauvoir, Simone de, 345
Beaver, Barry, 334
Bechet, Sidney, 10
Beck, Julian, 177
Beco, Mariette, 383
Becquerel, Henri, 131, 450
Bedford College, London, England, 122
Beech, Olive Ann, 88–89
Beech Aircraft Corporation, 88–89
Beecher, Catharine, 74–75, 110
Beecher, Henry Ward, 46
Beethoven, Ludwig van, 197–198, 202
Beeton, Isabella, 111
Begin, Menachem, 373
Behavioral differences between sexes, 17–18
Behn, Aphra, 215, 232, 453
Behnke, Catherine, 152
Béjart, Armande Grésinde, 173
Béjart, Geneviève, 173
Béjart, Madeleine, 173
Bell, Roseann P., 223

Bellamy, Mary Godot, 326
Bellew, Kyrle, 285
Bellgardt, Hildegard, 443
Bellisario, Marisa, 81
Bellon, Yannick, 189
Bellow, Susan Glassman, 269
Bellow, Saul, 269
Belzer, Elizabeth, 155
Bendig, Alice, 443
Benedict, Ruth, 113
Benham, Gertrude, 162
Benincasa, Catherine, 217
Bennet, John, 428
Bennett, Constance, 182
Bennett, Eileen, 409
Bennett, Estelle, 210
Bennett, Patricia, 210
Bennett, Veronica, 210
Benny, Jack, 182
Benoist, Marie Guillemine, 245
Bentley, Phyllis, 227
Ben-Yusuf, Zaida, 258
Beraud, Marthé ("Eva C."), 9
Berengaria, Queen of England, 7
Berg, Gertrude, 182
Berg, Patricia Jane ("Patty"), 404, 415
Bergen, Charlotte, 202
Bergman, Alan, 190
Bergman, Ingrid, 71, 191
Bergman, Marilyn, 190
Beringer, Esme, 172
Berlin, Irving, 180
Berlin Academy for the Science of Judaism, 391
Berlioz, Hector, 195, 199
Bermudez, Marion, 408
Bernard, Jessie, 443
Bernhardt, Sarah, 172, 175, 263, 276, 321, 328
Berning, Susie Maxwell, 416
Bernstein, Morey, 15
Berry, Mary Ada, 329
Bertha (collar), 283
Beruryah, 120
Bervoets, Marguerite, 28
Berwick, Margaret, 91
Besant, Annie Wood, 388
Bethune, Mary McLeod, 34, 455
Betterton, Mary Sanderson, 170, 176
Betterton, Thomas, 170, 176
Betts, Marina, 103
Bhatt, Ela, 455
Bheux du Pusieux, Jeanne-Emilie, 251
Biblical queens, 354
Bickerdyke, Mary Ann ("Mother"), 67
Bicyclists, 161, 418, 424; around-the-world, 160
Biegler, Martha ("Red Martha"), 158
Bierman, Gussie, 312
Big Bertha (gun), 156

Bigelow, Ruth, 86–87
Billboard magazine, 213
Billing, Baroness, 199
Binh, Nguyen Thi, 375
Biochemistry, 132, 133, 443, 445, 446
Biographers, 215, 224; Pulitzer Prizes, 448
Biographies of Famous Women (Liu Hsiang), 215
Biology, 445; pay, 130
Biophysics, 132, 443
Bird, Rose Elizabeth, 288
Bird Maidens, 354
Birth control advocates, early, 51, 71–72, 140, 186, 318
Birth name, use of, 333–335, 343
Birth statistics, males vs. females, 17
Births, unusual, 62–63; first Caesarean, 70
Bishop, Bridget, 310
Bishop, Elizabeth, 449
Bishop, Isabella Bird, 161
Bishop, Katherine S., 135
Bishop, first female in U.S., 390
Bissell, Emily, 446
Bittner, Merrill, 394
Bjerregaard, Ritt, 372
Blaché, Alice Guy, 186
Black, Barbara O., 141
Black, Cathleen, 230
Black, Georgia (George Cantey), 23
Black, Margaret Wears, 329
Black women, 33–34; actresses, 34, 442; African dance, 196; in the arts, 249, 254, 442; Blues singers, 207–208; businesswomen, 85–86, 87, 93; in civil rights fight, 26–27, 32, 288–289, 395, 444; entertainers, 34, 179–180, 207–209; fashion models, 279; in federal government employ, 102; field hands, 310–311; "first" achievements, various, 441–442, 444; first cabinet member, 442; first Congresswomen, 366, 442; first millionaire, 93, 442; first Olympic gold medal, 442; first Oscar, 442; first Pulitzer Prize, 442; in law, 287, 288, 290, 395, 442, 444; in medicine, 138–139, 441–442; in opera, 34, 204, 441, 442; in sports, 411, 419, 442; teachers, 34, 122, 124; writers, 34, 223–224, 333, 441, 442
Blackfoot woman warriors, 151

Blackwell, Alice Stone, 78, 339
Blackwell, Antoinette Brown, 390
Blackwell, Elizabeth, 4, 75, 136, 138, 344, 446
Blackwell, Emily, 75
Blackwell, Henry B., 336, 343, 344
Blackwell, Unita, 368
Blais, Madeleine, 447
Blake, Arthur, 181
Blake, Sophia Jex, 136
Blakesy, Jane von Edsinga, 154
Blanchard, Jean-Pierre, 164
Blanchard, Marie Madeleine Sophie, 164
Blankenship, Betty, 109
Blankers-Koen, Francina ("Fanny"), 404, 407
Blatch, Harriot Stanton, 78, 348
Blatt, Josephine Schauer, 407
Blaugdone, Barbara, 387
Blavatsky, Helena Petrovna, 388
Bleecker, Anne Eliza Schuyler, 218
Bliss, Lillie P., 253
Blitz, Ethel, 85
Block, Denise, 27
Blois, Natalie de, 257
Blood, Col. James H., 334
Bloomer, Amelia Jenks, 284
Bloomers, 284
Bloomfield-Moore, Clara Sophia Jessup, 429
Bloor, Ella Reeve ("Mother"), 67
Blossom, Violet, 298
Blossom Sisters, the, 74
Blue Belles, The, 210
Blue collar jobs, 100–101
Blues singers, 207–208
Blum, Arlene, 163
Blunschy-Steiner, Elizabeth, 372–373
Bly, Nelly (Elizabeth Seaman), 160
Blye, Birdie, 197
Boadicea (Boudicca), Queen of Britons, 144
Boas, Margaret, 135
Bobbed hair, 278
Boccaccio, Giovanni, 215, 239
Boggs, Jean Sutherland, 254
Boggs, Lindy, 365
Boglioli, Wendy, 63–64
Boillet, Colette, 385
Boisdechene, Josephine, 6
Boisseau, Juanita, 180
Boissevain, Inez Milholland, 325
Boivin, Marie Anne Victoire Gillian, 70
Bokassa, Jean, 359
Bokonyi, Susan, 4

Boleyn, Anne. *See* Anne Boleyn, Queen of England
Boleyn, Mary, 307
Bolger, Ray, 171
Bolin, Jane M., 290, 442
Bolivia, female head of state, 359
Bolling, Susanna, 148
Bolshoi Ballet, 194
Bolton, Frances Payne, 366
Bolton, Oliver Payne, 366
Bombeck, Erma, 222
Bonaparte, Pauline, 271–272
Bond, Carrie Jacobs, 29, 205, 433
Bond, Victoria, 202
Bondfield, Margaret, 371
Bonheur, Rosa, 245
Bonner, Theodolinda ("Dol," fictional character), 227
Bonny, Anne, 294
Book illustration, 246, 257, 258
Boone, Gray Davis, 230
Booth, Catherine Mumford, 343, 389
Booth, Evangeline, 452
Booth, John Wilkes, 285
Booth, Margaret, 185
Booth, William, 343, 389
Borden, Lizzie, 296
Borg, Arne, 420
Borgia, Lucrezia, 45, 68, 267
Boston Cooking School, 29, 111
Boston Opera Company, 197, 202, 204
Boston Symphony, 202
Boston University, 124, 202
Boswell Sisters, the, 74
Botanists, 134, 445
Botkin, Cordelia, 296–297
Botticelli, 250
Bottorff, Mary Cutter, 329
Boucher, François, 251
Boucherett, Emilia Jessie, 338
Boudinot, Col. Elias C., 323
Boulanger, Lili, 75, 200, 203
Boulanger, Nadia, 75, 200, 202
Boulogne, Geneviève de, 241
Boulogne, Madeleine de, 241
Bourke-White, Margaret, 259, 452
Boursier, Louise Bourgeois, 70
Bow, Clara, 188
Bowen, Ruth, 86
Bowers, Alice, 268
Bowling, 424
Bowser, Mary, 150
Box, Mary Hatt, 329
"Boxcar" Bertha, 158, 326
Boxing, 408; judges, 409
Boyd, Belle, 149, 267

Bozarth-Campbell, Alla, 394
Boze, Wilhelmina ("Billy") Connelly (Mrs. Manville), 56
Brabant, Honorine de, 320
Bracelli, Virginia, 385
Bracetti, Mariana, 346
Brachman, Helen Mahler, 87
Brackett, Leigh, 191
Bradford, Andrew, 89
Bradford, Barbara Taylor, 222
Bradford, Cornelia Smith, 89
Bradley, Mary Hastings, 134
Bradley-Martins, Mr. and Mrs., 264
Bradstreet, Anne Dudley, 215–216, 217
Bradwell, Myra Colby, 287
Braganza, Prince Miguel de, 262
Brand, Christianna (Mary Christianna Milne Lewis), 225
Brando, Marlon, 286
Branner, Martin, 108
Braque, Marcelle, 57
Brasch, Rose, 114
Brassieres, 273, 278, 282
Braun, Eva, 267
Bravery, 7, 25–26, 443
Braxton, Elizabeth Corbin, 360
Braziel, Maureen, 424
Breadheid, Janet, 310
Breast-feeding, 291–292
Brecht, Bertolt, 67
Breeskin, Adelyn, 254
Brennan, Patricia H., 87
Brent, Margaret, 287, 336
Bres, Elizabeth, 154
Bretécher, Claire, 255
Breteuil, Emilie de, Marquise du Châtelet, 128
Breuer, Joseph, 31
Breughel, Jan, 244
Brewer, Margaret, 151
Brezhnev, Leonid, 396
Bricci, Plautilla, 256
Brice, Donna Patterson, 420
Brice, Fanny, 178, 264
Brico, Antonia, 202, 206
Bridell-Fox, Eliza, 244
Brides: advice to, 51–52; payment for, 48
Bridgman, Laura, 29
Brigittine Order, 385
Brignoline Order, 385
Brill Building Sound, 210
Brine, Mary Dow, 434
Brinkley, Nell, 255
Brinton, David, 428
Bristoe, Billie, 185
Brittano, Susannah, 121–122
Britton, Barbara, 182
Britton, Nan, 46

Broadcasting, women in, 7, 81. *See also* Radio; Television
Broadwick, Tiny, 159
Brodt, Helen, 325
Broksopp, Joan, 386
Bronicka, Catherine de, 199
Brontë, Anne, 75, 332, 453
Brontë, Charlotte, 75, 332, 348, 453
Brontë, Emily, 75, 332, 453
Brook, Wendy, 422
Brooklyn Children's Museum, 254
Brooklyn Museum of Art, 248
Brooks, Angie, 374
Brooks, Caroline, 105
Brooks, Gwendolyn, 5, 442, 449
Brooks, Lala, 210
Brosby, Elizabeth, 455
Brothels, 42, 75, 91–92
Brough (Clapp), A. Louise, 412
Browder, Dolly, 104
Brown, Mrs. Caro, 447
Brown, Charles Brockden, 344
Brown, Clara, 103
Brown, Dee, 312
Brown, Dorothy, 138
Brown, Edmund G., Jr., 288
Brown, Eleanor McMillen, 281
Brown, Helen Gurley, 38, 87, 230
Brown, Jane (fictional character), 226
Brown, Jessica, 178
Brown, Jill E., 112
Brown, John Y., Jr., 280
Brown, Lesley, 63
Brown, Linda, 289
Brown, Louise, 63
Brown, Maggie Tobin (Molly), 219
Brown, Margaret (Old Mother Hubbard), 67, 283
Brown, Margery, 4
Brown, Marilyn V., 84
Brown, Olympia, 334, 390
Brown, Raymond L., 438
Brown, Rowine Hayes, 140
Brown, Mrs. Stephen, 102
Brown, Toni, 211
Brown, Mrs. V., 422
Brown Bess (musket), 156
Brown Betty (dish), 322
Brown v. *Board of Education of Topeka*, 289
Browne, Mary K., 404
Browning, Edward ("Daddy"), 51, 266
Browning, Elizabeth Barrett, 37–38
Browning, Florence ("Peaches"), 51, 266
Bruce, Josephine, 320
Brueschoff, Marianne, 451

Brulon, Angélique, 145
Bruntland, Gro Harlem, 372
Brusselmans, Anne, 28
Bryant, Lena Himmelstein, 282
Bryant, William Cullen, 229
Bryce, Emily (fictional character), 226
Bryn Mawr College, 126, 129, 403
Buba, Joy, 454
Buchenwald, 378
Buck, Carrie, 318
Buck, Doris, 318
Buck, Emma, 318
Buck, Pearl S., 488, 449, 452
Buckley, Daniel, 22
Buddha, 12
Bueno, Maria, 412
Buferd, Marilyn, 279
Bugg, Ima June, 329
Bulette, Julia, 91
Bum-roll, 272
Bump, Mercy, 4
Bunch, Madeline, 85
Bunch, Mother, 67
Bunford, Jane, 4
Burbidge, E. Margaret, 131, 446
Burch, Jo Ann, 456
Burdett-Coutts, Baroness, 453
Burke, Emily, 172
Burke, Mildred, 404
Burke, Yvonne Brathwaite, 366, 442
Burnett, Frances Hodgson, 223
Burney, Fanny, 232
Burns, George, 181
Burns, Lucy, 340
Burpitt, Susan Eatwell, 329
Burstyn, Ellen, 328
Burton, Beryl, 418
Burton, Isabel, 162
Burton, Richard (actor), 267
Burton, Sir Richard, 162
Busch-Lowman, Mary, 112
Buse, Renee, 225
Bushman, Francis X., 285, 286
Business Week, 80, 84
Business Woman's Journal, 93, 97
Business women, 86–91, 92–93; air travel statistics, 95; black women, 85–86, 87, 93; fashion and garments, 281–283; in management, 80–84, 96; product ideas, 86–87, 106–107
Bust improvers, 272–273
Bustle, 272
Buti, Lucrezia, 252
Buti, Spinetta, 252
Butler, Lady Elizabeth (Thompson), 246
Butler, Frank, 157
Butler, Jean Marie, 155

Butler, Nicholas Murray, 449
Butler, Samuel, 426
Butterworth, Jenny, 108
Byrne, Ethel, 71
Byrne, Jane M., 368
Byron, Augusta Ada, Lady Lovelace, 41, 330
Byron, Beverly, 366
Bryon, Catherine Gordon, Lady, 41
Byron, George Gordon, Lord, 41–42

Cabinet officers: Britain and Commonwealth, 371; European continent, 372–373; Middle East, 358, 373; U.S., 99, 370, 442
Cabrini, "Mother" Francesca, 386
Caddies, 417; origin of term, 402
Cade, Toni, 223
Cadwalader, Mrs. Richard, 263
Caesar, Julius, 12
Cagle, Myrtle T., 165
Cahill, Victor, 279
Calamity Jane (Martha Jane Cannary), 313, 439
Calderini, Novella, 76
Calderone, Mary Steichen, 140
Caldwell, Erskine, 259
Caldwell, Sarah, 4, 197, 202, 203, 204
Calenda, Constanza, 137
Caligula, Roman Emperor, 68, 377
Calkins, Mary Whiton, 141
Call, Hazel May, 329
Callas, Maria, 38, 320
Callinach, Mary, 160
Calliope (Muse), 12
Calloway, Jackie, 86
Calpurnia, 12
Calypso, 353
Cambridge University, England, 123
Camerawomen, movie, 185, 189
Cameron, Julia Margaret, 259
Camilla (ancient warrior), 143
Camp Fire Girls, 446
Campbell, Billie Jean, 270
Campbell, Georgina (Mrs. Manville), 56
Campbell, Glen, 270
Campbell, Mary, 7
Campbell-Walter, Fiona, 278
Canada: woman suffrage, 342; women in government, 371–372
Canadian Medical Association, 139
Cancer, 19, 314

Cannary, Martha ("Calamity") Jane, 313, 439
Cannon, Annie Jump, 131
Cannon, Sister Cathleen, 390
Cannon, Dyan, 189
Cannon, Isabella, 114
Cannon, Martha Hughes, 365
Canoeing, 418
Canova, Judy, 181
Cantey, George (Gloria Black), 23
Cantors, 389, 392
Capers, Valerie, 208
Capitol (Washington), sculptures of women in, 454
Captain and Tennille, The, 211
Car assembly workers, 100
Caraboo, Princess of Javasu, 8
Caraway, Hattie Wyatt, 366
Carbentus, Anna Cornelia, 244
Carbine, Pat, 230
Cardozo, Abbie, 103
Carlton, Jo Anne, 154
Carnarvon, Lady Evelyn, 7
Carnauba, Josimar, 62
Carnegie, Andrew, 64, 69, 298
Carnegie, Margaret Morrison, 64, 69
Carner, Joanne Gunderson, 416
Carney, Julia, 432
Caroline, Queen of England, 453
Carpenter, Kate, 325
Carpenter, Kathleen, 153
Carpenters, The, 210
Carradine, David, 326
Carrasco, Maria Victoria, 420
Carré, Mathilde ("The Cat"), 28
Carrier, Martha, 310
Carriera, Rosalba, 78, 241
Carrière, Mme. Alfred, 320
Carrol, Mary, 154
Carroll, Anna Ella, 153
Carroll, Diahann, 442
Carroll, John Alexander, 448
Carroll, Mary ("Molly") Darnall, 360
Carson, Rachel, 113, 452
Carter, A. P., 212
Carter, Ida Johnson, 289
Carter, Jessie, 112
Carter, Jimmy, 370, 396, 456
Carter, Mikele, 109
Carter, Mother Maybelle, 212
Carter, Philip Youngman, 225
Carter, Rosalynn, 364

Carter, Ruth Stapleton, 396
Carter, Susannah, 110
Carter Sisters, 212
Carteret, Elizabeth, 323
Cartland, Barbara, 36, 221
Cartoonists, 255–256
Carvajales y Camino, Laura Martínez de, 137
Carvic, Heron, 227
Cary, Mary Ann Shadd, 441
Cash, Johnny, 212
Cash, June Carter, 212
Cashibo people, Peru, 53–54
Cashman, Nellie, 5, 93
Caslavska-Odlozil, Vera, 425
Cassatt, Mary, 246, 446
Cassidy, Butch, 295
Casson, Herbert Newton, 343
Castellane, Count Boni de, 262
Castle, Barbara Anne, 371
Castle, Irene, 278
Castro, Inés de, 317
Catanei, Vannozza Dei, 7, 45
Cateechee (Isaqueena), 324
Cathcart, Linda L., 254
Cather, Willa, 446, 448
Catherine II, The Great, Czarina, 15, 38–39, 50, 244, 359
Catherine de' Medici, Queen of France, 357, 377–378
Catherine Howard, Queen of England, 308
Catherine of Aragon, Queen of England, 307, 308, 356
Catherine of Austria, 357
Catherine Parr, Queen of England, 245, 308
"Catherine wheel," 384
Catlett, Elizabeth, 249
Catt, Carrie Chapman, 337, 341, 447
Catteneo, Simonetta, 250
Cattle-rustlers, 295
Caurla, Lea (Leon), 23
Cavalieri, Lina, 266
Cavanagh, Kit, 146
Cave, Jennie F., 114
Cavell, Edith, 26, 439
Caven, Lorena, 159
Caxton, William 215, 427
Cecilia (Titian's model), 250
Cellier, Elizabeth, 70
Centennial Exhibition of 1876, female exhibitors at, 104–105
Center for the American Woman and Politics, 367, 369
Cerioli, Constance, 386
Certified Professional Secretaries, 98
Cézanne, Paul, 252
Chadwick, Alison, 163

Chadwick, Constance Cassandra, 298
Chadwick, Florence, 421
Chama people, Peru, 53–54
Chaminade, Cécile Louise Stéphanie, 200
Chamorro, Violeta Barrios de, 373–374
Chancellor, John, 185
Chandler, Dorothy ("Buffy") Buffum, 231–232
Chandler, Norman, 231
Chandler, Otis, 231–232
Chandler, Robin, 182
Chanel, Gabrielle ("Coco"), 281
Chantal, Jeanne de, 386
Chantels, The, 210
Chaplin, Charlie, 264
Chapone, Hester M., 429
Charisse, Cyd, 188, 328
Charles V, Holy Roman Emperor, 356, 357
Charles I, King of England, 171
Charles II, King of England, 20, 36, 171, 221, 252
Charles VII, King of France, 252, 277, 320
Charles VIII, King of France, 277
Charles IX, King of France, 357, 377–378
Charles, Nora (fictional character), 227
Charlotte, Queen of England, 65, 323
Charlotte, Princess of England, 277
Charlotte (slave), 311
Charlotte aux pommes (dish), 322
Charpentier, Constance-Marie, 243
Chase, Ann Baldwin, 360
Chase, Ilka, 182
Chase, Lucia, 193
Chase, Mary, 448
Chassler, Sey, 344
Chatauroux, Duchess of (Marquise de la Tournelle), 45–46
Châtelet, Marquise du (Emilie de Breteuil), 128
Chavez, Judy, 47
Chaworth, Mary, 41
Chayes, Antonia H., 153
Cheatham, Margaret, 269
Cheek, Alison, 394
Cheesecake, Anna Dumpling, 329
Cheeseman, Evelyn, 133
Cheltenham College for Young Ladies, England, 122
Chemistry, 134, 445, 446; Nobel Prize winners, 7, 132, 133, 450; pay, 130

Chen Li, 63, 145
Chen Muhua, 373
Cheney, Clara Imogene (Marcy), 78
Chenoweth, Alice, 334
Cher (Cherilyn LaPiere), 211, 326, 328
Cherokee Indians, 288
Chesler, Phyllis, 224
Chess, 424
Chesterfield, Lord Philip, 426
Chevalier, Adèle, 68
Chézy, Helmine von, 200
Chiang Ching, 328, 376
Chiang Kai-shek, Madame (Soong Mai-ling), 38, 75–76, 450
Chicago Lyric Opera, 203
Chicago Symphony, 347
Chicago Tribune, 231
Chichester, Sir Francis, 161
Chief Executive magazine, 230
Chiffons, The, 210
Childbirth: first Caesarean, 70; and sports, 63–64, 401, 405; unusual births, 62–63
Children's books, 223, 332
Ch'in Liang-Yu, 145
China: patron deities, 380–381; woman suffrage, 342; women in power, 373, 375–376
Chinchón, Countess Aña de, 329
Chiquita Banana, 95
Chisholm, Shirley, 366, 442
Choice Magazine Listening, 230
Chopin, Frédéric, 198–199
Choreographers, 193–196
Chorus Equity, 179
Chorus girls, 179
Chou En-lai, 376
Christian, Linda, 266–267, 269
Christian Science Monitor, 389
Christian Scientists, 30, 388–389
Christie, Dame Agatha, 11, 225
Christina, Queen of Sweden, 323, 434
Christina of Mergate, 240
Christine de Pisan, 215, 217
Chromosomes, X vs. Y, 18
Chulalongkorn, King of Siam, 122
Church, Ellen, 111, 112
Churchill, Peter, 27
Churchill, Lord Randolph, 261
Churchill, Sir Winston, 174, 240, 261
Churruca, Irene, 320
Chuter, Penny, 421
Chytilova, Vera, 189

Ci Xi (Tz'u Hsi), Empress of China, 360, 378
Ciencia (filly), 407
Cigarette smoking 292, 314
Cilèa, Francesco, 170
Cinders, Ella (comic-strip character), 108
Circe, 353
Circus managers, 88
Cissé, Jeanne Martin, 374
Citizens Party (1980), 365
City government, women in, 367–369
City planning, 256
Civil rights, 290–293; advocates, 26–27, 31, 32, 288–289, 395, 444. *See also* Women's rights
Civil Rights Act of 1964, 292
Civil Service Act of 1883, 102
Civil War, 7, 153; women disguised as men, 145; women spies, 149–150
Claflin, Avery, 201
Claflin, Dorothea Carroll, 201
Clairaut, Alexis, 130
Clairmont, Claire, 41
Clairvoyants, 13, 14
Clapp, Margaret, 448
Clara of Assisi, 385
Clark, Joe, 371
Clark, Petula, 5
Clark, Sarah Hatfield, 360
Clarke, Mary E., 151
Claudius, Roman Emperor, 68, 377
Clay, Mary (Marguerite von Graff), 9
Cleary, Catherine, 83
Cleopatra, 15, 36, 38
Clepsydra, 43
Clerical work, 96
Cleveland, "Baby Ruth," 330
Cleveland, Emeline, 124
Cline, Patsy, 213
Clio (Muse), 74
Clive, Kitty, 172
Clofullia, Mme. Fortune, 6
Clotho (Fate), 74
Cloyce, Sarah, 310
Clurman, Harold, 176
Clymer, Elizabeth Meredith, 360
Coachman, Alice, 442
Cobb, Gail A., 109
Cobb, Jerrie, 165
Cobden-Sanderson, Annie, 343
Cobham, Maria, 294
Cochran, Jacqueline, 151
Cock, Daisy Etta, 329
Cockburn, Catharine, 232
Cockrell, Lila, 368
Cocktail, invention of, 106
Coffal, Elizabeth, 109
Cogni, Margarita, 41

Cohen, Anna, 254
Cohen, Audrey, 422
Cohen, Geula, 373
Cohen, Ze'eva, 64
Cohn, Mildred, 443, 445
Coit, Lillie Hitchcock, 8, 104
Coit, Margaret Louise, 448
Coleman, Bessie, 442
Coleridge, Samuel Taylor, 426
Coles, Robert M., 449
Colette, 63, 78
Colettine Poor Clares, 385
Coligny, Comte Gaspard de, 40, 377–378
Collage, 247–248
College attendance, statistics, 127–128
Colleges. *See* Women's colleges
Collier, Constance, 201
Collins, Dorothy, 183
Collins, Judy, 212
Collot, Marie-Anne, 244
Colorado, woman suffrage in, 342
Colson, Elizabeth Florence, 445
Columbia University, 125–126, 131, 133, 135, 435
Columbian Exposition, Chicago, 246, 256, 346
Columnists, 75, 429, 430
Colvin, Margaret, 105
Comaneci, Nadia, 6
Comden, Betty, 233
Comédie Française, 170, 173
Comic-strip artists, 255
Comic-strip characters, 108
Commander, Lydia Kingsmill, 343
Commedia dell'Arte, 170
Commoner, Barry, 365
Communist party, U.S.A., 365
Composers, 29, 75, 77, 78, 199–200, 208; "Celebration of Women Composers'" benefit concert, 203; of popular songs, 204–205, 209, 210; precocious, 5, 197
Compton, Betty, 178
Computer sciences, 132, 330; pay, 130
Comstock, Anthony, 72
Conductors, 75, 197, 202–203, 208–209; all-girl groups, 206–207
Cone, Claribel, 252, 253
Cone, Etta, 252, 253
Cone, Honey, 211
Congo tribes, 53
Congregationalists: missionaries, 393, 394; ordination of women, 390 (*see*

also United Church of Christ)
Congress, members of, 365–367. *See also* U.S. House of Representatives; U.S. Senate
Conley, Kathleen, 155
Connelly, Cornelia Peacock, 385
Conner, Dale, 255
Conners, Carol, 190
Connie (comic-strip character), 108
Connolly Brinker, Maureen ("Little Mo"), 412
Cons, Emma, 176
Conscience, voices of, 31–32
Conselman, Bill, 108
Conservative Judaism, 392
Constant, Benjamin, 40
Constant Comment Tea Co., 87
Construction workers, 101
Contemporary Art Museum of Houston, 254
Cook, Beverly B., 289
Cook, Eliza, 433
Cook books, 79, 110–111
Cooke, Alexander, 171
Cooke, Barbara, 269
Cooke, Jack Kent, 269
Cooks, 29, 79, 110–111
Cool, Bertha (fictional character), 227
Coolidge, Calvin, 205, 279, 293, 363
Coolidge, Grace Goodhue, 363
Coolidge, Rita, 211
Coon Creek Girls, 212
Cooney, Joan Ganz, 451
Cooper, Bette, 279
Cooper, Gary, 440
Cooper, James Fenimore, 106
Copernicus, 121, 130
Copland, Aaron, 202
Copley, Helen Kinney, 232
Coppin, Fanny Jackson, 124
Corbett, James J., 285
Corbin, Margaret, 147
Corday, Charlotte, 267
Corey, Martha, 310
Cori, Carl F., 132, 450
Cori, Gerty T., 132, 135, 445, 450
Cornbury, Lord (Edward Hyde), 22
Cornell, Katharine, 232
Cornwallis, General Charles, 148
Corporate officers, 80–84, 127; film moguls, 192–193
Corrigan, Mairead, 27, 449
Corsets, 277–278
Corson, Juliet, 111
Corson, Mille Gade, 421
Corson, Richard, 276
Cory, Adela Florence, 333
Cory, Fanny Young, 255

Cosindas, Marie, 260
Cosmetics, 92, 271–272, 273–274, 329; do-it-yourself, 275–276; queens of, 276–277
Cosmopolitan magazine, 38, 87, 230
Costello, Catherine, 72
Costello, Della, 312
Costello, Patty, 424
Coston, Martha, 104–105
Costume design, 246, 247
Cosu, Alice M., 340
Cosway, Maria, 122
Cotton Club, Harlem, 179–180
Cotton gin, invention of, 106
Coudray, Angélique Marguérite Boursier du, 70
Council of Graduate Schools, 128
Countess of Huntingdon's Connexion, 387–388
Country Dance and Song Society of America, 194
Country music, 212–214
Country Music Association, 213
County government, women in, 367
Court, Margaret Smith, 412
Courtesans, 43–45, 218
Courtney, Janet Hogarth, 126
Coventry, Lady Maria, 271
Cowart, Juanita, 210
Cowley, Mary, 90
Cox, Gertrude Mary, 445
Craddock, Charles Egbert (pseudonym), 333
Craig, Judy, 210
Craig, Minnie, 365
Cramm, Baron Gottfried von, 55
Cramphorn, Lucy, 320
Crampton, Charlotte, 172
Crandall, Prudence, 31
Cranz, Christel, 424
Crawford, Cheryl, 176
Crawford, Ellis, 112
Crawford, Joan, 179
Crawford, Louisa Macartney, 433
"Crawford inheritance," 298
Cresswell, Old Mother, 67
Crews, Christine L., 152
Crick, Francis H., 133
Crime, women victims of, 314
Criminals, 66, 67, 68–69, 78; bandits, 295; murderesses, 68–69, 296–298, 299–300, 329; pirates, 294; statistics on women, 300; swindlers, 298–299; women on "most wanted" list, 299–300
Crimmins, Alice, 69
Crinoline, 273

Crocker, Anne, 320
Crocker, Betty, 94
Crocker, William G., 94
Crockett, Effie I., 205
Crockett, Linda, 154
Cronkhite, Bernice Brown, 444
Cronwright Schreiner, Samuel C., 334
Crosby, Caresse (Mary Phelps Jacobs), 278
Cross, Amanda, 227
Cross-country trips, 160–161
Crothers, Rachel, 232
Crow, Katie, 91
Crow Indians, 48; women warriors, 150, 151
Crowe, Sylvia, 257
Crumm, Agatha (comic-strip character), 108
Crump, Diane, 405
Cruz, Normita de la, 395
Cryer, Gretchen, 233
Crystals, The, 210
Cumming, Rose, 280
Cunitz, Maria, 130
Cunningham, Imogen, 259
Cunningham, Merce, 260
Curie, Marie S., 7, 77, 78, 131–132, 268, 450
Curie, Pierre, 131, 450
Curtis, Ann, 404
Curtis, Harriot, 415
Curtis, Hyacinth, 180
Curtis, Margaret, 415
Curtis, Tony, 171
Curtis Cup (golf), 415
Curzon, Lady, 261, 320
Curzon, Lord George, 261
Cushman, Charlotte Saunders, 172, 174, 451
Cushman, Pauline, 150
Cushman, Susan, 172
Cussons, Wendy, 320
Cuthbert, Betty, 417
Cybele (goddess), 380
Cyclists. *See* Bicyclists
Cynthiana, Ky., 323
Cyrene, 43
Cytology, 133

D'Agoult, Countess Marie Sophie de Flarigny, 198
Dahl-Wolfe, Louise, 259
Dahomey, Africa, 48
Daily Courant, 216
Daley, Richard, 368
Dalton, Adeline Younger, 66
Dalton, Isabella, 322
Daly, Lillian O'Malley, 154
Damrosch, Walter, 200
Dance, 170, 171, 193–196
Dandridge, Dorothy, 74, 180
Dandridge Sisters, the, 74, 180
Daniel, Margaret Truman, 452

Daniels, Bebe, 265
D'Annunzio, Gabriele, 44, 175
Dante Alighieri, 36, 226
D'Antonio, Angela, 268–269
Danzig, Allison, 411
Darchinger, Magda, 443
Dare, Precious Darling, 329
Dare, Susan (fictional character), 227
Dare, Virginia, 446
Darling, Candy, 180–181
Darling, Joan, 189
Darnell, Linda, 188
Darragh, Lydia, 148
Daubié, Julie Victoire, 126
Daughters: fathers', 76–77; legal treatment of, 288; mothers', 77–79
Daughters of Charity, 385, 386
Daughters of Liberty, 147
Daughters of Our Lady of Mount Calvary, 385
Daughters of St. Crispin, 99
Daughters Publishing, 228
Daura, Habe queen, 355
David, Jacques Louis, 243
Davidson, Karla, 192
Davies, Marion, 178, 264, 266
Davis, Angela Yvonne, 34, 299, 365
Davis, Bessie McCoy, 178
Davis, Bette, 7–8, 191
Davis, Cathy Ann ("Cat"), 408
Davis, Jefferson, 150
Davis, Lizzie, 158
Davis, Lynn E., 153
Davis Marguerite, 135
Davis, Ruth M., 153
Davis, Sammy, Jr., 86
Davison, Grace, 185
Davitashvili, Dzhuna, 396
Davona Dale (filly), 406
Dawes, Henry L., 32
Dawson, Mary Cardwell, 204
Day, Doris, 183, 328
Day, Dorothy, 71, 340
Day, Linda, 154
Deacons, 394
Dean, Ada Evans, 405
Dean, Debbie (comic-strip character), 108
Dean, Penny Lee, 422
Deason, Muriel (Kitty Wells), 212–213
Death of a Princess (film), 316
Deaths: causes of, statistics, 314; unusual, 15–16
Deborah (prophet), 143
De Carlo, Yvonne, 188
Decies, Fifth Baron, 262
Decker, Mary, 423
Declaration of Independence, 336; printer of, 77,

90; signers' wives, 360–362
De Claris Mulieribus (Boccaccio), 215, 239
DeCrow, Karen, 348
Dee, Sandra, 328
Degas, Edgar, 246
Degillio, Lynne, 100
De Grasse, Joseph, 186
De Havilland, Olivia, 191
De Horsey, Adeline Horsey, 329
De la Guerre, Elisabeth Jacquet, 199
De Laguna, Frederica Annis, 445
De la Hunty, Shirley S., 417
Delamare, Delphine, 218–219
Delauney, Robert, 115
Delauney, Sonia, 114–115
Deledda, Grazia, 449
Delrons, The, 210
De Luca, Ronnie, 420
De Lys, Gogo, 183
De Marco Sisters, the, 74
Demdike, Elizabeth, 309
Demetrius Poliorcetes, King of Macedon, 43
De Mille, Agnes, 194, 195
DeMille, Cecil B., 186
Demon, Barbara, 291
Demorest, Ellen, 92–93, 277
Deneuve, Catherine, 71
Deng Yingquiao (Deng Ying Chao), 376
Denmark: female succession, 357; woman suffrage, 342; women in government, 372
Dent, Jim, 417
Dentists, 77, 105
Department store heads, 81
De Pauw, Linda Grant, 107
DePeyster, Cornelia Lubbetse, 90
Depression (mental state), 19, 30–31
Derby, Pat, 159–160
DeSantis, Ann, 447
De Sopo, Philomena, 455
Desserts named for women, 322
Detective stories, 225–228, 332; female sleuths, 226–228
Deutsch, Helen R., 142
De Valois, Dame Ninette, 193
DeVere, Pearl, 91
Deveree, Jane, 6
Devi, Shanta, 15
Devlin, Bernadette, 71, 371
Dewey, Melvil, 125
de Wolfe, Elsie (Lady Mendl), 264, 280
Dexter, Elizabeth Anthony, 89
Dia, Countess de, 199
Diaghilev, Sergei, 193, 246

Diamond business, 85
Diamond Lil (West), 219
Diamonds, 265–267, 277
Diana Press, 228
Diaz, Eloiza (Inunza), 136
Dick, Nancy, 370
Dickinson, Emily, 232, 267, 446
Diderot, Denis, 242
Didion, Joan, 191, 325
Dienemann, Max, 391
Dietrich, Jan, 165
Dietrich, Marion, 165
Dietrich, Marlene, 16, 278, 328
Digby, Jane, Lady Ellenborough, 37
Dillard, Annie, 449
Diller, Phyllis, 113
Dillinger, John, 47
Dinesen, Isak, 113
Dingwall, Louise, 115
Diniz, Angela, 317
Dinning Sisters, the, 74
Dionne, Elzire, 62
Dionne quintuplets, 62, 315
Dior, Christian, 278, 282
Directors: documentaries, 189; movies, 186–187, 189–190; opera, 203–204; theater, 174, 176, 232
Directors Guild of America, 189
Discus throw, 418, 423
Dishes named for women, 320–322
Disney, Walt, 95, 184
Disraeli, Benjamin, 37
Disraeli, Mary Anne, 37
Divine (transvestite), 181
Divorce: no fault, 292–293; settlements, 269–270; statistics, 47–48
Dix, Beulah Marie, 185
Dix, Dorothea, 30
Dix, Dorothy (Elizabeth Meriwether Gilmer), 430
Dixie Cups, The, 210
Dixon, Edna, 340
Dixon, Jeanne, 14–15
Dixon, Mary, 146
Dixon, Mildred (Mrs. Duke Ellington), 180
Dmitriev-Mamonov, Alexander, 39
Doan Vinh Na Champacak, Prince, 55
Doane, Deborah B., 152
Dock, Lavinia, 340
Dockworkers, 101
Doctoral students, 127
Documentary directors, 189
Dod, Charlotte ("Lottie"), 410
Dodd, Sondra, 293
Dodge, Cindy, 157–158
Dodgson, Charles (Lewis Carroll), 219
Doe, Elizabeth, 313, 326
Dohrn, Bernardine Rae, 300

Dolin, Anton, 193
Dolle Minas (Dutch movement), 337
Dolly, Jenny, 74, 266
Dolly, Rosie, 74, 266
Dolly Sisters, the, 74, 178, 266
Dolores (Kathleen Rose), 177, 178
Domitien, Elizabeth, 359
Donahue, Phil, 344
Donnally, Mary, 70
Donnelly, Nell Quinlan, 282
Donner, Susan K., 155
Dorlhac, Helene, 373
Dorr, Nell, 259
Dors, Diana, 328
Douglas, Emily Taft, 367
Douglas, Helen Gahagan, 315, 367
Douglass, Frederick, 344
Doujebamo (Living Buddha), 383
Dove, Billie, 178
Dove, Lil Lovey, 329
Dowd, Nancy, 192
Dowden, Hester, 14
Downward Elizabeth Turner, 329
Dragon Lady (comic-strip character), 108
Drake, Jane, 94
Dramatists. *See* Playwrights
Draper, Dorothy, 280, 281
Draper, Elizabeth, 281
Draper, Margaret, 89
Drayton, Grace G., 255
Draz, Zelfa, 230
Dreamland Syncopators, 209
Dreams, clairvoyant, 12–13
Dress patterns, 92, 277
Dressler, Marie, 14, 179
Drew, Georgiana, 173
Drew, John, 173
Drew, Louisa Lane, 173–174
Driving, auto: cross-country, 160; race car, 7, 30, 159, 418
Droste, Marga, 443
Drucker, Wilhelmina, 337
Drug addicts, 313, 314
Drug tests, in athletic competition, 423
Druids, 49; priestesses, 13
Druschki, Frau Karl, 320
Dubofsky, Jean Everhart, 290
Duchemin, Catherine, 241
Duchesne, Rosa P., 122
Duck, Mary Rhoda, 329
Dudevant, Amandine Aurore Dupin. *See* Sand, George
Dudley, Dudley, 451
Duerk, Arlene B., 152
Duff, Mary, 41
Duff-Gordon, Lucille, Lady, 75, 178, 281

Dugan, Dixie (comic-strip character), 108
Dugès, Marie-Jonet, 70
Duke, Patty, 5
Duluth, Iris (fictional character), 227
Dulzaides, Rebecca G., 14
Dumas, Alexandre, 218, 321
Du Maurier, Daphne, 233
Du Maurier, George, 285
Dumée, Jeanne, 130
Dumm, Edwina Frances, 255
Dumont, Eleanore ("Madame Moustache"), 93
Duncan, Isadora, 195
Duncan, Maria-Theresa, 195
Dunham, Edna, 152
Duniway, Abigail Scott, 441
Dunkling, Leslie Alan, 329
Dunleavy, Rosemay, 194
Dunn, Dorothy, 185
Dunne, Irene, 178
Dunning, John, 296–297
Duperre, Laure, 199
Duplessis, Alphonsine Marie, 218
Durack, Fanny, 420
Durant, Alexia, 185
Durant, Ariel, 449
Durant, Henry, 125
Durant, Will, 449
Durbin, Deanna, 5
Dürer, Albrecht, 240
Duse, Eleanora, 175
Dustbooks, 228
Duston, Hannah, 25
Dvorak, Ann, 188
Dwyer, Virginia Alice, 82
Dyer, Mrs. Bob, 422
Dyer, K. F., 401
Dyer, Mary, 31
Dykstra, Candy, 100

Eagels, Jeanne, 179
Eakins, Thomas, 244, 258
Earhart, Amelia, 12, 15, 38, 348, 446, 452
Earl, Mary (pseudonym), 332
East, Mary (James How), 21
Easterling, Rita, 414
Eastman, Carole, 192
"Easy Aces" (radio show), 181
Eaton, Linda, 291
Eberhardt, Isabelle (Si Mahmoud), 21–22
Eberhart, Mignon G., 227
Eckman, Exira, 323
Ecologists, 445
Economists, 127; pay, 130
Eddy, Mary Baker, 30, 113, 267, 388–389
Eden, Barbara, 328
Eden, Elizabeth, 20
Ederle, Gertrude, 404, 420, 421
Edgerton, Winnifred, 131

Edison, Nancy Elliott, 69
Editors: magazine, 230, 332, 338; newspaper, 231, 441
Edmonds, Emma E., 150
Education, 120–128; higher, statistics (U.S.), 127–128, 136–137, 228; higher, statistics (USSR), 97; sex discrimination in, 123, 125, 126, 137–138, 435
Educators, 31, 75, 121–122, 124–126, 443–444; black, 34, 122, 124; handicapped, 29; Indian, 33; science faculties, 129, 131, 132, 152, 443; teacher statistics, 96, 97
Edward the Elder, King, 144, 240
Edward VI, King of England, 245, 306, 308
Edward VII, King of England, 44, 261, 266, 273, 439
Edwards, Bonita (Mrs. Manville), 56
Edwards, Joan, 183
Edwards, Marcelle (Mrs. Manville), 56
Egleston, Rita, 159
Eichler, Lillian, 430, 431
Eichtal, A. d', 199
Einstein, Albert, 250, 435
Eisenmann-Schier, Ruth, 299
Eisenberg, Celia, 312
Eisenberg, Harold (Holly Woodlawn), 181
Eisenhower, Ida Stover, 69
Eisenhower, Dwight D., 69, 370
Eisenhower, Mamie, 185
Eklund, Coy C., 345
Eleanor Crosses, 8
Eleanor of Aquitaine, Queen of England, 12
Eleanor of Castile, Queen of England, 8, 453
Elective office, 365–370; abroad, 371–374; candidates for U.S. president, 364–365. *See also* Government, women in
Elias, Anilu, 346
Eliot, George (pseudonym), 113, 332, 434, 454
Eliot, T. S., 230
Elizabeth I, Queen of England, 38, 245, 272, 275, 307, 308, 316, 320, 356, 359, 402, 439, 453
Elizabeth II, Queen of England, 357, 450
Elizabeth of York, Queen of England, 250, 453
Elizabeth, Queen of Bohemia, 453
Elizabeth-Charlotte, Princess of France, 322
Elk Hollering, 151

Elkins, Kathleen, 101
Elmira, N.Y., 323
Ellenborough, Lady (Jane Digby), 37
Ellery, Abigail Cary, 360
Ellington, Duke, 180, 208, 209
Elliot Medal, NAS, 133
Elliott, Maude Howe, 448
Ellis, Frank, 108
Ellstein, Abraham, 201
Elsie, the Borden cow, 94
El-Soud, Soad Abu, 346
Elstner, Anne, 183
Eltinge, Julian, 171
Embla (Norse legend), 3
Emerson, Alice B. (pseudonym), 332
Emerson, Mary, 90
Employment, 96–115; blue collar, 100–101; early factory conditions, 99, 312, 318; in government, 102 (*see also* Government); in management, 80–84, 96, 127, 192–193; pay, 80, 95, 96–97, 98, *table* 130, 292, 346; secretarial, 96, 98; sex discrimination in, 137–138, 287, 289, 291, 292, 315, 318, 346–347, 425; statistics, 96–97, 98. *See also* Working women
Empresses, 359–360
Encyclopaedia Britannica, 127
Ender, Kornelia, 420
Endor, the woman of, 13
Engels, Friedrich, 337
Engineering, women in, 100, 129, 256
English Channel swimmers, 421, 422
Englishwoman's Journal, 338
Englishwoman's Review, 338
Enheduanna (poet), 215
Enterprising Women, 230
Eon, Chevalier d' (Charles Eon de Beaumont), 22
Ephron, Delia, 78
Ephron, Nora, 78
Ephron, Phoebe, 78
Episcopal Church: missionary groups, 393; women priests, 389, 394–395, 444
Epitaphs, 437–438
Eppes, Bettie Jean, 109
Equal Credit Opportunity Act, 293
Equal Employment Opportunity Commission, 96, 290
Equal pay legislation, 80, 99, 292
Equal Property Law, in divorce, 269, 293
Equal Rights Amendment (ERA), 325, 337, 345, 347, 455

Equality League for Self-Supporting Women, 78
Erato (Muse), 74
Erdelyi, G. J., 401
Erdlen, Christina (Mrs. Manville), 56
Erskine, Catherine, 199
Erwin, Annabel, 222
Esau, Katherine, 445
Escobar, Virginia ("Cookie"), 101
Escot, Pozzi, 203
Esterhazy, Contess Caroline, 198
Esther, Queen, 354
Estrich, Susan, 288
Esty, Mary, 310
Etess, Elaine Grossinger, 79
Ethelfleda of Mercia, 144
Etiquette books, 429–430
Eubanks, Shirley B., 101
Eugénie, Empress of France, 322
Euphrosyne (Grace), 74
European Assembly presidency, 375
Euterpe (Muse), 74
Evans, Edith, 28
Evans, Herbert M., 135
Evans, Joan, 127
Evans, Mary Ann. *See* Eliot, George
Evanston College, 124
Evanti, Lillian, 442
Eve, 3, 454
"Evelyn and Her Magic Violin," 206
Everleigh, Ada, 75, 93
Everleigh, Minna, 75, 93
Evert Lloyd, Christine ("Chris"), 443
Evitt, Ardath, 115
Evrard, Clemence (Demoor), 137
Exner, Judith Campbell, 47
Explorers, 161–162; scientific, 133–134
Exter, Alexandra, 247
Eye, Shirley Foote, 329

Faber, Doris, 65
Failu, Gioacchino, 132
Fair, Charles, 92
Fairbanks, Avard, 454
Fairbanks, Douglas, Sr., 264
Fairfax, Beatrice (Marie Manning), 429
Faith healers, 30, 395–396
Falconet, Etienne, 244
Falsies, 272–273
Famous men, mothers of, 64–65
Fan clubs, 285
Fancher, Mollie, 14
Fannie Farmer Cookbook, The, 111
Fanny (rock group), 211
Fanny (slave), 310
Fansler, Kate (fictional character), 227

Farber, Bea, 405–406
Farenthold, Frances T. ("Sissy"), 365
Fargo, Donna, 211
Farmer, Fannie Merritt, 29, 111
Farnese, Giulia, 45
Farnsworth, Emma Justine, 258
Farr, Wanda Kirkbridge, 133
Farrar, Eliza W., 429
Farrar, Geraldine, 188
Farrell, Sister Carolyn, 368
Farrell, Warren, 344
Farrenc, Louise, 199
Farthingale, 272
Fashion design, 247, 281–282, 283, 284
Fashion models, 278–279, 281
Fashions: haute couture, 281; innovators, 277–278, 281–284; for the masses, 277, 282–283
Fates, Three, 68, 74
Fathers' daughters, 76–77
Father's Day, 293
Fatima, 383
Faulkner, Mignon, 63
Faulkner, Myrna, 63
Faversham, William, 285
Fawcett, Millicent Garrett, 338
Fawcett-Majors, Farrah, 279
FBI, 289; most wanted women, 299
Fears, Peggy, 178
Fede, Lucrezia del, 250
Federal judiciary, 290, 442; statistics, 289, 367
Federal Theatre Project, 176
Feigen Fasteau, Brenda, 334–335
Feigen Fasteau, Marc, 334–335, 344
Feine, Virginia Burns, 329
Feinstein, Dianne, 368
Feist, Ellen, 172
Feist, Emma, 172
Felicie, Jacoba, 137
Fell, Margaret, 343, 387
Fellows, Anna, 11
Felton, Rebecca Latimer, 366
Female Island, 353
Female Medical College of Pennsylvania, 136, 138, 139
Female Tatler (magazine), 216
Feminine Mystique, The (Friedan), 345
Feminist Press, 228
Feminist publishing houses, 228
Feminists, 30–31, 77, 78, 186, 333–335, 336–343, 345–346, 347–348; male

allies, 343–345. *See also* Suffrage movement
Fencing, 425
Ferber, Edna, 448, 452
Ferguson, Elizabeth Graeme, 218
Ferguson, Hilda, 178
Ferguson, James ("Pa"), 66, 369
Ferguson, Martrese Thek, 153
Ferguson, Miriam ("Ma"), 66, 369
Fermi Award, 132
Fern, Fanny (Sarah Payson Willis Parton), 429, 430
Fernande (Picasso's mistress), 57, 251
Ferrier, Kathleen, 320
Fichlander, Zelda, 177
Fickling, G. G. (Gloria and Forest E. Fickling), 228
Fiction. *See* Novelists
Field, Sally, 5
Field hands, 310–311
Field hockey, 402–403
Fields, Crystal, 414
Fields, Lew, 180
Fields, Dorothy, 180, 190
Fields, Mary, 99
Fighter pilots, U.S.S.R., 155
Figuer, Thérèse, 145
Figure skating, 404, 419
Filkins, Thora B., 13
Fillies, winning, 406–407
Fillmore, Abigail, 362
Fillmore, Mrs. Luther, 341
Film editors, 185
Film studio managers, 185
Finance, women in, 82–83
Financial Women's Association, 83–84
Finberg, Z. Willard, 393
Finch, Ruth Pinches, 329
Fine, Sylvia, 190
Finland: woman suffrage, 342; women in government, 372, 374
Finney, Mary (fictional character), 227
Firefighters, 103–104
Firnberg, Hertha, 372
First Women's Bank of Maryland, 83
First Women's Bank of New York, 81, 83, 84
Fischer, Emil, 347
Fischer, Helga, 268
Fisher, Anna L., 164
Fisher, Lucy, 192
Fisher, Mary, 387
Fisher, Mrs. Oakley, 320
Fisher, Welthy Honsinger, 122
Fishing, 420; shark, 422
Fiske, Minnie Maddern, 175
Fison, Evelyn, 320
Fitzgerald, Ella, 209
Fitzgerald, Frances, 449
Flack, Roberta, 434

Flagg, Sarah Ann, 434
Flagg, Wava White, 329
Flagler, Henry Morrison, 253
Flagmakers, 107
Flanagan, Elizabeth, 106
Flanagan, Hallie, 176–177
Flaubert, Caroline Fleuriot, 64
Flaubert, Gustave, 64, 218–219
Fleet, Thomas, 67
Fleming, Sir Alexander, 26
Fleming, Amalia, 26
Fleming, Peggy, 419
Fleming, Rhonda, 188
Fleming, Susan, 178
Fleming, Williamina, 131
Fletcher, Adele Whitely, 185
Fletcher, Maria, 280
Flexner, Simon, 132
Flight attendants, 112
Flocarline (filly), 407
Floyd, Isabella Jones, 360
Fock, Grete, 443
Fogarty, Ann, 281–282
Folies Bergère, 44
Follis, Ann, 345
Foltz, Clara Shortridge, 288
Fonda, Jane, 191
Fontane Sisters, the, 74
Foote, Lucinda, 435
Foote, Maria, 172
Forbes, Esther, 448
Force, Juliana, 249, 253
Ford, Anne McDonnell, 269
Ford, Betty, 451
Ford, Cristina, 269
Ford, Mrs. Ford Madox, 57
Ford, Gerald, 370, 456
Ford, Leslie (pseudonym), 332
Ford, Nancy, 233
Foreman, Elizabeth, 152
Fornarina, La, 252
Forrest, Carolyn, 451
Forstein, Dorothy, 12
Forten, Charlotte, 122, 223
Fortunato, Rita, 268
Foster, Elizabeth (Mother Goose), 67
Foster, Hannah Webster, 217
Foster, Joy, 6
Foster, Stephen C., 205
Foster mothers, 66
Fotheringham, Margaret, 340
Fouquet, Jean, 252
Fourcroy, Jean L., 141
Fourment, Helena, 250–251
Fowler, Lydia Folger, 138
Fox, Mrs. Caleb, 115
Fox, Carol, 203
Fox, David, 225
Fox, George, 343
Fox, Karen L., 391
Fox, Kate, 75

Fox, Margaretta, 75
France: woman suffrage in, 342; women in government, 373, 375
Franchise. *See* Suffrage movement; Voting rights
Francis, Elizabeth, 309
Franckowiak, Lucille, 110
Franco, Jennie, 312
Frank, Ray, 390
Frank Leslie's Lady's Magazine, 229
Frankenthaler, Helen, 444
Franklin, Anne Smith, 89
Franklin, Aretha, 86, 208, 210
Franklin, Benjamin, 89, 90, 121, 346, 360
Franklin, Deborah Read, 360
Franklin, Elizabeth, 90
Franklin, Rosalind Elsie, 132–133
Franks, Lucinda, 447
Fraser, Lady Antonia, 78, 227–228
Fratianne, Linda, 419
Fraunces, Phoebe, 148
Frazee Sisters, the, 74
Frazier, Brenda, 264, 278
Frederick II, the Great, King of Prussia, 138, 242
Frederick II, Holy Roman Emperor, 355
Frederick, Pauline, 456
Free Enquirer, 31
Freeman, Mrs. (actress), 172
Freeman, Elizabeth, 288–289
Freeman, Mary E. Wilkins, 220
Freemasons, 7
French, Alice, 220
French, Elizabeth, 105
French, Marilyn, 35
Frescobaldi, Dianora, 62
Freud, Amalie Nathanson, 64
Freud, Anna, 77, 142
Freud, Sigmund, 31, 64, 142
Freyja (goddess), 379, 454
Friday, Nancy, 224
Friedan, Betty, 83, 345
Friedman, Esther Pauline (Ann Landers), 75, 430
Friedman, Muriel, 141
Friedman, Pauline Esther (Abigail van Buren), 75, 430
Friend, Charlotte, 445
Frigga (goddess), 379
Frings, Ketti, 448
Frissell, Toni, 260
Frome, David (pseudonym), 332
Frontier women, 93, 99, 103; medical remedies of, 139
Frost, Alice, 182
Fry, Harriet, 112

Frykowski, Voyteck, 297
Fu Fei (goddess), 380
Fu Hao (Chinese consort), 375
Fugate, Caril Ann, 297
Fulbert, Arlette, 12
Fuller, Mrs. Eugene, 253
Fuller, Fay, 163
Fuller, Lillian, 115
Fuller, Loie (Marie Louise), 194–195
Fuller, Margaret, 76–77, 126
Fuller, Richard Eugene, 253
Fuller, Thomas, 426
Funk, Mary Wallace, 165
Furtseva, Yekaterina, 373
Fussell, Sarah, 183

Gable, Clark, 10, 286
Gabor, Zsa Zsa, 55
Gaches-Sarraute, Mme., 277
Gadd, May, 194
Gaea (goddess), 380
Gag, Wanda, 223
Gainer, Linda, 442
Gale, Zona, 448
Galizia, Fede, 240
Gallois, Germaine, 272
Gallup, Anna Billings, 254
Galvin, Catherine M., 141
Gamata, Habe queen, 355
Gamba, Juliet Seashell Moonbeam, 329
Gambling dealers, 93–94
Gampel, Lilit, 197
Gandhi, Indira, 358
Gandhi, Mohandas K., 122
Gandy, Evelyn, 370
Gannett, Deborah Sampson (Robert Sturtleff), 147
Gannon, Mary Louise, 141
Ganser, Margie, 210
Ganser, Mary Ann, 210
Gaprindashvili, Nona, 424
Garber, Mary, 425
Garbo, Greta, 267, 328
Garcia, Frances ("Frankie"), 14
Garden, Mary, 188, 201, 203
Gardener, Helen Hamilton (pseudonym), 334
Gardner, Ava, 328
Gardner, Erle Stanley, 227
Gardner, Isabella Stewart, 253
Garfield, James A., 362
Garfield, Lucretia Rudolph, 362
Garibaldi, Giuseppe, 145, 333
Garland, Judy, 5, 78, 184
Garner, Margaret, 68
Garnerin, Elisa, 164
Garnerin, Jacques, 163–164
Garret, Jackie ("Tonowanda"), 408
Garrick, David, 174
Garroway, Dave, 184, 279
Garthwaite, Terry, 211

Garzoni, Giovanna, 240
Gaston, Patricia (Mrs. Manville), 56
Gates, Reginald Ruggles, 50
Gatewood, Emma, 160
Gaudillon, Perrenette, 309
Gauss, Karl, 128
Gautier, Doña Felisa Rincon de, 367
Gautier, Judith, 77
Gautier, Théophile, 77
Gavard, Elise, 199
Gay, Samuel, 147
Gayle, Crystal (Brenda Gayle Webb), 213
Gaynor, J. C., 181
Gaynor, Mitzi, 328
Gaynor, William Jay, 160
Gayton, Zoe, 160
Gebhard, Hedwig, 372
Geiger, Emily, 148
Gelber, Jack, 177
Geller, Laura J., 391
Gelman, Polina, 156
Genauer, Emily, 447
General Association of German Women, 337
General Federation of Women's Clubs, 446
Genetics, 132, 445, 446
Genius of Liberty, 229
Gentileschi, Artemisia, 240–241, 315
Gentry, Bobbie (Roberta Streeter), 213
Genuine Risk (filly), 406–407
Geographic names, 322–325
George III, King of England, 9, 65, 130, 323
George, Phyllis, 280
George, Rosemary, 421
Gera, Bernice, 413
Gerard, Alice, 299
Gerard, Richard, 205
Gerke, Florence Holmes, 257
Germain, Sophie, 128
Germany: women physicians in, 136; woman suffrage, 342; women in government, 342, 372
Gerritsen, Cornelius Victor, 334
Gerstung, Martha, 420
Gertman, Stuart, 392
Gertrude, the Pocket Books kangaroo, 95
Gestring, Marjorie, 420
Gibb, Bridget, 57
Gibb, Marjory, 57
Gibbons, William, 228
Gibbs, Cecilia May, 255
Gibbs, Katherine, 113
Gibbs, Twinkle Starr, 329
Gibbson, Fredda, 183
Giblet, Eloise R., 446
Gibson, Althea, 411, 442
Gibson, Eleanor Jack, 444, 445

Giddens, Linda, 420
Giergon, Jolanta, 110
Gilbert, Grace, 6
Gilbert, Madonna, 33
Gilbreth, Lillian, 66
Gillespie, Larrian, 141
Gilliatt, Penelope, 192
Gilman, Charlotte Perkins, 30–31
Gilman, Dorothy, 227
Gilmer, Elizabeth Meriwether (Dorothy Dix), 430
Gilpin, Laura, 260
Gino, Habe queen, 355
Gioconda, Mona Lisa, 250
Giovanni, Nikki, 33, 223
Girardon, François F., 241
Girl Scouts, 446
Girling, Mary Anne, 388
Girls' Rodeo Association, 158
Giroud, Françoise, 373
Giroust, Marie Suzanne, 242
Girton College, England, 123
Gisela, Queen of Hungary, 240
Gish, Lillian, 259, 264
Gittelson, Natalie, 224
Gizirgizir, Habe queen, 356
Glad, Gladys, 178
Gladkowska, Konstancja, 199
Glamis, Elizabeth of, 320
Glasgow, Ellen, 220, 448
Glaspell, Susan, 232, 448
Glasse, Hannah, 110
Globe, Mrs. Samuel, 392–393
Globe Theatre, London, 171
Glover, Mrs. (actress), 172
Gluck, Heidi Yum-Yum, 329
Glueksohn-Waelsch, Salome, 446
Glyn, Elinor, 75, 220
Goddard, Mary Katherine, 77, 90, 346
Goddard, Paulette, 178, 188, 328
Goddard, Sarah Updike, 77, 89
Goddard, William, 89–90
Goddesses, 50, 379–381, 402, 454–455. See also Fates, Graces, Muses
Godey, William, 229
Godey's Lady's Book, 92, 153, 229, 293, 429, 430
Godiva, Lady, 25
Godwin, Frank, 108
Godwin, William, 338
Goelet, May (Duchess of Roxburghe), 262
Goeppert-Mayer, Maria, 133, 445, 450
Goethe, Katharine Elisabeth Textor, 64, 439

Goff, Armenia Funk, 329
Goffin, Gerry, 210
Gold, Rosalind, 392
Gold singles winners, 210–211
Gold Star Mothers, 446
"The Goldbergs" (radio show), 182
Goldhaber, Gertrude Scharff, 445
Golf, 115, 402, 403, 404, 415–417; caddies, 417
Golovkina, Sophia, 194
Goncharova, Natalia, 246, 247
Gone with the Wind (Mitchell), 220–221, 442
Gonne, Maud, 330
Gonzaga, Elisabeth, 50
Good, Dorcas, 310
Good, Nancy Hertz, 329
Good, Sarah, 310
Goodman, Benny, 207
Goodman, Ellen H., 447
Goodman, Linda, 222
Goodrich, Frances, 448
Goodrich, Sweet Clover, 329
Goodwin, Occo E., 141
Goolagong Cawley, Evonne, 412
Gordiyenko, Yekaterina, 423
Gordon, Ellen R., 81
Gordon, Laura de Force, 288
Gorelick, Sara Lee, 165
Gorga, William, 25
Goritscheva, Tatyana, 316
Gorman, Margaret, 279
Gorski, Gail, 112
Gott, Evie Ott, 329
Gottlieb, Leah, 283
Gouges, Olympe de, 337
Goughe, Alexander, 171
Goughe, Robert, 171
Gould, Anna (Duchesse de Talleyrand), 261–262
Gould, Helen, 262
Gould, Jay, 262
Gould, Lois, 15
Gould, Vivien (Baroness Decies), 262
Government, women in, 287, 288, 290, 365–370; Cabinet members (U.S.), 99, 370, 442; Cabinet officers abroad, 371, 372–373; Congress, 7, 315, 331, 365–367, 442; federal employees, 102, 290, 334, 369; female heads of state, 358–359; (*see also* Empresses; Queens); first, in England, 130; foreign nations, 358–359, 371–374, 376; governors, 66, 327, 367, 369; lieutenant governors, 369–370; mayors, 367–369; in Soviet Union, 97, 373; state legislators, 325, 365, 367, 369, 370; statistics, *table* 367
Gowdrie, Isobel, 310
Goya, Francisco, 251
Gozzadini, Bettisia, 287
Grabinska, Wanda G., 374
Grable, Betty, 440
Gracchus, Cornelia, 65
Graces, Three, 73–74
Graff, Marguerite von, 9
Graham, Betty, 87
Graham, Katharine ("Kay") Meyer, 231
Graham, Martha, 195, 196, 260
Graham, Philip L., 231
Grand Ole Opry, 213, 214
Grand Slam tennis winners, 412
Granny Smith apples, 330
Grant, Cary, 55, 286
Grant, Mrs. James (Annie McVicar), 204
Grant, Joan, 15
Grant, Micki, 233
Grant, Nellie, 185
Grant, Ulysses S., 150, 287
Granville, Christine (Countess Skarbek), 27
Grasso, Ella Tambussi, 369
Grau, Shirley Ann, 448
Grauman, Rosa, 440
Grauman, Sid, 440
Gray, Eileen, 256–257
Gray, Henry Judd, 297
Gray, Mary, 129
Gray Panthers, 115
Grayson, Katherine, 328
Great Britain: early women's colleges, 122–123; suffrage movement, 337–338; suffrage obtained, 342; women in government, 359, 371
Great Mother Wang (Hsi Wang Mu), 353, 379
Gredal, Eva, 372
Greece, ancient, prostitution in, 42, 43–44
Greeley, Horace, 126
Green, Adolph, 233
Green, Ann Catherine Hoof, 89
Green, Arda Alden, 135
Green, Constance McLaughlin, 448
Green, Hetty, 69
Green, Marty, 109
Greenberg, Florence, 87
Greenberger, Lillian, 185
Greene, Bella da Costa, 254
Greene, Catherine Littlefield, 106
Greene, Rev. John M., 125
Greene, Nathanael, 106, 148
Greenfield, Elizabeth, 441
Greenfield, Meg, 447
Greenhow, Rose O'Neal, 149
Greenwich, Ellie, 210
Gregory, Lady Isabella Augusta, 232
Gregory, John, 427
Grentz, Theresa Shank, 414
Grenville, Charles, 37
Grey, James (Hannah Snell), 146
Grey, Lady Jane, 306, 316, 438–439, 451
Grier, Mary Lynda Dorothy, 127
Grierson, Cecilia, 137
Griffin, Marion Mahony, 256
Griffin, Walter Burley, 256
Griffith, D. W., 186
Griffiths, Peggy, 180
Grimké, Angelina, 74, 343, 344
Grimké, Charlotte Forten, 122, 223
Grimké, Sarah, 75
Gripenberg, Baroness Alexandra, 372
Gris, Josette, 57
Griswold, Deirdre, 365
Gross, Kathy Jean, 319
Grossinger, Jenny, 79
Grover, Eve, 83
Groves, Penelope Palm Tree, 329
Gruber, Barbara, 393
Gruber, Judith, 393
Gruenberg, Louis, 200
Guadalupe, Our Lady of, 382
Gueiler Tejada, Lidia, 359
Guerin, Elsa Jane Forest, 21
Guicciardi, Countess Giulietta, 197–198
Guiccioli, Countess Teresa, 41–42
"The Guiding Light" (TV show), 300, 301
Guiliani, Marietta, 145
Guillemin, Roger C. L., 133, 450
Guinan, Texas, 113
Guinea, women in government, 374
Guinness, Mrs. Loel, 263
Guinness Book of World Records, 4, 6, 62, 268, 407
Guisewite, Cathy, 255–256
Gunness, Belle, 297
Gunning, Maria (Lady Coventry), 271
Guthrie, Helen, 309–310
Guthrie, Janet, 7
Gvinter, Anna, 340
Gwinnett, Ann Bourne, 360
Gwyn, Althea, 414
Gwynn, Edith, 182
Gwynne, Nell, 36, 252, 267
Gymnastics, 6, 425

Gynecology, 136, 138, 139, 140

H., Therese (German nurse), 443
Haas, Mary Rosamond, 446
Habe queens, 355–356
Hachen, Debra R., 392
Hachmeister, Louise, 346
Hackett, Albert, 448
Hadassah, 26
Haefker, Annedore, 424
Hagen, Kathleen I., 141
Haggard, Merle, 78
Hagman, Lucinda, 372
Hahn, Emily, 71
Hahn, Countess Ida von, 333
Hahn, Otto, 132
Haig, Alexander M., Jr., 151
Hairy women, 317
Hale, Lucretia P., 223
Hale, Sarah Josepha, 92, 229, 293, 429
Hall, Abigail Burr, 360
Hall, Carrie, 323
Hall, Florence Howe, 448
Hall, Gladys, 185
Hall, Gus, 365
Hall, Rachel C., 100
Hall of Fame, 451–452; Country Music, 213; Women's, 452
Halloway, Jean, 347
Hals, Frans, 243
Hamata, Habe queen, 355
Hambly, Loveday, 387
Hamer, Fannie Lou, 32
Hamill, Dorothy, 419
Hamilton, Alice, 75
Hamilton, Edith, 75
Hamilton, Emma, 37, 313
Hamlet, women in role of, 172
Hammarskjöld, Dag, 15, 249
Hammersley, Lilian Price ("Lily," Duchess of Marlborough), 261
Hammett, Dashiell, 228
Hammond, Leslie, 85
Hanaford, Phoebe A., 7, 113, 390
Hanau, Martha, 298–299
Hancock, Dorothy Quincy, 360–361
Hancock, Evelyn, 101
Hancock, John, 360–361
Handicapped women, 28–30, 208
Handler, Ruth, 86
Hangen, Ruth, 424
Hanging Gardens of Babylon, 8
Hankey, Mary Parsons, 435
Hanks, Nancy, 444
Hanlon, Maureen, 101
Hansberry, Lorraine, 224, 233, 442
Hansell, Ellen Forde, 410

Hansen, Patti, 279
Happiness of Womanhood (HOW), 347
Hardin, Lillian, 208–209
Harding, Florence DeWolfe, 363
Harding, Warren G., 46, 205, 363
Hardwick, Elizabeth, 219
Hardy, Thomas, 77
Harkness, Elizabeth, 320
Harlinde (needleworker), 239–240
Harman, Lillian, 343
Harper, Frances Ellen Watkins, 224, 441
Harpsichordists, 197, 199
Harrington, May Evans, 106
Harris, Addie, 209
Harris, Ann Sutherland, 245
Harris, LaDonna Cranford, 33, 365
Harris, Liz, 230
Harris, Patricia Roberts, 370, 442
Harrison, Annie Fortescue, 205
Harrison, Constance Cary, 220
Harrison, Elizabeth Bassett, 361
Harrop, Kathleen, 320
Hart, Deborah Scudder, 361
Hart, Jane, 165
Hart, Nancy (Civil War spy), 149–150
Hart, Nancy (Revolutionary War heroine), 148, 323
Hart, Pearl, 295
Hartford Female Seminary, 75
Hartley, Florence, 430
Hartopp, Dagmar, 320
Harvard Law Review, 288
Harvard University, 125, 131, 132, 141; first female faculty member, 75; Law School, 288; Medical School, 138, 140, 435, 443
Harwood, Fanny, 77
Haskell, Ella Louise Knowles, 288
Hasselman, Margaret, 318
Hathaway, Donny, 211
Hathor (goddess), 454
Haughery, Margaret, 29
Haughwitz-Reventlow, Count Kurt von, 54
Hauser, Rita F., 375
Haverman, Margareta, 241–242
Hawarden, Lady Clementina, 259
Hawke, Ivy, 421
Hawkes, Daphne Parker, 395
Hawkins, Erich, 260
Hawkins Lori, 417
Hawks, Howard, 191

Hawthorne, Alice (pseudonym), 332
Hayden, Sophia, 256, 346
Hayes, Helen, 175, 191, 250, 451, 452
Hayes, Janet Gray, 367–368
Hayllar, Edith, 77
Hayllar, James, 77
Haynie, Sandra B., 416
Hays, Mary, 147
Hays, Wayne, 47
Hayward, Susan, 440
Haywood, Spencer, 279
Hayworth, Rita, 328
He Zizhen, 376
Head, Bessie, 34
Head, Matthew (John Canaday), 227
Heads of state, 358–360. *See also* Queens
Health problems, 18–19
Hearn, Agatha, 286
Hearst, William Randolph, 231, 256, 264, 266
Heart disease, 19, 314
Hebrew Union College, Cincinnati, 390, 391
Hebrew Union College-Jewish Institute of Religion, 124, 389, 391, 392
Heck, Barbara Ruckle, 388
Hecuba, Queen of Troy, 65
Height records, 4–5
Heikel, Rosina, 136
Heine, Heinrich, 427
Heiss, Carol, 419
Held, Anna, 178, 272
Hellinger, Mark, 178
Hellman, Lillian, 233
Helme, Etta, 323
Héloïse, 36, 71
Hemans, Felicia Dorothea, 433
Hemingway, Hadley, 57
Hemingway, Mariel, 327
Hemingway, Pauline, 57
Henderson, Carolyn Rich, 180
Henderson, Florence, 184
Henderson, Marjorie ("Marge"), 255
Henie, Sonja, 404, 419, 440
Henin, Marie-Louise, 28
Henissart, Martha, 225–226
Henle, Gertrude, 446
Henneberge, Lady Margaret of, 62
Henri, "Citoyenne," 163–164
Henry VII, King of England, 123, 250, 453
Henry VIII, King of England, 121, 245, 307–308, 356
Henry II, King of France, 36, 271, 357
Henry III, King of France, 378
Henry IV, King of France and Navarre, 70, 145, 356

Henry, Maria Storer, 76
Hensel, Fanny Mendels-
sohn, 198, 200
Hepburn, Audrey, 184, 188
Hepburn, Katharine, 191,
450
Hepworth, Barbara, 249
Hera (goddess), 380
Herbert, Lady, 245
Herbst, Josephine, 220
Herford, Laura, 244
Heritage Dance Theater,
195
Herman, Woody, 209
Hernández, Amalia, 193
Heroic women, 7, 25–26,
443. *See also* War hero-
ines
Herrman, Eva, 255
Hershel, Caroline, 130
Hershey, Barbara, 328
Hesoid, 427
Hesperides, Garden of the,
353
Hetairae, 43
Heth, Joice, 9
Hewitt, Emily, 394
Heyward, Carter, 394
Heyward, Elizabeth Matth-
ewes, 361
Hiatt, Suzanne, 394
Hibbler, Gwen, 409
Hickey, Deirdre, 100
Hickok, Wild Bill, 439
Hicks, Helen, 415
Higby, Mary Jane, 183
Higgins, Marguerite, 447
High jump, 403, 417–418,
423, 442
High-wire artists, 157
Hildegard, Evelyn, 219
Hildegard of Bingen, 121,
199
Hill, Lord Arthur, 205
Hill, Bertha ("Chippie"),
207
Hill, Cassie, 103
Hill, Mildred J., 204
Hill, Patty Smith, 204
Hilles, Florence Bayard, 340
Hillis, Margaret, 202
Hills, Carla Anderson, 370
Hinderliter, Kim, 101
Hine (Polynesian legend), 3
Hip Chicks, The, 206
Hippolyta, Amazon Queen,
143
Hipponax, 426
Hirsch, Mary, 112
Historians, 121, 126, 127,
217, 225; Pulitzer Prize
winners, 127, 448
Hitchens, Dolores, 227
Hixson, Jean F., 165
Hobbs, Abigail, 310
Hobby, Oveta Culp, 151,
370
Hobhouse, Emily, 32
Hobos, 158
Hocq, Nathalie, 81

Hodgkin, Dorothy Mary
Crowfoot, 133, 450
Hoest, Bill, 108
Hoffman, Joyce, 420
Hoffman, Malvina, 249
Hoffman, Medora, 323
Hofmans, Greet, 357
Hogg, Ann Storer, 76
Hogg, Helen Sawyer, 131
Hokinson, Helen (Elna),
255
Holiday, Billie ("Lady
Day"), 207
Hollen, Andrea, 155
Hollenbeck, Mabelle, 65,
439
Holley, Sallie, 123
Holliday, Judy, 328
Holloway College, England,
122
Holly, Edna Mae, 180
Hollywood Girls' Club, 186
Holm, Eleanor, 404, 420
Holm, Hanya, 195, 196
Holmes, Oliver Wendell,
318
Holmes, Sophia, 102
Holst, Gustav, 203
Holst, Imogen, 203
Holt, Marjorie S., 366
Holtzman, Linda Joy, 392
Home, John, 426
Home economics, 134
Homemakers, 97
Homicide victims, 314
Hon-Cho-Lo, Madame, 88
Honeywell, Martha Ann,
28–29
Honorary degrees, 123, 131,
133, 443–444
Hooper, Ann Clark, 361
Hooton, Elizabeth, 386
Hoover, Annie, 65
Hoover, Herbert, 363
Hoover, J. Edgar, 65, 66
Hoover, Lou Henry, 363
Hope, Laura Lee (pseu-
donym), 332
Hope, Laurence (pseu-
donym), 333
Hope diamond, 263,
265–266
Hopi Indians, 48
Hopkins, Ann Smith, 361
Hopkins, Leola, 78
Hopkinson, Ann Borden,
361
Hopper, Grace Murray, 132
Horenbout, Susan (Susanna
Hornebolt), 240
Horizon magazine, 230
Horn, Kahn-Tineta, 33
Hornby, Leslie. *See* Twiggy
Horne, Lena, 34, 179
Horney, Karen, 142, 434
Horse-racing, 402, 404;
jockeys, 404–406; winning
fillies, 406–407
Horseshoe-pitching, 424
Horsford, Laura, 199

Horstmann, Dorothy Milli-
cent, 445
Horton, Gladys, 210
Horton, Irene, 420
Horvath, Kathleen, 411
Hosford, Mary, 123
Hosken, Fran P., 451
Hoskins, Jane Fenn, 387
Hosmer, Harriet, 248, 249,
325
Hostages, American, in
Iran, 319
Hotel business, 79
Housewives for ERA, 345
Housework, job elements
of, 97
Houssay, Bernardo A., 450
How, James (Mary East), 21
Howard, Catherine. *See* Ca-
therine Howard, Queen
of England
Howard, Libby, 101
Howard, Mary Woolley
Chamberlain, 367
Howe, Irving, 230
Howe, Julia Ward, 336–337,
434
Howe, Samuel Gridley, 29
Howell, Georgina, 265
Howie, Libby, 100
Hoxsey, Betty J., 347
Hoyt, Mary Francis, 102
Hrotswitha, 232
Hsi Wang Mu (Great
Mother Wang), 353, 379
Hsio-yen Shih, 254
Hubbard, Alice Cooper, 441
Hubbard, George F., 329
Hubbard, Old Mother
(Margaret Brown), 67,
283
Huber, Florence (Mrs.
Manville), 55
Huddleston, Myrtle, 421
Hudspeth, Pamela, 422
Huff, Tom, 332
Hufstedler, Shirley Mount,
370
Hughes, Mrs. (actress), 170
Hughes, Howard, 278
Hughes, Paula D., 84
Humbert, Thérèse, 298
Humes, Helen, 209
Humphrey, Doris, 195, 196,
260
Hungary water, 275
Hunt, Harriot K., 138, 435
Hunt, Mary E., 451
Hunt, Willy, 192
Hunter, Alberta, 209
Huntingdon, Countess of
(Selina Hastings),
387–388
Huntington, Anna Hyatt,
249
Huntington, Archer, 249
Huntington, Martha Devo-
tion, 361
Hurd, Dorothy Campbell,
415

Hurdlers, 403, 417, 423
Hurricanes, naming of, 331
Hurst, Fannie, 250
Hurston, Zora Neale, 224
Hurvich, Leo M., 444
Husband-beating, 314
Huston, Margo, 447
Hutchings, Florence, 325
Hutchinson, Anne, 31
Hutchinson, Isobel, 134
Hutton, Barbara, 54–55, 264
Hutton, Lauren, 278
Hutton, May Arkwright,
342
Huxtable, Ada Louise, 444,
447
Huysum, Jan van, 242
Hveger, Ragnild, 420
Hyams, Margie, 209
Hyde, Anne, 453
Hyfield, Hannah, 408
Hyman, Libbie Henrietta,
133, 445
Hypatia, 76, 120

Ian, Janis, 5
Ibsen, Henrik, 175
Idaho, woman suffrage in,
342
Illness, comparison between
sexes, 19
Imbs, Mrs. Bravig, 57
Impersonators, stage, 171,
172, 180–181, 201
Impostors, 8–9, 298–299;
men as women, 22–23;
women as men, 20–22,
146, 147, 294
Incas, 49
Income, women's, 96–97;
corporate officers, 80, 192;
entertainment industry,
185, 192; equal pay legislation, 80, 99, 292; in-
equalities, 80, 95, 96,
table 130, 292, 346; physicians, 136; scientists,
129–130; secretaries, 98
India, women in govern-
ment, 358, 374
Indiana University, 124
Indians (American): places
named for, 324; rights advocates, 32–33, 288; vic-
tims of, 311–312; women
warriors, 150–151
Infant mortality, male vs.
female, 17
Inglis, Elsie Maud, 138
Ingram, Margaret, 91
Inman (fashion model), 279
Innagari, Habe queen, 356
Intellectual differences between sexes, 17–18
Interior decorators, 280–281
International Amateur Ath-
letic Federation (IAAF),
423
International Association of
Policewomen, 109

International Olympic
Committee, 423
International Sweethearts of
Rhythm, 206, 209
International Women's Pro-
fessional Softball Associa-
tion, 414
International Women's
Year, 97, 345, 374
Inventors, 104–107
Iphigenia, 306
Iran: hostage crisis, 319,
371–372; woman suffrage,
342; women in govern-
ment, 373, 375
Iranian Organization of
Women, 346
Ireland: independence fight-
ers, 330; peace movement,
27; woman suffrage, 342
Irene, Byzantine Empress,
68
Irene (painter), 239
Iron, Ralph (pseudonym),
333
Iron Cross medals, 443
Iron Man Triathlon, 424
Irving, Sir Henry, 174
Irwin, June, 63
Isabeau of Bavaria, Queen
of France, 271
Isabella, Queen of Hungary,
275
Isabella, Queen of Spain,
446
Isabella II, Queen of Spain,
360
Isabelle I, Queen of Jerusa-
lem, 355
Isabelle II (Yolande de
Brienne), Queen of Jeru-
salem, 355
Isabelle of Cyprus, Queen
of Jerusalem, 355
Isaqueena (Cateechee), 324
Ishtar (goddess), 379, 454
Isis (goddess), 50, 379
Island of Fair Women, 353
Israel, women in govern-
ment, 358, 373
Italy: Order of Merit, 455;
woman physicians in,
136; women in govern-
ment, 373
Ivers, Alice ("Poker Alice"),
94
Ivri, Baronne C. d', 199

Jablonski, Wanda, 87
Jacklin, Carol Nagy, 18
Jackson, Carol, 159
Jackson, Elizabeth Hutchin-
son, 69
Jackson, Flora, 4
Jackson, Glenda, 191
Jackson, Helen Hunt, 32–33
Jackson, Mary, 90
Jackson, Stonewall, 149
Jackson, Vivian, 180
Jacobi, Lotte, 260

Jacobs, Aletta, 71, 75, 334
Jacobs, Charlotte, 75
Jacobs, Frederique, 75
Jacobs, Helen Hull, 404,
409, 412
Jacobs, Mary Phelps
(Caresse Crosby), 278
Jaeger, Andrea, 411
Jael, 144
Jaffa, Kathleen de, 200
Jaffe, Suzanne D., 84
Jaffee, Sandra S., 83
Jahl, Evelyn Schlaak, 418
Jahoda, Marie, 445
Jailed for Freedom (Ste-
vens), 340
Jamaica, women in govern-
ment, 375
Jamata, Habe queen, 356
James I, King of England,
309, 316, 453
James, Henry, 41, 200
James, Jessie, 295
James, Maud Merrill, 141
James, Naomi, 161
James, P. D. (Phyllis
Dorothy White), 225
James, William, 141
Jameson, Dorothea, 444,
445
Jane Seymour, Queen of
England, 121, 308
Jarcho, Alice, 85
Jarvis, Anna M., 293
Javelin throw, 403, 418
Jaynettes, The, 210
Jazz, women in, 208–209
"Jeanie with the Light
Brown Hair" (song), 205
Jeanne of Portugal, 317
Jefferson, Maria, 428
Jefferson, Martha, 120
Jefferson, Martha Wayles
Skelton, 267, 361
Jefferson, Thomas, 120, 122,
361, 428
Jellicoe, Ann, 233
Jemima, Aunt, 94
Jenkins, Elaine, 86
Jenkins, Mary, 91
Jennings, Elsie, 420
Jensen, J. Hans D., 133, 450
Jephthah, daughter of, 306
Jepsen, Myrna, 152
Jeritza, Maria, 10
Jerome, Jennie (Lady
Churchill), 261
Jerusalem, Crusader King-
dom of, 354–355
Jesus, women in life of, 381
Jewell, Sarah, 90
Jewett, Milo P., 125
Jewish freedom fighters, 26
Jewish Institute of Religion,
New York, 124, 389, 391,
392
Jewish Religious Union,
England, 390
Jezebel, Queen, 354
Jiang Xing, 328, 376

Joan, Pope, 21
Joan of Arc, 13, 145, 249, 265, 267, 309, 438
Joanna I, Queen of Naples, 359
Joanna (wife of Chuza), 381
Jobe, Mary L. (Mrs. Carl Akeley), 162
Jockeys, 115, 404–406
Joffrey Ballet, 196
Johansen, Linda, 155
Johns Hopkins University, 435; Medical School, 124, 132
Johnson, Alva, 112
Johnson, Barbara, 101
Johnson, Beverly, 163
Johnson, Josephine W., 448
Johnson, Judy, 405
Johnson, Justine (Mrs. Wanger), 178
Johnson, Lady Bird, 185
Johnson, Lillian, 319
Johnson, Lonnie, 207
Johnson, Lyndon B., 65, 69
Johnson, Mae, 180
Johnson, Opha, 153
Johnson, Rebekah Baines, 65, 69
Johnson, Vicki, 424
Johnson, Winnie, 180
Johnston, Frances Benjamin, 257, 258
Jokesters, habitual, 10
Joliot-Curie, Frédéric, 132, 450
Joliot-Curie, Irène, 7, 78, 132, 450
Jonas, Regina, 391
Jonasson, Olga, 139
Jones, Anna, 90
Jones, Annie, 6
Jones, Avonia, 172
Jones, Claudia, 112
Jones, Helen Carter, 212
Jones, Jean, 13
Jones, Jennifer, 188
Jones, Malinda, 172
Jones, Mary, 64
Jones, Mother (Mary Harris), 29, 348
Jones, Peaches, 159
Jones, Tiffany (comic-strip character), 108
Jones, Mrs. Zenith, 332
Joplin, Janis, 212
Jordan, Barbara, 113–114, 442, 451
Jordan, Jim, 182
Jordan, June, 224
Jordan, Marian, 182
Jorgensen, Christine, 19
Joséphine, Empress, 321, 322
Joshee, Anandibai, 136
Joslyn, Sarah H., 253
Jotti, Nilde, 373
Joubert, Rebecca, 408
Journalists, 34, 86, 88, 89, 103, 114, 126, 160, 185,

191, 216, 228–232; Pulitzer Prizes, 444, 447–448; sports, 7, 425. *See also* Magazines; Newspaper women
Joy of Cooking (rock group), 211
Joyce, James, 230
Joyce, Joan, 413–414
Joyce, Peggy Hopkins, 178, 269
Juana I, Queen of Spain, 359
Judd, Winnie Ruth, 297
Judiciary, 288, 289–290; first black women in, 290, 442; statistics, 289, 367
Judo, 424
Juilliard School of Music, 202; Dance Theater, 195
Juliana, Queen of the Netherlands, 357, 360
Juliet cap, 283
Juno (goddess), 380
Jury, women on, 290

Kabuki, 171; Onna, 170
Kahn, Bertha, 92
Kahn, Florence Prag, 366
Kai people, New Guinea, 48
Kali (goddess), 379–380
Kamin, Patty, 417
Kander, Lizzie Black, 111
Kanitovsky, Prince, 266
Kansi, 105
Kao-Tsung, Emperor of China, 377
Kaplan, H. Roy, 269
Karate, 408, 424
Karle, Isabella Lugoshi, 446
Karlin, Marsha, 190
Karvonen, Janet, 414
Kasebier, Gertrude, 257, 258, 260
Kashevarova-Rudneva, Varvara, 136, 138
Kassebaum, Nancy Landon, 365–366
Katherine Gibbs School, Inc., 81, 113
Katherine of Valois, Queen of England, 453
Kathryn Kuhlman Foundation, 396
Katz, Gloria, 192
Kauffman, Angelica, 6, 242
Kaufman, Irving R., 290
Kautsky, Karl Johann, 344
Kautsky, Luise, 344
Kazak people, Asia, 48
Kazickas, Jurate, 441
Kearse, Amalya Lyle, 290
Keckley, Elizabeth, 224
Keeler, Ruby, 178
Keen, Dora, 163
Keene, Carolyn (pseudonym), 223, 332
Keene, Laura, 176

Keller, Helen, 5, 29, 268, 446, 452
Keller, Inez, 112
Kellogg, Mary Fletcher, 123
Kelly, Betty, 210
Kelly, Denise, 418
Kelly, Dorothy, 26
Kelly, Fanny Wiggins, 311
Kelly, Grace, 7
Kelly, Jacquelin J., 152
Kelly, Nancy, 184
Kelsey, Frances O., 140, 452
Kemble, Adelaide, 173
Kemble, Charles, 173
Kemble, Fanny (Frances Anne), 173, 310
Kemble, Roger, 173
Kempe, Margery, 215
Kennedy, Caroline, 165
Kennedy, Florynce R., 348
Kennedy, Jacqueline Bouvier, 263, 268, 363
Kennedy, John F., 15, 47, 66, 69, 363, 374
Kennedy, Rose Fitzgerald, 66, 69
Kenner, Doris, 209
Kenton, Stan, 209
Kentucky Derby, 406–407
Kepler, Johannes, 130
Kepley, Ada H., 287
Kerns, Edith, 66
Keroualle, Louise de, 36
Kerr, Deborah, 184
Key, Francis Scott, 107
Khairi, Abla Adel, 421
Khajehnouri, Parivash, 346
Khashoggi, Soraya, 270
Khristova, Ivanka, 418
Khrushchev, Nikita, 165
Kiki of Montparnasse, 313
Kilgallen, Dorothy, 182
Kim Jin-Ho, 424
King, Billie Jean, 410, 412, 413, 414
King, Carole, 210
King, Coretta, 224
King, Dale, 115
King, Elizabeth, 147
King, Florence, 224
King, Henrietta Chamberlain, 88
King, Jean, 370
King, Louise, 185
King, Robert A., 332
King, Susan, 93
King and I, The (musical), 122, 184
King Sisters, the, 74
Kingsland, Florence, 430
Kingsley, Mary, 162
Kipling, Rudyard, 426
Kirkland, Caroline M. Stansbury, 229
Kissinger, Henry, 427
Kistler, Ruth, 62
Kitt, Eartha, 184
Klausner, Willette, 192
Klein, Charlotte C., 452
Klein, Evelyn Kaye, 206

Klein, Joan Dempsey, 289
Klotzman, Dorothy, 203
Knight, Gladys, 211
Knight, Dame Laura, 243
Knight, Margaret, 106
Knight, Sarah Kemble, 121
Koch, Ilse, 378
Koehler, Violet, 212
Koester, Marilyn, 82
Kollontai, Alexandra, 373
Kollwitz, Käthe, 243
Komarkova, Vera, 163
Koner, Pauline, 196
Könneritz, R. de, 199
Koob, Kathryn, 319
Kooiman-Van Middendorp,
    Gerarda, 224
Koontz, Elizabeth Duncan,
    375
Koppel, Barbara, 189
Korda, Reva, 82
Korjus, Miliza, 188
Kosmowska, Irene, 373
Kovaleva, Uelena, 423
Kovalevsky, Sonya Corvin-
    Krukovsky, 129
Kramer, Hilton, 246
Krantz, Judith, 222
Krenwinkel, Patricia, 297
Kreps, Juanita, 370
Krikker, Margaret Ann, 140
Kriloff, Maryse, 320
Kross, Anna Moscowitz,
    289–290
Krudner, Marie de, 199
Krüger, Augusta, 145
Krupa, Gene, 209
Krupsak, Mary Anne, 369
Kuan Yin (goddess),
    380–381
Kübler-Ross, Elisabeth, 451
Kudruavtseva, Nadezhda,
    423
Kuen-Luen (Kun-Lun), 353
Kufuru, Habe queen, 355
Kuhlman, Kathryn, 396
Kuhn, Maggie, 115
Kulakova, Galina, 424–425
Kumin, Maxine Winokur,
    449
Kunigunde, Abbess, 240
Kunigunde of Luxembourg,
    Empress, 240
Kunin, Madeline, 370
Kupla, Sarah, 312
Kurys, Diane, 189
Kusner, Kathy, 405
Kwannon (goddess), 380
Kynaston, Edward, 171
Kyteler, Dame Alice, 309

LaBelle, Patti, 210
LaBianca, Leno and Rose-
    mary, 297
Labille-Guiard, Adelaïde,
    242
Labor Firsts in America
    (U.S. Department of
    Labor), 99
Labor leaders, 29, 67, 337

Labor unions, 29, 98, 99
Labourne, Catherine, 382
Lacey, Beatrice C., 444–445
Lacey, John T., 444
LaChapelle, Marie-Louise,
    70
Lachesis (Fate), 74
Ladies Companion, 229
Ladies' Home Journal, 257,
    429, 450
Ladies Magazine, The, 229
Ladies' Professional Golf
    Association, 415, 416–417
Ladiesburg, Md., 323
Ladner, Joyce, 224
Ladnier, Tommy, 208
LaDuc, Lorena, 265
Ladyfingers, 322
"Lady Hell Cats," 153–154
"Lady in Red" (Anna
    Sage), 47
Lady Margaret Hall, Ox-
    ford, 123, 127
Lady of the Camellias, The
    (Dumas), 218
Lady's Magazine, 228
Lafarge, Marie, 296
La Flesche, Susette, 32
Lagerlöf, Selma, 223, 449
La Guardia, Fiorello, 290
Lais, 43
Lake, Baby, 266
Lakes named for women,
    324, 325
Lakey, Alice, 114
Lakshmi (goddess), 455
La Mama Experimental
    Theatre Club, 177, 234
La Marr, Barbara, 313
Lamarr, Hedy, 328
Lamb, Lady Catherine, 41
Lambelle, Princesse de, 265
Lamia, 43
Lamour, Dorothy, 328
Lancefield, Rebecca Craig-
    hill, 445
Landers, Ann (Esther Pau-
    line Friedman), 75, 430
Landon, Alfred M., 366
Landscape architecture, 257
Lane, Lois (comic-strip
    character), 108
Lane Bryant stores, 282
Lane Sisters, the, 74
Langdon, Dory (Mrs.
    Previn), 190
Lange, Daisy, 212
Lange, Dorothea, 259
Lange, Jean, 408
Langhorne, Nancy (Lady
    Astor), 262
Langrishe, May, 410
Langtry, Lillie, 10, 71, 92,
    262, 266, 272, 323, 328
Lannquist, Beverly C., 82
Lansbury, Angela, 184
Lansing, Sherry, 192
Lanskoy, Alexander, 39
Lantz, Grace, 184
Laperrière, Mme. Louis, 320

LaPiere, Cherilyn. *See* Cher
La Ponche, Anna-Marie,
    405
Larimer, Sarah, 311
Larionov, Mikhail, 246
La Rue, Danny, 181
Lassie (collie), 182
Lasuria, Khfaf, 4
Lathen, Emma (pen name),
    225–226
Latin scholars, 121
Latsis, Mary J., 225–226
La Tournelle, Marquise de,
    45–46
Latynina, Larissa Semyon-
    ovna, 425
Lauder, Estée, 276
Lauragais, Duchess of, 46
Laurencin, Marie, 246
Laverne, Lucille, 184
Lavinia (Titian's model),
    250
Lavoisier, Mme. Antoine,
    134
Law, women in, 76,
    287–290, 334–335; black
    women, 287, 288, 290,
    395, 442, 444; corporate
    law, 82, 192; firsts,
    287–288, 442; Indian
    rights, 33, 288; judge-
    ships, 288, 289–290, 442;
    statistics, 96, 103, 288
Law school, women in, 288
Lawler, Debbie, 5, 159
Lawrence, Andrea Mead, 63
Lawrence, Carol, 328
Lawrence, D. H., 76
Lawrence, Gertrude, 232
Lawrence, Mary Wells, 81
Lazarus, Emma, 75
Lazarus, Josephine, 75
Lazarus, Mel, 108
League for the Rights of
    Women, 345
Leah (slave), 310
Leakey, Mary D. Nicol, 134
Leasy, Emily, 325
"Leave It to the Girls"
    (radio program), 182
Lebewohl, Abe, 456
Le Corbusier, 253
Lecouvreur, Adrienne, 170
Ledford, Black-Eyed Susan,
    212
Ledford, Lily Mae, 212
Ledford, Rosie, 212
Ledoux, Leone, 183–184
Lee, Ann (Mother Ann), 67,
    388
Lee, Anne Pinckard, 361
Lee, Barbara, 210
Lee, Beverly, 209
Lee, Brenda, 5, 213
Lee, Dixie, 92
Lee, Ellen, 85
Lee, Gypsy Rose, 71, 178,
    328
Lee, Harper, 448
Lee, Peggy, 184

Lee, Dr. Rebecca, 441
Lee, Rebecca Tayloe, 361
Leech, Margaret, 448
Leepson, Marc, 401
Leg make-up, 276
Legal holidays, 293
Le Gallienne, Eva, 172, 176
Legend, first women in, 3, 379–380
Léger, Fernand, 247, 253
Leggett, Viola, 368
Legion of Honor, 145, 245, 411
Legislators: abroad, 371–373; in U.S., 365–367
Leigh, Augusta, 41
Leigh, Elizabeth Medora, 41
Leip, Hans, 205
Leiter, Marguerite ("Daisy," Countess of Suffolk), 261
Leiter, Mary (Lady Curzon), 261
Leitzel, Lillian, 157
Lele people, Congo, 53
Lely, Sir Peter, 252
Lemaire, Lyn, 424
LeMars, Iowa, 323
Lenclos, Ninon de, 40, 76, 439
Lenglen, Suzanne, 404, 409, 411
Lennon Sister, the, 74
Lenox, Anne, 154
Leo, Pope, 252
Leo Baeck College, London, 392
Leonarda, Isabella, 199
Leonardo da Vinci, 250
Leonowens, Anna, 122
Leopold, Estella Bergere, 445
Lepaute, Mme. Hortense, 130
Leporin-Erxleben, Dorothea, 136, 138
Lerner, Gerda, 145
Leslie, Frank, 88, 229
Leslie, Miriam ("Minnie"), 88, 229
Leslie's Weekly, 229
Lessing, Doris, 348
Lesur, Annie, 373
Letelier, Orlando, 316
Leverton, Irene, 165
Levi-Montalcini, Rita, 445
Levi-Tanai, Sara, 193
Levin, Jennie, 312
Levinthal, Helen Hadassah, 124, 391
Lewes, George Henry, 454
Lewinson, Minna, 447
Lewis, Alma, 34
Lewis, Edmonia, 105, 249, 442
Lewis, Elizabeth Annisley, 361
Lewis, Graceanna, 105
Lewis, Ida (journalist), 34
Lewis, Ida (lighthouse keeper), 25, 334

Lewis, Mrs. Lawrence, 340
Lewis, Mary Christianna Milne, 225
Lewis, Meriwether, 325
Lewis, Tillie, 86
Lewis and Clark Expedition, 63, 440–441
Leyster, Judith, 243
Lezcano, Marina, 406
Liaquat Ali Khan, Begum Ra'Ana, 455
Liberia, women in government, 374
Liberman, Paulette, 129
Librettists, 200–201; of musicals, 233
Liddell, Alice, 219
Lieberman, Nancy, 414–415
Lieutenant governors, 369–370
Life expectancy, female vs. male, 17
Life magazine, 191, 259, 282
"Lili Marlene" (song), 205
Lilith (Jewish legend), 3
Liliuokalani, Queen of Hawaiian Islands, 205
Limón, José, 195, 196
Lin Piao, 376
Lincoln, Abraham, 69, 153, 176, 220, 285, 293
Lincoln, Mary, 111
Lincoln, Mary Todd, 224, 267
Lincoln, Melissa Ludtke, 291, 425
Lincoln, Nancy Hanks, 69
Lind, Jenny, 93, 262, 321
Lindbergh, Charles A., 450
Lindgren, Astrid, 223
Linguistics, 103, 446; pay, 130
Lippi, Fra Filippo, 252
Liquid Paper Company, 87
Lisiewska-Therbusch, Anna Dorothea, 242
Lister, Sara, 153
Lister Institute, London, 135
Liszt, Franz, 40, 198, 200
Literature: Nobel Prize winners, 449; Pulitzer Prize winners, 448–449. *See also* Writers
"Little Annie Rooney" (song), 205
Little League All-Star Game, 414
Little Review, 230
Litvyak, Lilya, 155
Liu Hsiang, 215
Livia Drusilla, Empress (Julia Augusta), 376–377
Living Theater, 177
Livingston, Beulah, 185
Livingston, Christina Ten Broeck, 361
Livingstone, David, 324
Livingstone, Mary, 182, 328
Lizana, Anita, 411

Lloyd, Harold, 21
Lobbying groups, 84, 101
Local government, women in, 367–369
Lockett, Saint Charles, 86
Lockridge, Frances, 227
Lockwood, Belva Ann Bennett, 287–288, 364
Loden, Barbara, 189
Loeb, Marion, 230
Loehmann, Frieda, 282–283
Logan, Deborah Norris, 218
Logan, Mrs. John A., 293
Logan, Olive, 334
Lohman, Ann (Mme. Restell), 72
Lollipop Power, 228
Lombard, Carole, 10, 14–15, 328
London, Meyer, 340
London School of Medicine for Women, 138
Londonderry, Annie, 160
Long jump, 418, 423
Longbaugh, "Sundance" Harry, 295
Longevity records, 4
Longfellow, Henry Wadsworth, 229, 259
Longford, Countess of, 78
Loos, Anita, 5, 185
Lopez, Rita Lobato Velho, 136
Lopez-Melton, Nancy, 416
Lord, Mary, 375
Lorde, Audre, 224
Loren, Sophia, 440
Lorraine, Kay, 183
Lorraine, Lillian, 177
Lorrimer, Claire, 222
Los Angeles County Museum of Art, 245
Los Angeles Sentinel, 86
Los Angeles Times, 231–232
Loshetz, Nina, 188
Lottery winners, 268–269
Louis XIV, King of France, 199, 241, 265, 321, 322
Louis XV, King of France, 22, 37, 45–46, 251, 274, 321
Louise, Princess, 325
Louise, Tina, 179
"Love of Life" (TV show), 300
Lovedu queens, 356
Lovelace, Lady. *See* Byron, Augusta Ada
Low, Carrie, 415
Low, Juliette Gordon, 446
Lowell, Amy, 114, 449
Lowell (Mass.) *Sun,* 425
Loy, Myrna, 179
Luahine, Iolani ("Heavenly Bird"), 194
Luce, Clare Boothe, 233, 367
Lucid, Shannon W., 164
Lucy, Autherine, 26–27
Ludington, Sybil, 148, 446

Ludlam, Charles, 181
Luhring, Marie, 100
Lukens, Anna, 138
Lukens, Rebecca, 88
Lupino, Ida, 187, 189
Lutheran churches: missionary groups, 393; ordination of women, 394
Lynch, Hannah Motte, 361
Lynn, Janet, 419
Lynn, Loretta, 213
Lyon, Mary, 132
Lyon, Mary Mason, 124, 125, 451
Lyons, Enid Muriel Burnell, 371
Lyric String Quartet, 206
Lyricists, 204–205, 210; movie songs, 190; musicals, 233

Ma Bell (AT&T), 68
"Ma Perkins" (radio show), 183
Maaseen, Lieselotte, 443
Maass, Clara, 25, 446
Mabley, Jackie ("Moms"), 327
MacArthur, Mary Hardy, 64
McBain, Laurie, 222
McCabe, "Tough Willie," 178
McCambridge, Mercedes, 184
McCarthy, Patrick Henry, 160
McCartney, Judy and Era, 325
McCartney, Linda, 190
McCartney, Paul, 190
McClintock, Barbara, 445
McClintock, Elizabeth W., 339
McClintock, Mary Ann, 339
Maccoby, Eleanor Emmons, 18
McCoin, Lois Arline (Mrs. Manville), 56
McCollum, Elmer V., 135
McConnell, Lulu, 181
McCormack, John, 67
McCormick, Anne O'Hare, 447
McCormick, Macushla, 154
McCravey, Mary A., 82
McCrea, Margaret, 183
McCready, Irene, 91
McCullers, Carson, 233
McCullough, Colleen, 222
McDaniel, Hattie, 442
MacDonald, Flora (Canadian foreign secretary), 371–372
Macdonald, Flora (18th-century heroine), 25
McDonald, Mrs. Joe, 13
McDowell, Jane, 205
McElhone, Eloise, 182

McEvoy, J. P., 108
McEwan, Victor, 347
MacFarlane, Catharine, 139
McGee, Evelyn, 209
McGee, Fibber and Molly (fictional characters), 181, 182
McGinley, Phyllis, 449
MacGraw, Ali, 440
McGredy, Molly, 320
McGrory, Mary, 347, 447
McGuire Sisters, the, 74
Machree, Mother, 67
McHugh, Jimmy, 180
Macias, Edith, 154
McIntyre, Roberta, 154
McIvor, Flora, 320
McKean, Sarah Armitage, 361
McKee, Fran, 152
MacKenzie, Giselle, 183
MacKenzie, Len, 95
McKinley, Ida Sexton, 262–263
McKinley, William, 362
Mackintosh, Elizabeth, 226
Mackle, Barbara Jane, 299
McKnight, Marian, 279
MacLaine, Shirley, 179
McLaughlin, Eleanor, 394
McLean, Evalyn Walsh, 263, 266
Macleod, Fiona (pseudonym), 332
MacLeod, Louise, 115
McMillen, Inc., 281
McPartland, Jimmy, 209
McPartland, Marian, 209
Macphail, Agnes, 371
McPherson, Aimee Semple, 11, 395
MacPherson, Jeanie, 186
McWhinney, Madeline H., 83
Madame Bovary (Flaubert), 218–219
Madison, Cleo, 186
Madison, Dolley, 268, 364, 446
Madison, Helene, 404
Mae Wests, 284
Magazines, 228–230; women publishers, 89, 229–230, 332, 338; women's movement, 230, 338, 345
Magill, Helen, 124
Maguire, Molly, 329–330
Mahler, Henrietta, 87
Mahoney, Mary Elizabeth, 441
Maiden name, use of. *See* birth name
Maidenform, Inc., 282
Maillet, Antonine, 216
Mailly, Comtesse de, 45
Mailly, Louis de, Marquis of Nesle, 46
Maintenon, Marquise Françoise de, 321

Maitland, Agnes Catherine, 111
Maizel, Phyllis, 101
Make-up. *See* Cosmetics
Malcolmson, Ruth, 279
Male chauvinists, 346–347
Male feminists, 344–345
Male roles, women in: opera, 201; theater, 172
Malina, Judith, 177
Mallet, Elizabeth, 216
Mallon, Isabel A. (Ruth Ashmore), 429
Mallory, Molla, 412
Malone, Vivian, 26
Maltby, Margaret, 124
Maltese, Catherine, 312
Maltese, Lucia, 312
Maltese, Rosalie, 312
Mamas and the Papas, The, 211
Mamonova, Tatyana, 316
Man-of-War Nance, 91
Management, women in, 80–84, 96, 127; black women, 85–86; movie industry, 192–193
Manchester, Duchess Helena, 261
Manelli, Herminia, 145
Manet, Edouard, 246, 251
Manley, Joan D., 81
Manley, Mary de la Rivière, 216
Mann, Barry, 210
Mann, Carol B., 416
Mann, Mrs. Horace, 110
Manning, Ann Harned, 106
Manning, Marie (Beatrice Fairfax), 429
Mansfield, Arabella, 287
Manson, Charles, 297–298
Mantua, Princess of, 50
Manual dexterity, 17
Manuscript illumination, 240
Manville, Thomas, 55–56
Manzolini, Anna Morandi, 88, 136
Mao Zedong, 328, 376
Marasescu, Natalia, 423
Marble, Alice, 404, 409–410, 412
Marchant, Annie, 185
Marcia (painter), 239
Marco Polo, 353
Margaret, Duchess of Parma, 356
Margaret of Navarre, Queen, 121
Margaret of Valois, Queen of France and Navarre, 145, 321, 356
Margaret Rose, Princess of England, 5, 320
Margerum, Katy, 100
Margot (early tennis player), 410
Margrethe II, Queen of Denmark, 357

Maria Theresa, Hapsburg Empress, Queen of Hungary, 65, 359
Maria I, Queen of Portugal, 360
Marie, Queen of Rumania, 66
Marie Antoinette, Queen of France, 22, 65, 242, 264, 265, 267, 323, 439
Marie d'Avignon, 12–13
Marie de France, 216
Marie de Medici, Queen of France, 70
Marie de Montferrat, Queen of Jerusalem, 355
Marie Leszczynska, Queen of France, 321
Marijuana users, 314
Marillac, Louise de, 385
Marion, Frances, 185, 187
Marisol (sculptor), 249–250
Markova, Dame Alicia, 193
Marlborough, eighth Duchess of (Lilian Price Hammersley), 10, 261
Marlborough, ninth Duchess of (Consuelo Vanderbilt), 10, 261
Marlborough, Nancy, 100
Marozia, 45
Marple, Jane (fictional character), 227
Marquesas islanders, 53
Marriage: forms of, 52–54; keeping own name in, 333–335; statistics, 47–48; on terms of equality, 343–344
Married Love (Stopes), 51, 72
Marsden, Kate, 162, 346
Marsh, Dame Ngaio, 226
Marshall, John, 437
Marshall, Mary Randolph Keith, 437
Marshall, Paule, 224
Marston, Alice L., 100
Martel, Linda, 395
Martha (sister of Lazarus), 381
Martin, Cornelia Sherman (Mrs. Bradley Martin), 264
Martin, Margaret, 63
Martin, Susanna, 310
Martineau, Harriet, 439
Martinez, Julie, 66
Marvelettes, The, 210
Marx, Groucho, 159
Marx, Harpo, 178
Mary. *See* Virgin Mary
Mary Tudor (the Bloody), Queen of England, 245, 306, 307, 308, 356, 453
Mary II, Queen of England, 453
Mary, Queen of England (wife of George V), 123, 411

Mary of Burgundy, Empress, 277
Mary of England, Queen of France, 307
Mary Stuart, Queen of Scots, 78, 264, 267, 308, 321, 356, 402, 453
Mary, "the other" (mother of apostles), 381
Mary (sister of Lazarus), 381
Mary (wife of Cleophas), 381
Mary Janes (shoes), 284
Mary Magdalene, 381
Mashyane (legend), 3
Masiello, Alberta, 203
Massachusetts Institute of Technology, 134, 256, 259
Massek, Sue, 206
Masters, Natalie, 182
Masters, Sibella, 106
Mata Hari (Margaretha Zelle), 16, 267, 327, 439
Maternity fashions, 282
Mathematicians, 5, 41, 75, 76, 115, 120, 128–129, 132, 330, 346, 435, 445; ability, 18; pay, 130, 346
Mather, Cotton, 427
Mathieu, Simone, 411
Mathilda, Queen of England, 240
Matinée idols, 285
Matisse, Henri, 252, 253
Matisse, Mme. Henry, 57
Matsui, Hisako Higuchi, 416
Mattel Toy Company, 86
Matthews, Helen, 76
Matthews, Jean Flagler, 253
Matthews, Marjorie S., 390
Matthews, Patricia, 222
Maudgonning, 330
Maugham, Syrie, 280
Maugham, William Somerset, 280
Maximilian I, Holy Roman Emperor, 277
Maxwell, Elsa, 264, 265
Maxwell, Martha, 105
May, Elaine, 189
May, Saidie A., 253
Maya, Queen, 12
Mayans, 49
Mayer, Nancy, 224
Mayo, Virginia, 188
Mayors, 92, 114, 367–369
Mbongwe (Bantu legend), 3
MD Magazine, 136, 137
Mdivani, Prince Alexis, 54
Mead, Margaret, 15, 445, 450, 452
Means, Jacqueline, 395
Means, Lorelei, 33
Mears, Helen Farnsworth, 454
Mechler, Fanny Storer, 76
Meck, Nadejda von, 198

Medal of Science (U.S.), 455
Medea, 68
Medical school, women in, 128, 135–136, 441
Medicine, women in, 4, 67, 75, 105, 132, 135–142, 443, 444; Academy of Sciences members, 445, 446; birth control pioneers, 51, 71–72; black women, 138–139, 441–442; early, 137–138, 441–442; first licensed physicians, 136–137; income, 136; midwifery, 70, 138; Nobel Prizes, 133, 450; specialties, 136, 141; statistics, 96, 103, 136–137; surgeons, 124, 138, 139; teachers, 124, 138, 139; various firsts achievements, 139–140; 441–442
Medill, Joseph, 231
Medina, Lina, 4
Mei Baojiu, 171
Mei Lanfang, 171
Meir, Golda, 358
Meitner, Lise, 132, 347, 455
Melba, Dame Nellie, 322
Melbourne, Lady, 41
Mélisende, Queen of Jerusalem, 354
Mellanby, May, 135
Mellen, Joan, 224
Mello, Judy Hendren, 83
Melnick, Shari, 424
Melpomene (Muse), 74
Memorial Day, 293, 446
Men: advice to women, 427–428; famous, mothers of, 64–65; female-authored literature on, 224–225; feminists, 343–345; impersonated by women on stage, 172, 201; as imposters of women, 22–23; opinions on women, 426–427; women imposters of, 20–22, 146, 147, 294; in women's roles on stage, 171, 180–181
Menchik-Stevenson, Vera, 424
Mencken, H. L., 427
Mendelssohn, Fanny, 198, 200
Mendelssohn, Felix, 198, 200
Mendelssohn, Moses, 427
Mendoza, Gloria, 318
Menken, Mrs. S. Stanwood, 263
Menstruation and sports, 401
Mental problems, 19, 30–31
Mercator, Gerardus, 244
Mercer, Jacque, 279

Meredith, Beth, 185
Merici, Angela, 385
Meriwether, Lee Ann, 279
Merriam, Eve, 233
Merrilies, Meg, 320
Merrill, Helen, 209
Mertz, Lu Esther, 230
Messalina, Valeria, Empress, 377
Messenger-Harris, Beverly, 395
Messick, Dale (Dalia), 108, 255
Mesta, Perle, 265
Metalious, Grace, 221
Metalworkers, 101
Metcalf, Betsy, 106
Methodists: first in North America, 388; missionary groups, 393, 394; women ministers, 390, 394
Metropolitan Museum of Art, New York, 243, 249, 254
Metropolitan Opera, New York, 200–201, 204; Ballet, 193; conductors, 202, 203
Meurend, Victorine, 251
Meyer, Agnes E., 231
Meyer, Annie Nathan, 125–126
Meyers, Ann, 414
Michael, Moina, 446
Michener, James, 170
Michiko, Princess, 320
Middlebury Female Seminary, 124
Middleton, Mary Izard, 361
Midler, Bette, 5
Midwifery, 70, 138
Mikulski, Barbara, 366
Milbanke, Anne Isabella, 41
Military academy graduates, 155
Military forces, women in, 151–155, 447. See also War heroines
Mill, John Stuart, 344
Millay, Edna St. Vincent, 201, 449, 452
Miller, Albert, 333
Miller, Alice Duer, 348
Miller, Caroline, 448
Miller, Elizabeth Cavert, 446
Miller, Elizabeth Smith, 284
Miller, Irene, 163
Miller, Jordan, 344
Miller, Leo, 334
Miller, Marilyn, 5, 178, 264
Miller, Peggy, 104
Millman, Bird, 157
Mills, Ann, 146
Mills, Tarpe, 255
Milner, Brenda (Langford), 444
Mindell, Fania, 71
Miners, 101

Ministry, women in, 7, 30, 31, 113, 383–395; Christian churches, 389, 390, 394–395, 444; founders of orders, 385–386; founders of sects, 387–389; Quakers, 386–387; rabbis, 389, 390–392; statistics, 389
Minnelli, Liza, 78
Minor, Virginia L., 289
Mintz, Beatrice, 445
Miranda, Carmen, 5
Misha'al, Princess of Saudi Arabia, 316
Miss America, 7, 279–280
Missing persons, 11–12
Missionaries, 162, 393; Quaker, 386–387; women's groups and societies, 393–394
Missionary Sisters of the Sacred Heart, 386
Mistral, Gabriela, 449
Mitchell, Catharine, 447
Mitchell, Charlene, 365
Mitchell, David, 447
Mitchell, Jackie, 413
Mitchell, Joni, 212
Mitchell, Margaret, 220–221, 448
Mitchell, Maria, 77, 130–131, 451
Mitchell, Rebecca Brown, 342
Mitchell, Shirley, 181
Mitchell, William, 77
Moaning Minnie (mortar gun), 156
Mobley, Mary Ann, 280
Models: artists', 43, 44, 45, 250–252; fashion, 278–279, 281
Modern dance, 194–196
Modjeska, Helena, 174, 175
Moers, Ellen, 232
Moffitt, Ronni Karpen, 315–316
Mogridge, Mrs., 253–254
Mohammed, women in life of, 383
Moillon, Louise, 241
Molière, Jean Baptiste, 130, 173
Mollie Bailey's Show, 88
Molly (New York fire fighter), 103
Molly (slave), 311
Molly Maguires, the, 329–330
Mombron, Jaquette de, 256
Monaco, Princess Grace of, 7
Mondrian, Piet, 253
Money, Mary, 405
Monroe, Harriet, 229–230
Monroe, Marilyn, 171, 181, 225, 268
Mons Meg (cannon), 156
Montagne, Elizabeth, 319

Montagu, Lily H., 390
Montagu, Lady Mary Wortley, 432, 439
Montague, Harry, 285
Montez, Lola, 40, 275–276, 313, 348
Montezuma, Aztec Emperor, 14
Montfort, Jeanne de, 320
Montgomery, Edmund, 333
Montgomery, Garth, 95
Montgomery, Lucy M. (Maude), 223
Montour, Catharine, 324
Montoya, Mathilde, 136
Monzadellis, Cathy, 101
Moody, Anne, 224
Moody, Lady Deborah, 256
Moody, Helen Wills, 404, 409, 412
Moon Books, 228
Moore, Alla, 322
Moore, Anne (the Tutbury Marvel), 8
Moore, Grace, 188
Moore, Marianne, 449
Moore, Bishop Paul, Jr., 395
Moorefield, Marie, 394
Moran, Gussie, 410
Moran, Juliette M., 82
More, Sir Thomas, 121
Moreau, Jeanne, 189
Moreno, Rita, 188
Morgan, Barbara, 260
Morgan, Helen, 219
Morgan, J. P., 254
Morgan, Julia, 256
Morgan, Marabel, 347
Morgan le Fay, fairy queen, 353
Mori, Hanae, 282
Morini, Erica, 435
Morison, Samuel Eliot, 364
Morisot, Berthe, 245–246
Morland, Lady Ann, 453
Morland, Lady Carola, 453
Morland, Nigel, 227
Morley, Grace McCann, 254
Mormons, 41, 341, 342
Morning Star ceremony, of Skidi Pawnee, 306–307
Morris, Anita Stewart (Princesse de Braganza), 262
Morris, Esther Hobart, 341, 454
Morris, Jan, 19
Morris, Josie, 424
Morris, Kate Eugenia, 124
Morris, Mary Louise, 62
Morris, Mary Walton, 361
Morris, Mary White, 361
Morrison, Gertrude W. (pseudonym), 332
Morrison, Sarah Parke, 124
Morrison, Toni, 34, 224
Morton, Anne Justice, 361
Morton, Sarah Wentworth, 218

Moser, George Baker, 242
Moser, Mary, 242–243
Moses, Grandma (Anna Mary Robertson), 114, 446, 452
Moss, Lanny, 414
Mother (Mark I tank), 156
Mother Carey's chickens, 67–68
Mother Courage (Brecht), 67
Mother Goddam, 67
Mother Goose, 67
Mother Hubbard, 67, 283
Mother of Believers (Ayesha), 67, 383
Motherhood, 62–73; animals, 73; famous sons, 64–65, 69; foster mothers, 66; notable cases of, 62–63; oldest mother, 62; out of wedlock, 71; paeans to, 69; youngest mother, 4
Mothers, working, statistics, 96
Mothers' Clinic for Birth Control, London (1921), 51
Mothers' daughters, 77–79
Mother's Day, 293, 447
Motley, Constance Baker, 291, 442
Motor vehicle accidents, 314
Motorcyclists: cross-country, 161; stunt driver, 159
Mott, John R., 449
Mott, Lucretia Coffin, 336, 339, 447
Mount Holyoke Female Seminary (later College), 124, 125, 403
Mountain, Hannah, 104
Mountain climbing, 161, 162–163
Mountains named for women, 324, 325
Movie fan magazine writers, 185
Movie industry, women in: corporate officers, 192–193; directors, 186–187, 189–190; producers, 192–193; screenwriters, 185, 187, 189, 191–192, 233; "silent" era, 185–187, 188; song lyricists, 190
Mozart, Maria Anna, 197
"Mr. and Mrs. North" (radio and TV show), 182
Mrs. Whittelsey's Magazine for Mothers, 229
Ms. magazine, 203, 230; women to watch, 451
Muir, Karen, 6
Mujaji, title of Lovedu queens, 356
Mulcahaney, Norah (fictional character), 227
Muldaur, Maria, 211–212

Muldowney, Shirley, 418
Mulhall, Lucille, 157
Müller-Preiss, Ellen, 425
Muller v. *Oregon,* 99
Mullins, Priscilla (Mrs. John Alden), 65
Multiple births, 62–63
Mumford, Catherine, 343, 389
Mumtaz Mahal, Mughal Queen, 8
Munroe, Hector Hugh (Saki), 421
Munsel, Patrice, 188
Murasaki, Lady (Murasaki Shikibu), 215
Murat, Katrina, 103
Murderesses, 68–69, 296–298, 299–300, 329
Murdoch, Rupert, 231
Murdoch, Rachel (fictional character), 227
Murfree, Mary Noailles, ,333
Murphy, Bridey, 15
Murphy, Catherine, 248
Murphy, Charlotte, 290
Murphy, Dennis, 414
Murray, Anne, 211
Murray, Mae (actress), 178, 313
Murray, Pauli, 395, 444
Muses, Nine, 74
Museum careers, 253–254
Museum founders, 249, 253
Museum of Contemporary Crafts, New York, 253
Museum of Modern Art, New York, 250, 253, 259, 260
Musgrave, Thea, 200, 203
Musical groups, all-female, 206–207, 209–210, 211, 212
Musical writer/composer team, all-female, 233
Musicians, 75, 199–214; country, 212–214; Gold singles winners, 210–211; inspired by women, 197–199, 205–206; Jazz, 208–209; precocious, 5, 197, 200; rock 'n' roll, 209–212. *See also* Composers; Conductors; Harpsichordists; Opera; Pianists; Singers; Violinists
Musser, Vera, 104
Mussolini, Benito, 6
My Fair Lady (musical), 184
"My Friend Irma" (radio show), 181–182
Myerson, Bess, 279
Mydral, Alva Reiner, 374
Mystery novels, 225–228, 332
Mythical queens, 353–354

Naiad Press, 228
Nairne, Baroness Carolina, 204
Naismith, Barrie, 416
Nakayama, Omiki-San, 388
Nalachovskaya, Natalya, 316
Naldi, Nita, 178, 328
Names, 325–329; girls', 326–327; stars' real, 328–329; unusual, 325–326, 329
Nancy Drew books, 223, 332
Nanny (slave), 310
Napheys, George, 428
Napoleon Bonaparte, 40, 157, 271, 322, 439
Narcotics addicts, 313, 314
Nasatir, Marcia, 192
Nation, Carrie, 114
National Academy of Sciences, 131, 132, 133, 141, 445; women members, 445–446
National Association for the Advancement of Colored People (NAACP), 32
National Association of Colored Women, 32
National Association of Negro Musicians, 204
National Business Council for the ERA, 345
National Equal Rights party (1884, 1888), 364
National Foundation for Women's Health, 18
National Gallery of Canada, 254
National Negro Opera Company, 204
National Organization for Women (NOW), 345, 348
National Parks, 455
National Research Council, 128, 129
National Retired Teachers Association, 27
National Secretaries Association, 98
National Union of Women's Suffrage Societies (Great Britain), 338
National Woman Suffrage Association, 336, 337
National Women's Caucus, 345
National Women's Caucus for Art, 245
Navajo Indians, 53
Navratilova, Martina, 413
Navy Nurse Corps, 152
Nayar people, India, 52–53
Naylor, Hazel Simpson, 185
Nealey, Bertha West, 86–87
Needlework, 239–240
Nefertiti, Queen, 383
Nehru, Jawaharlal, 358, 374

Nellie Morse (filly), 407
Nelson, Lord Horatio, 37, 313
Nelson, Ingrid Karen, 85
Nelson, Lucy Grimes, 361
Nelson, Maud, 92
Nelson, Pamela, 82
Neovius, Dagmar, 372
Nero, Roman Emperor, 68, 377
Nesbit, E. (Edith Nesbit Bland), 223
Netherlands, the, 71; 75; queens of, 357; woman suffrage, 342
Neufeld, Elizabeth I., 446
Neumark, Martha, 391
Neuroanatomy, 455
Neurobiology, 445
Nevelson, Louise, 249
New Hall, England, 123
New Harmony, 31, 344
New Jersey, woman suffrage in, 341
New School for Social Research, New York, 124
New Seed Press, 228
New York City Ballet, 194
New York City Dance Company, 195
New York City Opera, 201, 203, 204
New York Daily News, 231
New York Evening Journal, 429
New York Herald-Tribune, 231
New York Infirmary for Women and Children, 75, 138
New York Journal, 429
New York magazine, 222, 230
New York Philharmonic, 202, 203
New York Post, 231
New York Pro Summer League, 415
New York Psychoanalytic Society, 142
New York Stock Exchange, 84; women members, 83, 85
New York Times, 185, 222, 246, 347, 425, 444
New York Tribune, 126, 231
New York Women's Symphony Orchestra, 206
New York World's Fair of 1965, 452
New Yorker magazine, 192, 255
New Zealand, woman suffrage, 342
Newman, Frances, 219
Newmar, Julie, 179, 188
Newnham College, England, 123
Newport Jazz Festival, 208

Newsday (Long Island), 31, 332
Newspaper women, 89–90; columnists, 75, 429, 430; first black, 441; publishers, 231–232. *See also* Journalists
Newsweek, 185, 192, 231
Newton, Grace, 295
Newton-John, Olivia, 210
Ney, Elisabet, 333, 348
Niagara Falls stunt women, 159
Nicholas, Cynthia ("Cindy"), 422
Nicholas, Harold, 180
Nichols, Ora, 184
Nicholson, Eliza, 88
Nielsen, Nielsine Mathilde, 136
Nightingale, Lady Elizabeth, 454
Nightingale, Florence, 162, 268
Nijinska, Bronislava, 193
Nineteenth Amendment, 341
Niobe, 65
Nixon, Hannah Milhous, 69
Nixon, Marnie, 184
Nixon, Patricia, 267, 363
Nixon, Richard M., 69, 267, 315, 363
Noble Prize winners, 7, 27,.. 78, 131–132, 133, 449–450
Noble, Jeanne, 34
Nochlin, Linda, 245
Noether, Emmy (Amalie), 129, 435
No-fault divorce, 292–293
Nolan, Mae Ella, 366
Nolan, Mary (inventor), 104
Nolan, Mary (suffragist), 340
Nolan, Michael, 205
Noland, May (Imogene "Bubbles" Wilson), 313
Norelius, Martha, 421
Norman, Karyl, 180
Norris, Kathleen, 10
North, Marianne, 134
North, Pamela (fictional character), 227
North London Collegiate School, England, 122
Norway: women in government, 372; woman suffrage, 342
Nouri, Farzaeh, 346
Nouvelle Revue, La, 332
Novak, Kim, 328
Novara, Sue, 418
Novelists, 30, 31, 74, 75, 77, 113, 219–222, 232, 233; advance royalties, 222; best-selling, 220–221; black, 34, 224, 333, 441; female models for, 218–219; first, 215, 217; mystery novels, 225–227,

332; Prix Goncourt, 77, 216; pseudonyms, 332–333; Pulitzer Prizes, 448; romance sales, 221–222
Novotna, Jarmila, 188
Nuclear physics, 132, 133
Nufer, Beth, 159
Nugent, Maude, 205
Nurse, Rebecca, 310
Nurses, 67, 162; first black, 441; heroines, 25–26, 443
Nursing mothers, 290–291
Nussbaum, Sadie, 312
Nuthall, Betty, 409
Nuthead, Dinah, 89
Nutrition experts, 134–135
Nutt, Emmma, 99
Nyad, Diana, 421–422
Nyro, Laura, 212

Oakes, Elizabeth, 334
Oakley, Annie (Phoebe Ann Oakley Moses), 5, 66, 157
Oatman, Mary Ann, 311
Oatman, Olive, 311
O'Bannon, Marsha A., 84
Oberlin College, 123, 390, 441
Oberon, Merle, 198
Obesity, 4, 19
Obie winners, 233
O'Bryant, Jimmy, 208
Obstetrics-gynecology, 136, 138, 139
O'Connell, Helen, 184
O'Connor, Eileen, 158
O'Day, Anita, 209
O'Day, Caroline, 366
Odets, Clifford, 175
Odier, Louise, 320
O'Donnell, Lillian, 227
Odysseus, 353
Oedipus complex, 64
Ofarim, Esther, 320
Office of Federal Contract Compliance Programs, 100
Oger, Mme. Pierre, 320
Ogino, G., 136
Ogygia (mythical island), 353
O'Hara, Maureen, 328
O'Hare, Kate Richards, 32
O'Keeffe, Georgia, 189, 247, 455
O-Kuni, 170
Olcott, Chauncey, 67
Old Mother Covington (cannon), 156
Old Vic Theatre, London, 176
Old West: bandits, 295; pioneers, 93, 99, 103
Oldfield, Ann, 438, 453
Olga, Lady, 6
Oliver, Joe, 208
Olivier, Fernande. *See* Fernande
Olivier, Sir Laurence, 171

Olsen, D. B. (Dolores Hitchens), 227
Olsen, Zoe Ann, 404
Olympic champions, 6, 29–30, 63, 403, 410, 417–420, 424–425; first black woman, 442; quantity of medals records, 417, 425
O'Murphy, Louise (La Morphise), 251
Onassis, Jacqueline Kennedy, 263, 268, 363
Oncologists, 445
One America, Inc., 86
O'Neal, Alice, 70
O'Neal, Tatum, 5
O'Neil, Kitty, 30, 159, 418
O'Neill, Eugene, 176, 200
O'Neill Logan, James, 334
Onna Kabuki, 170
Onnagata, 171
Onorato, Rosemary, 85
Opara, Christie (fictional character), 227
Opera, operetta: composers, 199–200; directors, 203–204; librettists, 200–201
Opera singers, 173, 200; black, 34, 204, 441, 442; challenging roles (soprano), 202; in movies, 188; women in male roles, 201
Ops (Rhea, goddess), 380, 455
Orchard, Sadie, 99
Orchestra conductors, 75, 197, 202–203
Ordway, Margaret, 185
O'Regan, Marilynn, 109
Originals, The, 210
"Orkney lad," 22
Orlando (Woolf), 20
Orloff, Katherine, 211–212
Orlov, Gregory, 39
Ormsby, Mrs., 62
Orr, Mary, 233
Orr, Martha, 255
Orrum, Eilley, 14
Orsini, Bette Swenson, 448
Osborn, Mary Jane, 446
Osborne, Mrs. John, 317
Osburne, Sarah, 310
Oscar winners, 5, 189, 190, 191; first black woman, 442
Ostergaard, Lise, 372
Ostfeld, Barbara, 392
O'Sullivan, Maureen, 185
Otero, Caroline (La Belle Otero), 44
Other Magpie, The, Crow warrior, 151
Otto-Peters, Luise, 337
Ouilmette, Archange, 324
Our Mims (filly), 406
Oury, Mme., 199
Out & Out Books, 228

Outerbridge, Mary Ewing, 402
Owen, Marabell Vinson, 419
Owen, Robert Dale, 31, 343, 344
Owens, Bethenia, 114
Owens, Ellen, 334
Owens, Rochelle, 233
Owens, Shirley, 209
Oxford, Lady, 41
Oxford University, England, 123, 128, 131, 435
Ozick, Cynthia, 348

Paca, Mary Chew, 361
Pachta, Jenny, 198
Page, Ann, 90
Paget, Debra, 188
Pahlavi, Ashraf, Princess, 375
Paine, Sally Cobb, 361
Paine, Thomas, 228
Painters, 76, 77, 239–248, 444; of antiquity, 239; early members of academies, 241–243: late starters, 114–115, 247–248; precocious, 6, 240–241; women's works misattributed to men, 243
Painters' models, 250–252
Pak, Esther Kim, 137
Palatine, Princess, 283
Palmer, Alice Freeman, 451
Palmer, Betsy, 184
Palmer, Stuart, 228
Palvanova, Bibi, 127
Panayotatou, Angelique, 137
Pandit, Vijaya Lakshmi, 374
Pandora, 3
Pankhurst, Christabel, 78, 338
Pankhurst, Emmeline Goulden, 78, 338
Pankhurst, Sylvia, 71, 78, 338
Pannier, 272
Pants for women, 278
Papal mistresses, 45
Pappenheim, Bertha, 31
Papuans, of New Guinea, 48
Paquin, Madame, 281
Para Olympics, 30
Parachutists, 115, 159, 164
Paranazin, Aztec Princess, 14
Parent, Gail, 192
Paris Conservatoire, 199, 202
Parish, Sister, 281
Park, Ida May, 186
Park, June, 320
Park, Mary Fettig, 209
Park, Patricia, 395
Parker, Bettye J., 223
Parker, Suzy, 278

Parkes, Bessie Rayner (Mrs. Belloc), 338
Parkhurst, Charlotte (Charley), 21
Parks, Rosa L., 32, 34
Parlor houses, 91–92
Parr, Catherine. *See* Catherine Parr, Queen of England
Parsa, Farrokhrou, 373
Parsons, Estelle, 184
Parton, Dolly, 5, 214
Parton, Sarah Payson Willis (Fanny Fern), 429, 430
Parvati (goddess), 380
Paschal, Margaret, 90
Paschall, Mary F. C., 258
Paston, Miss, 316
Pastrana, Julia, 317
Pastrana, Leonora, 317
Patchett, Jean, 278
Pathologists, 445
Paton, Lori, 289
Patrick, Ruth, 133, 445
Patterson, Alicia, 231
Patterson, Eleanor ("Cissy") Medill, 231, 262
Patterson, Joseph Medill, 231
Patterson, Shirley, 407–408
Patti, Adelina, 205, 262, 320
Pauker, Ana Rabinsohn, 373
Paul, Alice, 337, 340
Paul White Award, 456
Pauley, Jane, 185
Pawnee, Skidi, Morning Star Ceremony of, 306, 307
Pay. *See* Income
Payne, Freda, 211
Payne, Virginia, 183
Payne-Gaposchkin, Cecilia, 131
Payson, Joan Whitney, 413
Peace Nobel Prize winners, 27, 449
Peach, Dorothy, 320
Peach, Miss (comic-strip character), 108
Pearl, Minnie, 328
Peck, Annie Smith, 163
Peckett, Katherine, 403
Pediatrics, 136, 140, 445, 446
Pedro I, King of Portugal, 317
Peeters, Clara, 241
Peggy's Leg (toffee), 322
Peking Ballet, 194
Pelletier, Monique, 373
Pende people, Congo, 53
Pengelly, Bette Stephenson, 139
Penn, Susannah Lyma, 361
Pennell, Rebecca Mann, 124
Pennington, Mary)Engle, 134
Pennock, Mrs., 62

Pennsylvania Academy of Fine Arts, 244, 258
Pentagon policy makers, 153
Pentathlon, 418
Penthesilea, Amazon Queen, 143
People's party, 364
Pepperidge Farm Company, 107
Pereire, Mme. Isaac, 320
Pérez, Ernestine (Barahona), 136
Pericles, 43, 120
Perils of Pauline, 159
Perkins, Andy (Anne), 216
Perkins, Frances, 99, 370, 446
Perkins, Grace Martin, 11
Perkins, Ma, 66
Perkins, Mary (comic-strip character), 108
Perkins Institution for the Blind, 29
Perón, María Estela (Isabelita) Martínez de, 358–359
Perón, María Eva ("Evita") Duarte de, 358
Perrot, Catherine, 241
Perry, Antoinette, 177
Perry, Eleanor, 192
Pershing, General John, 151
Persson, Birgitta, 385
Petacci, Clara, 6
Peter I, the Great, Czar, 244
Peter III, Czar, 38, 39, 50
Peterkin, Julia M., 448
Peterman, Cornelia, 112
Peters, Jean, 188
Peters, Natasha, 222
Peterson, Charles J., 229
Peterson, Sylvia, 210
Peterson's Ladies' National Magazine, 229
Petit, Roland, 194
Petraglia, Minnie, 268
Petrova, Totka, 423
Petry, Ann, 224
Petty, Mary, 255
Pfeiffer, Jane Cahill, 81
Pfeiffer, W. A., 401
Pfizer, Beryl, 184
Pharmacology, 75, 140
Phidias, 43
Philadelphia Museum of Art, 254
Philanthropy, 29, 93
Philippa, Queen of England, 453
Phillips, Duncan, 253
Phillips, Marjorie, 253
Phillips Collection, Washington, D.C., 248, 253
Phipps, Joan, 405
Phipps, Marion (fictional character), 227
Photography, 103, 257–260
Photojournalism, 257, 259–260

Phryne, 44
Phylades of Cilicia, 171
Phyllis, Heather-Ann, 110
Physical differences between sexes, 17, 18
Physicians. *See* Medicine
Physics, 77, 120, 124, 131–133, 445, 446; Nobel Prize winners, 7, 78, 131, 133, 450; pay, 130
Piaf, Edith, 5
Pianists, 75, 78, 199–200, 208, 209; precocious, 197
Picard, Sophie, 129
Picard, Jeannette, 164, 394
Pickens Sisters, the, 74
Pickering, Edward, 131
Pickersgill, Caroline, 107
Pickersgill, Mary Young, 107
Pickett, Elizabeth P., 141
Pickford, Jack, 177
Pickford, Mary, 177, 187, 264, 440
Picon, Molly, 456
Pierce, Charles, 181
Pierce, Grace, 315
Pierce, Madeleine, 183
Pierry, Mme. du, 130
Pietropinto, Anthony, 224
Piggott, Emmeline, 149
Pignatari, Francisco ("Baby"), 266–267
Pilots, 112–113, 164–165; fighter, USSR, 155; first black woman licensed, 442; Iron Cross recipients, 443; WASPs, 151. *See also* Aviation
Pineda, Pat, 409
Pinkerton, Miss (fictional character), 227
Pinkham, Lydia, 88
Pintassilgo, Maria de Lurdes, 359
Pious, Minerva, 181
Pips, The, 211
Pirates, 294
Piscopia, Elena Cornaro, 121
Pitcher, Molly, 147, 447
Pitchers, baseball, 413, 414
Place, Etta, 295
Place names, 322–325
Plaisance, Queen of Jerusalem, 355
Planned Parenthood Foundation, 140
Platearius, Trotula, 137
Plato, 216, 426
Playwrights, 170, 215, 232–234; black, 224, 442;

Pulitzer Prize winners, 232, 448
Pleasant, Mary Ellen ("Mammy"), 91
Pleyel, Mme. Camille, 199
Pliny, the Younger, 49, 239
Plumb, Charles, 108
Pocahontas, 25, 446
Poderjay, Ivan, 11–12
Poe, Edgar Allan, 218, 334
Poetry magazine, 229–230
Poets, 75, 77, 114, 229, 232, 333, 334, 432–434; black, 5, 223–224, 441, 442; colonial, 217–218; first, 215, 216; Pulitzer Prize winners, 5, 442, 449; quoted in *Bartlett's,* 431–432; song lyricists, 204–205
Pointer Sisters, the, 74
Poiret, Paul, 246
Poirs Belle Hélène, 322
Poitiers, Diane de, 36, 271
Poker players, 94
Polak, Nicole, 85
Poland: woman physicians in, 136; woman suffrage, 342; women in government, 373, 374
Policewomen, 108–110, 115
Polis, Carol, 409
Political affairs, women in 217, 287, 353–376. *See also* Government; Voting rights
Political scientists, 124; pay, 130
Pollifax, Jane (fictional character), 227
Pollock, Jackson, 253
Polyandry, 52–54
Polygamy, 46, 341
Polygyny, 52
Polyhymnia (Muse), 74
Pompadour, Madame de, 36, 267, 283, 439
Pompadour hairdo, 283
Pons, Lily, 188, 323
Ponselle, Rosa, 203
Pontalba, Baroness Micaela Almonester, 256
Poor Clares, 385
Pope, Alexander, 171
Popova, Liubov Sergeevna, 247
Porter, Katherine Anne, 448
Porter, Sylvia, 451
Portia, Shakespeare's model for, 76
Portugal: female prime minister, 359; woman suffrage, 343
Possaner-Ehrenthal, Gabrielle, 137
Post, Emily, 430, 431
Postage stamps, 446–447
Postema, Pamela, 413
Potemkin, Gregory, 39
Potocka, Delfina, 199
Potter, Beatrix, 114, 223

Potts, Mary Florence, 105
Pougy, Liane de, 44
Pound, Ezra, 114, 230
Powell, Adam Clayton, 180
Powell, Eleanor, 440
Power, Katherine Ann, 300
Power, Tyrone, 269
Power of the Positive Woman, The (Schlafly), 347
Powers, Debra Ann, 77
Prall, Elizabeth Smith, 123
Pratt, Rebecca, 91
Praxiteles, 44
Preakness races, 407
Precocity, 5–6, 197; physical maturity, 4
Pregnancy: disability benefits, 290–291, 293; employment during, 291; and sports, 63–64, 401, 405
Preiskel, Barbara Scott, 82
Presbyterian churches: missionary groups, 393, 394; ordination of women, 394
Presidency, U.S.: female candidates for, 364–365; first ladies, 362–364
Presidents and vice-presidents, corporate, 80–82, 127; banks, 82–83; in film industry, 192–193
Presley, Elvis, 208
Press, Irina, 423
Press, Tamara, 423
Previn, Dory Langdon, 190
Price, Leontyne, 34
Priesand, Sally J., 391
Prima, Louis, 209
Prime ministers, 358–359
Primus, Pearl, 195–196
Princeton University, 133, 256
Printing, women in, 77, 89–90
Prinz, Deborah R., 392
Prison reformers, 32
Pritchard, Anne, 110
Pritchard, Hannah, 453
Prix Bordin, 129
Prix de Rome, 200
Prix Goncourt, 77, 216
Proba (poet), 215
Procne, 68
Procope, Ernesta G., 87
Proctor, Adelaide Anne, 433
Proctor, Barbara, 86
Proctor, Elizabeth, 310
Producers: movie, 192–193; theater, 177, 232
Professional Golfers' Association, 416–417
Professional Women's Bowling Association, 424
Property rights, 292, 344; in divorce, 269, 293
Prospectors, 93, 115
Prostitution: etymology of, 42–43; history of, 42; sta-

tistics, 314; prostitutes canonized, 381–382
Provincetown Players, 232
Provoost, Mary Spratt, 90
Pseudonyms, literary, 332–333
Psychiatrists, 136, 142
Psychics, 13–15, 396
Psychological differences between sexes, 18, 19
Psychologists, 120, 141–142, 445; pay, 130; winners of APA Distinguished Scientific Award, 444–445
Ptah, Merit, 137
Public health medicine, 140
Publishers, women, 86, 87, 88, 89, 92–93; list of feminist houses, 228; magazine, 87, 229–230, 332, 338; newspaper, 89–90, 231–232
Pugach, Burton, 317
Pugach, Linda, 317
Pugh, Bronwen, 278
Pulitzer Prize winners, 5, 127, 232, 442, 444, 447–449
Punneo, Giovanna, 109
Pure Food and Drug Act (1906), 114, 134
Pythagoras, 120
Pythia (Delphi oracle), 13
Pym, Mrs. (fictional character), 227

Quaker Fan, 91
Quakers, 31, 343, 386–387
Quant, Mary, 282
Queens, 359–360; African, 355–356; Biblical 354; of Crusader Kingdom of Jerusalem, 354–355; modern, 357; mythical, 353–354; 16th-Century, 356–357
Queen's College, England, 122
Queler, Eve, 204
Quentin, Patrick, 227
Quick, Flora, 295
Quimby, Edith Hinkley, 132
Quimby, Phineas P., 30
Quinine, 329
Quinton, Cornelia Bentley Sage, 254
Quintuplet births, 62, 315

Rabbinical studies, 120, 124, 389, 390–392
Rabbis, 389, 391–392
Rabier, Yvonne, 320
Rabin, Naomi, 393
Rachel (dish), 321
Racing-car drivers, 7, 30, 159, 418
Rackam, "Calico Jack," 294
Radcliffe, Ann (Harvard benefactor), 125

Radcliffe, Anne (novelist), 220
Radcliffe College, 125, 141; honorary degrees, 443–444
Radio shows, 181–184, 197; soap operas, 182–183; "Your Hit Parade," 183
Radio-Television News Directors' Association, 456
Railroad conductors, 100
Rainbow Books, 228
Rainer, Luise, 191
Rainey, Gertrude ("Ma"), 207
Raitt, Bonnie, 212
Raleigh, Sir Walter, 316
Rambert, Marie, 193
Ramborger, Annie, 105
Ramey, Venus, 279
Ramsey, Alice Hyler, 160
Ranavalona I, Queen of Madagascar, 360
Rand, Sally, 327
Randolph, Mary, 110
Rankin, Jeanette, 7, 366
Rankin, Judy, 416
Ranney, Helen M., 445
Rape, 315; statistics, 314
Raphael, 252
Rappe, Virginia, 313
Raskind, Richard. *See* Richards, Renee
Ratia, Armi, 283
Ratjen, Dora (Herman), 22
Ratner, Sarah, 445
Raunall, Sarah, 91
Rawlings, Marjorie Kinnan, 223, 448
Rawls, Elizabeth Earle ("Betsy"), 415, 417
Ray, Charlotte, 287
Ray, Dixy Lee, 327, 369
Ray, Elizabeth, 47
Ray, Man, 259, 313
Raye, Martha, 328
Raymond, Elinor, 257
Raymond, Evelyn, 454
Read, Gertrude Ross Till, 361
Read, Mary, 294
Reader's Digest, 230
Reagan, Nancy, 347
Ream, Vinita, 323
Reboul, Marie Thérèse, 242
Reconstructionist Judaism, 391, 392
Reconstructionist Rabbinical College, Philadelphia, 392
Red-light districts, 42
Reddy, Helen, 211
Redford, Robert, 286
Redgrave, Vanessa, 71
Reed, Barbara, 315
Reed, Donna, 188
Reed, Esther de Berdt, 147
Reed, James H., 295
Reed, Jessica, 177

Reed, Joseph, 147
Rees, Mina Spiegel, 129
Reese, Della, 328
Reeves, Martha, 210
Reform Judaism, 389,
390–392
Reformed Church: mission-
aries, 393; ordination of
women, *see* United
Church of Christ
Regan, Sylvia, 201
Regret (filly), 406
Reid, Dorothy Davenport
(Mrs. Wallace Reid),
186–187
Reid, Helen Rogers, 231
Reid, Inez Smith, 224
Reid, Mrs. John G., 415
Reid, Ogden M., 231
Reid, Wallace, 186
Reincarnation, 15
Reiner, Fritz, 347
Reinhoudt, Cindy, 407
Reitsch, Hanna, 443
Religious orders, founders
of, 385–386
Religious sects, founders of,
30, 387–389
Relinde (needleworker),
239–240
Rembrandt van Rijn, 251
Remus, George, 317
Remus, Imogene, 317
Renger, Annemarie, 372
Renoir, Pierre Auguste, 44,
252
Reparata and the Delrons,
210
Reps, Helen, 392
Resistance fighters, 26,
27–28
Resnik, Judith, 164
Restell, Madame (Ann Loh-
man), 72
Reuther, Rosemary, 394
Revere, Paul, 110
Revolutionary War,
women's contributions,
147–149; soldiers,
146–147
Reynders, Yvonne, 418
Rhea (goddess), 380, 455
Rhine Maiden (filly), 407
Rhoades, Lynn, 112
Rhoads, Esther Biddle, 122
Rhodes Scholars, 127, 155
Richard I, King of England,
7
Richards, Ellen Henrietta
Swallow, 134
Richards, Laura E., 448
Richards, Renee, 20
Richardson, Ethel
Henrietta, 333
Richardson, Gloria, 34
Richardson, Henry Handel
(pseudonym), 333
Richey, "Queen" Anne, 295
Richthofen, Else von, 76
Richthofen, Frieda von, 76

Richthofen, Johanna von,
76
Riddle, Theodate Pope, 256
Ride, Sally, 164
Riding: cross-country, 160;
and roping, 157–158, 424.
See also Jockeys
Riefenstahl, Leni, 189
Riggs, Bobby, 410
Riley, Bridget, 248
Rimini, Francesca da, 36
Rimsky-Korsakov, Ivan, 39
Rind, Clementina, 89
Rinehart, Mary Roberts,
226, 227
Rinehart, Terry London,
112
Ringler, Lorna, 279
Ritchie, Cheryl, 113
Rivers, Joan, 189
Road women, 158
Robbins, Ayn, 190
Robbins, Regina, 109
Roberts, Ann, 322
Roberts, Elizabeth Madox,
219
Roberts, Faline, 87
Roberts, Lydia, 135
Robertson, Alice Mary, 366
Robichaux, Jolyn, 85–86
Robichaux, Sheila, 86
Robinson, Julia, 445
Robinson, Mary (Mrs. Rob-
ert Dale Owen), 343
Robinson, Richard, 171
Robinson, Sugar Ray, 180
Rock groups, 209–210, 211
Rock 'n' roll, 211–212
Rock songwriters, 210
Rockefeller, Abby Aldrich
(Mrs. John D.), 253
Rockefeller, Barbara
("Bobo") Sears, 269
Roddy-Eden, Anita Frances
(Mrs. Manville), 56
Rodin, Auguste, 249
Rodnina, Irina, 419
Rodriguez de Tio, Lola, 346
Rodriguez-Dulanto, Laura
Esther, 137
Roe, Humphrey Vernon, 51,
72
Roebling, Mary, 83
Rogallo, Gertrude, 107
Rogers, Edith Nourse, 365
Rogers, Florence, 407
Rogers, Ginger, 179, 328
Rogers, Mrs. John, Jr., 340
Rogers, Karen, 406
Rogers, Mary Cecilia, 218
Rogers, Rosemary, 221
Rogstad, Anna, 372
Roland, Manon, 439
Roldan, Luisa, 248
Rolf, Ida P., 330
Rolfe, Lillian, 27
"Rolfing," 330
Roman Catholic Institute of
the Blessed Virgin, 385

Roman Catholics: first
woman preacher, 390;
poll on ordination of
women, 389
Rome, ancient: prostitution,
43; Vestal virgins, 49
Romeo, women in role of,
172
Ronettes, The, 210
Ronnell, Ann, 190
Rooney, Annie, 205
Roosevelt, Eleanor, 64, 363,
364, 366, 374, 447, 452
Roosevelt, Franklin Delano,
15, 64, 181, 231, 250, 364,
370
Roosevelt, Sara Delano, 64
Roosevelt, Theodore, 102,
205
Roper, Margaret More, 121
Rorer, Sarah Tyson, 111
Rose, Kathleen (Dolores),
177–178
Rose, Mary Swartz, 135
Rose hybrids, 320
Rosellini, Lynn, 425
Rosen, Julia, 312
Rosenbaum, Ruth Broem-
mer, 30
Rosenblatt, Jossele, 393
Rosenkowitz, Susan, 63
Rosenthal, Ida, 5, 282
Rosie and the Originals, 210
Roslin, Alexander, 242
Ross, Anne Lawler, 361
Ross, Diana, 181, 207, 209
Ross, Elizabeth ("Betsy")
Griscom, 107, 267, 447
Ross, Harold, 255
Ross, Sir James Clark, 324
Ross, Katharine, 188
Ross, Nellie Tayloe, 369
Rossetti, Dante Gabriel, 251
Rossi, Properzia de', 248
Roth, Lillian, 313
Rothschild, Baroness (rose),
320
Rothschild, Baronne Char-
lotte de, 199
Roulet, Lorinda de, 413
Rousseau, Jean Jacques,
337, 426
Rowing, 420–421
Rowlandson, Mary White,
217
Rowson, Susannah, 217
Roxburghe, Duke of, 262
Royal Academy of Art,
242–243, 244, 246
Royal Ballet Company of
Great Britain, 193
Royal Geographical So-
ciety, 161, 162, 346
Royal Society, 128
Royall, Anne Newport, 114
Royce, Josiah, 141
Rozanova, Olga Vladi-
mirovna, 247
Rubens, Peter Paul,
250–251

Rubin, Barbara Jo, 405
Rubin, Vera, 131
Rubinstein, Helena, 277
Rubirosa, Porfirio, 55
Rudd, Caroline Mary, 123
Rudkin, Margaret, 107
Rudolph, Wilma, 29–30, 419
Ruffian (filly), 406
Rumania, women in government, 373
Rumpff, Count Vincent, 261
Rumsey, Mary Ann, 323
Runners, 417; drug test disqualifications, 423; hurdles, 403, 417; Iron Man Triathlon, 424; relay, 417
Running Eagle, 151
Runyon, Brenda, 83
Rush, Barbara, 188
Rush, Julia Stockton, 361
Rusiecka, Salomea, 137
Ruskin, John, 77, 435
Russell, Arthur, 417
Russell, Bronwin, 417
Russell, Craig, 181
Russell, Lady Elizabeth, 453
Russell, Elizabeth (coachmaker), 90
Russell, Elizabeth Shull (geneticist), 445
Russell, Jane, 278
Russell, Lillian, 171, 328
Russell, Rosalind, 434
Russell, Stella, 82
Ruth, Babe, 413
Rutledge, Henrietta Middleton, 362
Rutt, Chris, 94
Ryan, Anne, 247–248
Ryan, Elizabeth, 409, 411
Ryskal, Inna, 424

S., Leni (Iron Cross recipient), 443
Saar, Betye, 248
Sabin, Florence Rena, 124, 132, 445, 452, 454
Sablière, Marguerite Hessein de la, 130
Sacajawea, 63, 440–441
Sachar, Ellen B., 84
Sachs, Nelly, 449
Sachs, Sadie, 317–318
Sacrifice, 49, 306–307
Sadler's Wells Ballet, 193
Sage, Anna, 47
Sage, Letitia, 163
Sager, Carole Bayer, 190
Sager, Ruth, 446
Sager, Sarah, 392
Sailing around the world, 161
St. Afra, 381–382
St. Anne's College, Oxford, 123
St. Audrey, 283–284
St. Catherine of Alexandria, 384
St. Catherine of Genoa, 384

St. Catherine of Siena, 217
St. Cecilia, 384
St. Clair, Sally, 147
St. Denis, Ruth, 195
St. Eugenia, 383
St. Galla, 6
St. Frances Xavier (Mother Cabrini), 386
St. Gregory the Great, 49
St. Hugh's College, Oxford, 123
St. John, Adela Rogers, 185
St. Joseph's College for Women, 386
St. Leger, Elizabeth, 7
St. Liberta, 6
St. Mary Magdalene, 381
St. Mary the Harlot, 381
St. Pelagia, 382
St. Thaïs, 382
St. Theodota, 382
St. Theresa, 267
St. Uncumber, 6
St. Veronica, 381
St. Werburga, 50
St. Wilgeforte (or Vigiforte), 6
St. Winefride, 384
St. Wulfhilda, 384
Saints, 6, 383–384; American, 386
Sakeeta, Queen of Egypt, 15
Salaries. *See* Income
Saleh, Salwa, 83
Salem, witches of, 310
Salemi, Sophie, 312
Salisbury, Countess Margaret, 308
Sally (slave), 310–311
Salmon, Mary, 90
Salome (follower of Jesus), 381
Salome (mother of apostles), 381
Salote Tubou, Queen of Tonga, 360
Saltykov, Sergei, 38
Salute to Women in Jazz, New York City, 208
Salvage, Lynn D., 81, 84
Salvation Army, 389
Sammuramat, Queen of Assyria, 144
Sampson, Agnes, 309
Samuel, Alice, 309
San Diego Union and Evening Tribune, 232
San Francisco Museum of Art, 253, 254
Sand, George (pseudonym), 38, 198, 321, 332
Sandamata, Habe queen, 355
Sandburg, Carl, 449
Sanderson, James, 343
Sanderson, Mary (Mrs. Betterton), 170, 176
Sandes, Flora, 146
Sandwina, Katie Brumbach, 407

Sanford, Leda Giovannetti, 230
Sanford, Maria, 454
Sanger, Alice B., 102
Sanger, Margaret, 71, 317–318, 452
Sanitation workers, 101
Sansom, Odette, 27
Sao Ch'ing Niang (goddess), 380
Sappho, 216, 455
Saqui, Madame, 157
Sarah (slave), 311
Sarasvati (goddess), 105, 378
Sarto, Andrea del, 250
Sasso, Dennis, 391
Sasso, Sandy, 391
Saturday Evening Post, 191, 255
Saud, King of Saudi Arabia, 87
Saunders, Allen, 255
Savage, Christina, 222
Sawyer, Sarah, 72
Sayers, Dorothy L., 226, 228
Saxe, Susan Edith, 300
Scanagatti, Louisa, 145
Scannell, Nancy, 425
Scepter Records, 87
Schäffer, Mary F.S., 258
Schally, Andrew V., 133, 450
Scharrer, Berta Vogel, 445
Schau, Mrs. Walter M., 447
Scheiblich, Christine, 420–421
Scheiss, Betty Bone, 394
Schelkanova, Tatyana, 423
Schenk von Stauffenberg, Countess, 443
Scherf, Margaret, 227
Schiaparelli, Elsa, 277
Schiff, Dorothy ("Dolly"), 231
Schimmel, Gertrude, 109
Schlafly, Phyllis, 347
Schmidt, Kathryn Joan (Kathy), 408, 418
Scholars, 120–121, 124, 126–135, 443–444
Schonberg, Harold, 203
School boards: woman members, 367; women's vote in elections, 341
Schreiber, Le Anne, 425
Schreiner, Olive, 333, 334
Schroeder, Becky, 107
Schubert, Franz, 198, 200
Schulz, Ilse, 443
Schumann, Clara Wieck, 198, 199
Schumann, Robert, 198, 199
Schumann-Heink, Ernestine (Mother of Doughboys), 67
Schuyler, Philippa Duke, 5
Schwitters, Kurt, 247
Scientists: 77, 88, 105, 120–121, 124, 129–135,

443–444; faculty members, 124, 129, 131, 132, 152, 443; honorary degrees, 131, 133, 443–444; late starters, 113; pay differentials, *table* 130. *See also individual sciences*
Scott, Barbara Ann, 404
Scott, Charlotte Angas, 129
Scott, Evelyn, 219–220
Scott, Gloria L., 375
Scott, Hazel, 197
Scott, Lady John (Alicia Anne Spottiswoode), 204
Scott, Peggy, 286
Scott, Sir Walter, 232
Screen Actors Guild, 187
Script writers: movie, 185, 186, 187, 189, 191–192, 233; TV, 233
Scruggs, Jeanne, 14
Sculptors, 105, 243, 244, 248–250, 323, 333, 442, 454; of antiquity, 239; models of, 43, 44, 45, 251
Seaman, Elizabeth (Nelly Bly), 160
Sears, Eleonora, 404
Seattle Art Museum, 253
Sebastian, King of Portugal, 357
Second Sex, The (Beauvoir), 345
Secretarial work, 96, 98
Seddon, Margaret Rhea, 164
Seeger, Ruth Crawford, 200, 203
Seers, 13–15, 66–67
Seeton, Emily (fictional character), 227
Segati, Marianna, 41
Segurane, Catherine de, 145
Selfridge, Gordon, 266
Semiramis, legend of, 144
Seneca Falls, 452, 455; Woman's Rights Convention (1848), 336, 338–339, 344
Senesh, Hannah, 26
Sennett, Ted, 187
Serban, Andrei, 234
Sergeant, William, 317
Serreau, Coline, 189
Serres, Olive, 9
Servis, Dorothy A., 82
Sessions, Lucy, 441
Seton, Elizabeth Ann, 386
Settlement houses, 30, 111
Seven Sisters (colleges), 125–126
Seventh-Day Adventists, 389
Sewall, Anna, 223
Sex, determination of, 18
Sex and the Single Woman (Brown), 87
Sex-change cases, 19–20
Sex discrimination, 346–347; alimony payment, 269,

291; in education, 123, 125, 126, 137–138, 435; in employment, 137–138, 287, 289, 291, 292, 315, 318, 346–347, 425; in pay, 80, 95, 96, *table* 130, 292, 346; in public affairs, 289, 336–340, 343, 367; social security benefits, 291; in sports, 404, 408, 414, 416, 418, 421
Sex Information and Education Council of the U.S. (SIECUS), 140
Sexton, Anne, 449
Sextuplets, 63
Sexual identity, in athletic competition, 22–23, 422–423
Sexual offenses, statistics, 314
Seymour, Mary, 93
Seymour, William, 316
Seymour sisters, 121. *See also* Jane Seymour, Queen of England
Shaftall, Beverly Guy, 223
Shah Jahan, Emperor, 8
Shakers (Shaking Quakers), 67, 388
Shakespeare, William, 76, 171–172, 175, 176, 283
Shakhovskaya, Princess Eugenie, 155
Shameless Hussy Press, 228
Shane, Eva, 409
Shane, Mary, 7
Shange, Ntozake, 224, 233
Shangri-Las, The, 210
Shanley, Estelle M., 425
Shannon, Julie, 103
Shanor, Karen, 224
Shark fishing, 420, 422
Sharp, William, 332
Shata, Habe queen, 355
Shattuck, Mrs., 146
Shaver, Dorothy, 81
Shaw, Anna Howard, 337, 390, 434
Shaw, Artie, 207
Shaw, George Bernard, 174, 175
Shaw, Ray, 250
Shawata, Habe queen, 356
Shawn, Ted, 195
Shearer, Kathleen, 101
Shearing, George, 209
Sheba, Queen of, 354
Sheba magazine, 230
Shelburne Museum, Vermont, 253
Sheldon, May French, 161
Shelley, Mary, 41
Shen Yunying, 145
Sheppard, Evelyn, 180
Sheppard, Sarah Hannah, 204
Sheraton, Mimi, 79
Sherman, Rebecca Prescott, 362

Sherman, General William Tecumseh, 67
Sherr, Lynn, 441
Sherwood, Mary E.W. (Mrs. John), 429, 430
Sherwood, Valerie, 222
Shevchenko, Arkady, 47
Shih Mai-yu, 136
Shiley, Jean, 403
Shinegger, Erike, 423
Shipp, Ellis, 138
Shipton, Ursula ("Mother"), 14, 66–67
Shirelles, The, 87, 209
Shirley, Anne, 327
Shofar blowers, 392–393
Shore, Dinah, 183
Shore, Jemima (fictional character), 228
Short women, 4–5
Shot put, 418
Shrimpton, Jean, 278
Shurtleff, Robert (Deborah Sampson Gannett), 147
Shuster, Joe, 108
Shuttleworth, Pam, 417
Si Ling-chi, Empress of China, 105–106
Sichelgaita of Lombardy, 144
Siddal, Elizabeth, 251
Siddons, Sarah Kemble, 172, 173, 174, 453
Siddons, William, 173
Sidney, Sylvia, 182, 188
Siebert, Muriel, 83
Siebold, Charlotte von, 70
Siebold, Regina von, 70
Siegel, Jerry, 108
Siegemundin, Justine Dittrichin, 70
Siemer, Deanne C., 153
Sigourney, Lydia Huntley, 229, 323
Silai, Ileana, 423
Silk manufacture, 106
Silks, Mattie, 91
Sillanpää, Miina, 372
Sills, Beverly, 184, 197, 202, 204, 451
Silver, Frankie, 296
Silver, Joan Micklin, 189
Silver, Maud (fictional character), 228
Silver Spoon (filly), 407
Simeoni, Sara, 418
Simmenauer, Jacqueline, 224
Simmons, Amelia, 110
Simmons, Maudine, 180
Simmons, Ruth (pseudonym), 15
Simms, Ginny, 183
Simon, Carly, 211
Simon, Norton, 82
Simon, Rita J., 300
Simone, Nina, 209
Simons, Vera, 164
Simpson, Thomas, 324

Simpson, Wallis Warfield (later Duchess of Windsor), 450
Sims, Lowery, 254
Sims, Naomi, 279
Sinatra, Dolly, 65
Sinatra, Frank, 65, 211
Sinatra, Nancy, 211
Singer, Maxine F., 446
Singers, 34, 78; Blues, 207–208; country music, 212–214; 50's and 60's groups, 209–210; Gold singles winners, 210–211; Jazz, 208–209; opera, 173, 188, 197, 200, 201, 441, 442; precocious, 5, 197; rock, 209–210, 211–212; Sister acts, 74, 210, 212; "Your Hit Parade," 183
Sinhalese people, 52
Sinkford, Jeanne Craig, 442
Sipila, Helvi Linnea, 374
Sirani, Elisabetta, 241
Sissle, Ethel, 180
Sisters, celebrated, 74–76, 210
Sisters of Charity, 386
Sisters of the Holy Family, 386
Sisters of the Road, 158
Six, Les, 200
Skarda (goddess), 402
Skating: figure, 404, 419; speed, 418
Star ceremony of, 306–307
Skiing, 402, 403; cross-country, 425; downhill, 423, 424
Skinner, Cornelia Otis, 44, 233
Skoblikova, Lidia, 418
Slave trade, 161
Slaves, field, 310–311
"Sleeping Lucy," 72
Slick, Grace, 71, 212, 326
Slide, Anthony, 185
Sloan, Jerry, 165
Slocumb, Mary, 147
Slowe, Lucy Diggs, 442
Smalley, Phillips, 186
Smart, Charles Selden, 334
Smedley-Maclean, Ida, 135
Smith, Ann, 90
Smith, Barbara Leigh (Mrs. Bodichon), 338
Smith, Bessie, 207, 209
Smith, Connie, 213
Smith, Doris, 76
Smith, Eleanor Armor, 362
Smith, Elizabeth Oakes, 334
Smith, Ethel, 183
Smith, Hazel Brannon, 447
Smith, Keely, 209
Smith, Madeleine, 296
Smith, Mamie O'Dell, 100
Smith, Margaret Chase, 364, 365, 452
Smith, Martha Turnstall, 90
Smith, Mary Ellen, 371

Smith, Mary Heathman ("Granny"), 70, 71
Smith, Patricia W., 422
Smith, Robyn, 405
Smith, Seba, 334
Smith, Shelley, 279
Smith, Sophia, 125
Smith, Mrs. Thomas, 330
Smith College, 124, 125, 403
Smithsonian Institution, 254, 266
Smoke, Marcia Jones, 418
Smyth, Dame Ethel Mary, 200
Snavely, Mary, 153
Snell, Hannah (James Grey), 146
Sniff, Alta Belle, 258
Snyder, Ruth Brown, 297
Soap operas: radio, 182–183; TV, 300–301
Social scientists, 124; pay, 130. *See also individual disciplines*
Social Security Administration, 291
Social workers, 30, 31, 75
Society and wealth, women of, 261–265
Society for Psychical Research, 9
Society for the Collegiate Instruction of Women, 125
Society for the Promotion of Employment of Women, 338
Society of Clinical Surgery, 139
Society of Friends, 343, 386–387
Society of Systematic Zoologists, 133
Society of the Holy Child Jesus, 385
Sociologists, 443; pay, 130
Socrates, 120
Söder, Karin, 372
Softball, 413
Soifer, Myra, 392
Soldiers. *See* War heroines; Warriors
Solís, Manuela, 137
Solomon, King, 354
Solomon, Beatrice R., 79
Solomon, Isker, 206
Solon, 42
Somerset, Sarah, Duchess of, 453
Somerville, Mary Fairfax, 115, 123, 128–129
Somerville Hall, Oxford, 123
Somogi, Judith, 203
Song lyricists, 190, 204–205, 210
Songwriters, 204–205, 209, 210
Sonny and Cher, 211, 326
Soong sisters, 75–76

Sophia, Sister (firefighter), 104
Sophy (slave), 310
Sorbonne, Paris, 132, 137
Sorel, Agnes, 252, 277, 320
Sorenson, Lennie Mettick, 113
Sorosis, 93
Soubirous, Bernadette, 382
Soups named for women, 320–321
Southern, Ann, 328
Southerne, Elizabeth, 309
Soviet Union, women in: artists, 246–247; education and employment, 97; fighter pilots, 155; in government, 97, 373; labor force, 97; physicians, 136; woman suffrage, 342
Spangberg-Holth, Marie, 137
SPARs, 151
Speed, Della Short, 329
Speed skating, 418
Spellman, Gladys N., 366
Speltarini, Maria, 159
Spencer, Anna W., 229
Spencer, Lily Martin, 65–66
Sperbeck, Florence, 115
Spewack, Bella, 233
Spewack, Sam, 233
Speyer, Leonora, 449
Spies, 12, 22; Civil War, 149–150; World War II, 27–28
Spinner, Francis Elias, 102
Spiritualists, 13–15, 75, 388
Spitalny, Phil, 206
Spivey, Victoria, 207–208
Sports, 7, 401–425; drug tests in competition, 423; late starters, 115; men in women's events, 22–23; money records, 413, 416, 419; myths about women, 401; Olympic champions, 6, 29–30, 63, 403, 410, 417–420, 424–425, 442; precocity, 5–6, 406, 410; pregnant women in, 63–64, 401, 405; sex discrimination in, 404, 408, 414, 416, 418, 421; sexual identity tests, 422–423; world records, 6, 30, 403, 407, 417–422. *See also individual sports*
Sports Illustrated, 291, 413, 425
"Sportsman of the Year," 413
Sportswriters, 425
Spottiswoode, Alicia Anne (Lady John Scott), 204
Spotts, Judy, 104
Spry, Constance, 320
Spychajowa-Kurkowska, Janina, 424
Spyri, Johanna, 223

Sri Lanka, 52; female head of state, 358
Staël, Madame de, 40, 434
Stafford, Jean, 448
Stalin, Joseph, 259, 373
Stanford, Sally (Marcia Busby), 92, 327, 367
Stanislas II, Poniatowski, King of Poland, 38–39, 321
Stanley, Henry, 324
Stanton, Elizabeth Cady, 78, 284, 336, 339, 348, 447
Stanwyck, Barbara, 178, 179
Starbuck, Mary Coffin, 387
Stark, Mabel, 157
Starkweather, Charles, 297
Starr, Belle ("Bandit Queen"), 78, 295
Starr, Brenda (comic-strip character), 108
Starr, Leonard, 108
Starr, Pearl, 78, 295
States, women in public affairs: governors, 66, 327, 367, 369; legislators, 325, 365, 367, 369, 370; lieutenant governors, 369–370; statistics, *table* 367; woman suffrage, 341–342
Statisticians, 445; pay, 130
Stavers, Susan, 106–107
Stead, Karen, 418
Steadman, Bernice Trimble, 165
Steers, Fanny, 432
Stein, Gertrude, 57, 201, 246, 252, 253, 439
Stein, Sarah (Mrs. Michael), 253
Steinbach, Sabina von, 248
Steinem, Gloria, 230, 345, 451
Steinman, Anne, 225
"Stella Dallas" (radio show), 183
Stepanova, Varvara, 247
Stephans, Ann, 229
Stephen, Sir Leslie, 77
Stephens, Helen, 404
Stereotype phrases, 23, 54, 79
Sterilization, forced, 318
Stern, Ava, 230
Steroid hormones, in sports, 423
Stettheimer, Florine, 246
Stevens, Doris, 340
Stevens, Risë, 188, 204
Stevens, Wallace, 230
Stevenson, Alice, 4
Stevenson, Nancy, 370, 451
Stevenson, Robert Louis, 77
Steward, Susan McKinney, 442
Stewart, Ellen, 177
Stieglitz, Alfred, 247, 258
Stimson, Julia C., 151

Stirling, Jane Wilhelmina, 199
Stockton, Annis Boudinot, 218, 362
Stoffels, Hendrickje, 251
Stojanova, Elena, 423
Stolle, Maria, 443
Stone, Constance, 136
Stone, Lucy, 78, 123, 333, 336, 343, 344, 447
Stone, Margaret Brown, 362
Stone, Paula, 182
Stoney, Mrs. W. M., 13
Stop ERA, 347
Stopes, Marie Carmichael, 50–51, 72
Storer sisters (actresses), 76
Stouse, Patty, 104
Stout, Rex, 227
Stovall, Thelma L., 370
Stowe, Emily Jennings, 136
Stowe, Harriet Beecher, 33, 74, 220, 429, 431, 452
Strange, Michael (pseudonym), 333
Strasberg, Lee, 176
Stratemeyer, Edna, 332
Stratemeyer, Edward, 332
Stratton, Alice Dale, 82
Straus, Mrs. Isidor, 16, 28
Strauss, Jean, 101
Street, Doca, 317
Streeter, Roberta (Bobbie Gentry), 213
Streisand, Barbra, 211, 268
Striano, Josephine Figliolia, 100
Strickland, Martha, 334
Striebel, John, 108
Stuart, Lady Arabella, 316, 453
Stuart, Helaine Meryl Zuckerman, 85
Stuart, Miranda (Dr. James Barry), 21
Student Nonviolent Coordinating Committee (SNCC), 32
Stumbough, Gene Nora, 165
Stunt women, 159–160
Stutz, Geraldine, 81
Subirana, Rosa Maria, 254
Subjection of Women, The (Mill), 344
Suckow, Ruth, 220
Suffolk, Frances Grey, Duchess of, 453
Suffolk, Marguerite, Countess of, 261
Suffrage movement, 26, 78, 88, 186, 200, 288, 289, 336–341, 358; British, 338; jailings, 338, 340
Suffrage Movement, The (Pankhurst), 338
Suggs, Louise, 404
Suicides, 313, 314
Suiko Tenno, Empress of Japan, 359

Sukey (slave), 311
Sullivan, Anne, 29, 446
Sullivan, Kathryn D., 164
Sullivan, Mary, 109
Sullivan, Mary Quinn, 253
Sullivan, Maxine, 209
Summer, Donna, 210
Summerskill, Edith, 371
Summerskill, Shirley (Shirley Samuel), 371
Sun Yat-sen, Madame (Soong Ching-ling), 75–76
Suplee, Hannah, 105
Supremes, The (original), 209
Surfing, 420
Surgeons, 124, 138, 139, 140
Susann, Jacqueline, 30, 221
Susanna (follower of Jesus), 381
Suttner, Bertha von, 449
Sutton, May, 409, 410
Suzman, Helen, 455
Svendsen, Caroline, 408
Swados, Elizabeth, 233–234
Swain, Louisa Ann, 341
Swanson, Gloria, 220, 263
Swanson, Katrina, 394
Swarthout, Gladys, 188
Sweden: woman suffrage, 342; women in government, 372, 374
"Sweet Adeline" (song), 205
Sweet Adelines, The, 206
Sweet Lips (cannon), 156
Sweets named for women, 322
Swift, Elizabeth Ann, 319
Swimmers, 6, 404, 419–420, 424; long distance, 421–422; male-female comparison, 401
Swindlers, 298–299
Switchboard operators, 99, 346
Switzerland: woman suffrage, 343, 372; women in government, 372–373
Swope, Alma, 153
Swynnerton, Annie Louisa, 243
Sybylle, Queen of Jerusalem, 355
Sylvester, Pamela, 151
Sylvia (veal dish), 321
Syms, Sylvia, 209
Szabo, Violet, 27
Szewinska, Irena Kirszenstein, 417
Szold, Henrietta, 26

Tabackin, Lew, 208
Tabei, Junko, 163
Tabor, Baby Doe, 313, 326
Tabor, Horace, 313
Taft, Helen Herron, 363
Taft, William Howard, 102, 363
Tai, wife of (mummy), 4

Tai Ai-lien, 194
T'ai Shan Mu (goddess), 381
Tailleferre, Germaine, 200
Taj Mahal, Agra, 8
Talbot, Henry, 172
Talbot, Mary Anne, 146
Tale of Genji, The (Murasaki), 215
Tall Bull, Cheyenne chief, 311–312
Tall women, 4
Talley, Madelon D., 83
Talley, Nedra, 210
Talleyrand, Duc Helie de, 262
Talmadge, Norma, 185, 440
Tandy, Anne Burnett, 81
Tapestry, 240, 242
Tapscott, Billie, 409
Tashman, Lilyan, 178
Tassi, Agostino, 315
Tate, Sharon, 297
Tauber-Arp, Sophie, 244
Taussig, Helen Brooke, 140, 444, 445
Tavern keepers, 90–91
Tawdry, origin of term, 283–284
Taylor, Alice Bemis, 253
Taylor, Ann (lyricist), 205
Taylor, Annie (missionary), 162
Taylor, Annie Edson, 159
Taylor, Avone (Mrs. Manville), 56
Taylor, Deems, 201
Taylor, Elizabeth, 5, 191, 267
Taylor, Harriet (Mrs. John Stuart Mill), 344
Taylor, James, 211
Taylor, Jane, 205, 432
Taylor, Joseph, 126
Taylor, Margaret (Mrs. Zachary Taylor), 267
Taylor Naomi Smith, 362
Taylor, Renee, 192
Taylor, Stella, 421
Taylor, Tom, 176
Taylor, Winifred, 109
Tchaikowsky, Peter, 198
Teachers, 96, 97, 121–122. *See also* Educators
Teasdale, Sara, 449
Tekakwitha, Kateri, 384–385
Tekgul, Ozcan, 456
Telephone operators, 99, 346
Television, 451, 456; script writers, 233, 347; soap operas, 300–301; "Today Show," 184–185, 279
Temple, Shirley, 6
Teneva, Daniela, 423
Tennille, Toni, 211
Tennis, 20, 404, 409–413, 442; attire, 409–410; earliest players, 410; Grand

Slam champions, 412; introduction to U.S., 402; precocity, 5, 6, 410
Tenri Kyo (Shinto sect), 388
Teoli, Camella, 318
Teresa, Mother, of Calcutta, 449
Tereshkova, Valentina, 165
Terling (Teerlinck), Lavinia, 245
Terman, Lewis M., 141
Terpsichore (Muse), 74
Terrell, Mary Church, 32, 124
Terry, Ellen, 174–175, 259
Terry, Hilda, 255
Terry, Lucy, 218
Tetrazzini, Luisa, 321
Tewkesbury, Joan, 189, 192
Textile design, 239–240, 244, 246, 247
Tey, Josephine (Elizabeth Mackintosh), 226
Thalia (Grace), 74
Thalia (Muse), 74
Thamyris (Timarete), 239
Thanksgiving Day, 293
Tharp, Twyla, 196, 327
Thatcher, Margaret, 359
Thaw, Alice Cornelia (Countess of Yarmouth), 262
Theano, 120
Theater, 170–177; design, 246, 247; directors, 174, 176, 232; managers, 176–177; men in women's roles, 171, 180–181; producers, 177, 232; women in men's roles, 172. *See also* Actresses; Playwrights
Théâtre de Danse, Paris, 193
Theia (Titan), 455
Theodora, mistress of Pope John X, 45
Theological colleges: enrollment statistics, 389; first women graduates, 124, 390
Theology, 121, 389–392; rabbinical studies, 120, 121, 124, 389, 390–392. *See also* Ministry, women in
Theoris, 43
Theosophical Society, 388
Thetford, Terri, 319
Thible, Elisabeth, 163
Thomas, Hociel, 207
Thomas, James, 126
Thomas, Lowell, 403
Thomas, Marlo, 455
Thomas, Martha Carey, 126, 435
Thomas, Olive, 177
Thomas, Pat, 210
Thompson, "Boxcar Bertha," 158, 326

Thompson, Clara Mabel, 142
Thompson, Kay, 183
Thomson, Virgil, 201, 246
Thoreau, Henry David, 426
Thorndyke, Helen Louise (pseudonym), 332
Thornhill, Claude, 209
Thornton, Alicia Meynell, 404–405
Thornton, Hannah Jack, 362
Thornton, Willie Mae ("Big Mama"), 208
Thrale, Hester L., 432
Throckmorton, Elizabeth, 316
Thun-Hohenstein, Mlle. de, 199
Thurber, Mame, 10
Tiberius, Roman Emperor, 376–377
Tibetan peoples, 53
Tiburzi, Bonnie, 113
Tichauer, Ruth W., 140
Tickey, "Blazin' " Bertha, 413
Tiegs, Cheryl, 279
Tillman, Georgeanna, 210
Tilton, Martha, 183
Tilzer, Harry von, 206
Timarete (Thamyris), 239
Time magazine, 81, 259, 425; "Men of the Year," 450
Times Change Press, 228
Timothy, Elizabeth, 89
Tintoretto, Marietta, 243
Tiresias (Greek legend), 20
Tir-Na-Mban, 353–354
Tissot, Janou, 424
Titanic, S.S., 16, 28, 219
Titian, 250
Tituba (Salem witch), 310
Tkacenko, Nadezhda, 418, 423
Toda people, India, 53
"Today Show" (TV), 184–185, 279
Todd, Jan Suffolk, 407
Toffana, Signora, 329
Toklas, Alice B., 57, 252, 434
Tolona, Khalilah, 269
Tom Paine Award, 455
Tomes, Robert, 428
Tomoe (samurai), 144
Tony Awards, 177, 234
Total Woman, The (Morgan), 347
Totino, Rose, 87
Tourret, Pat, 108
Towns named for women, 322–324
Townsend, Claire, 192–193
Townsend, Sally, 148–149
Track and field, 403, 404, 417–418; drug test dis-

qualifications, 423; male-female comparison, 401
Tracy, Faun, 207
Tranquilizer users, 314
Transvestites, 20–23, 180–181
Traubel, Helen, 188
Trautmann, Claudine, 418
Travel, 161
Travers, P. L. (Pamela), 223
Travolta, John, 286
Tree, Marietta, 375
Tree, Penelope, 278
Tremiar, Marian ("Tyger"), 408
Triangle Waist Company, 312
Trigère, Pauline, 83
Triplet births, 62
Tripp, Deborah and Susan, 4
Tropical storms, naming, 331
Troubadours, female, 199
Troubetzkoy, Prince Igor, 55
Troy Female Seminary, 124
Truckdrivers, 100
Truman, Harry S.; 69, 265, 374
Truman, Martha Young, 69
Trung-Nhi, 144
Trung-Trac, 144
Truth, Sojourner, 34, 65, 327–328
Tubman, Harriet, 26, 34, 447
Tuchman, Barbara W., 127, 449
Tucker, Sophie, 178
Tudor, Anthony, 193
Tufnell, Meriel, 405
Tufverson, Agnes, 11–12
Tules, Doña (Doña Gertrudis Barcelo), 93
Turgenev, Ivan, 199
Turnbull, Dora Amy Dillon, 228
Turner, Alice K., 222
Turner, Doris, 268
Turner, Tina, 328
Turrell, Jane Coleman, 217
Tussaud, Márie Gresholtz, 92
Tutbury Marvel, the, 8
Tweed, Karen J., 155
Twiggy (Leslie Hornby), 278, 329
Twilight Tear (filly), 406
Twin births, 62–63
Tyolajarvi, Pirkko, 372
Tyson, Cicely, 34
Tz'u Hsi (Ci Xi), Empress of China, 360, 378

Udaltsova, Nadezhda Andreevna, 247
Uhnak, Dorothy, 222, 226
Ulanov, Alexei, 419
Ullmann, Liv, 71

Ulmyn, Ruth, 23, 54, 79, 331
Umpires, 413
Undercover agents: American Revolutionary War, 148; Civil War, 149–150; World War II, 27–28
Underwear, 272–273, 277–278
Underwood, Charles G., 94
Undset, Sigrid, 449
Union Magazine of Literature and Art, 229
United Airlines, 95, 111
United Church of Christ, ordainment of women, 394
United Mineworkers Union, 29
United Nations, 249, 374–375; Convention on the Political Rights of Women (1952), 343; Declaration of Women's Rights (1967), 436–437; human rights awards, 455; women delegates at, 358, 364, 374–375
United Tailoresses Society (New York), 98
Universalists, women ministers of, 390
University degrees, first women recipients, 121; honorary degrees, 123, 131
University faculty positions, 129, 131, 202, 209; first, 75, 100, 124, 130, 132, 152, 287
University of Alabama, 26, 27
University of Bologna, 88, 136, 287
University of California at Berkeley, 135
University of Chicago, 124, 133
University of Maryland Art Gallery, 245
University of Michigan, 136, 455
University of Paris, 132, 137
Unmarried-and-living-together couples statistics, 47
Unmarried motherhood, 71
Unsinkable Mrs. Brown, The, 219
Upham, John B., 415
Urania (Muse), 74
Urban planning, 256
Urology, 141
Ursuline Order, 385
U.S. Air Force Academy, 155
U.S. Army, 151, 330
U.S. Coast Guard, 151
U.S. Coast Guard Academy, 155

U.S. Field Hockey Association, 403
U.S. Golf Association, 417; Women's Champions, 415–416
U.S. House of Representatives, women in, 7, 315, 331, 365–367; black women, 366, 442; unequal representation, table 367
U.S. Marine Corps, 151, 153–154
U.S. Medal of Honor, 7
U.S. Merchant Marine, 152
U.S. Military Academy, 155
U.S. National Tennis Open champions, 410, 411, 412, 413
U.S. Naval Academy, 155
U.S. Navy, 78, 132, 152; female ensigns, 154
U.S. Senate, women in, 365–366; unequal representation, table 367
U.S. Supreme Court, 32, 99, 367; first woman admitted to, 287; first woman to argue before, 287; women's rights decisions, 287, 289, 291, 292
Utah, woman suffrage in, 341–342
Utrillo, Maurice, 244
Uttar Pradesh, India, women of, 307

Vafardi, Kathe, 346
Valadon, Suzanne, 71, 244
Valentino, Rudolph, 187, 220, 285, 286
Valkyrie Press, 228
Vallayer-Coster, Anne, 242
Van Alstyne, Nancy, 146–147
Vanbrugh, Sir John, 426
Van Buren, Abigail (Pauline Esther Friedman), 75, 430
Van Buren, Adeline, 160–161
Van Buren, Amelia C., 258
Van Buren, Augusta, 160–161
Van Cott, Maggie Newton, 390
Vandellas, The, 210
Vanderbilt, Alva Smith (Mrs. William K. V.), 263–264
Vanderbilt, Consuelo (Duchess of Marlborough), 10, 261
Vane, Harriet (fictional character), 228
Van Gogh, Vincent, 244
Van Hooten, Leslie, 297–298
Vanilla Press, 228
Vanity Press, 228
Van Lew, Elizabeth, 150

Van Slyke, Helen, 222
Varda, Agnes, 189
Vare, Glenna Collett, 404, 415, 416
Varèse, Edgar, 195
Vasari, Giorgio, 250
Vashti, Queen, 354
Vasili, Count Paul (pseudonym), 332
Vassar, Matthew, 125
Vassar College, 122, 125, 131, 141, 403
Vassilchikov, Alexander Semeonovich, 39
Vassilet, Mme. Fydor, 62
Vaughan, Sarah, 209
Vecelli, Cecilia, 250
Vecelli, Lavinia, 250
Veder, Slava, 447
Veil, Simone, 375
Velakowsky, Freda, 312
Velez, Lupe, 187
Vennochi, Joan, 448
Venus, nomenclature of, 454
Verbal ability, 17, 18
Verdieu, Chevalier John Theodora, 21
Verdy, Violette (Nelly Guillerm), 194
Verhulst, Mayken, 244
Verne, Jules, 160
Verrette, Joyce, 222
Verushka (fashion model), 278
Vesley, Jane de, 407
Vestal, Madame (Lurline Monte Verde), 94
Vestal virgins, 49
Vestris, Lucia Elizabeth, 176
Viardot-Garcia, Pauline, 199–200
Victoria, Queen of England, 66, 70, 78, 360, 439; places named after, 324
Vien, Joseph Marie, 242
Vienna Conservatory, 435
Vigée, Louis, 76
Vigée-Lebrun, Elizabeth, 76, 242, 245
Vinciarelli, Lauretta, 257
Vindication of the Rights of Woman (Wollstonecraft), 337
Vining, Elizabeth Gray, 122
Vintimille, Comtesse du Luc de, 45
Violinists, 197, 435
Vionnet, Madeleine, 281
Virgin Mary, 16, 68, 381; appearances of, 382–383; models for artists, 252
Virgin wives, 50–51
Virginity, meanings of, 48–50
Visitation Order, 386
Visual-spatial coordination, 18
Vlad, Santa, 423

Vogue, 191, 260, 278
Volleyball, 424
Volner, Jill Wine, 153
Volpe, Ray, 416
Voltaire, 128
Volz, Anita M., 84
Voting rights, 290, 336–343, 345; "arguments" against, 339–340; denial of, 289, 336–340; granting of (dates), 341–343. *See also* Suffrage movement
Vreeland, Diana, 279

WACs, 151, 260
Wagner, Cosima, 203
Wagner, Jane, 189
Wagner, Richard, 198, 203
Wagner, Siegfried, 203
Wagner, Winifred Williams, 203
Wain, Bea, 183
Waitressing, 96
Waitz, Grete, 423
Wak Wak (mythical land), 354
Wake, Nancy (Lucienne Carlier), 27
Wakefield, Priscilla, 82
Wakefield, Ruth, 107
Wald, Patricia McGowan, 290
Waldron, M., 171
Waleska (Warluskee), 324
Walewska, Marie, 71, 439
Walker, Edwin C., 343
Walker, Jimmy, 178
Walker, Lucy, 161
Walker, Maggie Lena, 82–83, 442
Walker, Mary E., 7, 333
Walker, Mary Richardson, 160
Walker, Sarah Breedlove, 93, 442
Walker, Valerie, 113
Walkers, long distance, 160, 162
Wallace, DeWitt, 230
Wallace, George C., 26, 369
Wallace, Lila Acheson, 230
Wallace, Lurleen, 369
Wallace, Michele, 224
Wallace, Sippie, 207
Walsh, Joan, 319
Walsh, Julia M., 84
Walsh, Stella, 404
Walters, Barbara, 185, 451
Walters, Margaret, 225
Walton, Dorothy Camber, 362
Walzama, Habe queen, 355
WAMs, 151
Wang Tuan, 5
Wanger, Justine Johnson, 178
War heroines, 7, 26, 27–28, 144–152, 443; leaders and officers, 145–146, 151–152
Ward, Elizabeth S. P., 222

Ward, Mrs. H. O. *See* Bloomfield-Moore, Clara Sophia Jessup
Ward, Irene, 371
Ward, Lillian, 159
Ward, Mary, 385
Ward, Sybil, 172
Ware, Dawn Fraser, 420
Warhol, Andy, 180, 181
Warner, Emily, 112
Warner, Susan Bogart, 105
Warner Corset Company, 278
Warren, Mercy Otis, 126, 217
Warrenton, Lulu, 186
Warriors: legendary, 143–144; Indian women, 150–51
Warwick, Dionne, 87, 211
Washburn, Margaret Floy, 141, 445
Washington, George, 9, 148
Washington, Isabel, 180
Washington, Martha, 147, 267, 447
Washington, Ruth, 86
Washington Evening Star, 257
Washington Herald, 231
Washington Post, 231, 425
Washington Star, 425
Washington Times, 231
WASPs, 151
Water skiing, 420
Waterbury, Ruth, 185
Waterlow, Lady, 320
Waters, Ethel, 179, 180
Waters, Maxine, 451
Watseka (Potawatomi), 324
Watson, Clarissa, 229
Watson, Ella ("Cattle Kate"), 295
Watson, James D., 133
Watson, Lucille, 180
Watson, Thomas E., 366
Watson, Vera, 163
Watson-Schütze, Eva Lawrence, 258
WAVES, 151, 442
Wealthy women, 261–265, 268, 442
Weapons, female nicknames for, 156
Weathermen, 300
Webb, Mrs. (actress), 172
Webb, Aileen Osborn, 253
Webb, Beatrice Potter, 99, 453
Webb, Brenda Gayle (Crystal Gayle), 213
Webb, Clifton, 65, 439
Webb, Electra Havemeyer (Mrs. J. Watson), 253
Weber, Carl Maria von, 200
Weber, Lois, 186
Weber, Max, 76
Weber and Fields, 180
Webster, Ben, 78
Webster, Margaret, 78

Webster, Martha C., 422
Wee-hun-ga (Indian queen), 324
Weichel, Maria, 311–312
Weidman, Charles, 195
Weierstrass, Karl, 129
Weight lifting, 407–408
Weight records, 4
Weil, Cynthia, 210
Weil, Mathilde, 258
Weill, Claudia, 189
Weinstein, Paula, 193
Weiser, Norman, 182, 188, 199
Weiss, Betty, 210
Weiss, Louise, 375
Weiss, Mary, 210
Weld, Theodore, 343, 344
Wellesley College, 125, 141, 403
Wells, Alice Stebbins, 109
Wells, Delilah, 323
Wells, Gwen, 101
Wells, Jane, 105
Wells, Kitty (Muriel Deason), 212–213
Wells, Sarah, 323
Wells-Barnett, Ida B., 34
Welty, Eudora, 448
Wentworth, Patricia (Dora Amy Dillon Turnbull), 228
Werner, Johanna, 91–92
Werner, Mary Lou, 447
Wertheim, Mitzi, 153
Wertmüller, Lina, 189–190
Wesendonck, Mathilde, 198
West, Dottie, 213
West, Honey (fictional character), 228
West, Mae, 5, 219, 284, 286, 428
West, Rebecca, 71
West, Sarah Pearson, 69
West Point graduates, 155
Westendorf, Jennie Morrow, 205
Westendorf, Tom, 205
Westminster Abbey, women buried in, 453
Westover, Cynthia, 106
Westover, Russ, 108
Wethered, Joyce, 404
Wharton, Edith, 31, 447, 448
Wharton, Electra Waggoner, 263
Wheatley, Phillis, 34, 217, 441
"When a Girl Marries" (radio show), 183
Whimsical (filly), 407
Whipple, Catharine Moffat, 362
Whistler's Mother, 67, 447
Whistling Chorus of Agnes Woodward, 206
White, Ellen Gould, 389
White, Phyllis Dorothy, 225

White, Mrs. William Allen, 447
White House, employment at, 102, 224, 346; Honor Guard, 152
Whitely, Opal, 9
Whitlock, Charles, 173
Whitlock, Elizabeth Kemble, 173
Whitman, Bert, 108
Whitman, Marina von Neumann, 127
Whitney, Eli, 106
Whitney, Gertrude Vanderbilt, 249, 253
Whitney, Helen, 262
Whitney, Payne, 262
Whitney Museum, New York, 248, 249, 253
Whittelsey, A. G., 229
Whittle, Anne, 309
Whitty, Dame May, 78
Whitworth, Kathrynne Ann ("Kathy"), 416
Widdemer, Margaret, 449
Widerstrom, Karolina, 136
Wieck, Clara, 198, 199
Wiesenfeld, Paula, 291
Wife-beating, 314
Wife prices, 48
Wightman, Hazel Hotchkiss, 410–411
Wightman Cup, 410–411
Wigman, Mary, 194, 195, 196
Wigner, Eugene, P., 133, 450 .
Wilcox, Ella Wheeler, 434
Wild West shows, 157
Wilde, Jennifer (pseudonym), 222, 332
Wilde, Oscar, 14, 175
Wilder, Laura Ingalls, 223
Wilhelm II, Kaiser, 66
Wilhelmina, Queen of the Netherlands, 357, 360
Wilhelmina (incarnation of Third Person of the Trinity), 383
Wilkinson, Elizabeth, 408
Wilkinson, Tudor, 178
Willard, Emma H., 124, 433, 452
Willard, Frances Elizabeth, 26, 124, 348, 447, 452, 454
William the Conqueror, 12, 240
Williams, Betty, 27, 449
Williams, Cicely D., 135
Williams, Elizabeth, 387
Williams, Esther, 311
Williams, Eunice, 311
Williams, Ivy, 288
Williams, Mary Lou, 209
Williams, Mary Trumbull, 362
Williams, Roger, 31
Williams, Shirley, 371, 444
Williams, Spencer, 207

Williams, William Carlos, 230
Willis, John Henry, 334
Wills, Frances, 442
Wills, Lucy, 135
Willum, Persis (fictional character), 228
Wilmore, Jack, 401
Wilson, Cairine, 371
Wilson, Edith, 364
Wilson, Eileen, 183
Wilson, Harriette, 46
Wilson, Imogene ("Bubbles"), 313
Wilson, Jessie, 64
Wilson, Lena, 158
Wilson, Luzena, 103
Wilson, Margaret, 448
Wilson, Margery, 186
Wilson, Marie, 181–182
Wilson, Mary, 209
Wilson, Meredith, 219
Wilson, Rachel Bird, 362
Wilson, Ruth, 101
Wilson, Sandra, 159
Wilson, Teddy, 207
Wilson, Thomas Woodrow, 64, 337, 364
Wilson, William Heard, 334
Wimauma, Fla., 324
Wimbledon champions, 409, 410, 412, 413
Winbourne, Rebecca M., 107
Winkle, Winnie (comic-strip character), 108
Winn, Dilys, 226
Winnemucca, Sarah, 33
Winner, Septimus, 332
Winslow, Ola Elizabeth, 448
Winsor, Jackie, 250
Winsor, Kathleen, 221
Winston-Salem Journal, 425
Winters, Shelley, 191
Witcher, Frances Miriam Berry ("Frank"), 333
Witches, 308–310
Withers, Hildegard (fictional character), 228
Withers, Josephine, 245
Witherspoon, Elizabeth Montgomery, 362
Withy, Widow, 91
Witkin, Evelyn Maisel, 446
Wittgenstein, Princess, 198
Wittig, Nancy Constantine Hatch, 394
Wodzinska, Maria, 198, 199
Woffington, Peg, 174
Wolcott, Laura Collins, 361
Wolf, Rosalie J., 84
Wollstonecraft, Mary, 41, 71, 337–338
Woman Chief (Crow), 150
Woman in the Nineteenth Century (Fuller), 126
Womanpriest (Bozarth-Campbell), 394
Woman's Medical College of Pennsylvania. *See* Fe-

male Medical College of Pennsylvania
Woman's Symphony of Chicago, 206
Women and Russia (magazine), 316
"Women Artists in Washington Collections," 245
"Women Artists 1550–1950" (exhibit), 245
Women in Government (lobbying firm), 84
Women in Jazz (album), 208
Women Itinerants' Hobo Union, 158
Women Working in Construction (lobbying group), 101
Womenfolk, The, 206
Women's Bureau, Department of Labor, 99, 375
Women's Christian Temperance Union (WCTU), 26
Women's colleges: first, in England, 122–123; Seven Sisters, 125–126
Women's Intercollegiate Debating Society, 288
Women's Jazz Festival, Kansas City, 208
Women's liberation movement, 230, 345–346
Women's magazines, 228–229, 230
Women's Organization of Egypt, 346
Women's Professional Basketball League, 414–415
Women's rights: advocates, 3, 32, 75, 287–289, 336–346, 347–348; court decisions, 287, 289, 290–292, 318; credit opportunity, 293; education, 123–126, 293, 345, 433; employment, 289, 291, 292, 315, 318; legislation on, 99, 287, 292–293, 341–342; pay, 80, 99, 292; pregnancy benefits, 290–291, 293; property, 292, 293, 344; U.N. Convention (1952), 343; U.N. Declaration (1967), 436–437. *See also* Voting rights
Women's Rights National Historical Park, 455
Women's Social and Political Union (Britain), 200, 338
Wong, Marion E., 185
Wood, Maria, 325
Wood, Natalie, 329
Wood, Peggy, 179
Wood, Ruby Ross, 281
Wood, Sarah (Mrs. Roger Kemble), 173
Woodhull, Victoria Claflin, 46, 334, 364

Woodiwiss, Kathleen, 221, 222
Woodlawn, Holly, 181
Woods, Josephine ("Josie"), 91
Woodward, Agnes, 206
Wooley, Hannah, 110
Woolf, Virginia, 20, 77
Woolfolk, Sally D., 152
Woollcott, Alexander, 175
Woolson, Constance Fenimore, 220
Wooten, Anita Carter, 212
Wordsworth, Elizabeth, 123
Workers World party, 365
Working women, 96–115; business proprietors, 85–91, 92–93; firsts, 98–100; in professions, 96, 103 (*see also* Law; Medicine); sex discrimination, 287, 291, 292, 315, 318, 346–347; statistics, 96–97, 98. *See also* Employment
Working Women–National Association of Office Workers, 98
Workman, Fanny Bullock, 161
World Meteorological Organization, 331
World records, athletic, 6, 30, 403, 407, 417–422
World War I, 151, 153, 155, 161
World War II, 153; Iron Cross Recipients, 443; undercover agents, 27–28; USSR fighter pilots, 155; women services, 151, 153–154
World's Anti-Slavery Convention, London (1840), 336
World's Columbian Exposition, Chicago, Woman's Building at, 246, 256, 346
Worthing, Helen Lee, 313
Wren, Christine, 413
Wrestling, 404
Wright, Mrs., 146
Wright, Deedee, 210
Wright, Frances, 31
Wright, Frank Lloyd, 256
Wright, Mabel Osgood, 258
Wright, Martha C., 339
Wright, Mary Kathryn ("Mickey"), 415, 416
Wright, Patience Lowell, 248
Wright, Susanna, 218
Wrinkle removers, 275
Wrist-wrestling, 424
Writers, 75, 78, 126–127, 215–234; advance royalties, 222; advice columnists, 75, 429, 430; black, 34, 223–224, 333, 441, 442; children's books, 223, 332; colonial,

217–218; etiquette books, 429–430; female pseudonyms, 332; feminist, 345; handicapped, 29; Indian, 32–33; late starts and second careers, 113, 114; literary firsts, 215–216; male pseudonyms, 332–333; on midwifery, 70; of mysteries, 225–227, 332; precocious, 5; Pulitzer Prizes, 447–449; religious, 387; screen, 185, 186, 187, 189, 191–192, 233; teachers, 121. *See also* Autobiographers; Biographers; Historians; Journalists; Novelists; Playwrights; Poets
Wu Chao, Empress of China, 359, 377
Wu Chien-Shiung, 77, 133, 445
Wunderlich, Frieda, 124
Wunk, Elfrieda, 443
Wurdemann, Audrey, 449
Wyeth family, 77
Wyler, Gretchen, 179
Wyman, Anne C., 448
Wynette, Tammy, 213–214, 329
Wynn, May, 328
Wyoming, woman suffrage in, 290, 341, 454
Wyse, Lois, 81
Wythe, Elizabeth Taliaferro, 362

Yaffe, James, 227
Yakumo, Habe queen, 355
Yakunya, Habe queen, 355
Yale University, 100, 216, 435; Law School, 290
Yalow, Rosalyn S., 133, 445, 450
Yanbamu, Habe queen, 356
Yarmouth, Earl of, 262
Yeats, Mary, 91
Yeats, William Butler, 230, 330
Yeh, Chun, 376
Yeroyanni, Thekla, 346
Young, Ann Eliza Webb, 46
Young, Billie, 332
Young, Brigham, 46
Young, Loretta, 188
Young, Margaret W., 102
Young, Wanda, 210
Younger, Cole, 295
"Your Hit Parade," 183
Yourcenar, Marguerite, 216
Youth, Aliyah, 26

Zaharias, Mildred ("Babe") Didrikson, 403, 404, 452
Zaitsev, Aleksandr, 419
Zackrzewska, Marie, 138
Zalkind, Ronald, 211
Zama, Habe queen, 356
Zane, Betty, 149

Zarubin, Victoria, Regina, 329
Zaturenska, Marya, 449
Zavadovsky, Peter Alexeyevich, 39
Zelle, Margaretha. *See* Mata Hari
Zenger, Anna Catherina Maul, 89
Zenger, John Peter, 89

Zenobia, Queen of Palmyra, 144
Zetkin, Clara, 337
Ziegfeld, Florenz, 177, 178, 281, 285
Ziegfeld Follies, 177–178, 281, 313; standards, 285
Zimmerman, Helena (Dutchess of Manchester), 261

Zimmerman, Jan, 451
Zöetmans, Madame, 320
Zola, Emile, 298
Zoology, 133, 445
Zubata, Salma, 266
Zubov, Plato, 39

As the author of twelve works of nonfiction, and a textbook editor, Marjorie P. K. Weiser has been writing and editing books for more than twenty years, among them *Ethnic America, Museums U.S.A., Fingerprint Owls and Other Fantasies* and, with Jean Arbeiter, *Pegs to Hang Ideas On.* A graduate of Hunter College, she lives with her family in New York City. She first met Jean Arbeiter when they were both working for the same publishing house, Weiser as associate editor and Arbeiter as publicist, and they have been friends ever since.

Jean Arbeiter has been a publicist for Funk & Wagnalls, World Publishing, the Family Service Association of America, the National Association of Social Workers and *Human Nature* magazine. A Vassar College and New York University graduate, she and her family live in Leonia, New Jersey.